Google Apps Hacks

First Edition

Philipp Lenssen

O'REILLY®

BEIJING • CAMBRIDGE • FARNHAM • KÖLN • PARIS • SEBASTOPOL • TAIPEI • TOKYO

GOOGLE APPS HACKS

by Philipp Lenssen

Published by Make:Books, an imprint of Maker Media, a division of O'Reilly Media, Inc.
1005 Gravenstein Highway North, Sebastopol, CA 95472.

O'Reilly books may be purchased for educational, business, or sales promotional use.
For more information, contact our corporate/institutional sales department:
800-998-9938 or *corporate@oreilly.com*.

Print History
April 2008
First Edition

Publisher: Dale Dougherty
Associate Publisher: Dan Woods
Editor: Brian Jepson
Creative Director: Daniel Carter
Designer: Anne Mellinger
Production Manager: Terry Bronson
Copy Editor: Nancy Kotary
Indexer: Patti Schiendelman
Cover Photograph: Daniel Carter

ISBN-10: 0-596-51588-X
ISBN-13: 978-0-596-51588-1

To D. & C.

CONTENTS

CHAPTER 3: THE GOOGLE DOCS FAMILY: GOOGLE SPREADSHEETS 52

CHAPTER 4: THE GOOGLE DOCS FAMILY: GOOGLE PRESENTATIONS 82

CHAPTER 5: BECOME A GMAIL POWER USER 98

CHAPTER 9: MANAGE YOUR PHOTOS AND VIDEOS WITH PICASA AND YOUTUBE 210

CHAPTER 10: CREATE YOUR OWN HOME PAGE, BLOG, OR GROUP 236

CHAPTER 11: DIVE INTO GOOGLE MAPS, GOOGLE EARTH, AND SKETCHUP 3D 280

FOREWORD

Google. That's the search place, right? Not anymore. Today, Google is like a megastore offering products and services of all types. Sure, it still has search—but it doesn't stop there. Google can be your office; your answering service; your secretary. It can bring you the news each day, report on how your business is performing, and provide you with entertainment when the day is done. Best of all, virtually all of these services are free—and that's beginning to dramatically change our lives.

I remember the shock of how expensive my first computer was when I bought it in 1985—and how shock turned to horror as I contemplated the cost of software. As a college student, I couldn't afford it. I *borrowed* copies, like so many others. After college, I started buying my own software. But even with a good job, it was an expensive outlay to equip myself with a word processor and a spreadsheet, as well as an electronic organizer. Expensive database software? Forget it. But without software, our computers are lumps of metal and plastic. Software is what lets us harness a computer's power to do many things faster, better or more creatively than without digital help.

Enter Google. If I were in college today, I'd no longer need to borrow word processing software. Google gives it to me, free of charge. And spreadsheets. And notepads. And a calendar, and an email address book—not to mention nearly unlimited storage of my actual email. Heck, using Google's products and services, I can start a business on a shoestring budget.

The birth of the personal computer liberated millions from the "priesthood" of programmers that watched over the big mainframes of the past. PCs (IBM PCs, Windows machines, Macs, and computers running other operating systems) let ordinary people tap into a computer's power. But the liberation movement didn't end with the PC. The emergence of the Web let millions slip around the gatekeepers of big publishers and media outlets. Anyone could speak out and develop a strong voice at little to no cost. Liberation continues as part of the web application movement. Free web apps—software requiring no painful installation process—let millions create information and access it from anywhere. Quality tools no longer have to be obtained at high cost. The price barrier, like the computer priesthood and the media gatekeepers, has been swept aside—and much credit goes to the charge that Google has led.

The glorious revolution hasn't produced utopia, however. The downside to Google offering so many products in such a short time is that you may find that they're missing features you want. But because as free apps they don't generate revenue through a process of continual upgrades, it can take a long time for features to appear. I'm still waiting for the feature that lets me see more than 100 emails at one time in Gmail—how hard can it be?

Enter this book. If the software's not doing what it should, hack it! Find a workaround, a patch, or an add-on. Philipp Lenssen has assembled an amazing number of ways to make Google Apps do what you want—or to do things you didn't know you wanted them to do until he showed you how. In addition, he also takes the apps further by combining them. Google's many apps are almost like having access to a web-based Erector Set. You can link pieces of apps together to create new and unusual creations.

Viva the revolution! Viva the revolutionary's manual! Get hacking!

— Danny Sullivan, Chitterne, UK

Danny Sullivan is the editor of the popular news site SearchEngineLand.com and organizer of the SMX: Search Marketing Expo conference series. He's been involved in covering search engines dating back to the pre-Google era of the mid-1990s.

PREFACE

0.15 seconds. That's the time it just took Google to return 100 search results from the Web for a random word. Google searches through billions of documents, and it has masses of people using it every second.

13 minutes, 48 seconds. That's the time it just took Microsoft Windows to return 100 search results on this PC for the same random word. My Windows searches through thousands of documents, and it has only a single user today (me).

More than 13 minutes' difference is a long time; if you're working in a hurried office, it's the crucial separation between "Yeah, it works," and "I'll just try to find the document myself."

What separates the first process from the second? It's not only the number of smart engineers caring about search engine technology. It's also the fact that when you're using Google, you're not using your own computer, but the earth's biggest supercomputer instead. This supercomputer is itself made up of tens or hundreds of thousands of smaller computers, spread all over the globe; many perhaps resembling your own computer in power. But connect them, and you end up with the ultimate tool to run applications. Search, it turns out, is just one of these applications—and the Google engineers realized this too, a while ago.

Google's Apps—a Google Office, or a Google OS?

Today, Google is growing its apps suite to what people have started to call a Google Office, or even a Google Operating System. It actually has features of both. There's a platform called *iGoogle* to run your own small programs (which in turn are called *gadgets*). There's a word processor (Google documents) and a kind of online Excel (Google Spreadsheets). There's a filesystem explorer that's found in the Google Docs program. The Google Gears program expands your browser so that you can use web applications even when you're offline. Google Calendar lets you manage your events. Gmail lets you manage your email. Google SketchUp lets you create 3D scenery. Google's YouTube hosts your video collection. Google Maps shows you information mapped in space, using satellite imagery, driving directions, and even detailed street view photos. And there's much more in this Google apps suite.

However, most of these aren't desktop applications you install: they're hosted online. This approach brings with it some pros and cons. On the upside, not only won't you need to install these web applications; you don't need to care about getting the latest software patch, either. Also, as is the case with most of Google's web apps, they're free to use (as they're partly ad-financed). And these online tools are very collaborative in nature—instead of editing the Word file all on your own, Google Docs allows you to edit along with others, simultaneously. And when you're finished creating a document, you won't save it locally to send out the attachment, but instead can simply point someone to the URL of where your document is hosted.

There are some downsides too. Microsoft (among others who provide office suites), although not a leader in searching, has immense experience in desktop applications. Excel, PowerPoint, Outlook, and others are feature-rich, and thanks to the advanced desktop model, the interface can support many tricks and niceties that are still hard to emulate in the browser.

Google can certainly be expected to expand their tools over time. But today, almost universally across applications, Microsoft Office wins when it comes to the sheer quantity of features.

And that's where this book comes in. There's a long tradition in computing that when there's a missing feature, you apply a hack to make the program do what you want. After all, software—the desktop model, or the new online model—is supposed to do the work for you, not the other way round.

In *Google Apps Hacks*, we'll be presenting you with a wide array of hacks that guide you through getting more out of this new application suite. From easier workarounds (how do I attach a Google document to an email?), to more advanced tips (how do I skin my Gmail client?), to programming guides (how do I use the `importXml` function in my spreadsheet?). We'll also introduce the more exotic programs of the Google apps suite, like Google Notebook, and provide you with approaches to apply to your projects. Google apps, it turns out, have their own "13 minutes" problems every once in a while; hopefully, by using these hacks, you'll be able to route around some of them.

How to Use This Book

You can read this book from cover to cover if you like, but each hack stands on its own, so feel free to browse and jump to the different sections that interest you most. If there's a prerequisite that you need to know about, a cross-reference will guide you to the right hack.

How This Book Is Organized

This book is intended to be a compendium of tricks and tricks for life in the age of (Google) web apps. Beyond this, we hope you will gain a broader understanding of how the various parts of the "Google office" interconnect (indeed, although the great variety of Google tools offered allows you to tackle tasks in many different ways, this same variety can also be confusing). *Google Apps Hacks* is organized into 12 chapters:

Chapter 1, Meet the Google Docs Family

Google Docs is the name for the Google suite that includes document, spreadsheet, and presentation editing. In this chapter, you will find information related to all three of them, as well as the Google Docs explorer tool in general. You learn how to make the best use of document sharing, how to connect Google Docs to your desktop, how to do backups, and more.

Chapter 2, The Google Docs Family: Google Documents

The Google document editor is the Word of web apps. Formerly named Writely, this application allows you to create all kinds of documents, with a focus on sharing and team editing capabilities. In Chapter 2 you will find out about things like replacing text using regular expressions, file conversions, and Cascading Style Sheets to prettify your document.

Chapter 3, The Google Docs Family: Google Spreadsheets

Google Spreadsheets is Google's spreadsheet web editor. Along with numerous functionalities that you may know from desktop tools such as Microsoft Excel, Google Spreadsheets also allows you to connect cells to live information contained on the Web, which Chapter 3 discusses—among many other hacks.

Chapter 4, The Google Docs Family: Google Presentations

The web tool that's code-named "Presently" is the new kid on the block of Google Docs. While it's a rather fresh addition lacking features of more powerful tools like PowerPoint, it already offers some solid base features. We'll take a look into some of the base features, as well as advanced uses of the presentations app.

Chapter 5, Become a Gmail Power User

Gmail was originally released on April 1, 2004, causing many people to believe that its then 1 GB of storage must be a joke. Since that day, many people have started to use Gmail as their main email application, and some of these users also built their own functionality on top of Google Mail using Greasemonkey scripts. We'll discuss these scripts as well as other Gmail hacks, like user stylesheet editing, in depth.

Chapter 6, Customize Your Google Home Page

The iGoogle variant of the Google home page is a bit of a fridge door on which you can stick all kind of magnets: a calendar, your latest mail, your to-do list, a photo, or something else plain fun. In Chapter 6, you'll find out how to program gadgets and create them using wizards, as well as how to create custom themes. We'll also show many of the interesting available gadgets.

Chapter 7, Manage Your Events with Google Calendar

This chapter offers hacks on such subjects as creating a to-do list, sharing and finding of calendars, taking the quick add box of GCal with you, and connecting your mobile phone to your events.

Chapter 8, Keep Up on News with Google Reader

If you haven't used an "RSS reader" before (or if you are considering switching from your current one), you might want to give Google Reader a try. Some of the advanced uses and hacks are illustrated in Chapter 8. You'll learn about Google Gears, which adds offline capabilities to Reader, package tracking and Wikipedia article tracking, alerts, and the many locations at which Google offers feeds for their tools.

Chapter 9, Manage Your Photos and Videos with Picasa and YouTube

Chapter 9 covers Google's Picasa Web Albums, Google-owned YouTube, and Google Video. If you want to find out more about how to add your pics and videos to the Web, you might find useful hacks like linking to a specific time within a Google Video, adding subtitles to a video, displaying the lyrics for a music video, "geotagging" your photos, and more.

Chapter 10, Create Your Own Home Page, Blog, or Group

Creating and maintaining your own site is a topic that could span a whole book. Or perhaps a whole bookshelf. In Chapter 10, we've picked some of the most interesting use cases for hacking Google's Blogger, Google Groups, and Google Page Creator. You also get to know Google Sites, the former JotSpot, which allows you to set up wiki-style intranet or Internet destinations.

Chapter 11, Dive into Google Maps, Google Earth, and SketchUp 3D

Google Maps and its desktop sibling Google Earth squeeze the Earth—and the universe, as http://sky.google.com shows—into your browser. This chapter discusses ways to embed a Google map onto your own site; tips on using Google SketchUp 3D, which allows you to add models to Google Earth; programmatically creating Keyhole Markup Language layers on top of maps; and more.

Chapter 12, Google Analytics and Beyond: Market Your Site, Track Visitors

What's the best publication without visitors to see it? A very lonely publication, I guess. By analyzing your traffic with Google Analytics, you can optimize your site for your visitors, whether you built a traditional home page, a weblog, or anything else. In Chapter 12, you will find out how to track iGoogle gadget traffic, how to customize your Google Analytics dashboard, how to add a live chat to get to know your visitors better, and more.

For every set of apps, a Beyond Google section gives you a broad overview for some of the valuable tools in the area offered by the Google competition.

Conventions Used in This Book

This book uses the following typographical conventions:

Italic
Used to indicate new terms, URLs, filenames, file extensions, directories, and folders.

`Constant width`
Used to show code examples, verbatim searches and commands, the contents of files, and the output from commands.

Pay special attention to notes set apart from the text with the following icons:

This icon indicates a tip, suggestion, or general note. It contains useful supplementary information or an observation about the topic at hand.

This icon indicates a warning or note of caution.

The slider icons, found next to each hack, indicate the relative complexity of the hack:

Easy:
Intermediate:
Expert:

Using Code Examples

This book is here to help you get your job done. In general, you may use the code in this book in your programs and documentation. You do not need to contact us for permission unless you're reproducing a significant portion of the code. For example, writing a program that uses several chunks of code from this book does not require permission. Selling or distributing a CD of examples from O'Reilly books does require permission. Answering a question by citing this book and quoting example code does not require permission. Incorporating a significant amount of example code from this book into your product's documentation does require permission.

We appreciate, but do not require, attribution. An attribution usually includes the title, author, publisher, and ISBN. For example: "*Google Apps Hacks*, by Philipp Lenssen. Copyright 2008 O'Reilly Media, Inc., 978-0-596-51588-1."

If you feel your use of code examples falls outside fair use or the permission given here, feel free to contact us at *permissions@oreilly.com*.

Acknowledgments

Thanks to everyone at O'Reilly who helped make this book happen, including Brian Sawyer, who was there in the earliest phase; Dale Dougherty; Nancy Kotary, copyeditor; Terry Bronson, production manager; Patti Schiendelman, indexer; Anne Mellinger, designer; and Daniel Carter, cover designer. A hat tip to Tim O'Reilly. My biggest thanks of all goes to Brian Jepson for his terrific and extensive work in editing the book. Brian's not only an expert wordsmith, but also has a great technical understanding, and he molded this book into a true O'Reilly publication.

Thanks to Motti Strom (Mobile Software Engineer at Google UK), Piotr Konieczny (http://blog.konieczny.be), Adam Sah, Bryan Burkholder, and Siggi Becker (http://siggibecker.de), who all sent tips for the book. Ionut Alex. Chitu from Romania also sent pointers, and his blog (http://googlesystem.blogspot.com) continues to be a terrific resource for all kinds of Google-related tips and tricks. For their hack contributions, a big thanks to Tony Hirst, Reto Meier, and Chris Riley. Thanks to my wife and family for the support.

Special thanks to everyone at Google Blogoscoped for sharing news and tips via email and in the forum or helping out otherwise, including, but by far not limited to, Haochi Chen, Search-Engines-Web.com, Ionut (again), Brinke Guthrie, TomHTML, Luka, Peter Dawson, Colin Colehour, David Hetfield, Mathias Schindler, James Xuan, Hebbet, Manoj Nahar, Juha-Matti Laurio, Tadeusz Szewczyk, Sohil, Mambo, Mrrix32, Art-One, IanF, Stefan2904, Roger Browne, Martin Porcheron, Niraj Sanghvi, Kirby Witmer, Mysterius, Seth Finkelstein, Alek Komarnitsky, Rohit Srivastwa, Josue R., Orli, Beussery, Veky, JohnMu, Hong Xiaowan as well as all Chinese translators of Google Blogoscoped, Jared, Keith Chan, and Ramibotros (a longer list is at http://blogoscoped.com/forum/personrank.html). Last not least, thanks to the Google Blogoscoped co-editor Tony Ruscoe from Sheffield, UK. When others take a coffee break, you can find him digging around Google source code to find noteworthy bits and pieces.

We'd Like to Hear from You

Please address comments and questions concerning this book to the publisher:

O'Reilly Media, Inc./Maker Media, Inc.

1005 Gravenstein Highway North

Sebastopol, CA 95472

(800) 998-9938 (in the United States or Canada)

(707) 829-0515 (international or local)

(707) 829-0104 (fax)

We have a web page for this book that lists errata, examples, and any additional information. You can access this page at: http://www.makezine.com/go/gappshacks.

To comment or ask technical questions about this book, send email to *bookquestions@oreilly.com.*

Maker Media is a division of O'Reilly Media devoted entirely to the growing community of resourceful people who believe that if you can imagine it, you can make it. Consisting of Make Magazine, Craft Magazine, Maker Faire, and the Hacks series of books, Maker Media encourages the Do-It-Yourself mentality by providing creative inspiration and instruction.

For more information about Maker Media, visit us online:

MAKE: www.makezine.com

CRAFT: www.craftzine.com

Maker Faire: www.makerfaire.com

Hacks: www.hackszine.com

Google Apps Hacks

First Edition

Philipp Lenssen

01 MEET THE GOOGLE DOCS FAMILY

Google Docs (http://docs.google.com) is the title of Google's text, spreadsheet, and presentation editor, similar in style to Microsoft's Word, Excel, and PowerPoint programs, but with fewer features, and a stronger focus on collaboration. With Google Docs, you can write letters, recipes, tutorials, a diary, book chapters—I'm using it to write this book—or anything else.

You can also create web pages, thanks to the export options that Google Docs provides. Google Spreadsheets, on the other hand, allows you to perform spreadsheet calculations; you can keep any numeric or textual data organized—from the prices of items in your antique collection to the age and address of your employees, and so on. Google Spreadsheets provides you with a variety of formulas to perform calculations within a spreadsheet. You can also create neat visualizations using the chart tool. Google Presentations, the last of the trio, is useful for creating presentation slides for online or offline use.

To sign up for this service, as is the case with most other Google services described throughout the book, you need a Google Account.

HACK 01: How to Get Your Google Account

You can create a Google Account through many of Google's services. The easiest way is to go to http://www.gmail.com and click the "Sign up for Gmail" link. (Note that if you already have Gmail, you also already have a Google Account.) During the sign-up process, you provide your first and last name and your preferred username, along with other information, as shown in Figure 1-1. Once you agree to the Terms of Service and complete the sign-up by clicking the "I accept" button, you'll see a Congratulations page. Now you can log in to most Google services using your email + password.

If your email address is a gmail address, such as "officehacks@gmail.com", it's enough to enter just "officehacks" (along with your password) when you want to log in to your Google Account.

Log In to Google Docs

Now you can go to http://docs.google.com and log in to Google Docs. After you log in, you will see your file explorer, pictured in Figure 1-2. On the left side you can find different views of your items, and you can also see a list of people you have shared your items with; on the right side, you will see your files, if you have any.

To create a new document—"document" is Google's name for a word processing file—click the New button in the top left and pick Document. A new browser window with the document editor appears, as shown in Figure 1-3—now you can start writing, inserting images, creating tables, and more. Click anywhere on the document title to change its name, and then save the file. By default, unless you

Figure 1-1.
Creating a Google Account

Google Mail BETA

Create a Google Account - Google Mail

Change Language: English

Create an Account

Your Google Account gives you access to Google Mail and other Google services. If you already have a Google Account, you can sign in here.

Get started with Google Mail

First name:

Last name:

Desired Login Name: @googlemail.com

Examples: JSmith, John.Smith

check availability!

Choose a password: Password strength:

Minimum of 6 characters in length.

Re-enter password:

☑ Remember me on this computer.

Creating a Google Account will enable Web History. Web History is a feature that will provide you with a more personalized experience on Google that includes more relevant search results and recommendations. Learn More

☑ Enable Web History.

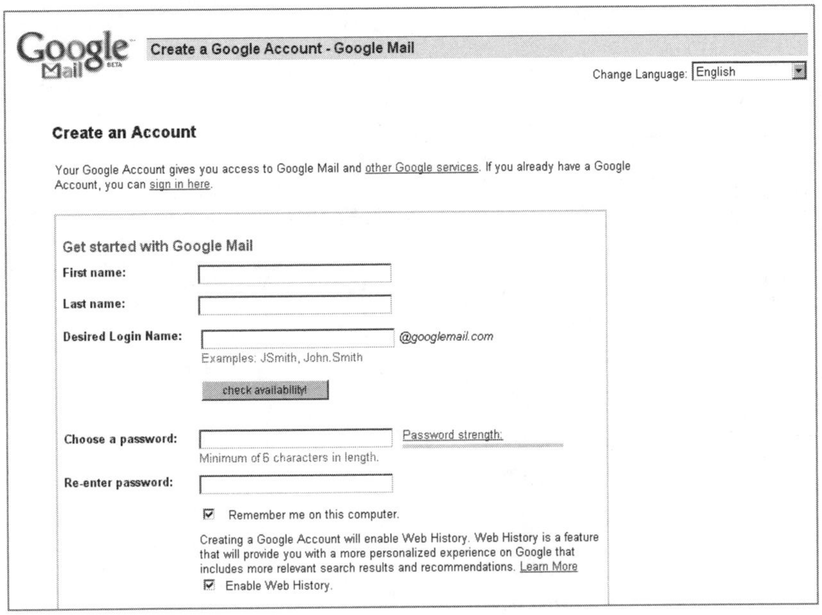

Figure 1-2.
The Google Docs file explorer

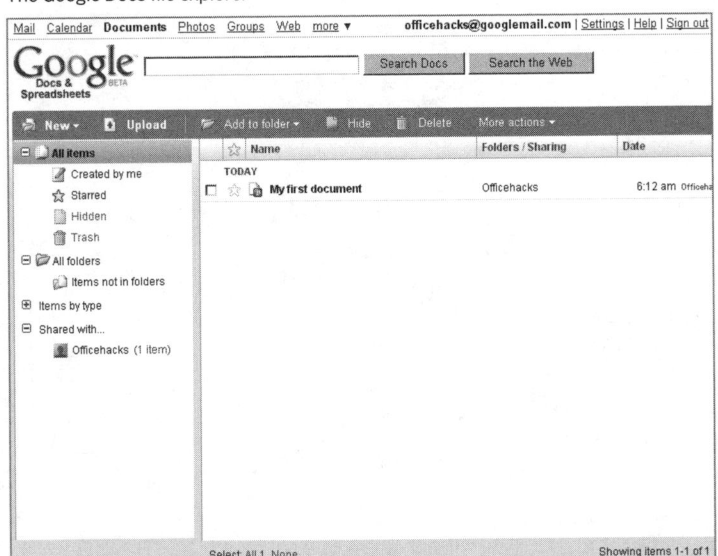

share the file with others, your document is private. It is, however, stored on Google's servers. (It would also be visible to anyone who's able to guess your password, so make sure that you use a strong password—more than just a single word, for instance.)

Google Spreadsheets, shown in Figure 1-4, has a similar look and feel to the Google document editor. One key difference is that it automatically saves your changes as you make them.

Google Presentations, pictured in Figure 1-5, allows you to prepare a new presentation and, to some extent, import an existing Microsoft PowerPoint presentation. It reuses interface elements from the document and spreadsheets editor.

Figure 1-3.
The Google Docs editor

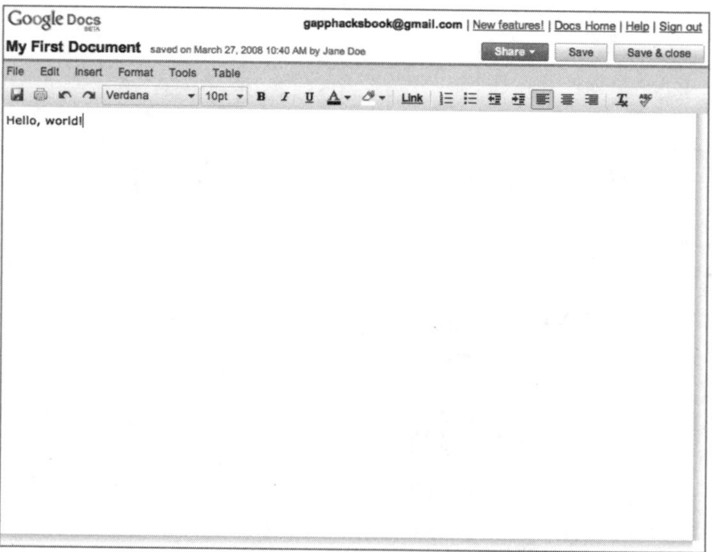

Figure 1-4.
The Google Speadsheets editor

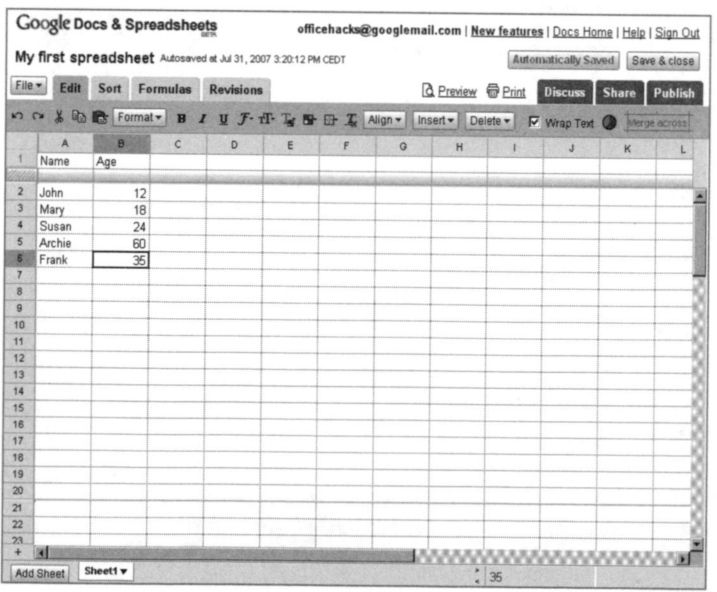

Figure 1-5.
The Google Presentations editor

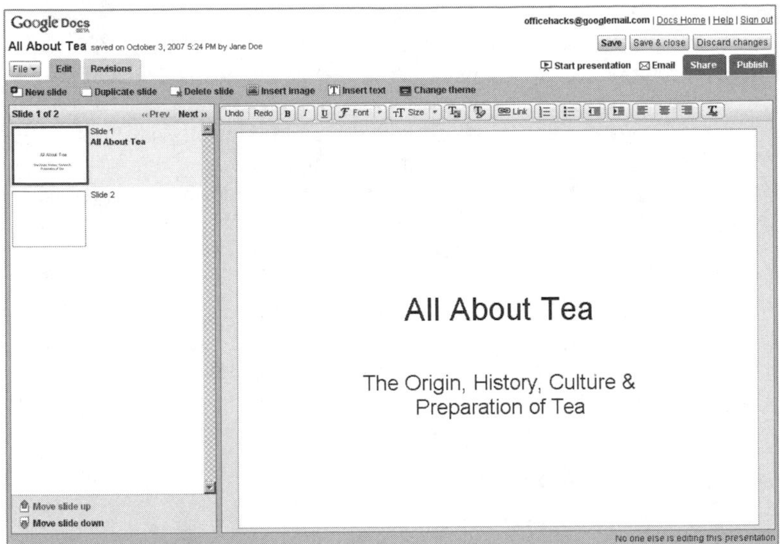

Sometimes you may not instantly see the document you saved when you switch back to the Google Docs file explorer. To refresh the window, click your browser's refresh button, and you will find your documents view has been updated.

If you have a problem with Google documents, Spreadsheets, or Presentations, the best place to find help—after you've checked the Google Docs help file, that is—is the official Google help group on the subject. Go to http://groups.google.com/group/GoogleDocs, click the "Join this group" link, and pose your question in one of the different sections, like "How do I . . . ?" (for general questions) or "Something is Broken" (when you think you've discovered a bug). If a Google employee answers, you will find a square "G" icon next to the member's name, but advice from nonemployees can be superb too.

HACK 02: Collaborate with Others Through Google Docs

With Google Docs, you can collaborate with others on the same document at the same time, and make documents accessible to the world within seconds by publishing them on the Web.

Online applications are born to be collaborative—the program and the data it works on are already potentially accessible from all over the world. Plus, every user will see the same version of that program without having to worry about whether they've installed all the latest patches, because the software runs on Google's servers, which automatically pick up the latest bug fixes and new features.

This collaborative approach requires you to do a bit of rethinking if you're used to desktop office tools. Instead of sending someone an attachment, invite them to a Google document. Instead of discussing a spreadsheet via the phone, email, or instant messenger, use the chat function that's built into Google Spreadsheets (see "Sharing a Spreadsheet," later in this hack). Instead of setting up third-party screen sharing software, you can invite others to your presentation URL and flip the slides for them.

Ironically, by being centralized, the data acts more as if it's decentralized; as the files are stored on Google's servers, which are already accessible to others who provide the needed credentials (their Google Account), Google ensures that you don't need to create a copy of a file to have someone else see it. So instead of dozens of Microsoft Word files scattered around your team's PCs (or in different folders on your intranet), the Google document exists only in that virtual "computing cloud." And Google Docs tracks who edits it, can alert you of changes, and allows you to compare document revisions.

Get Feedback on a Document You're Working On

One common use of collaboration is to ask for feedback on a document you're editing. Your friend, colleague, editor, or boss can add comments to your document, which you can work with in turn. All your collaborator needs for this is a Google Account, as discussed in the beginning of this chapter. (Without a Google Account, others can only view your documents—they cannot modify them.)

Let's start by creating a Google Docs document at http://docs.google.com. Name it "Thai Chicken Recipe." To get the initial recipe, you can go to Google Base at http://base.google.com and click the Recipes link; next, select the cuisine, main ingredient, and more from the drop-down menus, as pictured in Figure 1-6, and choose your preferred dish. You can highlight, copy, then paste the full page content directly into your empty Docs document as shown in Figure 1-7.

If you like to eat but you're no master cook, you can now invite your master cook friend to the document to proofread it. (None of your friends can cook Thai? Visit Google's social network at http://orkut.com and join the 6,500+ member-strong "Thai food lovers" community.) To invite

Figure 1-6.
Google Base stores user recipes, among other structured data

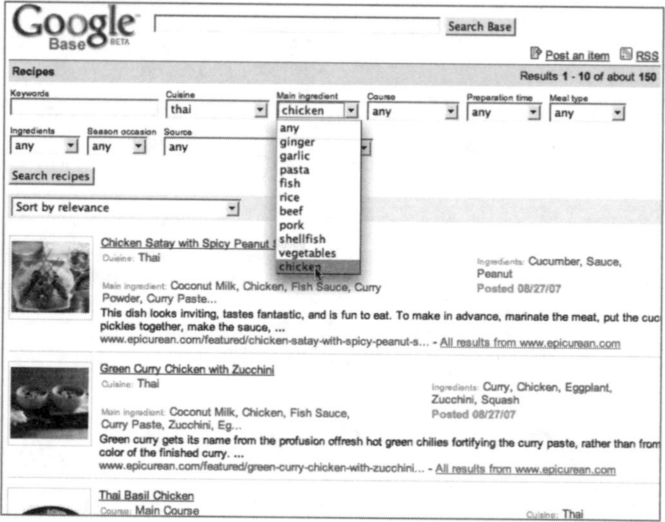

Figure 1-7.
After copying the Thai Basil Chicken recipe into the Docs editor

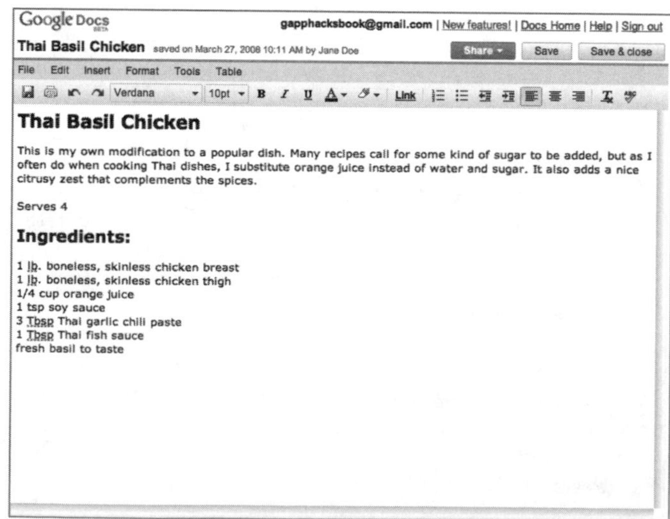

your friend, click Share→"Share with others" on top of the editor. Enter your friend's email address—preferably their Gmail address—into the invitation box. (And uncheck the "Invitations may be used by anyone" box, just in case someone else manages to get their hands on the invitation.) When you click the "Invite collaborators" button, your friend gets an email message, shown in Figure 1-8, and can start to edit along.

When you have a document open, you can see if someone else is editing it at the same time, thanks to the orange "Also editing now . . ." message at the bottom. Almost instantly, when someone else updates the document, the document you're viewing will change as well, as shown in Figure 1-9. If you're not happy with a revision, you can switch to File→"Revision history" and click the link of the last revision you agreed with; that revision will come up in the Google Docs editor for you to review, and you can click the "Revert to this one" button if you'd like.

You can also remove collaborators at any time, using the Share settings.

> Although you cannot directly chat with your collaborators within the Google Docs document editor, you can visit http://talk.google.com to open a separate, browser-based chat window for background discussions.

A NOTE OF CAUTION

By using the Revision history, collaborators with whom you share a document will also be able to see versions of the document made before you shared it. If you want to avoid this, you can make a copy of your document, and then only share the copy.

Figure 1-8.
An invitation to edit along in the same Google document

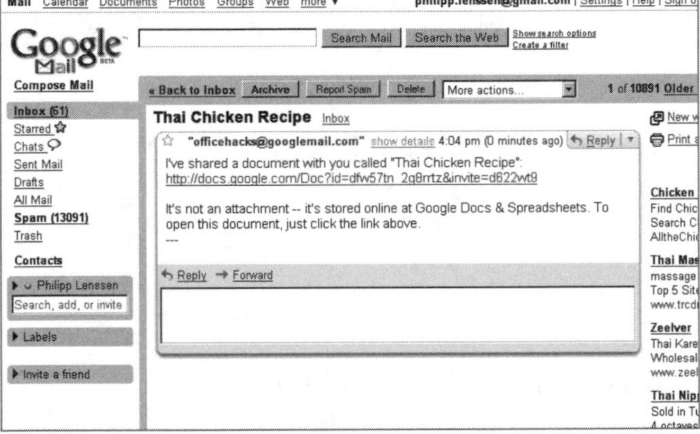

Figure 1-9.
A collaborator removed some of the original recipe text

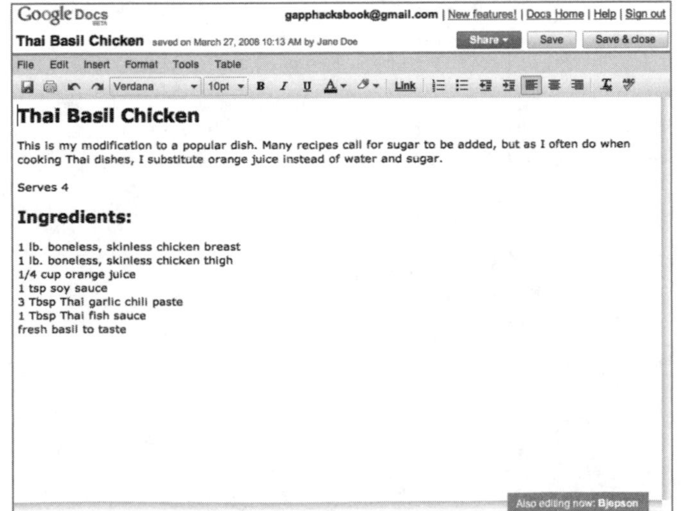

Publishing a Document for All to See

Instead of granting some people permission to modify your document, you can also publish a document for the whole world to see by clicking Share→Publish as web page→Publish document. You will then be provided with a URL like the following:

```
http://docs.google.com/Doc?id=dfp37tn_2g8xrtz
```

Depending on what you choose, this web page will now either host a static version of the document from the time you published it, or it will be up-to-date to reflect your latest changes (see the "Automatically re-publish . . ." checkbox in the "Share" settings). Readers don't need a Google account to view this plain web page.

Sharing a Spreadsheet

Spreadsheet sharing is even more powerful than sharing a document, because not only will others be able to edit the data with you simultaneously, there's also a chat box attached to the right side of the spreadsheet. To share the document, you first invite collaborators from your contacts via the Share button; after they've clicked on the link in the invitation email that they received, you can switch to the Discuss tab on top to chat with them, as shown in Figure 1-10.

Also, the cell your collaborator is working on at the moment is highlighted in a different color. It's almost as if your spreadsheet turned into a wiki—though even wikis (like the online encyclopedia Wikipedia.org) usually don't show this much real-time information regarding what others are doing!

For another Google tool supporting real-time group collaboration, give Google Notebook **[Hack #14]** a try.

Presenting to a Group

Google Presentations has a chat feature similar to the one that Spreadsheets offers. Plus, with Presentations you can take control of the document and move from one slide to the next, so people can follow along in their own browser in real-time.

Figure 1-10.
Editing and chatting alongside a spreadsheet

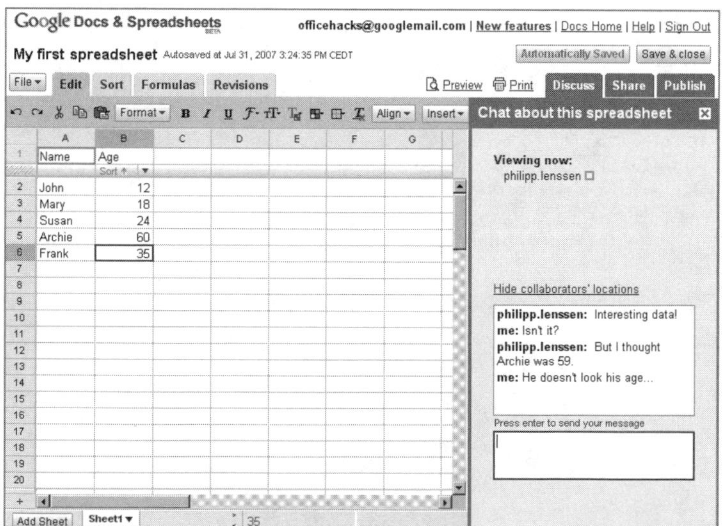

To share a Presentation with a group, first save the file. Now click Share→Publish as web page→ Publish document. Or, if you want to share the document with only a select few, pick "Share with others" instead, and invite the other members. If you decide to publish, you will end up with a document URL like the following:

```
http://docs.google.com/Present?docid=dfx37tn_24fxbtdz&fs=true
```

Going to this address will show the presentation on the left side and a group chat on the right. As owner of the document, you'll see a button labeled "Take control of the presentation." Click it, and you can move the slides for others once they choose to follow you, as shown in Figure 1-11.

Figure 1-11.
Watching a presentation within the browser; the slide to the left, the chat to the right

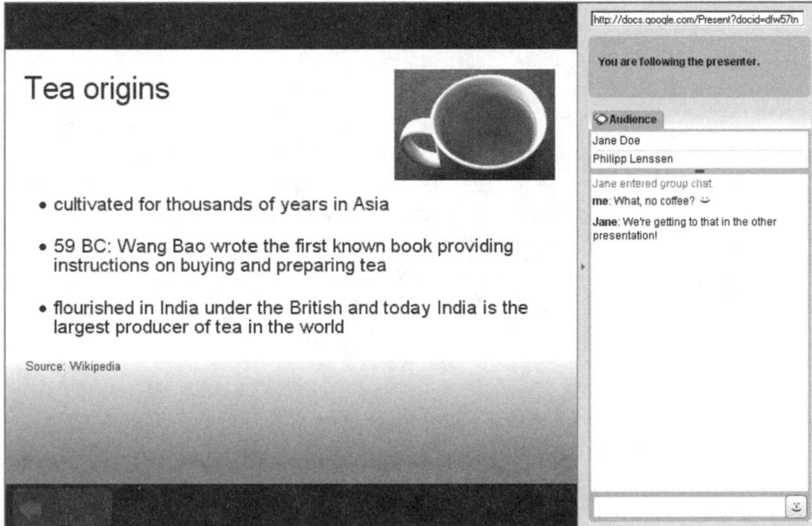

HACK 03: Make a Desktop Icon to Create a New Document

You launch desktop programs from the desktop. Why not launch Google programs from the desktop, too?

If you want to open up Google Spreadsheets to create a new file, you can point your browser to http://www.google.com and choose "Documents" from the "more" menu on top, then click New→ Spreadsheet. A quicker way to do this is to use a bookmark, but Motti Strom, Mobile Software Engineer at Google UK, suggests an even better way: create a desktop icon to launch Google documents, spreadsheets, or presentations.

Windows

Start by right-clicking any free spot on your Windows desktop and selecting New→Shortcut from the context menu, as shown in Figure 1-12. Type the following address for the shortcut:

```
http://spreadsheets.google.com/ccc?new
```

Save your shortcut, and name it "New Google Spreadsheet."

Figure 1-12.
Creating a new desktop shortcut

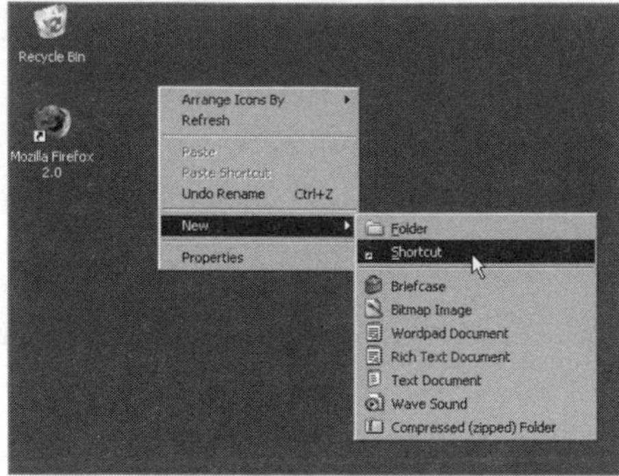

Mac OS X

Whether or not you use Safari, open it up. Create a new bookmark (Bookmarks→Add Bookmark) for whatever page opens up; it doesn't matter because you're going to change it in a moment. Give the bookmark the name "New Google Spreadsheet." Next, select Bookmarks→Show All Bookmarks, and edit the bookmark you just created to replace the URL with http://spreadsheets.google.com/ccc?new. Now, drag this bookmark to your desktop. If you don't want to keep the bookmark in Safari, you can delete it now, because you have a copy on the desktop.

Try It

This shortcut will let Google launch a new unnamed Spreadsheet for you. Give the icon a try by double-clicking it. Note that you may be required to log in to your Google account if you aren't already.

You can create a second desktop shortcut for Google Documents. Use the same method, but pick the following URL for the shortcut:

```
http://docs.google.com/?action=newdoc
```

Save the shortcut, name it "New Google Document," and give it another try.

For a Google Presentations shortcut, use the following URL, naming it "New Google Presentation":

```
http://docs.google.com/?action=new_presentation
```

Changing the Icons

You can improve on this hack by using nicer icons than the default. Enter the following URL in your browser's address bar to access the Google Spreadsheets icon:

```
http://www.google.com/images/spreadsheets/favicon.ico
```

This is a so-called "favicon," a 16 x 16 pixel image that the browser displays in bookmarks or the address bar when you visit a web site. But because it's an *.ico*—icon—file type, you can reuse it as an icon for your short cut. If your web browser didn't automatically download it for you, right-click the image to download it to your computer. Once you have downloaded the icon, rename it *spreadsheets.ico*.

Repeat the same process with the Documents and Presentations icons at the following two addresses, and give it the name *documents.ico* and *presentations.ico*:

http://docs.google.com/favicon.ico
http://docs.google.com/presently/images/favicon.ico

Now go back to the three desktop shortcuts that you created to add these icons. On Windows, right-click your "New Google Spreadsheet" shortcut, select Properties from the context menu that appears, switch to the Web Document tab and click the "Change Icon" button. Browse to find your icon named *spreadsheets.ico* and click OK to use it.

On Mac OS X, download the program img2icns from http://www.shinyfrog.net/en/software/img2icns/ and drag the *.ico* file onto it to create a proper Mac OS X icon file. Switch to the Finder, click to highlight the icon file that img2icns created (img2icns puts files on the Desktop by default), and select Edit→Copy. Right-click on your "New Google Spreadsheet" shortcut, and choose Get Info. Click the icon in the upper left, and press Command-V to paste the icon in. After you've done this, you can delete the *.ico* file and the icon you created, if you want to.

Voila! You can do the same for your "New Google Document" and "New Google Presentation" icons by using the *documents.ico* and *presentation.ico* files instead of the one for spreadsheets. You will now have icons based on the Google Docs graphics, as shown in Figure 1-13.

Figure 1-13.
The shortcuts appear in the official Google Docs design now

Adding a Keyboard Shortcut

On Windows, you can attach a custom keyboard shortcut to desktop shortcuts. To do so, just right-click your shortcut named "New Google Spreadsheet" and click into the Shortcut key field. Enter Ctrl-Alt-S—or another shortcut, though some shortcuts are reserved by Windows and cannot be chosen—and approve the dialog. Now, you can press Ctrl-Alt-D anywhere in Windows to launch a new spreadsheet with Google.

You can repeat the same process for your "New Google Document" and "New Google Presentation" shortcuts. Pick Ctrl-Alt-D, or Ctrl-Alt-P, or any other keyboard shortcut you can easily remember, and you will now be able to quickly launch Google Docs word processing and presentation documents from Windows.

Create a Shortcut Icon for an Existing Document

You can also create a shortcut to any existing Google document of yours. Maybe there's a shared To Do list for your project at work, and you access it quite regularly; speeding up the launch process would be nice.

First, open up your document in the browser as usual by going to http://docs.google.com and clicking its title. Most browsers will now display the "favicon" icon at the left side of the address bar. Drag and drop this favicon onto your desktop, and the shortcut will be created for you automatically. You can close the document now and double-click the icon later on to launch it again. (Be aware that if you already have the document opened in your browser, clicking this shortcut will create a second window with your document.)

For further ways to integrate Google web apps into the desktop, take a look at the Mozilla Prism project at http://labs.mozilla.com/featured-projects/#prism.

HACK 04: Embed a Dynamic Chart into a Google Document or a Web Page

Copy the URL of a Google Spreadsheets chart into your document—or a web page—and configure it so that it automatically updates whenever you change the underlying data.

Debora runs an ice cream shop in London. London is not the warmest location in the world, which might hurt her sales, but Debora knows one way to get the word out to make more people come to her shop: an amazingly cool web site. For her site, she prepares historical articles on the subject of ice cream, and also wants to include a near real-time chart of the most popular flavors she's selling that week. Debora can create the flavor sales chart in Google Spreadsheets, but how can she include this chart in a Google Docs document so that it's automatically updated?

Start by creating a new spreadsheet **[Hack #1]**. Fill the left column with flavors and the right column with sales numbers. You can then include a chart by selecting all filled cells and clicking the chart icon on top. In the "Create chart" dialog that appears, pick your preferred design (such as a a three-dimensional pie chart) and click "Save chart." Your spreadsheet will now look similar to the one pictured in Figure 1-14.

Next, right-click the chart and choose "Publish chart" from the menu that appears. A window will appear with the code you need to embed this chart in an HTML page. Highlight this code and copy it. You can now insert this image in a Google Docs document. Instead of using the Insert Picture menu, switch to Edit→Edit HTML and paste the code into a paragraph, as in the following code sample:

Figure 1-14.
A spreadsheet listing ice cream sales, with a 3D pie chart

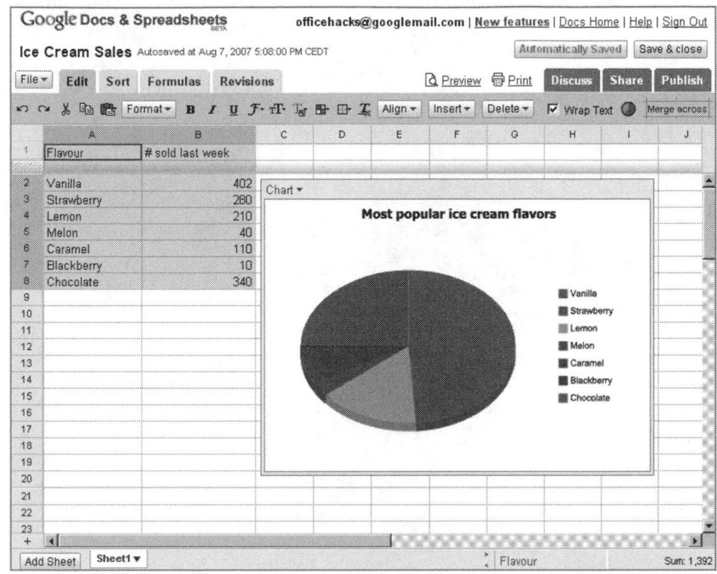


```
<p style="float: right; margin: 30px 0 30px 30px">
<img src="http://spreadsheets.google.com/pub?key=pLPFsG-ujjlXByXdTYUGLYA&oid=3&output=image" />
</p>
```

In preceding example, there is an additional style definition **[Hack #18]** to position the image to the right of the text. The margin values are provided in the clockwise order of top, right, bottom, left.

If you switch to the normal editing mode and then back to Edit HTML mode, you'll notice that Google has entity-escaped the URL for you (changing `&` to `&`). This is nothing to worry about, and in fact it will make sure your document is valid HTML.

Note this method of embedding the chart also works with any other webpage, such as a blog post.

To publish the Google document as a web page, choose Share→"Publish as web page"; select "Automatically re-publish . . ." here too, if you want to ensure that all your future edits will be reflected in the document. Note that you should not pick the automatic republishing option if you don't want people to see your changes in real time. Instead, wait until you're done with your revisions, click Share→"Publish as web page", and then click "Re-publish document."

To everyone except those with editing rights for your document, the result will look as pictured in Figure 1-15. (If editing rights are available, the document will appear inside a Google Docs editor.) And now, whenever you change any of the underlying flavor sales data in the original spreadsheet, this web page will automatically display the latest version of the pie chart, as shown in Figure 1-16—there's a slight loss on the vanilla front, but Debora has this well covered with increased chocolate sales!

The Google Charts Image Generator

Another way to embed charts into a web page or a Google Docs document is to use the Google Charts API, a standalone service not connected to Google Spreadsheets. "API" is short for Application Programming Interface, but there's usually no programming needed to get the Google Charts API to work—it's just a straightforward way of creating a special image URL, which you then include in your page.

Figure 1-15.
The original chart, published in a Google Docs document exported as a web page

Ice Cream

Mrs. S. T. Rorer says, "If you wish to pack ice cream and serve it in forms or shapes, it must be molded after the freezing. The handiest of all of these molds is either the brick or the melon mold.

After the cream is frozen rather stiff, prepare a tub or bucket of coarsely chopped ice, with one-half less salt than you use for freezing. To each ten pounds of ice allow one quart of rock salt. Sprinkle a little rock salt in the bottom of your bucket or tub, then put over a layer of cracked ice, another layer of salt and cracked ice, and on this stand your mold, which is not filled, but is covered with a lid, and pack it all around, leaving the top, of course, to pack later on. Take your freezer near this tub. Remove the lid from the mold, and pack in the cream, smoothing it down until you have filled it to overflowing. Smooth the top with a spatula or limber knife, put over a sheet of waxed paper and adjust the lid. Have a strip of muslin or cheese cloth dipped in hot paraffin or suet and quickly bind the seam of the lid. This will remove all danger of salt water entering the pudding. Now cover the mold thoroughly with ice and salt.

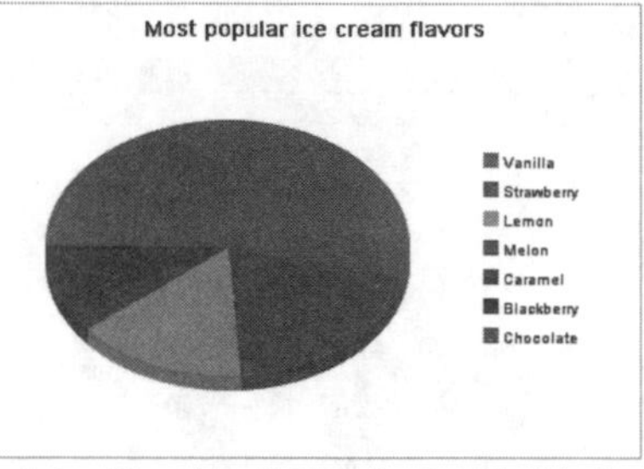

Make sure that your packing tub or bucket has a hole below the top of the mold, so that the salt water will be drained off. If you are packing in small molds, each mold, as fast as it is closed, should be wrapped in wax paper and put down into the salt and ice. These must be filled quickly and packed.

Molds should stand two hours, and may stand longer."

Figure 1-16.
The chart on the document automatically updated after changing the underlying spreadsheet numbers

Ice Cream

Mrs. S. T. Rorer says, "If you wish to pack ice cream and serve it in forms or shapes, it must be molded after the freezing. The handiest of all of these molds is either the brick or the melon mold.

After the cream is frozen rather stiff, prepare a tub or bucket of coarsely chopped ice, with one-half less salt than you use for freezing. To each ten pounds of ice allow one quart of rock salt. Sprinkle a little rock salt in the bottom of your bucket or tub, then put over a layer of cracked ice, another layer of salt and cracked ice, and on this stand your mold, which is not filled, but is covered with a lid, and pack it all around, leaving the top, of course, to pack later on. Take your freezer near this tub. Remove the lid from the mold, and pack in the cream, smoothing it down until you have filled it to overflowing. Smooth the top with a spatula or limber knife, put over a sheet of waxed paper and adjust the lid. Have a strip of muslin or cheese cloth dipped in hot paraffin or suet and quickly bind the seam of the lid. This will remove all danger of salt water entering the pudding. Now cover the mold thoroughly with ice and salt.

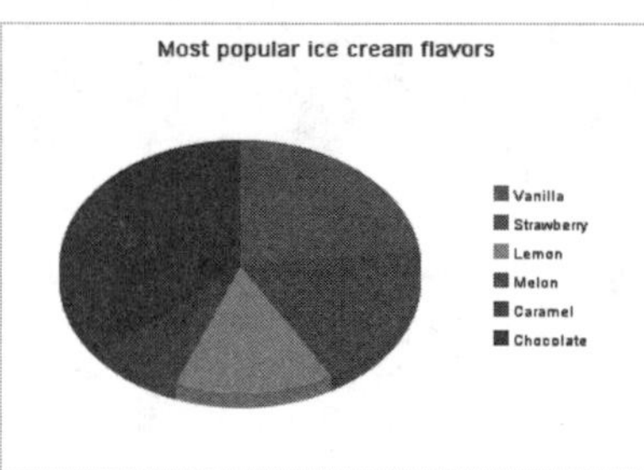

Make sure that your packing tub or bucket has a hole below the top of the mold, so that the salt water will be drained off. If you are packing in small molds, each mold, as fast as it is closed, should be wrapped in wax paper and put down into the salt and ice. These must be filled quickly and packed.

Molds should stand two hours, and may stand longer."

Here's an example chart URL, which generates the 3D pie chart shown in Figure 1-17 as a PNG file; another type of chart image is shown in Figure 1-18:

http://chart.apis.google.com/chart?cht=p3&chd=t:90,49&chs=350x150&chl=Foo|Bar

Give this a try by entering the URL into the browser address bar.

Now, if you break down the URL into its parameter components, you will better understand how it works:

» **cht=p3** tells the image that the chart type wanted is a pie chart in 3D ("p3").
» **chd=t:90,49** are the actual chart values, separated by a comma, in text format (the "t").
» **chs=350x150** defines the resolution of your chart; in this case, a width of 350 pixels and a height of 150 pixels.
» **chl=Foo|Bar** indicates the text that labels each section of the pie chart.

 Note that the Chart API is limited to 50,000 requests per day—if you expect to generate more requests than that, you may want to cache the image on your server instead of issuing a request each time someone visits your page.

Figure 1-17.
The image generated by the Google Charts API

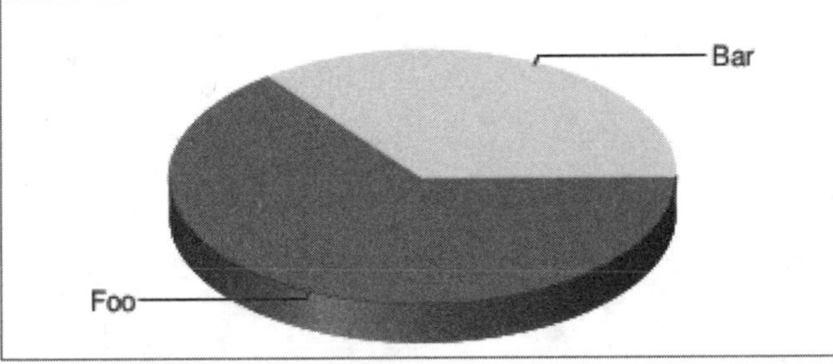

Figure 1-18.
Another image from the Google charts generator

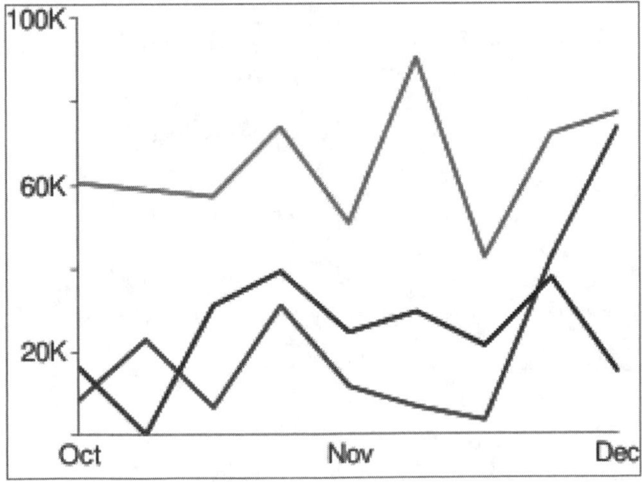

The API can do much more than this, though. You can choose from many different chart types, or customize colors, line styles, and fills, to name just a few of the available options. For a full list of features, take a look at Google's documentation available at http://code.google.com/apis/chart/.

HACK 05: Share Documents with a Group

If you find yourself sharing many documents with the same group of people, adding all their names each time can be tiresome.

The Share tab of Google Docs has a nice feature that's easy to overlook: custom invitation groups. If you need to invite the same people over and over, this one is for you. The solution presented here was originally laid out by Ionut Alexandru Chitu, a Google expert and blogger (http://googlesystem.blogspot.com) from Romania, who wanted an alternative to an otherwise tedious process.

To give this a try, create a new document by going to http://docs.google.com and choosing New→Document (or Spreadsheet or Presentation) from the menu. Enter some text and save your document. Now switch to Share→"Share with others". Instead of typing the names of the people you want to invite, click the "Choose from contacts" link. Select All Contacts from the dropdown menu (it defaults to Most Contacted) in the new window that appears, and select all the people you want to share the document with, as shown in Figure 1-19.

Although you can't directly edit or delete a group within Google Docs, all groups are shared with Gmail—See **[Hack #39]** for more information. So to edit a group, visit Gmail at http://gmail.com and click the Contacts link to the left.

Depending on your browser and browser settings, Google's prompts—like the one asking you to name your contact group—may not immediately appear. This may happen, for instance, on Windows Internet Explorer 7, where a yellow bar on top of the window alerts you with a warning, suppressing the Google prompt. To permanently disable this security warning when working with Google Docs in Internet Explorer 7, select Tools→Internet Options from the menu. Switch to the Security tab and select the Trusted Sites icon. Now click the "Sites" button and add "http://docs.google.com" to the list of web sites (uncheck the "Requires server verification" box if necessary).

Figure 1-19.
The Google Docs contacts dialog

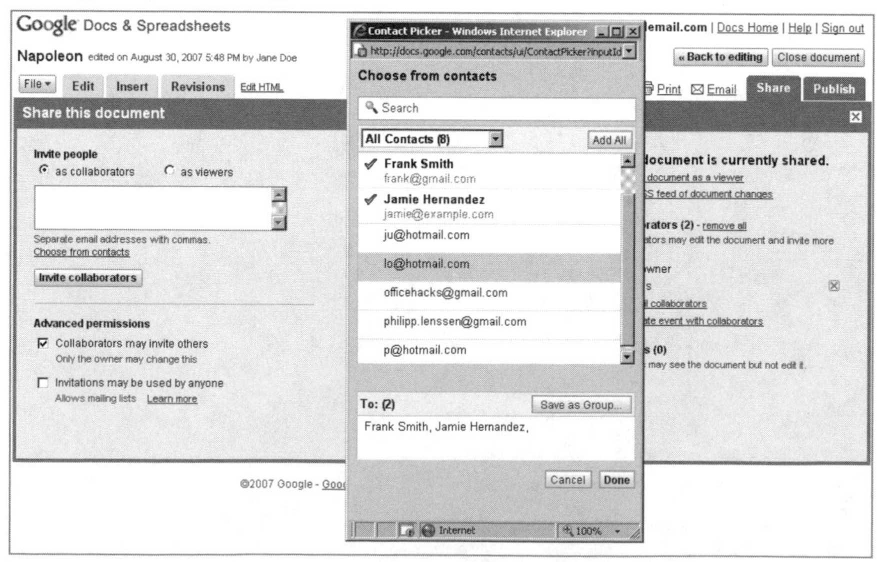

Instead of clicking Done right away in this dialog, click the "Save as Group" button. A new prompt asks you to name this group, so provide a name like Colleagues or Family. Now when you close the dialog via the Done button, the names you selected will be entered into the invitation box for you. But the next time you want to share a document, you can just click the "Choose from contacts" link, select your custom group from the drop-down menu at the top of the window (the same menu that defaults to Most Contacted), and press the "Add All" button to invite all of them at once.

HACK 08: Automatically Open Local Files with Google

Wouldn't it be neat to automatically open a local Office file with Google Spreadsheets? Actually, you can!

By default, those files you open in the Google Docs file listing at http://docs.google.com will open in Google's editor. Local files on your hard disk, however, are likely to be associated with an offline program like OpenOffice.org or Microsoft Office. But there's a way to associate these files with Google's tools. All you need is the Google Toolbar for your browser.

For this hack, you need Firefox 1.5+. If you don't have the Firefox browser yet, you can get it for free at http://firefox.com. Then point your browser to http://toolbar.google.com and click the "Download Google Toolbar" button to get the Google toolbar, as pictured in Figure 1-20.

During installation, you need to approve several confirmation dialogs, and finally restart your browser. Once the setup is complete, you will notice the toolbar at the top of your browser. Select Settings→Options from the toolbar menu to the right, as pictured in Figure 1-21.

In the dialog that opens, select the Docs checkbox, and click the "File Settings . . ." button below it; now check the "Double-click a file icon" option and confirm the dialogs by clicking OK, as shown in Figure 1-22.

Figure 1-20.
The Google Toolbar home page

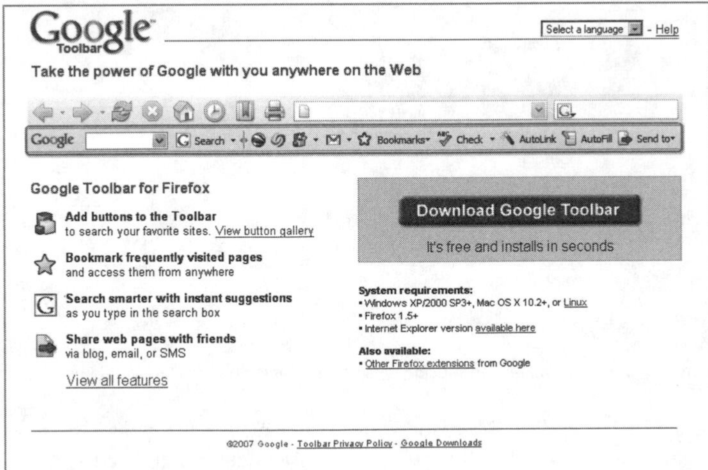

Figure 1-21.
Accessing the Google Toolbar's options

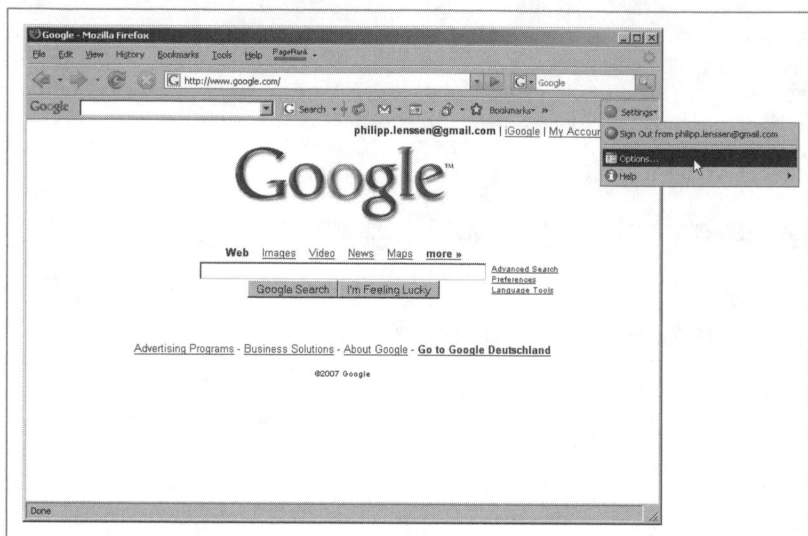

Figure 1-22.
The Docs→File Settings dialog of the Google Toolbar

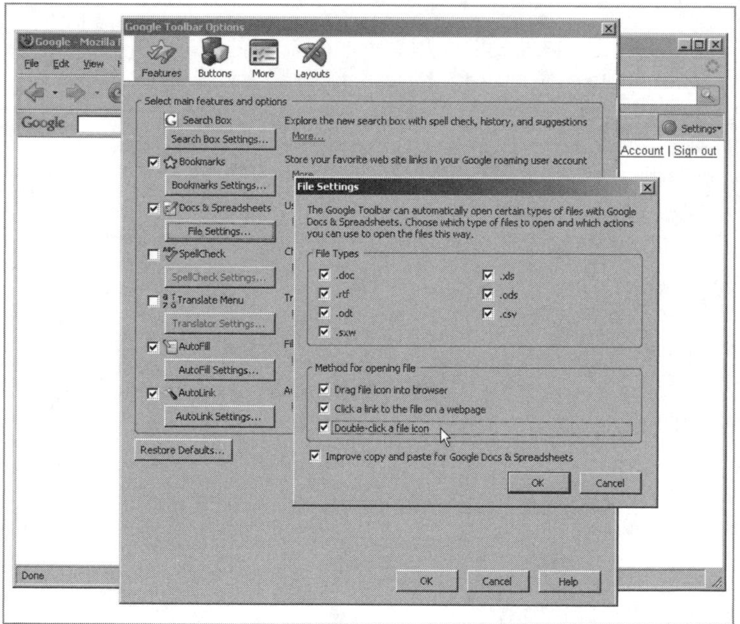

At the time of this writing, the "Double-click a file icon" option was not available on Mac OS X or Linux.

Now, files with extensions like RTF, ODS, or XLS—Microsoft Office or OpenOffice file types—will automatically open with Google. Give it a try by locating an XLS file on your computer, or create a new one. The first thing you will notice is that the icon has changed. Double-click the file (or drag it into Firefox), and you will see it open in your browser, as shown in Figure 1-23. Also, the file will be automatically added to your Google Docs file listing.

Figure 1-23.
Opening a Microsoft Excel file from your desktop with the Google Spreadsheets editor

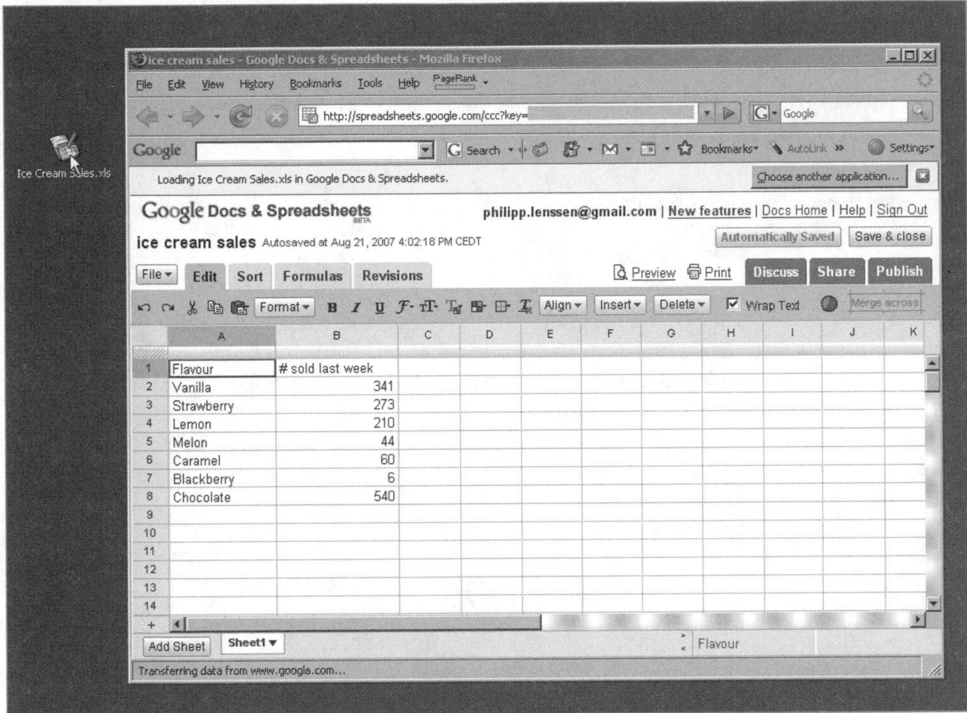

Note that what you opened now in the browser is a redundant Google Docs copy of the document; changes you are making here will *not* be saved back to the document on your hard drive, unless you decide to export the document again to overwrite the old, local version. In other words, while you did open the local file (i.e., you uploaded and saved it to Google Docs and loaded it in the editor), all editing and saving will happen to the new online file.

 Not all of your original files may survive the transition to Google Docs. For instance, a chart graphic included in an Excel file may not show any more once the file is opened in Google Spreadsheets.

HACK 07: Google Docs on the Run

If you carry a mobile phone with a web browser, then you carry parts of Google Office, too—without having to install anything.

When you're on the go, viewing your Google Docs documents works best on a laptop, ultramobile PC, or web tablet. However, in some circumstances you might want to have a quick look at one of your documents without busting out any of these devices. In those situations there's a fallback plan waiting for you at http://docs.google.com/m: Google Docs mobile.

The mobile variant of Google Docs, a light 'n' lean version of the Docs web site optimized for cellphones, as pictured in Figure 1-24, lets you view your file listings as well as some of the file contents. Exactly what you will see depends on your type of mobile phone, but in general, if your phone supports rich browsing, you can:

- View a list of all of your files
- Search for specific files
- Open Docs folders
- Open spreadsheets in HTML view
- Open spreadsheets as Excel files (if your phone supports the XLS Excel spreadsheet format)
- Open word processing documents

When you open Google Docs mobile on your cellphone, you will be required to log in if you're not authenticated. To save some time writing your full username, you can—as is the case with the desktop version of Google Docs—enter "officehacks" instead of the full "officehacks@gmail.com" (for example). This trick works only with Gmail addresses, though.

Opening a word processing document in Google Docs mobile will just show the file as it would appear on a web site. (Presentation files cannot be opened on anything but iPhones at the time of this writing.) The rendering for spreadsheets, on the other hand, is a little more advanced in its optimization for small screens. You will by default see only a single column, and you can jump to specific rows or columns. You can also view the contents of a single cell on its own by entering its coordinates in the column/row search box, as shown in Figure 1-25, and then selecting the "Go to Cell" button.

Figure 1-24.
The Google Docs mobile home page

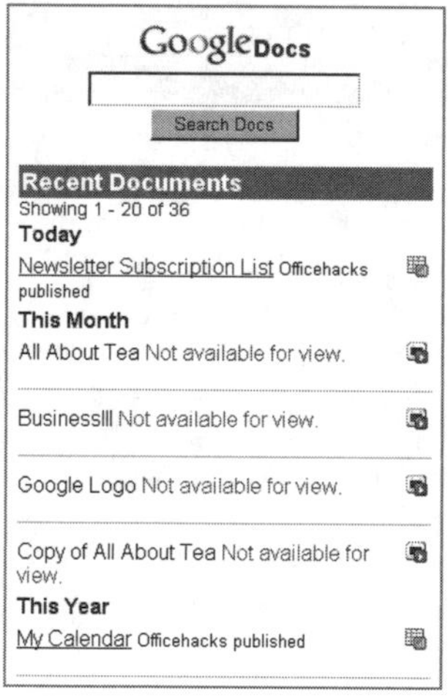

Figure 1-25.
Viewing an ice cream sales spreadsheet

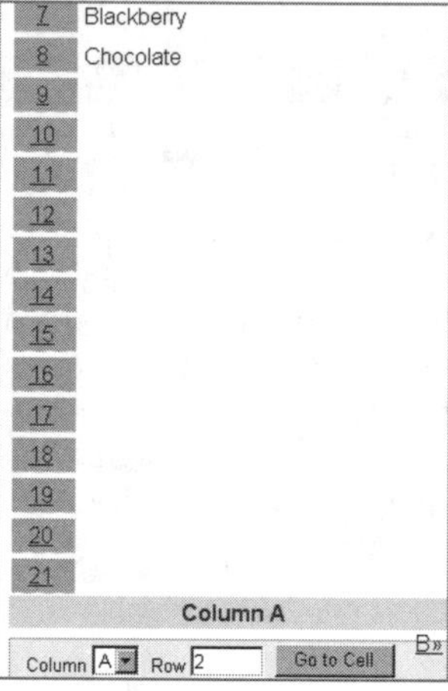

HACK 08: Back Up All Your Google Docs Files

Make your backups before something bad happens, not afterwards.

Google no doubt backs up your Google Docs data on some of their many servers. And old versions of your document still live on through their revision history. But when you delete a document, there's no getting it back. You can minimize the damage of such accidents by storing copies of Google Docs documents on your hard disk (from which you can burn them on CD, copy them to your USB stick, upload them to other storage services or your own server, and so on).

Backing Up a Small Number of Files

If you have only a couple of word processing documents or presentations to back up, here's what you can do. Log in to Google Docs and in the file listing pane, select all of your files of a single type—only documents, or only presentations—one by one. Then open the "More actions" menu on top and pick "Save as HTML (zipped)." You can now select a folder on your hard drive and let the download begin.

However, this method is very limited, at least at the time of this writing. For one thing, Google Docs won't let you select different file types for download (like a mixture of word processing documents *and* presentations). Also, downloading won't work if you select more than a single spreadsheet at once.

Backing Up All Your Files

But there's an alternative, robust approach to backing up all documents. The detailed steps are as follows. For this to work, you need the Firefox browser, the Greasemonkey extension, the DownThemAll Greasemonkey script, and the GoogleDocsDownload Greasemonkey script. This solution was originally described by Ionut Alexandru Chitu in his blog Google Operating System at http://googlesystem.blogspot.com.

Here are the steps in detail—note that whenever you are asked to restart your browser after installations, you must do so before continuing:

1. Install Greasemonkey by clicking the Install Now button at https://addons.mozilla.org/en-US/firefox/addon/748. (Restart your browser after the installation, and you will see a smiling monkey head icon in the bottom right of your browser.)

2. Install DownThemAll by clicking the Install button at http://downthemall.net and following the instructions. DownThemAll is a tool that allows you to download multiple files contained in a web page at once.

3. Install GoogleDocsDownload by typing http://1st-soft.net/gdd/googledocdownload.user.js in your address bar and pressing Return or Enter. Follow the instructions that appear.

You now have all the tools to start the actual backup process, which you can repeat anytime you want to create a backup:

1. Log in to http://docs.google.com.

2. Select all documents. This is trickier than it may seem, because if you have more than 50 documents, you first need to repeatedly scroll down the file listing pane, then wait a bit, then scroll down again, in order to make Google show all files. Afterwards, next to the "Select" label, click the link reading "All *X*" files (where *X* is the number of your files).

3. In the top right, you will notice a menu entry reading Download Selected Documents. (This link appears thanks to the GoogleDocsDownload script you previously installed.) Open this menu and choose Microsoft Office Files, as shown in Figure 1-26.

Figure 1-26.
All documents are selected, so it's time to click "Download Selected Documents"

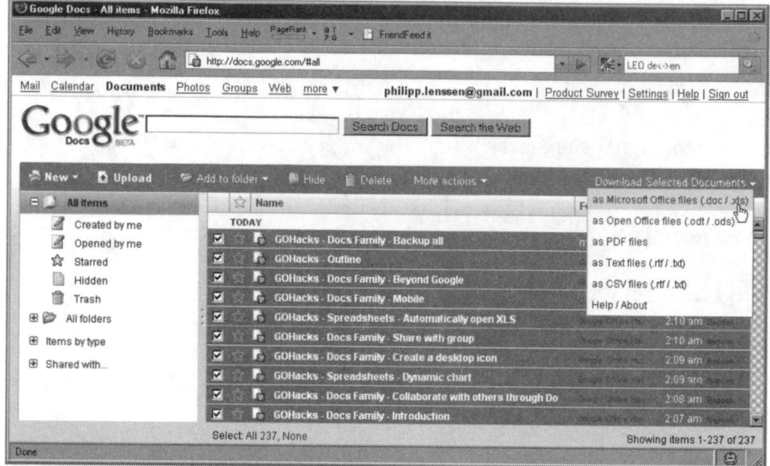

Figure 1-27.
Opening DownThemAll to download a list of links all at once

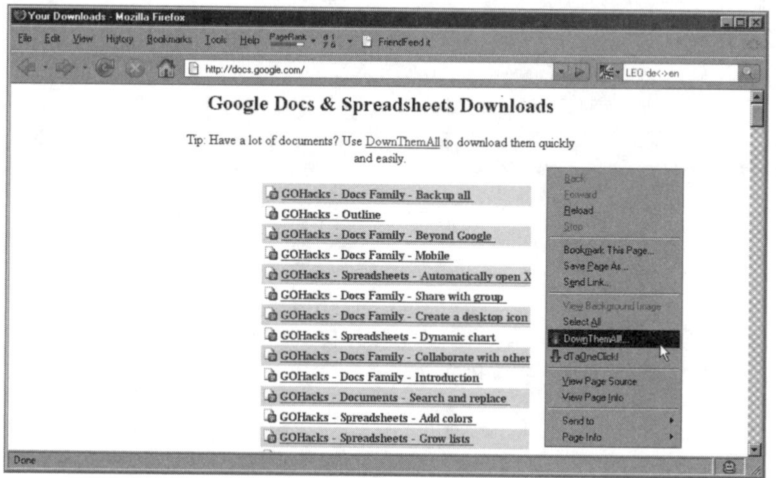

4. A new browser window opens containing links to all of your Google Docs files. Downloading them individually is tedious, but thanks to DownThemAll, you can now right-click the page to select "DownThemAll! . . ." from the context menu, as shown in Figure 1-27.

5. In the DownThemAll dialog that pops up, as shown in Figure 1-28, check the "All files" box, and then specify a place to download to by clicking the folder icon. Hit the Start button to begin downloading. Wait for the download to finish and you're done!

You now have all your documents in different formats on your hard disk. Spreadsheets are available as XLS files, and can be opened with programs like Microsoft Excel, OpenOffice Calc or, again, Google Spreadsheets **[Hack #6]**. Word processing documents get the *.doc* extension. And presentations are available as a ZIP file that contains the needed HTML, stylesheet, and image resources.

If you don't mind fiddling around at the command prompt, there's an advanced method for backing up files using a Python script. Take a look at GDataCopier at http://code.google.com/p/gdatacopier/.

Figure 1-28.
Configuring DownThemAll to start the download of all files

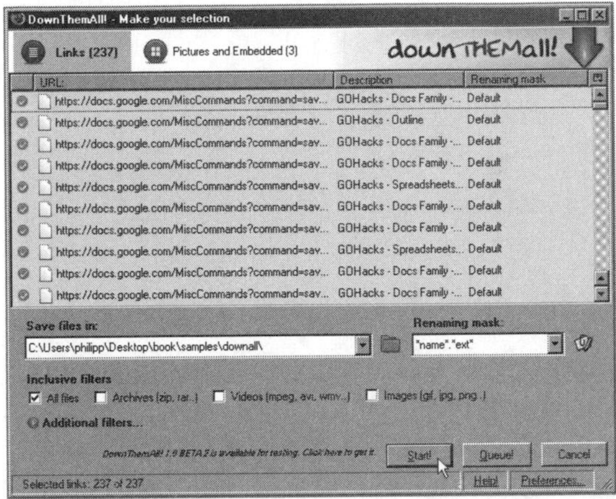

HACK 08: Beyond Google: Create Documents with Zoho, EditGrid and more

If you're not completely satisfied with the Google Docs product family, or you just want to explore other offerings to find alternative features, take a look at Zoho, EditGrid, and others.

Zoho: Online Office Suite

Zoho, similar to Google Docs, is a free online office application suite. It comes complete with a rich text editor (Zoho Writer), a spreadsheet editor (Zoho Sheet), a presentation editor (Zoho Show), and more. You can register for an account at http://zoho.com, shown in Figure 1-29.

After signing up, you'll get an email with a confirmation link. Click the link, and you are ready to create your first document. In Figure 1-30, you can see a spreadsheet listing people's ages and occupations. The average age was calculated using the AVERAGE formula. The chart graphic was inserted using the Add Chart toolbar icon, then choosing the Stacked Column 3D type. As with Google Docs, after preparing your document, you can share it with a selected group of people, or publish it as a web page for all to see.

With Zoho Writer, you can create word processing documents, as shown in Figure 1-31. You can style your document in a variety of ways, include images or smileys, run a spellchecker, or graphically create tables, to name just a few of the options. A toggle HTML source toolbar icon (labeled as "<>") allows you to edit the source of the document. You can then publish the finished document as a web page or embed it in your blog.

EditGrid: An Alternative to Google Spreadsheets, Excel, or OpenOffice.org

EditGrid, available at http://editgrid.com and shown in Figure 1-32, also allows you to create spreadsheets online. It is available as a free version as well as a more powerful "Organisation

Figure 1-29.
Zoho.com, an online alternative to the Google office suite

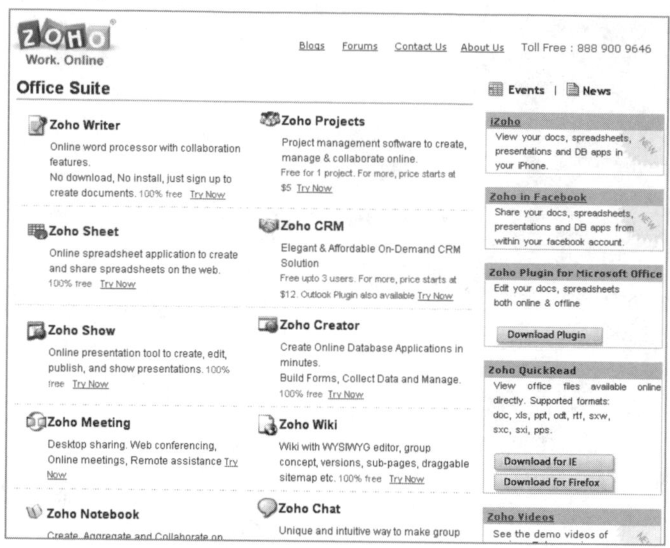

Figure 1-30.
The Zoho Sheet editor, with a list of your documents to the left

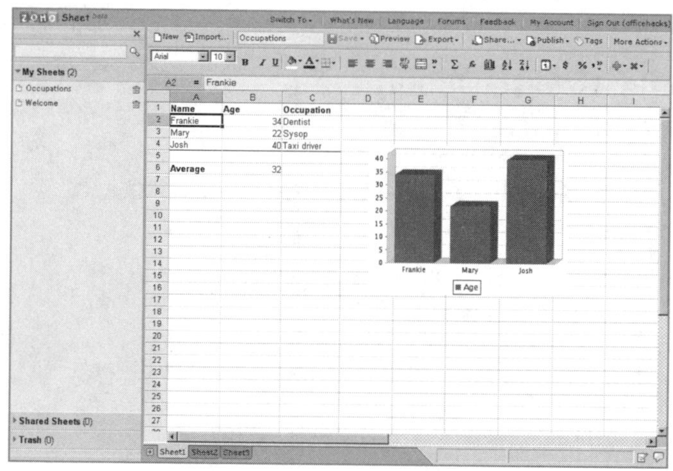

Account." Using EditGrid, you are able to create spreadsheets with 516 different formulas (that's about as many as Google Spreadsheets), and then collaborate on your data with others. Chart graphics are supported as well, as pictured in Figure 1-33. Also, EditGrid supports an API (Application Programming Interface) for developers to connect data to their own applications, similar to what Google does with their Google Spreadsheets Data API.

On top of all that, you can include data from other sources by launching the Remote Data wizard by selecting Data→Manage Remote Data. You can pick from any of the three categories: Stock Quote, Currency Exchange, and Web Data.

EditGrid's Web Data feature is particularly interesting, as it allows you to grab data from any public webpage. At http://editgrid.com/tnc/cliff/Pressure_Tracker, the EditGrid team posted an example of this functionality. The goal of the spreadsheet sample is to get the pressure value from a Hong Kong weather web page. After opening the HTML source code of the weather web page, you will see the relevant part that prints the pressure value, which goes something like this:

Figure 1-31.
Creating a document with the Zoho Writer editor

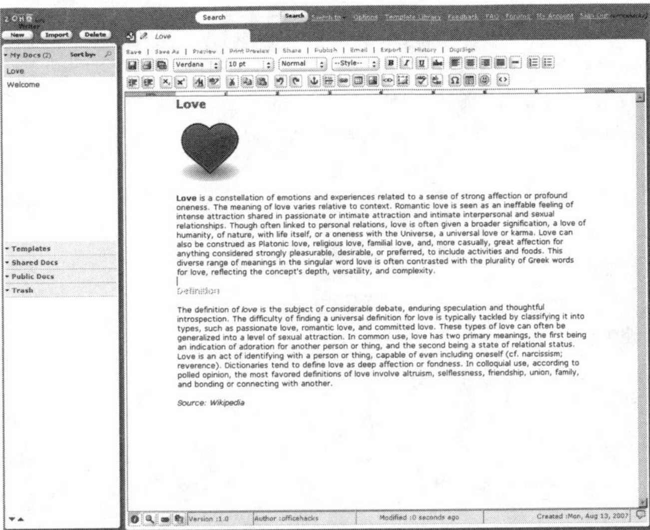

Figure 1-32.
The EditGrid home page

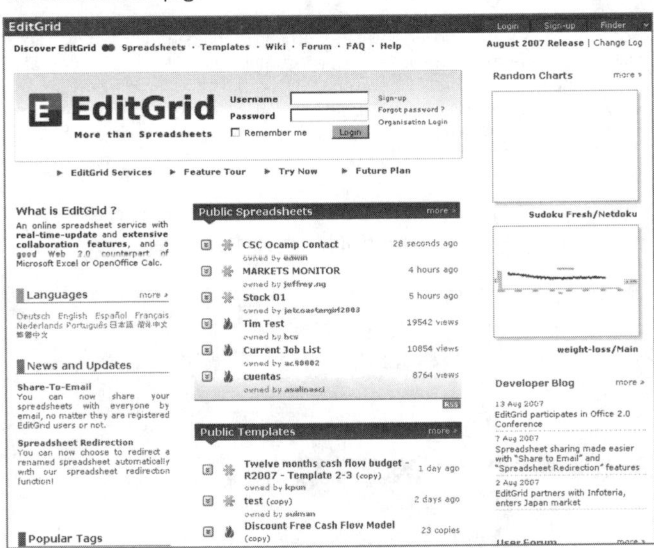


```
<HTML>
<HEAD>
 ...
<TD VALIGN="top"  CLASS="obsTextA">Pressure:</td>
<TD><IMG SRC="http://image.weather.com/web/blank.gif" ...></td>
<TD VALIGN="top"  CLASS="obsTextA">29.68 in.
<IMG SRC="http://image.weather.com/web/blank.gif" ...>
 ...
</body>
</HTML>
```

But all you need is the highlighted value "29.68". At this point, you can use the following regular expression **[Hack #13]**:

```
(?!nbsp:)Pressure:</td>.*
```

Figure 1-33.
The EditGrid main editor view

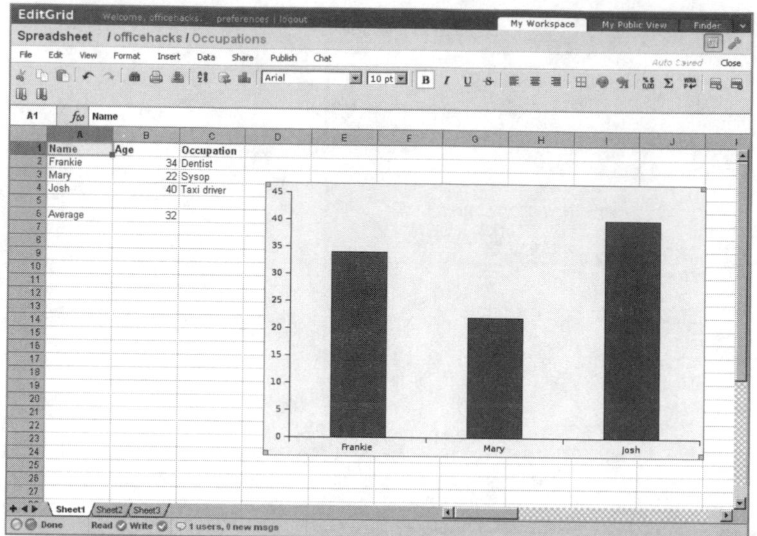

> Note that this act of so-called "screenscraping" as used by the Web Data feature is somewhat error-prone, as your regular expression may become invalid whenever the site you're scraping updates their HTML template. Additionally, it may be against a site's Terms of Service or *robots.txt* declaration file to use automated screenscraping mechanisms. If the web site has an official API, you should use that and become familiar with its Terms of Service. This is not to say that using an API is completely maintenance-free (APIs sometimes get discontinued, or change their protocol in such a way that you'll need to rewrite your applications).

This expression retrieves a much smaller portion of the full HTML page. You can now use EditGrid's RIGHT function to get just the number in question and have it display in another spreadsheet cell of yours, as shown in Figure 1-34.

Figure 1-34.
Accessing live data from web sites using EditGrid's Web Data feature

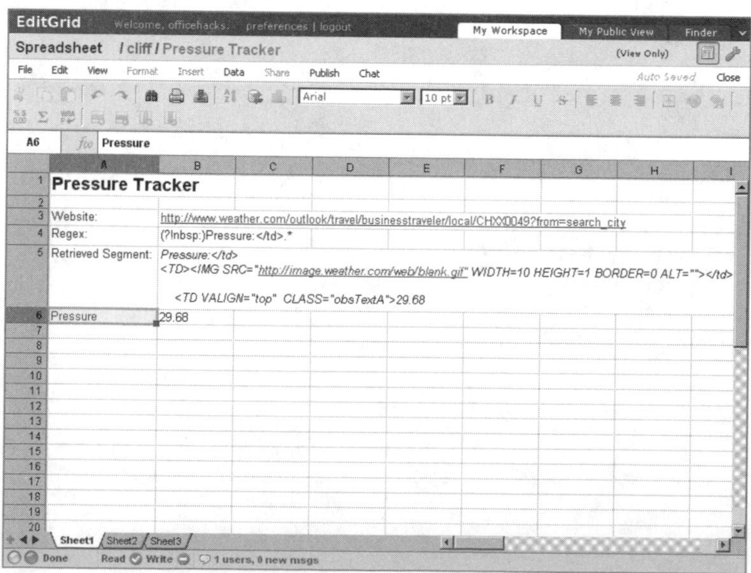

ThinkFree's Online Office Suite

ThinkFree (http://www.thinkfree.com) is another online application provider, offering free online word processing, spreadsheet, and presentation editors. ThinkFree's programs come in two flavors each: Quick Edit and Power Edit. The quick editing lacks some features that competitor's tools may have, but the power editing is a more complete application, and it looks a lot like Microsoft's Office suite. Note that the Power Edit mode needs to install a set of Java files on your machine before you edit the first time.

As you can see pictured in Figure 1-35 (a word processing document in Quick Edit mode) and Figure 1-36 (a spreadsheet in Power Edit mode), both program variants show advertisements on the righthand side of your document.

Figure 1-35.
The ThinkFree word processing editor: Quick Edit mode

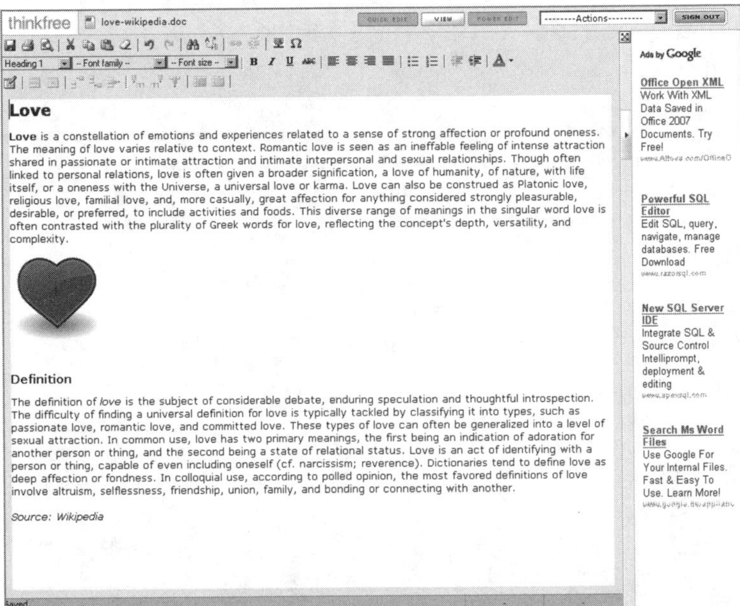

Figure 1-36.
Editing a spreadsheet with ThinkFree: Power Edit mode

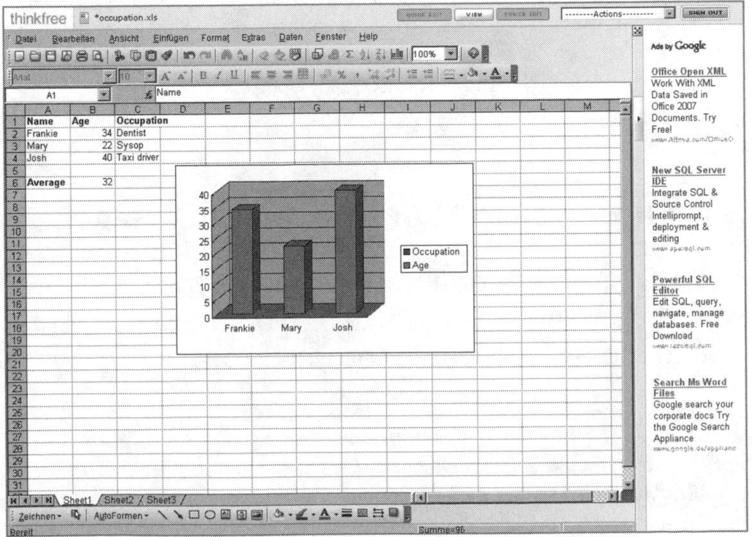

02 THE GOOGLE DOCS FAMILY: GOOGLE DOCUMENTS

Writing on paper—like the kind made from the papyrus plant and used in ancient Egypt, or the kind you'd buy in a store today—may seem old-fashioned, but compare it to your typical digital word processor today (like Microsoft Word, or OpenOffice.org Writer)...

On paper, you can use any type of symbol, without having to worry about installing fonts. You can easily include your drawings without increasing the file size. You can get together with a small group to scribble along on the same paper in real time. You can underline, strikethrough, and use arrows and quick charts without knowing a single shortcut or location of a menu entry. Also, paper won't ask you to register before using it.

What does Google documents (see Chapter 1 for an overview and introduction) have that paper doesn't, anyway? Besides not requiring trees to be felled in production, that is. Here's an overview:

- With Google documents, you can view the editing history of a file. This means that if you want to, you can compare the current state of the document with one from two months ago, and replace the new version with the old version if necessary.
- With Google documents, you can collaborate in real time with a group of people who are not in the same room, or even in the same country.
- You can check the spelling of the document, get a count of all the words in the document, or search and replace within the text.
- Google documents allows you to let someone else see your file without you having to make a copy of it—they will simply be referred to your source document, provided you grant them access to it.

Now, papyrus paper would last about 200 years in European conditions. It's hard to tell how long your Google documents writings will last. Writely, the predecessor to Google documents (before Google acquired Upstartle, the creators of Writely), has only been around for two years. But if you're suspicious about the longevity of this medium, there's still the option to print out any Google document.

HACK 10: Let Others Subscribe to Your Document Changes

Using Google Docs' RSS feed of document changes, you can let others keep up with the revisions you make to a public document. All they need is a feed reader application or web browser.

Say you're using Google Docs to write a project to-do list **[Hack #68]** for a group. There are two items on the list already, as shown in Figure 2-1: *1. Have someone get the milk*, and *2. Unscrew the light bulb.* You now want to add a third item. Docs already allows you to let others see your document, or edit along if you like. But how do they know when you've changed the document?

Figure 2-1.
A project to-do list for your team

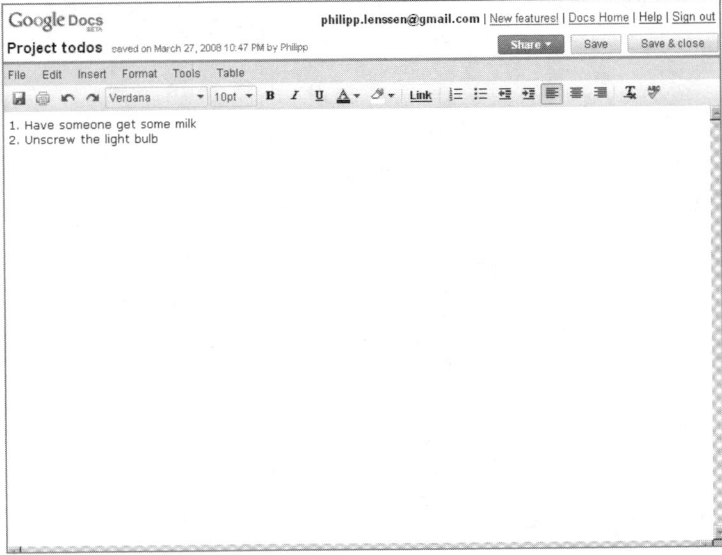

One way to keep everyone up to date is to publish your document changes via an RSS feed. An RSS feed is a web-based subscription format that allows the browser or a separate client program (the RSS reader) to display frequently updated content, like a blog, a news site—or your Google document's change log.

Before you can publish the RSS feed, your document must be published. Publishing a document doesn't that mean you make it fully public; only those who know the document address will be able to access it, and this address won't automatically be listed in search results (and the address is not easy to guess either).

To make your document public, hit Share→"Publish as web page" and click the "Publish document" button. You should also activate the "Automatically re-publish when changes are made" checkbox.

 Anyone you send the document URL to can also pass it on for others to see (and if someone posts it on a discussion board, it might even start appearing in search results). Public documents aren't password-protected—use Share→"Share with others" to share confidential docs with only the users you specify.

Note that you can stop publishing later at any time.

Now you need to find the RSS feed's address. Click Share→"Share with others" and the link starting with "View RSS", as pictured in Figure 2-2. A new window opens, from which you can bookmark or copy the URL. Send the URL to your collaborators and let them subscribe to it. Your collaborators can subscribe via their browser's native feed reader option, or you can point them to a standalone RSS reader like Google Reader (see Chapter 8) at http://reader.google.com, as shown in Figure 2-3—and you're done. You can now add a third item to your list (for example, *3. Get help in case unscrewing of the light bulb goes wrong*), and others will be alerted of your changes when they check their RSS reader. Your team can also set up a program like rss2email at http://rss2email.infogami.com to automatically get an email whenever the RSS feed changes.

Figure 2-2.
The Share mode, including the "View RSS feed . . . " link

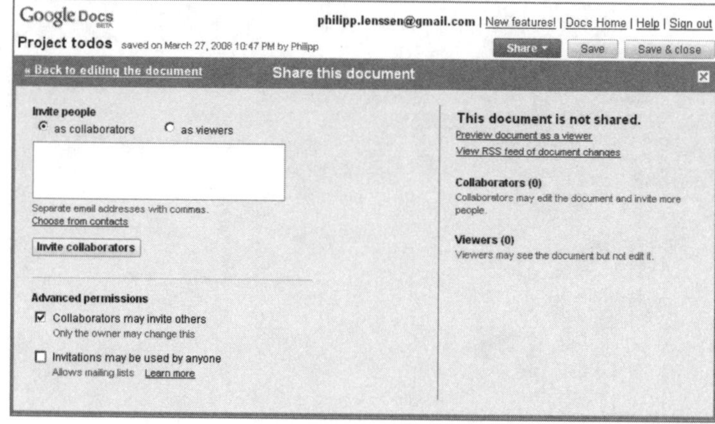

Figure 2-3.
Google Reader, now subscribed to the to-do list's change history

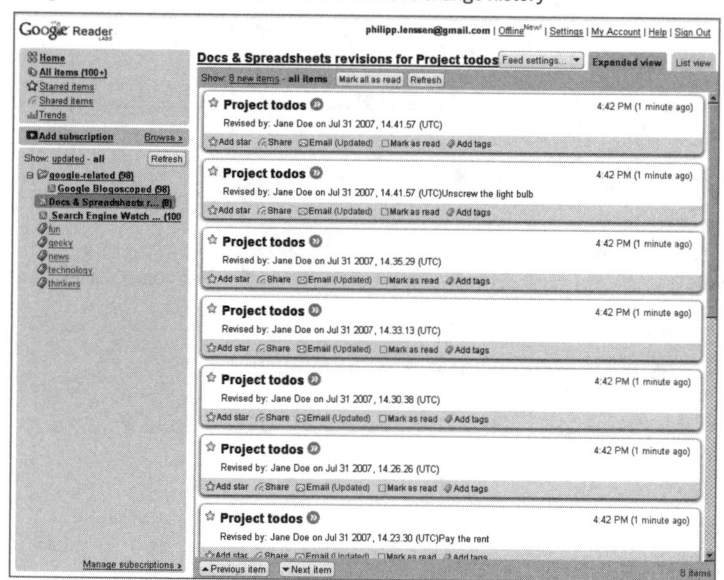

HACK 11: Blog with Google Docs

With the help of Google Docs' publishing options, you can use the Docs editor to blog.

A blog helps you to communicate with a group of people at once (see Chapter 10). It's your very own newspaper, or, if you prefer, your public diary. Done right, blogs (short for "web logs") are more of a two-way conversation than a monologue. People can comment on whatever you write, and if you integrate the comments into your existing and future posts, the blog becomes a form of dynamic, collaborative writing. Blogs can also be a great way to get your head around any subject; blog about something, and you might end up becoming an expert in this field. However, don't expect to talk with a large audience immediately, or to end up as expert in a field after a week—both parts take time and dedication, and even the best blogging tool in the world can't automate this effort.

Blogging tools always come with a built-in editor; that's how they make web publishing as easy as possible. But you can also use Google Docs as an alternative blogging editor.

Let's create a Docs-powered blog. For this example, I'll create a movie review site.

First, you need to sign up with Google's Blogger at http://blogger.com to create a blog. You can use your Google Account login for this service, then choose a display name, and accept the Terms of Service, as shown in Figure 2-4. Now click the "Create your Blog . . . " button and set up a blog with your preferred title, address, and template, as shown in Figure 2-5.

Figure 2-4.
Signing up for Blogger

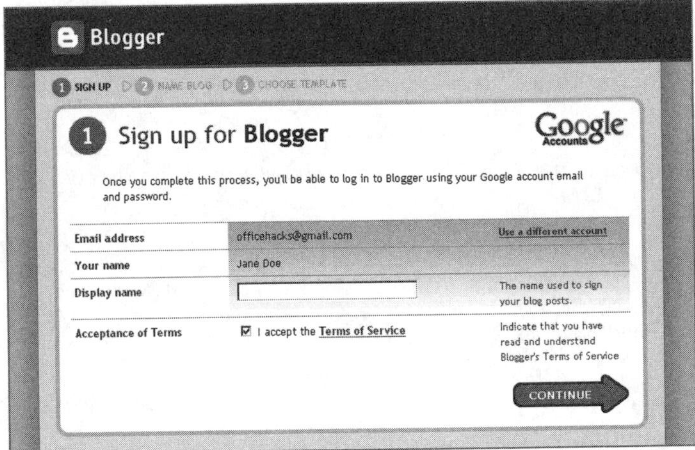

Figure 2-5.
Picking a blog title and address

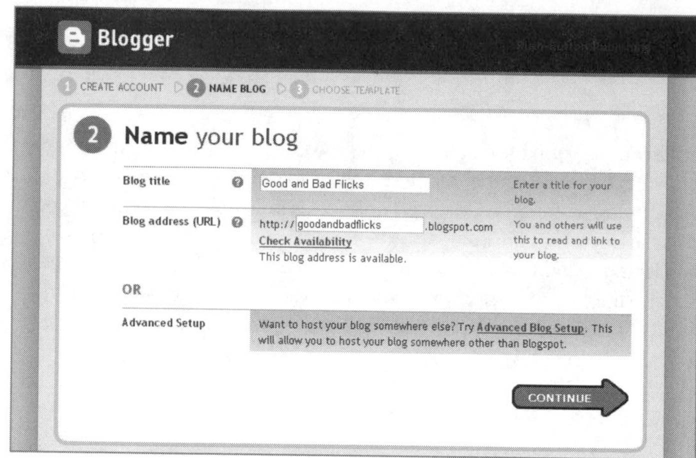

By default, your blog will be hosted at Blogspot.com. In this case, the blog is named "Good and Bad Flicks" and its address is http://goodandbadflicks.blogspot.com. If you prefer, you can make the blog invitation-only, which means you get to choose who can read it. To do this, use the Settings→Permissions→Blog Readers options; otherwise, everyone can read your blog.

Now that your blog is created, you can go to Google Docs at http://docs.google.com and create a new document as usual, including images, headlines, links, and more, as shown in Figure 2-6.

When you're done creating the document, click the "blog site settings" link in the "Publish as web page" dialog. Enter your username and other information exactly like you did when you signed up with Blogger. Or, if you're using another blogging tool like LiveJournal or WordPress **[Hack #114]**, use your credentials from that service.

Confirm by clicking OK. You can now click the "Post to blog" button and view the result on your blog, as pictured in Figure 2-7!

In case you are using your own server or domain for your blog, you can also select "My own server/custom" on top of Google Docs' Blog Site Settings dialog, and provide your blog's API Access URL. MovableType, for instance, uses the URL http://YOURBLOG/PATH/TO/mt-xmlrpc.cgi for this. A more extensive list of Access URLs can be opened by following the link reading "Click here for yours" in Google's dialog.

Figure 2-6.
Blogging a movie review in Google Docs

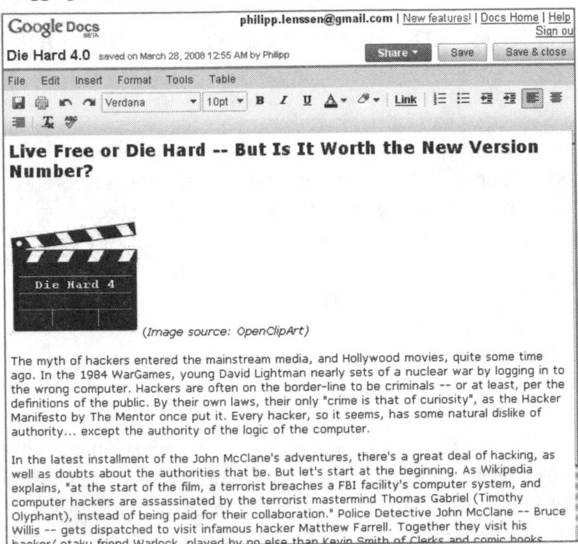

Figure 2-7.
The review is now live at the blog

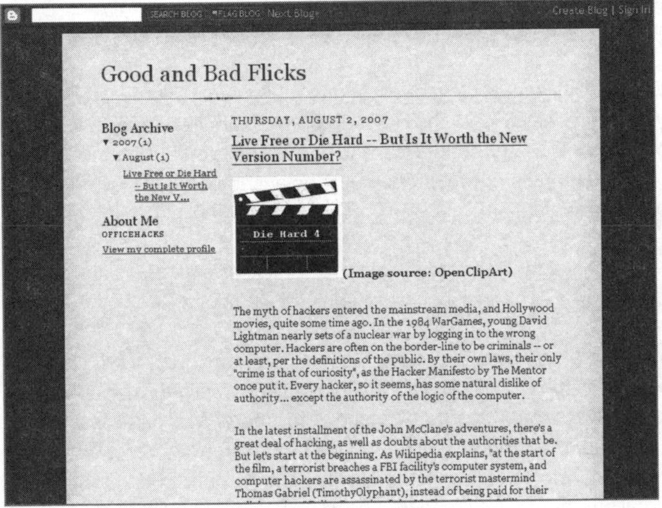

HACK 12: Insert Special Characters Into Your Documents

Find out about Unicode characters, and how you can use them in your Google Docs documents.

There are more letters around than the ones you see on the keyboard. In fact, there are more keyboards around than the one you're used looking at. In Germany, for instance, the top letters row starts with "QWERTZ" instead of the English "QWERTY," and you'll find the "umlaut" character keys Ö, Ü, and Ä on the right side.

But when the character you want isn't on your keyboard at all, you need to look into software to get what you need. Chinese users, for instance, use IMEs (Input Method Editors), which allow you to enter basic letters (Pinyin), which are then "transliterated" into the Chinese symbol. Google also offers an IME of their own for free download at http://tools.google.com/pinyin/.

On Mac OS X, when you need to enter a special character, click the input menu, which is a flag icon in the menu bar (if it's not visible, go to System Preferences→International→Input Menu and select "Show input menu in menu bar") and select Show Character Palette. You can search for characters using this palette, and double-click on the desired character to insert it. In Windows, you can see this character table by going to Start→Programs→Accessories→System Tools→Character Map. You can switch to different groups in this list, and copy any letter to then paste it into your document.

> On Windows, you can also type special characters in Google Docs, or any other text editor, by holding down the Alt-key on your keyboard and pressing a number combination on your numpad; Alt-0169 results in ©, and Alt-0165 results in ¥.

To accommodate all the special characters across languages, and to make sure that the letter you typed is also seen the same way on the receiving end, the Unicode Consortium (a nonprofit made up of representatives from the computer industry, academia, and community) created the Unicode character listing in the early 1990s, and many programs today use the accompanying Unicode Transformation Format (UTF) for text transfer.

Google Docs also has a native Unicode character list for you to pick from. Pick Insert→"Special characters" from the editor menu. A dialog like the one shown in Figure 2-8 will appear.

You can select any character from the dialog to paste it into your document, or you can switch to one of the other groups—"Asian characters," "Wingdings" (visible only on Internet Explorer on Windows, at least among the browsers we tested), and "Advanced"—for more. Wingdings is a font, originally created by Microsoft, made up of symbols like a telephone or a mailbox. And the advanced dialog gives you the option to choose any Unicode character you like. The number 8634 results in a circular arrow ↺. The hexadecimal number 0x2665 shows a heart ♥. The number 9835 shows a note ♫, and 9730 an umbrella ☂. Typing the hexadecimal value 0x2603, on the other hand, and increasing the font size quite a bit, results in the following:

Figure 2-8.
The Google Docs text editor offers you a list of special characters to pick from

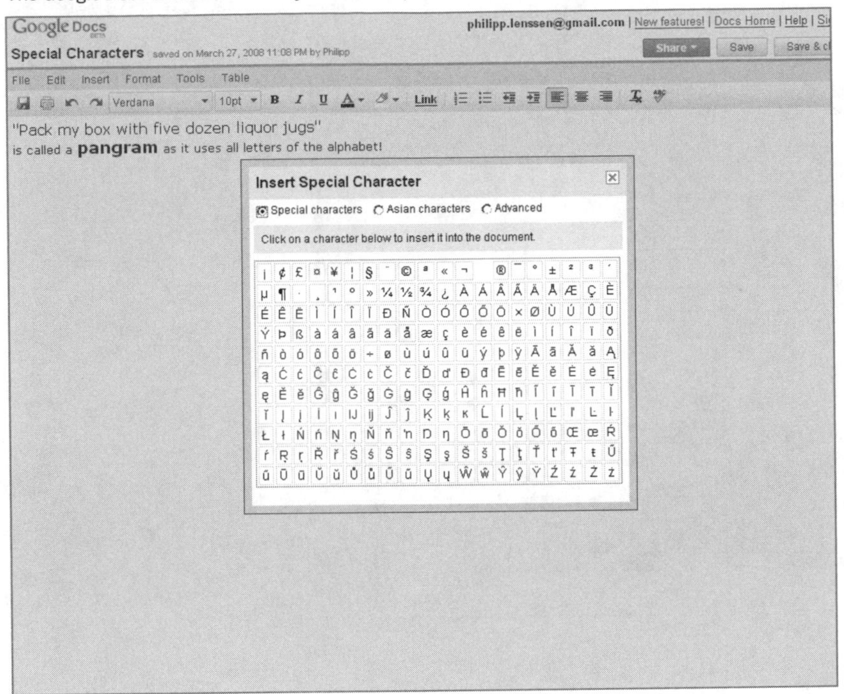

HACK 13: Search and Replace Text Using Regular Expressions

Want to go beyond basic search and replace? Hack up some "regex" wizardry.

Google Documents allows you to search and replace text in your document by selecting File→Find and replace (see Figure 2-9). But this feature permits more than plain replacement of one snippet with another. You get the full range of so-called *regular expressions* (select the "Regular expression" checkbox), a mini programming language that deserves (and has) a book's worth of coverage; Jeffrey E. F. Friedl's *Mastering Regular Expressions*, Third Edition (O'Reilly) goes into this topic in great detail. The regular expression (also known as *regex*) syntax may seem cryptic at first, but once you learn it, it offers a quick and powerful way to replace text in your documents.

Here are some regular expression replacement scenarios, along with an explanation of the syntax so that you can adapt this for your own needs.

 You cannot use Undo to roll back changes made with Google's search-and-replace function. Save your document before making a change if you're unsure about the results. Sometimes replacements—especially using regular expression syntax—may do more than you expected them to do. For instance, unless the "Match whole word" option is checked, replacing "federation" with "federations" would also change "confederation" to "confederations".

Additionally, be aware that you also cannot always roll back a change by closing the document to reopen it, because sometimes Google Docs documents will be autosaved even when you don't choose to save it (for instance, this happens when you switch to the "Edit HTML" mode, but it also happens in other circumstances). In that case, you need to revert to an older version of your document by switching to File→Revision history.

Figure 2-9.
The Find/Replace function for Google documents. This feature was in Alpha mode at the time of writing, meaning it's even less reliable than a Beta release.

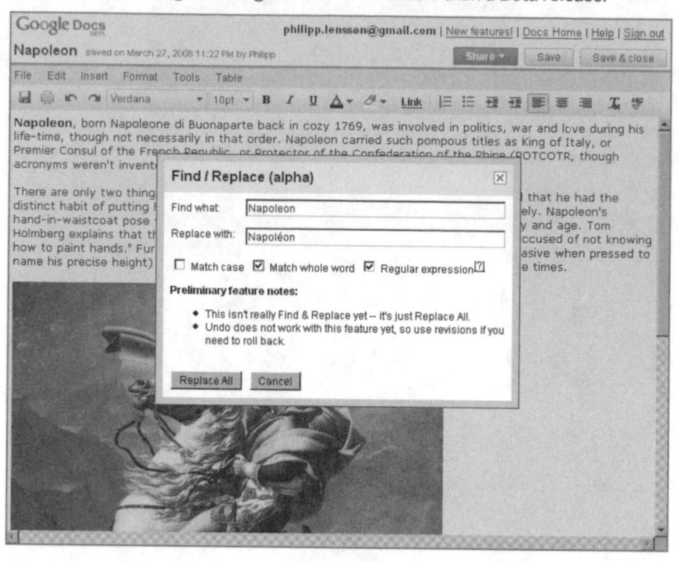

A plain non–regular expression replacement
Find: `Napoleon`
Replace with: `Napoléon`
Explanation: Although the search-and-replace function supports regular expressions, you don't need to use the special regular expression syntax. You can simply enter two plain text strings. In this example, all occurrences of the word "Napoleon" are replaced with "Napoléon".

Removing references to endnotes
Find: `\[\d+\]`
Replace with: *leave blank*
Explanation: Given a text containing references to endnotes in square brackets, such as "[1]", how would you go about removing everything in square brackets? Removing the notes is easy, as you can just select the end portion of the document and hit the delete key. The answer to removing any digits surrounded by square brackets is shown in this regular expression. In this regex, you have to escape the square brackets using `\`, because as you'll see in "Replacing obfuscated email addresses with real ones," the square brackets would otherwise have a special meaning. Within the brackets, the `\d` indicates any digit, and the + specifies "one or more".

Replacing obfuscated email addresses with real ones
Find: `([A-Za-z0-9_\+\.]+) at (\w+) dot (\w+)`
Replace with: `$1@$2.$3`
Explanation: Sometimes, email addresses found on the web use special syntax like "someone at example dot com" to defend from spammers. In this case, the real email address behind the obfuscated one would be **someone@example.com**.

This regular expression automates the process by looking for a sequence of characters that are acceptable in an email address username: all alphabetic characters (`A-Z` and `a-z`), numbers (`0-9`), and some symbols (+ and `.`). The + and `.` symbols need to be prefixed with the *escape character* (`\`) so that they are not interpreted as a special character. All of these characters are grouped in brackets, which denotes they are a *character class* (that is, they can match any one of these symbols). The + immediately following the character class specifies that they can match one or more of these characters. After the email username, the regular expression matches a few more things: the word "at" surrounded by spaces, one or more alphanumeric characters (`\w` is an abbreviation for `[A-Za-z0-9_]`), the word "dot" surrounded by spaces, and finally one or more alphanumeric characters.

The replacement uses numeric references to items that the regular expression "captured": anything within parentheses is stuffed into `$1` (for the first set of parentheses), `$2` (for the second), `$3`, and so on.

This regular expression can match only one particular type of obfuscated email address, and even so, it has its limits. What if the email address were "someone at mail dot example dot com"? Perhaps after studying the regular expressions in this hack, and reading up some more on the topic, you'll be able to solve that problem.

Changing a date format
Find: `((Jan|Feb|Mar|Apr|May|Jun|Jul|Aug|Sep|Oct|Nov|Dec).*) (\d\d?), (\d{4})`
Replace with: `$3 $1, $4`
Explanation: If you want to replace one date format with another, this expression comes in handy. It looks for all occurrences of the format "MONTHNAME DAY, YEAR" to replace them with "DAY MONTH, YEAR". The portion of the regular expression that matches the month uses a feature called *alternation*: various alternatives are expressed between the pipe (`|`) symbol. So the first grouping (`$1`) will match Jan or Feb or Mar, and so on. In order to match either the three-letter abbreviation or the full name, the alternatives are followed by `.*`, which could match anything, including "Mary" or "Octal". What we're banking on here is that anything of the form specified (a word, a number, a comma, and another number) is very likely to be a date.

Did you notice that we skipped a number in the replacement expression? That's because the second grouping (`$2`) refers to the second set of parentheses, which are also the same parentheses that separate the alternatives. So if `$1` matched "January", `$2` would have only matched "Jan".

Removing all HTML tags
Find: `</?[^>]*>`
Replace with: [leave blank]
Explanation: Suppose you have some text that is full of unwanted HTML text, like `<p>` or `<em>`. This regular expression removes all those tags for you. It looks for any string that:

- Begins with an opening less-than sign (such as `<p>` or `<p align="left">`)
- Optionally (the `?` that follows `/` indicates the `/` is optional) has `/` as the second character (as in `</p>`)

Then it grabs everything (any character except a greater-than sign: `[>]*`) up to the closing greater-than sign (>). Because Google Docs works line-by-line, it is unable to remove tags that span more than one line, such as:

```
<p align="left"
   class="note">
```

Preceding all domain names with "http://"
Find: `(([-\w]+\.)+[-\w]+)`
Replace with: `http://$1`
Explanation: If your text contains a lot of references to domain names, like "Please go to www.acmeinc.com to see our product page," you can automatically add the string "http://" before each of them. This regular expression works by first looking for groups of letters and numbers (`\w`, which is shorthand for `[0-9a-zA-Z_]`) and hyphens, followed by a period, such as "foo.", "www.", and "mail-server." Then it looks for a group of letters, numbers,

and hyphens without a period (a top-level domain name such as com, edu, or net). So this regular expression would match www.oreilly.com, using the following steps:

www.
oreilly.
com

As you've seen earlier, the `$1` refers to the group matched by the first (in this case, outer) set of parentheses. The inner set of parentheses could be referred to by `$2`, but it's not needed because it's a subset of what you're interested in.

Note that when matching hyphens, the `-` needs to come at the beginning of the `[ ]` group or be escaped with `\` because it has special meaning within `[` and `]`, as you saw in "Replacing obfuscated email addresses with real ones."

Hacking the Hack

Sometimes you want to replace not just within the visible text, but also within the underlying HTML source. However when you switch to the HTML mode for a document, the Edit→Find and replace menu disappears. But you can work around this limitation by using a *bookmarklet*, a browser bookmark containing JavaScript. JavaScript also natively supports regular expressions.

First, create a new bookmarklet as described in **[Hack #16]**. The basic JavaScript needed for this is the following replacement function, where "a" is the (regular expression–based) string to find, and "b" the string to replace with:

```
javascript:(function(){
    var ta = document.getElementById("wys_textarea");
    ta.value =ta.value.replace("a", "b");
})()
```

To execute this function, create a bookmarklet for it and click the bookmark while in the "Edit HTML" mode of your document.

But you can take this much further by specifying a function in place of "b". Every time that "a" is matched, the function will be invoked, and the value that it returns will replace "a". For example, suppose you want to look for all occurrences of an <h3> tag to then insert a new anchor tag in the form of `<h3><a name="#header1"></a>`, where "1" will be incremented throughout the document. You can use a JavaScript bookmarklet to do this. First, initialize a variable called `counter`. Then, create a function that adds 1 to the counter and returns the replacement string. Then, instead of specifying "b", put in the name of the function (`getNextH3` in this example):

```
javascript:(
  function() {
     counter = 0;
     function getNextH3() {
       counter++;
       return "<h3><a name=\"#header" + counter.toString() + "\"></a>";
     }
    var ta = document.getElementById("wys_textarea");
    ta.value =ta.value.replace(/<h3>/g, getNextH3);
})()
```

Note that instead of a search term of the form "a", the term comes in between / and /. This another way to specify a regular expression in JavaScript ("a" and `/a/` are equivalent). Using these characters allows you to put a modifier at the end of the regular expression, in this case "g", which specifies global search-and-replace. (Otherwise, you'd replace only the first match).

For more information on regular expressions in JavaScript, see Danny Goodman's *JavaScript & DHTML Cookbook*, Second Edition (O'Reilly).

—Brian Jepson and Philipp Lenssen

HACK 14: "Google Docs Light" for Web Research: Google Notebook

Set up your Google Notebook to copy snippets and jot down thoughts while surfing the Web.

You can think of Google Notebook as a lightweight sibling of Google Docs. As both a browser extension and a feature added to your Google search results, a Google Notebook is something you "carry around" while surfing; it lets you save small pieces of text or links for future reference. You can also use it as a collaborative tool for projects in which a whole team is doing research on a specific topic.

Let's just imagine our topic at hand is pets and pet food, for our new web site PetFoodInfo.example.com, and that we want to acquire more information in preparation for building the site. We'll start by heading over to the Google Notebook home page at http://google.com/notebook to install Notebook. After signing in with your Google Account **[Hack #1]** and agreeing to the terms of service, the download for the Google Notebook browser extension will start. (Accept the security dialog if one pops up, and reopen all browser windows if you're asked to.)

At the time of this writing, the browsers currently supported are Internet Explorer 6 and later (Windows XP only) and Firefox 1.5+ (Windows XP and Vista, Mac OS X, and Linux).

Now when you visit the Notebook home page, you can create a new notebook and title it "Pets and pet food." Notes that you add here are saved as you go, as shown in Figure 2-10.

What's more, you now have a Notebook gadget added right to your browser, which you can expand to add notes to while browsing any web page. Check the bottom right of your browser for the "Open Notebook" icon; clicking it expands the menu, as pictured in Figure 2-11. From the Yahoo! Pets home

Figure 2-10.
The Google Notebook homepage after signing in

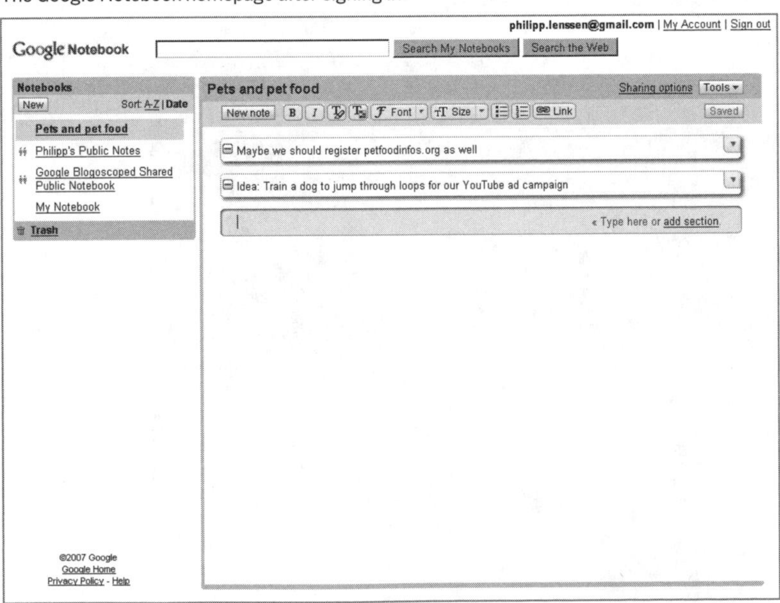

page, a note reading "We need more cat content!" was added. The link below the note was generated by dragging and dropping a link from that page into the note; in similar fashion, you can also copy text found on any page.

Also, on Google search result pages, you will now find a link reading "Note this" below snippets, as shown in Figure 2-12. Click it and the link turns into a "Duly noted" message, and a Notebook window pops up adding the result link and snippet as a new note (on Google results pages, this works even when you don't have the Notebook browser extension installed).

Collaborative notes

To share your notes with friends, family, or other members of your team, select your notebook on the Notebook home page and click the "Sharing options" link on top. You can then invite collaborators by listing their emails one by one (comma-separated) and clicking the "Save Settings" button. (Note that people you invite do not need the Notebook browser extension, though they do need a Google Account to sign in.) Jane, the user I've invited in Figure 2-13, will now receive an invitation email and can then edit along in the same notebook, at the same time I do. After a short delay (a few seconds, or whenever you select Tools→Refresh), any changes made are synchronized on both ends.

Converting a Notebook to a Google Docs document

If you want to, you can convert your Google Notebook to a Google Docs text document at any time. Select Tools→Export to Google Docs from the Notebook menu and a new document opens, which you can then edit as usual. (Note that your new Docs text will not inherit the sharing options of the Notebook, so you will have to configure them again if you want the same users to have access to the new document.)

Figure 2-11.
Opening the Google Notebook (bottom right) on the Yahoo! Pets home page to add a note

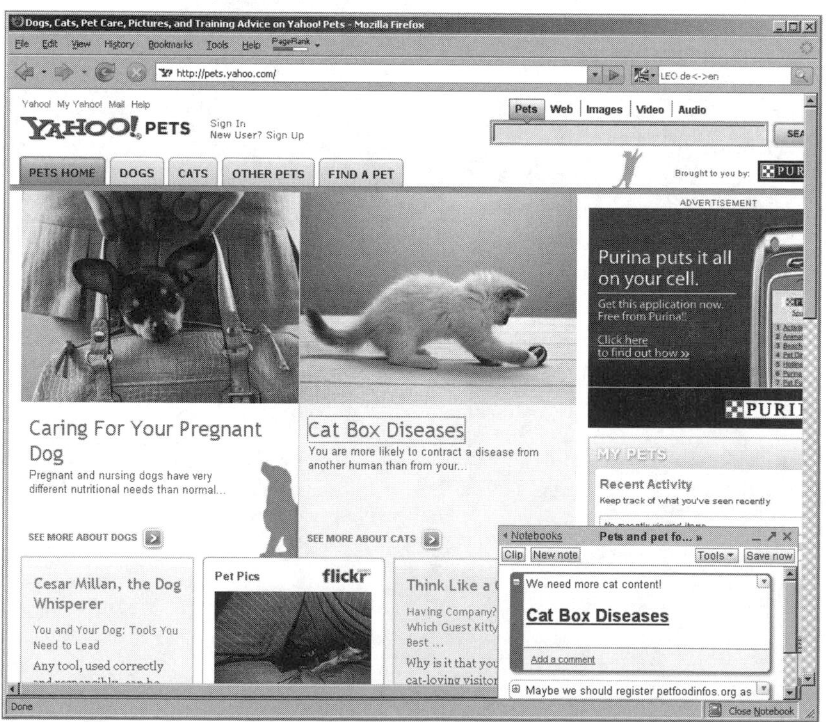

Figure 2-12.
Noting the third web result in a search for pet food

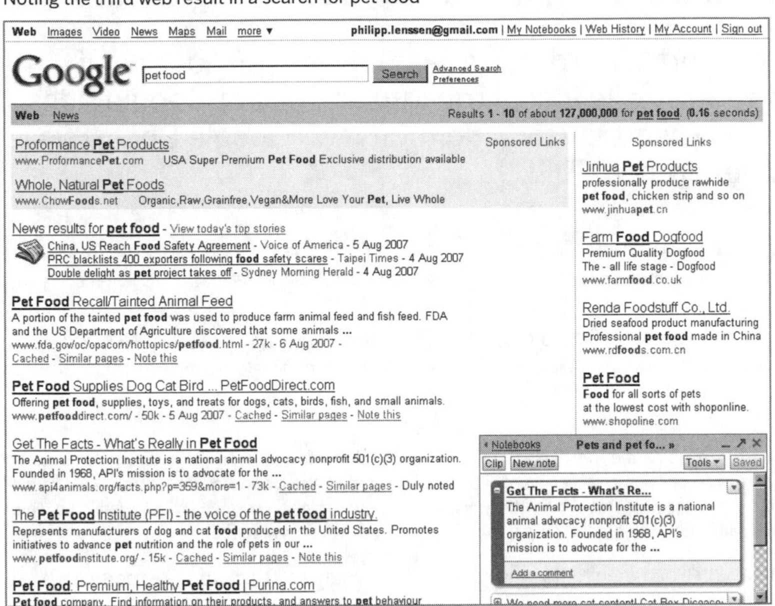

Figure 2-13.
Jane added comments to the notes; as a collaborator, she can also edit any note itself, or add new notes to this Notebook

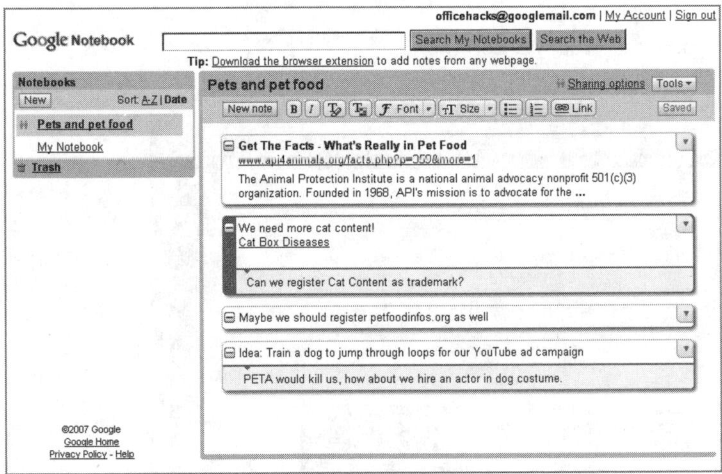

HACK 15: Convert a Word File Into a PDF with Google Docs

If you need to convert a Word document into a PDF—or one of many other formats—take it on a trip into and out of Google Docs. Even if you have no need to store it or edit it on Google Docs, this is a quick way to generate a PDF!

Google Docs has both import and export functionality. Using the two in combination means that you can convert documents; for instance, you can upload a Word document and save it as a PDF file.

To upload a Word file, go to the Google Docs home page (http://docs.google.com) and select Upload. In this example, I'm uploading a Word file containing a story by the Grimm Brothers, as pictured in Figure 2-14.

> The maximum size of an uploaded Word file, including embedded images, was 500 KB at the time of this writing. If you need to convert a larger Word file, consider installing Adobe Acrobat, the free CutePDF (http://www.cutepdf.com), or the free OpenOffice.org (http://www.openoffice.org), which can also save documents as PDFs. Mac OS X can create PDFs natively from any application that can print.

After the upload finishes, you'll be taken to the newly uploaded document. Click the File menu and select Save as PDF as shown in Figure 2-15. You will now be able to download the PDF, as shown in Figure 2-16. How well the layout survives the conversion greatly depends on the document. For simple documents, the results are usually good, but for more complex ones you will see some layout changes.

Figure 2-14.
The source document in Word (with an illustration by Elisabeth Maria Anna Jerichau-Baumann)

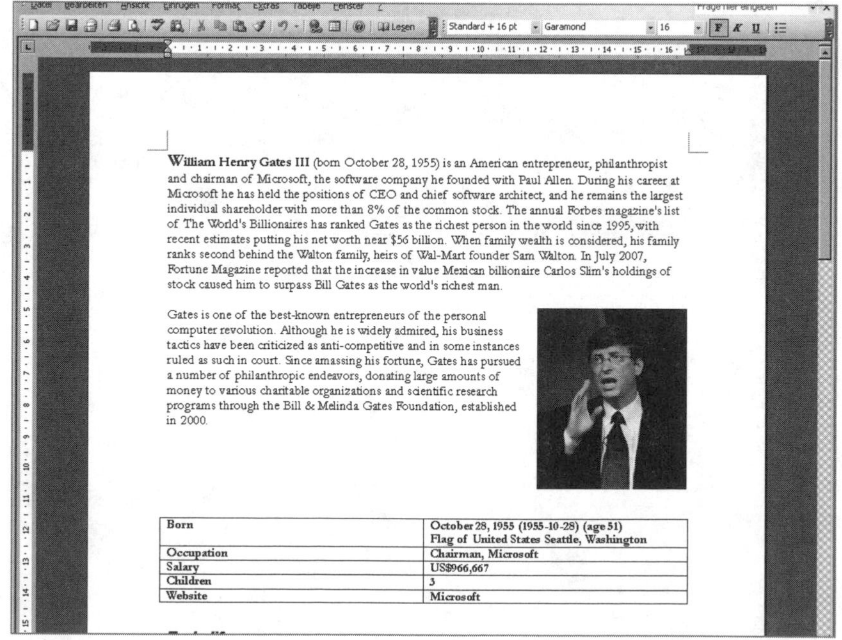

William Henry Gates III (born October 28, 1955) is an American entrepreneur, philanthropist and chairman of Microsoft, the software company he founded with Paul Allen. During his career at Microsoft he has held the positions of CEO and chief software architect, and he remains the largest individual shareholder with more than 8% of the common stock. The annual Forbes magazine's list of The World's Billionaires has ranked Gates as the richest person in the world since 1995, with recent estimates putting his net worth near $56 billion. When family wealth is considered, his family ranks second behind the Walton family, heirs of Wal-Mart founder Sam Walton. In July 2007, Fortune Magazine reported that the increase in value Mexican billionaire Carlos Slim's holdings of stock caused him to surpass Bill Gates as the world's richest man.

Gates is one of the best-known entrepreneurs of the personal computer revolution. Although he is widely admired, his business tactics have been criticized as anti-competitive and in some instances ruled as such in court. Since amassing his fortune, Gates has pursued a number of philanthropic endeavors, donating large amounts of money to various charitable organizations and scientific research programs through the Bill & Melinda Gates Foundation, established in 2000.

Born	**October 28, 1955 (1955-10-28) (age 51) Flag of United States Seattle, Washington**
Occupation	**Chairman, Microsoft**
Salary	**US$966,667**
Children	**3**
Website	**Microsoft**

Figure 2-15.
The same document imported into Google Docs

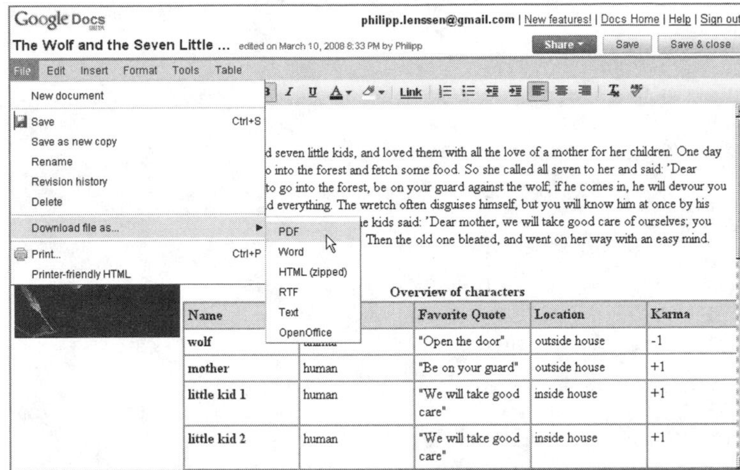

Figure 2-16.
And finally, the document as PDF

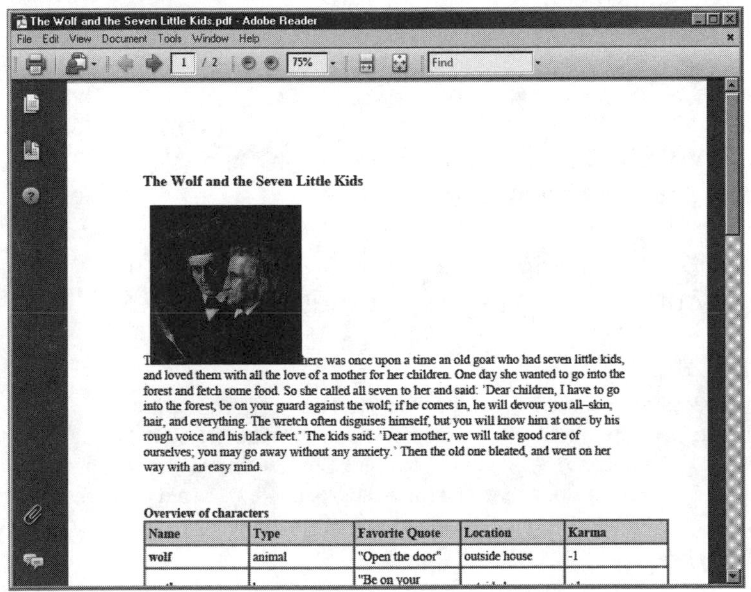

Google Docs supports a number of document formats, and the list of supported formats changes from time to time. Here's the list that was current as of the time of this writing:

File types you can *import* into **Google Docs documents**:

- HTML, text, Microsoft Word, Rich Text Format, OpenOffice document, StarOffice

File types you can *export* from **Google Docs documents**:

- HTML, text, Microsoft Word, Rich Text Format, OpenOffice document, PDF

File types you can *import* into **Google Spreadsheets**:

- Comma-Separated Values files, Microsoft Excel, OpenOffice spreadsheet

File types you can *export* from **Google Spreadsheets**:

- HTML, text, Comma-Separated Values files, Microsoft Excel, OpenOffice spreadsheet

File types you can *export* from **Google Presentations**:

- HTML

File types you can *import* into **Google Presentations**:

- Microsoft PowerPoint (PPT and PPS)

HACK 16: Write a JavaScript Bookmarklet to Transmogrify Your Documents

Use some JavaScript trickery to generate tables of contents for your Google Documents and perform other complex text manipulations.

When you create a word processing document in Google Docs, you can turn any line into a headline by clicking the Style button to select Header 1 (for the main headline), Header 2 (for subsequent headlines) and so on. You can then publish the document by using Share→"Publish as web page". But what if you've created a document so long that it needs a table of contents to aid your readers? Long web pages often use a linked table of contents at the top of the document; the reader clicks on it, and is automatically taken to the section of interest.

Creating such a table of contents manually in Google Docs can be a tedious job. You would have to select your headlines one by one and choose Insert→Bookmark for each. Then, you would need to click the link icon, select the Bookmark option, find your bookmark, and enter the headline's text—again, one by one.

But there's an easier way to do this: by using the power of bookmarklets. A *bookmarklet* is a small JavaScript function you can add as a browser bookmark to then run on any web page. Bookmarklets can do smaller jobs like advanced search and replace, counting how often a word occurs on a page, or changing the page color. And they can also be used to create a table of contents.

To try this, create a new document. I'm creating one about the phenomenon of synesthesia. I style the main headline on top as Header 1 using the Style button. All other headlines will be styled as Header 2, as shown in Figure 2-17.

If you check the source of the document (you can do this by clicking Edit→Edit HTML), you will notice that the Header 2 is an "h2" element. And this is where the bookmarklet comes in: it will look

Figure 2-17.
The original document, containing headlines and paragraphs

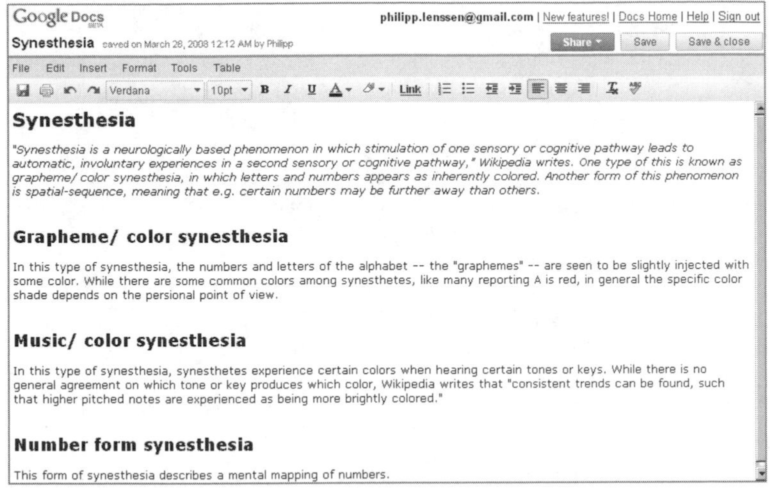

for any occurrence of this element and add an ID to it. (It ignores "h1" with the assumption that h1 is used for the chapter title; you can also expand the script if you want to "catch" elements other than h2.) The ID in turn will be linked to the table of contents, which you can create as an unordered list element "ol," inserted right before the first h2.

Here's the JavaScript code accessing the HTML Document Object Model, with spacing, line breaks, and comments added for clarity:

```
javascript:(function(){
    // grab the <iframe> Google uses, then grab all <h2>'s in it
     var doc = document.getElementById("wys_frame").contentWindow.document;
     var headlines = doc.getElementsByTagName("h2");
     if (headlines.length >= 1) {
         // insert an empty Table of Contents list element if none exists
         var toc = doc.getElementById("toc");
         if (!toc) {
             toc = doc.createElement("ol");
             toc.setAttribute("id", "toc");
             headlines[0].parentNode.insertBefore(toc, headlines[0]);
         }
         toc.innerHTML = "";
         // add an id to every <h2> & link it from the ToC
         for (var i = 0; i < headlines.length; i++) {
             var id = "toc" + (i + 1);
             toc.innerHTML += "<li><a href=\"#" + id + "\">" +
                     headlines[i].innerHTML + "</a></li>";
             headlines[i].setAttribute("id", id);
         }
     }
})()
```

Modern browsers support linking to IDs. For other browsers, you can use HTML like the following when generating the Table of Contents: `<h2><a name="toc1"></a>Number form synesthesia</h2>`.

To add this code as bookmarklet, you must compress the JavaScript into a single line, removing most spacing, comments, and post it on a web page as a link so you can drag it to your bookmark bar. You can find the bookmarklet at http://blogoscoped.com/googleappshacks/bookmarklets.html—just drag and drop the link into your bookmarks collection. To easily find a bookmarklet when you need it, consider adding it to your link toolbar, or creating a special "bookmarklets" folder in your bookmarks.

Now that you have the bookmarklet, you can run it when you edit your document, as shown in Figure 2-18. Once clicked, a new linked list appears before your first Header 2. Clicking the Create ToC bookmarklet again updates the list in case your headers changed in the meantime. You can then save the document and publish it for others to see.

> Everyone with editing rights for your document (including you) will see an editor instead of a normal web page at the URL that you used to publish the document. To see the same plain HTML page others see, log out of your Google Account by clicking "Sign out" at the top right of Google Docs, or temporarily switch to another browser with which you didn't log in to Google.

Hacking the Hack

You can also get creative, and write bookmarklets that do other things to your documents. For instance, the following JavaScript—with spacing and line breaks added again (you will need to make it one line to turn it into a bookmarklet)—will add a black one-pixel border to all images contained within your document (overriding other styles that may exist for images):

```
javascript:(function(){
    var doc = document.getElementById("wys_frame").contentWindow.document;
    var elements = doc.getElementsByTagName("img");
    for (var i = 0; i < elements.length; i++) {
        elements[i].setAttribute("style", "border: 5px solid #000");
    }
})()
```

Figure 2-18.
Running the "Create ToC" bookmarklet

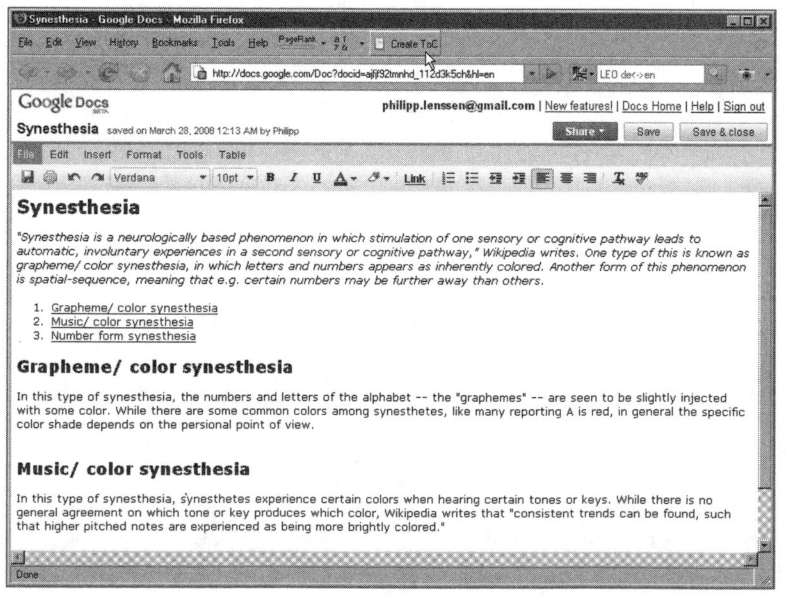

HACK 17: Remove Formatting Before Pasting Text Into a Document

When you pull in text from other sources, here's how you can do it without dragging in all of its original formatting.

Sometimes you want to spice up your Google Docs document by copying and pasting a quote, source code, headline or any other piece of text from the Web. There's only one problem with that: the material you paste in will bring along formatting from the original document. This can lead to colors and fonts that don't match your document, and it's sometimes tricky to remove this unwanted formatting using just the Docs toolbar. (Editing the HTML in its source code view is often the only reliable alternative to get back your native document styling.)

This problem may also appear when you are copying content from one Docs document to another; suppose you move the headline of your document into a table of contents document, but you don't want it to appear large and bold there. So wouldn't it be nice if the text pasted uses your native document styles, and nothing but?

Google offers a Remove Formatting button to the right side of its Docs editor toolbar—it's the letter "T" with a small red "x" next to it—but this feature doesn't always work. But here's a simple alternative method: before pasting your clipboard into your document, paste the clipboard text into the browser address bar above your document, just as though you were typing in a URL (it's basically a big text area that you can use as a scratchpad). Now, select the text that's in the address bar and copy it back to the clipboard. In doing so, your clipboard contents will have changed from rich text to plain text—and you can now safely paste it into your Docs document!

You are also able to use any other plain text editor for this job of freeing your clipboard text from exotic formatting, but the browser address bar is the one place always right within reach, even when you're sitting at a kiosk in an Internet café, hotel, or airport, where the only application you can run is a web browser. However, note that the address bar hack works only for clipboard content that fits on a single line; for content spanning multiple lines, you need to use a plain text editor of some kind—or, if none is in reach, jump over to any online plain text area—like the one presented at http://google.com/language_tools—to copy and paste into and out of.

Google employee Matt Cutts suggests the "Copy Plain Text" Firefox extension as an alternative. You can get it at https://addons.mozilla.org/en-US/firefox/addon/134.

HACK 18: Prettify Your Document with Inline Styles

Invoke the awesome power of Cascading Style Sheets to add style to your Google Docs document.

The lack of formatting options in Google Docs can be both blessing and curse. It's a blessing, because the Docs interface is remarkably uncluttered, which makes it easier to use for casual writing; you can clearly see that it doesn't carry the legacy of a product that saw the introduction of many rarely used exotic options. If, on the other hand, you'd like to tweak the document layout a bit more, you might miss some of the menu and toolbar entries available in programs such as OpenOffice.org Writer or Microsoft Word.

One way to overcome the formatting limitations that Google Docs imposes via its simplified menus is to switch to the Edit HTML mode for advanced editing. Instead of a what-you-see-is-what-you-get interface, here you will be presented with the document source represented as

HTML source. It's more confusing to wade through, but it allows you to make use of a feature called *inline styles*. HTML uses CSS (Cascading Style Sheets) for styling, and an inline style is simply a portion of CSS included right within the HTML.

Suppose that you want to restrict the line length of documents. By default, Google Docs expands to fill the whole browser window; if you want to share a document with a colleague, however, you may want to give them a better reading experience, as full-width paragraphs can hurt readability. For this example, I'll use an article on the superhero Superman. As pictured in Figure 2-19, the line length covers the full browser width, and there's little padding to the editor's left and right borders.

To restrict the line length, click Edit→Edit HTML above the toolbar. Unless you imported the document or previously styled it using the Google Docs layout options, the HTML you will see now is rather minimalist and consists mostly of paragraph tags—and "strong" for bold and "em" (emphasis) for italic—like the following:

```
<p>
<strong>Superman</strong> is a comic book character created by Joe
  Shuster and Jerry Siegel. Originally spawned in 1932 and sold to
  DC (Detective Comics) in 1938, Superman went on to become one of
  ...
</p>
```

To apply your own style, wrap the whole document with a "div" (division) element like the following:

```
<div>
<p>
<strong>Superman</strong> is a comic book character created
      ...
</p>
<p>
     ...
</p>
...
</div>
```

This serves as container to which you can apply the stylesheet, which you do by adding a "style" attribute with the width and padding definitions:

```
<div style="width: 600px; padding: 30px">
  ...
</div>
```

When you click the "Back to editing the document" link, you will find the layout of your text changed to something more readable, as shown in Figure 2-20. Now that your text is wrapped with a container, some browsers will let you select it and adjust the width visually using the mouse.

> For a full list of layout changes that you can apply using CSS, take a look at the official language specification at http://w3.org/TR/CSS21/. Note, however, that not all styling is allowed in Google Docs; Google employs a "white list" of CSS properties, meaning that anything not on the white list is prohibited and will be removed from your document. (Because Google documents are hosted on http://google.com, there are certain security restrictions with the HTML you produce.) To see such a CSS white list, take a look at http://google.com/apis/maps/documentation/mapplets/infowindowallowed.html. Although not specifically about Google Docs, that help page gives you a good idea of what's allowed in Google Docs.

More Ways to Change the Layout of Your Document

Add an image border: At the moment, Google doesn't offer you a menu entry to put a border around an image you include via Insert→Picture. But switch to the HTML view after inserting an image, and modify the "img" tag to include a style like the following:

```
<img src="..." alt="" style="border: 1px solid rgb(0,0,0)" />
```

Figure 2-19.
The article's line length fills the whole window, hurting readability unless the browser window is resized

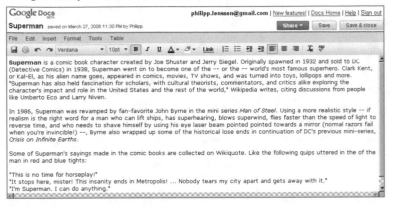

Google Docs BETA philipp.lenssen@gmail.com | New features! | Docs Home | Help | Sign out

Superman saved on March 27, 2008 11:30 PM by Philipp Share Save Save & close

File Edit Insert Format Tools Table

Verdana 10pt B I U Link

Superman is a comic book character created by Joe Shuster and Jerry Siegel. Originally spawned in 1932 and sold to DC (Detective Comics) in 1938, Superman went on to become one of the -- or the -- world's most famous superhero. Clark Kent, or Kal-El, as his alien name goes, appeared in comics, movies, TV shows, and was turned into toys, lollipops and more. "Superman has also held fascination for scholars, with cultural theorists, commentators, and critics alike exploring the character's impact and role in the United States and the rest of the world," Wikipedia writes, citing discussions from people like Umberto Eco and Larry Niven.

In 1986, Superman was revamped by fan-favorite John Byrne in the mini series *Man of Steel*. Using a more realistic style -- if realism is the right word for a man who can lift ships, has superhearing, blows superwind, flies faster than the speed of light to reverse time, and who needs to shave himself by using his eye laser beam pointed pointed towards a mirror (normal razors fail when you're invincible!) --, Byrne also wrapped up some of the historical lose ends in continuation of DC's previous mini-series, *Crisis on Infinite Earths*.

Some of Superman's sayings made in the comic books are collected on Wikiquote. Like the following quips uttered in the of the man in red and blue tights:

"This is no time for horseplay!"
"It stops here, mister! This insanity ends in Metropolis! ... Nobody tears my city apart and gets away with it."
"I'm Superman. I can do anything."

Figure 2-20.
A new layout for the article

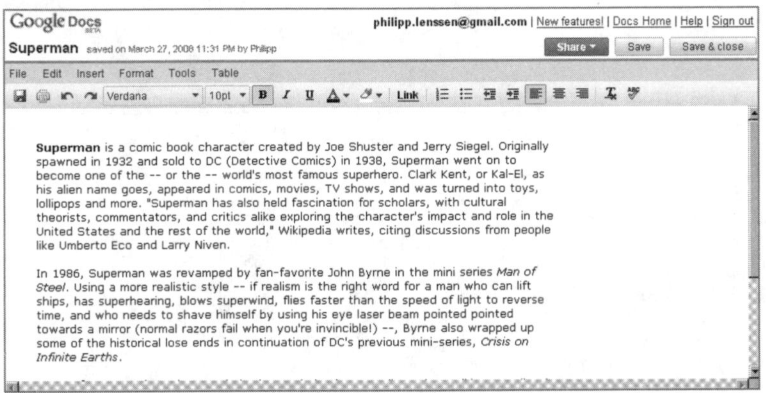

Google Docs BETA philipp.lenssen@gmail.com | New features! | Docs Home | Help | Sign out

Superman saved on March 27, 2008 11:31 PM by Philipp Share Save Save & close

File Edit Insert Format Tools Table

Verdana 10pt B I U Link

Superman is a comic book character created by Joe Shuster and Jerry Siegel. Originally spawned in 1932 and sold to DC (Detective Comics) in 1938, Superman went on to become one of the -- or the -- world's most famous superhero. Clark Kent, or Kal-El, as his alien name goes, appeared in comics, movies, TV shows, and was turned into toys, lollipops and more. "Superman has also held fascination for scholars, with cultural theorists, commentators, and critics alike exploring the character's impact and role in the United States and the rest of the world," Wikipedia writes, citing discussions from people like Umberto Eco and Larry Niven.

In 1986, Superman was revamped by fan-favorite John Byrne in the mini series *Man of Steel*. Using a more realistic style -- if realism is the right word for a man who can lift ships, has superhearing, blows superwind, flies faster than the speed of light to reverse time, and who needs to shave himself by using his eye laser beam pointed pointed towards a mirror (normal razors fail when you're invincible!) --, Byrne also wrapped up some of the historical lose ends in continuation of DC's previous mini-series, *Crisis on Infinite Earths*.

Switch to a different font or font size: The document editor already includes a font menu allowing you to select a font and font size, but its options are limited and you may want to go for yet another font and size. (It's worth noting that a font available on your computer may not be available on someone else's computer, and as fonts are not embedded into Google Docs files, another computer may show a different fallback font.) Again, you can use a "div" container wrapped around your full document, like the following:

```
<div style="font-family: helvetica, arial, sans-serif; font-size: 14px">
  ...
</div>
```

> A static font size unit like "px"—pixels—can create accessibility problems on certain systems where the user requires a bigger font. If you want to use a font that scales better with the user preferences, and looks good on very large resolutions, consider using a relative font size, such as "font-size: 120%".

But there's one hurdle left yet for certain documents. Google also inserts its own stylesheets into any document you create, and if you have paragraph elements within your text, Google's stylesheet will override your own style, meaning that your font definition is ignored! To solve this, you can remove all "p" tags in the HTML view and include two breaks between any two paragraphs, like the following:

```
<br /><br />
```

Figure 2-21.
The text is now justified, and it uses an increased line-height and font size

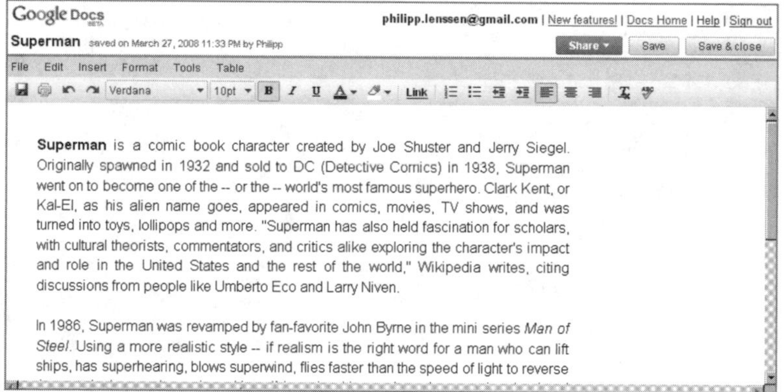

Justify your text: If you set the alignment of your text through the Docs editor toolbar, you are restricted to left alignment, center alignment and right alignment. One alignment you can't select is fully-justified text, as shown in Figure 2-21. Use the following inline style for your "div" container to achieve this:

```
<div style="text-align: justify">
  ...
</div>
```

Increase the line height: To increase the line height of your document, as shown in Figure 2-21, add the following style:

```
<div style="line-height: 1.4em">
  ...
</div>
```

The "em" unit represents the font height currently in use for your document. It's a relative unit, so it's a bit more flexible than static ones like "px".

Output your whole text in uppercase: To convert all your writing into uppercase letters, use the following style on your "div" container:

```
<div style="text-transform: uppercase">
  ...
</div>
```

Increase the letter or word spacing: To increase the space between any two letters of your text, use a style like the following:

```
<div style="letter-spacing: 2px">
  ...
</div>
```

Negative values like "–1px" are allowed as well. If, on the other hand, you want to increase the spacing between two given words of your text, use the following style on your "div" container:

```
<div style="word-spacing: 1.5ex">
  ...
</div>
```

(The "ex" unit refers to the height of a lowercase "x" in your current font.)

Float text/images around other text/images: If you want to position one element to the left or right of another element, you can use tables and include your element within a table cell. Or you can use the "float" style property, as shown here applied to a paragraph:

```
<p style="float: left; width: 250px">
  ...
</p>
<p>
   ...
</p>
```

Use the same layout for multiple documents

When you defined advanced layout options using inline styles, it can be handy to reuse the same template for several documents. There are two basic ways to do this: you can copy the HTML of a "div" container somewhere to store it (for example, in a Google Docs document itself), and then copy and paste it into new documents when you create them. There's an even easier way: you can open an existing document that is already styled, and then select File→"Copy document" from the menu. (If your previous document was shared, you will see a dialog asking whether to keep the existing sharing settings for the copied document; click "Cancel" if your new document should remain private at first.)

03 THE GOOGLE DOCS FAMILY: GOOGLE SPREADSHEETS

Spreadsheets can be used for managing all kinds of information. You might think finance and accounting are the most common uses for a spreadsheet, but Joel Spolsky, one of the developers behind Microsoft Excel 5.0, found out (as he tells in his great book, *User Interface Design for Programmers*, which is also available online), merely keeping *lists* is what most people do with them. You can keep lists of your books, for instance, with the book title in the left column of the spreadsheet table and your rating, expressed as number from 1 to 10, in the right column.

Google Spreadsheets, part of the Google Docs suite (see Chapter 1 for an overview and introduction) supports much more than lists, but it is not as feature-rich as competing desktop products like Microsoft Excel. However, as a web application, it does contain some built-in niceties that traditional desktop programs may not have, such as:

- A chat program next to the spreadsheet, in which you can discuss the document with your friends and colleagues
- A revision history that allows you to go back to a document from minutes, days, weeks, or months ago (or just compare changes)
- Easy multiauthor editing, including color indicators showing who is currently editing what
- Formulas that access real-time data—financial or otherwise—from other web sites and services
- Sharing documents in real time with others without having to make redundant, soon-to-be-outdated copies
- Embedding dynamic spreadsheets in a web page or blog post

Google Spreadsheets has a few interesting tricks up its sleeves. Read on to learn how to make it do all kinds of things.

HACK 19: Add Live Data to Your Spreadsheet

Wouldn't it be nice if some of your spreadsheet data automatically created and updated itself? Actually, it's very simple with the GoogleLookup and GoogleFinance functions.

Here's a quick question: when was Matt Groening, creator of *The Simpsons*, born?

The correct answer is February 15, 1954. Admittedly, I didn't know that either until I just looked it up on Google, using a feature called Google Q&A (for "Questions & Answers"). Try it out yourself by entering *matt groening birthday* into Google. On top of the results you will find what's called a *onebox* containing the information, as shown in Figure 3-1.

Figure 3-1.
Matt Groening's date of birth: February 15, 1954, apparently

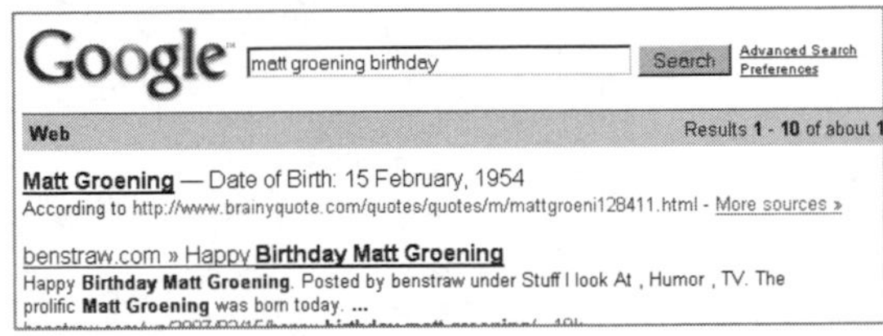

Google Q&A is good for more than just researching Matt Groening's birthday—it can turn up a variety of other information and trivia. These results are not provided by a human: instead, a Google program automatically scours the Web to find this information on sites like Wikipedia, Brainyquote.com, and many more. Here are a couple of other queries that result in direct answers:

- The search *sylvester stallone birthplace* results in "Sylvester Stallone—Place of Birth: New York, New York, USA"
- The search *berlin population* results in "Berlin—Population: 3,405,000 (11/2006)"
- The search *length of the amazon river* results in "Amazon River —Length: 6,400 KM (4,000 MI) approx."
- The search *mass of betelgeuse* results in "Betelgeuse—Mass: 14 [solar masses]"
- The search *barry lyndon director* results in "Barry Lyndon—Director: Stanley Kubrick"
- The search *catch-22 author* results in "Catch-22—Author: Joseph Heller"

Google used to provide a lot more "fun" queries, like "real name of Superman"; alas, many of them have been removed by now. When you rely on the Google Q&A feature, know that sometimes queries return wrong answers; that answers aren't always structured alike (one answer for a birthplace question may be "San Francisco," while another may be "Sherman Oaks, CA," listing the state as well); and that certain questions may not be answered at all.

All these queries can be broken into the two basic pieces: *entities* and *attributes*. For instance, "Matt Groening," "Berlin," and "Amazon river" are the entities. And "birthday," "birthplace," and "length" are the accompanying attributes. To issue a query from within a spreadsheet, you must be able to express it in terms of entity and attribute. This is where the Google Spreadsheets' GoogleLookup function comes in.

GoogleLookup, Google's Q&A data for your spreadsheet

To include Q&A data in your spreadsheet, use the GoogleLookup function. Let's create a spreadsheet containing celebrity information; you'll provide the celebrity name, and GoogleLookup provides the results for the other fields. Open a new spreadsheet at http://docs.google.com and enter several celebrity names in the first column. Leave the second and third columns, titled "birth date" and "birthplace" empty for now, as shown in Figure 3-2.

Figure 3-2.
Creating an automated celebrity information spreadsheet

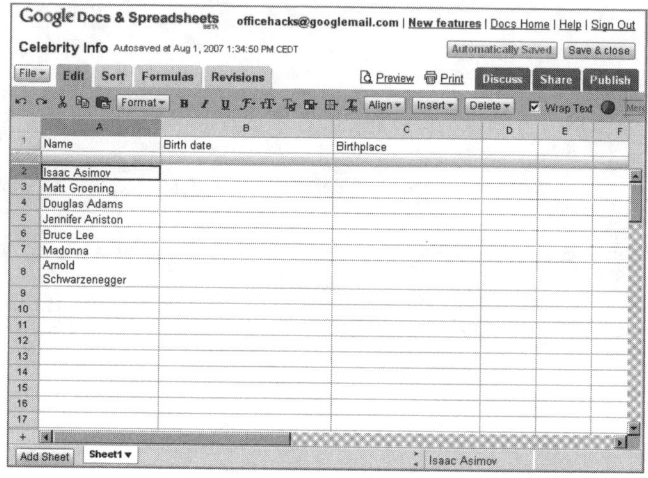

The GoogleLookup formula has the following structure:

```
=GoogleLookup(entity, attribute)
```

So, you can select the cell next to Isaac Asimov and enter:

```
=GoogleLookup("Isaac Asimov", "Birth date")
```

As soon as you hit the Return key, this cell's value is calculated for you; after a brief "loading" message, the cell now contains the value "January 2, 1920" (in this case, the value is of static nature, but other values like "population" may change over time). Hover your mouse over any cell containing a GoogleLookup function to see what web sources Google used for the data.

You can now fill the rest of the cell with this formula, but it would be a bit redundant to type the entity value into every cell. Go back to the cell containing Mr. Asimov's birthday and double-click the cell to edit it. Select the entity value ("Isaac Asimov") in the formula and type `$A2` (the `$` in front of the `A` keeps `A` from changing to `B` if you were to copy or autofill cells from the Birth Date to Birth Place column). Your formula should now look like this:

```
=GoogleLookup($A2, "Birth date")
```

Instead of hard-wiring the name, you've replaced it with a variable pointer (you could also replace "Birth date" in the formula with `B$1`; the `$` keeps `1` from changing to `2`, `3`, etc. if you copy or autofill downward). Now you're ready to automatically fill the other cells. Copy the cells containing the formula by pressing Ctrl-C, then select the other cells below it and press Ctrl-V to paste. Repeat the same process with the third column (but use "Birthplace" for the attribute), and voilà—you've created an automatically updated celebrity information spreadsheet, as shown in Figure 3-3!

You may need to use Ctrl-C and Ctrl-V on the Macintosh platform, because Command-C/V sometimes invokes the operating system's Copy/Paste commands rather than the ones build into Google Spreadsheets. But Google Spreadsheets has its own copy/paste handlers wired up to Ctrl-C and Ctrl-V, and because these don't have a function on Mac OS X, they are more reliable.

Figure 3-3.
The date and place values have been automatically filled in

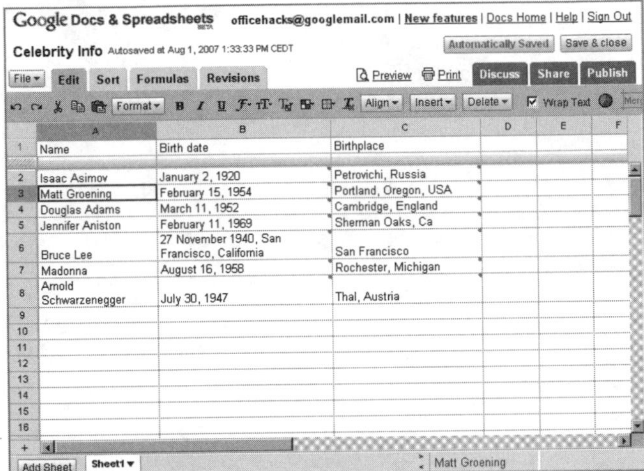

At the time of this writing, Google allows a maximum of 250 GoogleLookup functions per spreadsheet.

Using the "Publish" tab, you can even turn this data into a web page, or embed the table in your homepage (Publish→More Publishing Options) **[Hack #21]**.

Using GoogleLookup Values as Arguments for Other Calculations

You can also take results returned from the GoogleLookup function and use them inside other formulas in your spreadsheet. Sometimes it's necessary to clean up the values returned by GoogleLookup, though. In the table shown in Figure 3-4, the following formula—with a hat tip to the helping soul of the Google Docs groups, André "Ahab" Banen—strips unwanted text out of population values to get an actual number:

```
=IFERROR( VALUE(LEFT(B2, FIND(" ", B2))), IFERROR(VALUE(B2)) )
```

In this formula, the FIND function looks for the first occurrence of a space character within the text contained in the A2 cell. That's because the space character signals the end of the numeric value (in Figure 3-4, B2 contains "107,449,525 (July 2006 est.)").

If the space is found, the LEFT function trims the B2 text down to all the characters up until the space, and VALUE converts the result into a number. If there is no blank available in the number cell, an error is thrown, which is caught by the IFERROR function, which returns the second parameter if the first parameter returns an error. And this second parameter takes whatever is in B2—you know by then that it didn't contain a space character—and returns it as a number using the VALUE function (another IFERROR wrapper is used in case the string can't be turned into a number for some reason).

This trick enables you to retrieve the sum of the populations—here, Mexico and Japan—by using the formula "=C2+C3".

Another function, named GoogleFinance and explained in the following section, returns values that are a little more structured.

Figure 3-4.
Adding up GoogleLookup values

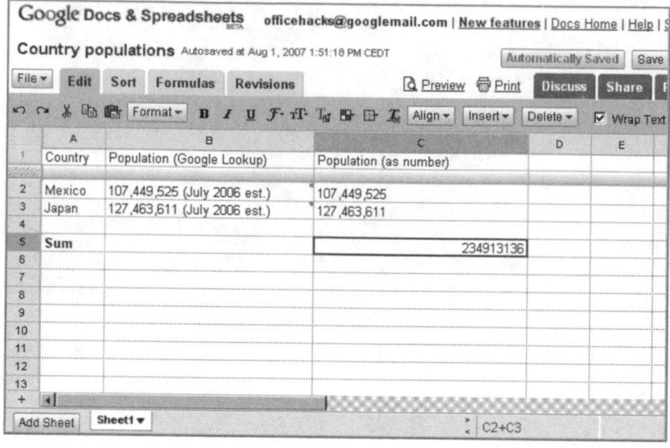

Get Real-Time Finance Data

The GoogleFinance function is essentially GoogleLookup's older sibling, but it provides finance data only. As with GoogleLookup, you need to provide two values, but they're called *symbol* and *attribute* this time:

```
=GoogleFinance(symbol, attribute)
```

For instance, to find out the current price of Yahoo stock, you would write:

```
=GoogleFinance("YHOO", "price")
```

This function returned "23.25", as shown in Figure 3-5.

The stock price value comes with a delay of up to 20 minutes, according to Google. Some of the other attributes you can use are:

- **priceopen:** The opening price of the stock for the day
- **high:** The highest price the stock traded for the day
- **low:** The lowest price the stock traded for the day
- **volume:** The number of shares traded of this stock for the day
- **marketcap:** The current market cap of the stock
- **tradetime:** The last time this stock traded
- **high52:** The 52-week high for the stock
- **low52:** The 52-week low for the stock
- **shares:** The quantity of shares outstanding for the stock
- **currency:** The currency in which the stock is traded

For a full list of available attributes, you can search the Google Docs help file for "GoogleFinance."

Figure 3-5.
"Where's my stock at?" answered by GoogleFinance

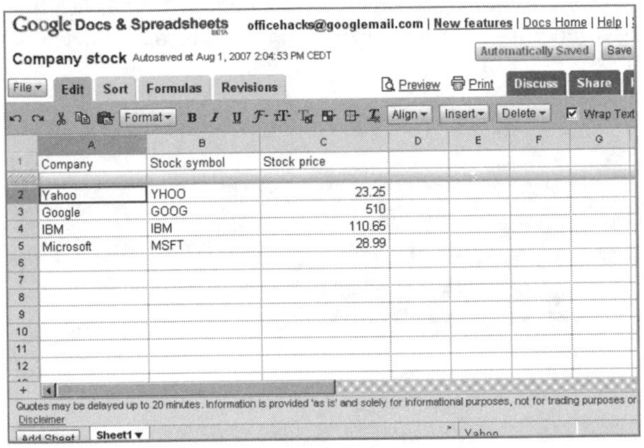

Company	Stock symbol	Stock price
Yahoo	YHOO	23.25
Google	GOOG	510
IBM	IBM	110.65
Microsoft	MSFT	28.99

HACK 20: Pick a Winner at Random

Use the RAND function in combination with sorting to pick first-, second-, and third-place winners from a list.

Google Spreadsheets gives you many formulas. To view all of them—242, at the time of this writing—open a new spreadsheet at http://docs.google.com, switch to the Formulas tab, and click the "more" link to the right. You can now scroll through the different groups and jump to a help entry for a particular formula by selecting the "more" link next to them. The INT function, for example, rounds a given number down to its integer component, turning a 2.7 into a 2. SEARCH returns the position of a text segment within a longer string. The GoogleLookup function polls data from the Web **[Hack #19]**.

Another interesting function is RAND, which returns a random number between 0 and 1. Inspired by David and Raina Hawley's "Random Sorting" hack in *Excel Hacks*, 2nd Edition, here's how you can use RAND to pick a winner from a list of participants. First, create a list of participants by adding a Name and a Rank column. Fill the Name column with a list of names, as shown in Figure 3-6.

Now, select the field next to the first participant, type `=RAND()` and hit return (or pick the RAND function from the Formulas menu). On some systems, you can now select the field and copy it (Ctrl-C or right-click and select Copy), and select all the other fields next to the participants and paste it (Ctrl-V or right-click and select Paste). However, on other systems, this will copy the result value and not the function; to avoid this result, click the bottom-right edge of the source cell, and then drag it over the other cells for RAND to be automatically filled in for them.

> You may need to use Ctrl-C and Ctrl-V on the Macintosh platform, too, because Command-C/V sometimes invokes the operating system's Copy/Paste commands rather than the ones build into Google Spreadsheets. But Google Spreadsheets has its own copy/paste handlers wired up to Ctrl-C and Ctrl-V, and because these don't have a function on Mac OS X, they are more reliable.

Each contestant from the list now has a random number next to it, and you can now sort the list by this number. To do so, click the divider line just below the Rank to get the sort option to appear. Next, sort the column (it doesn't matter whether you choose A–Z or Z–A, because what you're after is a random result). Additionally, you can include a result section that reports the top three cells (using =A2, =A3, and =A4 respectively) to show the winners, as pictured in Figure 3-7. Each time you click the Sort option, a new random list of winners is generated, since the RAND function calculates a new value every time you perform an action.

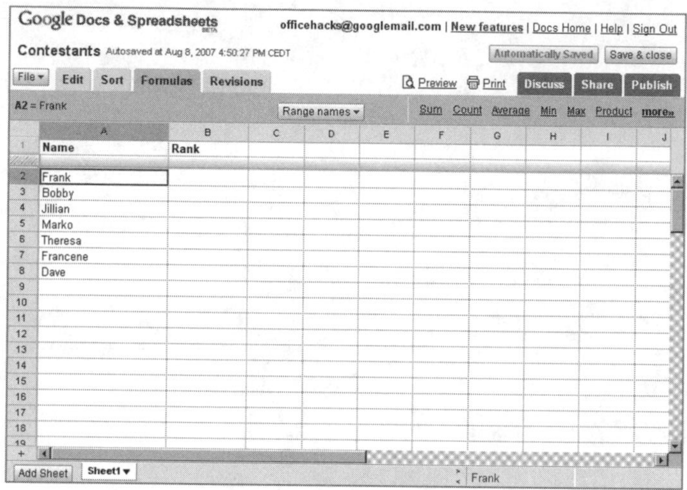

Figure 3-6.
A Google Spreadsheets list of contestants

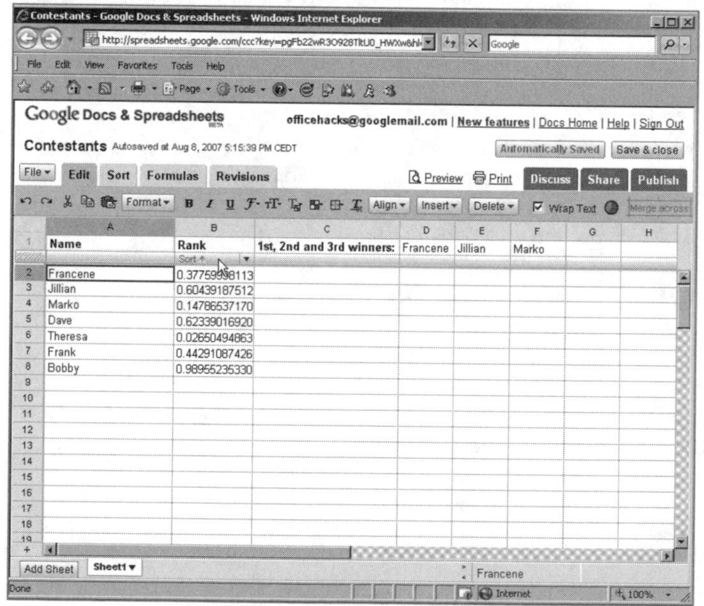

Figure 3-7.
Francene is randomly picked as the first winner

HACK 21: Embed Your Spreadsheet in a Web Page

You can export a Google Spreadsheet to an embeddable HTML format, which you can then include in your blog or any other web page.

There are different ways to include spreadsheet data in a web page, such as a blog posting. You can export the spreadsheet to HTML and copy that into your web site's HTML editor, for instance. This is a good quick and dirty way to do it, but as you'll see, there are better ways.

Let's start with a spreadsheet listing album releases of the Beatles, as shown in Figure 3-8.

> I compiled the Beatles discography data with a little help from the Google Music service, which you can find by performing a Google.com web search for "beatles" and then clicking on the album image shown in the results. You can find the spreadsheet at http://spreadsheets.google.com/ccc?key=pvm6FPiylicL8KMnPUNzCcw—this is a read-only view of the data, but you can make a copy by choosing File→Copy spreadsheet.

To export the discography data as HTML, select File→Export→HTML from the Spreadsheets menu. A new browser window will open; view the HTML source of the page, and look for the second opening "table" tag. Copy everything from (and including) this tag, up to (and including) the corresponding closing "table" tag. If you're using a rich text editor for your web page or blog, switch to HTML editing mode (Blogger's HTML editing mode is shown in Figure 3-9). Next, paste the table you copied into the editor, as shown in Figure 3-9. Figure 3-10 shows the spreadsheet data embedded in a Blogger blog.

> If you find that the HTML source appears as one long line, you can save the HTML file to your hard drive, and use the HTML Tidy utility (http://tidy.sourceforge.net) to format the source in a more human-friendly way.

The HTML for this post, however, is bloated, and also doesn't automatically update when you update your spreadsheet data source. A more direct way to embed a spreadsheet is to choose the Publish

Figure 3-8.
Your spreadsheet discography

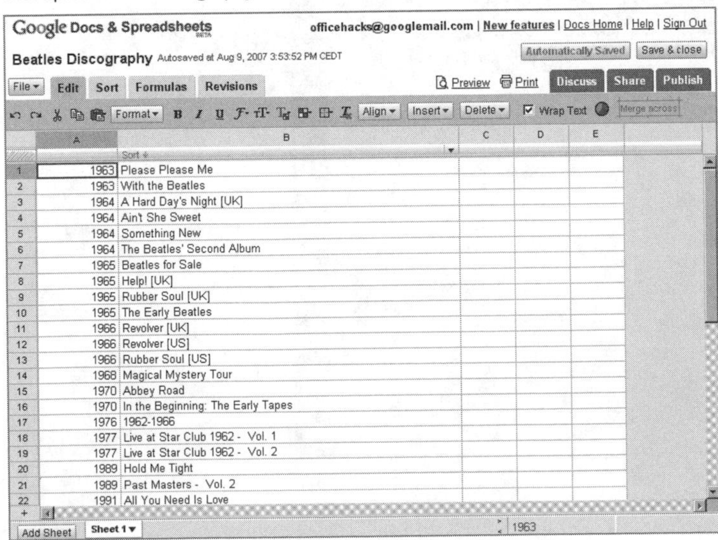

tab in Google Spreadsheets to click "Publish now" (check the "Automatically republish . . . " option, too). You can now select the "More publishing options" link and in the dialog that opens, pick "HTML to embed in a webpage," as shown in Figure 3-11. After clicking "Generate URL," paste the code snippet provided to you into your blog's HTML editor and publish the post, as shown in Figure 3-12.

Figure 3-9.
Using the "Edit HTML" view of Blogger, you can paste the HTML source from any page

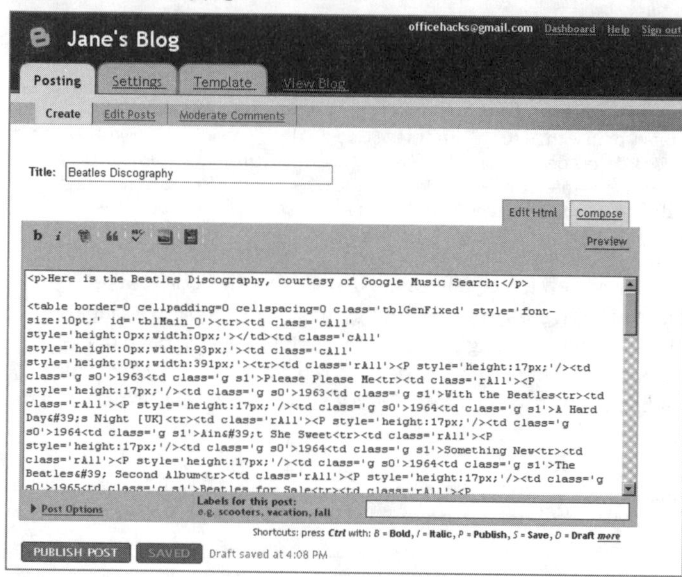

Figure 3-10.
The published blog post, showing the discography table

 Google will offer you a so-called "Iframe" to paste into your web site. An *Iframe*, or *inline frame*, is a browser window within the browser window, showing another web page. If you are posting the spreadsheet to a blog, it's possible that the Iframe will not be visible in some RSS readers. Also note that depending on your web page template, you may need to adjust the Iframe's "width" property so that the scroll bars to the right side will not be cut off.

For yet another way to add spreadsheets data to your web sites, have a look at how to use Spreadsheets as a Content Management System **[Hack #22]**.

Figure 3-11.
The publishing options dialog

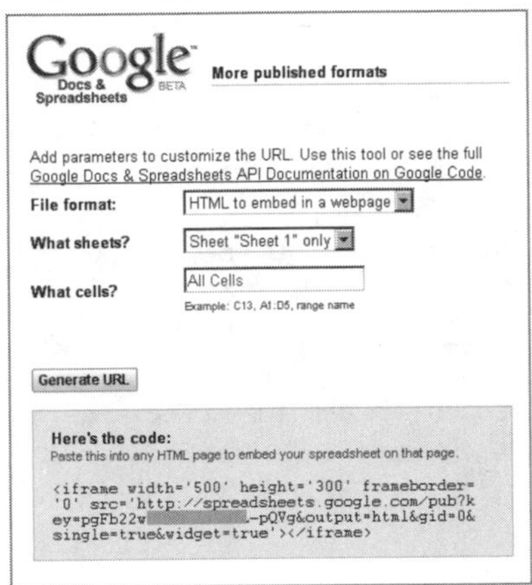

Figure 3-12.
The Beatles discography included as embeddable HTML

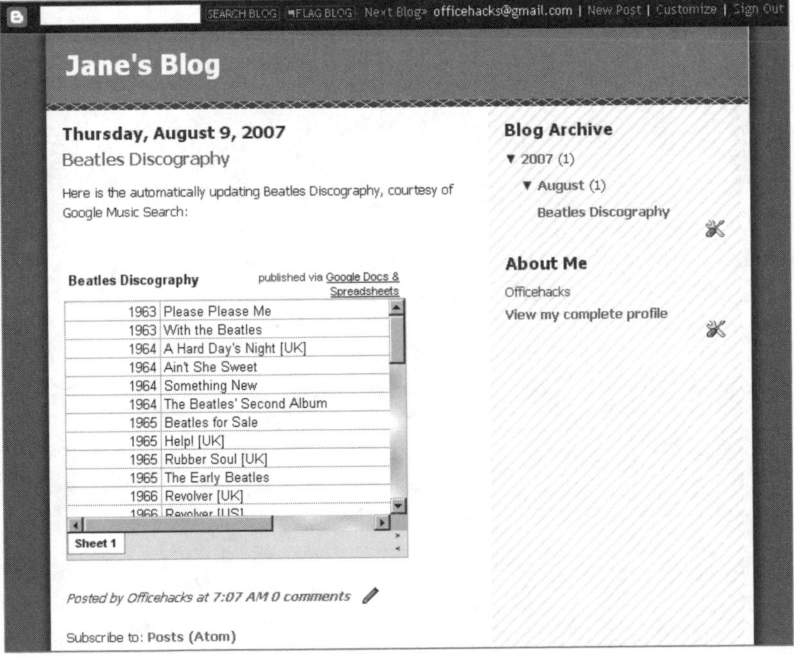

HACK 22: Use Google Spreadsheets as a Content Management System

By automatically populating your web page with values from Spreadsheet cells and addressing them via JavaScript, you can create a mini-CMS.

Do you want to enable your friend or colleague to quickly edit some text on your home page, but don't want to set up a big content management system (CMS)? Use a Google Spreadsheet as data source, an idea first presented by Todd Huss at http://gabrito.com.

To get started, create a new spreadsheet at http://docs.google.com and insert two column titles: one labeled "name", the other "content". Then create two sample rows, using the names "headline1" and "paragraph1", as shown in Figure 3-13, and fill the content fields with some text of your choice.

You probably already have an HTML page where you want to include these values now. I'll pick a company I'm calling "Wine for Sale 2000." Right now the web page is a static file that I haven't yet connected to the spreadsheet, as shown in Figure 3-14.

To embed the dynamic headlines into the HTML page, you first need to publish the spreadsheet via the "Publish" tab. Select the "Automatically re-publish . . . " option as well. The spreadsheet will now have a public address like the following:

```
http://spreadsheets.google.com/pub?key=pgFb21wR3090hBx3GJULx0Q
```

I highlighted the "key" part because you'll need it now. Include the following snippet in your HTML, and replace the key value, highlighted again, with the key from a spreadsheet you've published. Give identifiers to the headline and paragraph you want to fill automatically. Use values from the name column of the spreadsheet, as shown here (headline1 and paragraph1):

```
<h1 id="headline1"></h1>
<p id="paragraph1"></p>
<script type="text/javascript">
```

Figure 3-13.
Your data spreadsheet containing a list of name/content pairs

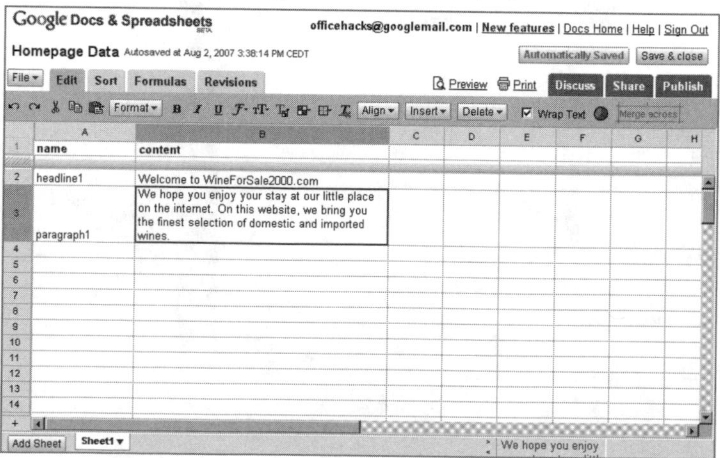

```
function displayContent(json) {
    document.getElementById('headline1').innerHTML = json.feed.entry[0].gsx$content.$t;
    document.getElementById('paragraph1').innerHTML = json.feed.entry[1].gsx$content.$t;
}
</script>
<script type="text/javascript"
src="http://spreadsheets.google.com/feeds/list/pgFb21wR3090hBx3GJULx0Q/od6/public/
values?alt=json-in-script&callback=displayContent">
</script>
```

What does this JavaScript do? It requests a *JSON* data packet from the Google server and asks for this data to be sent to the "displayContent" function you created. JSON is short for "JavaScript Object Notation," and it's a data exchange format useful for JavaScript and other languages.

Now you can refresh the page and see that your headline and paragraph automatically adjust to the spreadsheet values. And when anyone changes the spreadsheet data, your page will update itself too!

 You should only share the spreadsheet with people you trust, because they can include HTML, and even JavaScript, into your document. To protect yourself against undesirable HTML and JavaScript you can use a JSON parser library at http://json.org/json2.js, which comes with usage examples right in the file.

Hacking the Hack

There's only one problem with using JavaScript: it executes inside the browser (on the client side) and is therefore less accessible than static HTML. For instance, search engine bots will not be able to see your text and correctly index it; also, some mobile browsers may not render your page fully.

Figure 3-14.
For now, the sample home page displays static headlines only

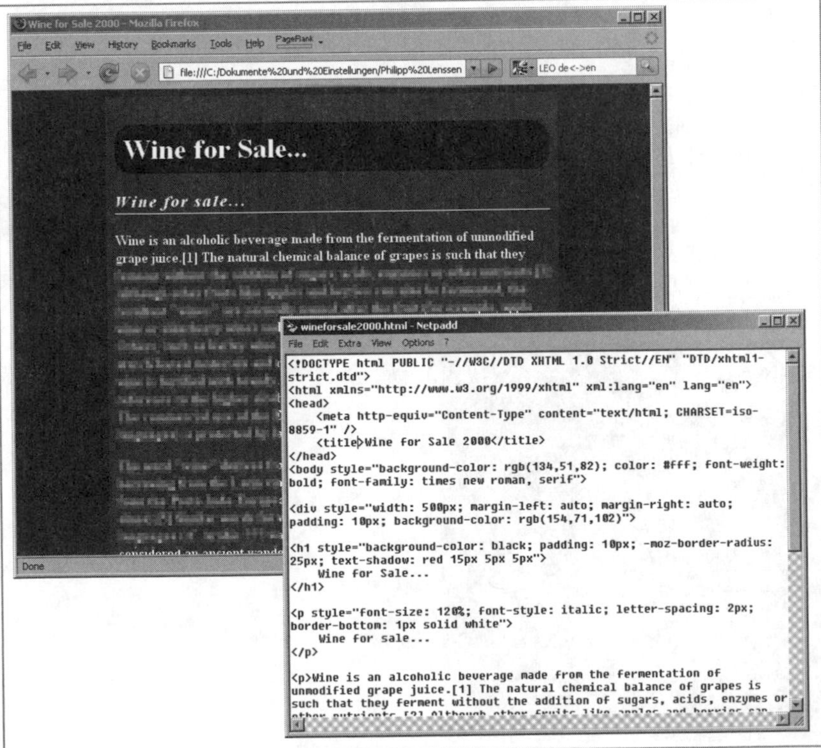

To overcome this barrier, you can create the HTML on the server side, using a language like Python or PHP. For example, the latest version of PHP supports the JSON data format. You can also use the comma-separated values (CSV) output of Google Spreadsheets:

```
name,content
headline1,Welcome to WineForSale
paragraph1,"We hope you enjoy your stay at our little place on the internet. On..."
```

This is the accompanying PHP snippet to parse this data (replace the key value highlighted here with your own):

```
<?
// Parse the CSV data into an associative array
$spreadsheet = array();
$handle = fopen(
  'http://spreadsheets.google.com/pub?key=pgFb21wR3090hBx3GJULxOQ&output=csv&gid=0', "r");
while ( ( $data = fgetcsv($handle) ) !== false ) {
    $spreadsheet[$data[0]] = $data[1];
}
fclose($handle);
// Output the values below, but filter against HTML
?>
<h1 id="headline1"><?= htmlEntities($spreadsheet['headline1']) ?></h1>
<p id="paragraph1"><?= htmlEntities($spreadsheet['paragraph1']) ?></p>
```

You don't need to restrict your spreadsheet values to manually edited ones, by the way. Using the GoogleLookup function **[Hack #19]**, you can also access live data pulled from the Web. If you give one row the name "`brazil population`" and use the formula `=GoogleLookup("Brazil", "population")` for its content, you can access the result with the following PHP, producing the output shown in Figure 3-15:

```
<p>Brazil, with a population of
<?= htmlEntities($spreadsheet['brazil population']) ?>,
has several wine regions, including Andradas, Caldas,
and Serra Gaucha.</p>
```

Figure 3-15.
The wine shop, now with dynamic headlines delivered via Google Spreadsheets

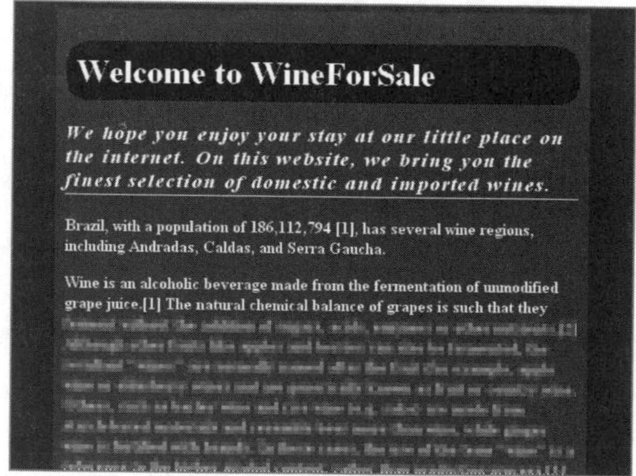

HACK 23: Show Elapsed Time as Days and Hours

Using a formula, you can convert values such as "186 hours" into the more readable "7 days 18 hours." Inspired by the hack "Show Total Time as Days, Hours and Minutes" from David and Raina Hawley's *Excel Hacks*, 2nd Edition, I decided to try this out in Google documents.

To set up for this hack, create a simple time management table, as shown in Figure 3-16. The left column contains the tasks—designing, programming, debugging, and so on—and the right column contains the hours spent for this task. The overall time spent on the project is currently displayed in hours, as shown in Figure 3-16, using the following formula:

```
=sum(B2:B12)
```

This adds up all numbers between cells B2 and B12. In this case, the result is 186 hours. Type "186 hours in days" without quotes into a Google web search, and the Google calculator will tell you that this equals 7.75 days.

> For a full feature list of what the Google calculator can do for you, including answering such queries as "17 * 22 – 3," "200 USD in EUR," or "42 in Roman numerals," see http://google.com/help/calculator.html.

You can get your spreadsheet to display a more readable sum, too. To do this, replace the SUM formula you used earlier with this one (select the hours sum cell, double-click or press F2, replace the formula with what you see here, and press Return or Enter):

```
=INT( SUM(B2:B12) / 24 ) & " days " & MOD( SUM(B2:B12), 24 ) & " hours"
```

The first part of the formula adds up all hours, divides this by 24 (the number of hours in a day), and rounds the number down to the nearest integer. The second part of the formula uses the MOD function

Figure 3-16.
The development tasks spreadsheet sums the list of tasks to a total of 186 hours

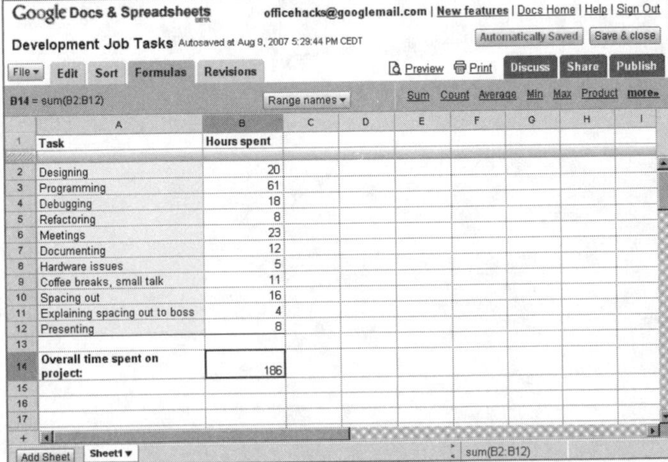

(modulo arithmetic), which takes two parameters, divides the first parameter by the second, then returns the remainder. The result will display as "7 days 18 hours," as shown in Figure 3-17.

Hacking the Hack

This approach works fine, but you can make it more readable through the use of a *named range*, an easy-to-remember label assigned to a specific range of cells. In Google Spreadsheets, switch to the Formulas tab (located toward the top of the page), click "Range names," and select "Define new." Name your range by using a label like "hours_spent" and select the range of cells (B2:B12). (See Figure 3-18.) Save the new range and close the dialog, and you're ready to replace your existing formula with the following:

```
=INT( SUM(hours_spent) / 24 ) & " days " & MOD( SUM(hours_spent), 24 ) & " hours"
```

Or, to return the number of weeks, you can use the following formula, which expands the former one:

```
=INT( SUM(hours_spent) / 24 / 7 ) & " weeks " & INT( MOD( SUM(hours_spent) / 24, 7 ) ) &
" days " & MOD( SUM(hours_spent), 24 ) & " hours"
```

Alternatively, you may also want to print an overview of the total hours spent in multiple formats, such as seconds, minutes, hours, days, weeks, and years. You can name result cells of calculations using the range names feature to simplify this step, as pictured in Figure 3-19, which also shows the formulas being used (in the neighboring gray cells). For instance, the weeks are calculated using the following formula (instead of INT, you can use FLOOR to round down to a precise date—the level of precision is indicated by the second parameter):

```
=FLOOR(days / 52.18, .01)
```

Figure 3-17.
Here is a much more readable representation of the time you spent on various tasks

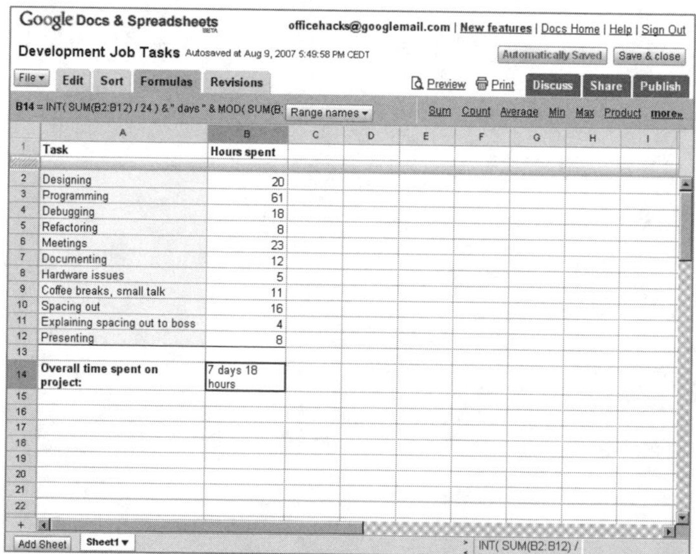

Figure 3-18.
Creating a new range name

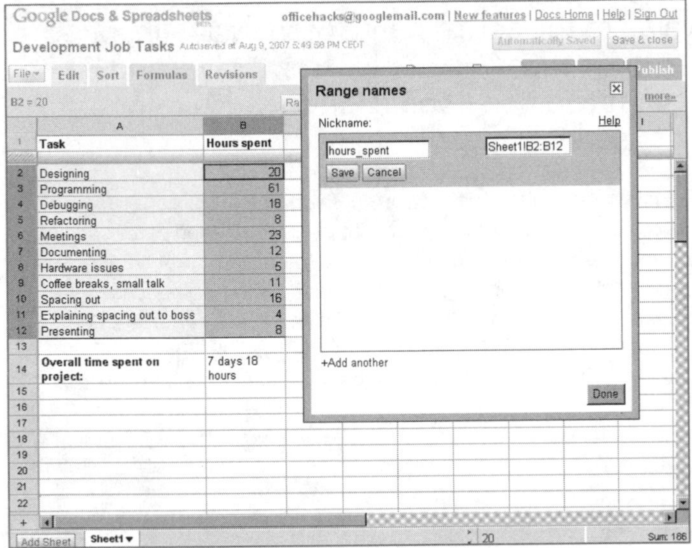

Figure 3-19.
Simultaneously showing the total time in different formats

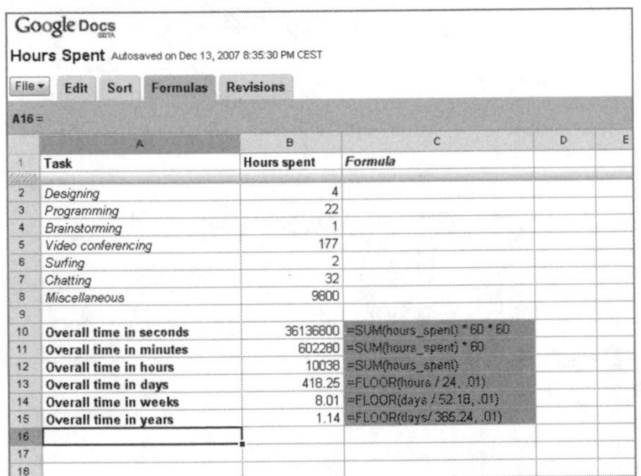

HACK 24: : Show the Weekday or Month of a Date

To get from a date value to the actual name of the day—inspired by the hack "Return the Weekday of a Date" from David and Raina Hawley's *Excel Hacks*, 2nd Edition—you need to press a couple of different functions into service.

Among Google Spreadsheet's functions are a few that let you get the name of the day or month for a given date value. Take a look at the sample spreadsheet with user registration dates shown in Figure 3-20. To the left side, you can see a list of usernames; next to them, you can see the date on which each user registered for the service. Dates are easy enough to get into a spreadsheet, but to get the spreadsheet to print out the weekday in every row, you'll need to use some functions. The functions you need to pick the weekday are called WEEKDAY and CHOOSE. The WEEKDAY function returns a number from 1 to 7, where 1 is Sunday, 2 is Monday, 3 is Tuesday and so on.

> Wondering how to calculate the number of days the user has been registered so far? Check out **[Hack #25]** for complete details.

Try it out yourself by entering the following into any cell:

```
=WEEKDAY(B2)
```

This formula shows that April 21, 2004 (the value in B2), is a "4", which means Wednesday. (A quick jump over to Google Calendar at http://calendar.google.com verifies this.) But that isn't very readable—you still need to convert this number into the name of the weekday. To do this, use the CHOOSE function, which takes an index value as first parameter, and then decides on any of the following parameter values provided based on that index. This becomes clear when you look at the formula necessary to return the verbose weekday:

```
=CHOOSE(WEEKDAY(B2), "Sunday", "Monday", "Tuesday", "Wednesday", "Thursday", "Friday",
"Saturday" )
```

If the first parameter is 1, the function will choose "Sunday"; if it's 2, it will chóose "Monday," and so on. Put this formula into the "Weekday registered" field in each column, and it will correctly display

Figure 3-20.
A user registration dates table in Google Spreadsheets

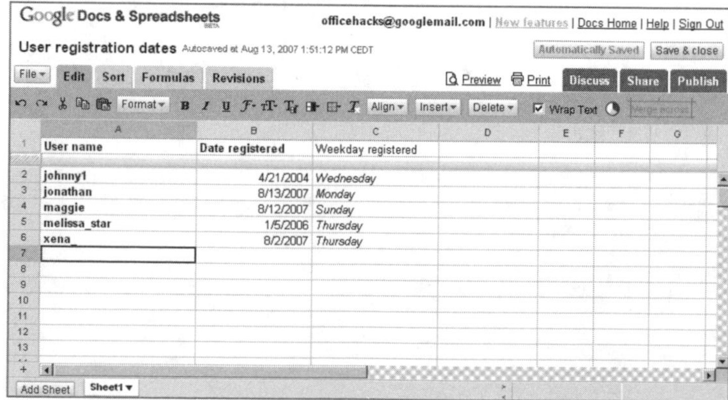

the day names as shown in Figure 3-20. And if you prefer the weekday to be shown in abbreviated form, like "Sun," "Mon," and "Tue," you can wrap this whole formula in the LEFT function, which takes two parameters (a text string and the number of letters to print):

```
=LEFT( CHOOSE( WEEKDAY(B2), "Sunday", "Monday", "Tuesday", "Wednesday", "Thursday", "Friday",
"Saturday" ), 3 )
```

Similarly, if you want to show the name of a month, you can use the MONTH function:

```
=CHOOSE( MONTH(B2), "January", "February", "March", "April", "May", "June", "July", "August",
"October", "November", "December" )
```

Although these examples and the Google Spreadsheets formula documentation show all function names written in uppercase, you can also write them in lowercase or mixed case.

HACK 25: Show the Difference Between Two Dates

Solve the question "how long ago?" with a straightforward formula.

Suppose you want to find out the number of days since a given date, such as when a user registered. Given a spreadsheet listing the dates, as shown in Figure 3-21 (see [Hack #24] for the weekday calculation), this is a straightforward subtraction between two dates; the current date, which you can access via the NOW function, minus the old date (B2 for the first data cell):

```
=INT( NOW() - B2 )
```

The INT function cuts off the fraction of the number by rounding it to its nearest integer. This way, only full days will be printed out. Change "B2" to the corresponding cell when you enter the formula into other fields, or click the cell with this formula (D2 in Figure 3-21) to highlight and drag the handle in the lower right to copy the formula. You can now click the sort bar below the "# days registered" cell to find out that user "johnny1" has been the most loyal registrant to date, being with us for for 1,209 days already.

Figure 3-21.
User registration dates in Google Spreadsheets

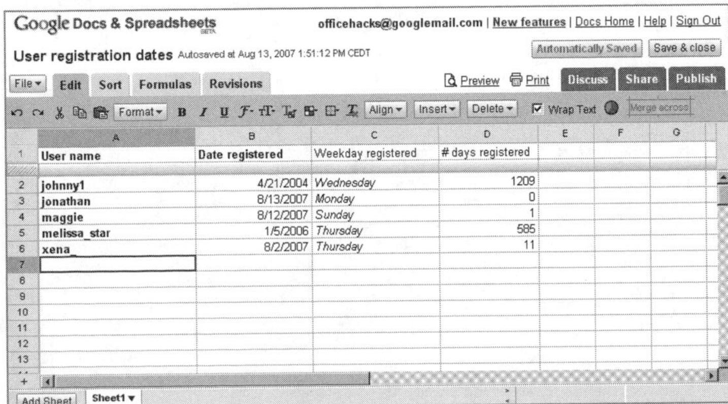

	A	B	C	D	E	F	G
1	User name	Date registered	Weekday registered	# days registered			
2	johnny1	4/21/2004	Wednesday	1209			
3	jonathan	8/13/2007	Monday	0			
4	maggie	8/12/2007	Sunday	1			
5	melissa_star	1/5/2006	Thursday	585			
6	xena_	8/2/2007	Thursday	11			

HACK 28: Automatically Complete Lists of Related Items

Google Spreadsheets is smart enough to finish lists of information for you, and can even go beyond what Excel or OpenOffice.org can do.

It's not unusual to find lists of related values in a a spreadsheet. For instance, you may come across a list of weekdays. To fill out such a list, you can start by typing the first three:

```
Sunday
Monday
Tuesday
```

You can automatically grow the list to include the other weekdays. You might have encountered this feature (*auto-fill*) in Microsoft Excel. Select your list cells, and then drag the handle in the bottom-right corner down over empty cells. Thanks to this feature, your list now reads:

```
Sunday
Monday
Tuesday
Wednesday
Thursday
Friday
Saturday
Sunday
Monday
Tuesday
...
```

This trick works with other sequential list data too, like *1, 2, 3* or *A, B, C* and more. When Google Spreadsheets is not able to continue the list data, it will just repeat the existing data in a loop for the repeated cells.

Hacking the Hack

You can even grow arbitrary lists with a different feature: Magic-Fill. Open a new spreadsheet and type the following superhero names into the cells:

```
Batman
Superman
Wonder Woman
```

Expanding this list as usual will just repeat the list. But here's a trick: instead of just dragging the handle in the bottom-right corner down, as shown in Figure 3-22, this time hold down the Control key (Option on the Mac) while doing so. The list that appears will now show something like the following:

```
Batman
Superman
Wonder Woman
batman
wonder woman
superman
green lantern
spiderman
jla
aquaman
the flash
```

Figure 3-22.
Continuing a list with the Magic-Fill feature

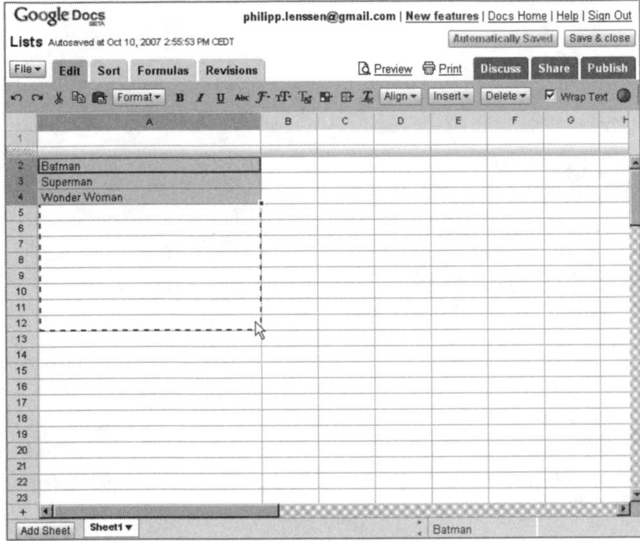

The Flash is a superhero; so is Spider-Man, and the JLA is the Justice League of America, a superhero group. But holy batarang, how on earth was Google able to tell that you are looking for new superhero names? This is certainly more than you might be used to from Excel. The answer to this feature lies in a member of the Google Labs service array called *Google Sets*. Give the tool a try by visiting http://labs.google.com/sets and enter the names *George Clooney, Brad Pitt*, and *Harrison Ford* into the first three boxes, as pictured in Figure 3-23. Press the Large Set button, and you will see a list like this one:

```
brad pitt
george clooney
harrison ford
tom cruise
angelina jolie
johnny depp
julia roberts
matt damon
bruce willis
jennifer lopez
britney spears
...
```

Not all among the results returned are male Hollywood actors, as the original names might have suggested, but Google seems to have understood your seed list contained U.S. celebrity names. You can try this with any other seed list, too (though Google in certain cases won't be able to find good results for you). Here are some example lists that you can try growing in Google Spreadsheets or Google Sets:

```
ford, hummer, bmw, ...
martin scorsese, stanley kubrick, todd solondz, ...
big mac, hamburger, cheeseburger, ...
theory of relativity, quantum theory, ...
```

Figure 3-23.
Google Sets, the basis for Magic-Fill

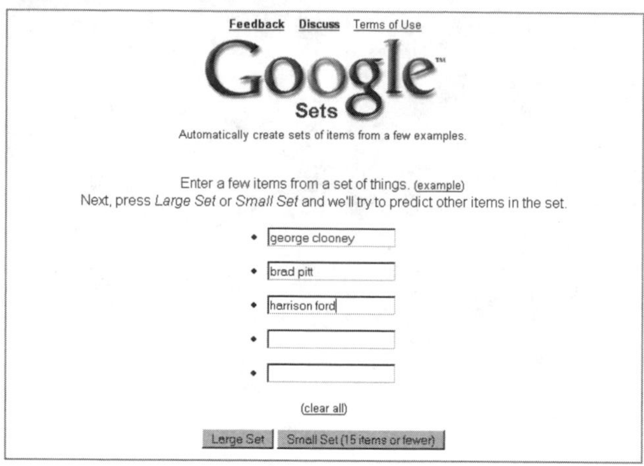

HACK 27: Import Data from Web Sites

Screenscrape bits and pieces from any web page for automated inclusion in your spreadsheets.

Google Spreadsheets offers you a set of default functions to look up financial data, or trivia from their Q&A database **[Hack #19]**. But you can go beyond this feature and access custom data from any web page, such as a list of links from a blog, or a list of titles or ISBN numbers from a bookseller's web site.

There are four key functions that can import external web data: *importXml*, *importData*, *importHtml*, and *googleReader*. The most flexible of these is *importXml*, as it turns any kind of HTML into structured data.

Suppose that you want to automatically add a list of book titles on the subject of extreme sports. Head over to a bookseller's web site, like Barnes & Noble (http://barnesandnoble.com) and perform a search for "extreme sports"; copy the address of the results page, shown in Figure 3-24. This URL might look like the following:

```
http://search.barnesandnoble.com/booksearch/results.asp?WRD=extreme+sports
```

Now you hold the first part to successfully use the importXML function: the URL of the source page. The second part of the equation is to tell your spreadsheet specifically which HTML part of that page you want, by using XPath, a language for specifying subsets of an XML (or XHTML) document. Open the HTML source of the Barnes & Noble page by right-clicking the page and picking "View Page Source" from the context menu. Check for the HTML structure in which the book titles are listed on the page. In this case, the surrounding HTML looks like the following (with indention and line breaks added for clarity):

```
<div class="bc-desc">
<h2>
<a href="isbnInquiry.asp?z=y&amp;EAN=9780316155601&amp;itm=5">
      Maximum Ride
...
```

One way to describe the position of the title is thus to say: *anywhere in the HTML, within a div tag of the class "bc-desc", there's an "h2" tag, and in it an "a" tag—extract the text within it.* In XPath syntax, this is expressed as:

```
//div[@class='bc-desc']/h2/a/text()
```

To explain, the double slashes in the beginning mean "anywhere within the structure," whereas a single slash means "a child node immediately below the current structure." The `@` character denotes an attribute. And `text()` grabs the text node itself, though it's optional for the importXml function (still, it's good practice to use it in case you use XPath in other environments).

To summarize, the cell content you want to paste into your spreadsheet is the following (all on one line):

```
=importXml("http://search.barnesandnoble.com/booksearch/results.asp?WRD=extreme+sports",
"//div[@class='bc-desc']/h2/a/text()")
```

Insert this formula into a cell, press Return or Enter and wait a few seconds. The result is a list like the following, also shown in Figure 3-25:

```
Extreme Sports
How Angel Peterson Got His Name
Winterdance
No Nest for the Wicket (Meg Langslow Series #7)
Maximum Ride
Bruce Lee's Fighting Method
Maximum Ride
Extreme Danger (Hardy Boys Undercover Brothers #1)
The Contest
The Summit (Everest Series #3)
```

You can now share this list **[Hack #2]**, embed it in a blog **[Hack #21]**, or do anything you could do with any other spreadsheet values.

Figure 3-24.
The Barnes & Noble search result page offers semistructured HTML data, which you can access in Google Spreadsheets

Figure 3-25.
Using the importXml function, there's now an automatically created list of book titles

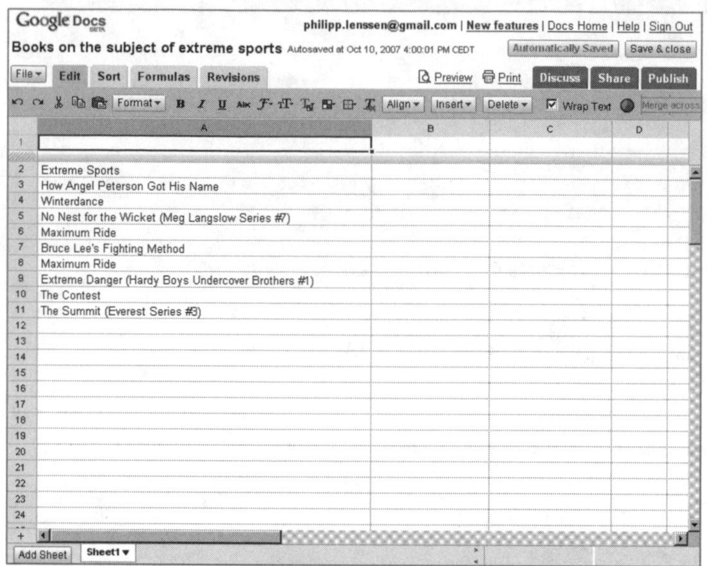

As soon as the external web site's HTML layout changes, your XPath—and with it, your automated spreadsheet list—might break. It makes sense to check your list every now and then to see whether it's still stable. Also, try to find an XPath that balances precision (so you don't find elements you don't need) with fuzziness (so that you don't nest your structure too deeply and precisely, as that makes the XPath more prone to break when the external HTML output changes).

Overview of the Data Import Functions

Here is an overview of Google Spreadsheet's data import functions, further described at http://docs.google.com/support/spreadsheets/bin/answer.py?answer=75507:

importXML

```
=importXml(URL, XPath-query)
```

Access an external XML or HTML file to return structured data via an XPath query.

The following example code retrieves the book titles as shown previously:

```
=importXml("http://search.barnesandnoble.com/booksearch/results.asp?WRD=extreme+sports",
"//div[@class='bc-desc']/h2/a/text()")
```

importData

```
=importData(URL)
```

Access an external CSV (comma-separated values) or TSV (tab-separated values) file. In fact, this works with any arbitrary URL, though the data returned may not be too useful; for instance, using importData to poll an HTML page might return a list of elements, each filling a single cell.

Here is example code, accessing the output of another spreadsheet (restricted to that other spreadsheet's cell range named "mainTable"):

```
=importData("http://spreadsheets.google.com/pub?key=pvm6FPiylicLvKQbERrGJVQ&output=csv&gid=0&range=mainTable")
```

importHtml

```
=importHtml(URL, "list" | "table", index)
```

Grab an external web page's table or list elements. The index parameter indicates the position of that table/list.

The following example retrieves the table values from a blog post, as shown in Figure 3-26, to convert them to cells of a Google Spreadsheet, as shown in Figure 3-27:

```
=importHtml("http://blogoscoped.com/archive/2007-09-10-n74.html", "table", 1)
```

Whenever your formula is showing an error, hover the mouse over the cell to see the details for this error.

Figure 3-26.
The source blog posting from Google Blogoscoped . . .

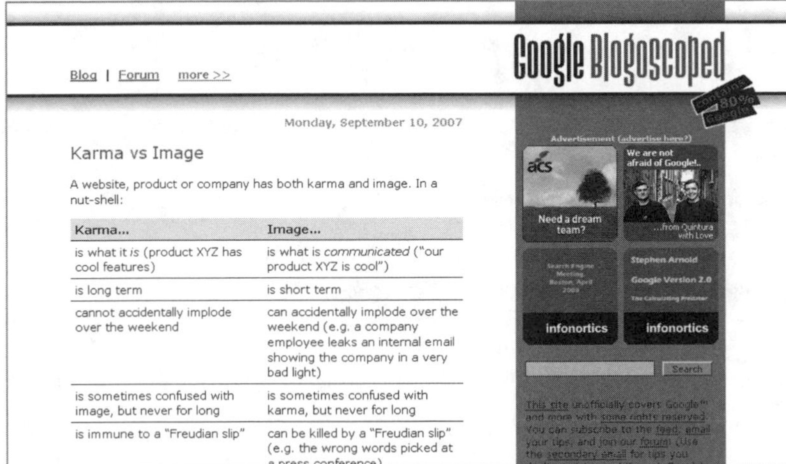

Monday, September 10, 2007

Karma vs Image

A website, product or company has both karma and image. In a nut-shell:

Karma...	Image...
is what it *is* (product XYZ has cool features)	is what is *communicated* ("our product XYZ is cool")
is long term	is short term
cannot accidentally implode over the weekend	can accidentally implode over the weekend (e.g. a company employee leaks an internal email showing the company in a very bad light)
is sometimes confused with image, but never for long	is sometimes confused with karma, but never for long
is immune to a "Freudian slip"	can be killed by a "Freudian slip" (e.g. the wrong words picked at a press conference)

Figure 3-27.
. . . and the blog posting's table, automatically turned into a spreadsheet

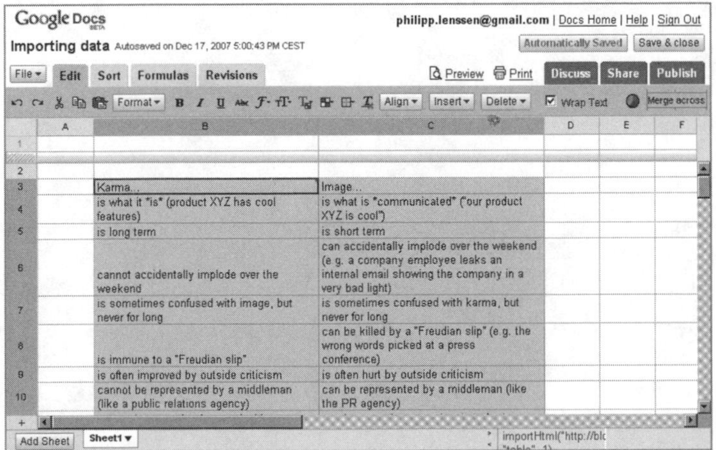

	A	B	C
1			
2			
3		Karma...	Image...
4		is what it "is" (product XYZ has cool features)	is what is "communicated" ("our product XYZ is cool")
5		is long term	is short term
6		cannot accidentally implode over the weekend	can accidentally implode over the weekend (e.g. a company employee leaks an internal email showing the company in a very bad light)
7		is sometimes confused with image, but never for long	is sometimes confused with karma, but never for long
8		is immune to a "Freudian slip"	can be killed by a "Freudian slip" (e.g. the wrong words picked at a press conference)
9		is often improved by outside criticism	is often hurt by outside criticism
10		cannot be represented by a middleman (like a public relations agency)	can be represented by a middleman (like the PR agency)

importFeed

```
=importFeed(URL, [feed-query | item-query], [headers], [number-of-items])
```

Import an RSS or Atom feed. The optional feed/item query parameter tells the function which parts of the data to return, accepting the values "feed", "feed title", "feed author", "feed description", "feed url", "items", "items author", "items title", "items summary", "items url", or "items created". The third parameter will be a Boolean value ("true" or "false") specifying whether you want column headers. The fourth parameter limits the number of returned items. This example code pulls the first four items from a blog's RSS feed:

```
=importFeed("http://sethf.com/infothought/blog/index.rdf", "items", , 4)
```

The following example code pulls all item titles from a feed, as shown in Figure 3-28:

```
=importFeed("http://waxy.org/links/index.xml", "items title")
```

This example gathers information about a feed, displaying column headers such as title, description, and URL:

```
=importFeed("http://feeds.feedburner.com/Googlified", "feed", true)
```

Figure 3-28.
Using the importFeed function to display RSS or Atom items

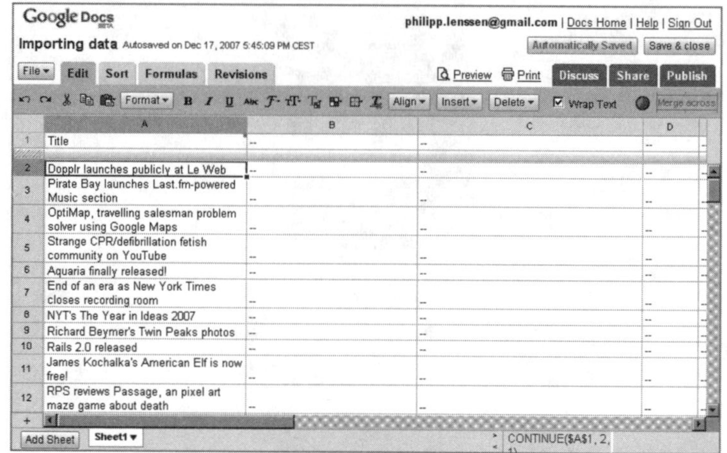

HACK 28: Format Cells According to Their Values

Add a little color to your spreadsheets to better visualize data.

Google Spreadsheets allows you to add conditional formatting to cells. This means that you can command your spreadsheet, for instance, to show every number greater than 1000 in green, or to use a yellow background color to highlight cells containing the word "John".

To get this feature to work for you, create a new spreadsheet or open an existing one. For sample purposes, I am creating a spreadsheet to collect newsletter subscribers, containing columns with the subscriber's name, age, and profession as shown in Figure 3-29. Once you've set up your spreadsheet, select all the columns you want to apply your conditional formatting to. They will appear highlighted in blue. Right-click them, and select "Change format with rules . . . " from the context menu, as shown in Figure 3-29.

In the dialog that appears, you can now specify your custom constraints, and the appropriate formatting. Let's say you want to highlight in red all those cells where the age of the user listed is below 18. In the drop-down box of the dialog, select "Less than," and in the value box enter "18" (without quotes), as shown in Figure 3-30. This custom color is applied to all cells that meet the criteria as soon as you hit the "Save rules" button. The formatting will also appear in published versions of spreadsheets.

Conditional formatting is also applied to cells containing dynamic values created with spreadsheet formulas.

Adding Gradients

Conditional formatting can help you visualize ranges of numbers in longer listings. Let's create a new column to the right titled "Yearly income in €" and add values for average income to the newsletter subscriber list. Suppose that you want to color lower incomes in red and higher incomes in green—and every income figure in between using some other color.

Figure 3-29.
The Google Spreadsheets context menu offers to let you change the cell formatting based on custom rules

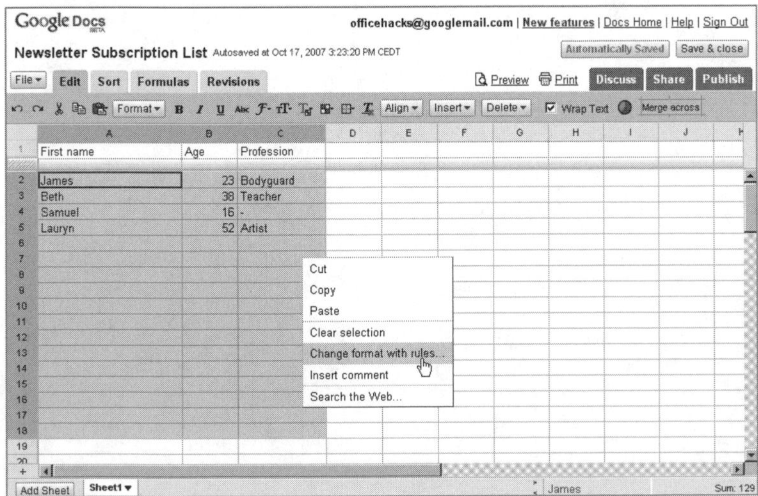

Figure 3-30.
Adding a special formatting rule for younger newsletter subscribers

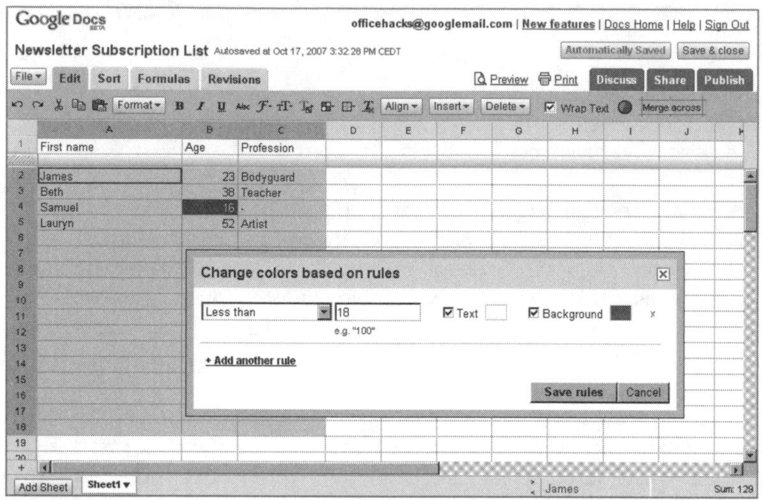

Figure 3-31.
A sample image serves as color reference

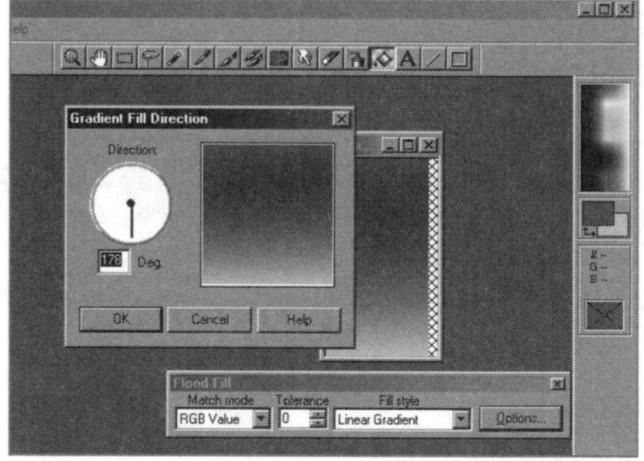

To help me pick the right in-between colors, I created a reference color gradient between red and green using a paint program that I referred to as I set up the formatting rules. You can use many different image editors for this purpose, like Photoshop, PhotoPaint, GIMP, or PaintShop Pro (which you see in Figure 3-31). You can, of course, simply wing it and not generate a gradient at all.

Now you can select your income data cells and add all the rules you need. Google Spreadsheets will apply the first rule it finds to be true, ignoring subsequent ones down the list, so you can simply define the rules in the following order, for a result as shown in Figure 3-32:

- Greater than 120,000: use light green
- Greater than 60,000: use green
- Greater than 30,000: use yellow/light orange
- Greater than 10,000: use orange
- Greater than –1: use red

Figure 3-32.
Creating a color gradient for your spreadsheet

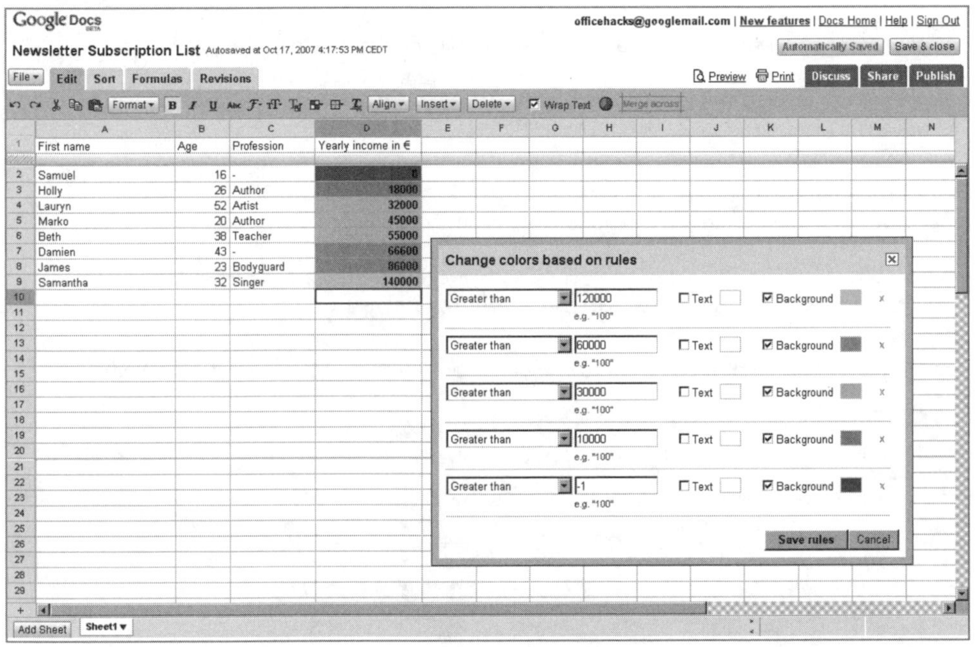

HACK 29: Convert Currencies Within Your Spreadsheet

Use a little screenscraping magic to convert one currency into any other.

Google Spreadsheets' importXml function pulls external web site data into your spreadsheet **[Hack #27]**. You can use this feature for currency conversion, too.

Suppose that you have a table with payments made to you from a variety of companies, just like the sample table shown in Figure 3-33. There are three columns: Company, USD, and EUR. The sample payments are provided in USD; Universal Exports, for instance, paid $200. It would be tedious if you had to convert the values into Euros manually for every row, but there's a way to automate this.

First, you need to find a good online currency converter to use for the importXml function. To recap, the Google Spreadsheets importXml formula uses two parameters:

```
=importXml(URL, XPath)
```

There's a variety of currency converters, but you must pick one that can be accessed using URL parameters (so that you can provide a URL containing the dollar amount and the "from" and "to" currencies to the importXml function), and that also returns HTML that is easy to parse (because you will need to write a little XPath query to retrieve the result). Google, too has currency conversion in search results, but they are not always formatted plainly enough. However, a service from Yahoo! Finance fits your needs perfectly. A URL like the following one:

```
http://finance.yahoo.com/currency/convert?amt=750&from=USD&to=EUR
```

returns a result as shown in Figure 3-34. The conversion results are embedded in an HTML table of the class "yfnc_datamodoutline1." This contains the Euro value in the second row, third column (508.5435 in Figure 3-34). Hence, the XPath to query for this number is:

```
//table[@class='yfnc_datamodoutline1']//tr[2]//td[5]
```

The complete importXml function call is (this should all be kept on one line):

```
=importXml("http://finance.yahoo.com/currency/convert?amt=750&from=USD&to=EUR", "//table[@
class='yfnc_datamodoutline1']//tr[2]//td[5]")
```

To make the formula more flexible, you need to replace the values 750, USD, and EUR with their respective cell names, as shown here for the "Acme Inc" row:

```
=importXml("http://finance.yahoo.com/currency/convert?amt=" & B2 & "&from=" & B1 & "&to=" &
C1, "//table[@class='yfnc_datamodoutline1']//tr[2]//td[5]/b")
```

Repeat this formula for all the other cells in your spreadsheet, using the correct cell names.

Figure 3-33.
The original table does not include € values yet

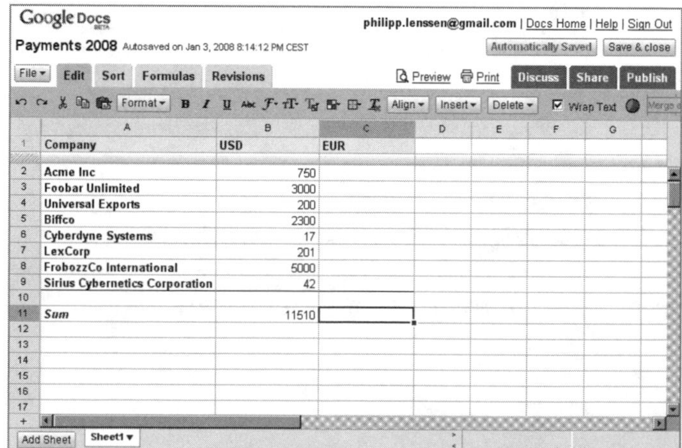

	A	B	C
1	Company	USD	EUR
2	Acme Inc	750	
3	Foobar Unlimited	3000	
4	Universal Exports	200	
5	Biffco	2300	
6	Cyberdyne Systems	17	
7	LexCorp	201	
8	FrobozzCo International	5000	
9	Sirius Cybernetics Corporation	42	
10			
11	*Sum*	11510	

Notice in Figure 3-35, that the Euro values are automatically filled in for you! Whenever you change a USD value on the left side, the values will automatically update, too. Also, you can replace EUR with, say, GBP for British Pounds, and the values will again be updated within seconds.

To find the correct currency abbreviation—from the Solomon Islands Dollar "SBD" to the Vietnam Dong "VND"—you can go back to the Yahoo! Finance page and inspect the values contained in the drop-down box.

There's currently a limit of 50 importXml operations in a spreadsheet.

Figure 3-34.
The Yahoo! Finance currency converter is the brains behind our operation

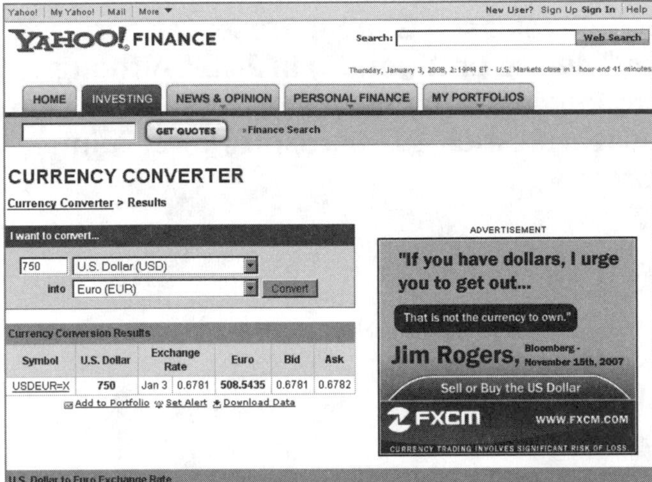

Figure 3-35.
The values calculated by importXml, utilizing Yahoo! Finance

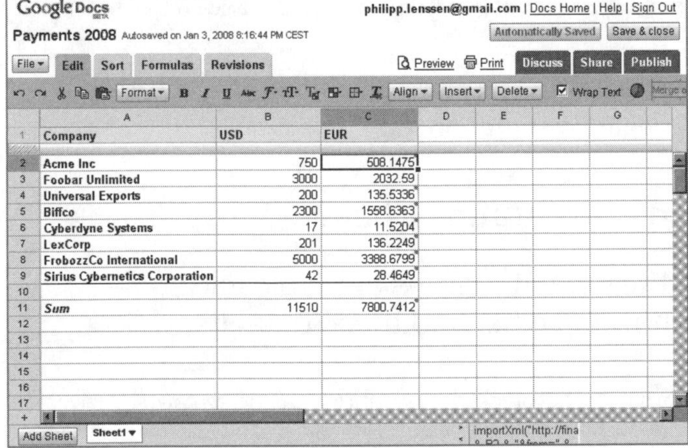

	A	B	C
1	Company	USD	EUR
2	Acme Inc	750	508.1475
3	Foobar Unlimited	3000	2032.59
4	Universal Exports	200	135.5336
5	Biffco	2300	1558.6363
6	Cyberdyne Systems	17	11.5204
7	LexCorp	201	136.2249
8	FrobozzCo International	5000	3388.6799
9	Sirius Cybernetics Corporation	42	28.4649
10			
11	*Sum*	11510	7800.7412

04 THE GOOGLE DOCS FAMILY: GOOGLE PRESENTATIONS

(Slide 1: Introducing Google Presentations.)

Twenty years after the release of the first version of the beloved and feared PowerPoint (codenamed "Presenter" during production), Google released Google Presentations (codenamed "Presently" during production) in 2007. Although the two products fit broadly in the same space, Google Presentations is not as feature-rich as Microsoft PowerPoint or OpenOffice.org Impress yet.

At the time of this writing, the browser-based Google Presentations editor allowed you to:

- Create slides with rich text and images
- Use themes (including specific color schemes, fonts, and background images)
- Import PowerPoint (PPT) files, with some limitations
- Use the revision history to review and revert to older versions of a presentation
- Share a presentation as a web page
- Export a presentation as a static HTML document
- Print a presentation

Another feature of Presentations is collaboration, and at least in that regard, it offers more than some of its desktop competitors do. Not only can you edit a presentation with someone else, seeing the changes they make reflected in your document in real time, but you can also present to a group online [Hack #2].

(On to Slide 2: Hacking Google Presentations...)

HACK 30: Add a Custom Presentation Theme

Don't limit yourself to the default themes available in Google Presentations. Here's how to go beyond those defaults.

Google Presentations offers only a small set of predefined layouts for your presentation. But what if you want to do something unique, such as getting your company logo and background colors on every slide of the presentation?

The "Change Background" Dialog

One way to do this is to right-click a blank part of any slide, and then select "Change background" from the context menu. A dialog like the one shown in Figure 4-1 will pop up. Click the "Insert image" link to upload an image or click the color bucket icon to pick a new background color. When done, check the "Apply background to all slides" checkbox, and click Save.

Figure 4-1.
The Change background dialog

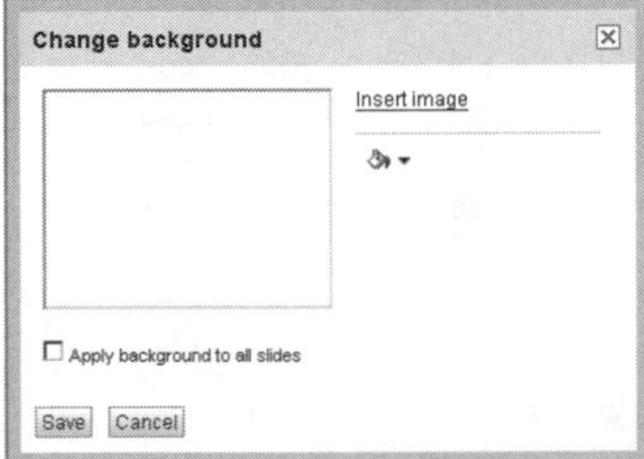

Directly Adjusting the Stylesheet

Another way to tweak your presentation's background image and colors is to export the presentation as a ZIP file, and then adjust the theme's stylesheet.

To do so, open an existing presentation, or create a new one. Now, select Change Theme from the top menu and pick the Gradient White theme (though other themes work as well), as pictured in Figure 4-2. Then choose File→Save as ZIP from the menu and pick a location on your computer. If you extract the ZIP file and open the folder, you will notice that Google provided you with a set of HTML files, stylesheets, and images, as well as JavaScript library files. Open the HTML file in the main folder—in the case of my sample presentation, it's called *All_About_Tea.html*—in your browser to have a look.

Figure 4-2.
Select one of the predefined themes in Google Presentations

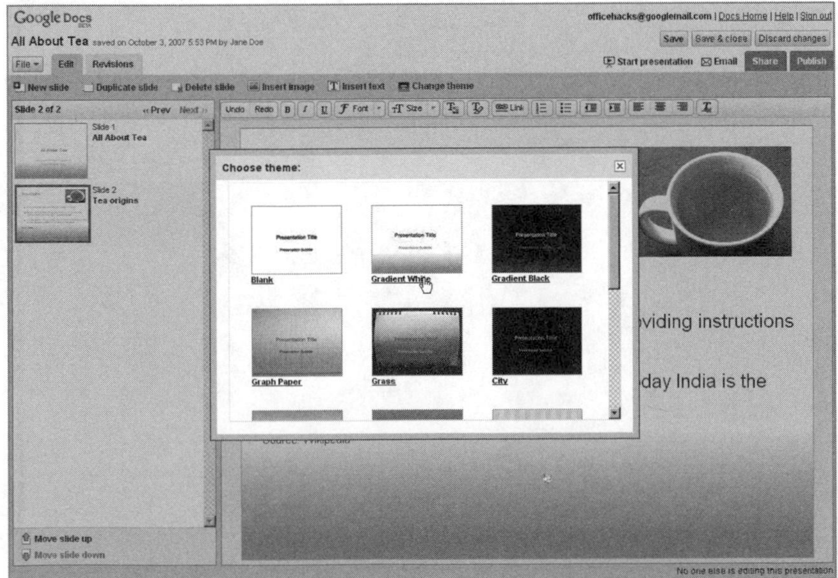

Next, locate the main background image of your presentation by opening the folder *files/themes/gradientwhite*. In it, you will find the picture *gradientwhite_sm.png*; open it in an image editor, replace it with your design, and save the image (but don't change the filename). You can create an image from scratch, as long as you give it the dimensions 800 x 600 and save it over the old image location in PNG format. Check the resulting presentation in the browser to see if you're happy with the design.

You can now upload the presentation folder to a web server, and send the link to other people. You could also zip the presentation up and send it to others as an email attachment.

In order to not replace the background image over and over whenever you export a new presentation, next time just copy your presentation's specific HTML file and folder to your server's presentation framework folder. For instance, if your presentation is called "All About Tea," then just move the files *All_About_Tea.html* and the accompanying folder *All_About_Tea_images* into your prepared main presentations folder. That folder, which you can call (for example) *Presentations*, now stores all of your exported presentations. There's a nice bonus to this approach: anytime you now make a change to the theme stylesheet, every presentation on the server will automatically adjust to the new layout—as long as all the presentations use the "gradientwhite" theme that you overrode.

This hack comes with a couple of caveats. Probably the most serious issue when exporting a presentation is that you're losing the capability to collaborate on it with others, or make later changes to it via Google Docs, as the ZIP file was simply a static copy of what your presentation looked like at the time of the export. Also, another, general issue with background images for themes is that they don't smoothly scale for any resolution; for instance, your company logo may appear "jaggy" if scaled up to resolutions higher than 800 x 600.

Hacking the Hack

Other than just changing the background image, if you know a bit about CSS syntax, you can also tweak fonts and colors to your liking. Open your theme's CSS file (*files/themes/gradientwhite/theme.css*) with a simple text editor and make the desired changes. For instance, the file contains the following code:

```
/* Default Body Content */
 .goog-presently-theme-gradientwhite {
   font-family: Helvetica, Arial, sans-serif;
   color: #333;
   background-color: #333;
 }
```

If you amend the color properties to read as follows, your presentation font will appear in dark red instantly—on every slide, as shown in Figure 4-3:

```
...
color: rgb(137,1,18);
background-color: rgb(215,210,179);
...
```

Figure 4-3.
Your presentation after customizing the theme

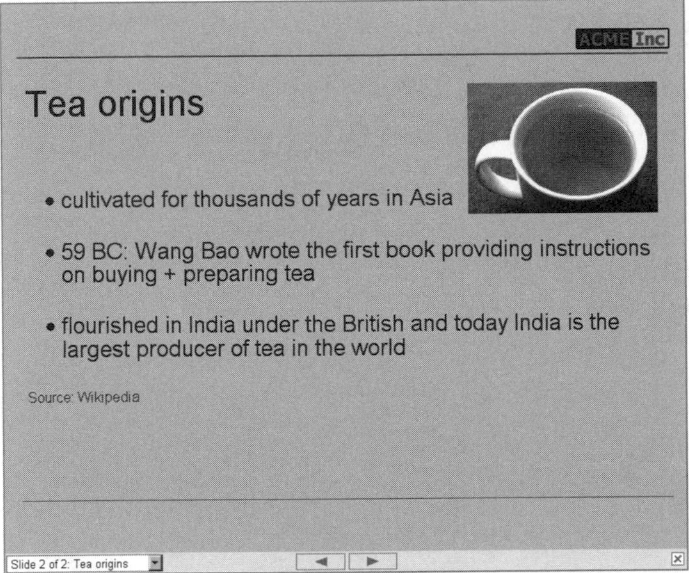

HACK 31: Find Images for Your Presentation

Not an artist or great photographer yourself, or just in a hurry to find the right image to help get your point across? Look for work with special free-to-share licenses.

If you want to spice up your Google Presentation with a telling visual, and you don't have a graphic designer to provide you with a custom-made one, you might be tempted to head straight to Google Images to perform a search. Unfortunately, it's not always easy to determine the copyright status of images you find on Google Images, and determining what is within your "fair use" rights for republishing copyrighted images can get complicated and may require legal advice (and obtaining permission to use a copyrighted image is usually rather time-consuming).

One way to make sure you are allowed to use a given picture is to look for it in public domain resources. For instance, very old pictures may be in the public domain, which is essentially a copyright-free zone. There are also websites dedicated to offering you public domain clip art, like the extensive http://www.openclipart.org.

The Creative Commons

But what about finding high-quality and recent photos? Enter the Creative Commons initiative (http://creativecommons.org). Creative Commons is a licensing scheme that allows the publisher of a work to choose from among a set of "some rights reserved" licensing terms. For instance, a photographer may allow anyone to reuse a photo in noncommercial contexts, as long as the photo source is appropriately credited.

Many web sites offer Creative Commons licensed material, but your first stop should be the photo-sharing web site Flickr. Instead of entering through the front door, which offers only a general photo search, point your browser to http://flickr.com/search/?l=cc for the Creative Commons–only search engine. Enter a keyword, such as "skyscraper," and look through the results for a fitting image, as shown in Figure 4-4. You can also visit http://www.flickr.com/creativecommons/, select just a single variant of the Creative Commons license, and search for photos that use this license.

Figure 4-4.
Searching for Creative Commons–licensed photos on Flickr

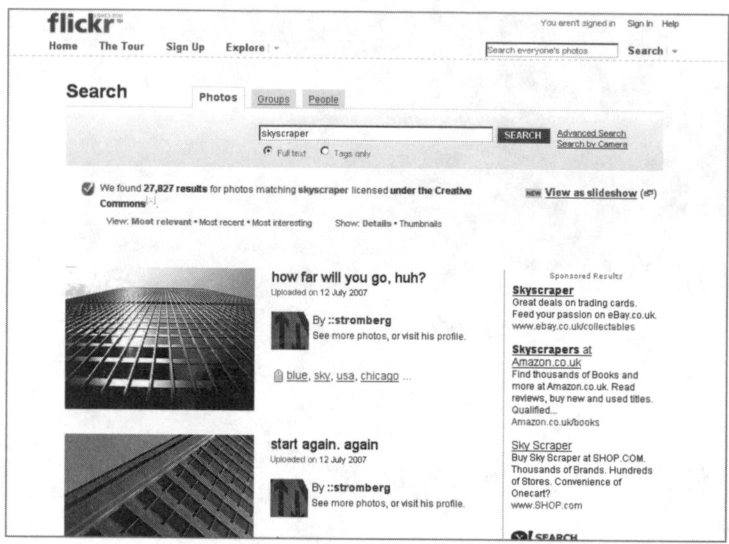

When you go to the photo detail page, you will find the specific licensing terms in the righthand navigation bar. Click on the "Some rights reserved" link to find out what exactly you can and can't do with the work.

For instance, if the photo has a "share alike" condition, then you must also license your presentation under the same or similar Creative Commons license; if you're comfortable with those terms, go to http://creativecommons.org/license/ to pick a compatible license. It's nice to share and may even give your presentation additional exposure. If the photo has an "attribution" condition, then you must credit the photographer. Pay attention to the various combinations of Creative Commons license terms. For example, "Attribution-NoDerivs" allows you to reuse the photo, but it does not allow you to create derivative works from it.

Note that when including an image from the Web in your presentation, you may need to open it in an image editor, and save in a lower resolution or lower quality format so that your presentation doesn't take a long time to load **[Hack #32]**.

HACK 32: Shrink Your Presentation for Easy Sharing

Don't leave it to Google to optimize the file size of your presentation.

Whether you're exporting a presentation to send to someone, or sharing a Google Docs presentation URL online, it makes sense to optimize the size of the file, so that you can reduce the amount of time it takes to download or view your presentation. The most frequent cause of bloated presentation file sizes are large images. They may also slow you down when you're editing your presentation—the same is true for Google documents, too.

> If you are a user of Adobe Photoshop or the free GIMP (http://www.gimp.org) graphics editor, you can use the Save for Web feature to save files in a nice compact format that also looks good online. Save for Web perform all of the steps described in this hack. In Photoshop, choose File→Save for Web. In GIMP, you'll need to download and install the Save for Web plugin from http://registry.gimp.org/node/33 before you can use GIMP's File→Save for Web option.

A photograph that you've taken or an image you've downloaded from the Web **[Hack #31]** may be too large to be efficiently embedded in a web page. Although you can resize the image within the presentation, Google still stores the original file in its original size, which means that the person viewing your presentation is downloading the full image file. Instead, when using large files, it's better to load the image file into your favorite image editor and export it using optimized settings; try to find the best image type and compression method, reduce the image resolution, and (for certain image formats) reduce the number of colors.

Find the Optimum Image Type and Compression Quality

There are many image formats you can choose from. The **JPEG** format is good for photos and certain images with complex multicolor shapes, as shown in Figure 4-5. Your photo editor may offer you different quality settings for saving, so choose the lowest quality that you're comfortable with; don't go too low on the quality, or your photo will contain the kind of heavy JPEG artifacts shown in Figure 4-6. Note that if your source file already contains heavy JPEG noise, you cannot remove it by just resaving with a higher quality setting.

Figure 4-5.
Photos are often best saved as JPEGs

> Avoid flat red color areas when saving as JPEG. This particular image compression algorithm often creates heavy, noisy artifacts for red.

The **PNG** format is optimized for line art, certain types of screenshots that don't contain large photos, and other less "complex" pictures, as shown in Figure 4-7. PNG is a so-called *lossless* compression format, so the image doesn't lose detail when it's saved; JPEG, on the other hand, will typically lose a bit of its quality every time you save it with different compression settings. To better help the PNG compression reduce your file size, you can also reduce the number of colors in your image to 256 (also known as 8-bit). Your image editing program should allow you to do this.

Figure 4-6.
The JPEG quality settings for saving this photo were too low, creating an unpleasant end result

GIF is a bit of an older format, similar to PNG files; here, the reduction to 256 colors—or 16 colors, or 2—is a must. In most circumstances, you should choose PNG over GIF. GIF allows only a single transparent color from the palette, whereas PNG supports varying ranges of transparency.

Figure 4-7.
Screenshots often fare well when saved as PNGs

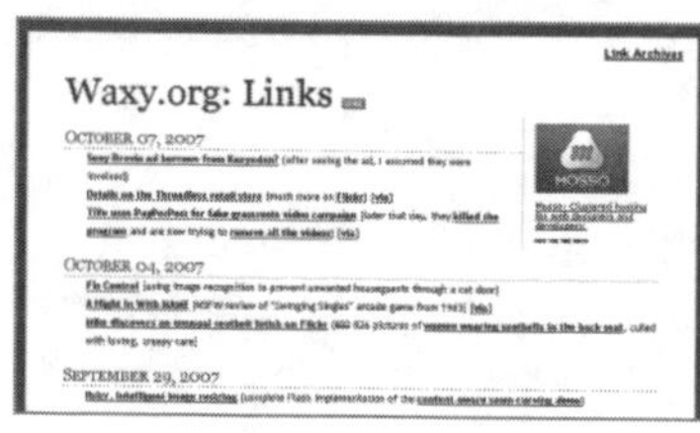

If in doubt about which image type to choose, try going for PNG first and check whether the image file size is acceptable; if the image ends up below 40 KB, for instance, this will do fine for most purposes. If the PNG ends up being too large, try to save as JPEG instead and compare file sizes.

> Some of Google's presentation themes use background images, like the Grass or Rustic themes. Although these images aren't dramatically big, if you want to fine-tune your presentation for best performance, you can also use a theme that doesn't use a background image.

Good Resizing and Color Reduction

There are different ways to resize an image, and to reduce its colors (useful for the PNG and GIF formats). Note that the terminology for these varies from one image editor to the next, but the underlying approaches are similar.

Resizing versus resampling: Sometimes when downsizing the resolution of a photo, you are offered to resize it, or to resample it. Resampling returns smoother results, as it "merges" the colors of adjacent pixels. It may only be offered in your photo editor if the image you are working on uses more than 256 colors; convert your image to a high-color format first if that's not the case. After resampling, you can decrease the amount of colors again before saving.

Dithering versus nondithered: When you reduce the number of colors for an image, your photo retouching application may offer you different methods for this. One of them is called *dithering* or *error diffusion*. This means that a "color spray" effect is used to create the impression of a higher color range. For instance, if you wanted to convert an image with a high range of gray tones to a black and white image, intermingling black and white pixels could be used to create the impression of different tones of gray, as shown in Figure 4-8. Although in general, dithering creates smoother results, it can also be detrimental to the file size, as PNG and GIF compression algorithms are better at optimizing larger same-color areas.

Figure 4-8.
A two-color image can use dithering to emulate gray areas

HACK 33: Use PowerPoint Templates

Load a presentation template into Google Docs. And don't take the wrong file extension for a "no."

When you export a presentation, you can tweak the images and stylesheets to fit your needs **[Hack #30]**. But if you have a PowerPoint template that you want to use (or if you find one online), there's a way to import those into Google Presentations.

To find a theme, search the Web for keywords such as *powerpoint themes* or *powerpoint templates*. For example, one site that popped up during my search was http://brainybetty.com/MENUPowerPoint.htm, which offers free ZIP files of Microsoft PowerPoint presentation templates. After I downloaded and unzipped them, I found that they contained files with the .pot extension (like *BusinessIII.pot*).

Google Presentations doesn't officially support PowerPoint templates, but if you make it think that the file is a PowerPoint document, you can get it to load. Change the file's *.pot* (PowerPoint Template) extension to *.ppt* (PowerPoint Document), open up Google Docs, and click the Upload button. Browse for your *.ppt* file, hit Upload File, and wait a bit. Your presentation will now consist of two or so slides, and you can multiply any slide by right-clicking a slide thumbnail and selecting "Duplicate slide" from the context menu, as shown in Figure 4-9.

If you have Microsoft PowerPoint or OpenOffice.org available on your local computer, you can create a new blank presentation, pick a template of your choosing, and then save the document as a .ppt. Then you can import it into Google Presentations.

Figure 4-9.
A PowerPoint template from BrainyBetty.com imported into Google Presentations

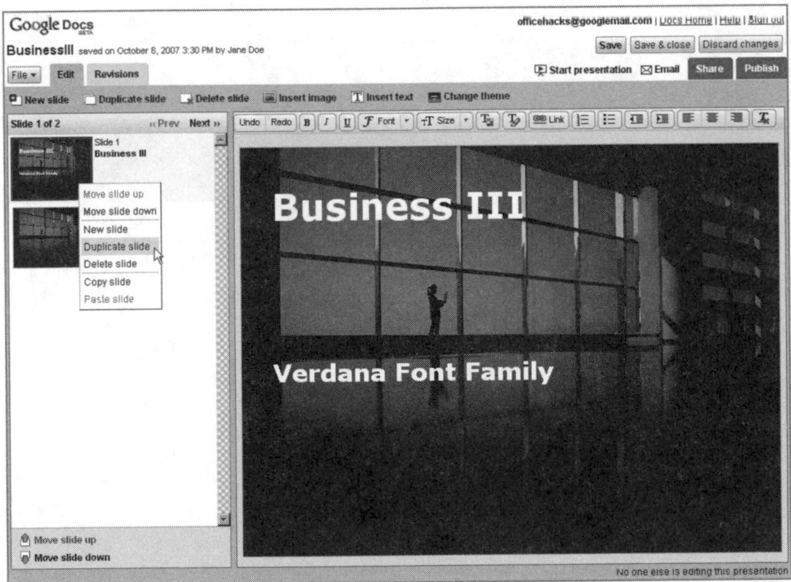

HACK 34: View Your Presentation on a Mobile Phone

Want to take a presentation with you?

As of this writing, Google did not offer a way to view presentations on a mobile phone. However, many mobile devices, especially so-called "smart phones," can view PDF files. If you've got a mobile device that supports PDF, you can generate a PDF version of your presentation by selecting File→ Export as PDF, and then send the PDF to your phone using Bluetooth, the synchronization software that came with your phone, or by putting it on the phone's memory card. Figure 4-10 shows a Google Presentation PDF on a Nokia Series 60 mobile phone.

There is at least one mobile device that can view PDFs, but which has no user-accessible file storage: the iPhone. To view a PDF on the iPhone, you can either post the PDF on a web site that you later access with your iPhone's web browser, or email it to one of the email accounts you can read on your iPhone.

If your mobile device does not support PDF, you may still be able to view it. The pdftohtml utility (see http://pdftohtml.sourceforge.net) can convert PDF files to HTML. This utility will turn a PDF into a collection of HTML and image files that you can transfer to a web server and view from any HTML-capable device. You'll need to experiment with pdftohtml's settings to optimize the generated HTML to fit the capabilities of your mobile device.

— Brian Jepson

Figure 4-10.
Viewing a presentation on the go
(the 34% indicates the document scale)

HACK 35: Make Your Presentations Easy to Read

Enhance the accessibility and readability of your presentation.

The World Wide Web is far from WYSIWYG—what you see is usually not what you get. What you see on your browser is only one rendering of the many possible ways a web page may appear to users. This flexibility isn't necessarily a bad thing, as it allows HTML to be converted to speech, to fit on small mobile screens, be spidered by search bots, or be rendered by nongraphical browsers. It also allows the reader of a document to make changes in their browser options to adjust the document—for example, a sight-impaired person might want to increase the document font size. Catering for all these kinds of devices and user needs is called *accessibility*.

Accessibility in part depends on the tools you use to generate the HTML. In the case of Google Presentations, you don't control the HTML during creation—it's possible that the presentation as generated by Google just won't adjust to a mobile phone display, for instance. However, you can still ensure that you use certain fonts, colors, and other design elements so that the presentation is clearly decipherable when viewed. Here are some tips to help you achieve this.

Note that some fonts may not be installed on the target system. As HTML typically doesn't embed fonts for viewing, the browser tries to find the font on the local system. If it's not there, it picks another font. At the time of this writing, Presentations allow you to choose from the fonts Arial (called "Normal"), Courier New, Georgia, Trebuchet, and Verdana. As these are rather common fonts, you should be generally safe with those. (And even if a fallback font is displayed on another browser, it's not the worst thing that could happen, although it can sometimes lead to strange overlapping between lines of text.) Know though that some characters you may be using, like Chinese characters or special symbols [Hack #12], may not be installed on the target system.

Choose a high-contrast color scheme. When your presentation is projected on a screen, it might become brighter, look washed-out, or lose some colors. A formerly perfectly tuned, subtle color scheme can suddenly become unreadable. To prepare for this in advance, use strong contrasts. For example, bright yellow text on a white background should be avoided, whereas black on white will always work. Some of the themes offered by Presentations, like the one named Bubbles, are already borderline in this regard. You should also make sure the line weights on your fonts are heavy enough to stand out well (fonts with thin weights tend to get lost).

Consider download times for your audience. Google Presentations are web pages, so they need to be downloaded to the browser before they are displayed. To create fast-loading presentations, try not to include giant images. Sometimes, choosing the right image file type, compressing the images, and reducing the number colors can go a long way toward improving download speed [Hack #32].

Try not to convey information by color alone. If you use colors to make a point, it makes some sense to also include the relevant information in another way, as color blind people may have difficulty with the combinations of colors you have selected. For instance, if you display a graph that distinguishes items using color, you should also use a secondary cue, such as patterns or thickness.

> The Trace Research and Development Center includes links to sites and tools that will help you adapt your color scheme choices for color blind users. See http://trace.wisc.edu/world/web/#dis_web_use.

If writing for a global audience, don't expect a full grasp of the English language. This is more about readability than accessibility: using simpler wording can sometimes allow your readers to get your point quickly, as they won't need to look things up in a dictionary. (A thesaurus, like the one found at http://thesaurus.com, comes in handy when looking for simpler word alternatives.) Granted, sometimes a more exotic word just gets the point across more elegantly, and may be the best choice . . . and even members of a foreign audience might be interested in learning new words. Often, a balance between the two approaches can achieve good results.

HACK 36: Embed a Presentation in Your Web Page

Go small with your presentation.

If you have a blog or other web site, you can either point people to the presentation by linking to it—or, if you want to make things quick and easy for your visitors, just embed the so-called Mini Presentation Module.

To use it, first make sure your presentation is published. In Google Presentations, switch to the Publish tab and click "Publish document" (you can unpublish the document later if you change your mind). A box appears with an HTML snippet like the following:

```
<iframe src='EmbedSlideshow?docid=dfw57tn_31g8h2k4' frameborder='0' width='410' height='342'></iframe>
```

Copy and paste this into the your blog or web page using the HTML view of your editor. In Figure 4-11, I'm using Blogger.com. The result, as shown in Figure 4-12, is a miniature version of the presentation, styled not unlike the YouTube video player. Back and forward buttons allow the visitor to go through your slides.

Figure 4-11.
Preparing a blog post in Google's Blogger; note that the HTML snippet needs to be entered into the Edit HTML tab, not the Compose tab of the editor

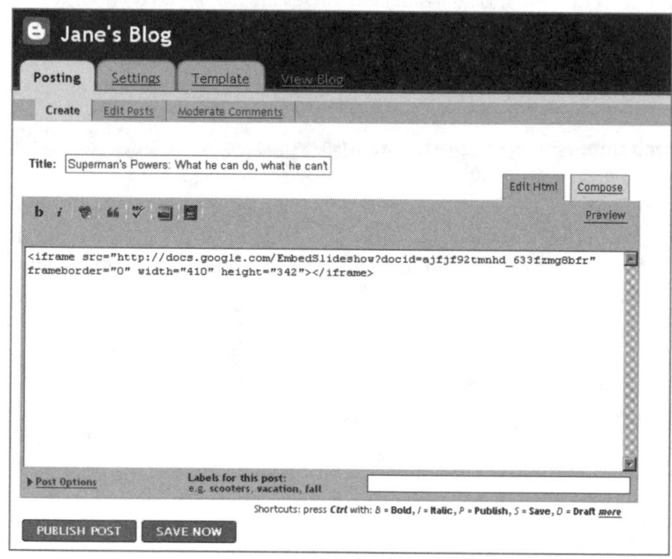

Note that at the time of this writing, you cannot successfully change the width and height attributes of the HTML snippet—your mini presentation will always remain fixed at 410 x 342 resolution.

If you care about HTML accessibility, include a plain link to the published presentation between the opening and closing iframe tags like this: <iframe ...><a href="...">My presentation</a></iframe>. This link lets your readers find your presentation even if they are using a tool that doesn't support inline frames—say, certain RSS feed readers (tools and browsers that do support iframes will just hide your alternative link). And if you care about HTML validation, note that you need to make sure your HTML document conforms to the "transitional" document type for the iframe element to be valid. To try validating your site, point your browser to http://validator.w3.org and enter your site's URL. (Not every error pointed out by the World Wide Web Consortium's validator will cause troubles in popular browsers, though some of the errors may do so.)

Any kind of widget embedded in your web site may slow down the loading time of your page; this includes mini presentations. Don't shy away from using widgets, but do test your site every now and then, and try not to include too many of them.

Figure 4-12.
The result is an embedded Google presentation, with all images and text scaled down for miniature reading

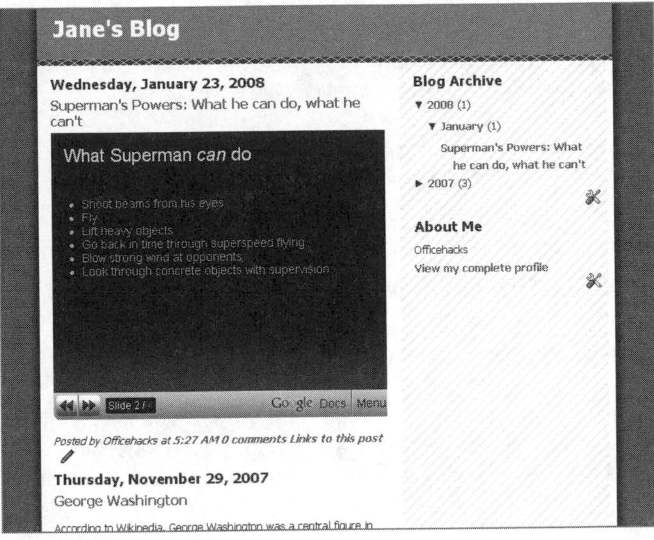

HACK 37: Drag and Drop Images from Other Web Sites

Include another site's images without saving them locally first.

This feature of Google Presentations is a bit of a rarity among web applications, so it could easily get lost, although it's really useful: you can drag and drop images from other web sites into your presentation, as shown in Figure 4-13. Just open two browser windows side by side, click and hold the left mouse button on the picture, and drag it into a blank spot within your presentation slide. (Note that this creates a copy of the original image on Google's servers, so the original server will not need to bear the bandwidth burden when people view the image in your presentation.)

Figure 4-13.
Dropping the Flickr image into the slide

If you plan to publish your presentation, make sure you are within your rights to use the image: either ensure that you are working within the principles of Fair Use (web sites such as http://copyright.gov/fls/fl102.html and http://fairuse.stanford.edu have extensive information on Fair Use) or choose an image that has a license permitting you to share it **[Hack #31]**. For instance, the photo I'm using in the figure is by Hildo Trazo, who was nice enough to release it under a Creative Commons Attribution license. The license requires me to add the necessary credits within the presentation before publishing it.

> The image file size will remain the same as the source file, even if you resize the image within your presentation, so you may be better off saving it locally first and resizing it **[Hack #32]**.

HACK 38: Save Your Presentations as Video

If a picture tells a thousand words, a video tells a million.

When you convert your presentation to a video, you can upload it to sites like YouTube for easy embedding and viewing. A video presentation also allows you to add sound such as music and voiceovers. But how do you go from a web page (remember, every Google presentation is essentially a web page) to video format?

Windows Movie Maker is a free program by Microsoft that lets you create videos. It's included with Windows XP and Vista (Start→All Programs→Windows Movie Maker). You can cut the video, add sound, use subtitles, and more. Similarly, Mac OS X has iMovie, installed by default on every Mac (for a quick and easy slideshow, iPhoto will do the trick). Whether you're on Mac OS X or Windows, you need to turn your presentation into a sequence of images before you can make a movie. There are two ways to do this. But first, use File→Save as PDF to get a PDF of your presentation.

Break a Presentation up Into Images Using Screenshots

Using an image editor—like Photoshop, PhotoPaint, PaintShop Pro, or the GIMP—you can take screenshots from the PDF view of the presentation.

On Windows, you can make a screenshot of each PDF page by pressing the PrtScrn button to put the entire screen into your clipboard. Then, paste the screenshot into your image editor. In your image editor, crop the screenshot to the exact size of the slide, as shown in Figure 4-14. Save each slide as *1.png*, *2.png*, *3.png* and so on. On Mac OS X, press Command-Shift-4, and the mouse cursor will turn into a crosshair. Click and drag to select a slide, and Mac OS X deposits a screenshot on your desktop named *Picture 1.png*. Repeat for each slide, and you'll have *Picture 2.png*, *Picture 3.png*, and so on.

Break a Presentation Into Images Using ImageMagick

ImageMagick is an open source suite of image manipulation tools that let you convert, crop, and style images—and that's naming just a few of its capabilities. You can also use ImageMagick to turn a PDF into a sequence of images. Go to http://www.imagemagick.org to download and install the version of ImageMagick for your operating system.

To use ImageMagick, you need to get yourself to a command line prompt. On Windows, this is called the Command Prompt, and can be found via the Start menu (or you can press Windows-R, type `cmd`, and then press Enter). On Mac OS X, open the Finder, make your way to the Applications directory, and then into the Utilities directory under that. Run the Terminal program.

Now you need to `cd` (change directory) to where your PDF is. Assuming it's on your desktop, here's what you type to do it on Windows:

```
cd %HOMEDRIVE%%HOMEPATH%\Desktop
```

Figure 4-14.
Generating individual slideshow images

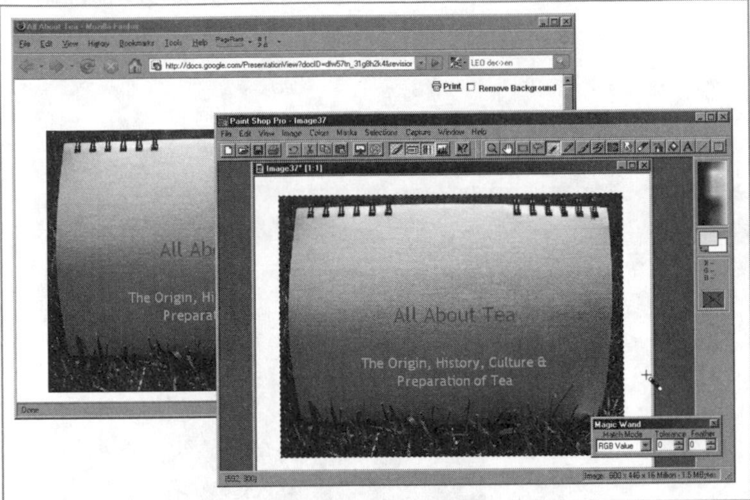

On Mac OS X, type:

```
cd ~/Desktop
```

Now, you need to run the *convert* command on your PDF. A `%d` in the output filename tells ImageMagick to generate a series of numbered images. You'll need to replace "All About Tea.pdf" with the name of your PDF:

```
convert "All About Tea.pdf" slide_%d.png
```

Windows has its own command-line utility named convert. If you've installed ImageMagick, it should have set things up so you run its convert utility instead of the Windows one. If you need to run the Windows convert utility, try the command `%SYSTEMROOT%\SYSTEM32\convert /?`. If you find that the Windows convert utility is running instead of ImageMagick's, try `"C:\Program Files\ImageMagick-6.3.8-Q16\convert.exe"`. (The exact name of the ImageMagick directory may be different depending on which version you installed.)

When you're done, you'll have a series of images on your Desktop: slide 1 will be named *slide_0.png*, slide 2 will be named *slide_1.png*, and so forth. Now you are ready to drop your images into the movie.

Alternatively, if you'd like an animated GIF, ImageMagick would be happy to oblige. Specify a GIF as the output filename without the `%d`, and specify a delay in seconds, as in: `convert -delay 5 "All About Tea.pdf" "All About Tea.gif"`.

Making the Movie

After completing the previous steps, run Windows Movie Maker (Windows) or iPhoto (Mac OS X). If Movie Maker is not on your Windows computer already, point your browser to http://microsoft.com/windowsxp/downloads/updates/moviemaker2.mspx to find out more about how to get it.

After starting Movie Maker or iPhoto, you can select all of your individual PNG images at once and drag and drop them into the program.

If you're using Windows Movie Maker, you should first adjust the presentation speed by going to Tools→Options→Advanced and setting the picture duration. Arrange the images on the storyboard as shown in Figure 4-15. You can give the video a test drive now and add titles, subtitles, effects, image transitions and sound, and then save it by choosing File→Save Movie File. The generated video format is WMV, short for Windows Media Video, which is also supported as an upload format on Google's YouTube.com.

When you want to upload your presentation clip to a video sharing site, it is advisable that you use the highest quality export settings in Movie Maker, as YouTube and others will compress the video to a smaller file size later anyway.

Figure 4-15.
The slideshow images are now imported to Windows Movie Maker

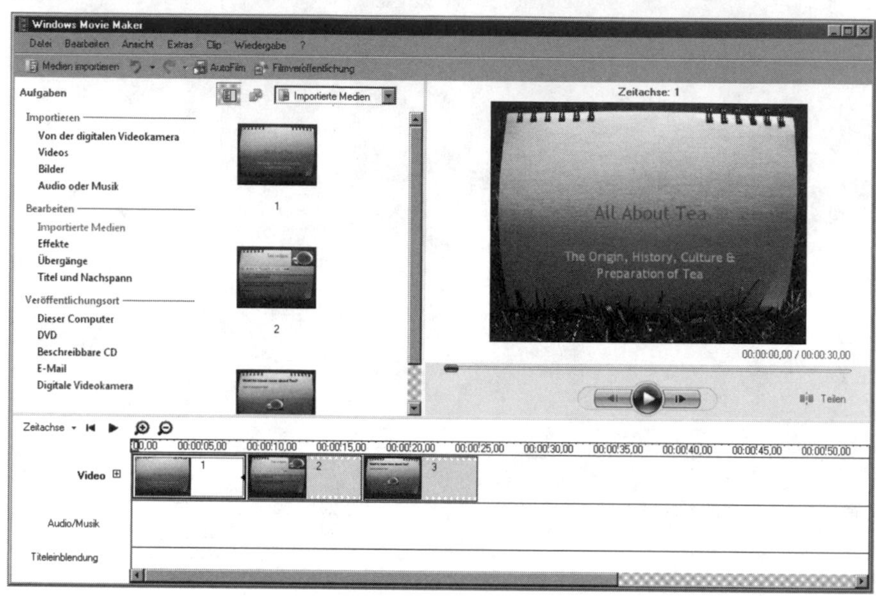

On Mac OS X, select the images in iPhoto, choose File→Export, and then pick QuickTime. Choose the desired options (including background music, image size, and how long to display each image) as shown in Figure 4-16, and click Export.

You can record your own voice to add as a sound layer for the presentation, which will enable you to guide the viewer through the slides. Or, if you want to add music but you don't have anyting appropriate on your computer, you can search Google for keywords like `royalty-free music, dramatic music, public domain mp3s, creative commons music` and so on (make sure that the music you find is indeed royalty-free). If you want to add sound to your presentation on Mac OS X, import your slideshow video into iMovie first. iMovie has many more options than iPhoto.

— Brian Jepson and Philipp Lenssen

Figure 4-16.
Exporting slideshow images to a video on Mac OS X

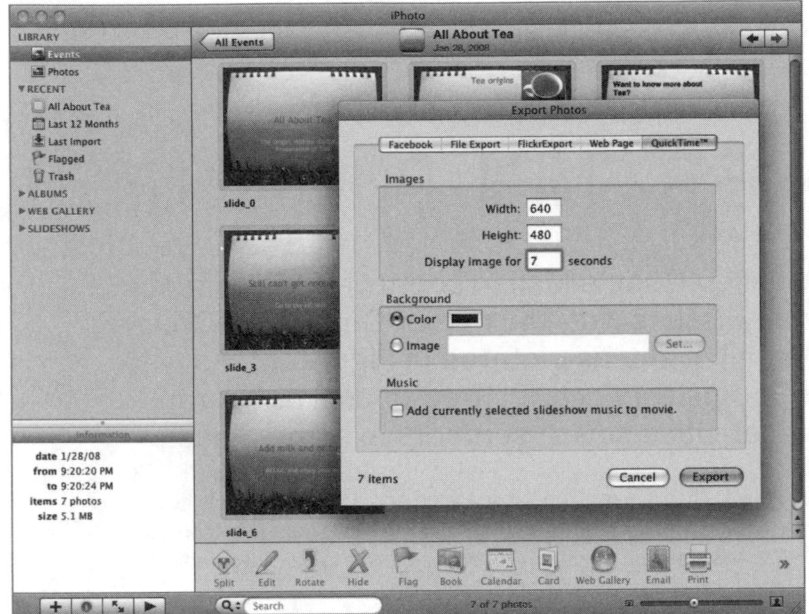

05 BECOME A GMAIL POWER USER

Gmail—also called Google Mail in countries where there were trademark issues with the name "Gmail"—is Google's web-based email client, as pictured in Figure 5-1. As with many other Google services, it's free to use, but comes with context-sensitive advertisements in some places.

Gmail made quite a splash when it arrived on the scene on April 1, 2004, not only because of its then 1 GB of storage, which many people first believed was an April Fool's hoax (Microsoft's Hotmail, in comparison, had only 2 MB at the time), but also because the interface reinvented some aspects of what we usually expect from email clients. Today, Gmail has:

- A conversation view that sorts replies to your mails into a single thread.
- Built-in chat functionality, allowing you to switch between email and Google Chat.
- An inbox that instantly displays after signing in (other email clients often show the inbox only after an extra click).
- Labels instead of folders, meaning that you can attach multiple keywords to a single email.
- An expandable storage plan, where you can buy some extra gigabytes if in need (and share the extra storage with other Google applications, too).
- A search function that returns results within split-seconds. Paul Buchheit, one of the inventors of Gmail, said "Everyone here [at Google] had lots of email. This company is a little bit email crazy. I get 500 emails a day. So there was a very big need for search."[1]

While Gmail can do a lot already, people expanded it over time with homemade tools and tricks. One popular approach is to use Greasemonkey scripts. A Greasemonkey script expands your Firefox browser to get a web page to do more than its makers intended it to do **[Hack #42]**. You can also hack Gmail by adding a user stylesheet **[Hack #41]**. And there's an abundance of advanced native features that you can use, like the Gmail search operators **[Hack #44]**—useful even if you get fewer than 500 mails a day—and third-party tools that connect to Gmail **[Hack #45]**.

To sign up for Gmail and get an address in the form of *janedoe@gmail.com*, go to http://gmail.com and log in with your Google Account (see Chapter 1). Figure 5-1 shows a Gmail inbox.

WHAT'S WITH ALL THESE ADS?

Gmail displays advertisements that are targeted to your emails. This means that when you or your friends talk about, say, indoor sundials (a special device utilizing a rotating lamp to show the time even when the sun's not shining!), the advertisement next to the message may read "Buy cheap indoor sundials" with a link to the sponsor. When Gmail was launched, this stirred up some controversy because people realized that Google's machines would read their email in order to target the ads. The truth is, all web-based email clients must access your

continued on next page

1 *Founders at Work*, Jessica Livingston (Apress, 2007).

Figure 5-1.
The Gmail inbox, currently using 0% of the available 2888 MB.

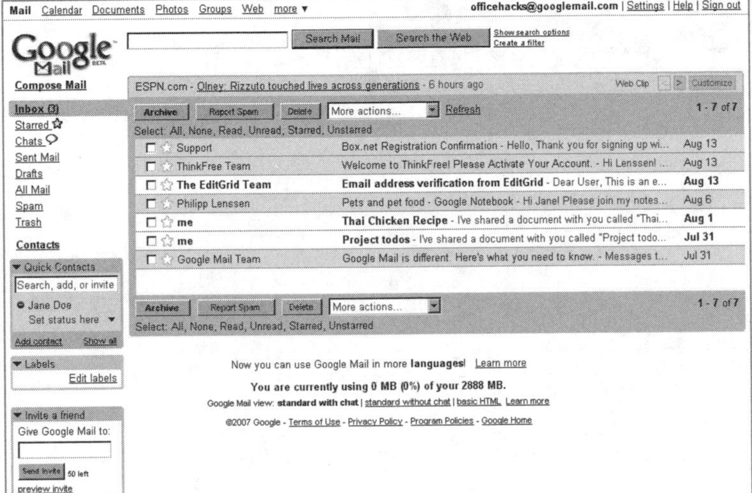

HACK 39: Send Mail to Several People at Once

Do you find yourself addressing the same group of recipients over and over? It can be quite monotonous to enter all their email addresses every time. There is an easier way to achieve this.

If you haven't gotten around to checking out the Contacts functionality in Gmail, have a look by clicking on the lefthand "Contacts" link in Gmail. You will now see a list of your contacts with whom you exchange mail frequently, as well as a complete list of contacts, and your contact groups. For every contact, you can provide address or telephone details, along with other private notes on the contact. You can also add a small photo for every contact, or add a contact group.

Creating your own contact group has one major advantage: you will then be able to just type the group name in the Gmail To: field, and see it expand to the full list of recipients. Not only will this save you time typing, it also decreases the chance that you'll accidentally address the wrong person (sending potentially private information) because two of your contacts share the same first name.

To create a new group, switch to the Contacts dialog. Click the button with a plus sign and two people at the top of this box to add a group (see Figure 5-2). Name the group—like "Family" or "Colleagues." Then, select "All Contacts" again, and place a check mark next to those you want in the group. Click on the Groups button, and select your new group from the drop-down "Add to ..." list. Now, when you compose a new message by clicking Compose Mail or hitting **c [Hack #46]**, you can just enter the first letters of the group name and hit Return or Tab to expand the name to all email addresses of this group automatically as shown in Figure 5-3.

WHAT'S WITH ALL THESE ADS?

continued from previous page

mail content in order to store, process and display it, but Google decided to display targeted instead of untargeted ads. The rule of thumb is: as email may contain a lot of private information on you and your friends, only use email clients from companies which you trust to handle this information with care. This is true for Gmail, Windows Live Mail, Yahoo! Mail and even email that's not web-based: email messages that are sent and received must pass through an email server that's under the control of whomever provides you with email service.

Figure 5-2.
Adding a Gmail contact group

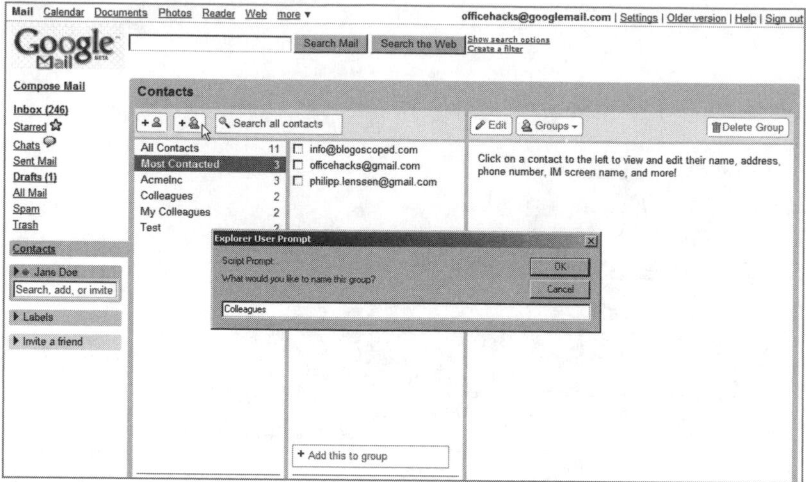

Figure 5-3.
Gmail's autocompletion feature in action

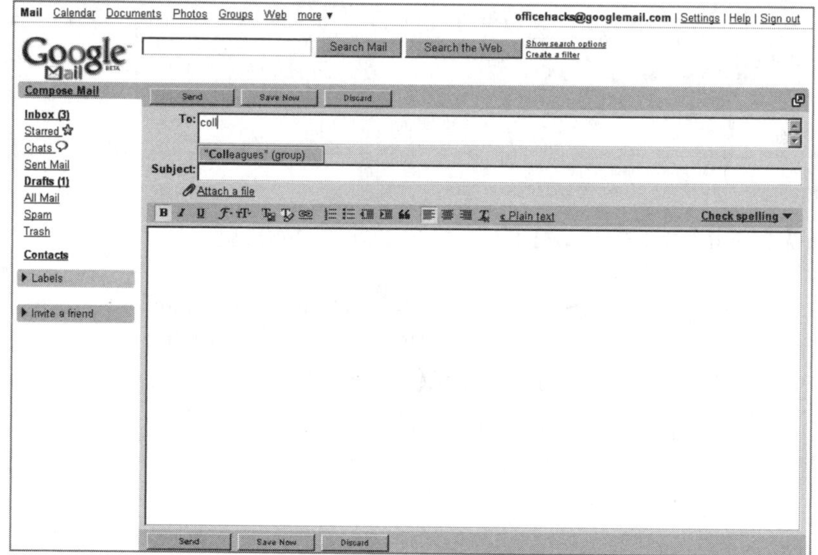

HACK 40: Import Contacts from Other Email Programs

If you moved from another email client to Gmail, you lost all of your existing contact addresses. Or did you?

Gmail allows you to import and export your contact data. The file format for this is a comma-separated values (CSV) file. To import a CSV file, log in to Gmail and click the Contacts link to the left. Now click Import (at the time of this writing, located at the bottom of the screen), click Browse to select your CSV file, and click Import.

But how do you get Outlook Express, Hotmail, Thunderbird, or Mac OS X Mail to create such a file for you? Here is how to do it in these programs; other email clients have similar export options.

Outlook Express

In Outlook Express, choose File→Export→Address Book... from the menu, as shown in Figure 5-4. In the dialog that follows, select "Text File (Comma Separated Values)" and click the Export button. Choose a location for the CSV file and select the fields you want to export, or just leave these checkboxes on their default selection.

If you are curious, this is what the saved CSV file may look like if you were to open it in a simple text editor (with some of the many fields snipped for brevity):

```
Name,E-mail Address,Home Street,Home City,Home Postal Code,...
Frank Smith,frank...@gmail.com,,London,,...
Daniel Clowes,daniel@example.com,,Oakland,,...
Jaime Hernandez,jamie@example.com,,,,...
...
```

As you can see, the first line contains the field names, and the other lines contain the field values in sequential order. You can also open a file like this in Excel, Google Spreadsheets, or any other program supporting CSV.

Figure 5-4.
Exporting an address book in Outlook Express

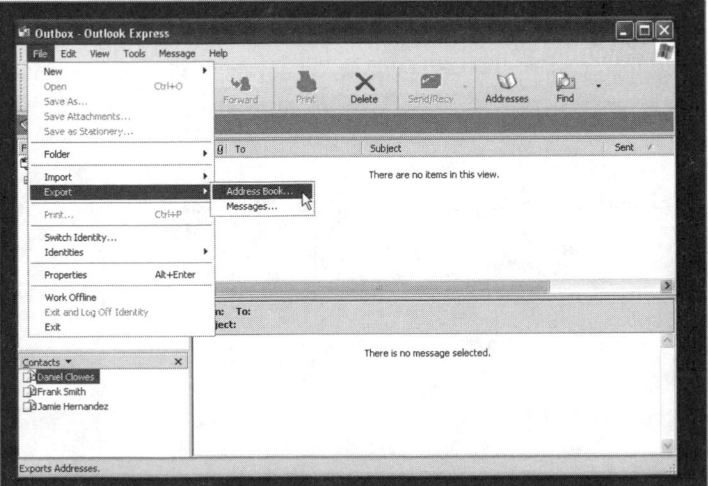

To import this file into Gmail, open Gmail and choose Contacts→Import, as shown in Figure 5-5. Note that after a successful import, you may need to switch from "Most Contacted" to "All Contacts" to see the new contacts (and to further edit them in Gmail, as you see fit).

Hotmail

If you have signed up with Windows Live Hotmail but you want to switch to Gmail, you can take your address book with you as well. Start by logging in to Hotmail.com. Click the Contacts button to the left side, and then choose Options→Export contacts from the top-right menu. Click the "Export contacts" button to start the file download. Save the CSV file somewhere, and import it into Gmail by choosing Contacts→Import from within Gmail.

Figure 5-5.
Importing the address book into Gmail

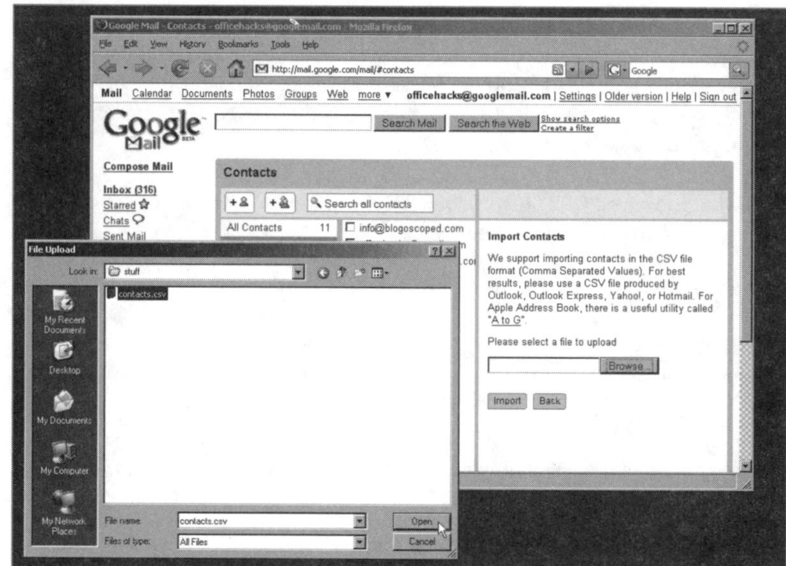

Mozilla Thunderbird

If you are using Thunderbird as your mail client, you can export your contacts by opening up the address book and selecting Tools→Export from the menu, as shown in Figure 5-6. In the save dialog, choose Comma Separated as file type. Pick any file name, like "contacts", and save. Open the saved file by choosing Contacts→Import in Gmail.

Mac OS X Address Book

If you use Apple's Mail program, all your contacts are probably in Apple's Address Book application, which cannot export CSV on its own. However, the free A to G utility, available at http://bborofka.com/atog/, can do this for you.

Figure 5-6.
Exporting Thunderbird's address book

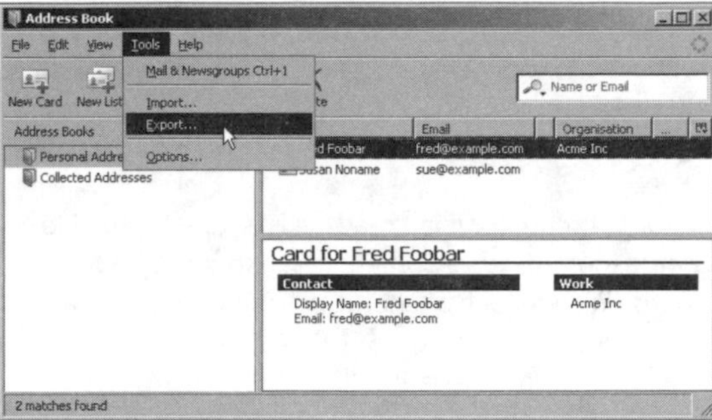

HACK 41: Adjust Your Gmail Layout

By adding a user stylesheet to your browser, you can tweak the design of any web page, including Gmail.com.

The default Gmail layout is already good, but you might want to adjust some details to improve on it. For instance, you might think the font size of messages is too small to comfortably read. One thing you can do is press Ctrl-+ (Command-+ on the Macintosh) in your browser (this works in Internet Explorer 7 or Firefox 2, among others). But, depending on your browser, this technique may also change other web pages that you read.

Another approach to tweak the Gmail layout is to add a user stylesheet. Stylesheets—or CSS (short for "cascading style sheets")—come in two flavors: *user stylesheets* and *author stylesheets*. An author stylesheet is created by the webmaster and delivered to you from the server. (In theory, the webmaster can create several author stylesheets, one for each medium—printed hard copy, mobile devices, computer screen, and so on.) A user stylesheet, on the other hand, is stored locally on your computer, and can override the settings of the author stylesheet. Together, the two styles will be merged into what you will see displayed in the browser.

Let's use a simple stylesheet that will turn the background of every web page (not just Gmail) gray:

```
body {
     background-color: gray !important;
}
```

The CSS syntax is always written in the order *selector* (`body`), *property* (`background-color`), and *value* (`gray`). The `important` keyword just makes sure the author stylesheet delivered by the server is overridden.

Internet Explorer

To add a user stylesheet in Internet Explorer 7, first create a new text document on your computer. Use Notepad or your favorite text editor. Just be sure to save the file as plain text without any formatting. Open it and type the stylesheet code in the previous example into it. Save your file as *user.css*. Next, select Tools→Internet Options→General→Accessibility→"Format documents using my style sheet." Click Browse to select your *user.css* file. To stop using this stylesheet, uncheck the box labeled "Format documents using my style sheet."

> Internet Explorer caches your stylesheet. You may want to rename it and reselect the stylesheet every time you make a change to it, so that your latest CSS is used.

Firefox

In Firefox on Windows XP or Vista, use a text editor to create (or if it already exists, to edit) the file *%APPDATA%\Mozilla\Firefox\Profiles**foldername**\chrome\userContent.css*, add the CSS to it, and restart Firefox. Note that ***foldername*** is a random sequence of characters followed by *.default* (for example, *dph0cj4b.default*) that is different for each Firefox user. *%APPDATA%* is a Windows variable that you can type into the Explorer location bar, the "File name" field in file save/open dialogs, and the Command Prompt. It expands to the full path of your Application Data folder, such as *C:\Users**username**\AppData\Roaming*.

For Firefox on Linux, the path to your user stylesheet is usually *~/.mozilla/firefox/foldername/chrome/userContent.css.*

For Firefox on Mac OS X, it usually is the *Library/Application Support/Firefox/Profiles/**foldername**/chrome/userContent.css* folder in your home folder.

To stop using this stylesheet, delete the lines you added from the *userContent.css* file, delete the file, or move it out of the way (like into another folder). For a little more luxury in managing stylesheets in Firefox, you can also download an extension called Stylish **[Hack #72]**. To stop using the stylesheet, click "None Selected" on the Style Sheet pop-up menu.

Safari

If you're using Safari, choose Safari→Preferences→Advanced. Choose Other from the Style Sheet pop-up menu and select the *user.css* file that you created.

Admittedly, a gray background on every web page isn't too pretty, but as you can see, your change took effect immediately. For a more subtle change of design, you need to define a more precise *selector* (this determines which HTML elements the new styling is applied to) than just `body` (which selected everything). To do so, open the HTML source of the Gmail page. In Firefox, you can simply select a portion of the page, right-click, and select "View selection source," as shown in Figure 5-7. At the time of this writing, the HTML preceding a Gmail message had the following format—but as with any web page, this is subject to change over time, so you will need to view the source of a Gmail web page to see exactly where things are these days:

```
<td class="cbln">
<div class="mb">
<div id="mb_5">
<div style="direction: ltr;">
                Hello Jane!
                ...
```

In the user stylesheet, you can now specify the classes highlighted in the example to increase the font-size:

```
.cbln .mb {
     font-size: 17px !important;
 }
```

This CSS means that any element of the class `mb` that is nested within an element of the class `cbln` is selected, applying a font size of 17 pixels. The use of the `important` keyword ensures that styles defined elsewhere are being overruled. The default Gmail font size, as shown in Figure 5-8, will now be increased for you, as shown in Figure 5-9. You might also want to tweak the font size to a relative font size: "95%" will make the font 95% the size of the default.

Figure 5-7.
Selecting a portion of the page to view the source HTML behind it

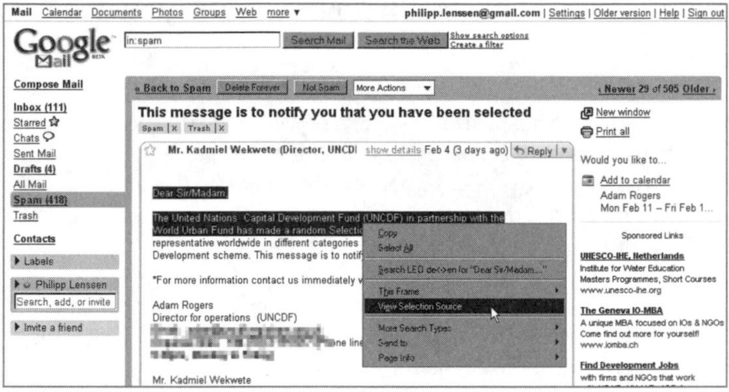

Figure 5-8.
Gmail at its default font size

Figure 5-9.
Gmail with an increased font size after applying a user stylesheet

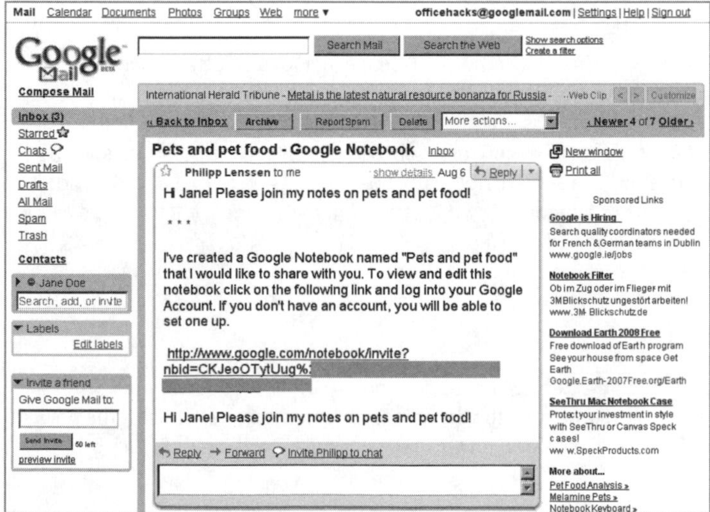

HACK 42: Change the Appearance and Behavior of Gmail

Gmail already has plenty of options. But with this hack, you can add plenty more.

Greasemonkey is a Firefox browser extension that allows anyone to provide code that adds some bells and whistles to web applications—including Gmail. If you've ever felt like you hit the limits of Gmail's native functionality, you might want to give Greasemonkey a try. To install this add-on, point your Firefox browser to http://greasespot.net and click the "Download Greasemonkey" link. Select the Install Now button to be guided through the installation process.

After restarting your browser, Greasemonkey is now active for you, indicated by a smiling monkey icon in the bottom right of your browser (click the monkey head at any time to make it frown—this deactivates Greasemonkey until you click the monkey again).

Greasemonkey on its own will not do anything in particular; you still need to add some custom scripts. This is where http://userscripts.org comes in. It's a giant directory of user-submitted Greasemonkey scripts. A query for "gmail" using the site's search engine returns dozens of results, some of which are described in detail here.

To install any of the user scripts, just click the "Install this script" button on the script detail page and close and reopen any browser windows that you expect to be affected by the script. To uninstall a script, select Tools→Greasemonkey→Manage User Scripts from the Firefox menu, mark the scripts you want to uninstall, and click the "Uninstall" button.

Make sure that you trust the creator of a Greasemonkey script, as a script may take partial control over your browser. Also note that it may be against the terms of service of some web applications to perform any automation against their web site. In general, though, Google seems to be okay with people Greasemonkeying their apps, and even Google employees have been publishing add-on scripts on their personal blogs.

Unfortunately, because Greasemonkey scripts rely on the specifics of a site's underlying HTML and JavaScript, they may stop working if the site in question changes the structure of their web site significantly. Some of following Greasemonkey scripts, while functional at the time of this writing, may not work when you try this, making it necessary to try look for a replacement script by another author, or a newer version of the script you're trying.

Here are some cool things you can do with Gmail and Greasemonkey:

Gmail with different attachment icons
URL: http://userscripts.org/scripts/show/7056

When you open your Gmail inbox, you can tell whether a message includes an attachment. But you won't be able to immediately see what file type the attachment is, because Gmail always uses the same paperclip icon. Not so with this Greasemonkey script. After adding it and opening Gmail, you will notice an image icon for images, a PDF icon for Adobe Acrobat files, and so on, as shown in Figure 5-10. (Note that because this is a screenshot of my spam box, I had to make all the rude subjects invisible!) If the file type is not supported by this Greasemonkey script or if there are multiple attachments, the paperclip icon is displayed.

Gmail super clean
URL: http://userscripts.org/scripts/show/7646

This Greasemonkey script performs an extensive beautification on Gmail. If you're already used to the default Gmail layout, this will take some time to get used to, but as the title promises, the new look will indeed be super clean (and full of smooth cyan shades, too), as pictured in Figure 5-11!

Folders4Gmail
URL: http://userscripts.org/scripts/show/8810

At the time of this writing, Gmail uses labels instead of the more traditional mail folders. A label is similar to a folder, in that it allows you to organize your messages. And unlike with traditional folders, you can also associate several labels with a message at once in Gmail. However, you cannot create nested hierarchies of labels at this time. That's where more traditional folders can be of help, and the Folders4Gmail script provides them.

After adding the script, you can now create a hierarchy of labels. Let's say you want to have a folder "Job" that includes the subfolders "Boss," "Important," and "Jokes." Open Gmail and switch to Settings→Labels, and create a new label "Job." Now add another label named "Job\Boss." The

Figure 5-10.
The attachment file type is now indicated by a special icon—even before you open the message

aw-confirm@ebay.com	2:59 pm
uuu你好！ 你有未_上_市_股_	2:58 pm
Melvin Bragg	2:55 pm
Caspar Andrews	2:54 pm
Aimee Chase	2:53 pm
ªñ ¿Ë ¬Û «Á	2:51 pm
susan henk	2:51 pm
gstotal	2:49 pm
Humberto G. Patrick	2:47 pm
Iva Masters	2:47 pm
Earlene Noel	2:34 pm
AloChile.com (2)	2:06 pm
Berton Daniels	2:02 pm
18th WSCTS World Congres.	1:57 pm
greace_john@terra.es (2)	1:55 pm
Rex Huffman	1:54 pm
Piotrek	1:48 pm
Lush Entertainment	1:46 pm
Jasmine R. Land	1:41 pm
Replicator	1:36 pm
Renato Mendes	1:34 pm
Teddy Mckenna	1:28 pm

Figure 5-11.
The Gmail inbox with the "Gmail super clean" Greasemonkey script

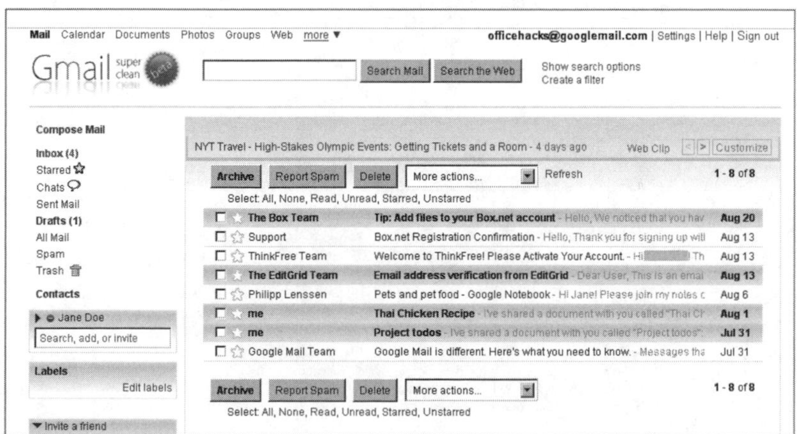

backslash you are using for that name tells the Folders4Gmail script to put the "Boss" folder into the "Job" folder, as shown in Figure 5-12. Using this special syntax, you can now create your own nested label/folder system in Gmail.

Gmail HTML Signatures

URL: http://userscripts.org/scripts/show/20887

Gmail allows you to add a signature to your messages, but it will not allow you to use more than one signature, or to use HTML in your signature. With this script you can define an HTML signature for each email address that you use with Gmail.

To define a signature, start a new message, or reply to one, then click the Create Signature link that appears to the right of your email address, as shown in Figure 5-13. An edit box will appear to let you type in your HTML (see Figure 5-14). Once you've set up your HTML signature, you'll see that

Figure 5-12.
Nested labels, made possible by the Folders4Gmail Greasemonkey script

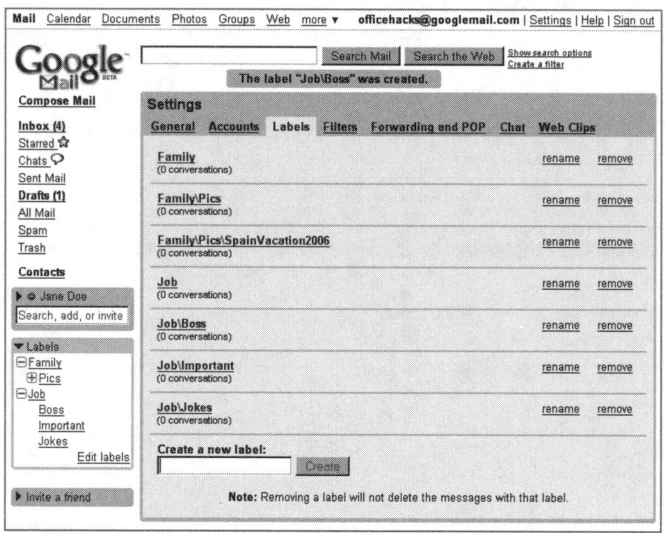

Figure 5-13.
Click Create Signature to create a new signature

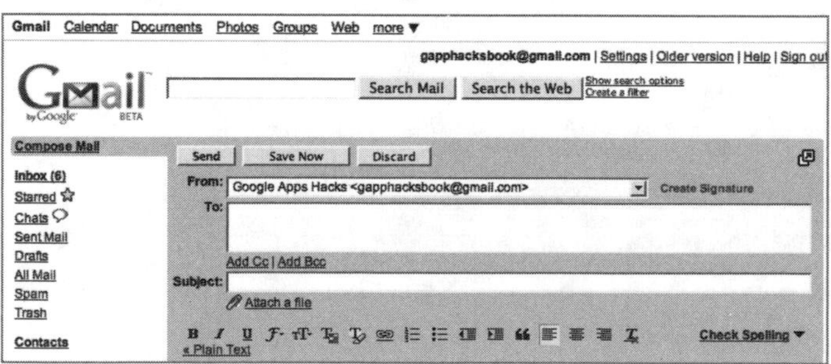

signature at the bottom of each new message, as shown in Figure 5-15. Note that even though there is a line break in the HTML, the two lines are run together. If you want them on separate lines, use a `<p>` or `<br>` element.

Gmail Conversation Preview
URL: http://userscripts.org/scripts/show/1554

Do you get so many messages every day that even the act of *opening* a message takes too much time? Maybe you're in need of the Gmail Conversation Preview script. After installing, you can right-click any subject line in your inbox to open a speech-bubble-like instant preview, as shown in Figure 5-16. Assuming that opening a message usually takes you 2 seconds, and further assuming you get 50 mails a day, this will save you almost 10 hours every year . . . enough to watch the complete *Godfather* trilogy with your friends!

Figure 5-14.
Creating a new HTML signature

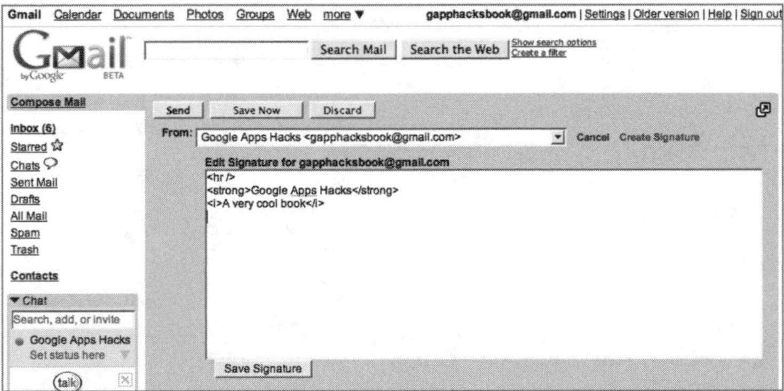

Figure 5-15.
Using your new HTML signature

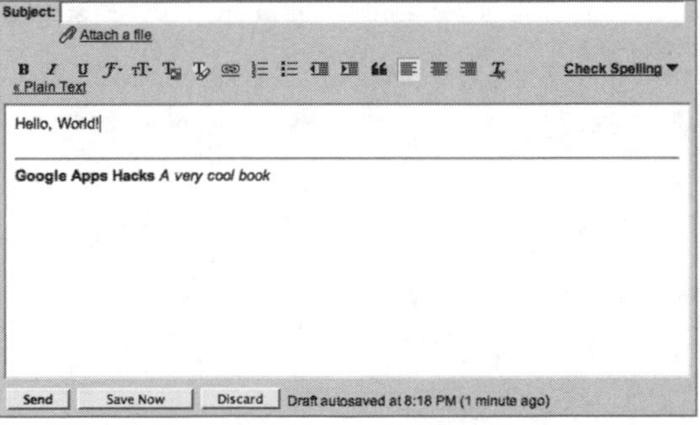

Figure 5-16.
The Gmail Conversation Preview script in action

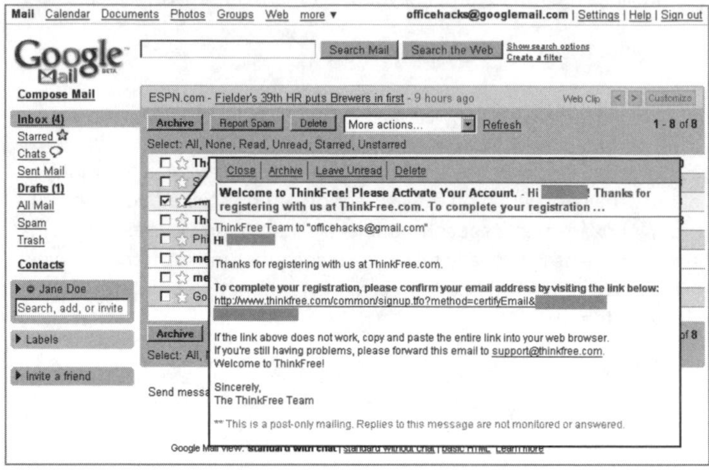

HACK 43: Read Gmail on Your Mobile Phone

Wouldn't it be nice to access your mail wherever you are? Online applications are made for this.

You don't necessarily need a notebook and Wi-Fi to access your email on the go (in a train, at the shore, on the bus). Your mobile phone may let you access Gmail, either through its built-in web browser or through support for Java applications. And if your monthly cellular plan gives you access to mobile data for a reasonable metered price (per KB or MB) or better yet, your plan allows unlimited data access, you have several options to add Gmail to your phone.

Cellular data plans are either unlimited or billed on a per-KB basis. If you are unsure of what cellular data plan you have, be sure to check with your cellular carrier before trying this hack. Be careful using any cell phone application that accesses the Web, as it is possible to rack up large charges if you have not set up an affordable cellular data plan.

The Gmail web site allows you to choose between two different main flavors: an advanced version with all the bells and whistles, as well as a more basic HTML version. Although the basic HTML version lacks many features, it's also more accessible on older browsers, and it's likely to work better with the stripped-down or slower browsers you find on smaller devices.

To switch to the basic version at any time—whether you're accessing Gmail from your desktop computer, or anywhere else—just click the "basic HTML" link at the bottom of Gmail. In the basic version, you may notice that the application needs less resources and may load faster for you. It also comes with some accessibility enhancements. The major downside with this version is the lack of autocompletion of email addresses. Some advanced mobile browsers already work fine with the basic version of Gmail. For other devices, it's not yet basic enough.

A leaner variant of Gmail is Gmail mobile, which you can access by visiting http://gmail.com from your mobile browser (if it doesn't appear, visit http://m.gmail.com). Google should automatically detect that you're browsing from a mobile device and show you a web page that's optimized for your device's capabilities. Figure 5-17 shows how Gmail appears in the Nokia N95 web browser. If you don't like your phone's existing mobile browser, you can give Opera Mobile or Opera Mini (http://opera.com) a try.

In Gmail mobile, as shown in Figure 5-18, you see only the sender names and titles of emails, as well as a few navigation links and a search box below them. By default, Gmail mobile won't show your labels, but you can click the "more" link at the bottom to activate some of them.

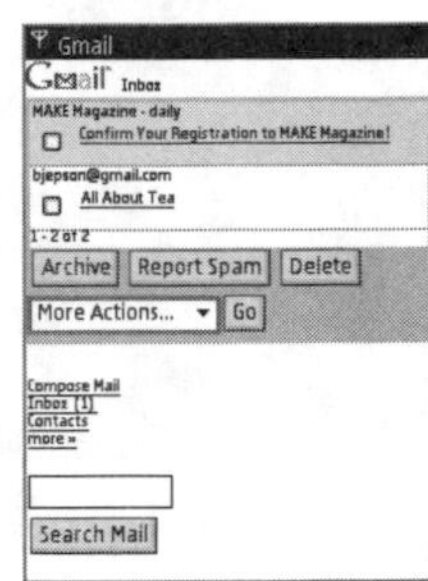

Figure 5-17. One of Gmail's mobile variants

But Gmail mobile doesn't just mobile-optimize your messages. When you click on an outgoing link someone sent you within an email, Google will also display that web site in a version adapted for your phone. Figure 5-19 displays how Google displays the popular blog Boing Boing (http://boingboing.net) by filtering its text and images through a proxy (an extra server placed between your browser and Boing Boing's server) which cuts & chops everything into smaller, more edible pieces.

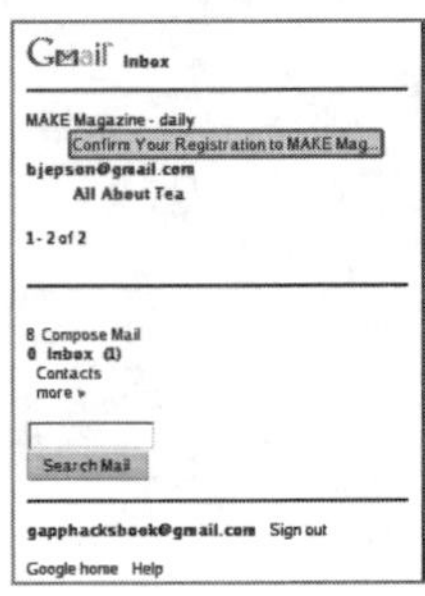

Figure 5-18. Gmail mobile

Yet another option for email reading is to download a mobile Gmail program. If your phone supports the Java framework, you can point your phone browser to http://gmail.com/app to get started with this. (Although the downloadable program looks nicer on some phones, on other phones, it may also cause problems—like too-small font sizes.)

> Java is an application platform that lets software developers create programs that can run, with (theoretically!) little or no modification, on different operating systems, including mobile device operating systems. It is available on many modern mobile phones.

As if four options to access your emails weren't enough, Google offers a fifth: POP or IMAP access to your email. POP and IMAP are short for Post Office Protocol and Internet Message Access Protocol, respectively; both are standards for sending mail. For this alternative to work, your phone needs a built-in email application supporting POP or IMAP access (if you're unsure, please refer to your phone's manual or built-in help files to find out whether this is supported). You also need to enable POP in Gmail. Log in to Gmail.com and click Settings→Forwarding and POP/IMAP. Select either the Enable POP or Enable IMAP radio choices, and hit the Save Changes button.

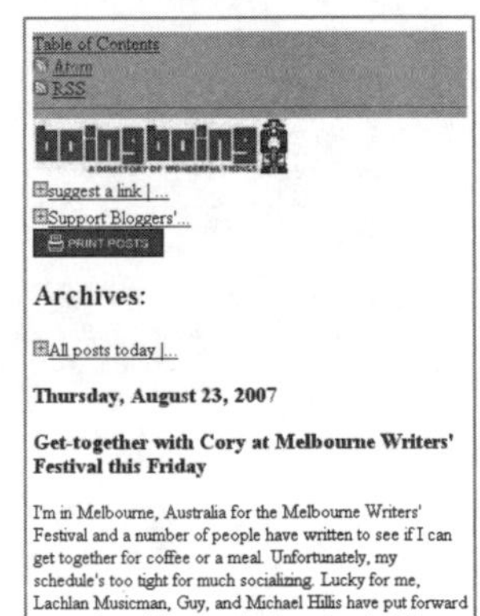

Figure 5-19. BoingBoing.net displayed through Google's mobile proxy

If your phone supports IMAP, that's the best choice, because IMAP treats Gmail as a remote collection of folders, and what you see on your phone is in sync with what you'd see if you opened Gmail via a web browser. Gmail's IMAP even makes all your labels appear as remote folders, and you can move a message from the Inbox into an IMAP folder to apply that label to it. POP, on the other hand, pulls down copies of the messages that arrive on the Gmail server, so the view you get on your device and the view you get on the web are not in sync.

Now if only there were as many ways to get rid of spam mail!

HACK 44: Organize Messages as They Arrive

If you get a lot of messages every day, a little Gmail automation can go a long way toward staying organized.

Our hypothetical Gmail user Beth gets a lot of emails at her office, where she's using Gmail—about a hundred, every day, from all kinds of people: friends, family, colleagues (and complete strangers offering all kinds of commercial endeavors; hopefully these make it to her spam folder). She's using a variety of tricks to maintain control of her mails; she's subscribed to a jokes mailing list, for instance, but because she refuses to open PowerPoint jokes, all jokes with that attachment type go straight to her trash can. She also started working on a new project developing fluorescent keyboards to type at night, and all mails in relation to that project are grouped together nicely under one label. When her biggest client, Albert, emails her, she automatically has his messages starred. Plus, whenever she gets mails from her family, she forwards them to her home address.

Gmail's Search and Filter Syntax

To make all of this possible, you can use Gmail filters, which are based on Gmail's search syntax. A basic search in Gmail looks for exact matches in the whole of an email; its subject, its "from" field, "to" field, message body, and more. The following search returns all mails containing the words "invitation" and "inquiry":

```
invitation inquiry
```

If you want to find emails containing either of each word, use the OR operator. Make sure to write the operator in all uppercase—although keywords used in searches are not case-sensitive, this operator is:

```
invitation OR inquiry
```

In the following search, the pipe character "|" is a synonym for OR, and parentheses group the terms together (this means that the | applies only to those two grouped terms). To exclude certain words, use the minus operator, as before "join":

```
(invitation | inquiry) -join
```

Quotes ensure that only the entire phrase is found:

```
subject:"partnership offer"
```

A slight variation of the previous query, shown here, searches for both words in the subject line but not necessarily as a full phrase. Note that there's no space after the colon:

```
subject:(partnership offer)
```

Use the `from:` or `to:` operators followed by a colon to search only among sender or recipients:

```
from:arthur OR from:tricia.mcmillian@example.com
```

Similarly, you can use the operators `subject:` to only search in email subjects, `filename:` to search for attachment names and extensions, or `cc:` and `bcc:` to search in the carbon copy and blind carbon copy fields. The following search finds messages that are either from Mike, or that include the word "inquiry" in the subject and have an attachment with a TXT extension:

```
from:mike OR(subject:inquiry filename:.txt)
```

Note that by default, your queries do not search through the spam or trash boxes, even when you use the search box while in your spam or trash box. To include those two in a search, click "Show search options" on top and pick "Mail & Spam & Trash" from the Search drop-down menu.

Create a New Filter

With the Gmail search operators in mind, you can now create *filters*. A filter is applied to emails as soon as they arrive in your email account. Among other actions, you can forward a message, star it, or apply a label to group it with other mails.

To create a new filter, log in to Gmail and click "Create a filter" on top. You now have several input fields to choose from to compose a search, but you can also simply use your custom advanced search syntax in the "Has the words" field. Enter the following, for instance:

```
from:miguel OR from:jenny
```

and hit the "Test search" button, as shown in Figure 5-20. If you see the kind of results you wanted to target, click the "Next Step >" button and choose your action, or a combination of actions. For this example, I picked "Skip the inbox" and "Apply the label: Office." Save the filter by clicking the "Create Filter" button, and you're done. You can edit or completely remove a filter at any time by choosing Settings→Filters from the Gmail menu.

How Beth Handles Her Filters

But back to Beth; here's how she achieves her different email organization tricks. To avoid any PowerPoint attachments from her jokes mailing list, Beth uses the following filter and checks the "Delete it" box:

```
subject:jokes filename:ppt
```

To group all mails in relation to her fluorescent keyboard project, she created the label "fluorescent" and then created the following search filter, choosing the "Skip the Inbox" and "Apply the label: fluorescent" options:

```
fluorescent OR keyboard OR FluoKeys3000
```

To add a star to all of Albert's mail to make sure she can respond in time, Beth uses this filter (and checks the "Star it" box):

```
from:albert@example.com
```

And to forward her family mail to her private email account, she uses the following search filter, while providing her home address in the "Forward it to" field:

```
from:(joey OR meredith OR paula OR sammy OR ruthbert)
```

Figure 5-20.
Creating a Gmail filter

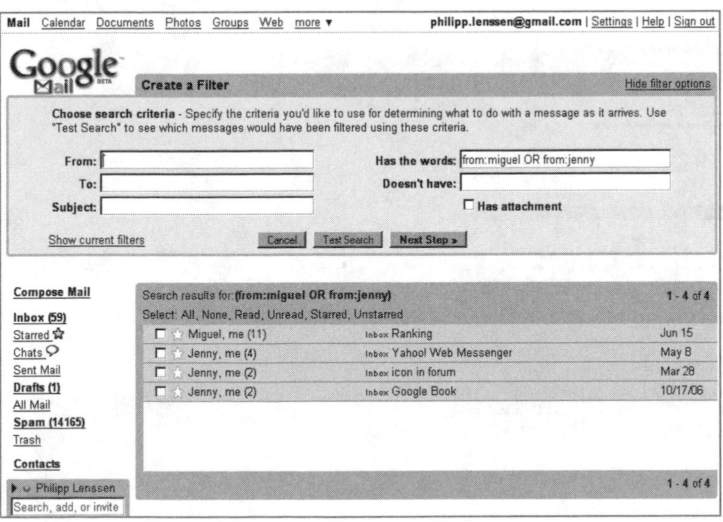

HACK 45: Gmail Drive, Your Online Hard Drive

There's a long-rumored Google product called Gdrive, a virtual storage system that lets you access your files from anywhere. Google employees already use Gdrive internally. But there's a second, unofficial product out there for the rest of us that already brings Gdrive functionality . . . by kidnapping Gmail.

If you're in need of more storage space than your hard disk offers, you can buy a new one—or outsource some of the space to an online drive. One way to do so is by installing Gmail Drive, a third-party product that handles your files by sending them to Gmail behind the scenes.

Gmail Drive may cease working anytime that Google decides to block it or change the workings of their Gmail program. Also note that Gmail Drive requires you to enter your Google Account credentials; always do this only if you sufficiently trust the author of any program, and understand enough about the program's security model to trust it to keep your credentials secure.

Please note there's a serious caveat to using this Gmail Drive program—a caveat big enough that you may decide you may not want to try this hack at all, or use it only on a Google account that doesn't contain highly important data! **The caveat here is the fact that Google may lock the accounts of people who use file storage software on top of it.** For more information on this please refer to the Gmail terms of use, as well as the help entry at http://mail.google.com/support/bin/answer.py?answer=43692.

To install Gmail Drive, you need Windows XP/2000 or Vista. Open http://viksoe.dk/code/gmail.htm and look for the download link at the bottom. After downloading and running the setup files, you will find that your Windows Explorer→My Computers folder has a new item: Gmail Drive. Click on it and you are required to enter your Google Account login name and password, as shown in Figure 5-21. You can check the "Auto Login" option if you want to, or access further options via the "More" button.

Figure 5-21.
Logging in to Gmail Drive

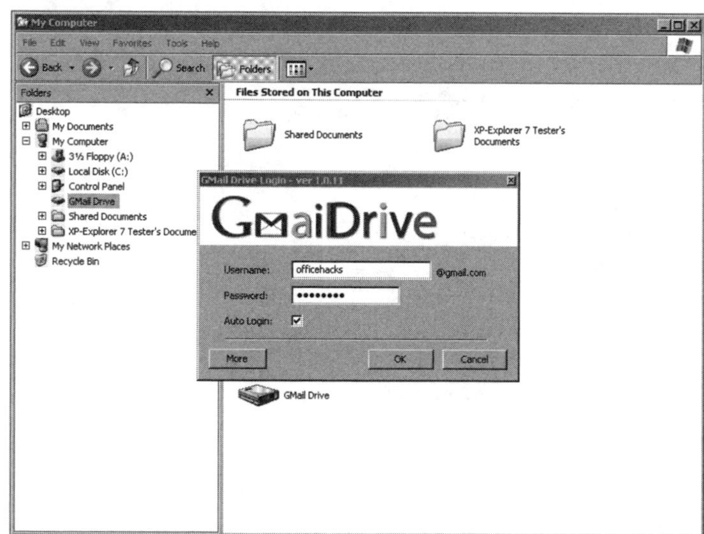

If you logged in successfully, you can start to use your Gmail Drive folder almost like any other folder. Give it a try by dragging and dropping a file from elsewhere on your computer into this folder. The copy process may take a while. I copied a file called *netpadd.zip*, for instance, as shown in Figure 5-22.

What actually happens here is that Gmail Drive sends your file as an attachment to your Gmail account. You can see this for yourself by logging in to Gmail, as shown in Figure 5-23. A new email starting with the subject "GMAILFS" appears in your inbox; you can open that email and download the attachment, if you want to.

Figure 5-22.
Gmail Drive now stores two ZIP files

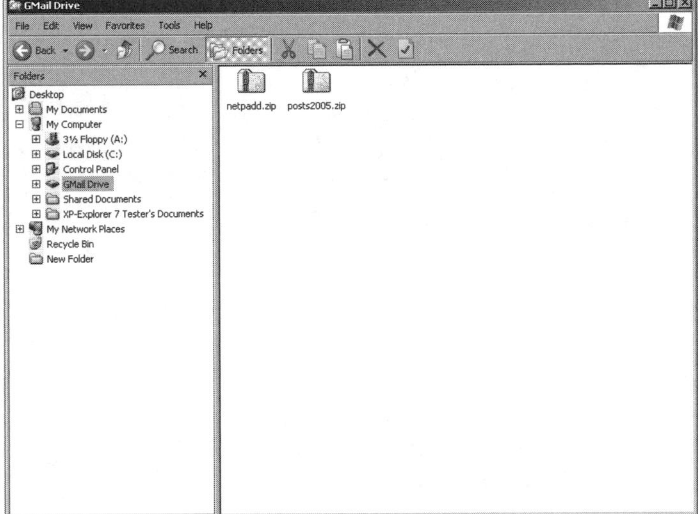

Figure 5-23.
The file you copied to your Gmail Drive will appear as an attachment in Gmail

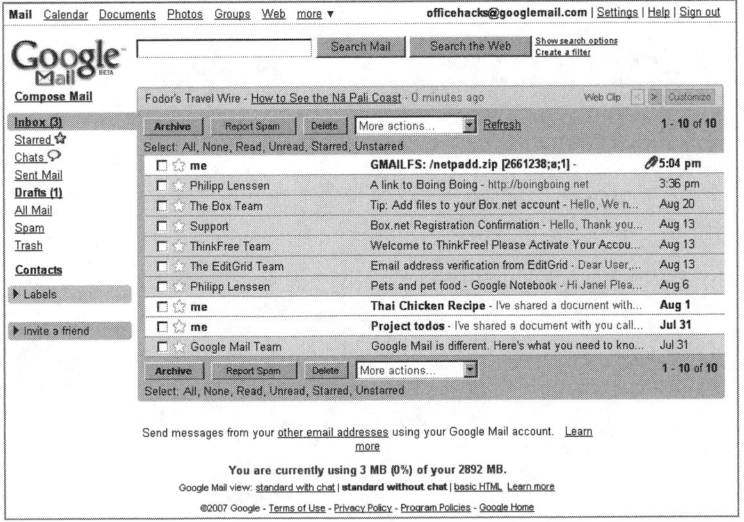

However, to hide the messages sent to you by Gmail Drive, you can add a filter **[Hack #44]**. Click "Create a filter" and enter the word "gmailfs" in the subject input box. Click "Next Step" and check the "Skip the Inbox" and "Apply the Label. . . " options. Create a new label named "Gmail Drive" (or any other name that you prefer). Now save your filter and you're done, as shown in Figure 5-24.

By storing your text documents, spreadsheets, ZIP files, movies, music, and other files this way, you can access them from any desktop computer or laptop around the world, as long as it's got Gmail Drive installed. And even if you are on a computer that doesn't allow you to install new programs, like in an Internet café, you can go back to your Gmail account to find your files. Your only limitation with this approach is the storage limitation of Gmail itself. If you want to increase your email storage, take a look at http://google.com/accounts/ManageStorage to buy additional GB of storage.

An Alternative: GmailFS

Another option for storing files with Gmail is GmailFS, the Gmail Filesystem. This mountable Linux filesystem requires some system administration and development knowledge to set up, as it's based on the Python programming language and other technologies. A full installation guide for GmailFS is located at http://richard.jones.name/google-hacks/gmail-filesystem/gmail-filesystem.html. Mac OS X users can consult the guide at http://blog.macos.fr/post/2007/01/18/GMailFS-for-Mac-OS-X.

The same caveats mentioned earlier apply to GmailFS—be aware that Google may lock Gmail accounts of people using file storage apps on it!

Figure 5-24.
Creating a filter to group all Gmail Drive messages under one label

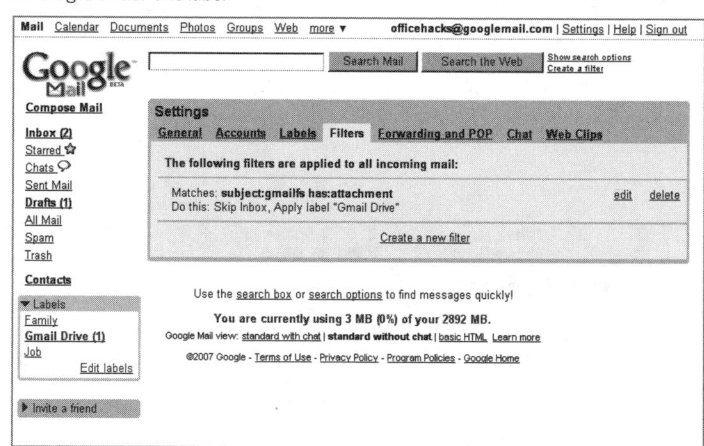

HACK 48: Know Your Gmail Keyboard Shortcuts

Want to work even faster in Gmail? Consider switching from mouse to keyboard for certain repetitive tasks.

Although browsers offer a range of default keyboard shortcuts, for quite some time it wasn't common for web applications to make use of their own advanced shortcuts. That was the realm of desktop software—the kind of software that ships in a box and requires you to install it, but that also has a traditionally much richer interface. But as time progressed, so did the richness of web applications. Google is one of the companies stretching the limits of what's possible in online interfaces. Sometimes that results in longer waiting times for your application to load, or other accessibility hurdles. At other times, it may allow you to get your work done faster . . . as is the case with keyboard shortcuts.

What follows is an overview of the most important Gmail shortcuts, shown in Table 5-1. Before you use them, make sure that you have shortcuts enabled. In Gmail, go to Settings, check the "Keyboard shortcuts on" option, and click the Save Changes button. Note that in order to avoid

Table 5-1.
Gmail keyboard shortcuts

KEYSTROKE	DESCRIPTION
c	Compose a new email message. Use Shift-c to open the current message in a new window. Opening a new window may take a few seconds.
r	Reply to a message that you've opened. Use Shift-r to open the reply in a new window.
j	Move the focus to the next conversation. To the left of your mail messages, you will see a small arrow indicating which message has focus.
k	Move the focus to the previous conversation.
Enter	Open the currently focused conversation.
Shift (while selecting messages)	Select several messages at once. Let's say you see 20 new spam mails in a row in your inbox and you want to mark them as spam, accordingly. Just check the box of spam mail 1, hold down the Shift key, and then check the box of spam mail 20 down the list. You will find that messages 2–19 have now been selected for you as well.
Shift (while opening a message)	Holding down the Shift key when you click on a new message results in the message being opened in a new window. Note that this feature, as well as the previous one for message selection, works even if you've disabled shortcuts.
u	When reading a conversation in detail view, this shortcut returns you to the inbox.
x	Toggles the state of the checkbox to the left of the currently focused conversation.
m	Mutes one or more conversations (either the conversation you currently have open or conversations you have selected with the checkboxes to the left). If a conversation is muted, all new messages added to it later on will be automatically archived for you—skipping the inbox so you can easily ignore them, but still have them available when you search for them. This is a special shortcut for special circumstances; it's mostly useful for when you are subscribed to a mailing list and you want to ignore a specific thread. Note that messages directly addressed to you still make it into your inbox as usual, even when they are part of a muted conversation.
!	This shortcut flags a mail as spam. As with other shortcuts, you can undo the operation immediately afterwards by clicking "Undo."
/	Takes you to the search box. You can now start typing any search query **[Hack #44]** and hit Return.

interference with your normal writing, these shortcuts work only when your cursor is outside of a new email composition box, the search box, or any other input area. However, you can leave an input field at any time by hitting the Escape key.

For a complete list of Gmail shortcuts, see http://mail.google.com/support/bin/answer.py?answer=6594. If you've enabled shortcuts in your settings, you can also press the ? key anytime to open a cheat sheet of available shortcuts, and you can close that sheet with the Escape key.

And in case you're not satisfied with all the existing shortcuts, you can also add your own via the unofficial Gmail Macros Greasemonkey script offered by Google's Mihai Parparita. The script can be found at http://blog.persistent.info/2007/11/macros-for-new-version-of-gmail.html. Note as the Macros hack relies on Greasemonkey **[Hack #42]**, it works only in Firefox.

HACK 47: Make Gmail Better

This hack is for the brave of heart Firefox users who don't mind completely overhauling their Gmail interface and functionality—through the use of a single add-on.

Better Gmail 2 is a Firefox extension that collects an abundance of individual Greasemonkey add-ons **[Hack #42]** all under one hood. Go to https://addons.mozilla.org/en-US/firefox/addon/6076 to download the extension, and restart Firefox. It was developed by Gina Trapani, editor of the Lifehacker blog (http://lifehacker.com), where you can often find updates and other information about Better Gmail.

Once installed, open Gmail, and then open the Better Gmail settings in Firefox via Tools→Better Gmail 2. A tabbed options dialog, as shown in Figure 5-25, will appear. Check any of the features you would like to see added to your Gmail client and reload Gmail to see them take effect. Here are some of the available options:

- Make all email-to links on web pages instantly open Gmail
- Use a fixed-width font to display messages
- Show the attachment file type as an icon
- Switch to the "Super clean" Gmail theme, among others
- Hide the spam counter

and many more.

But the best option of all may be "Force encrypted Gmail connection." Although Gmail uses a secure connection when you are logging in with your username and password, it uses an insecure connection when you are reading your email, which means it is possible for an eavesdropper connected to your wireless or wired network to snoop on your email.

 Due to the changing nature of Gmail, or any other web application, not all Greasemonkey add-ons will work exactly as expected. You can disable the Better Gmail extension at any time by selecting Tools→Add-ons→Better Gmail 2: Disable.

Figure 5-25.
The options dialog of Better Gmail 2, the unofficial extension for advanced Gmail behavior and appearance control

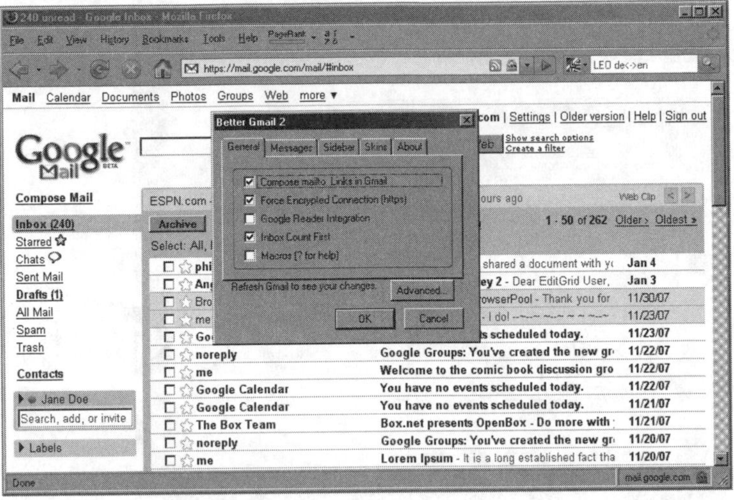

HACK 48: Back Up Your Email

Google claims that you never have to delete your emails again with Gmail. But what if you delete something accidentally—or you delete it because you want to make more storage available, but you realize later that you want it back?

To back up all your Gmail emails—just in case!—you can install the free email client Mozilla Thunderbird (or another similar program), download all your messages, and then back up the file that contains all your email. You can then burn this file onto a CD, DVD, or copy it to a hard drive—anywhere where you can keep it safe. Then you can restore it at any time, even if you've deleted the messages in Gmail, or even if you no longer have the Gmail account. Here are the steps involved:

1. Activate POP in Gmail

For this hack to work, you need to activate POP in your Gmail. POP is short for Post Office Protocol, and it's a standard way to retrieve messages from an email server. Go to Gmail and click Settings→ Forwarding and POP. Check the "Enable POP for all mail" box and save your changes. You are now ready to access your Gmail messages with a desktop client, such as Thunderbird.

2. Install and run Thunderbird

To install Mozilla Thunderbird, point your browser to http://mozilla.com/thunderbird/ and click the Download Thunderbird button. You will be asked to save an executable file on your disk. Run the installer and complete the setup.

Now start the Thunderbird program. During launch, you will be guided through an account wizard where you provide your Gmail credentials. Just choose Google Mail or Gmail from the list of selections and enter your name and email address in the dialog that follows, as shown in Figure 5-26.

Afterwards, provide your Gmail password, and your email from your Gmail account will begin downloading (even though this says Inbox, it really is the contents of your Gmail "All Mail" folder). If you have a lot of email, this can take a long time. Figure 5-27 shows a Gmail inbox in Thunderbird.

Figure 5-26.
Providing your Gmail login credentials in Thunderbird

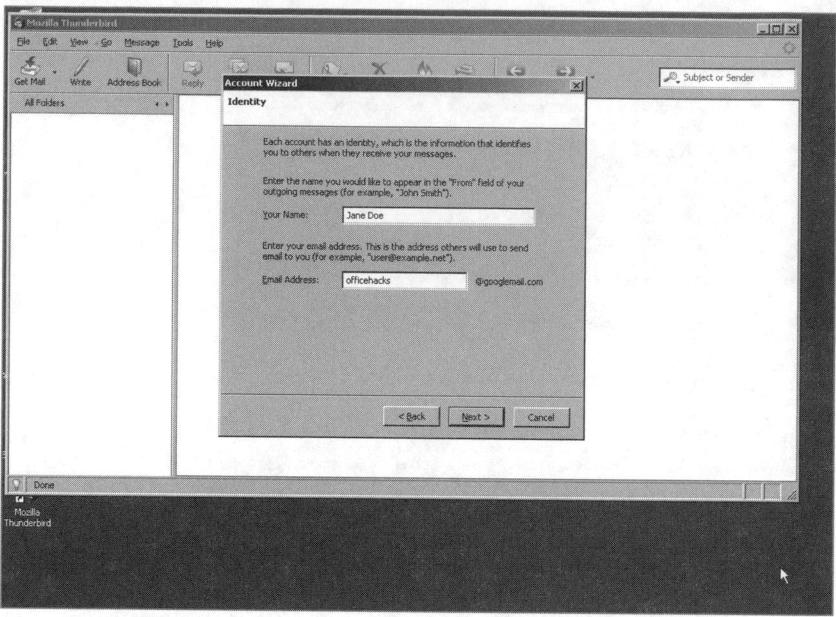

Figure 5-27.
Accessing your Gmail messages in Thunderbird

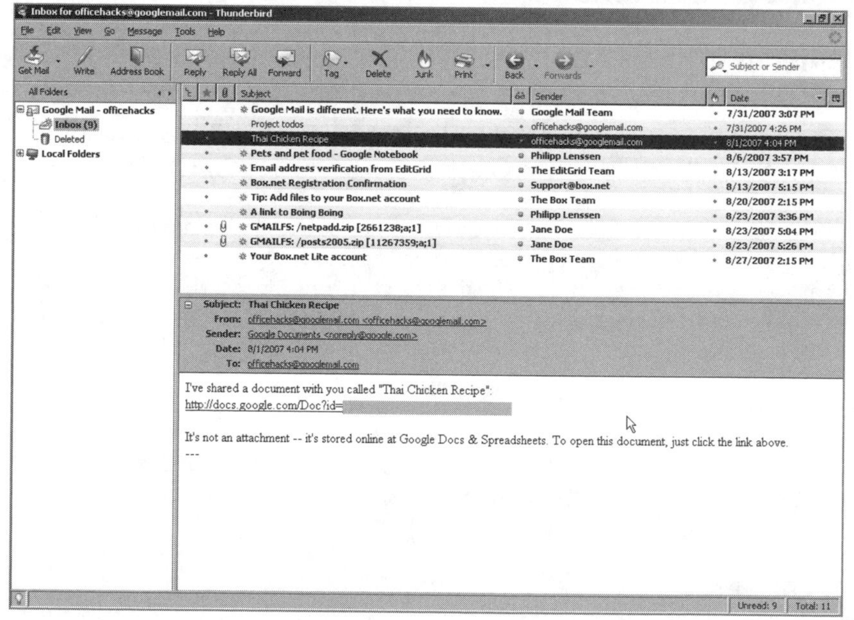

3. Find your Gmail inbox file

Now you need to find the file where Thunderbird stored your Gmail messages. This file uses a standard mailbox format, mbox, that is supported by many email programs. To find the file, you'll first need to locate your Thunderbird profile directory. Open up a command-line terminal program: Terminal on Mac OS X (go to Applications in the Finder and look in the Utilities subdirectory); Command Prompt on Windows (click Start→All Programs or Programs, then choose Accessories→Command Prompt); and xterm or similar on Linux.

If you have more than one profile configured in Thunderbird, you'll need to first `cd` to the *Profiles* directory, then poke around using `cd` and `ls` (Mac OS X or Linux) or dir (Windows) to figure out which profile contains your Gmail messages. The one you're looking for will have a *pop.gmail.com* subdirectory under the profile's Mail directory.

Next, use the `cd` command to "change directory" (switch to the folder) where Thunderbird stores its mail.

On **Mac OS X**, type the following:

```
cd ~/Library/Thunderbird/Profiles/*/Mail
```

On **Windows**, type the following (you can also use the pathname, minus the "cd" in Explorer:

```
cd %APPDATA%\Thunderbird\Profiles\
```

Then type `cd`, followed by a space, and press Tab. The command will expand to include your profile directory. For example:

```
cd 2punitlu.default
```

Next, type:

```
cd Mail
```

On **Linux**, type the following:

```
cd ~/.mozilla-thunderbird/*/Mail
```

Press the Return or Enter key after you type a command. Now, leave your command-line window open, and proceed to the next step.

4. Copy your inbox to a local folder

Now you're ready—or nearly ready—to make a backup copy of all your Gmail messages. First, make sure that Thunderbird is done downloading all your Gmail. This could take quite some time, so be sure to double-check.

If you want to make absolutely sure that you've downloaded all your mail, compare the number of messages reported by Thunderbird (look at the lower right of the Thunderbird window for the Total: field) to the number of messages in your Gmail All Mail folder (click All Mail, and look in the upper-mid-left of the Gmail window for something like "1–25 of 11449" or however many messages you should have).

When you've downloaded all your mail, quit Thunderbird. Return to the command-line window where you changed to the Mail directory. Use this command to back up your Gmail folder on the Mac or Linux:

```
cp pop.gmail.com/Inbox Local\ Folders/
```

Or, on Windows:

```
copy pop.gmail.com\Inbox "Local Folders\"
```

Remember to press Enter or Return after you type the command.

Now, start Thunderbird up again, and you should see two folders with identical contents: one in the Gmail folder, the other in the Local Folders collection, as shown in Figure 5-28 (you may need to press the + symbol to the left of Local Folders to show this). Now you can tell Thunderbird to delete the Gmail account (choose Tools→Account Settings→Gmail, then click Remove Account). and you'll still have a copy of the messages.

If you want to back this file up to CD or DVD, follow the preceding instructions to locate the file, and copy it to another location, then burn it. If you find it easier to work with the Mac OS X Finder or Windows Explorer, you can open the folder quickly from the command line. On the Mac, use the preceding instructions to navigate to the folder at the command line, then type this command and press Enter:

```
open .
```

On Windows, use this command:

```
start .
```

Google already promises to store backups of your emails in multiple locations—and it's not known to randomly crash, like your computer may—but better safe than sorry, especially considering that you could accidentally delete an email yourself!

— Brian Jepson and Philipp Lenssen

Figure 5-28.
Your Gmail messages, all backed up

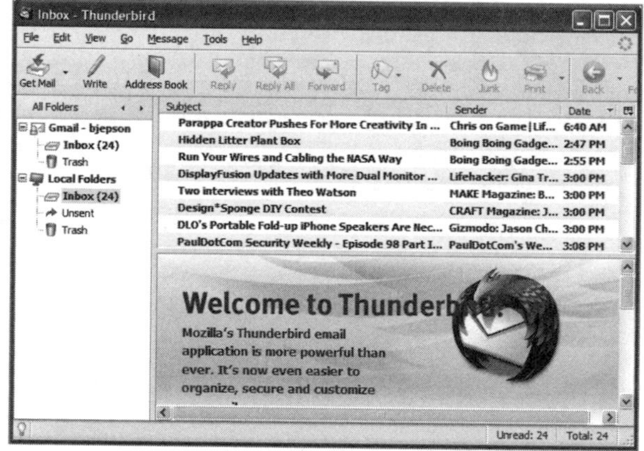

HACK 49: Attach a Google Docs Document to Your Email

There are many ways to send a Google document. Here are the alternatives at your disposal.

You just created a new text document in Google Docs discussing the life and times of Napoleon Bonaparte, as shown in Figure 5-29. How do you send this file to someone else to have a look at, too? There are several ways to accomplish this, each with their own pros and cons.

Option 1: Attach a Word file

You could save the file as Word in Google Docs, and attach the Word file to your email message. Go to Google Docs, open your document from the file list, and choose File→Export as Word. . . from the menu. Save the Word file, and head over to Gmail to compose a new message. Click "Attach a file," select the Word file you want to send, and click Send.

Pros: People are already used to receiving Word attachments, and they do not need a Google Account to edit your file.

Cons: When you export your Google document into the Microsoft Word format, some formatting details may be changed after the conversion. Also, when you send a document as an attachment, you are sending a mere copy; any edits the recipient makes to the document are not automatically reflected in your document. Reintegrating changes into your source document stored at Google Docs can be a hassle.

> If you select the attachment before typing your email, you will save some time, because Google starts uploading the file to its server while you are typing the message. Also, this way there is less of a chance that you'll mention an attachment in your mail but actually forget to attach it, a common mistake that happens to many of us.

Figure 5-29.
A Google document discussing Napoleon Bonaparte

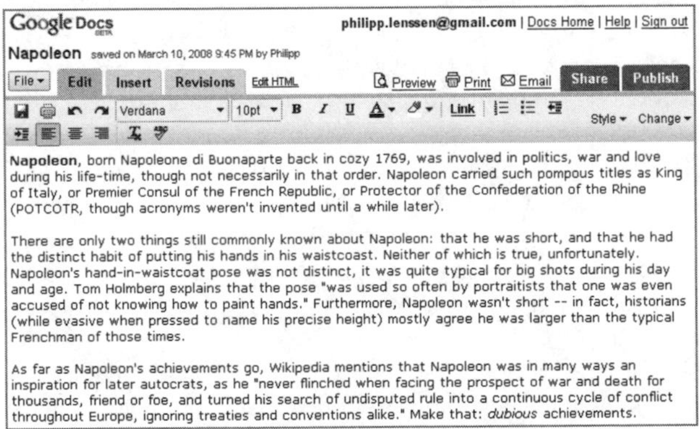

Option 2: Share the Document with One Person or a Small Group

Sharing a Google Docs document means giving another Google Account user the right to access your document. However, you need not create a copy of the file in order to do so; both you and the recipient will be editing the same file, potentially at the same time **[Hack #2]**.

To share a document, open it in Google Docs and switch to the Share tab. Enter the recipient (or group of recipients), and uncheck "Invitations may be used by anyone" if you want only this single recipient (or group) to access the document. Click "Invite collaborators" and you are offered the opportunity to write a custom invitation message. Afterwards, you're done and the recipient will get a link to your document in their email inbox.

The recipients do not need a Google account to see the document, though they do need one to edit it. If the recipients are logged in to Google, they are presented with a full Google Docs editor; if they are not logged in, they will just see an uneditable, simpler web page with a footnote link reading "Edit this page (if you have permission)."

If you uncheck the "Collaborators may invite others" box, the people you invite won't be able to grant access to other users. This setting also forces anyone who wants to read this document to log in to their Google account first. Now the document is also not easy to forward any more. Keep the box checked, however, and your document will be available on an unlisted URL (a URL that is almost impossible to guess by outsiders).

Pros: By sharing a document you can use the full range of Google Docs collaboration features. Google will show you when someone else edits the document; you will see changes on the other end reflected in the document on your end in near real-time; there will be a revision history for the document, and so on.

Cons: If recipients want to edit the document they receive, they must have a Google Account, like a Gmail account, or must sign up for one **[Hack #1]**. And if they want to forward your document to someone else, they must first understand the concept of Google Docs sharing. For some, just handling an attachment may be easier.

Option 3: Paste the Document Into the Message Body

With this option, you just copy the full content of the Google document. Open your Google document, select the full page, and press the copy shortcut—Control/Command-C. Then, open a compose window in Gmail and switch to rich-text editing mode (if you aren't already in this mode) by clicking "Rich formatting." Paste the document in, click Send, and your recipient will receive your text.

Pros: The recipient of your email will be able to start reading your text immediately, without opening any additional files, or signing up for a Google Account. By hitting reply in their email client, recipients may also cite from parts of your text to add their comments below it, as is typical in email conversation. The recipient can also decide to forward parts of your document to someone else by using a forward option, removing selected parts from the email body.

Cons: Not all email clients handle display details similarly, so some of the formatting may end up wrong. For instance, many email clients do not directly show images until a special button or link is clicked. Also, your recipient won't be able to directly collaborate with you on the document, as they could with a shared Google document, and any subsequent changes you make to the document are not reflected on your recipient's end. If you realize later on that a part of your text needs a correction, you have to resend the file.

> Why do email clients often hide images in messages, unless you actively approve showing them? One reason is your privacy and safety; if an image within an email is not sent with the mail but stored on another server, then that server's owner might know when you open the email—their web server log is updated each time a file is retrieved from it, so they can determine when you loaded the picture they sent to you. If they gave the picture a file name unique to each recipient, they can precisely know who read the email they sent, and when. This could be potentially abused by a bulk junk mail sender to verify that a recipient email address is indeed active, which could lead to further junk mail.

Option 4: Publish the Google Document as a Web Page to be Seen by Many

If your document's content is not of a very private nature—the text on Napoleon's life is not, despite his affairs!—you can also publish it as a web page. Open your Google Docs document and click Publish. Check the "Automatically re-publish when changes are made" box and click "Publish document." Alternatively, you can also publish the Google Docs document as a blog post **[Hack #11]**. Now you can compose a new message and manually paste the link of your published page into the mail.

Pros: If you want your document to be truly public, this is the easiest alternative. The recipient of your document can now easily forward the link you sent to others. For reading your document, no Google Account is needed for this.

Cons: Though the URL of your document may not be known by everyone, the file is also not completely private. Use this option for public documents only.

HACK 50: View Unread Messages

Quickly find outstanding messages that might need a reply.

If you receive a lot of email messages every day, you might not be able to read each of them in a timely manner. Over some weeks, unread messages may pile up in your inbox—but there is no lefthand navigation entry in Gmail to see all of them. Instead you may find yourself moving through page after page of your inbox to find the messages you still wanted to read, and possibly reply to.

But there's an easier way to do this. Enter **`is:unread label:inbox`** into the Gmail search box, and you will find all unread messages in the results. This syntax is part of the advanced Gmail search syntax **[Hack #44]**.

Now, a search such as "**`is:unread label:inbox`**" is slightly hard to remember. However, you can bookmark any search results you're seeing in Gmail. To have the bookmark always in view, you can add it to your bookmark bar. For example, the URL of the preceding search result will be:

```
http://mail.google.com/mail/#search/is%3Aunread+label%3Ainbox
```

> If you're using an older version of Gmail (normally, you must click Older Version at the top of the Gmail screen to enable this older version), you will notice that searches cannot be bookmarked, because they don't have their own distinctive URL. In that case, try the Persistent Searches Greasemonkey script by Google employee Mihai Parparita at http://gmail-greasemonkey.googlecode.com/svn/trunk/scripts/gmail-saved-searches.user.js.

HACK 51: Insert Pseudographical Email Signatures

Surprise your recipients by adding some pseudographical glitz to your email signature.

Google's email client doesn't ship with a native way to add graphic signatures. Even if it would, most email clients receiving your message are configured so that they won't display graphics by default anyway (at least not if the image is externally hosted, instead of being included in the mail itself). But there's a workaround for this: you can use Unicode symbols **[Hack #12]**, which render as graphics but are just text characters.

Finding the Right Unicode Character

You can use any Unicode character you want, but a couple of symbols create especially good-looking signatures. The easiest way to find them is to copy and paste the character you like from a character table found online. Here are some good pointers to get you started digging for the right "icon":

Miscellaneous symbols (Figure 5-30)
URL: http://en.wikipedia.org/wiki/Miscellaneous_Symbols

Arrow symbols (Figure 5-31)
URL: http://en.wikipedia.org/wiki/Arrow_%28symbol%29

"Dingbat" characters (Figure 5-32)
URL: http://en.wikipedia.org/wiki/Dingbat

Miscellaneous technical symbols (Figure 5-33)
URL: http://en.wikipedia.org/wiki/Miscellaneous_Technical_%28Unicode%29

Figure 5-30.
Miscellaneous symbols

Figure 5-31.
Arrow symbols

Figure 5-32.
Dingbat symbols

Figure 5-33.
Technical symbols

Some symbols work better than others when displayed in smaller fonts. The telephone symbol, for instance, may be hard to make out in rather small font sizes, and a character like a cross, bullet point, smiley, or arrow is more flexible in different contexts.

Adding the Character to Your Signature

Once you have some good characters, log in to Gmail and click the Settings link on top. Copy and paste your symbols, along with your normal signature data (like your blog/home page address or your telephone number) into the signature box and press the Save Changes button. You will now find a result similar to the one shown in Figure 5-34 on outgoing emails.

Creating Larger Unicode Art Pieces

Not satisfied creating one- or two-liner signatures? Well, you can combine multiple Unicode characters to form a larger picture, as shown in Figure 5-35. The following Unicode set comes in handy for this task:

Box drawing characters (Figure 5-36)
URL: http://en.wikipedia.org/wiki/Box_drawing_characters

Experiment with the kind of pseudographics effects you can achieve using these symbols. However, note that you should not mix normal characters into the "Unicode art" you create—not even blanks, or Unicode symbols from other sets—because that will render your pictures indiscernible in email clients that use a proportional font to display messages. Furthermore, restrict your signature length to a maximum of 72 characters per line, so that it won't get cut off by line breaks in certain email clients.

To get more signature inspiration, you can also do a Google search for the phrase "ASCII art," resulting in finds like the one shown in Figure 5-37.

Thanks to Piotr Konieczny of http://blog.konieczny.be for sending along the inspiration for this hack.

Figure 5-34.
An example of a Unicode signature in Gmail

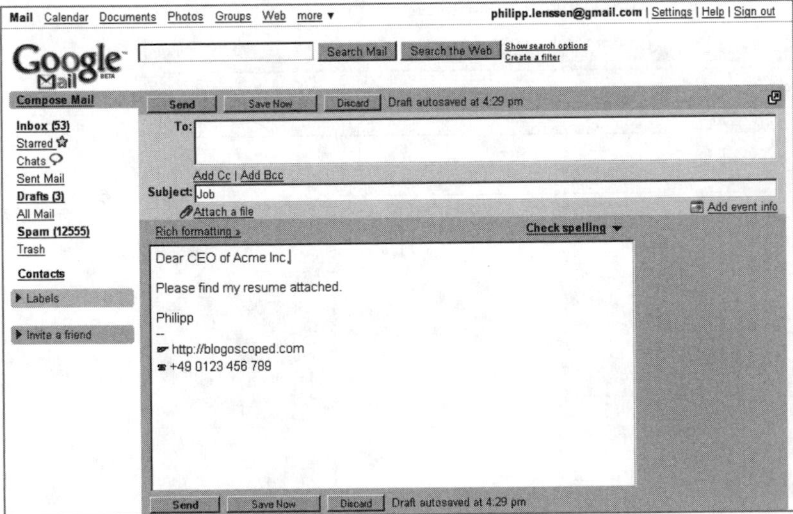

Figure 5-35.
Multiple Unicode characters—10, in this case—form a single larger shape

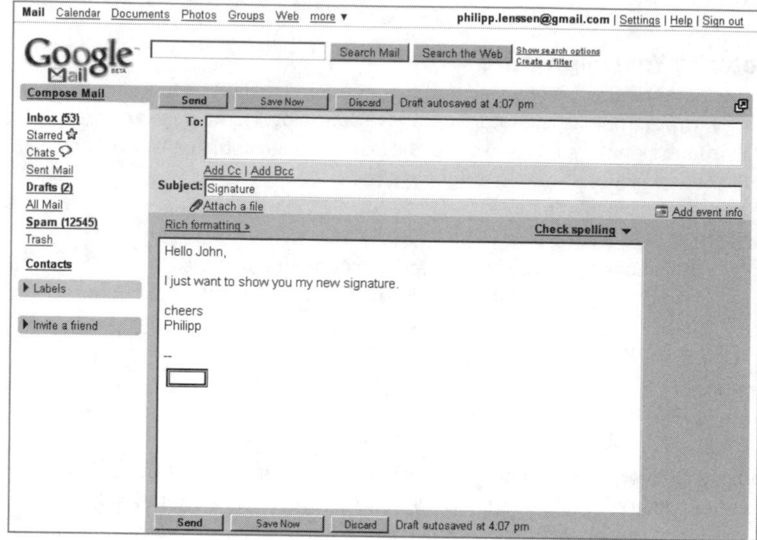

Figure 5-36.
Box drawing characters

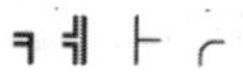

╕ ╣ ├ ╭

Figure 5-37.
A full-blown ASCII/Unicode art piece

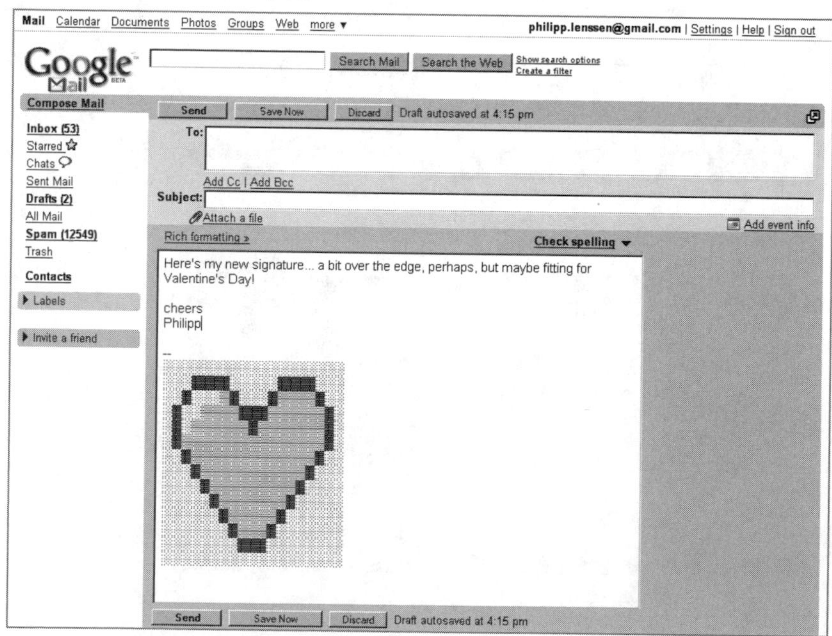

HACK 52: Forward Messages to Your Cellphone

If your cellphone provider offers an email address to receive SMS messages, you can kidnap this address to forward certain messages to your mobile phone as text messages.

Thanks to Bryan Burkholder for suggesting this hack.

Depending on your mobile phone provider, you may be able to forward selected email messages to your cell phone via SMS. For instance, let's say you are a webmaster for the large web site Example.org. Whenever the server gets traffic peaks that cause the server CPU to work overtime, you want to get an alert right away. You don't always check your email, but you always carry your cellphone with you, and a sound alerts you when a new text message arrives—a message like "There's a traffic peak at Example.org, please check soon!"

But just how do you get Gmail to contact your phone? Here's how; first, you need to determine which messages you want to forward. In the case of above example, you should first make sure that the status messages sent from your server to your Gmail account will always be using the keyword [cellphone alert] somewhere in the subject. You'll have to configure this on your server, or whatever device is sending you notifications.

Now, you can define a filter **[Hack #44]**. In Gmail, click "Create a filter" next to the search box. In the Subject field, enter "cellphone alert" or "[cellphone alert]" and click the Test Search button to check the results, as shown in Figure 5-38. If it is correct, click Next Step, and in the new dialog page check the "Apply the label" box, and create a new label named "Sent to cellphone." Also, check the "Skip the Inbox" field. In the "Forward it to" box, enter the email address your cellphone provider offers you, like *yournumber@message.alltel.com*, as shown in Figure 5-39. Check with your phone provider's technical support if you want to find out if such an address scheme is offered in their service, and how you can determine or create your address.

Pingdom.com offers a similar (paid) alert service and can be configured to send you an email or SMS during server downtimes.

Figure 5-38.
Step 1 of 2 in setting up a forward filter

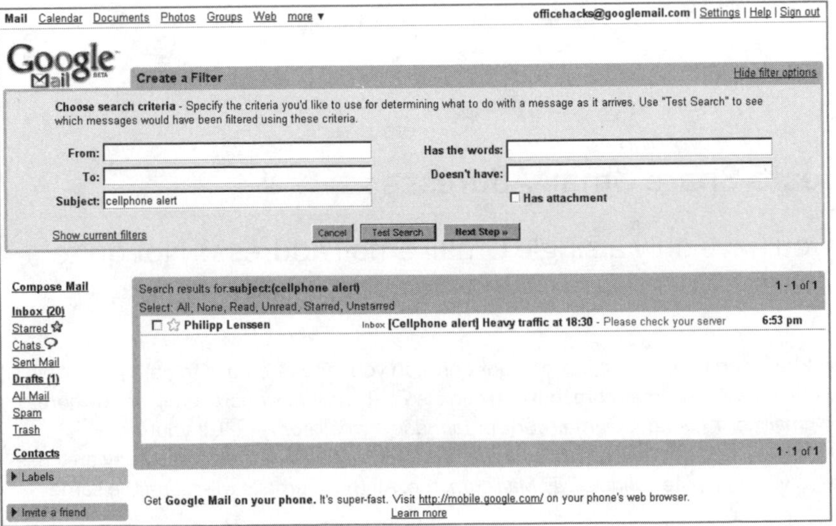

The Wikipedia page on SMS Gateways has a list for many major cellular carriers: http://en.wikipedia.org/wiki/SMS_gateways. Here are a few. Be sure to double check your carrier's web site or contact tech support, because this information is subject to change:

- AT&T Wireless: number@txt.att.net
- Fido: number@fido.ca
- Rogers: number@pcs.rogers.com
- Sprint: number@messaging.sprintpcs.com
- Sprint Nextel: number@page.nextel.com
- T-Mobile USA: number@tmomail.net
- Verizon Wireless: number@vtext.com

Approve the dialog by hitting the Create Filter button, and your phone is ready to receive those Example.org server status alerts! Each alert that's being sent will additionally be archived in Gmail under the label "Sent to cellphone," so you can find it later if needed.

Figure 5-39.
Step 2 of 2 in setting up a forward filter—your cellphone is now ready to receive SMS alerts for specific emails

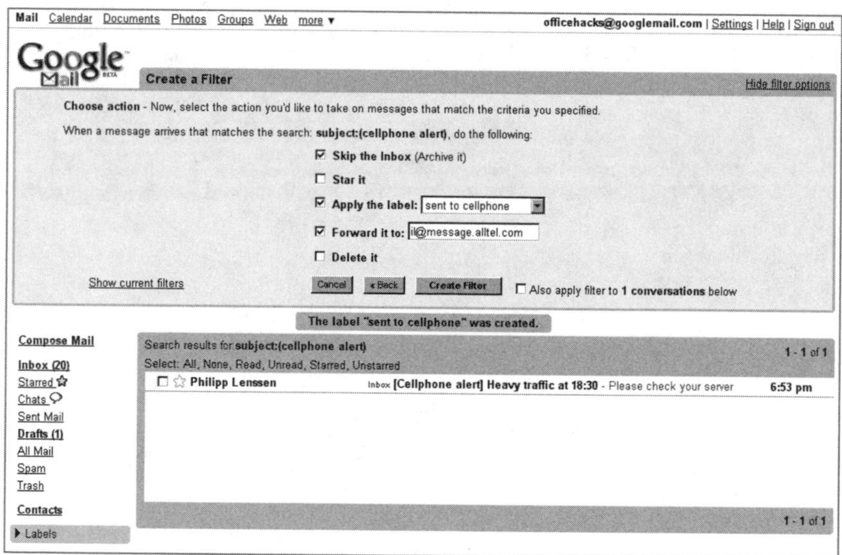

HACK 53: Create Spare Gmail Addresses

You think you have only a single Gmail email address? Not quite true—you've got a nearly unlimited number already.

Gmail's email address scheme is quite flexible. Not only can you receive emails to both *johndoe@gmail.com* and *johndoe@googlemail.com*, but you can also put a dot anywhere at all, or nowhere, as in *john.doe@gmail.com*, *j.ohndoe@gmail.com*, or *johndoe@gmail.com* (well, if your name is indeed John Doe, that is; please replace accordingly). As usual with email addresses, they are case-insensitive too, so you can write *JohnDOE@gMail.com*, too. All those emails will reach the same inbox—yours.

There's another way to form the email address though, and it's perhaps the most useful. You can add a plus along with a keyword to your email name. Like the following examples:

```
johndoe+family@gmail.com
johndoe+job@gmail.com
johndoe+spam@gmail.com
```

These addresses will all be sent to your normal Gmail inbox. This can come in very handy if you want to hand out separate email addresses for separate needs: perhaps one address for your office colleagues or your boss, another address for public mailing lists, one for registering at web sites you don't know that well, and yet another one for family members.

Although you can receive emails containing dots anywhere, when you log in to your Gmail account you still need to provide the dots exactly where you put them (if you included any) during your initial account signup.

Once you separate your emails with these keywords, you can go ahead and filter **[Hack #44]** incoming mail accordingly. Just go to Gmail and click the "Create a filter" link on top. Then in the To: field, enter the address you've handed out, as pictured in Figure 5-40, and click Next Step. You can then select the Skip the Inbox field and choose Apply the Label, creating a new label by the name "Job," as shown in Figure 5-41. Click Create Filter to confirm.

Now, whenever you get a new mail sent out to *johndoe+job@gmail.com* (*johndoe* being your chosen username, and *job* being the keyword of choice), it will be automatically sorted into the Job folder/label which you can access from the bottom left of Gmail.

Figure 5-40.
Setting up the filter by providing a special To: address

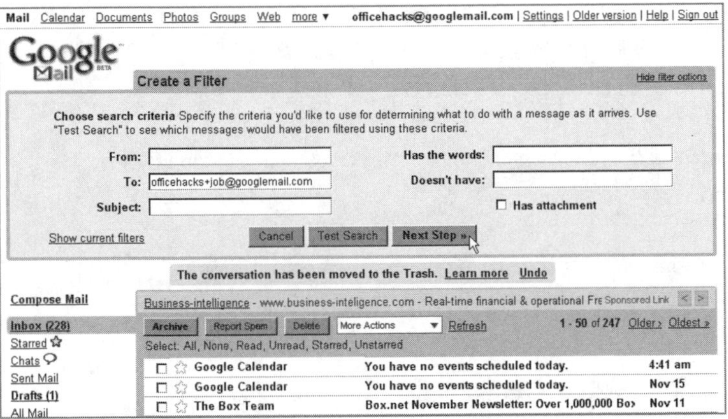

Figure 5-41.
Creating a new label "Job" to filter specific mails

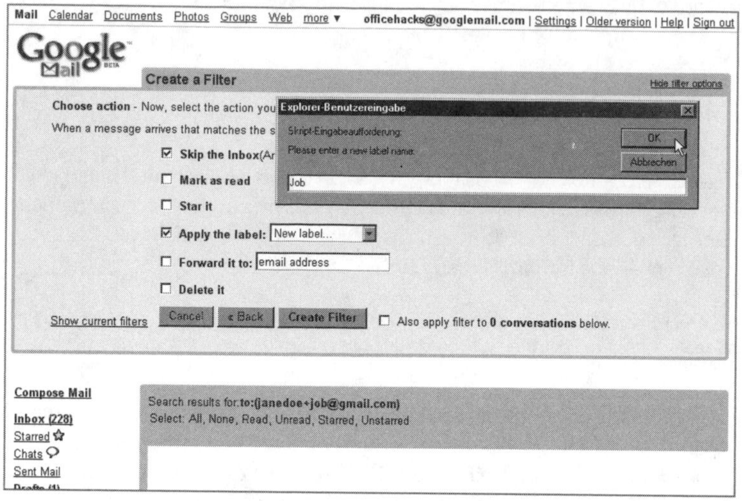

HACK 54: Search for a Specific Language

Sometimes Google releases undocumented features. At the time of this writing, Gmail's `lang` operator is one such undocumented feature—but that shouldn't stop you from using it!

Gmail.com has a hidden search feature allowing you to find messages in one language only. The operator at hand is used in web searching, too: "lang", as in the following searches (which find German, French, and Italian messages, respectively):

```
lang:de
lang:fr
lang:it
```

If you search for "lang:de" for instance (no quotes), you will see all your messages in German. Note that the labeling might not always be 100% accurate. You can also combine your language-restricted search with a normal keyword query, such as:

```
lang:de zahlung
```

You can also combine the language operator with filters **[Hack #44]**.

If you are unsure about what abbreviation to use for a given language, Google's advanced search dialog (http://google.com/advanced_search) can help. In the select box next to the "Return pages written in" label, choose any language. I'm picking Arabic, as shown in Figure 5-42. Also, enter a keyword at the top, and then hit the Google Search button. In the URL now showing in your browser, there's a parameter named "lr" with a value like "lang_ar"—the last two letters are the abbreviation you need to search in Gmail, such as *lang:ar*.

Hat tip to Alan/Garett Rogers at Googling Google, http://blogs.zdnet.com/Google/

Figure 5-42.
Google's advanced search dialog can help you find language abbreviations

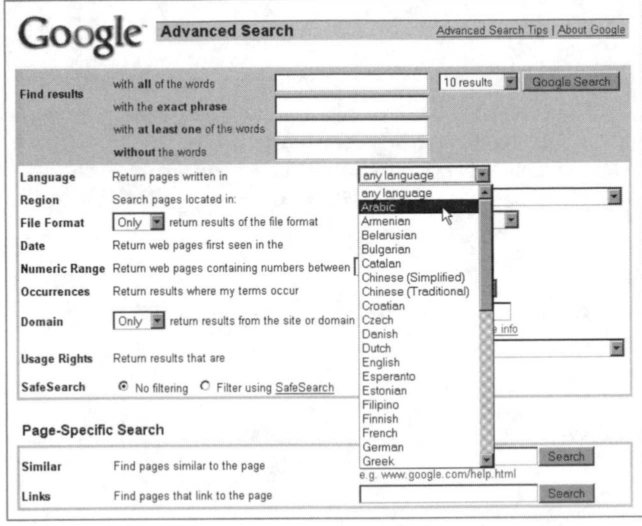

HACK 55: Link to Conversations, Searches, Labels, and More

Use the power of Gmail's permalinks.

Many of today's web applications are optimized to dynamically load new content into the current page you're on instead of forwarding you to another page. This fix can offer faster loading times, but it often comes with a problem: your browser's back button won't work the way you expect it to, and if you create a bookmark, it usually brings you to the main page rather than the content you were interested in.

Gmail.com offers a more accessible version of the default service, which you can switch to by choosing the footer link reading "basic HTML." This service not only uses an interface with fewer features, but behaves more like a traditional web application in many respects. But even in its default version—a dynamic web application—Gmail allows you to use the URL shown in your browser's location bar to link to specific content.

Linking to Specific Conversations

For instance, when you open a conversation thread in Gmail, the location bar contains a URL similar to this one:

```
http://mail.google.com/mail/#inbox/11623a4bda0eea2f
```

Imagine that you're emailing about an upcoming event with your friend, and you now want to add this information to Google Calendar. Instead of copying all the details into the Calendar event description manually, you can now just add the URL of the thread, and click through to the conversation details when you need more information.

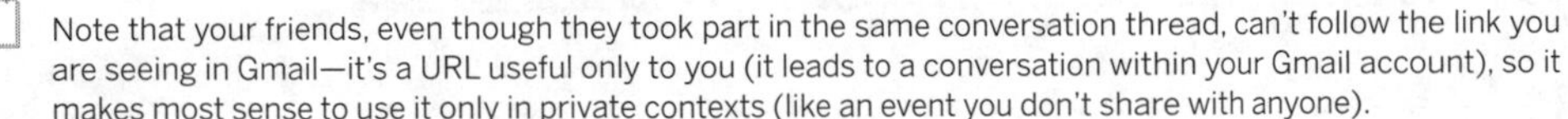
Note that your friends, even though they took part in the same conversation thread, can't follow the link you are seeing in Gmail—it's a URL useful only to you (it leads to a conversation within your Gmail account), so it makes most sense to use it only in private contexts (like an event you don't share with anyone).

Linking to Searches to Allow Easy Retrieval of Threads

You can also link to searches. A search for "horses," for instance, generates the following address:

```
http://mail.google.com/mail/#search/horses
```

This, too, can be useful—like when you want to point a friend to a specific conversation that the two of you had. You can now pick some rather distinct words or a phrase from the message (such as "John, attached find the meeting details"), search for it, and copy the generated URL to send it to your friend or colleague. They will now be able to easily retrieve the thread you are referring to, assuming that they are also using Gmail, and that they haven't deleted the message.

Linking to Labels

You can also link to specific labels that you've set up. Let's say one of your labels is called "job," for all job-related mails. Clicking on the label link will take you to a page with the following URL, which you can bookmark for later reference:

```
http://mail.google.com/mail/#label/job
```

CREATE BOOKMARK SHORTCUTS

If you're using Firefox as your default browser, you can also set up a special bookmark keyword. Open the Bookmark menu, find your job bookmark and right-click it to open its properties from the context menu. In the Keyword box, enter "job", as shown in Figure 5-43. Approve the dialog by hitting the OK button. Now whenever you enter the word "job" into the browser address bar in Firefox, you will be immediately taken to your mails filtered into the job label/folder. You can use this trick with any bookmark.

Figure 5-43.
The Firefox bookmark properties dialog

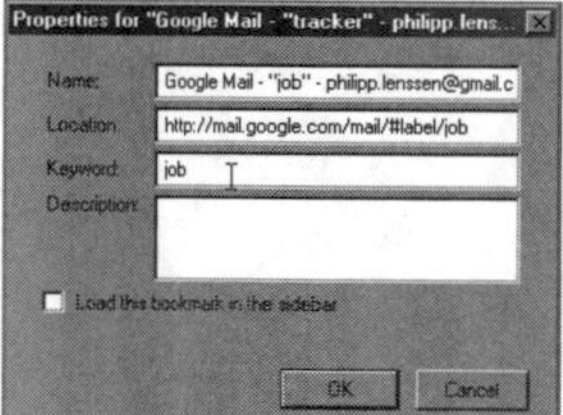

Creating a "Compose" Shortcut

Another way to use Gmail's permalink-style URLs is to add a shortcut for composing a new mail to the browser toolbar (the term "permalink" comes from the world of blogs, though note that not all Gmail URLs are necessarily quite as permanent). For instance, in Internet Explorer, it's the Links bar; in Firefox, it's called the Bookmarks Toolbar. In Safari, the name is Bookmarks Bar. The address for composing a new mail is:

```
http://mail.google.com/mail/#compose
```

Go to that link, then drag and drop the URL onto your bookmarks toolbar. Rename the link title to something shorter, like "Compose mail." Now when you click it, as shown in Figure 5-44, you will instantly open a new Gmail compose window.

Figure 5-44.
Following a "Compose mail" toolbar shortcut (I rearranged the toolbar layout in Firefox so the buttons take up less space)

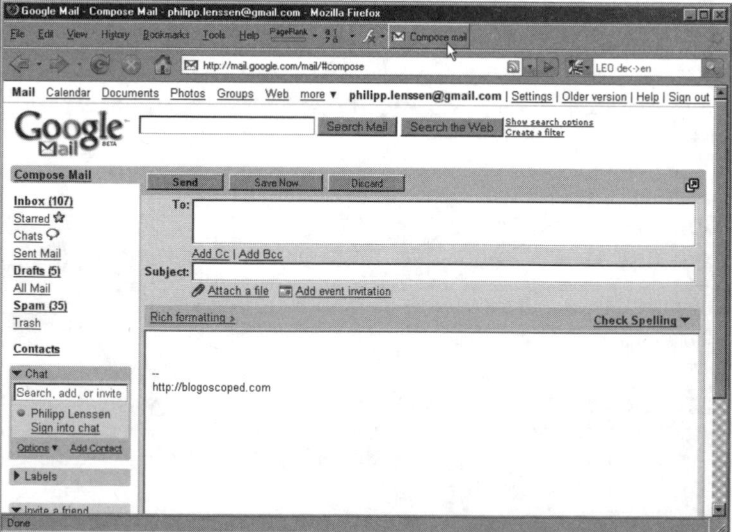

Curious about how to save button space at the top of Firefox, as shown in Figure 5-44? You might use a bookmarks toolbar or the Google Toolbar, but you can also move the buttons from those further up—to then make the bars disappear. Right-click a toolbar and select Customize from the context menu. You will now be able to move any button from a toolbar onto the top bar (to the right side of the Firefox menu) via drag and drop. Once finished, click the Done button. Now right-click a toolbar again and uncheck it in the context menu to make it disappear.

HACK 58: Beyond Google: Yahoo! Mail, MS Hotmail, and More

Is Gmail getting on your nerves, for some reason or other? Well, it's not the only web mail application out there, so you might find yourself giving Google's competition a try, too.

Two of the most popular free email clients out there are Yahoo! Mail and Microsoft Windows Live Hotmail, the successor to Hotmail. You may also prefer a desktop mail client, like Thunderbird, to the web-based kind.

Switching web email clients is the easiest when you have an address like yourname@yourserver.com which merely forwards to your web mail client address, like your Gmail address. If you have your own hosting provider then you can usually log in to the hosting provider's control panel to set up addresses like these (please consult your hosting support or help files for the details). If you don't yet have one, you can try to search Google for "get domain", "web hosting" and similar to find a service.

Once you set up your email adress this way, you don't need to hand out a new address to friends and colleagues whenever you switch to another email application. In the Gmail settings Accounts tab, you can also change your Reply-To address to e.g. "yourname@example.com", meaning other people will never reply directly to the Gmail address. This adds an extra layer of flexibility.

Once you set up your email adress this way, you don't need to hand out a new address to friends and colleagues whenever you switch to another email application. In the Accounts tab under Gmail settings, you can also change your Reply-To address to *yourname@example.com*, so that other people will never reply directly to the Gmail address. This adds an extra layer of flexibility.

Yahoo! Mail

Yahoo's email offering is especially tempting if you're used to desktop programs like Microsoft Outlook or Outlook Express, as it shares some of the look and feel of these applications. To sign up for Yahoo! Mail, visit http://mail.yahoo.com. If you don't already have a Yahoo! ID, click the "Sign up" button to create one. You will be required to pick a username and password, provide your first and last name, gender, and more. Your email will end up being of the format *YourUserName@yahoo.com*.

After logging in to your mail account, you will be greeted with a page collecting news, calendar events, and special messages and advertisements, as shown in Figure 5-45. If you switch to your inbox, you will find that you can drag and drop messages into the trash in the lefthand navigation pane. You will also notice that messages you open will show in a new tab within the browser.

Microsoft Hotmail

Hotmail—or Windows Live Hotmail, as it's fully titled—can be reached at http://hotmail.com. Sign up for an account if you don't have one already; note that you can also use an MSN Messenger or Passport account as your so-called Windows Live ID for this purpose. Sign in with your username and password. As opposed to Gmail and Yahoo Mail, you need to provide your full email address during login (for example, *YourUserName@hotmail.com* instead of just *YourUserName*).

After signing in to Hotmail, the program opens with an intro page containing news, miscellaneous information, and ads, as pictured in Figure 5-46, but you can access your inbox by following the link to the left. Hotmail also offers a calendar application and an address book. As with Gmail, the

Figure 5-45.
Yahoo! Mail has the look and feel of a desktop application

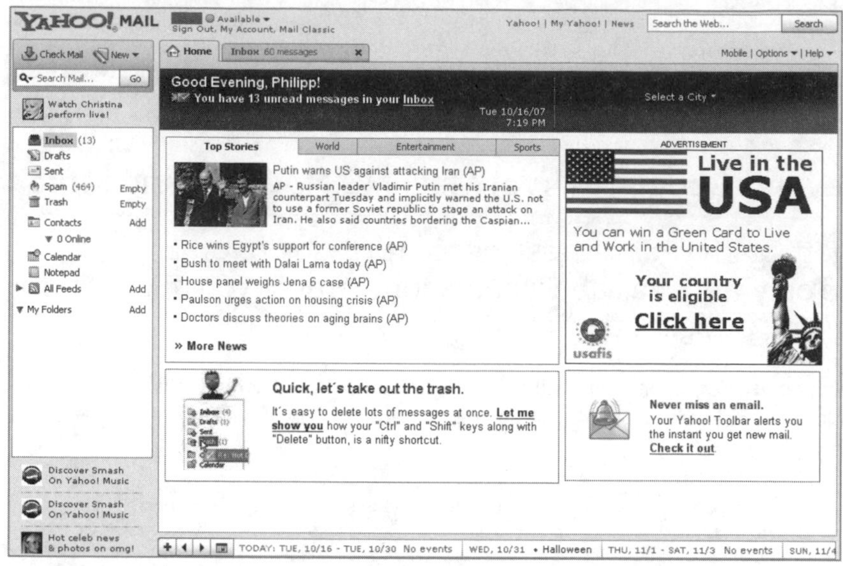

Figure 5-46.
Welcome to Hotmail!

amount of email storage varies over time, but at the time of this writing, Hotmail offered 5 GB. Furthermore, Hotmail allows you to switch the interface theme **[Hack #47]** via the Options menu.

Mozilla Thunderbird

Thunderbird is the sibling of the Firefox browser, with a focus on handling email instead of web pages. Pictured in Figure 5-47, it's a lean "offline" client that you can download at http://mozilla.com/thunderbird/ and install for free **[Hack #48]**—and even use to access your Gmail email, if you want to, using POP or IMAP **[Hack #52]**.

Figure 5-47.
The Thunderbird email inbox

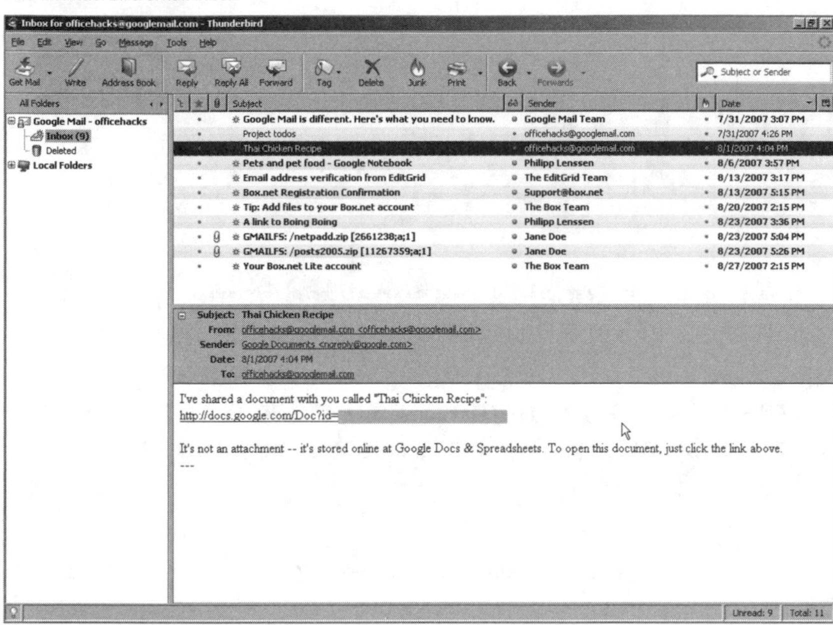

06 CUSTOMIZE YOUR GOOGLE HOME PAGE

iGoogle is the name of Google's personalized home page, which you can reach by clicking "iGoogle" on the Google home page, or by going straight to http://igoogle.com. iGoogle is not a single feature of the Google home page; rather, it's an alternative flavor of it, displaying a variety of so-called "gadgets," as shown in Figure 6-1.

If you like the simplicity of the current Google home page, you don't need to switch. But if you're looking for ways to add more spice to Google, consider the move—and you can also switch between the two flavors, depending on what you need to do. You will then be able to see weather gadgets, interactive maps, miniature versions of special search engines, your Gmail inbox, and much more, right on Google.com. You can set your own background image for Google as well.

To use iGoogle fully, you need a Google account (see Chapter 1). This way you will be able to add your own tabs and gadgets. An iGoogle tab is just a collection of multiple gadgets, and you can add several different tabs. A gadget, on the other hand, is . . . *anything* really. Think of it as a web page or web application but in miniature form.

Figure 6-1.
iGoogle: your customized and widgetized version of the Google home page

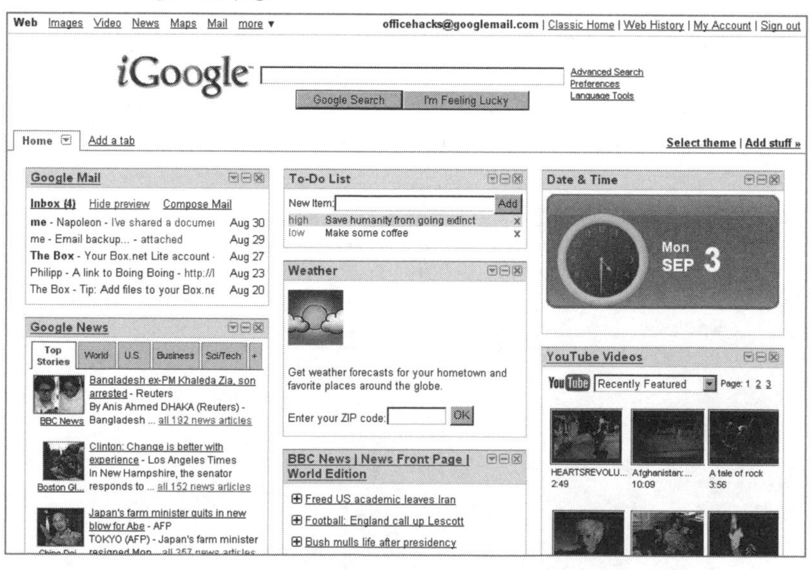

Here's a short overview of the kind of gadgets available today in the Google gadget directory—from little helpers and applications to games, from the very useful to the merely entertaining, and everything in between:

- Weather forecasts for your location
- A Wikipedia search box, restricting results to pages from this large, human-edited online encyclopedia
- A colorful box showing the current date and time
- The Einstein quote of the day, or the Jon Stewart quote of the day
- Brain teasers to start your day
- Your own ToDo list
- A search box for a dictionary or thesaurus
- An information box showing your IP address
- Your Google Calendar events for the month
- The Buddhist thought of the day, or a painting masterpiece of the day
- A "falling blocks"-style puzzle game, playable right within your browser
- The top stories from Google News
- A countdown ticker for your birthday (or New Year's Day)
- A Mario-style jump-and-run game, or a Pac-Man-like maze game
- Hotmail or Yahoo! Mail
- The Garfield or Dilbert cartoon of the day
- An eBay tracker to watch out for bargains for you
- Google Talk, so you can chat with others right from Google.com
- A market summary, courtesy of Google Finance, or a stock chart of your choice
- The latest headlines from CNN.com, Reuters, ESPN, *Time*, or FOX
- The latest headlines from any RSS-enabled blog or news site of your choice

and much more!

Behind each of these gadgets is an XML file containing HTML, CSS, and JavaScript defining what the gadget should do; how it reacts to your input, which data sources it is supposed to pull, and which preferences you set for this gadget. A gadget can also simply refer to another web site, whose contents are integrated into your Google home page. Also, gadgets can communicate with each other using gadget-to-gadget communication. You can create your own gadgets, too, with no, little, or lots of programming—whatever you prefer. So without further ado, let's take a look at how to hack the Google home page using iGoogle as well as how to hack iGoogle itself (by going beyond its native scope of features).

 Some older gadgets may require you to "inline" them. An inlined gadget has access to more of your Google settings than regular gadgets. When it comes to gadgets that require inlining, only add those you consider safe and trustworthy. In general, however, inlining is not required in the first place; what's more, Google deprecated the inlining feature, so gadgets developed these days cannot use inlining.

GOOGLE DESKTOP

Some Google gadgets—the so-called *universal gadgets*—also run on the desktop instead of the browser, as part of Google Desktop (and as a side-note, some gadgets also run in social networks like Orkut, by way of Google's OpenSocial library). The Google Desktop setup is available for Windows Vista/2000/XP, Mac OS X 10.4+, and Linux, and can be downloaded from http://desktop.google.com. Google Desktop offers more than gadgets: it also lets you search your computer, or bring up a quick search box for the Web when you hit the Ctrl/Command key twice.

If you want gadgets on your desktop, but don't need all of Google Desktop, look into Amnesty Generator (http://www.amnestywidgets.com), which can convert Google Gadgets into Mac OS X Dashboard widgets or Windows Vista Sidebar gadgets. Also, Mac OS X users can choose to download just the portion of Google Desktop that embeds gadgets in Dashboard (click "Choose your own features" on the download page.)

HACK 57: Add Google Tools to iGoogle

You can search for new content or browse the Google directory, adding individual gadgets as you come across them. But you can also add several gadgets all at once.

The iGoogle home page (http://igoogle.com) is the perfect place to organize your Google apps suite, like Google Calendar, Gmail, Google Reader, or Google Docs. It offers helper gadgets that showcase your inbox, your calendar events, and your current documents. You can go to iGoogle and click "Add stuff" to search for these Google gadgets one by one, or you can add the whole lot of them in one semiautomated swift swoop.

To automatically add these gadgets, click on "Add a tab" on top. Inside the dialog that shows up, enter the tab name "Google Tools". Keep the "I'm feeling lucky" checkbox selected when pressing OK. After a few seconds, you will end up with a new tab collecting all kinds of gadgets.

Because this selection is automated, it may not be exactly what you require. At this time, some of the useful gadgets that are added were (this may change in the future):

- Google Reader, to keep up on your RSS subscriptions
- Google Talk, to chat with friends, family, and colleagues
- Google Notebook for writing down smaller notes **[Hack #14]**
- A Google Maps search
- A ToDo List
- Google Groups (if you are a member of any)
- A Google Docs files overview
- Google Docs
- Gmail

But some of the gadgets may not be useful to you, and some that you may find useful are probably missing. To fine-tune Google's preselection, go ahead and remove all those gadgets that you do not want by clicking the "x" button of each. For instance, I removed the ToDo list and Google Groups gadgets, among others. Now select "Add stuff" and look for others, and especially these gadgets:

- Search for "Google Bookmarks" to get the official Google bookmarks gadget.
- Search for "Picasa Web Photos" to display your Picasa photos.
- Search for "Google News customized" to get the latest headlines for your topic of choice; for instance, I've entered "Yahoo". You can pick any topic you like to track for your job project or your personal interest.

Once you've added these, you can also change your tab layout. Click the arrow icon next to your tab name "Google Office," and choose "Edit this tab." Select a new layout from the list of options for a result as shown in Figure 6-2.

To save you the time it takes to add these gadgets, you can also just integrate the shared tab we provide at http://blogoscoped.com/googleappshacks/link/apps-tab. (To share a custom tab of your own, select "Share this tab" from the tab menu.)

Figure 6-2.
Your Google office home page

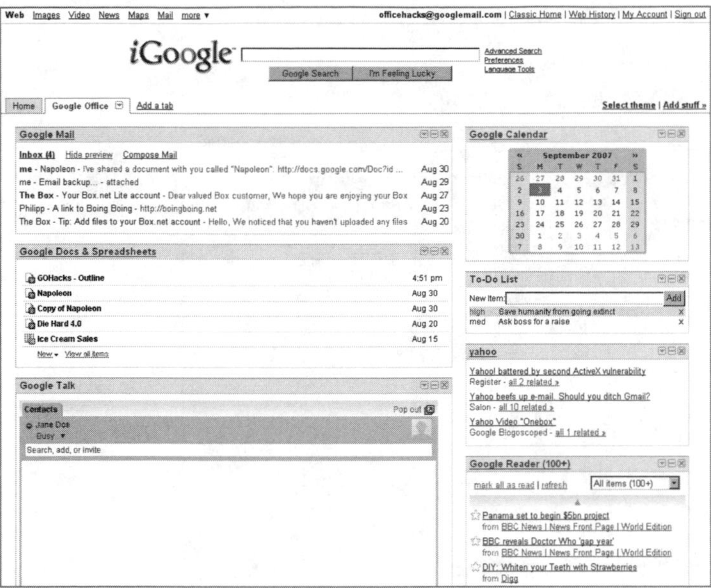

HACK 58: Chat from iGoogle

You don't need to leave your seat, or the Google home page, to talk to others.

Google offers different tools for you to chat with your friends or colleagues. Among them are:

1. The Google Talk client, a desktop application. This requires you to download and install a file from http://google.com/talk. At the time of this writing, it's the only variant of Google Talk that is voice-enabled, allows file transfers, and notifies you when you receive new mail in Gmail.

2. The web-based Google Chat program, integrated with Gmail (http://gmail.com).

3. The Google Talk web page. You can launch a new chat window at http://google.com/talk.

4. The Google Talk web page gadget. Starting off at http://igoogle.com, you can add the gadget to your personalized Google home page.

One of the easiest ways to chat is to use the standalone web version of Google Talk, either running in its own window or as a gadget. To add the gadget, click the "Add stuff" link at the top of iGoogle. Search for "Google Talk" and choose the official Google Talk gadget (it will say "By Google"). Click "Add it now" and your iGoogle page now contains an instant messenger, as shown in Figure 6-3.

To get started, simply enter your friend's Gmail address into the top box. They may not appear in the list until they've confirmed you as a contact. Chatting is now as easy as typing something and hitting Return, as you would do in any other instant messenger client. There are a number of special symbols, so called emoticons or smileys, that you can type to display a graphic icon to your friend:

```
:D      Smile
=)      Smile
:)      Smile
=D      Smile
```

Figure 6-3.
The Google Talk gadget on iGoogle

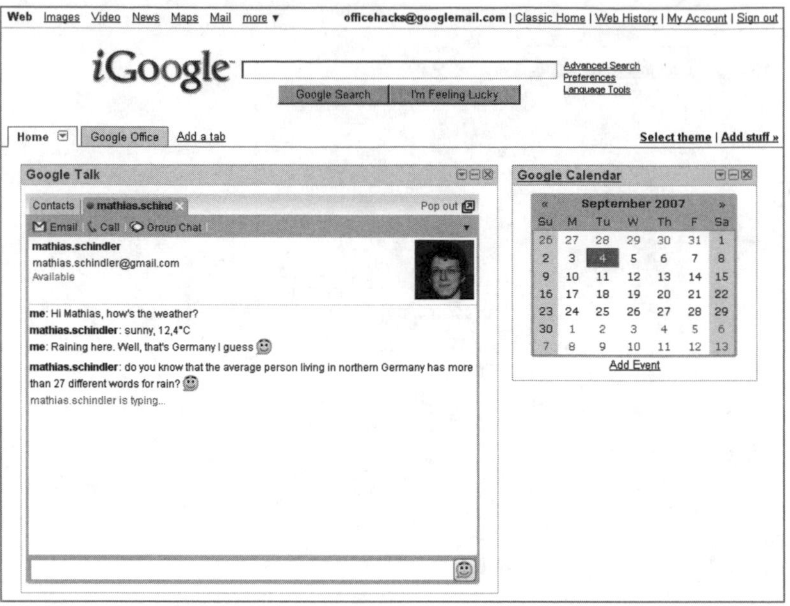


```
:-)     Smile
;)      Wink/irony
;-)     Wink/irony
:-O     Surprise
x-(     Angry
B-)     Glasses/cool
:'(     Crying
:-|     Neutral
:-/     Disappointed/skeptical
:p      Sticking tongue out
<3      Heart/love
</3     Heartache
:(|)    Monkey
\m/     Hand/rocking
}:)     Devil/evil
```

You can use any other emoticon (see http://en.wikipedia.org/wiki/Emoticon) not on this list, but it will not be converted to a graphic by Google Talk.

 If your chat partner uses a non-Google chat client, or Gmail chat, your symbols may show as different icons or remain plain text.

Google's gadget framework also allows you to include a Google Talk gadget on your web site or blog. Open the menu of the gadget by clicking its arrow icon on top and select "About this gadget." On the page that follows, click "Embed this gadget" (look in the section of the page labeled "for Webmasters"). You can then change the title and layout of the gadget and click the "Get the code" button, as shown in Figure 6-4. Copy and paste the resulting HTML and include it on your website. If you add the code to a blog post, make sure you are in the Edit HTML, not the Compose/Rich Text/ WYSIWYG mode. Figure 6-5 shows how the gadget appears on a blog post.

Figure 6-4.
Get the code to embed the Google Talk gadget

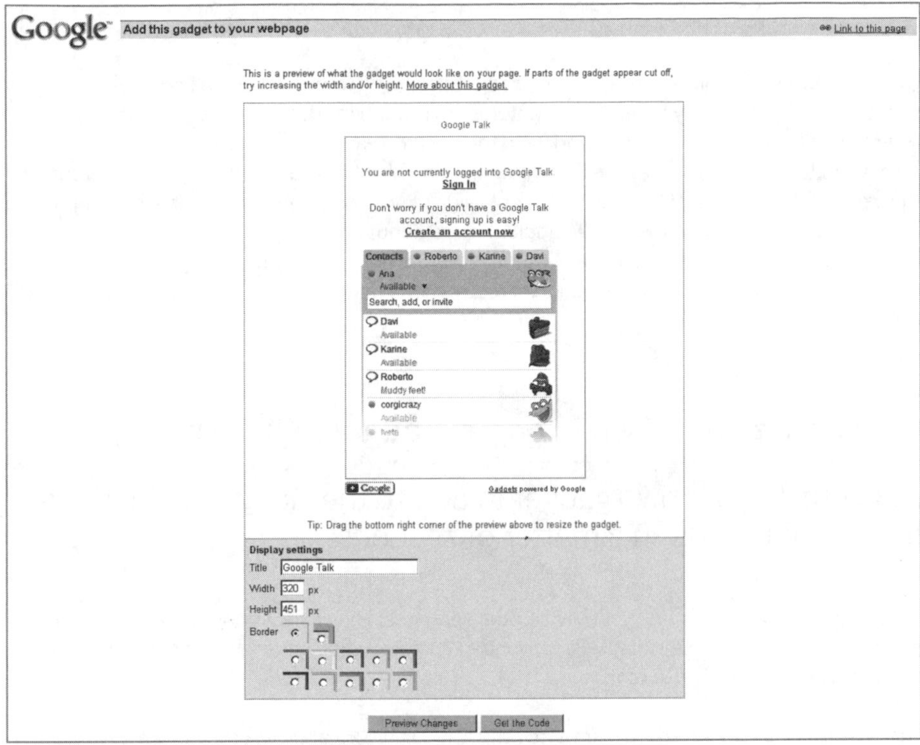

Figure 6-5.
The Talk gadget embedded in a Blogger blog

Please note that due to security restrictions, embedding the Google Talk gadget into a web page works with many but not all browsers. Internet Explorer 7, for instance, may not allow users to sign in to the gadget if it's included on your blog or other web page.

But wouldn't it be nice to take control over the gadget design as well? Creating a user stylesheet **[Hack #41]** might come in handy here, though (interestingly enough) this will not work with the online version of Google Talk, but it will work with the desktop variant. The reason is that the gadget version of Google Talk actually uses the Flash plug-in instead of being a plain web page, whereas the desktop version of Talk uses HTML and JavaScript to display its contents. Google Talk desktop also comes with a set of predefined themes. To find out more about hacking the desktop Talk CSS, take a look at http://kylehayes.info/blog/index.cfm/2006/4/1/Hacking-Google-Talk-Themes. To download a selection of ready-made new themes, point your browser to http://gtalk.anthonysottile.com.

HACK 59: Create Your Own iGoogle Gadgets Quickly

You can create your own gadget to add to the Google home page or share with friends, in a matter of seconds.

There are two basic ways to create your own iGoogle gadgets. The easiest and quickest way is to use Google's wizard, described in this hack. For advanced customization, you can also create the XML for the gadget from scratch **[Hack #60]**.

To launch the iGoogle gadget wizard, sign in to http://igoogle.com and click the bottom link reading "Create your own gadget," which will lead you to the page shown in Figure 6-6. At the time of this writing, you could choose from seven different gadget types:

1. A photo or series of photos
2. A "GoogleGram," which is a gadget you can share with friends or family, and which displays a different message and illustration every day
3. The "Daily Me" gadget showing others what you are up to at the moment
4. A free-form gadget to showcase any kind of text and image combination
5. A gadget to display a YouTube video channel for friends
6. Your personal top ten list
7. A custom countdown ticker gadget

Suppose that you want to create a Daily Me gadget. Pick "Get started" and fill out the form in the dialog that follows, as shown in Figure 6-7. You can add a photo of you from any public address on the web or upload an image from your computer, or choose a photo from one of your Picasa albums. Press the "Create Gadget" button when you're finished with the form, and enter a list of recipients to send this gadget to. You can then decide to make this gadget public or not—if this is just for friends, there is no need to publish it within the Google gadget directory—and hit the Save button. You and others (everyone who confirmed your invitation, that is) will now be able to see the gadget on iGoogle, as shown in Figure 6-8.

By default, the gadget is added to the currently active tab. However, you can move any gadget into any other tab by dragging and dropping it over another tab.

Figure 6-6.
The different choices for making your own gadget

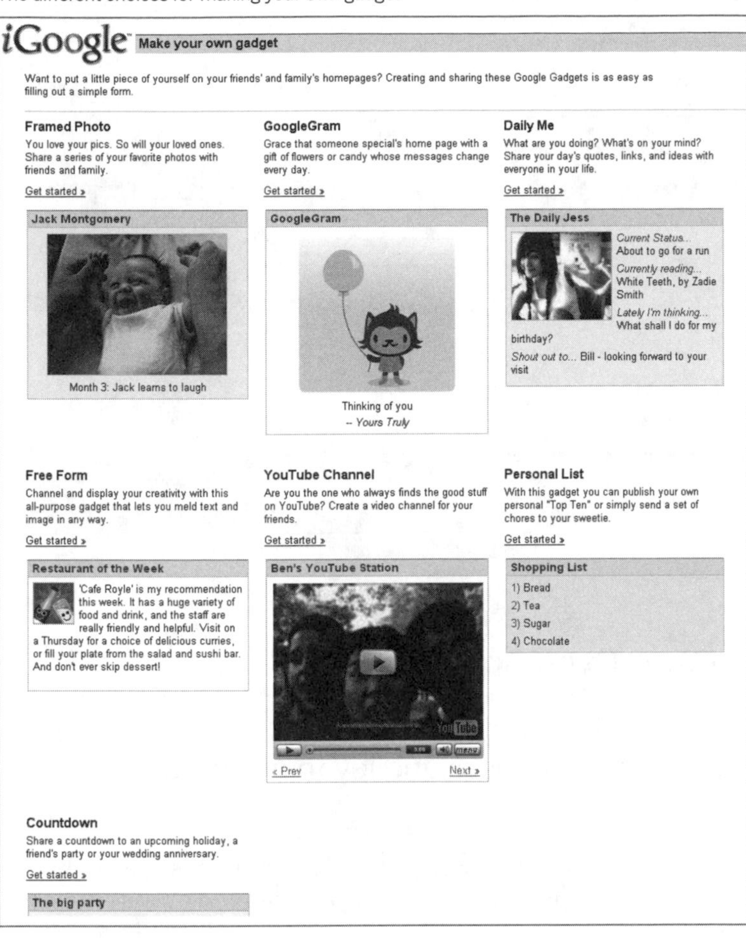

Figure 6-7.
Preparing a "Daily Me" gadget to share with others

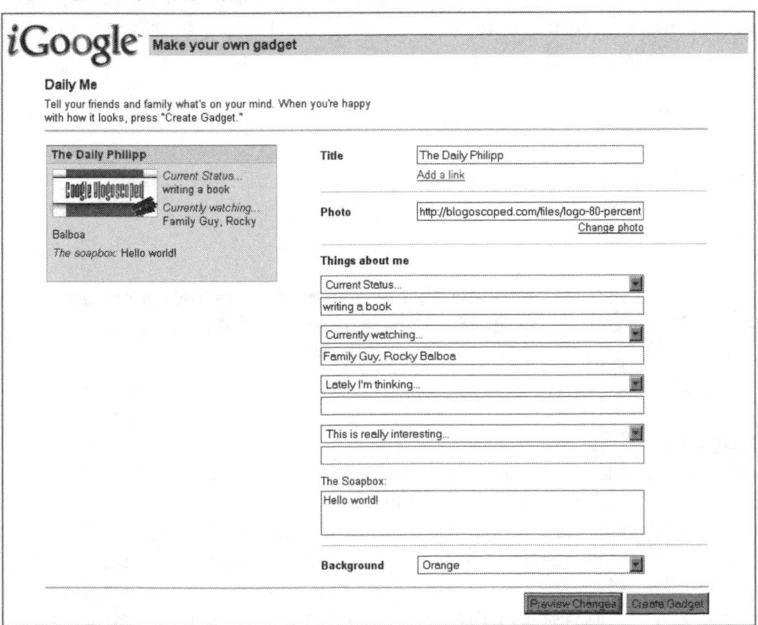

Figure 6-8.
A homemade gadget included on someone else's iGoogle. Note that the settings menu of this gadget will only show up on the iGoogle homepage of the gadget creator.

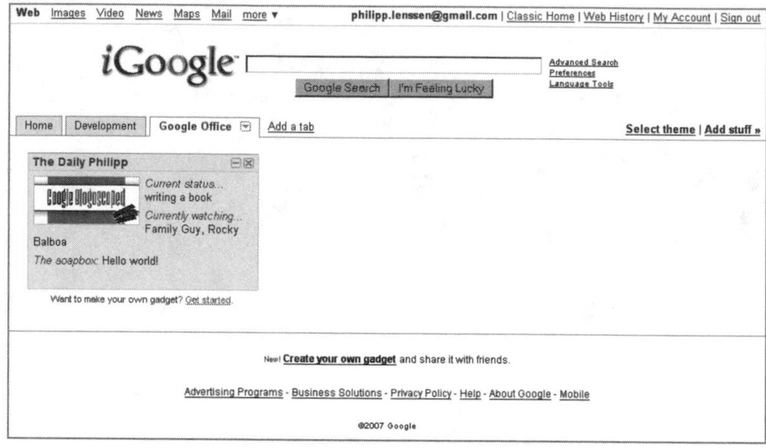

HACK 60: Program Your Own iGoogle Gadget

You can add almost any functionality to the Google home page. Helpful tools can spread usefulness and joy to others, and they can even promote your web site.

As long as you have basic web development skills and you know some HTML, CSS, and JavaScript, you can create your own custom gadgets from scratch. If not, you can also create a gadget using Google's gadget maker **[Hack #59]**.

Broadly speaking, a Google gadget—also called a *widget*, or *module*—is just a small web page. It can be a little helper tool, a Flash game, a special search engine, or anything else you can think of or find online. Furthermore, gadgets meeting certain criteria are not limited to being placed on iGoogle, but may also be included on blogs or other web sites, or within Google Desktop.

Every gadget is made up of an XML (eXtensible Markup Language) document that defines its inner workings. This definition can include all of its HTML, CSS, JavaScript, and so on—or it can just instruct iGoogle to display information from another web page. Furthermore, the Google gadget framework stores user settings for you, if you need them, and comes with additional JavaScript functions you can use in your own code.

Let's get started by creating a gadget that does nothing more than display the message "Hello world, this is my first gadget!" After that, I will outline a more complete gadget utilizing PHP5, XHTML, CSS, and a database.

The Hello World Gadget

A Google gadget is an XML text file that you can create on your computer and upload to a web server. You can also use the official Google Gadget Editor (see http://code.google.com/apis/gadgets/docs/gs.html#GGE), which comes complete with hosting (a place to store your files online) and color-coding capabilities. To set up your own gadget development framework, go to iGoogle at http://igoogle.com and click "Add a tab" to create a new tab named "Gadget Development" (be sure to uncheck the "I'm feeling lucky" option **[Hack #57]**). Now click "Add stuff" to the right and select the

"Add feed or gadget" option. Enter gge.xml to add the Google Gadget Editor, and enter developer.xml to add a developer helper gadget. Next, click "Back to iGoogle Home" to go to your new tab.

By rearranging the gadgets, you can set up a development environment as pictured in Figure 6-9. (To make the Google Gadget Editor wider, click the down-pointing arrow to the right of the tab name, choose Edit This Tab, and pick a two-column layout that gives more width to the leftmost column.)

Technically, the Hello World sample is already finished now, because Google preloaded this sample into the editor! Click on the Preview tab of the gadget editor to see this as it would appear live. Next, click Editor, then take a look at the source code of the gadget:

```
<?xml version="1.0" encoding="UTF-8"?>
<Module>
<ModulePrefs title="hello world example" />
<Content type="html"><![CDATA[
     Hello, world!
]]></Content>
</Module>
```

The XML declaration on top defines the character set, UTF-8 **[Hack #12]**. The root element is called `Module`, as gadgets were previously (and still occasionally are) called "modules" by Google. The `ModulePrefs` element stores your settings for this gadget, such as its title; a `UserPref` element, not shown in this short example, can store the custom user settings. The actual content of your module is the HTML section, wrapped within the `CDATA` part.

Change the content from "Hello, world!" to anything else, and include some simple (X)HTML, like the following:

```
...
<Content type="html"><![CDATA[
<p><img src="http://google.com/logos/conan_doyle.gif" alt="" />
<p>Hello world, this is my first gadget!</p>
]]></Content>
...
```

Figure 6-9.
The Google Gadget Editor, along with the "My Gadgets" gadget, helps you with the development process

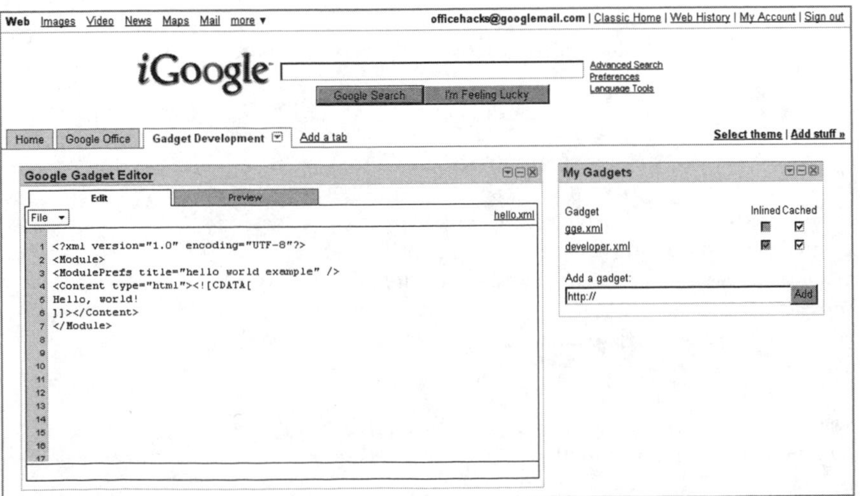

Preview the gadget, and if you like the results, save it by selecting File→Save As from the editor gadget menu. You can opt to use Google's hosting solution for this. Choose any filename for your sample, like `hello2.xml`. You will see this filename displayed in the top right of your editor. Click the link to open the URL in a new window, and the address may look similar to the following:

```
http://hosting.gmodules.com/ig/gadgets/file/122710312740571178902/hello2.xml
```

Copy the address you are seeing and paste it into the box within the developer helper gadget (the gadget titled "My Gadgets"). Clicking the Add button will now show your gadget on the iGoogle page. At this point, you can share the gadget with anyone else, or read through Google's tutorial at http://google.com/apis/gadgets/docs-home.html to find out more about the gadget syntax. You can also load further samples into the gadget editor to see what they are made of. To do so, select New from the Google Gadget Editor's File menu.

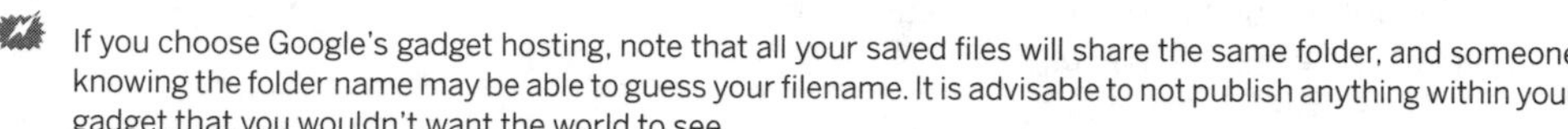
If you choose Google's gadget hosting, note that all your saved files will share the same folder, and someone knowing the folder name may be able to guess your filename. It is advisable to not publish anything within your gadget that you wouldn't want the world to see.

Google does not declare any HTML document type when rendering gadgets to the browser. Although you can implicitly use XHTML or HTML (Strict or Transitional) in your gadget, the lack of doctype makes some browsers switch to a so-called "quirks mode." This may bring with it some subtle differences in regards to how CSS is displayed, among other issues.

The Daily Product Image Gadget

Suppose that you want to create a gadget that displays a different image from your product database every day. Note this section requires a basic understanding of the technologies involved—the gadget syntax, Apache/PHP/MySQL, CSS, and XHTML—and gives just a broad overview of how you can put the individual pieces together.

The first choice you face when deciding how to set up your gadget is whether to embed your code in the gadget XML, or just have the XML point to a page on your server. The former approach has the benefit of using the Google gadget framework's native caching capabilities. Google polls your XML definition every once in a while but then serves it from their own servers to gadget users, saving you bandwidth. This hack uses code embedded in an XML file instead of a pointer to your webpage.

If your hypothetical database table "products" has the fields *id, title, price*, and *image*, then you could create a second table "products_random" with the fields *id, product_id*, and *date* and fill it once with product image IDs using a script, or add to it daily using a `cron` job on your server. Please note that if you're not comfortable with using a SQL server table, an alternative approach to define the product data is listed shortly as well.

Whether you are using SQL or not, the PHP file to show the daily image is as follows:

```
<?
 header('Content-Type: text/xml; charset=UTF-8');
 echo '<' . '?xml version="1.0" encoding="UTF-8" ?' . '>' . "\r";
 ?><Module>
<ModulePrefs title="Acme Inc's Daily Product Image"
     title_url="http://example.com"
     description="Shows a new Acme Inc product everyday!"
     author="Jane Doe"
     author_email="officehacks@gmail.com"
     author_affiliation="Acme Inc"
     author_location="Chicago"
     screenshot="http://example.com/gadget-screenshot-280x250.png"
     thumbnail="http://example.com/gadget-thumbnail-120x60.png"
/>
```

```
<Content type="html"><![CDATA[
<style type="text/css" media="screen">
  /* if you have additional CSS... */
</style>
<script type="text/javascript"><!--
   /* if you have additional JavaScript... */
   // --></script>
<p><img src="<?= getProductImageUrl() ?>" alt="" />
</p>
]]></Content>
</Module>
```

The function to get the product image (using SQL) could be as follows (note that other functions referenced here are not listed for this sample—if you want to try this out without setting up the SQL database, try the next version of this function):

```
<?
function getProductImageUrl()
{
    $url = 'no-image.jpg';
    $database = openDatabase();
    $query = 'SELECT products.image AS productImage FROM products ' .
            'LEFT JOIN products_random ' .
            'ON products.id = products_random.id ' .
            'WHERE date = ' . smartQuote( getIsoDate() ) . ' LIMIT 1';
    $rows = mysql_query($query) or die('Error');
    while ( $c = mysql_fetch_array($rows) ) {
        $url = $c['productImage'];
    }
    closeDatabase($database);
    return 'http://example.com/images/' . $url;
}
?>
```

If you'd rather not use SQL for now, you can also use a function that stores your product data in an array. In the following code, several cover image IDs from the O'Reilly catalog are listed. Using the `day()` function, you get a number representing the day of the year—0 for January 1, 42 for February 12, and so on. The modulus operator (%) now gives you the remainder of `dayOfYear` divided by the amount of covers available. This `coverIndex` number can be used to grab a specific cover ID—for every new day a different number is picked (rotating back to the beginning of the array if no more new covers are available):

```
<?
function getProductImageUrl()
{
    $coverIds = array(
            '9780596528348',
            '0596527209',
            '0596007795',
            '0596100604',
            '0596101538');
    $dayOfYear = date('z');
    $coverIndex = $dayOfYear % count($coverIds);
    $coverId = $coverIds[$coverIndex];
    return 'http://oreilly.com/catalog/covers/' . $coverId . '_cat.gif';
}
?>
```

As you can see in these example functions, the returned image URL is an absolute URL; that's because even though the XML is initially hosted on your server, it will later be served by Google through the gmodules.com domain.

In order to have your script be recognized by your web server as a PHP script, you will probably need to give it a filename such as *product-gadget.php*. If you are using the Apache server with `mod_rewrite` enabled, you can make it look like an XML file by using syntax like the following inside an *.htaccess* file on your server:

```
RewriteEngine On
RewriteRule ^product-gadget\.xml  product-gadget.php
```

This would let you use a URL like http://example.com/product-gadget.xml. Your gadget is now ready to be submitted at http://google.com/ig/submit!

> Note that an alternative to this approach is to have your product image script emit an RSS/Atom feed, as iGoogle users can also add any feed as a gadget. This way, you would also support RSS readers, RSS-enabled screensavers, and mobile devices that support RSS.

HACK 61: Create an iGoogle Theme

Is the plain white background of the Google home page boring you?

When you click the Select Theme link at iGoogle.com, you are forwarded to the themes directory to pick one of the many available looks for your Google home page. You'll find choices like Lollipopland, Hong Kong (pictured in Figure 6-10), or Darts. Some of the themes are provided by Google; others are homebrewed. Certain themes will also change with the time of the day, and may include Easter eggs—special surprises showing at specific times of the day.

> Pssst: not keen on waiting for hours on end to glance at the Easter eggs? Take a look at UK developer Tony Ruscoe's hack to make them appear instantly at http://ruscoe.net/blog/2007/03/google-personalized-homepage-easter.asp.

If you want to create your own theme, Google has a detailed one-stop tutorial to the Themes API for you at http://code.google.com/apis/themes/docs/dev_guide.html. Basically, each theme consists of an XML file that lists different "skins," which define things like link colors, text colors, and background images. (Note that although you can choose between the different available iGoogle logos, you are not allowed to completely remove the logo.)

igThemer

Even more direct than going through the Google tutorial to develop a theme is to use igThemer. Available at http://hawidu.com/themes/, this third-party tool presents a form listing the various available options. I've clicked on the color picker for the header background, for instance, and after making a selection, pressed the Refresh button at the top of the form. This resulted in the look shown in Figure 6-11.

Hit the Create button at the end of the form when you're done customizing, and igThemer will host the XML for you at a URL similar to this one: http://hawidu.com/themes/public/theme021208093859.xml.

The iGoogle Theme Editor Bookmarklet

Another very interesting option for theme creation is the bookmarklet developed by Japan's Yoshiomi Kurisi, at http://chris4403.blogspot.com (thanks to Ionut of http://googlesystem.blogspot.com for suggesting this hack). A bookmarklet is a short piece of JavaScript, stored as a

Figure 6-10.
Google's Hong Kong theme for iGoogle paints the background as cityscape

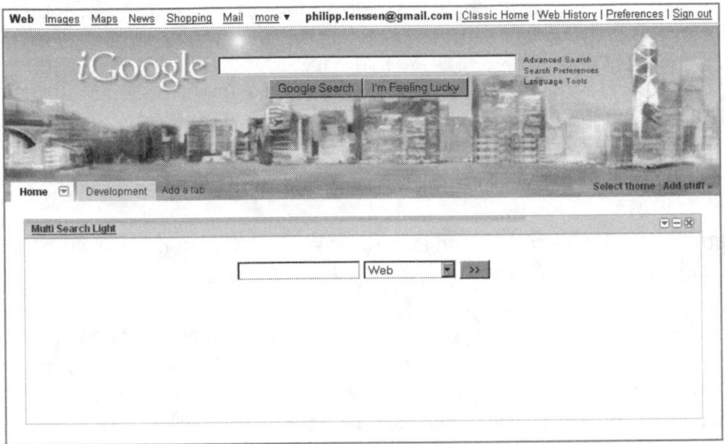

Figure 6-11.
igThemer takes you through creating an iGoogle theme

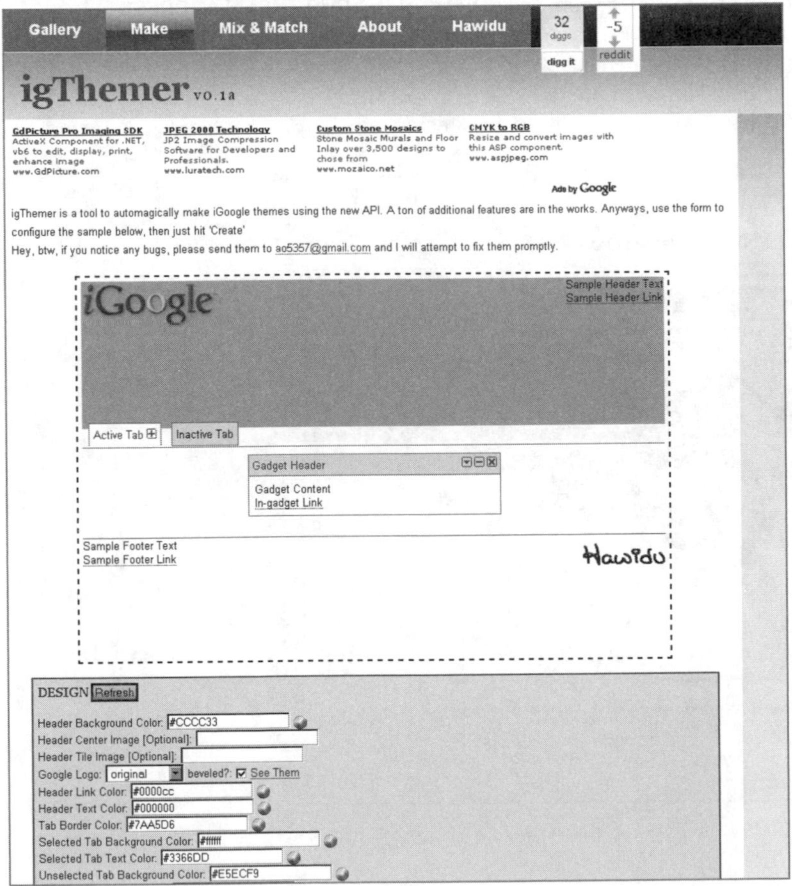

browser bookmark, that you can execute on any web page **[Hack #16]**.

To get started, create a bookmark from the Edit iGoogle Theme link found at http://blogoscoped.com/googleappshacks/bookmarklets.html. This is the code behind the bookmark address, if you're interested (though you do not need to understand the code to use it):

```
javascript:var s=document.createElement('script');s.id="igteid"; s.type="text/javascript";s.
src= "http://igoogle-theme-editor.googlecode.com/svn/" +"trunk/iGoogleThemeEditor/dist/ige.
js?lang=en&" +new Date().getTime(); document.body.appendChild(s);void(0);
```

Now click this bookmarklet while at iGoogle.com to bring up a neat WYSIWYG editor, as shown in Figure 6-12. Expand the dialog's groups, like Header Area, to adjust specific values.

Click Create XML if you like the result. You can now copy the code out of the text box that comes with the dialog, and paste it into somewhere more permanent. Note that the iGoogle Theme Editor, unlike igThemer, does not do the hosting for you. If you don't have your own server, one way to store the XML is to copy and paste it into the Google Gadget Editor **[Hack #60]**, then click File→Save As from its menu. The resulting public URL will be similar to this one: http://hosting.gmodules.com/ig/gadgets/file/115456851207031 82/mytheme.xml.

To test the stored theme, go to iGoogle.com and append `?skin=`**YOUR-THEME-ADDRESS** to the URL in the browser address bar, as in this snipped example: `http://www.google.com/ig?skin=`**http://hosting.gmodules.com/ig/...mytheme.xml**.

Once your theme is created, you can submit it to the directory at http://google.com/ig/skin_submit.

Figure 6-12.
The iGoogle theme editor bookmarklet in action

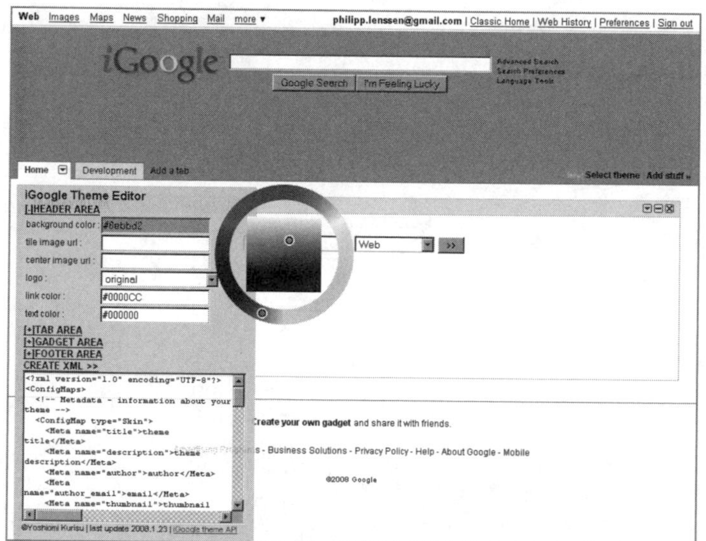

HACK 62: Add Google News to iGoogle

There's more ways than one to get Google News on iGoogle . . . in fact, there are at least six.

Google News (http://news.google.com) is Google's mainstream news (and partially, blog) aggregator. According to a test I conducted in 2006, over 10,000 selected news sources are indexed in the US version alone. News stories from sites that are part of Google News are often indexed within mere minutes. By splitting up various stories into content clusters, Google helps you track developments of breaking news.

There are different ways to put Google News onto your iGoogle home page. Following are explanations for each of them. To add one of these gadgets, go to http://igoogle.com and select Add stuff→Add feed or gadget; then paste in the gadget's XML URL.

> Have a blog you want to submit for inclusion in Google News? Try http://www.google.com/support/news_pub/bin/request.py to see whether it will be accepted by Google's editors. There's no guaranteed way to get inside the program, but it should be easier if you have multiple bloggers on board along with an editor, turning your blog into more of a group effort at news, rather than a form of personal expression.

The Tabbed Google News Gadget

You will find this official Google gadget (see Figure 6-13) at: http://www.google.com/ig/modules/tabnews.xml. Different tabs categorize news into Top Stories, U.S., World, and more. You can also add your own categories via the settings dialog, which you can access by clicking the down-pointing arrow icon on top of the gadget. You can customize how many items are displayed per tab and whether to show image thumbnails. You can also switch to another country's version of Google News.

A Custom RSS Feed

On iGoogle, you can subscribe to any RSS or Atom feed, including the ones offered by Google **[Hack #77]**. The URL for the Google News feed is the following, where "mozart" needs to be replaced by your own keyword or keywords (use a + character as separator): http://news.google.com/news?hl=en&ned=us&ie=UTF-8&output=rss&q=**mozart**.

> Note that this gadget can be included on other web pages, too (as is the case with many, but not all gadgets). To do so, expand the options dialog by clicking the arrow icon and select "About this gadget." On the gadget page, follow the "Embed this gadget" link and you'll see some code that you can embed in your web page.

Figure 6-13.
The tabbed Google News gadget

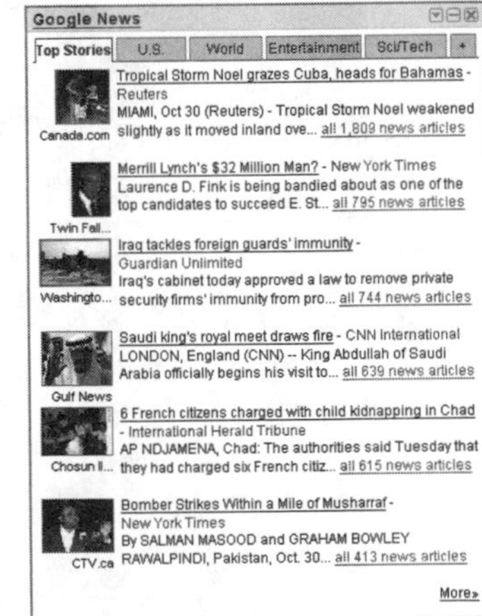

The result is a simple list of new items from the feed, as pictured in Figure 6-14, where each item can be expanded to show its snippet.

Figure 6-14.
The Google News RSS feed

mozart - Google News
⊞ And Will You Tap Dance to Mozart's Requiem? - New York Times
⊞ Mozart's music was 'key' - Christian Science Monitor
⊞ Cash is the best - Times of India

You can also subscribe to a category rather than a search. Just use the navigation to the left of the Google News home page to jump to a specific section. Then, copy the RSS feed from there, like the following ones:

- Business: http://news.google.com/?ned=us&topic=b&output=rss
- Entertainment: http://news.google.com/?ned=us&topic=e&output=rss

The Whole Google News Home Page

When switching to the wide-column layout in your iGoogle tab options, you can even comfortably include the Google News home page itself—by wrapping it in an XML gadget. You can create such a wrapper from scratch **[Hack #64]** or use the existing wrapper at the following address, for a result as shown in Figure 6-15: http://blogoscoped.com/home page/google-news-default.xml.

Figure 6-15.
The Google News home page itself, included as a gadget

The Non-Tabbed Google News Gadget

An older, but also official gadgetized version of the Google News home page is available at the following URL: http://www.google.com/ig/modules/builtin_news_customized.xml.

The gadget will show three stories—or more, if you edit the settings—on any chosen keyword, as shown in Figures 6-16 and 6-17.

There are also a couple of topic-specific standalone gadgets available from Google, such as:

- Top stories: http://www.google.com/ig/modules/builtin_news_topstories.xml
- Tech news: http://www.google.com/ig/modules/builtin_news_technology.xml

The Mobile Variant of Google News

Just as you can include the full Google home page as described earlier, you can also include the mobile-optimized version (pictured in Figure 6-18). You can find a gadget wrapper for it at the following address: http://blogoscoped.com/home page/google-news.xml.

Personalized News Recommendations

Google also has a Recommended News gadget available for you. You can find it located at: http://www.google.com/ig/modules/recommendations/recommended_news.xml. This widget is tailored to your personal Google News usage. For instance, if you are searching for "classical composers" a lot, then you might get a new recommendation for a news story on Bach. Figure 6-19 shows how the gadget looks when I include it on my page (I'm getting a story on Google Inc. because I read a lot about Google on Google News).

Figure 6-16.
At first, the Google News gadget will ask you for a keyphrase

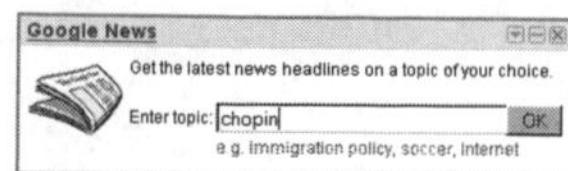

Figure 6-17.
After you've provided the topic, several up-to-date story clusters will appear

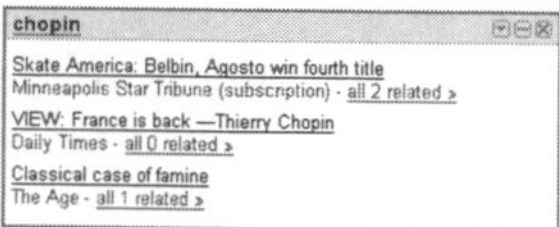

Figure 6-18.
The Google News mobile gadget

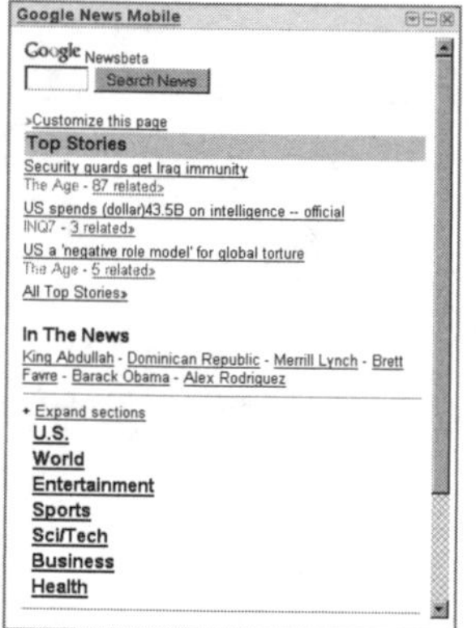

Figure 6-19.
The news recommendation widget asks you if you like a particular recommendation; the blue-on-white arrow button at the top right allows you to page through to the next story

HACK 63: Embed Content from Any Web Site in a Gadget

Fetch content from any other web site in near real time to stay up-to-date on iGoogle.

Some sites offer an API (Application Programming Interface) for you to grab their data. But using so-called *screenscraping*, you can grab almost any web site's content—independent of whether the site offers an API to developers. This hack comes in handy to collect snippets of information from dynamically updated, information-heavy web sites.

The iGoogle framework makes fetching web site content very easy through the `_IG_FetchContent()` function. This function accepts two parameters: one is the URL to be fetched, and the other is the function to execute when the content is returned.

As an example, let's say you want to measure the number of times blogs recently linked to your company home page (or your personal blog, or any other web site). You can use the Google Gadget Editor to create a new gadget **[Hack #60]**, as shown in Figure 6-20. The first step is to set up the "skeleton" of your gadget, and include a "Loading" message:

```
<?xml version="1.0" encoding="UTF-8"?>
<Module>
<ModulePrefs title="Fetch Content Example" />
<Content type="html"><![CDATA[
<p id="content">Loading...</p>
]]></Content>
</Module>
```

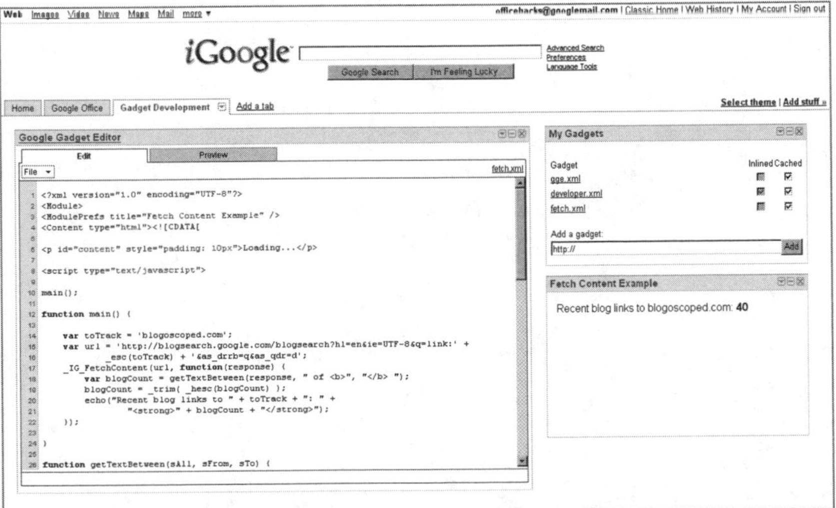

Figure 6-20.
Scripting an iGoogle module using the Google Gadget Editor

This way, until your script finishes, a "Loading. . . " message is displayed. Now go over to Google Blog Search at http://blogsearch.google.com, and perform a search that's restricted to mentions from the past week (or day, or month) while using the "link:" operator to find links to your site only. For instance, you can search for `link:example.com` or `link:blogoscoped.com`, as shown in Figure 6-21. Between the words "Results 1 – 10 of" and "linking to" to the top right of Google Blog Search results, you can see the number of links to the blog. You can now fetch this value for the gadget using a JavaScript block. Insert the following below the line that reads "`<p id="content">Loading...</p>`":

```
<script type="text/javascript">
main();
function main() {
    var toTrack = 'blogoscoped.com';
    var url = 'http://blogsearch.google.com/blogsearch?' +
              'hl=en&ie=UTF-8&q=link:' +
             _esc(toTrack) + '&as_drrb=q&as_qdr=w';
    _IG_FetchContent(url, function(response) {
        var blogCount = getTextBetween(response, " of <b>", "</b> ");
        blogCount = _trim( _hesc(blogCount) );
        echo("Recent blog links to " + toTrack + ": " +
                "<strong>" + blogCount + "</strong>");
     });
}
```

This script first calls the `main()` function. It then defines a domain to track—*blogoscoped.com*, in this case—and constructs the Google Blog search URL needed. (Instead of screenscraping a Google domain, you can also access any other URL, from nasa.gov to digg.com, and more.) Afterwards, `_IG_FetchContent()` is called with that URL. Within the response text, you can now look for the HTML immediately surrounding the target text you want to display. The `_hesc` function escapes this value, converting it from HTML to text, and `_trim` removes blanks from the left and right. Finally, the `echo()` function outputs the result into the gadget body. Here are the `getTextBetween()` and `echo()` functions that make up the rest of the script block. If you prefer, you can also use a regular expression for `getTextBetween` **[Hack #13]**. Insert these just before the line that reads "`]]></Content>`":

Figure 6-21.
The results of a Google Blog search

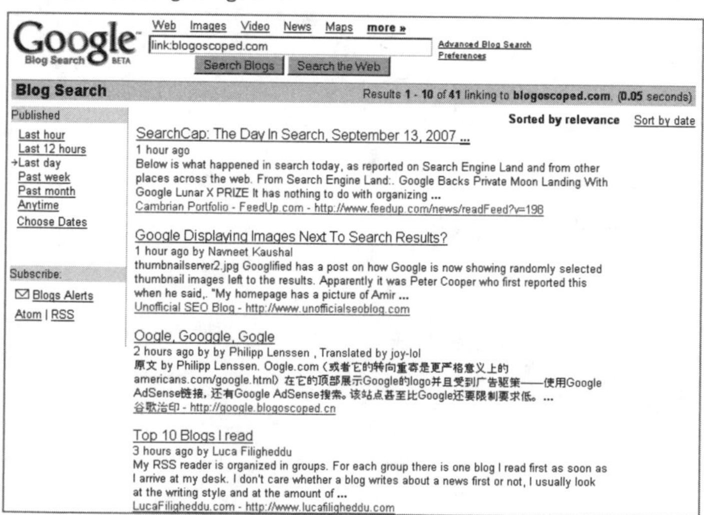

```
function getTextBetween(sAll, sFrom, sTo) {
    var sPart = "";
    var iFrom = sAll.indexOf(sFrom);
    if (iFrom >= 1) {
        var iTo = sAll.indexOf(sTo, iFrom);
        iFrom += sFrom.length;
        if (iTo >= 1) {
            sPart = sAll.substring(iFrom, iTo);
        }
    }
    return sPart;
}

function echo(s) {
    var elm = _gel("content");
    if (elm) {
        elm.innerHTML = s;
    }
}
</script>
```

You can also go with the following alternative. Instead of the `getTextBetween` call, write:

```
var blogCount = getMatch(response, " of <b>([^<]*)</b> ");
```

Now include the `getMatch` function:

```
function getMatch(sAll, sExpr) {
    var regex = new RegExp(sExpr);
    var matches = regex.exec(sAll);
    return (matches && matches[1]) ? matches[1] : "";
}
```

Your gadget will now display something like "Recent blog links to *example.com*: 40," where *example.com* is the domain you searched for. The iGoogle gadget framework will cache these results for one hour per URL, so you won't see data from the last few minutes, but the value is recent enough to provide you with a good daily overview of activity.

Note that if you want less caching for speedier results, you can use the `refreshInterval` parameter defining a caching time frame in seconds, as illustrated in the following line, which is set to 10 minutes:

```
_IG_FetchContent(url, function(response) {
    var blogCount = getTextBetween(response, " of <b>", "</b> ");
    blogCount = _trim( _hesc(blogCount) );
    echo("Recent blog links to " + toTrack + ": " +
            "<strong>" + blogCount + "</strong>");
}, { refreshInterval: (60 * 10) });
```

You can even set this parameter to a value of `0` to disable caching completely, but you should avoid using such frequent intervals, as it puts too much traffic stress on the target servers.

– Philipp Lenssen & Brian Jepson

HACK 64: Add Any Flash Game as a Gadget

Not content with adding games available in the official Google gadgets directory? A little trick allows you to add almost any Flash game you can find.

Google gadgets come in two main flavors: those that are self-contained, including the necessary HTML and JavaScript within the gadget XML itself, and those that simply point to an outside URL to display content. Using the latter format, you can have the gadget point to a game created for the Flash plug-in, too. The nice thing about most Flash applications is that they resize dynamically, perfectly fitting your chosen gadget size.

To look for Flash games, enter **flash games** into a Google search. You will stumble upon many directories, most of them presenting loud and wildly animated games. Once you discover the Flash game you want to add, open the HTML source of the page it's embedded on and search for occurrences of the extension ".swf". For sample purposes, I picked a simple mouse-based shooting game, perfect to balance your stress level during lunch, from a site called FlashGames247.com. Opening the HTML page, I can see that the source URL is http://flashgames247.com/13770/games/blastem/blastem.swf.

With that URL in hand, it's now time to create your gadget. Open the Google Gadget Editor **[Hack #60]** or any other editor of choice and start with the "hello.xml" sample framework. Notice that the main part of the gadget currently reads the following:

```
...
<ModulePrefs title="hello world example" />
<Content type="html"><![CDATA[
 Hello, world!
]]></Content>
...
```

Figure 6-22.
Creating a gadget that points to another URL

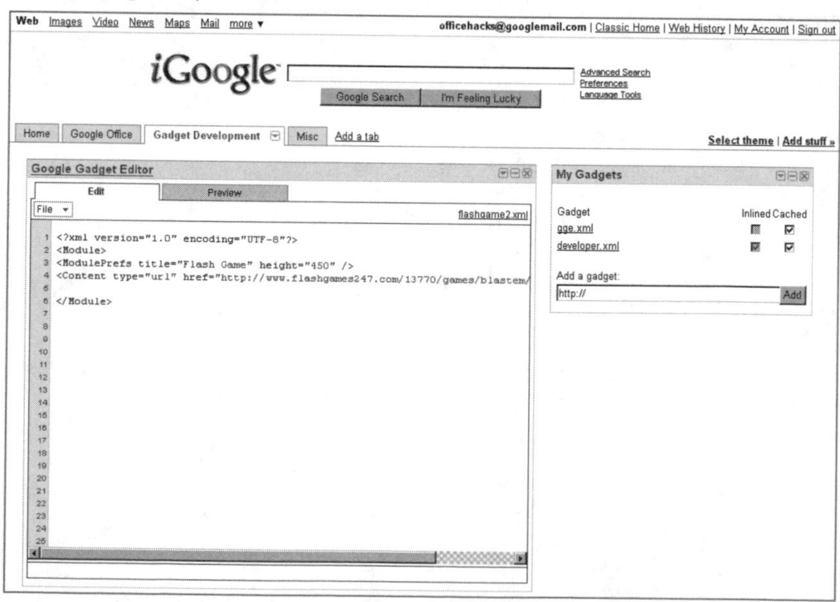

This format is for self-contained gadgets, and as you can see, it comes complete with some HTML. But you want to switch this type of gadget to one that points to an external web site, so you need to amend the example code to read as follows, as shown in Figure 6-22:

```
...
<ModulePrefs title="Flash Game" height="450" />
<Content type="url"
href="http://flashgames247.com/13770/games/blastem/blastem.swf" />
...
```

Note that you are completely removing the `<![CDATA[]]` and also dropping the closing `</Content>` tag. Also note that a `height` attribute was added to the `ModulePrefs` element and set to 450 pixels to allow more display space for the game. Save your gadget, copy the URL of the XML file, and add it to iGoogle. You can create a new tab dedicated to just the game, and edit the tab properties to allow your gadget to use the full browser size, as shown in Figure 6-23. Happy gaming!

> You can also add any HTML page as a gadget, not just SWF files. Often, mobile variants of home pages are sized especially well for gadget use. You can also experiment with turning a home page that doesn't have a mobile variant into a gadget-sized page by filtering the URL through a mobile proxy, such as http://phonifier.com or http://www.google.com/gwt/n.

Figure 6-23.
The Flash game included as a gadget

HACK 65: Beyond Google: Netvibes, Pageflakes, and More

Get a different, non-Google flavor of gadgetized home pages.

There are many more personalized home page tools out there than just iGoogle.com, with different feature sets and styles.

Netvibes

From France comes a service called Netvibes, which you can find at http://netvibes.com. As you can see from their home page, as pictured in Figure 6-24, Netvibes arrives chock-full of handy gadgets in their default mix. They've got everything from weather information to email wizards, web search utilities, sticky notes, and news items from different providers.

You can get a first taste of Netvibes without registering. However to keep your settings and the content you added from its widget directory—called "Ecosystem" in Netvibes—you need to register. Registering requires only your email address and a password of your choice.

Figure 6-24.
The Netvibes home page

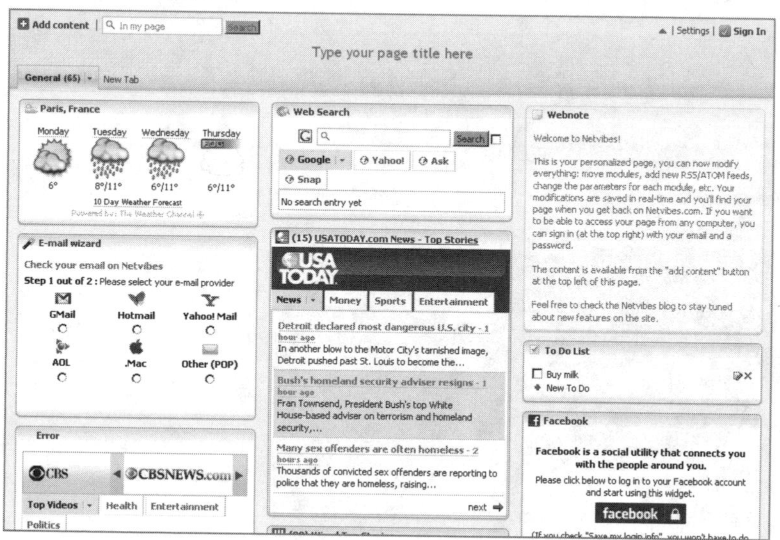

Pageflakes

Pageflakes describes their service as "your home page with your favorite news, weather, sports, entertainment, photos, videos, music, email . . . and much more, all in one place." When you get started with them at http://pageflakes.com, a wizard dialog lets you pick some topics of choice, like news, sports, music, food, gossip, and more. You can also provide your location.

The page created for you, as shown in Figure 6-25, then contains different relevant widgets, called "Flakes" in this service. By clicking the orange flakes icon at the top right, you can open a directory with many more widgets to add to your page.

Figure 6-25.
Pageflakes after completing the setup wizard

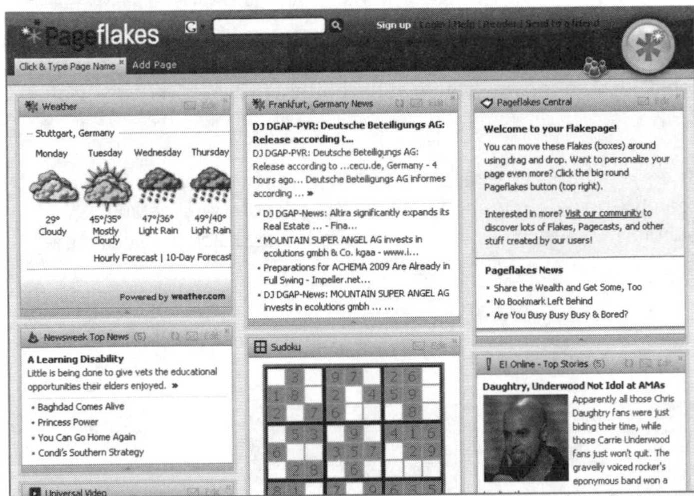

As with iGoogle, you can also share your widget setup—here, as a so-called Pagecast. There's even a Pagecast directory, as shown in Figure 6-26. As another interesting feature, Pageflakes allows you to get connected to other users of the service via their people directory. Everyone can share their photo or avatar picture, list their interests, and tell the world a bit about them. For every person, you can also find people with similar interests through a sidebar.

Figure 6-26.
A directory for sharing topic-specific configurations of Pageflakes tabs

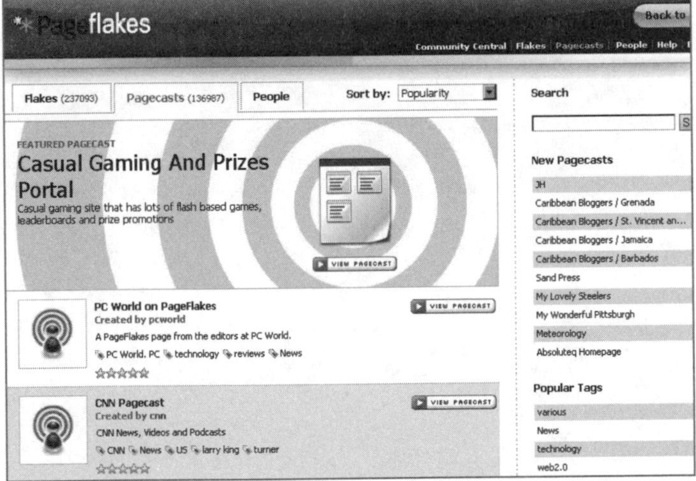

Protopage

Like iGoogle, Netvibes and Pageflakes, Protopage (http://protopage.com) is a personalized start page. However, its layout differs substantially from the aforementioned services. Instead of a rigid grid layout, Protopage allows you to freely move your widget windows around on the page, as shown in Figure 6-27. You can also enable the auto-arrange option at the bottom to avoid overlapping of gadget windows.

At the top right of Protopage, there is a search box that expands when you hover over it; from Amazon search to Wikipedia search, Google, eBay, and Yahoo, there's a lot of useful default engines provided. If this isn't enough for your taste, you can also add to this dialog by clicking the "Customize list" link at its bottom.

Figure 6-27.
The Protopage home page

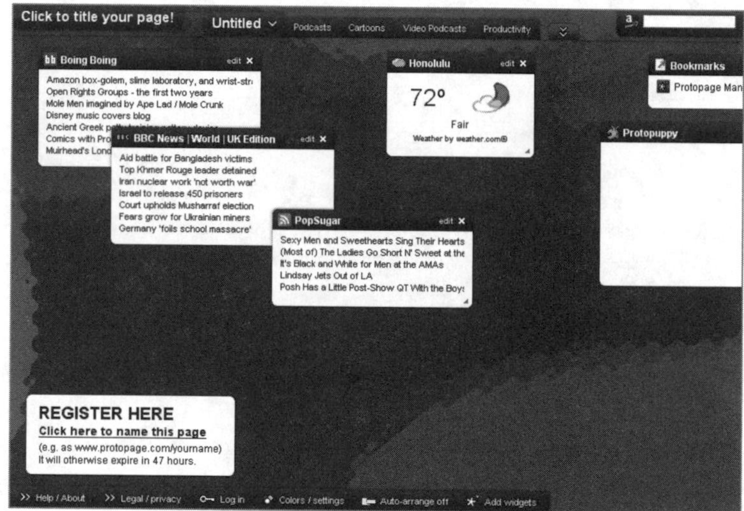

07 MANAGE YOUR EVENTS WITH GOOGLE CALENDAR

Google Calendar lets you track your events—from a doctor's appointment to the family picnic—and share them with others. You can also subscribe to the public calendars of other people, organizations, or information such as moon phases or U.S. holidays.

Now this would not be Google if this tool weren't web-based. Furthermore, Calendar is integrated into some other Google tools; for instance, you can quickly add an event from within Gmail. Also, Gmail automatically turns certain phrases into Calendar events.

To get started with Google Calendar, point your browser to http://calendar.google.com. If you already have a Google Account (see Chapter 1), you can enter your credentials now to sign in. After providing your username and your time zone, you will see your calendar in its default view, as shown in Figure 7-1. Click anywhere in the calendar to add an event quickly; a bubble pops up to let you enter what your event is about. You can provide just a title, or make full use of the Quick Add syntax **[Hack #73]**. You can then click either Create Event or "edit event details." The dialog for editing the details allows you to choose many options, as shown in Figure 7-2.

You can also add events by clicking the Create Event or Quick Add links shown just below the Google Calendar logo. You can search for public calendars by entering keywords, like the name of your city. If you are subscribed to or have created more than one calendar, you can control how they are displayed: check the box next to the calendar name to show it, and click the down-pointing arrow to the right of the calendar name to choose which color it uses. That's not all you can do on Google Calendar: you can also invite others to your events, import and export calendar data, view the calendar on your cell phone, and much more.

Figure 7-1.
Your own online calendar, courtesy of Google

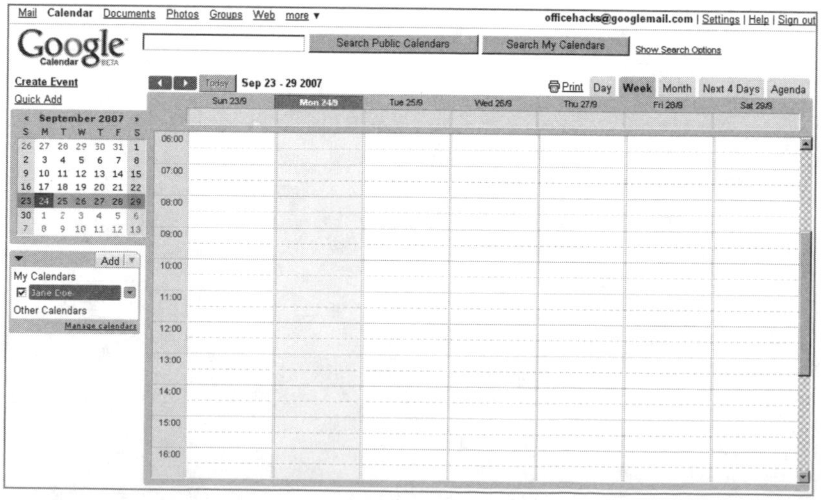

Figure 7-2.
Adding an event

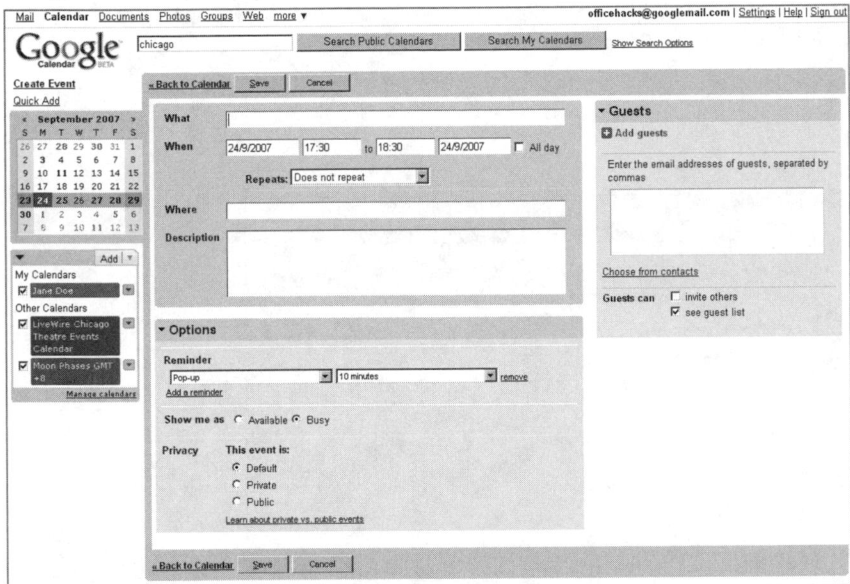

HACK 66: Access Your Calendar from a Mobile Phone

If you never want to miss another appointment, consider subscribing to SMS alerts for appointments, or using Google Calendar's mobile version.

If you've never missed a meeting before, consider yourself lucky—or very gifted. Maybe it's enough to just check your calendar every few days. For the rest of us, these alerts are one way—in addition to email alerts—to be reminded of an upcoming event. And if you want to peek at your calendar on the go, you can access a light version of Google Calendar on your cell phone.

 Check your cell phone bill to determine how many messages you have each month: some cellular carriers charge for incoming as well as outgoing SMS; it can get expensive if you go over your limit.

Calendar SMS Alerts

To set up your SMS alerts, log in to your calendar and click the Settings link on top. Switch to the Mobile Setup tab, as shown in Figure 7-3, input your country and phone number, and check whether your carrier is supported. For example, at the time of this writing, over 30 different carriers in the U.S. are supported; from Alaska Communications Systems to Western Wireless.

Click the Send Verification Code button, and seconds (or minutes) later, you will have a new message on your phone, that reads something like the following:

```
Your Google Calendar verification
code is 23456
```

Enter the number you received back into the verification field at the end of the online form and click "Finish setup." You will now be able to configure how you would like to be reminded of alerts on a calendar-by-calendar basis. By default, each calendar is configured to notify you using a pop-up notice, but these pop-ups appear only when you have the Google Calendar web site open. Choose the "SMS" option from this drop-down and specify how many minutes before an event you would like to be reminded. You can configure additional reminders (such as email) by clicking the "Add another reminder" link. Click the Save button, and you're all set.

Figure 7-3.
Setting up mobile alerts

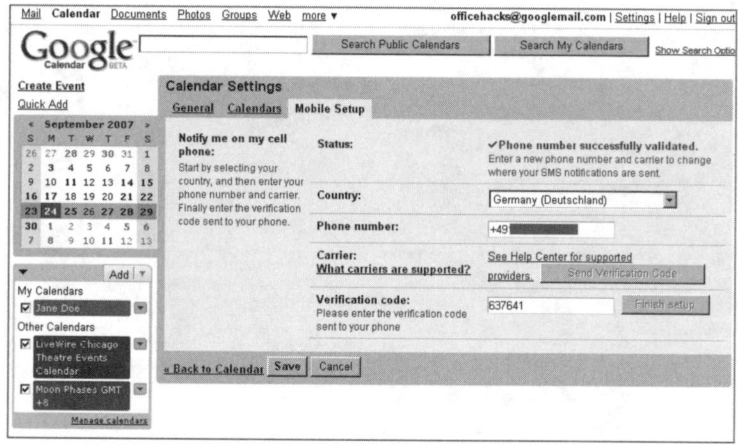

Figure 7-4.
Your latest events on your mobile phone

Google Calendar BETA
Prev Today Next
Tue Sep 25
12:00 Meet John for lunch
Thu Sep 27
Full Moon at 03:35 HRS
Fri Sep 28
03:00 The Collector (Plays)
the side project theatre (map)
Sat Sep 29
03:00 The Collector (Plays)
the side project theatre (map)
Sun Sep 30
00:00 The Collector (Plays)
the side project theatre (map)
03:00 The Collector (Plays)

To change your settings later, click the down-pointing arrow next to your calendar name in the list of calendars that appears on the left side of the screen, and select the Notifications option.

View Your Calendar on the Go

Another way to keep up-to-date is to view Google Calendar on your mobile phone. Just access http://calendar.google.com on your mobile browser and you will see the latest events, as shown in Figure 7-4. This isn't a full calendar application—for instance, you will not be able to delete items—but you can still add events. To do so, scroll down to the Quick Add box and enter, for example, "picnic with Mary at 4pm tomorrow."

> Note that if you're accessing Google Calendar from the iPhone, you will see a special version of the mobile variant, as shown in Figure 7-5.

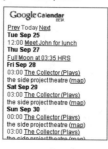

Figure 7-5.
Google Calendar on an iPhone

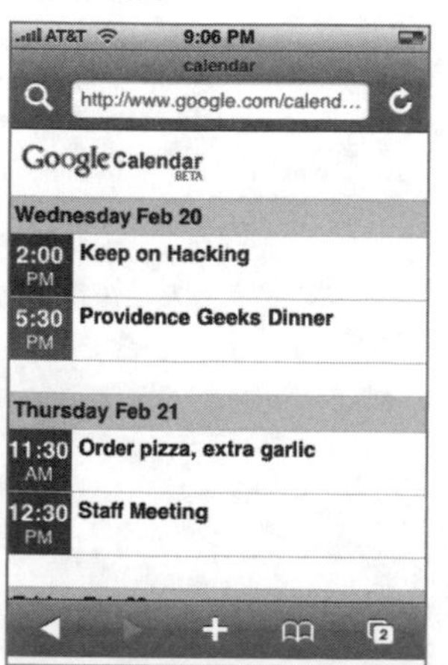

Add and Request Events via SMS

If you're in the United States, you can also create new events on your mobile phone by sending an SMS to the number 48368 ("GVENT"). This feature supports the full Quick Add syntax, such as "dinner with niraj on saturday at 8pm" **[Hack #73]**. Additionally, you can ask the GVENT number to send you an SMS detailing your next event (send "next", without the quotes, to 48368), today's full schedule (send "day"), or tomorrow's schedule (send "nday"). For this to work, ensure you've configured your calendar via Settings→Mobile Setup as outlined earlier in this hack.

HACK 67: Subscribe to Public Calendars

Suffering from information overload? Then you'd better not try this hack at home—here's a way to create the ultimate calendar.

Google Calendar allows you to mix your own calendar with calendar events created by others. This can help you to discover happenings in your neighborhood, keep track of festivals in other countries, or follow the schedule of a celebrity or politician, to name just a few uses.

There are two basic ways to get new calendar content. One is to search, and the other to explore. If you already have a clear picture of what type of calendar you want, give the search functionality a try. Go to http://calendar.google.com, enter a keyword in the search box on top, and send it off by clicking the Search Public Calendars button. For instance, if you enter the name of your home town, you might be able to find calendars listing nearby events; I've entered "stuttgart", as shown in Figure 7-6. Another option is to enter the name of your favorite band or musician—say, "Loudon Wainwright III"—as you might sometimes stumble upon a concert calendar. Click Add Calendar next to calendars that catch your interest, and they will be displayed on your calendar in their own unique color.

 As these public calendars are maintained by third-party providers, there's no telling whether the information contained within them is correct.

Instead of searching, you can also explore the existing third-party calendars. Click the arrow icon next to the Add button and select "Add a public calendar." Switch to the Browse Calendars tab in the dialog that opens up, and select calendars from the list. You will be able to add moon phase calendars, calendars containing local holidays, and more.

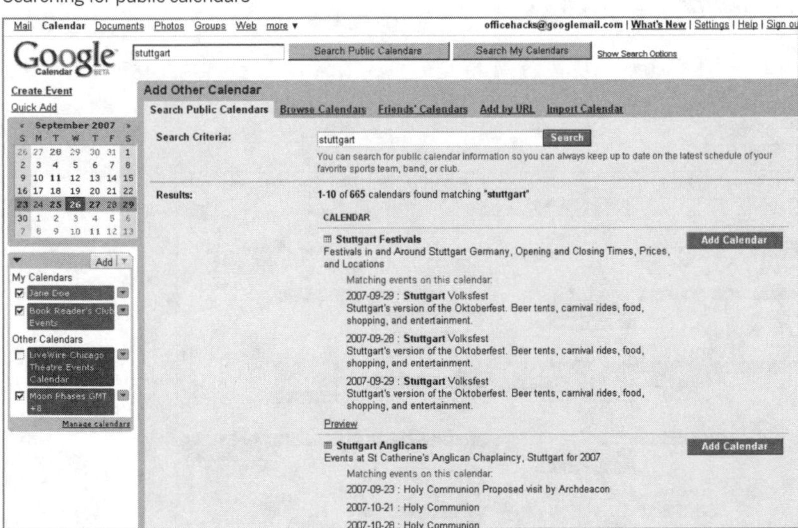

Figure 7-6.
Searching for public calendars

If you regularly send email to business contacts and friends overseas, it's interesting to know what holidays they might be having this week, and just what it is they're celebrating.

A more luxurious way to discover new calendars is the Google Calendar gallery, which you can find at http://google.com/calendar/gallery, shown in Figure 7-7. Here are some of the calendars you can add:

- Tour calendars
- A Netflix calendar of DVD rental availability dates
- Music events for specific cities
- Dates of local festivals
- Sports events in your hometown
- The scheduled time of your favorite TV show

Note that much of the content of the Google Calendar gallery is U.S.-specific, making it a less valuable resource if you're not living in the United States. But if you find things you like, and you don't mind the extra loading time before your calendar shows up, you can mix and mash your own calendar, as shown in Figure 7-8.

Figure 7-7.
The Google Calendar gallery

Figure 7-8.
A Google Calendar subscribed to several other public calendars

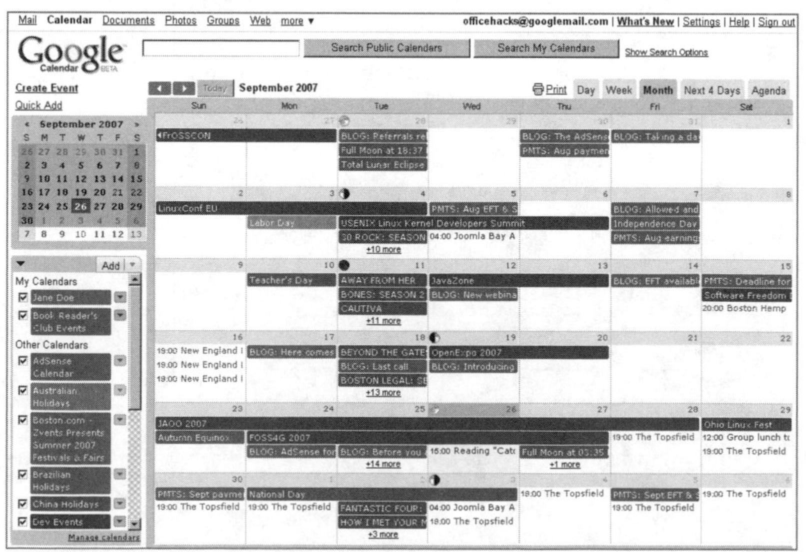

HACK 68: Create a To-Do List in Google Calendar

You might find a calendar application the right place to maintain your to-do lists.

If you need a very simple to-do list, there's a Google gadget that you can add to your iGoogle home page. Just go to http://igoogle.com, click "Add stuff" to the right, search for "todo" (see Chapter 6), and pick the To-Do List gadget that was created by Google.

Alternatively, to integrate a to-do list with your calendar, complete with due dates and other details, you could add events as usual in Google Calendar and use them as your to-do items. But there are a couple of other tools you can use to enhance Google Calendar with a real to-do list.

A Greasemonkey To-Do List for Calendar

One way to add a real to-do list to Calendar is with the Google Calendar TODOlist Greasemonkey script. To run this script, you need to be using the Firefox browser, with Greasemonkey installed **[Hack #42]**. Once installed, point your browser to http://userscripts.org/scripts/show/9179 and click the "Install this script" button. After the installation is complete—make sure that the Greasemonkey icon in your browser bar at the bottom is smiling and showing in full color (and not frowning in shades of gray), indicating that it is enabled—log in to Google Calendar.

You will now find a new to-do list widget to the left side of your calendar, as shown in Figure 7-9. You can add new items by clicking the + icon in the to-do list, and you can edit the text of a to-do item by clicking its name and typing the new text. Click the checkbox next to an item, and it will be displayed with a strikethrough, indicating the item is successfully completed (see the "Reinstall Windows" to-do in Figure 7-9). When you click the "Flush closed" link at the widget's footer, all completed tasks will be removed from view.

> Note that you can access the same to-do list across different computers, provided that you log in with the same Google Account credentials, and have installed Firefox, Greasemonkey, and the TODOlist user script. But what if you're on a computer without this setup—and possibly, a computer disallowing you to install your own software? In that case, a little time travel will do: the to-do list items are actually stored as normal events. . . back in the wild psychedelic year of 1969! To see the items, just click Show Search Options and in the "Date from. . . to" boxes, enter "1969" and "1970," respectively.

Figure 7-9.
A Calendar to-do list, brought to you by a Greasemonkey script

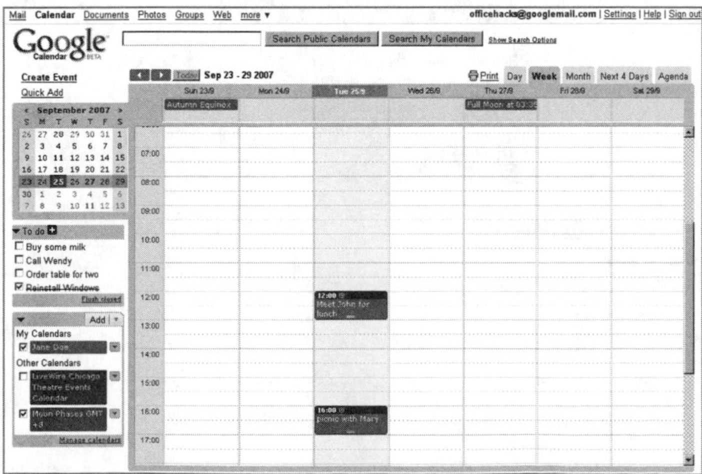

Remember the Milk's To-Do List

Another to-do list add-on for Google Calendar is offered by the web site Remember the Milk. To use this widget, you must first sign up with the free service at http://rememberthemilk.com. Click the Signup button, provide your information, confirm the registration email that you receive, and you're set. You can find the widget by clicking Remember the Milk's Help link or going directly to http://rememberthemilk.com/services/googlecalendar/. Now, add the Remember the Milk widget by clicking the Google Calendar button, as shown in Figure 7-10.

> Before you sign up for Remember the Milk, you might want to install Google Gears **[Hack #76]**. That's because Remember the Milk can use Google Gears to store information locally so you will be able to use it offline.

Now you will find a special check mark icon on top of each day in Google Calendar. Click this icon, and a dialog like the one shown in Figure 7-11 opens. In this dialog you can click the "+" icon next to the Today label and define a new task. Next time you log in to Google Calendar, this task is still visible. Once the task is finished, you can click its arrow icon and select Complete. To get an overview of all your items, you may also want to log in to the Remember the Milk home page itself.

> Wondering how the Remember the Milk gadget implements this enhancement of Google Calendar? You can also create your own icons and dialogs like it does **[Hack #71]**.

You can also add locations, which your Calendar To-Do widget will then render on a map when you switch to its Map tab. To add a location, click the Locations link on top of Remember the Milk's web site and search for a location on the Google Maps gadget. Once you've named and saved a location, you will be able to select it from the Location drop-down when you create a task in Google Calendar.

> With Remember the Milk's gadget pop-up, it's easy to click the wrong link to add a date-dependent to-do; always click the "+" icon next to the Today label, and avoid the "Add task" link in the pop-up, as the latter will not connect the to-do item to the specific date you picked. (Use the "Add task" link only if you want to add a general to-do unconnected to any date.)

To remove the Remember the Milk add-on, switch to your Google Calendar settings page and select the Calendars tab. Look for the Remember the Milk calendar and click the trash can icon to its right.

Figure 7-10.
You can add Remember the Milk's widget by clicking the "Google Calendar" button to the right

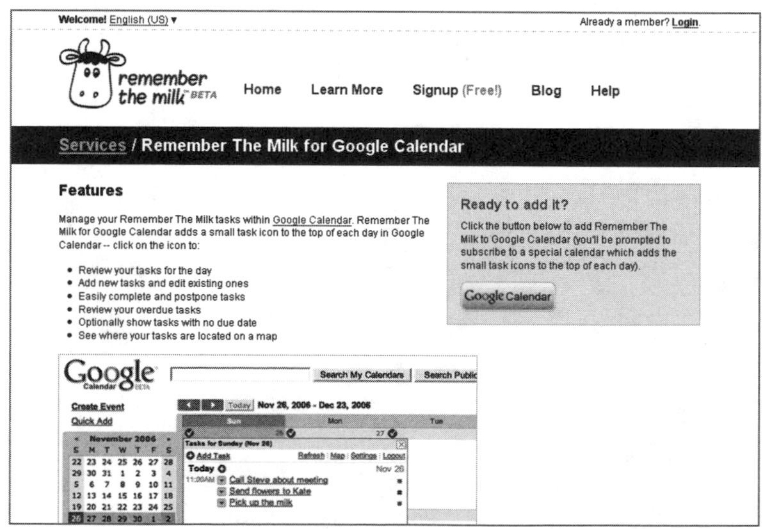

Figure 7-11.
The Remember the Milk widget in action on your Google Calendar

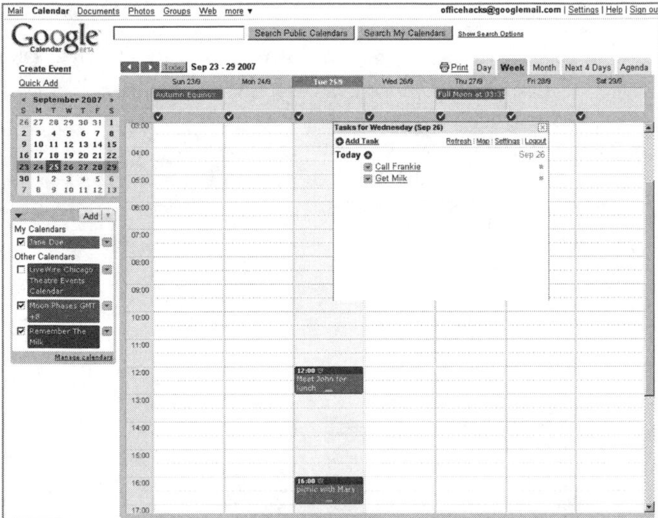

HACK 69: Share Calendars

Calendars can be shared with collaborators—or the whole world.

Do you want to create a community-maintained public calendar? With Google Calendar, you can; after all, more minds can tackle a task faster and better. And even if you're the only person maintaining the dates and descriptions, it's often useful to share specific events with a group of friends or colleagues.

To implement a publicly viewable and group-maintained calendar, sign in to Google Calendar, click the Add button to the left, and select "Create a new calendar" from the menu. For this sample, I will create a calendar for a local book reading group, naming it "Book Readers' Club Events," as shown in Figure 7-12. If you like, check the "Share all information on this calendar with everyone" option—everyone will now be able to search for your calendar, too, so choose this only for truly public events—and click the "Create calendar" button.

Figure 7-12.
Creating a new public calendar

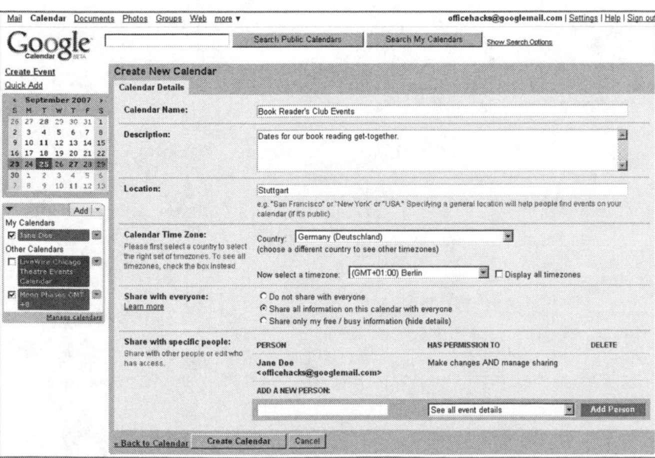

Now when you add a new event in your Google calendar, you can toggle the calendar selection box to "Book Reader's Club Events," as shown in Figure 7-13. You can invite specific guests or add comments to the event.

If you have a blog or other web page, you can also include a special button so that others can easily add this event to their own calendar. To do so, click the "Publish this event" link in the event details dialog. Copy the embed HTML code you are provided with and paste it into your site publishing editor—like Google's Blogger **[Hack #11]**. Make sure that you've switched to the Edit HTML tab when pasting the snippet, as shown in Figure 7-14. Others reading your blog post will be referred to their own Google Calendar when they click your button, pictured in Figure 7-15, enabling them to instantly copy the event details to their own schedule.

Figure 7-13.
Selecting the appropriate calendar when adding an event

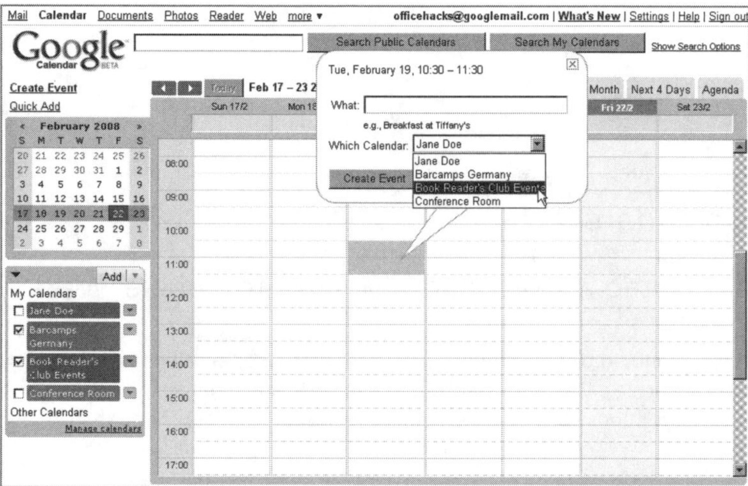

Figure 7-14.
The Calendar invite button HTML snippet in Google's Blogger

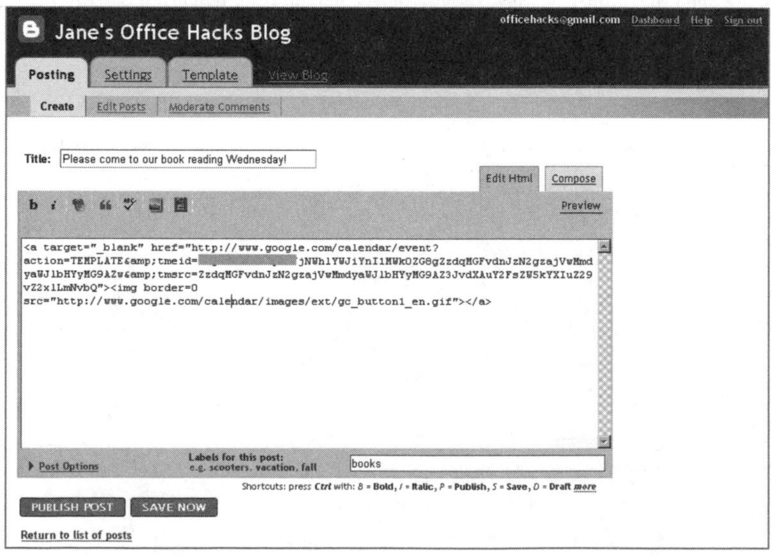

Figure 7-15.
The Google Calendar button allows other visitors to quickly add an event to their own calendar

Embed a Full Calendar

You can even embed the calendar itself on your blog or home page. In Google Calendar, open the calendar drop-down by pressing the arrow icon next to the calendar name, and click "Calendar settings." On the dialog that appears, you will find two small blue buttons reading "HTML"; click the one that appears under "Calendar Address," and another dialog with the calendar address will open. As you want to embed this instead of just point to it, click the link reading "configuration tool." A new browser window or tab will open up to allow you to configure the layout for the calendar widget, as shown in Figure 7-16. You can set the calendar to a new width, toggle which elements you want to be visible, and switch to another background color, among other layout options.

When you're done with the calendar widget wizard, copy the HTML snippet from the top box, and paste it into your web site, as shown in Figure 7-17. Others can now not only look at your calendar on your home page, but also add this calendar to their own Google Calendar by clicking the "Add to Google" button within your widget.

But there's still one thing left: the option for others to create new events on your calendar, too.

Invite Others to Edit Events in the Calendar

To fully share the calendar with someone else, including giving them the rights to add or delete events on it, open the calendar drop-down menu found next to the calendar name and select "Share this calendar." You will see a box to add a new person; enter the Gmail email address of your friend, family member, or colleague—like `officehacks@gmail.com`—and choose the option "Make changes

Figure 7-16.
Google's embeddable calendar helper

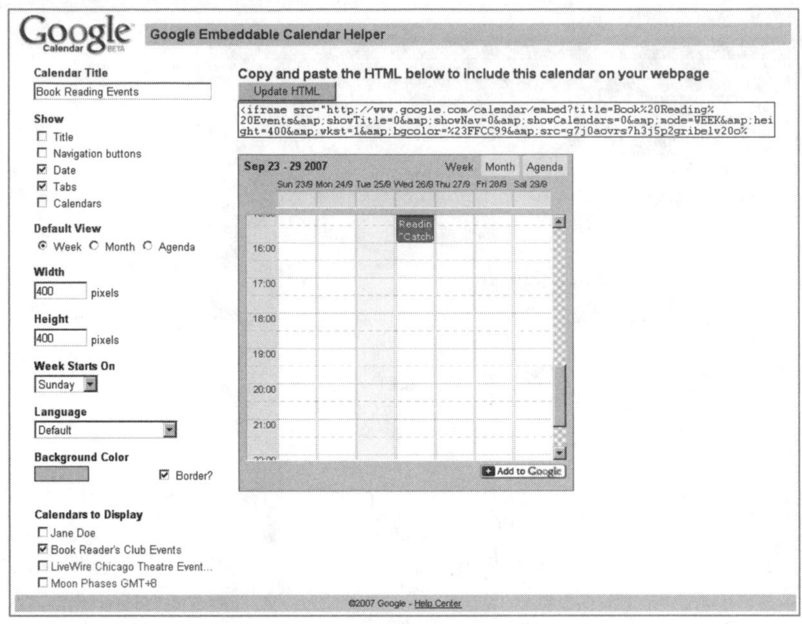

Figure 7-17.
Jane's book reading events calendar, shared with the world through her Google Blogspot blog

to events" before hitting the Add Person button. Confirm this dialog with the Save button, and the other person can now edit your calendar. Events which are changed or added will automatically update in other instances of the calendar, such as the embedded calendar on a blog.

Now, no more excuses to miss the local group meetings—especially when you've set up calendar alerts, too **[Hack #66]**!

HACK 70: Put a Calendar XML Widget in Your Blog

Beyond the official Google Calendar widget, there's an easy way to feature the latest events of any shared calendar in your blog's sidebar or elsewhere.

Google Calendar already ships with a widget that displays a full-color, full-featured calendar on other web pages [Hack #69]. But there's another way to embed calendar events in more minimalist, but also more customizable fashion: connect the calendar's Atom feed to the feed widget.

First, you need to locate your calendar's XML feed. Make sure your calendar is set to be public, and that you don't have any events intended to be private in it. Now locate your calendar's feed address; click the down-pointing arrow next to the calendar name and select Calendar Settings from the list, as shown in Figure 7-18. Click the first orange XML button (the one under "Calendar Address") in that dialog and copy the URL that Google provides for you. It will look something like the following (split into two lines for easier reading):

```
http://www.google.com/calendar/feeds/g7j0aovrs7h3j5
    p2gribelv20o%40group.calendar.google.com/public/basic
```

If you look at this address in your browser, you will find it's actually an Atom feed for others to subscribe to. It will automatically stay up to date with your calendar events, sorted by the time you added them, with newest additions on top. (Note that the events are *not* chronologically ordered by their actual event date and time.) Here are some of the fields that you might find in a feed:

```
Group lunch to chat
Book Reader's Club Events
When: Sat Sep 29, 2007 12pm to 1pm CEST
Event Status: confirmed
Reading "Catcher in the Rye"
Book Reader's Club Events
```

Figure 7-18.
Opening your calendar settings

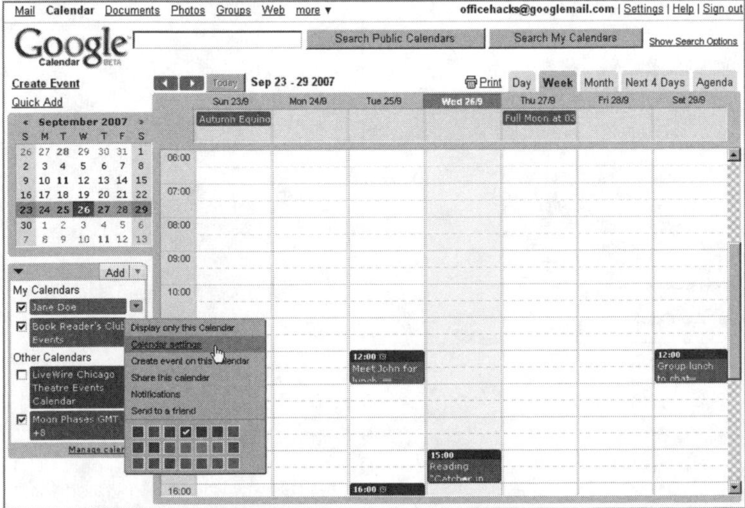

```
When: Wed Sep 26, 2007 3pm to 4pm CEST
Event Status: confirmed
Reading a comic book
Book Reader's Club Events
When: Thu Sep 27, 2007 7pm to 8pm CEST
Event Status: confirmed
```

Grabbing the Feed to Use Elsewhere

With this feed in hand, others can keep up to date on your latest calendar additions via a feed reader, such as Google's own Google Reader. Plus, you can convert any feed to an iGoogle home page gadget. Just point your browser to http://igoogle.com and click "Add stuff," then "Add by URL." A small dialog opens, in which you can copy and paste your calendar feed URL to add it to your personalized Google home page, as shown in Figure 7-19.

Now, unlike other gadgets, you can't directly embed feed-based gadgets onto any web page. What you can do here, however, is to use Google's AJAX Feed API. Go to http://code.google.com/apis/ajaxfeeds/ and click the "Sign-up for a Google AJAX API key" link on top. After agreeing to the terms of service, you can generate an API key. Write it down for future use, and copy Google's sample code into a plain text editor.

Let's look at Google's sample HTML code, line by line. First, there's the HTML opening portion, including the document type declaration, the head tag and a character encoding definition. Furthermore, there's a link to Google's JavaScript library; it includes your unique API key, highlighted in bold (and split into multiple lines for display):

```
<!DOCTYPE html PUBLIC "-//W3C//DTD XHTML 1.0 Strict//EN" "http://www.w3.org/TR/xhtml1/DTD/
xhtml1-strict.dtd">
<html xmlns="http://www.w3.org/1999/xhtml">
<head>
<meta http-equiv="content-type" content="text/html; charset=utf-8"/>
<title>Google AJAX Feed API - Simple Example</title>
```

Figure 7-19.
The calendar feed as an iGoogle gadget

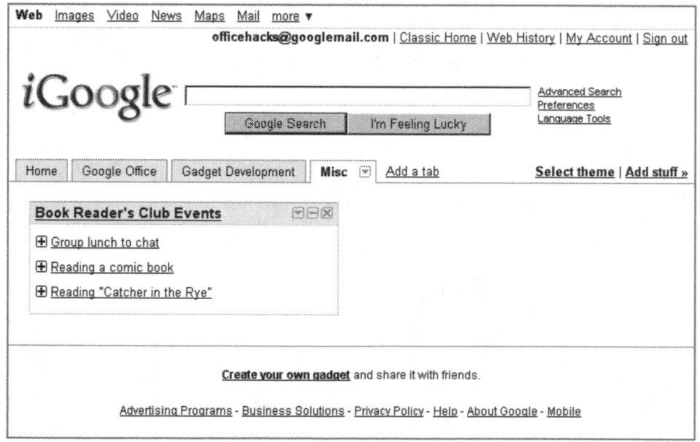

```
<script type="text/javascript" src="http://www.google.com/jsapi?key=ABQIAvAApH2nqapCL4bg4uRTR
VvfzRR1JzaEnpQZ7YiBBUK6oRrqkchPJMd0Nf2npnhREFa8-1ypJu1y-cB4DQ"></script>
```

Next, still in the head portion of the HTML, there's an inline JavaScript snippet.

```
<script type="text/javascript">
    google.load("feeds", "1");
    function initialize() {
      var feed = new google.feeds.Feed("http://www.digg.com/rss/index.xml");
      feed.load(function(result) {
        if (!result.error) {
          var container = document.getElementById("feed");
          for (var i = 0; i < result.feed.entries.length; i++) {
            var entry = result.feed.entries[i];
            var div = document.createElement("div");
            div.appendChild(document.createTextNode(entry.title));
            container.appendChild(div);
          }
        }
      });
    }
    google.setOnLoadCallback(initialize);
</script>
</head>
```

Finally, the body element of the HTML shows a `div` (division) element container to hold the output of the JavaScript:

```
<body>
<div id="feed"></div>
</body>
</html>
```

The `initialize` function of the JavaScript example portion is the most interesting here. It first loads an RSS feed from social news web site Digg.com. If the feed loaded correctly, and did not encounter errors, the container element in the HTML body will be selected. Now, a `for` loop iterates through all the different news elements of the Digg feed, highlighted in bold in the example. For each individual feed entry, another `div` element is created within the so-called DOM, the tree-structured HTML Document Object Model. This `div` element will receive some text content in the form of the particular Digg news headline, to then be appended to the main container in the body section.

The result? Several headlines from Digg, displayed below each other. Now to use your calendar instead of the sample feed by Digg, replace the URL http://www.digg.com/rss/index.xml, shown in italic in the example, with your calendar feed URL. Load the resulting web page in your browser and you will see a result similar to the one shown here:

```
Group lunch to chat
Reading a comic book
Reading "Catcher in the Rye"
```

Naturally, you can now also take the necessary HTML and JavaScript code to paste them into an existing web site of yours, like in your blog's sidebar.

Tweaking Google's Sample Code to Suit Your Needs

Instead of just accessing the feed item's title, you can also access the `content` or `contentSnippet` properties in the `for` loop. I've changed the code slightly in the following example to concatenate an HTML string, apply some reformatting, and then output it to the browser as shown in Figure 7-20. In bold here again is the `for` loop that iterates through the individual feed items (note that the feed URL

Figure 7-20.
Displaying a reformatted events feed on a web page

Coming up:

>> **Group lunch to chat**
Sat Sep 29, 2007 12pm to 1pm CEST

>> **Reading a comic book**
Thu Sep 27, 2007 7pm to 8pm CEST

>> **Reading "Catcher in the Rye"**
Wed Sep 26, 2007 3pm to 4pm CEST

itself is split into two strings for display here, but the + combines them into one):

```
function initialize() {
  var feed = new google.feeds.Feed("http://www.google.com/calendar/feeds/" +
    "g7j0aovrs2h3j3p2gEibelv20o%40group.calendar.google.com/public/basic");
  feed.load(function(result) {
    if (!result.error) {
      var container = document.getElementById("feed");
      var s = "";
      for (var i = 0; i < result.feed.entries.length; i++) {
        var entry = result.feed.entries[i];
        s += "<p><strong>&gt;&gt; " +
            "<a style=\"color: #339\" href=\"" + escapeXml(entry.link) +
             "\">" + escapeXml(entry.title) + "</a></strong><br />";
        var content = entry.contentSnippet;
        content = content.replace(/<br>/g, " ");
        content = content.replace("Event Status: confirmed", " ");
        content = content.replace("When: ", " ");
        s += escapeXml(content) + "</p>";
      }
      container.innerHTML = s;
    }
  });
}

function escapeXml(s) {
    // Converts characters to entities for XML/(X)HTML output
    s = s.replace(/&/g, "&amp;");
    s = s.replace(/</g, "&lt;");
    s = s.replace(/>/g, "&gt;");
    s = s.replace(/"/g, "&quot;");
    return s;
}
```

As the calendar will inherit your blog's Cascading StyleSheet settings, you can fine-tune its layout. See http://w3.org/MarkUp/Guide/Style and **[Hack #18]** for more information on CSS.

HACK 71: Embed All Kinds of Content in Calendar Events

Using Google Calendar, you can create an event that has a date, a title, a description, comments, and so on. But how about an event that contains an image—or even a full web application?

Google Calendar accepts external calendars in two different formats: the XML-based Google Calendar Data API format, and the cross-industry iCalendar or "iCal" format. iCal is just a simple text file that follows some straightforward syntactic rules. Following is an example calendar, which you can create as a plain text file using an extension like **.ical* and then upload to your web site:

```
BEGIN:VCALENDAR
CALSCALE:GREGORIAN
X-WR-CALNAME:Book Reader's Club Events

BEGIN:VEVENT
DTSTART;VALUE=DATE:20070929
DTEND;VALUE=DATE:20070930
SUMMARY:Book Reader's Club Meeting
END:VEVENT

END:VCALENDAR
```

As you can see, the iCal calendar is split up into several lines, each of which is in itself split up into name/value pairs separated by a colon character. The calendar starts with the line "BEGIN: VCALENDAR" and ends with "END:VCALENDAR". In between, you will find more information on this calendar—here, the calendar name "Book Reader's Club Events"—as well as the specific events, along with dates and titles. The date format is `YYYYMMDD`, so `20070929` means September 29, 2007.

Adding Web Content Events to iCal

So far, the iCal file contains nothing that you aren't able to reproduce by creating a new calendar from within Google's native Calendar interface. But there's more to it: with iCal, you now have the ability to add what are called *web content events*. These can be used to link a date to an image, or a static web page, or a full-blown web application—like a small web-based game. The lines needed to add external content to a VEVENT entry are displayed in bold here:

```
...
BEGIN:VEVENT
DTSTART;VALUE=DATE:20070929
DTEND;VALUE=DATE:20070930
RRULE:FREQ=WEEKLY
SUMMARY:Book Reader's Club Weekly Game
X-GOOGLE-CALENDAR-CONTENT-TITLE:Play a linguistic game!
X-GOOGLE-CALENDAR-CONTENT-ICON:http://blogoscoped.com/googleappshacks/calendar-icon.gif
X-GOOGLE-CALENDAR-CONTENT-URL:http://www.gamesforthebrain.com/gadgetized/game/anagramania/
X-GOOGLE-CALENDAR-CONTENT-TYPE:text/html
X-GOOGLE-CALENDAR-CONTENT-WIDTH:300
X-GOOGLE-CALENDAR-CONTENT-HEIGHT:350
END:VEVENT
...
```

These new lines tell the calendar to associate September 29, 2007, with an icon stored on http://blogoscoped.com and a game hosted on http://www.gamesforthebrain.com. The event will repeat weekly. The icon here is a 16 x 16-pixel 256 color GIF, and the game is a small-display optimized game. Any other third-party web site that displays well on a mobile phone or within a gadget can be used this way, and of course you can also create your own HTML file to be displayed here. Instead of HTML, you can also show an image; to do so, replace the value for `X-GOOGLE-CALENDAR-CONTENT-URL` with the image URL, and instead of the content-type `text/html`, use (for example) `image/gif`.

Let's see what this will now look like in Google Calendar! Log in to your calendar and open the Add drop-down that appears above the list of your calendars. Select Add by URL and enter your calendar's full URL (remember, you must have saved the file in iCal format and uploaded it to a server somewhere). After clicking Add and then the OK button and waiting a few seconds for Google to load and display your file, you will see the icon on top of a day in the calendar default display. Click on the icon, and it expands to showcase the content from the URL you specified, as shown in Figure 7-21.

Google caches the iCal file that you provide to it. If you are still testing your calendar and you make changes to the iCal file, you can upload it under a new filename, like *my2.ical* instead of *my1.ical*. You can also append an arbitrary parameter to the URL, like "my.ical?v=2", to make sure that Google won't be accessing its old copy of your file. Note, however, that Google does not cache web pages that you link to in the iCal file—such as the URL of the game shown earlier—so you may want to implement caching on your own if the content is hosted on your server and is generated by a CPU-intensive script.

The location of your iCal file must be publicly crawlable, so it must not have any *robots.txt* directive disallowing spidering by external bots. This would, for instance, prevent you from using the Google Spreadsheets text export option to create an iCal file with Google Docs, as all spreadsheets are disallowed from external crawling.

Hacking the Hack: Dynamic iCal Files

Naturally, you are not restricted to serving static, manually written iCal files. One way to serve dynamic iCal files is to use a server-side scripting language, like Python or PHP. For instance, you might want to offer different web content event for every day of the year, and link it to a URL that passes the actual date as a query string. The following file content might be hosted at a URL, like http://example.com/ical.php5:

```
...
X-GOOGLE-CALENDAR-CONTENT-ICON:http://example.com/default.gif
X-GOOGLE-CALENDAR-CONTENT-URL:http://example.com/web-event.php5?date=2007-09-29
...
```

That PHP script can now query a database, like a MySQL table containing date stamps for each row, to define the HTML output, such as a product image of the day linked to the product web page.

Figure 7-21.
Opening the web content event, like this anagram game

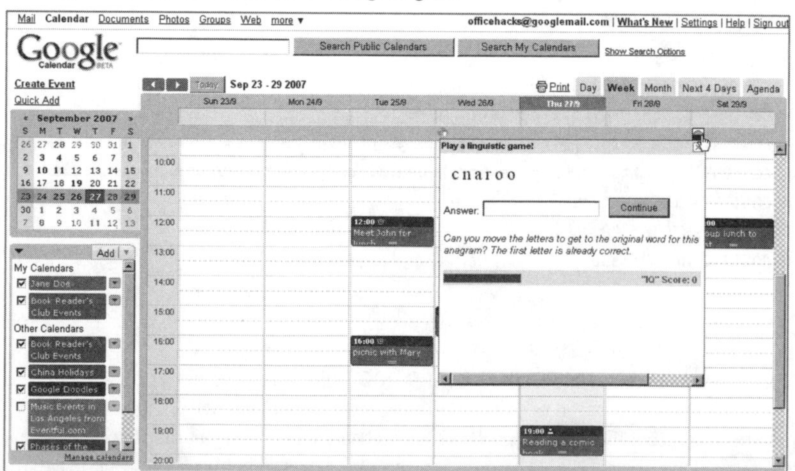

HACK 72: Style Your Calendar

Bored by the same old Google Calendar layout, day in and day out? Don't despair: you can create a custom skin or download third-party skins.

You can skin any web site with *user stylesheets*, home-made CSS (Cascading Style Sheets) files that override the default layout options for any web site. You can manage these files yourself for most browsers **[Hack #41]**. But if you're browsing with Firefox, you can also get a little help in the form of a Firefox extension called Stylish.

Installing and Using Stylish

To install Stylish, point Firefox to https://addons.mozilla.org/en-US/firefox/addon/2108. Click the Install Now button, confirm the setup, and restart your browser.

You will now see an icon in the bottom right of Firefox. Now sign in to Google Calendar, click the Stylish icon, and select Manage Styles from the menu. In the dialog that opens, click the Write button. You can now enter a description, like "My Calendar Skin." In the code field, enter the following CSS for your user stylesheet (the first line is split to fit here):

```
@-moz-documenturl-prefix(http://www.google.com/calendar),
              url-prefix(https://www.google.com/calendar) {
  body {
      background-color: gray !important;
  }
}
```

This URL prefix syntax restricts your style to Google Calendar only. Within that scope, you defined a gray background color for the whole page (pretty, this may not be—but it's just an example!). The `!important` keyword is needed to ensure that existing author stylesheets of the web page are overridden. Click the preview button, and you will see this user stylesheet in action, as shown in Figure 7-22. Hit Save if you like it, and experiment with further layout changes. Stylish is not just for Google Calendar; it works with other web pages too.

Figure 7-22.
The Stylish extension helps you define custom stylesheets for any web page

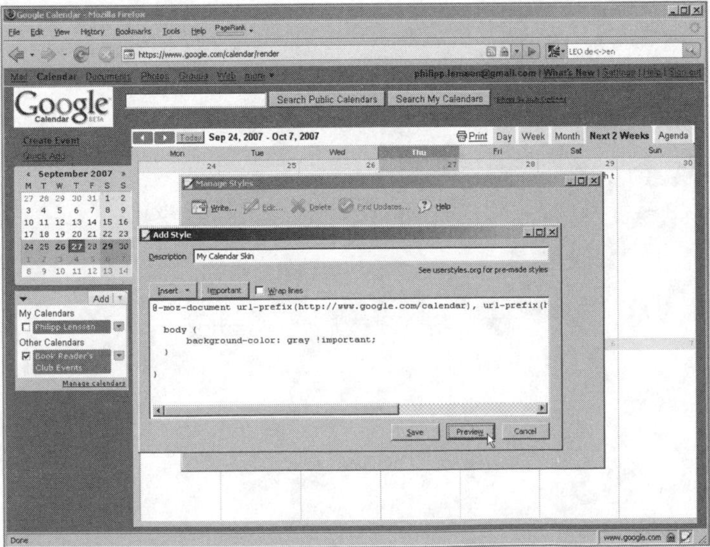

Adding Third-Party User Stylesheets

Creating a custom stylesheet takes time, development skills, and an eye for design. Part of the challenge is to determine the right CSS *selectors* so that your style will be applied to the correct parts of the underlying HTML page. However, there's help: http://userstyles.org is a directory where you can find ready-made stylesheets to grab and run.

The easiest way to access Google Calendar styles in this directory is to just click the Stylish button and select "Find Styles for this Page" while viewing your calendar. You may not always find all the styles available for a given page, so an additional search at http://userstyles.org for "google calendar" will also retrieve good results.

For example, suppose you've located the style named "Slate Series." In its details page, scroll down an click the "Load into Stylish" button. You'll probably want to amend this stylesheet by adding support for non-HTTPS calendar connections; all this takes is a minor tweak to the URL prefix syntax. Click the Stylish icon, select Manage Styles, then select Google Calendar ("Slate Series") and click Edit. Change the following line:

```
@-moz-document url-prefix(https://www.google.com/calendar),
               url-prefix(https://www.google.ca/calendar) {
```

to:

```
@-moz-document url-prefix(https://www.google.com/calendar),
               url-prefix(https://www.google.ca/calendar),
               url-prefix(http://www.google.com/calendar),
               url-prefix(http://www.google.ca/calendar) {
```

Click Save, and the result is the dramatic layout change pictured in Figure 7-23!

Figure 7-23.
Google Calendar after applying the "Slate Series" user stylesheet

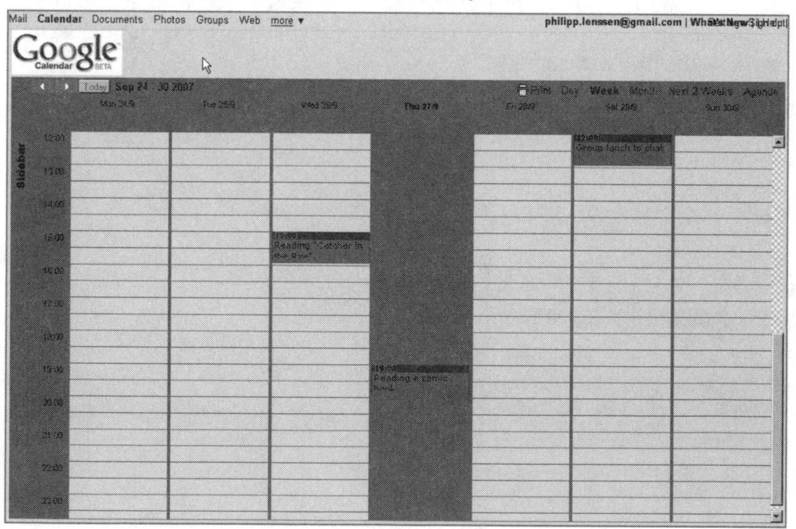

HACK 73: Quickly Add Events from Anywhere

Google's Quick Add functionality can be accessed from outside Google Calendar, too.

You might have come across the Quick Add feature at the left side of Google Calendar, pictured in Figure 7-24. It's like a freestyle text input field to create a new event, and accepts sentences like the following:

```
meeting with Frank 7pm tomorrow
call julia at 1pm
family lunch next Tuesday at 14:00
ski trip 10/20 - 10/26
Japanese language course every Thursday 7-8pm for 6 months
```

> If you're on a supported U.S. cellphone carrier, you can also send sentences like these to Google from your cell phone. As shown in **[Hack #66]**, you can send a message like "next" or "day" to the short code 48368 and retrieve calendar entries. Configure Google Calendar for mobile phone support as described in that hack, and then try sending a sentence like the example ones to 48368.

You can also press the shortcut `q` while in Calendar to bring up the Add box. But what's even quicker than opening Google Calendar to add a quick event? Not opening the calendar, and still adding a quick event! And if you use Firefox to browse the Web, you're lucky. Elias Torres' Quick Add extension runs under Firefox and lets you open a Quick Add prompt whenever you need it, no matter which web site you're on.

Figure 7-24.
Quick-adding your events in Google Calendar

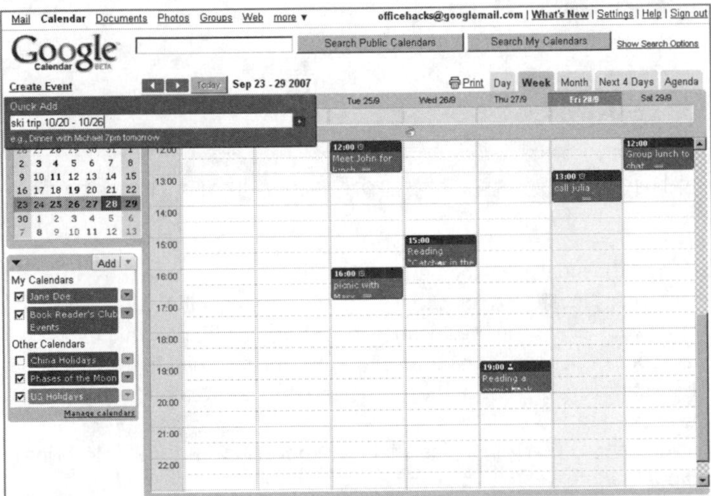

To install this extension, point Firefox to http://torrez.us/code/quickgooglecal/quickgooglecal.xpi and follow the installation prompts. After restarting your browser, you will find a new menu entry in your browser's Tools menu reading "Google Calendar Quick Add." You can now click this menu entry from anywhere on the web, or—even better—press the shortcut Control-Q to open a quick-add box, as shown in Figure 7-25. Enter the event in a Google Calendar–friendly syntax as listed earlier in this hack, confirm it by hitting the Return key, and the event will be added for you. If there are any problems saving your event, go to http://calendar.google.com, make sure you are logged in to Google Calendar, and try again.

Figure 7-25.
After spotting a date on any web page, you can quickly add it to Calendar

HACK 74: Know the Weather

Your planned picnic: huge success or soggy, rained-out disaster?

To add weather forecasts to Google Calendar, click the Settings link and scroll down to the entry that reads "Show weather based on my location." Pick either Celsius or Fahrenheit. If you haven't done so already, you should enter your location in the Location input box (like "Paris, France", without the quotes, or a U.S. zip code). Click the Save button, and you'll be returned to the Calendar home page. In the left pane that lists calendars, check the box next to the new Weather entry.

You will now see weather icons at the top of days in the calendar, as shown in Figure 7-26. Hovering over the icon brings up a tooltip with more weather information.

> Note that removing this calendar again can be confusing, at least if you try to take the same route for removing it as you would with other calendars. At the time of this writing, neither hiding nor deleting the calendar in the Settings→Calendars tab works; although the calendar will be briefly gone, it reappears next time you log in. Instead, to remove the calendar, switch to Settings, check the "Do not show weather" option located toward the bottom of the page, and click Save.

Figure 7-26.
Weather icons integrated with your calendar

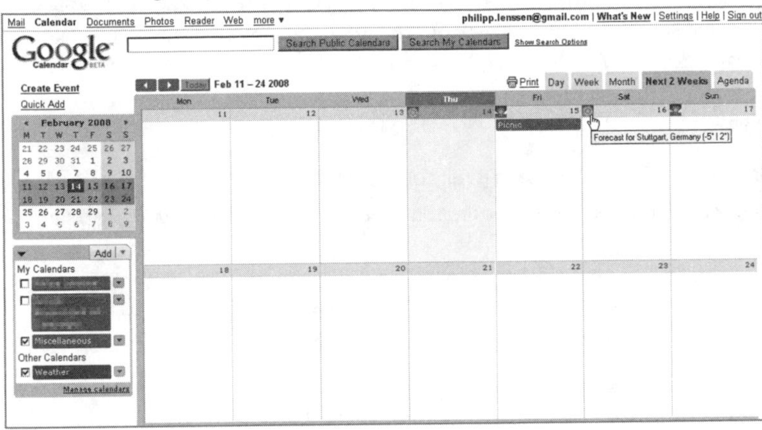

HACK 75: Beyond Google: Yahoo! Calendar and Others

Give the GCal competition a spin.

There are different approaches to planning your 24/7. Although Google Calendar is an efficient tool—beating mental notes by several square pixels, unless you happen to be a professional memory magician—other scheduling web apps are worth a look as well.

Yahoo! Calendar

If you're looking for an alternative to Google Calendar, give Yahoo! Calendar a try. You can find it at http://calendar.yahoo.com. Log in with your Yahoo! account (you can create an account for free if you haven't got one yet), and you'll be presented with a layout similar to the one shown in Figure 7-27.

Figure 7-27.
Yahoo! Calendar: the "Play Pool" event has been added

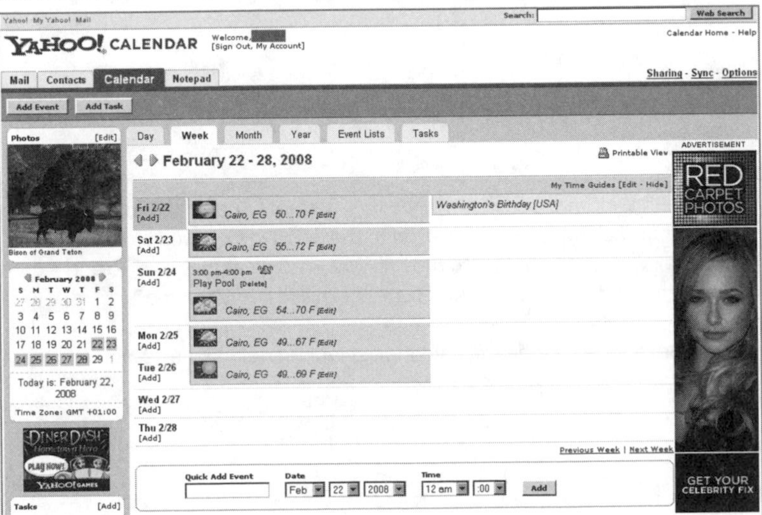

As you can see in the top tabs, this calendar app is part of the Yahoo! suite, which also gives you a mail and contacts service (and as usual, there are ad banners showing). I've switched to the weekly view, and added an event for Sunday reading "Play Pool." The other date information shown, like weather and holidays, was added by Yahoo.

Here are some of the features of the Yahoo! calendar:

- You can share a calendar with friends (or make it fully public for everyone to see).
- You can set your time zone, preferred daily view, first day of the week, your daily working hours, and more in the options.
- You can set up email alerts for your events, or opt to have a daily calendar view be sent to you; you can also receive reminders in Yahoo! Messenger or on your mobile phone.
- A program called Yahoo! Autosync synchronizes your calendar with Outlook, Outlook Express, or Palm Desktop.

Yahoo's calendar also integrates a to-do list, accessible through the Tasks tab, shown in Figure 7-28. And just for fun, you can also show a monthly photo to the left by picking from different themes like *animals* or *abstract*.

Figure 7-28.
Yahoo! Calendar's task list feature

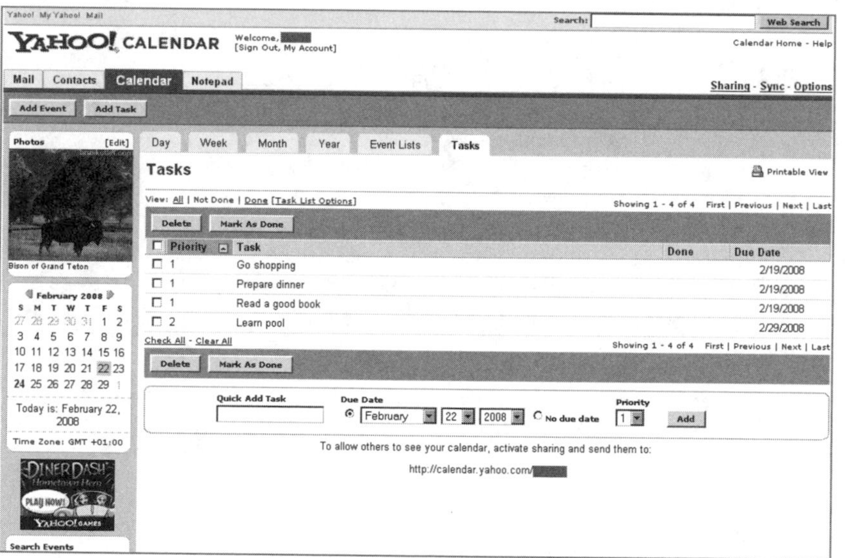

Microsoft's Calendar

Hotmail, also known as Microsoft Windows Live Hotmail, has an integrated calendar application, too. Log in to http://hotmail.com and click the Calendar button to the left. I've switched to the weekly view in Figure 7-29. Note the full view does not fit into the browser window at that size. To add a date, you can double-click a cell in the calendar and then enter a subject, like "Go for a ride."

Features of Hotmail's calendar include sharing the calendar, selecting default views, and setting up reminders.

30 Boxes

After registering for the free calendar app 30 Boxes (http://30boxes.com), you'll receive a registration email that you need to confirm. Once you set up your calendar by providing optional details like your blog URL or your MySpace ID, you'll see a neat full-size grid as shown in Figure 7-30.

Figure 7-29.
The Hotmail calendar service

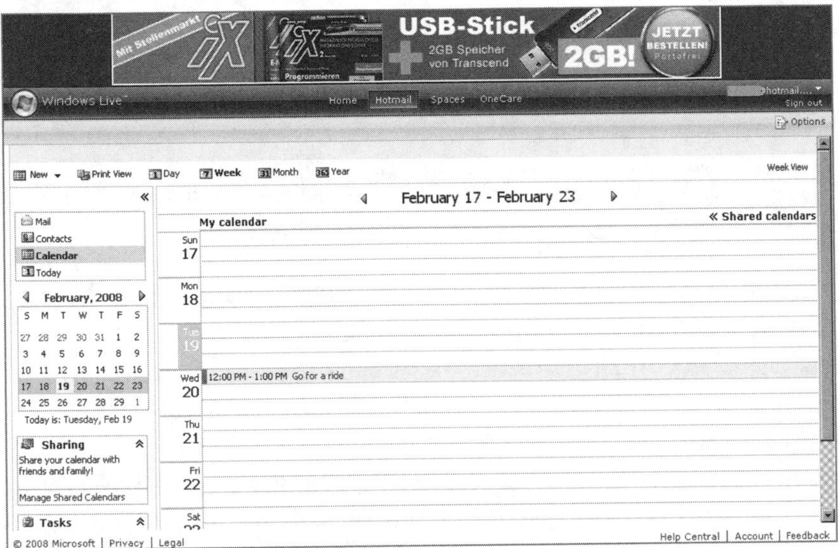

Adding an event is simple—either enter something like "lunch thursday 1pm" or "play pool sunday 15:00 repeat weekly" in the input box on top, or click a day box to open up an editing dialog (the close button for that box is in the bottom right, not at the top right where you might expect it).

30 Boxes allows you to share the calendar, set up email reminders for your events, include holiday calendars for some countries, and more. You can also add a 30 Boxes calendar widget to your MySpace page, iGoogle, a TypePad blog, and other places.

Figure 7-30.
A rather minimalist design approach is taken by 30 Boxes

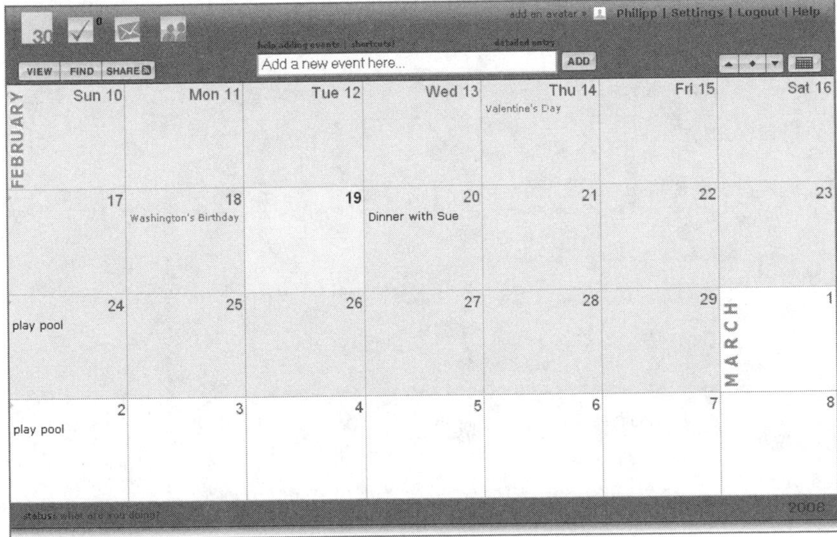

08 KEEP UP ON NEWS WITH GOOGLE READER

Google Reader is Google's "feed reader" web application. Most blogs, but also many traditional news sites, have an accompanying feed, which contains the site's latest entries in a computer-readable syndication format. By subscribing to a feed using a feed reader, you can keep up to date with this web site without ever having to actually visit it again—because the post arrives in your feed reader. Similar to how things work in an email inbox, any unread posts show up in bold to the left.

There are two flavors of these feeds: RSS and Atom. One way to subscribe to them is to use Google Reader. All you need is a Google Account **[Hack #1]**. Point your browser to http://reader.google.com and log in. To get you started, Google provides instructions, and gives you the chance to subscribe to several preselected feed bundles in various categories—from News to Sports, Fun, Geeky, Thinkers, Finance, and more (Figure 8-1).

Bloggers and everyone else publishing a feed can decide whether they want to offer a full feed or a partial feed. A full feed means that you, as the reader, never have to leave Google Reader to get the full article. This can bring with it several advantages, and depending on your likes and dislikes, you may

HTML AS A FEED?

Like feeds, HTML itself can also be parsed by software. However, HTML has grown more complex over time; for instance, it often includes layout definitions right within the main file, as opposed to an external stylesheet. Also, HTML doesn't yet have a clearly defined and agreed-upon structure to denote specific articles within a page. Efforts in the form of drafts are underway to change this, like XHTML 2 and HTML 5. XHTML 2, for instance, proposes to include a `<section>` element, and the option to write, for example, `<h role="rss:title">...</h>` for headings. HTML 5, on the other hand, has an `<article>` element. But these drafts take time to be finalized, if ever, and then to become supported by browsers or feed readers, so they pose no present alternative to RSS or Atom feeds.

Figure 8-1.
Upon signup for Google Reader, you can select from a couple of topic bundles. Each bundle contains a selection of blog or mainstream news feeds.

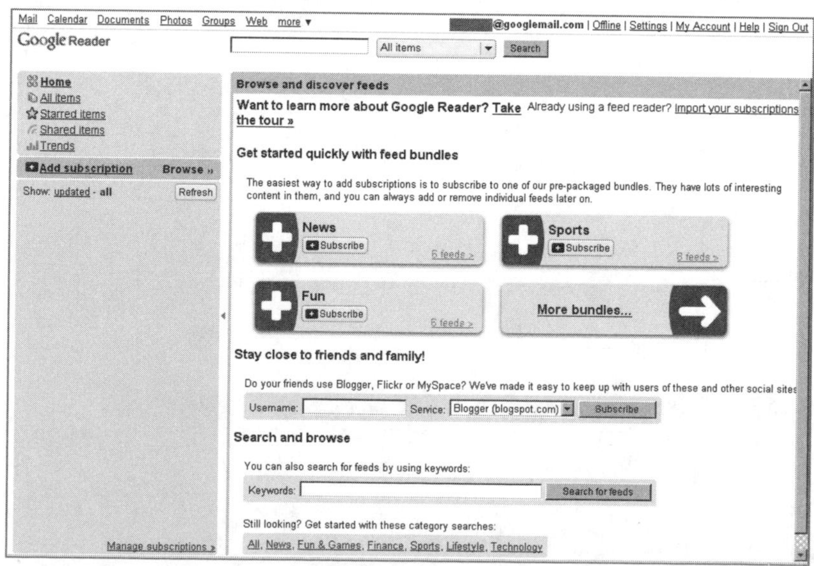

Figure 8-2.
Reading a blog (in this case, Fury.com) through Google Reader

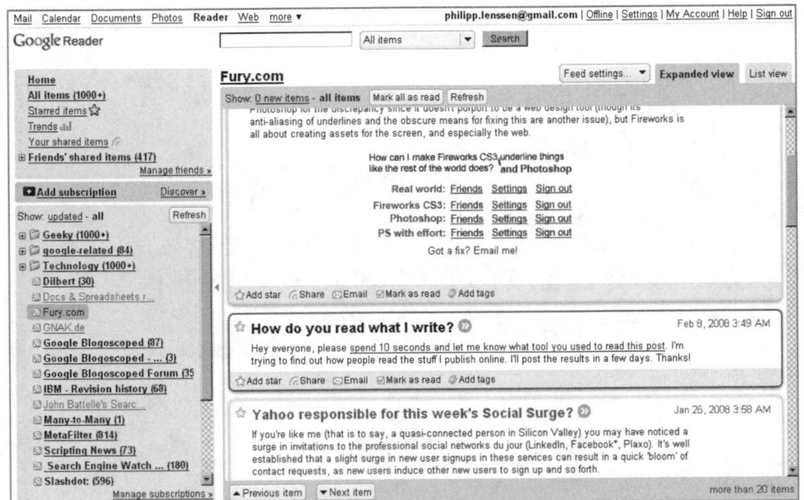

start to prefer reading everything from Google Reader: there may now be fewer ads, less navigation, less clutter, but instead, faster loading times. Also, every blog will appear in the same font and font size (see Figure 8-2). By its nature of displaying a stripped-down version of the site, feed readers on the other hand impose some restrictions on what an article can contain. Sometimes, if special content or styling is included in an article, you might still need to visit the original page to see it.

Finding New RSS Feeds

If you want to go beyond the default bundles that Google offers you upon signup, you can search for more feeds. One way to do so is to check whether your favorite home pages and news sites already provide a feed (and every good blog will have a subscription feed, too). Look for an orange feed icon or anything else that says "RSS," "XML," or similar (see Figure 8-3); also, your browser may help you locate the feed by displaying a special icon on such pages.

Figure 8-3.
If you spot this icon, the RSS or Atom feed usually isn't far away. An alternative icon often used is an orange button reading "XML."

Another way to find new feeds is to use Google Blog Search at http://blogsearch.google.com. Despite its name, Blog Search finds more than just blogs—it actually digs for any kind of RSS/Atom feed. Enter a topic you're interested in such as "history" or "stamp collection," and Google will show you results for both individual posts as well as blogs or other sites covering these topics. Searching for "history," for instance, returns sites like History.com or HNN.us, the History News Network. You don't necessarily need to find the address of the feed itself, as you can also just copy a URL like http://www.hnn.us and paste it into the "Add subscription" box in Google Reader. Google will attempt to automatically locate the feed for you.

In addition to using Google Blog Search, you can search for feeds within Google Reader. Click the Discover link to the left and enter your keywords in the "Search and browse" box at the bottom. Happy reading!

HACK 78: Use Google Reader Offline

Google Reader is called an "online application." But that doesn't mean that you have to be online to use it.

Google Gears is a Google-powered open source project aiming to allow web site publishers to make a part of their application available offline. Not too many web sites have this feature enabled yet, but those that do allow you to use some parts of their application even when you're not connected to the Internet. Google Reader is one of the applications that is partially Gears-enabled.

To give this feature a try, log in to Google Reader at http://reader.google.com. You need to have the Firefox 1.5+ browser to get this to work, or, on Windows XP/ Vista, you can use Internet Explorer 6+ as well. In Reader, click the Offline link on top. You will be taken through a Google Gears installation. Follow the instructions, as shown in Figure 8-4. You may be required to download a browser add-in, run it, and then restart the browser.

Figure 8-4.
Installing Google Gears, a browser extension that allows websites to take parts of their functionality offline

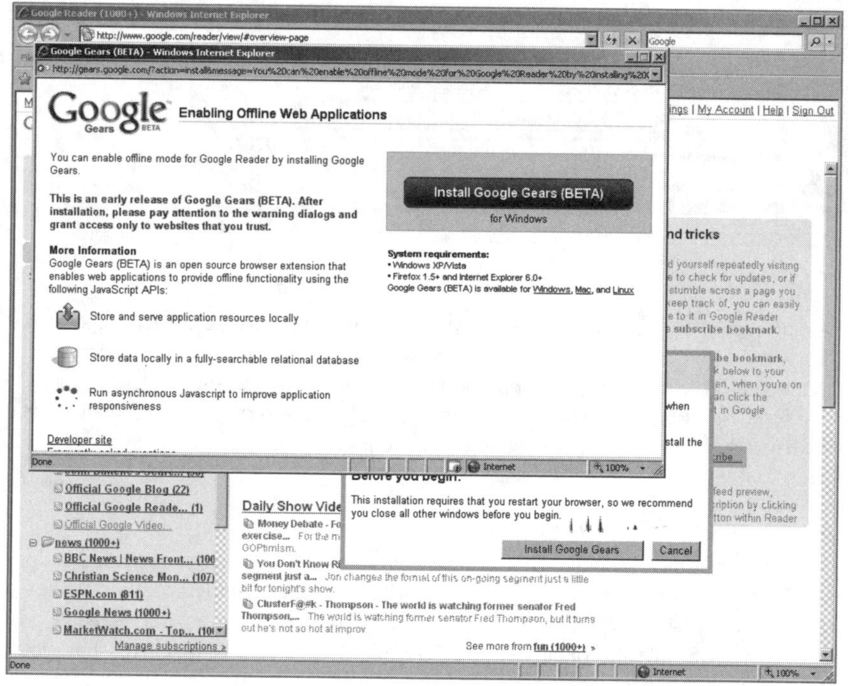

After installation, go back to Google Reader. You will notice a new green arrow in the top navigation bar. This means that you're in online mode—click the arrow to go into offline mode. The first time you switch into offline mode, up to 2,000 articles from your subscribed Google Reader feeds will be downloaded for you. After the download is done, you can disconnect from the Internet and still read some of your feeds.

Note that because Google Gears is a browser extension and not just a feature of the web site, you need to install Gears on every computer on which you want to use these offline capabilities.

HACK 77: Subscribe to Google's Feeds

Interconnect the Google office by subscribing to different info feeds Google offers.

There is a staggering number of RSS and Atom feeds available all over the Web (see the introduction to this chapter). Not surprisingly, Google's own properties have plenty of feeds as well. Hooking up Google Reader to other services of Google helps you keep up to date.

Subscribe to a Google Blog Search

Go to http://blogsearch.google.com and search for any keyword. At the left side of the search results—which you can sort by relevance (the default) or date—you will find a link named Atom, which you can add to Google Reader. On most browsers, this link can also be accessed by clicking the orange feed icon located nearby or within your browser address bar.

Subscribe to Google News

Go to http://news.google.com and search for any keyword. For instance, you might want to subscribe to alerts for the name of yourself, or your company, or your web site. You can also subscribe to a specific domain which is indexed in Google News, such as "site:cnn.com" (no quotes)—useful if the site itself doesn't offer an RSS feed already. To the left of the Google News results, you will always find the link "RSS," which you can subscribe to with Google Reader.

Subscribe to Google Video

Similar to other types of search engines, Google Video (http://video.google.com) offers a link named "RSS" on its search results pages.

> Google Video searches through different video sites, including YouTube, Google Video itself, MetaCafe, and Break.com. To find Google Video–filtered results for only a single one of these sites, use the site operator along with your search query, as in "site:break.com soccer" (without the quotes) to find only soccer-related material from Break.

Subscribe to Google Web Search

When you perform a Google web search query, you will not find any RSS or Atom feed link on the results page. However, there's help available, in the form of Google Docs.

Create a new spreadsheet at http://docs.google.com. In the first cell, use the `importXml` formula **[Hack #27]** as follows—replace "horse+riding" with your own keywords, using the plus symbol where you would usually put a space in the search query:

```
=importXML("http://www.google.com/search?q=horse+riding",
          "//a[@class='l']/@href")
```

The first parameter in this function is the Google result URL. The second parameter is the XPath. In this case, the XPath translates to "Find all anchor elements 'a' in the source document that have the class name 'l', and grab their link parameter 'href'." As a Google result by default has 10 result links, that's also the number of URLs appearing in your Google spreadsheet now.

As a second step, publish the spreadsheet and check the "Automatically re-publish . . . " box. Click "More publishing options" and pick Atom from the file format drop-down. Click the Generate URL button, and copy the resulting URL as shown in Figure 8-5 to add to Google Reader . . . and voilà, you are now subscribed to a Google web search result.

Figure 8-5.
Publishing the results of importXml, wrapped around a Google search result, as an Atom feed

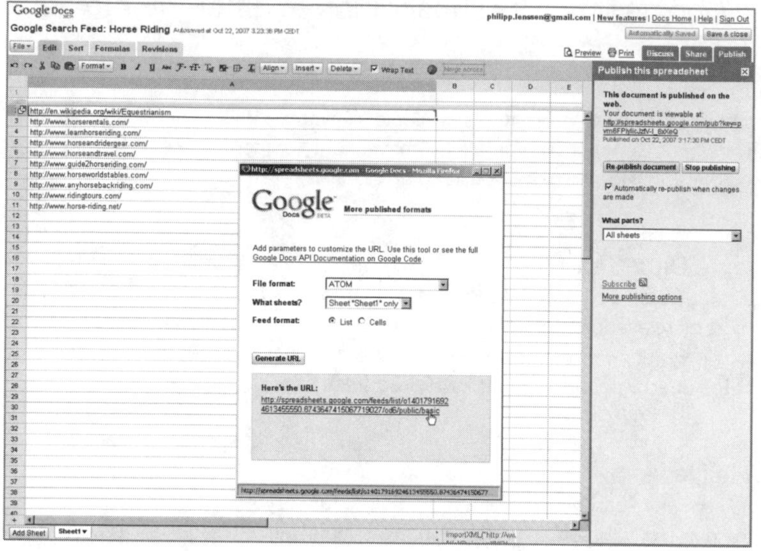

Subscribe to Gmail Messages

Gmail does have an RSS feed at http://mail.google.com/mail/feed/atom (see Chapter 5). However, this feed requires authentication, as it contains your private data, so you can't subscribe to it using Google Reader (even when you try using the format https://username:password@gmail.google.com/gmail/feed/atom). You might be able to access it using other RSS readers, though; for instance, the Windows desktop program SharpReader at http://sharpreader.net supports this. As with any application that asks for your Google Account credentials, provide these details only when you trust the program's creators, as well as whatever security model they use to protect your credentials.

Subscribe to Google Docs

To see newly published documents, spreadsheets, or presentations, you can access the Google Docs **[Hack #1]** feed. Go to http://docs.google.com and click the Settings link on top. Switch to the RSS Feeds tab and click the "view feed" link to add it to Google Reader. By default, only public Docs documents will reveal their title along with a snippet, although you can change this setting in the RSS Feeds tab.

In addition to subscribing to a general feed covering all your documents in Google Docs, you can also open a single document and subscribe to its RSS feed, which you will find in the Publish tab; the link is named Subscribe and is accompanied by the orange feed icon.

This document-specific feed acts as a kind of change log, which is especially useful if the document is very important to you.

Subscribe to Google Notebook

You can also subscribe to your Google Notebook **[Hack #14]** to keep up to date on this collaborative notes-sharing tool. Log in to your notebook at http://google.com/notebook/. If the notebook in question isn't already shared, click "Sharing options" and under the "Publish this notebook" label, check the Yes option and click the Save Settings button.

If your notebook is published, click the View link above it. A new browser window or tab opens, containing an HTML page of your notes. If your browser doesn't automatically offer you a link to subscribe to the RSS feed contained within this HTML page, open its source and look for the part reading `alt=rss` and copy the URL you see to add it to Google Reader. The format of the feed URL will be similar to this one:

```
http://www.google.com/notebook/feeds/12341500972093356787/notebooks/BDRRESwoWkbdw5vMh?alt=rss
```

Subscribe to Google Groups

Google Groups (http://groups.google.com) is Google's Usenet discussion group display service. You can navigate to any group, then subscribe to it using the orange XML button at the bottom of the page, which will take you to a page displaying different feed formats.

For instance, the feed for the Usenet group *rec.arts.comics.misc* (miscellaneous discussion of comic books as part of the recreation/arts groups hierarchy) looks like this:

```
http://groups.google.com/group/rec.arts.comics.misc/feed/atom_v1_0_msgs.xml
```

Subscribe to Picasa Web Albums

Picasa is Google's online photo storage and display service. Navigate to http://picasaweb.google.com and then to any one of your albums or to the albums of others, and you will find an RSS link at the bottom right of the page. You can subscribe to it using Google Reader to track the list of new photos being added to the album over time.

Subscribe to YouTube Videos

To get the RSS feed for any Google YouTube tag result, replace the bold part in the following URL with your own keyword or set of keywords (use a plus character as a separator between keywords):

http://youtube.com/rss/tag/**japanese+show**.rss

This will provide you with a list of videos, and as shown in Figure 8-6, you can instantly play them within Google Reader.

For a list of other feeds offered by YouTube—including recently added, top favorites, and most viewed today—check http://youtube.com/rssls.

Figure 8-6.
A YouTube feed displayed in Google Reader

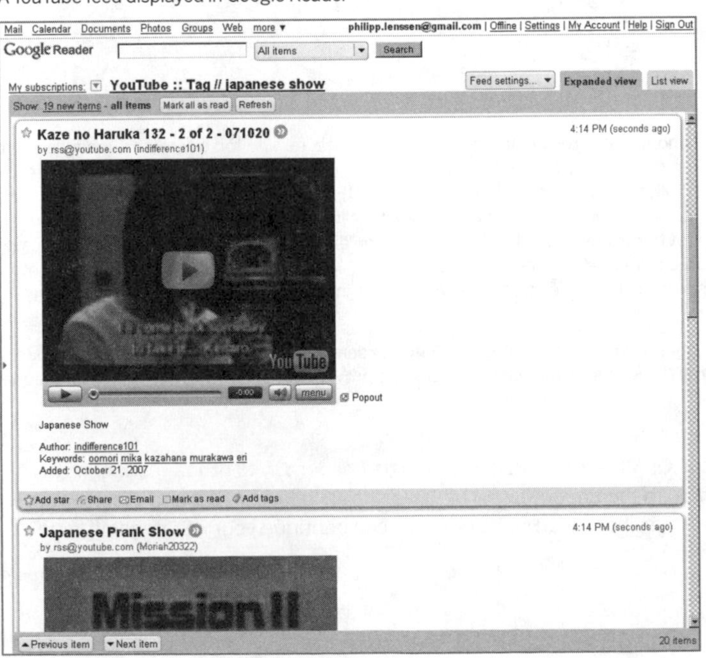

HACK 78: Take Your Old Subscriptions with You

Switching your feed reader doesn't need to cause a lot of headaches.

If you were using another feed reader before Google Reader, you might want to take your old subscriptions with you. Wouldn't it be nice to move all of them at once instead of having to resubscribe to feed URL after feed URL? Luckily, there's a perfect format for just that, called OPML. OPML, the Outline Processor Markup Language, collects several RSS feed addresses within a single file.

For instance, if your old feed reader is Bloglines (http://bloglines.com), log into it and in the lefthand navigation, click the "Export Subscriptions" link, pictured in Figure 8-7. An OPML download will be offered to you; save it to your computer. If you are curious, you can open the download file with a plain text editor, and you will see something along the lines of the following—a structured list of feed URLs in XML format:

```
<?xml version="1.0" encoding="utf-8"?>
<opml version="1.1">
<head>
<title>Bloglines Subscriptions</title>
    ...
</head>
<body>
<outline title="John Battelle's Searchblog"
        text="John Battelle's
        Searchblog" htmlUrl="http://battellemedia.com/" type="rss"
        xmlUrl="http://battellemedia.com/index.rdf" />
<outline title="Fury.com"
        text="Fury.com" htmlUrl="http://fury.com/"
        type="rss" xmlUrl="http://fury.com/index.rss" />
<outline title="MetaFilter"
        text="MetaFilter" htmlUrl="http://www.metafilter.com/" type="rss"
        xmlUrl="http://xml.metafilter.com/atom.xml" />
   ...
</body>
</opml>
```

> The OPML format is easy enough that you could add new items with a text editor, or create such a file from scratch. Note that if you manually add URLs containing the "&" (ampersand) character, you need to escape these so they are a proper XML entity by writing "&" instead (OPML is an XML application). This escaping of ampersand characters is actually even needed when you include links in HTML, though the HTML format is usually more forgiving about this issue, and will still render in popular browsers (it will fail the test when using validator programs). To check whether you created a well-formed XML document, try dropping the file into a browser like Firefox and see if it correctly loads, or throws an error message.

> For details on export options from a variety of other feed readers, like Firefox Live Bookmarks, iGoogle, Newsgator, Netvibes or myYahoo, check the handy list Google provides at http://google.com/help/reader/faq.html#export.

Now that you've exported the OPML file, import it into Google Reader. Go to http://reader.google.com and click Settings. Switch to the Import/Export tab, as shown in Figure 8-8, and provide your file in the OPML upload box. After the upload succeeds, you can continue your RSS reading with your complete list of feeds.

Figure 8-7.
Feed reader Bloglines offers an export function to the left side

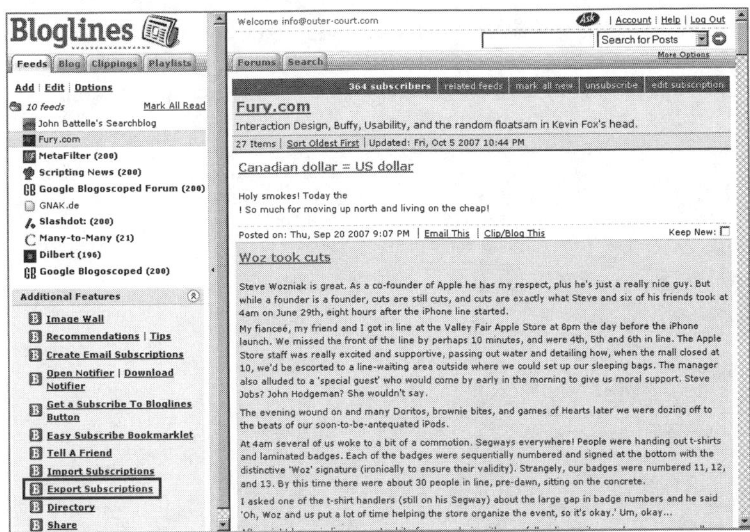

Figure 8-8.
Google Reader's import dialog

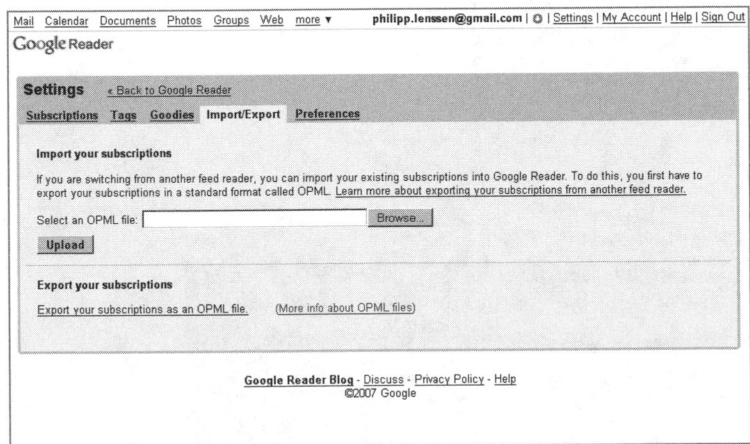

HACK 79: Get Alerts for New Blog Posts

Display the number of unread Reader items in your browser status bar. It's the fastest way—hands down—to catch the latest news.

You can check Google Reader for new items by just visiting it at http://reader.google.com—or, if you're using the Firefox browser, you can install a little notifier to tell you how many new items are waiting for you.

To get this add-on, point Firefox to https://addons.mozilla.org/firefox/3977 and click the Install Now button. After installation, you are required to restart your browser. When you do this, an options dialog from the new Notifier extension will greet you, as shown in Figure 8-9. If you trust this extension's author and are confident that he will keep your information private, you can now provide your Google Account username and password. You can leave the other options set to their default values for now and confirm the dialog by hitting the OK button.

In the bottom right of Firefox, notice the new icon pictured in Figure 8-10. It indicates the number of currently unread posts in Google Reader, and shows some more context information when you hover over it. Click on it to be taken to Reader, or click with your middle mouse button to refresh the display (you can also hold down the Ctrl key while clicking). If you don't manually refresh the display, it will be updated every five minutes by default. To change the refresh rate, or any other options, right-click the notifier display to be taken to the options dialog.

Figure 8-9.
The Google Reader Notifier preferences

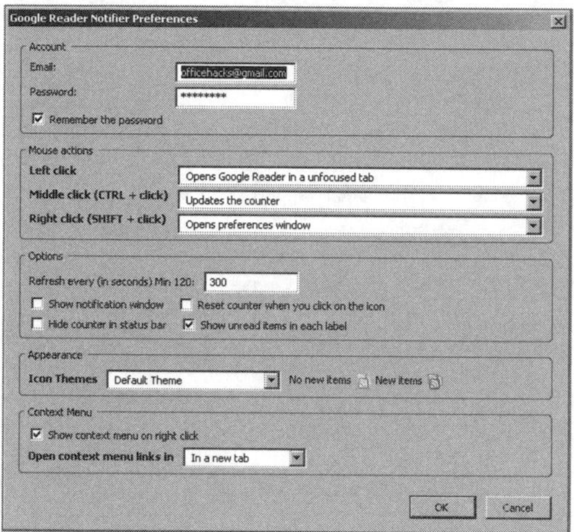

Figure 8-10.
Outside of Google Reader, you can still see how many new messages demand your attention via Google Reader Notifier

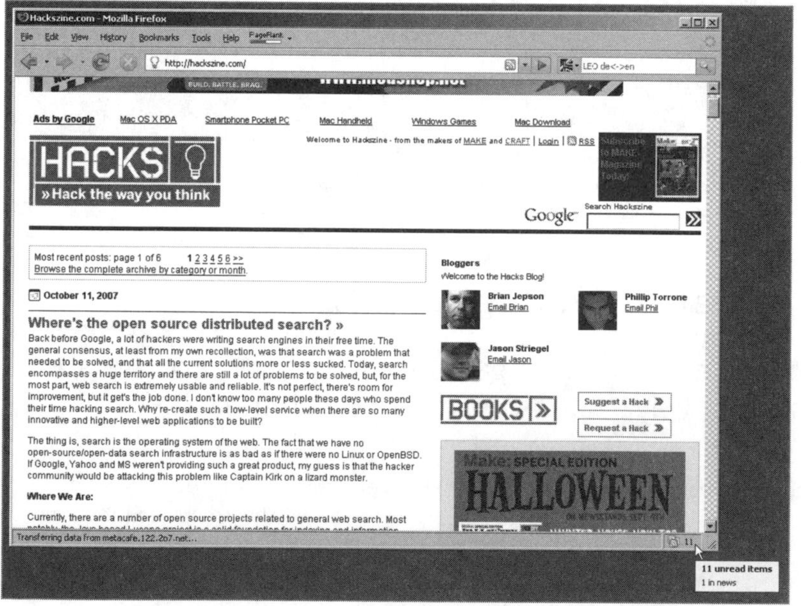

HACK 80: Share a Post with a Single Shortcut

Sharing items as so-called "clips" is easy; here's how.

If you already have a web site or blog, you can integrate a small "blog posts of interest" section for it using a Google Reader feature called clips.

To give this a try, visit Google Reader (http://reader.google.com) and click on the "All items" navigation link to the left side, or select any other view, like a folder in your subscription list. When you are scrolling through the list of blog posts, notice that the post in focus has a blue border, whereas posts out of focus have a gray border. Whenever you feel that a post currently in reading focus is worth sharing, hit the shortcut Shift-S on your keyboard, or click the Share icon below the post, which flags the post as being shared. Repeat this for every post you want to share.

To publish the clip of your shared items, go to the Reader Settings page and select the Tags tab. In it, next to the row labelled "Your shared items" click the "add a clip . . ." link. A new browser window opens, as shown in Figure 8-11. If you want to, adjust the layout options for the clip widget. Then copy the relevant HTML snippet out of the text box. Paste the snippet into the template of your blog or other home page, publish the template, and you're done—the clip gadget will now automatically display new items you shared from within Google Reader!

Figure 8-11.
The Google Reader clip gadget

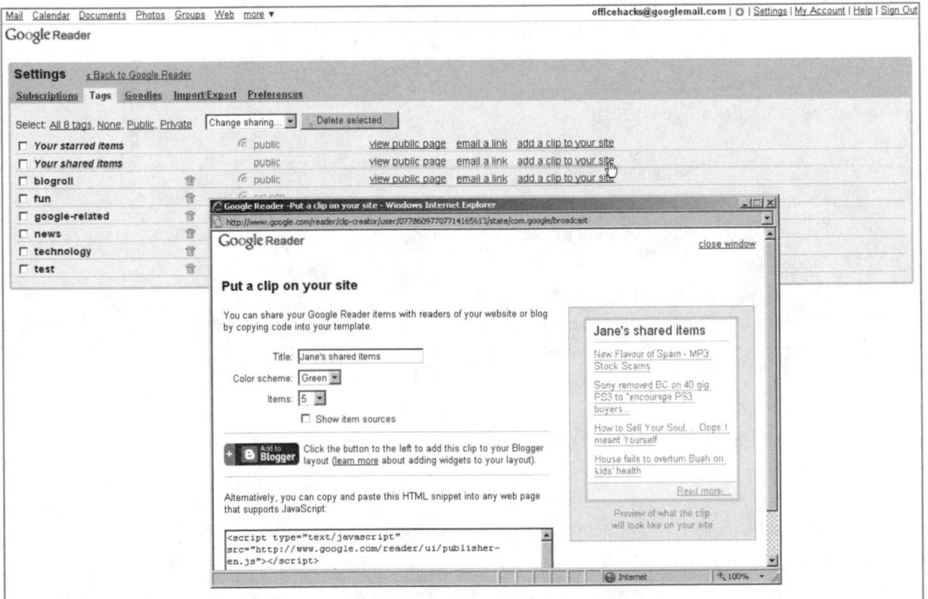

QUICK HACK 

OTHER USEFUL GOOGLE READER SHORTCUTS

Shift-S isn't the only handy keyboard shortcut in Google Reader. Here are some more:

KEY	DESCRIPTION
j	Move down to the next post
k	Move up to the previous post
s	Star an item
m	Mark a post as read or unread (hit Shift-A to mark a complete subscription as read)
l	Add tags to a blog post in focus
v	Open the currently focused post in a new window, at its original location
u	Collapse the lefthand navigation to view the posts in full-screen mode

HACK 81: Use Google Reader's Mobile Version

Put your feed items on your cellphone, or on iGoogle.

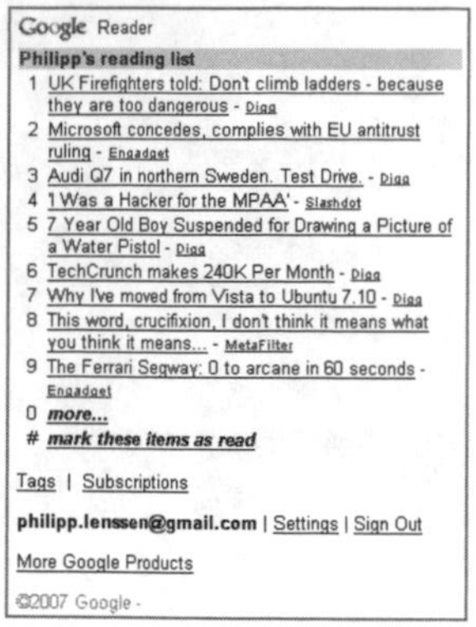

Figure 8-12.
Google Reader mobile

As is the case with many to most Google products, Google Reader is available in a special mobile-friendly version. Point your phone's web browser to http://google.com/reader/m to access your items, as shown in Figure 8-12. You will see a list of the latest titles, as well as their source publications, and you can navigate to specific tags or feed subscriptions. To increase the length of this reading list, switch to the mobile settings page and adjust it.

If your phone supports it, you can press the numbers 1–9 as shortcuts to jump to an item. Each individual post will be rendered through Google Reader again, optimized for smaller displays. If you don't like the reformatting, you can also disable this option in the Google Reader mobile settings. A link named "See original," below the post—accessible by pressing 1—takes you to the source. If you want to keep the item for later review on the desktop, you can also star it by pressing *.

Kidnap Mobile Reader to Display as an iGoogle Gadget

If you want to display Google Reader as a gadget for your personalized Google home page at http://igoogle.com, you have two options. First, there is an official gadget for this purpose. Log in to iGoogle and click "Add stuff" on the right side. Search for "google reader" and add the official gadget from Google to your home page.

As a second option, you can also create your own iGoogle gadget wrapper around any URL you find. Mobile-optimized web sites, as well as Flash files **[Hack #64]**, are an especially good fit. Open a plain text editor on your computer or start the Google Gadget Editor **[Hack #59]**. Now type the following XML for your gadget—change the author information to reflect your own details:

```
<?xml version="1.0" encoding="UTF-8" ?>
<Module>
<ModulePrefs title="Google Reader mobile"
    title_url="http://www.google.com/reader/"
    description="Displays Google Reader mobile as gadget"
    author="Jane Doe"
    author_email="officehacks@gmail.com"
    author_affiliation="Google Office Hacks"
    author_location="Example Town, Sampleonia"
    height="240"
/>
<Content type="url" href="http://www.google.com/reader/m/view/" />
</Module>
```

The most important part of this XML file has been highlighted in bold; it's the line referring the external Google Reader mobile URL. Once you save this file on your server or with the Google Reader Gadget, click the link "Add stuff" on the iGoogle home page and select Add by URL. Provide your gadget's address and click Add. As shown in Figure 8-13, you now have two gadgets to display Google Reader content: the official one to the left, and the unofficial one you created to the right.

> Alternatively, you can also add any RSS or Atom feed as a Google gadget on its own. Just switch to the "Add by URL" dialog and provide the feed URL.

Figure 8-13.
The Google Reader iGoogle gadget on the left, and your Google Reader mobile wrapper on the right.

HACK 82: Track What Wikipedia Says About You

"You are what people think you are"? Well, not quite . . . but public perception is important feedback to what you do. Why not track it?

If your company, school, organization, or favorite football team (or perhaps even you?) happen to be big enough to have an entry in online encyclopedia Wikipedia, it might be worthwhile for you to see which changes are being made to it. This way you can keep up on the public perception—and occasionally public misconception—of whatever entity it is you care about. All you need to do is to find the RSS/Atom feed for the Wikipedia entry, and you can subscribe to it using Google Reader. Thanks to Mathias Schindler, Wikipedian (http://mathias-schindler.de) for suggesting this hack.

First, check to see whether Wikipedia contains an entry on whatever you're interested in. You can start with a Google search using the query "Acme Inc site:wikipedia.org" (no quotes), where "Acme Inc" is the name of your company, organization, school, and so on. If you don't find anything among the first few results, try visiting http://wikipedia.org directly to use its native search functionality.

Once you found the entry, copy the page name as shown in the URL; if the URL is http://en.wikipedia.org/wiki/Acme, your page name would be "Acme". Then use the following feed URL, again replacing "Acme", highlighted in bold here, with the name of your chosen subject:

```
http://en.wikipedia.org/w/index.php?title=Acme&action=history&feed=atom
```

(If you were looking at a non-English entry, replace "en" with your country code as you found it on Wikipedia.)

You can now head over to Google Reader (http://reader.google.com) and subscribe to the feed by clicking "Add subscription," pasting the URL into the input box, and clicking the Add button. The feed is a history of old and new revisions that the article in question undergoes. So whenever someone somewhere changes the Wikipedia entry, you will be among the first to know via your feed reader, as shown in Figure 8-14.

Figure 8-14.
Subscribing to the change log for IBM

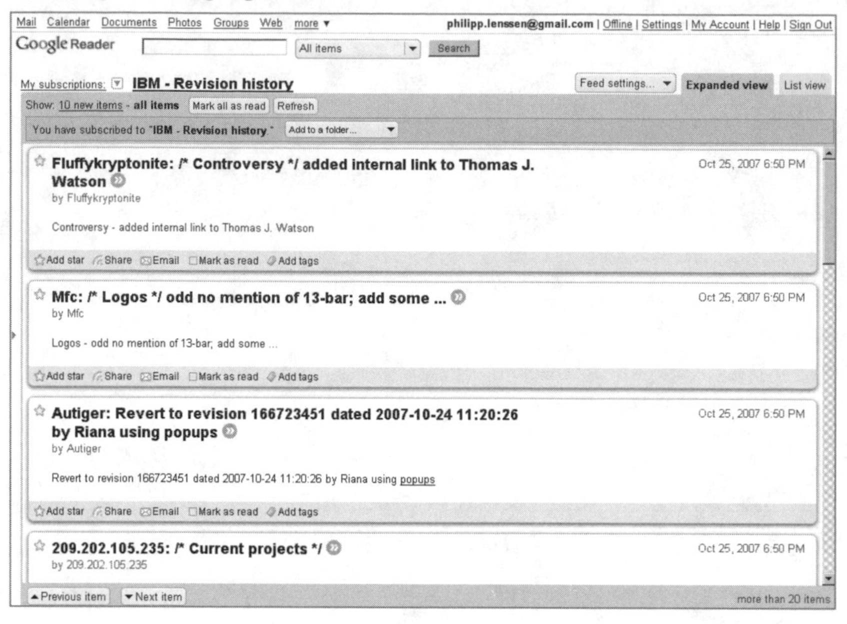

To track Wikipedia changes to an article outside of Google Reader, use the Wikipedia watchlist feature. First, make sure you're logged in to Wikipedia (click the "Log in/create account" link at the top of any Wikipedia page). Above most articles, you will now find a tab that reads Watch. Click it to add the article to your watchlist. You can view this watchlist by clicking the "my watchlist" link on top. (If you want to unsubscribe from a watched item, either click "unwatch" on top of the article in question, or—and this works better if you want to unsubscribe from multiple items—follow the link "View and edit watchlist" or "Edit raw watchlist" shown on your watchlist page.) As for your privacy, note that although—according to Wikipedia's help files—normal users won't see which pages you've added to the watchlist, developers who have access to the servers holding the Wikipedia database may see that list.

For a way to keep track of changes on any web page—not just Wikipedia—check out web page change detection services **[Hack #104]**.

HACK 83: Track Your Package

Waiting for a delivery to arrive? Let Google's feed reader keep you up-to-date.

Nellie just ordered half a dozen memory sticks from her favorite online shop. She's not the impatient kind but she's really curious when the package will arrive, because she needs those sticks. Well, luckily for her, she can subscribe to the package via Google Reader. OK, not the package itself, but an RSS feed automatically polling status information from providers like UPS, FedEx, USPS, or DHL/Airborne!

Here's how it works if you like to do the same (thanks to LifeHack.org and Stephen Tordoff for discovering this hack). First, get your package tracking number ready; it might be contained within your order confirmation email, for instance. Then point your browser to http://isnoop.net/tracking/ and paste that number into the input box. I'm entering 1Z039AF20304071510 for this example. Now hit the Track It! button and you will find a map showing the route your delivery took so far, as shown in Figure 8-15. This extremely cool map is created using the Google Maps API, by the way **[Hack #115]**.

Figure 8-15.
The package has arrived already, as the UPS tracker shows

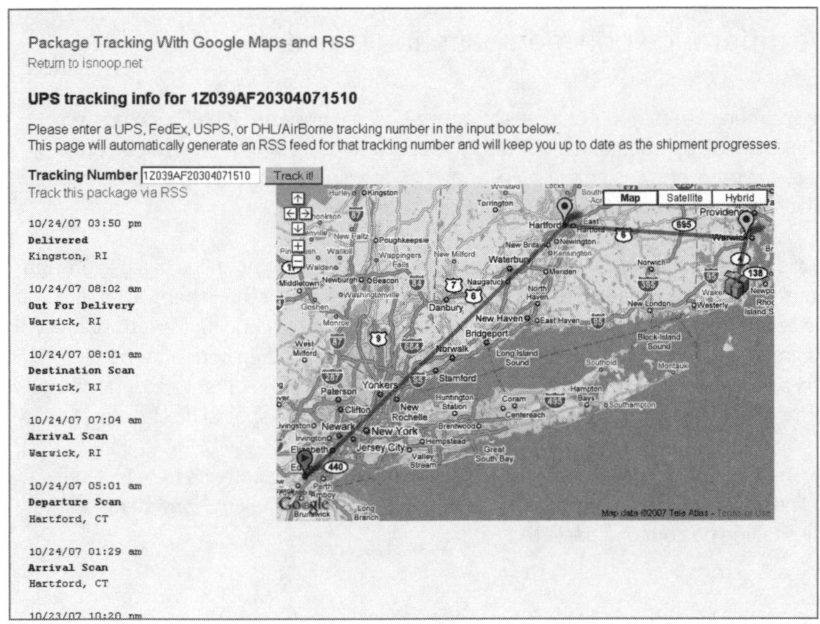

Furthermore, isnoop.net offers you an RSS link on your tracking status page. Right-click the URL and select Copy Link Location (or similar option) from the popup menu. Now go to Google Reader at http://reader.google.com. Click the Add subscription link, and add the URL you copied into the box. Confirm via the Add button—and that's it! You will now be able to see the route your package takes, as pictured in Figure 8-16.

Figure 8-16.
The package status; as usual, RSS readers display items in reverse-chronological order, meaning that the latest event is at the top

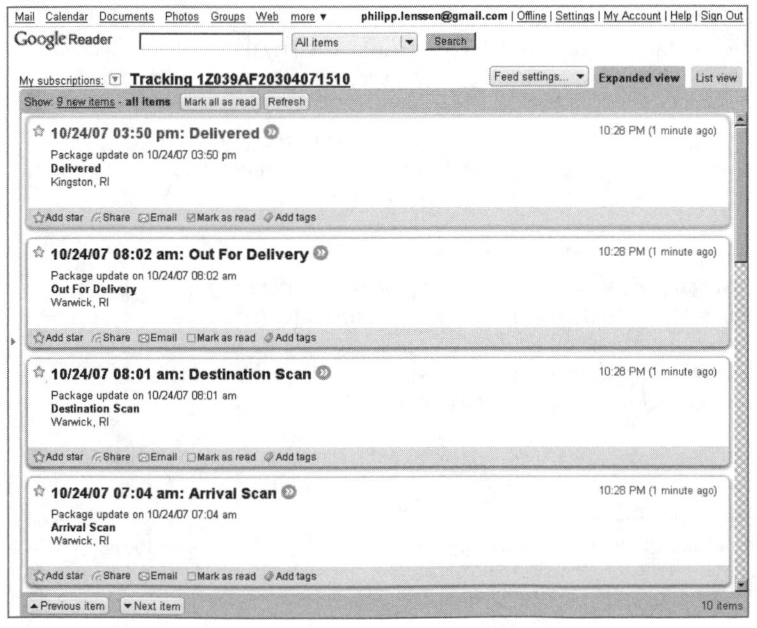

HACK 84: Compare Two Posts to See the Changes

Visualize the difference between past and present.

When a news blogger makes substantial changes to a blog post a while after it has been posted, netiquette says that the blogger should mark or disclose changes accordingly. This can be done by adding an update to the post, or by using the `<del>` and `<ins>` tags in the post to mark up deletions and insertions, which typically render as strikethrough and italic, respectively.

The reason for this is that every blog post can grow to become part of a larger online discussion, and when other bloggers reference a post or the post collects comments, and it then changes behind the scenes, things become confusing. Although your mileage may vary, amending the introductory sentence of a post from "Adam stole my car" to "Adam bought my car" half an hour after posting (for example) would be a potentially confusing change if left unmarked; if, on the other hand, you correct a mere spelling error a couple of minutes after posting, it may not justify a special disclosure.

On the other hand, behind-the-scenes changes, such as the removal of a sentence to hide it, are hard to pull off online anyway. Or, as *NewsRadio*'s Joe Rogan once put it, "Taking something off the Internet? That's like taking pee out of a pool."

> **OTHER WAYS TO COMPARE**
>
> For news site Google Blogoscoped (http://blogoscoped.com), I'm polling the various official Google blogs, as well as some non-feed-enabled Google pages (like a press images page) for changes every few minutes. This is done using what's called a *cron job* on my server. It's a scheduling service that launches different tracking scripts. If a blog post is changed, the changed version will be saved in the database in addition to the old version, allowing me to check the differences if I want to. New blog posts and other changed pages are then emailed to my Gmail account using a special keyword in the subject, which allows me to filter these messages into a specific label section **[Hack #44]**. The result is a bit of a mixture between email, page change detection service **[Hack #104]**, and feed reading.

Retrieving the Older Version of the Article

If you read something in Google Reader or elsewhere but suspect a change, there are several ways to investigate. The first question is—how do you retrieve an earlier version of the post? Unless you set up a tracker—see sidebar—you'll likely not have saved an earlier version yourself.

One way to retrieve an older version of a post is the Google cache. If the post URL is http://example.com/2008/foobar.html, for instance, you would search Google for exactly that URL. If you're lucky, the top result will be the post in question, containing a link reading Cached below it. Click the link and you can copy the older version (though it may well not be the first version of the post).

Yahoo! has a very similar feature; if the Google cache turns out to be missing, or if the cached version by Google is too new (already reflecting the latest version of the post), try a search at Yahoo.com.

Another way to retrieve older pages is the Wayback Machine, which you can find at http://archive.org/web/web.php. In the input box on top, enter the URL (such as http://example.com/2008/foobar.html) and click the Take Me Back button. If the URL was indexed by the Wayback Machine, you will be able to see links to older versions. Follow a link and copy the page you find.

Your Google Reader version of the post may itself be an older version already, as Google caches posts. Other blog readers may have cached older versions as well. For instance, try logging in to Bloglines.com; if you've subscribed to the blog there, you can look for the specific post and copy the text for reference.

If nothing turned up yet using those methods, try searching Google or other engines for longer quotes from the blog using a phrase search (with quotes before and after the words, that is). It might be that this way, you stumble upon other blogs who posted longer quotes from the source article. A trick to find particularly long quotes is to search for several quotes from different, scattered locations of the source article all at once, like this search:

```
"monday, adam said he" "wednesday, mary then called * and" "in the end adam resigned"
```

> The more distant each phrase is from another in the source article, the better the chances that you'll find a more complete quote, not just a partial one. And the more distinct the quotes are, the better the chances that you'll retrieve pages related only to the article in question. Note you are limited to a maximum of 32 words in a Google search, but you can "compress" some space using the wild card character, an asterisk (*).

Comparing Two Versions of a File

Now, if you managed to copy the old version from somewhere, go to the live version of the post (such as http://example.com/2008/foobar.html) and copy it as well. You now have two copies of the article, but how do you compare them?

The best solution to this is decisively simple in retrospect, but nothing you'd necessarily think of automatically—Amit Agarwal of the highly informative tips and tricks blog Digital Inspiration (http://labnol.org) did, though.

Open a Google Docs document at http://docs.google.com by selecting New→Document from the menu. Give the document a fitting title, like "Foobar," and paste the oldest version of the blog post that you recovered into it. Save the document. Now select all text within the document and paste the newest version of the blog post over it. Then jump to the Revisions tab of the document, check the boxes next to the old and new versions (Figure 8-17), and click Compare Checked. The result is a nicely color-highlighted formatting of whatever word or sentence changed in the article, as shown in Figure 8-18. (Note that although the algorithmically selected highlights are not always in the most intuitive places, usually you will get an idea of what was changed.)

This approach of file comparison works with any other text document, too. If you want more features than the Google comparison offers you, you can look into desktop comparison tools—like Beyond Compare (http://scootersoftware.com/moreinfo.php)—but for a quick comparison, Google Docs works fine.

Figure 8-17.
Selecting the two relevant versions in the Google Docs Revisions tab

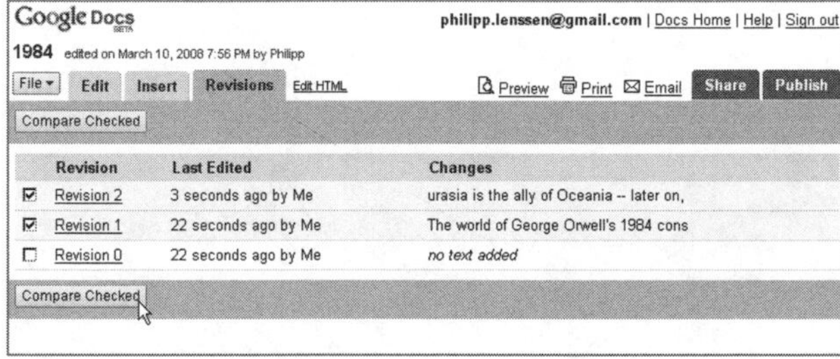

Figure 8-18.
Google Docs highlights the differences of old and new

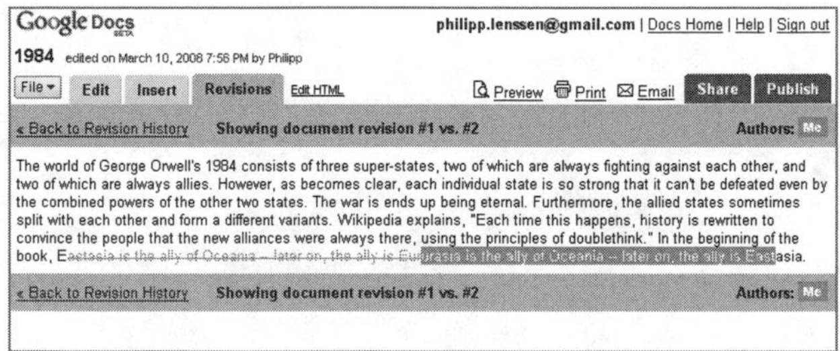

HACK 85: Beyond Google: Bloglines, Kinja, and Other Feed Readers

RSS readers usually come in two flavors: online applications and desktop applications. They also span different media, including your home computer and your mobile phone. And if you prefer, you can also channel feeds through other tools, such as email, or your browser bookmarks. Following are a few alternatives to Google Reader. Sometimes they have more features, sometimes less, and sometimes they are just different . . . and possibly, more to your taste.

Bloglines

Bloglines is one of the most well-known web-based feed readers. You can register for a free account at http://www.bloglines.com. After logging in, you will see your subscriptions to the left side and the posts to the right side, similar to what you may be used to in Google Reader (Figure 8-19). Note that as opposed to Google Reader, at Bloglines items will become read even if you haven't scrolled them into view yet (you can use the Keep New checkbox to retain items that you've loaded). Bloglines allows you to subscribe directly to package tracking numbers **[Hack #83]** and other nonfeed items.

Figure 8-19.
Bloglines, a competitor to Google Reader, with a similar basic layout

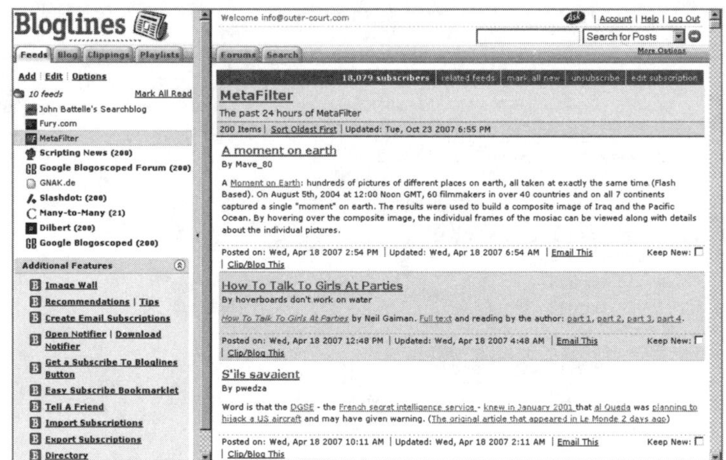

SharpReader

SharpReader is a Windows-based desktop feed reader. You can download the program for free at http://sharpreader.net; note that the .NET framework is required, so if you don't have it on your machine yet, you need to install it first from http://windowsupdate.microsoft.com.

After running the setup, the program shows in a basic three-pane view—a list of your subscriptions in the left pane, a list of posts in the top right pane, and the post itself in the bottom right pane, as shown in Figure 8-20.

NetNewsWire

NetNewsWire is a popular free feed reader for Mac OS X. You can download it from http://newsgator.com/Individuals/NetNewsWire/. NetNewsWire can use the NewsGator online feed reader to keep your RSS subscriptions in sync across multiple computers. Figure 8-21 shows NetNewsWire in action.

Figure 8-20.
Desktop feed reader SharpReader

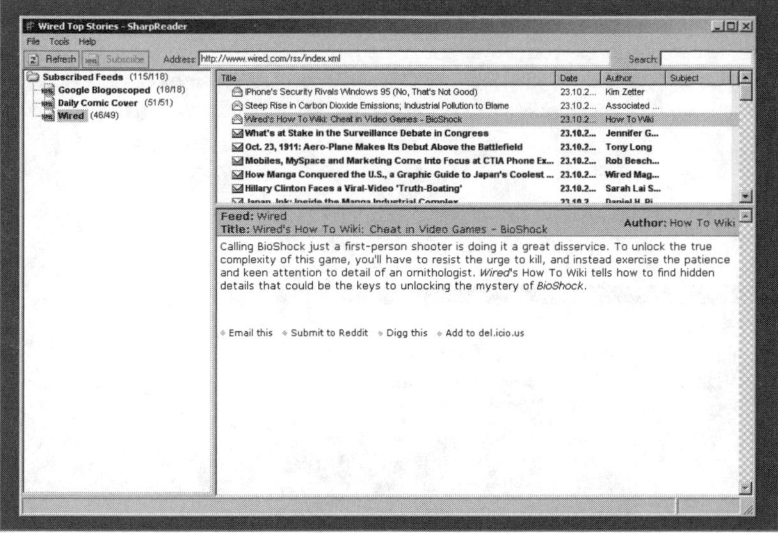

Figure 8-21.
The NetNewsWire feed reader

The big con of a desktop application is that you need to install it on every machine you are using, and you can't easily share items from your subscriptions (other than storing an OPML export of your subscription online; luckily, SharpReader and NetNewsWire do support OPML). But desktop readers also have some pros compared to web apps like Google Reader. For one thing, desktop readers will pop up notifications when new items have arrived, whether or not you have a web browser window open in the first place. It's also more common for desktop readers to enable you to access password-protected feeds, a feature available in NetNewsWire but not Google Reader.

SendMeRSS

Even if you don't want to leave your email client, you can keep up with feeds. A service named SendMeRSS, available at http://sendmerss.com/, allows you to subscribe to any feed via email; that is, new posts will be sent to a mail address you provide. Just input the blog feed of choice along with your email address into the web site, as shown in Figure 8-22, and click the Subscribe button. Now check your email inbox and approve the SendMeRSS confirmation by clicking the link in the message.

Figure 8-22.
SendMeRSS sends new posts of RSS feeds to your email address

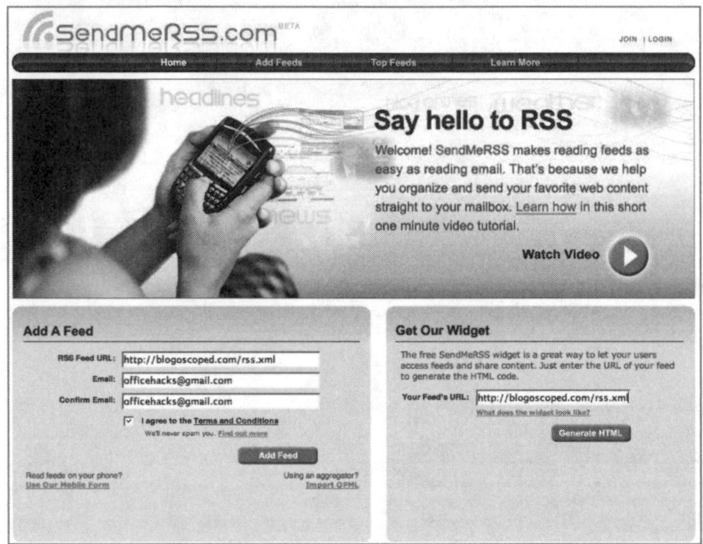

Kinja

Kinja is a feed reader with a good-looking, rather minimalist interface. After registering for free at http://kinja.com and making your choice of subscriptions, new posts from any of your feeds will be mixed with each other to create a single news page, as shown in Figure 8-23. By default, you will see only a snippet of every post—even if the feed is published with full content—so you can quickly scan posts. The "read more . . ." link attached to every item takes you to the article's source.

Figure 8-23.
Kinja's personalized feed stream

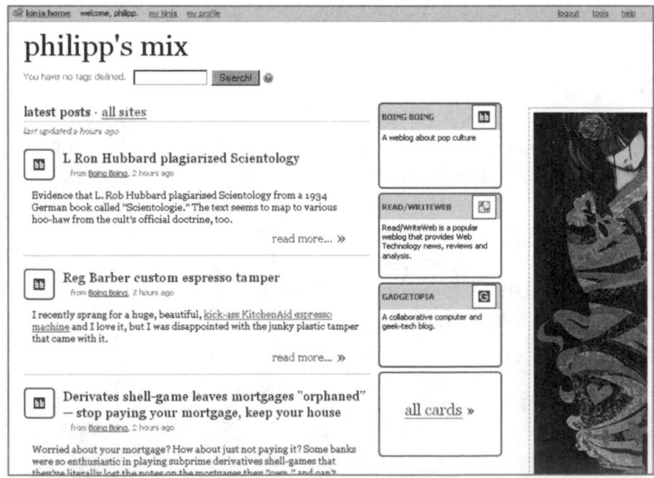

Kinja also publishes an RSS feed for your subscription mix; look for that link at the bottom of your reading list when you're logged in. This is called "feed splicing" and means that you can subscribe to the specific mix in yet another feed reader.

FriendFeed

FriendFeed (http://friendfeed.com) allows you to plug in several of your friend's RSS feeds at once—like their blog feed, their Amazon wishlist, their shared Google Reader items, their favorite YouTube videos, or whatever feeds they've defined in their profile. (And for people who don't have

Figure 8-24.
FriendFeed showing new items from people you subscribed to

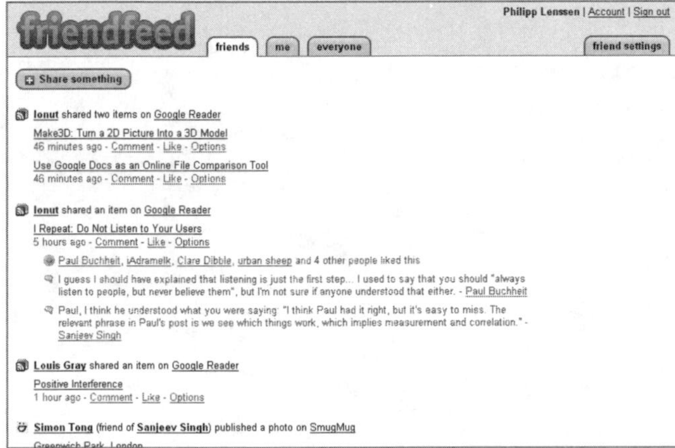

a FriendFeed feed profile configured, you can set up your own "imaginary friend" profile.) You will then get a stream of their activity, which you and others can comment on, as shown in Figure 8-24. Thanks to the "Share something" button, you can also use FriendFeed as your microblogging app. Simple, social, and addictive!

Netvibes

Netvibes (http://netvibes.com) is both a personalized home page—in the style of iGoogle (see Chapter 6)—as well as one of the many ways to digest RSS. After registering with the site, click "Add content" in the top left and select the "Add a feed" link. You can now provide a single RSS or Atom feed, or the URL of a home page containing such a feed, or you can browse for an OPML file on your disk that contains your existing subscriptions **[Hack #78]**.

Blog feeds or other feeds that you subscribe to will show as little gadget boxes on your Netvibes home page, as pictured in Figure 8-25. Clicking an item will take you to the Netvibes feed reader shown in Figure 8-26.

Live Bookmarks

If you are using Firefox as your browser, you can subscribe to any feed using the Live Bookmarks feature. To do so, open the drop-down box displayed on a feed that you're viewing in Firefox, select Live Bookmarks, and click the Subscribe Now button. If you check your bookmarks, you will now find a new folder containing the latest items from this subscription. As the name indicates, Live Bookmarks will change over time to add new items as they are published, so it's quite different from a traditional static bookmark.

Note that you can also display Live Bookmarks in your navigation toolbar for quick access, as shown in Figure 8-27.

Figure 8-25.
The Netvibes home page, customized to display your feeds selection

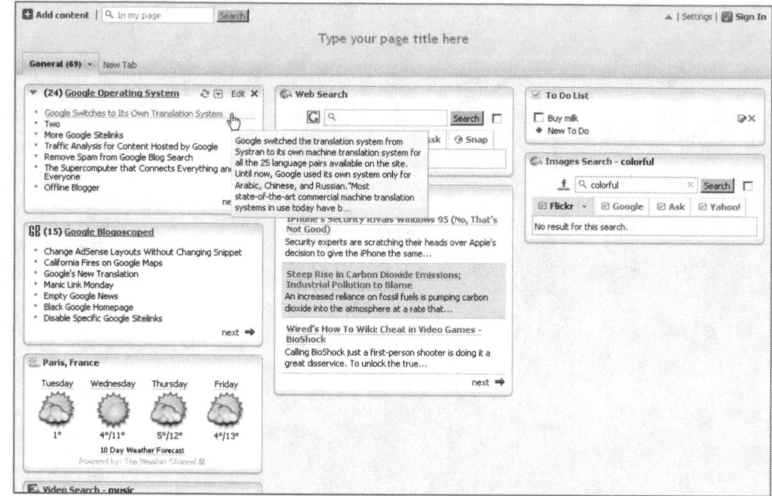

Figure 8-26.
The Netvibes feed reader post view

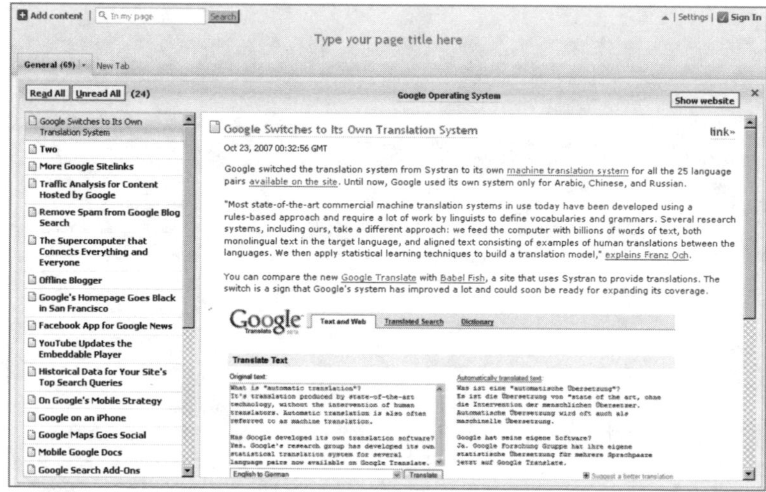

Also, Internet Explorer 7 and the Mac OS X Safari browser both allow you to add RSS bookmarks by clicking the orange RSS icon that appears to the right of the URL in the browser's location bar.

Figure 8-27.
Live Bookmarks expanded in the bookmarks toolbar in Firefox

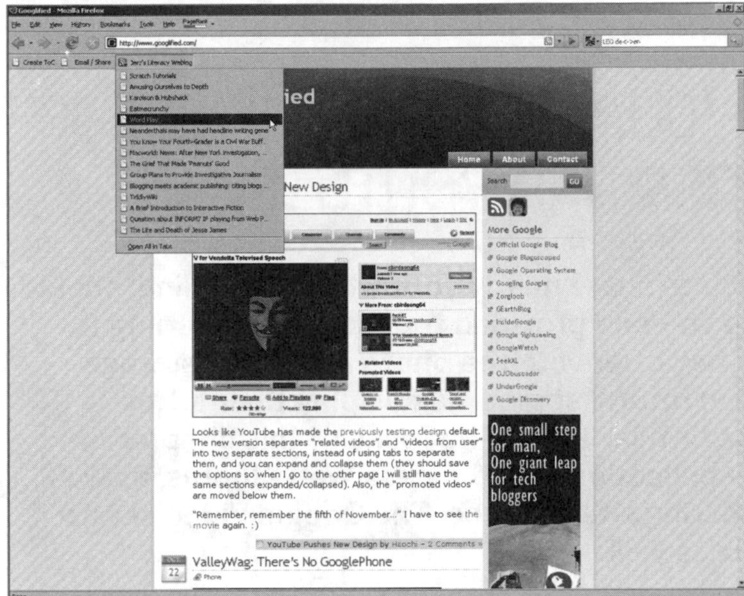

09 MANAGE YOUR PHOTOS AND VIDEOS WITH PICASA AND YOUTUBE

Google allows you to share nearly your whole life online, should you decide to do so—and provided that you are recording it with a camera. They offer you free photo and video storage capabilities and in return, sometimes display their advertisements on top or near them. The focus of this chapter is Google's photo application called Picasa Web Albums, as well as their video-sharing site YouTube. The Google Video service is part of the mix as well.

Sign Up for YouTube

YouTube, shown in Figure 9-1, is a video-sharing site with many community-oriented features: you can subscribe to a friend's video channels, privately share videos, comment on videos, or add videos to your list of favorites and then share them with others.

If you don't have a YouTube account yet, you can use your Google account to sign up **[Hack #1]**. Visit http://youtube.com and click the "Login with your Google account" link. Enter your Google account credentials if requested. You will then be asked a few details for your YouTube account creation, such as your preferred username, your country, and your postal code. Complete this step of the registration and you're in.

Figure 9-1.
The YouTube home page. The top section to the left shows videos being watched at the time by other users.

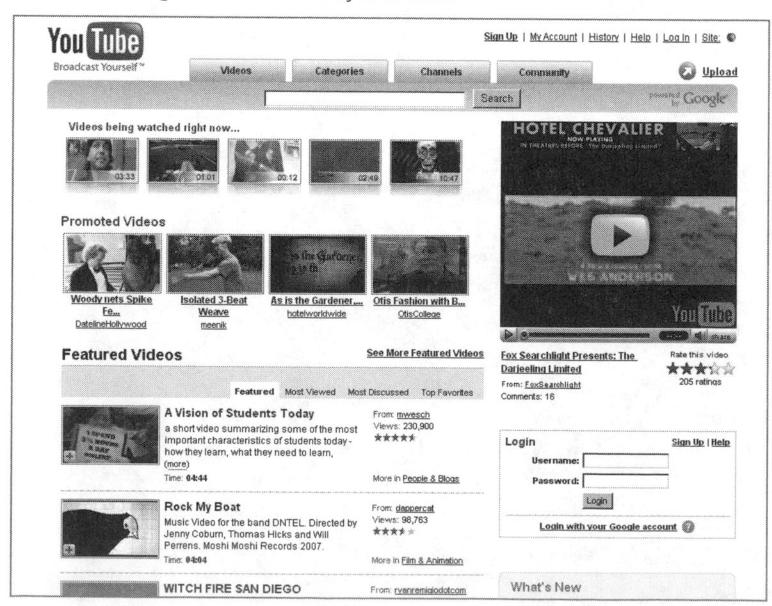

Take some time to browse through the different YouTube tabs on top showing categories and channels, or use the YouTube search box to find content on your favorite topics—from origami tutorials and tech talks to student pranks or music videos. Also check out your My Account page linked at the top; this is your personal control center to modify profile settings or go back to videos that you've added.

To upload a video, click the Upload button and provide your video details, such as tags (related keywords for your video), description, and title. You can then either record a video with your webcam, or pick an existing file from your hard disk to upload and convert. YouTube supports the file formats WMV, MPG, MOV, and AVI.

When you add videos, YouTube warns that they don't allow you to upload copyrighted content but also note that under U.S. laws, you have certain "Fair Use" rights to use some copyrighted material.

> To find out more about Fair Use laws when remixing other people's content, http://copyright.gov/fls/fl102.html is a good start. Also check out what the Creative Commons initiative might have to offer for your needs **[Hack #31]**.

In any case, you will not be able to upload videos that are longer than 10 minutes, which is one of the ways that YouTube tries to protect against the sharing of copyrighted movies. Also, the video file size is restricted to 100 MB, though if you find yourself ending up with too-large files, try compressing them using tools such as Apple iMovie or Windows MovieMaker.

> Can't see the actual videos? Some proxies—think of a proxy as a layer between your company or school's network and the free-roaming Internet outside—disallow Flash content, but Flash is required for YouTube playback. If you experience problems, the best thing may be to ask your network administrator to allow Flash.

> Do you have precise control over the video format you're recording? If so, YouTube suggests that for the highest-quality results, you save the file as MPEG4 (DivX, Xvid, SQV3) at 320 x 240 pixels, with a 64k mono MP3 audio track.

YouTube versus Google Video

Google Video (http://video.google.com) also allows you to upload your videos at this time, though Google has decided to de-emphasize this feature and turn Google Video, pictured in Figure 9-2, into a "meta" video search engine instead of a personal video sharing site. However, give Google Video a try to see if it's to your liking. It has certain native features, like subtitling of videos **[Hack #90]**, or downloading them for the iPod and PlayStation Portable, which the Google-owned YouTube lacks. Plus, you can reuse your Google Account credentials as usual to log in.

Sign Up for a Picasa Web Album

Google's photo manager, Picasa, comes as a desktop application as well as a web app called Picasa Web Albums, shown in Figure 9-3. You can find it at http://picasaweb.google.com, and you can log in with your Google Account. After accepting the terms of service, start by clicking the Upload Photos button.

Figure 9-2.
The front page of the Google Video search engine

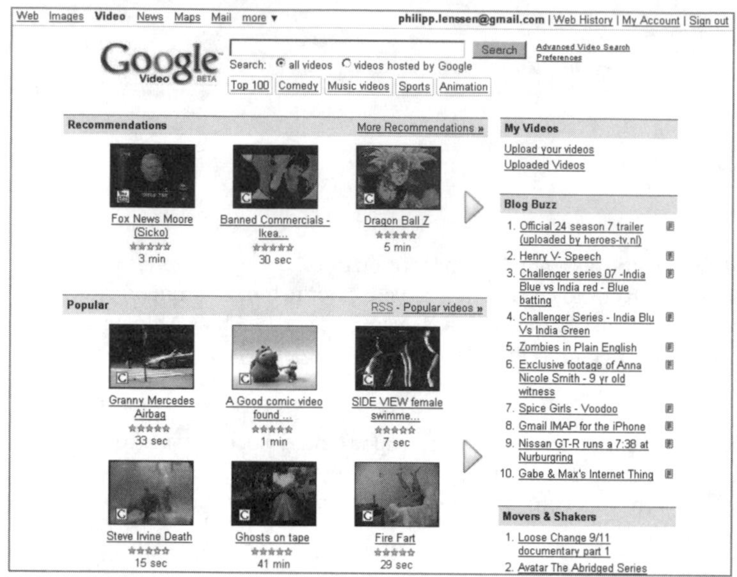

Figure 9-3.
An album in Picasa

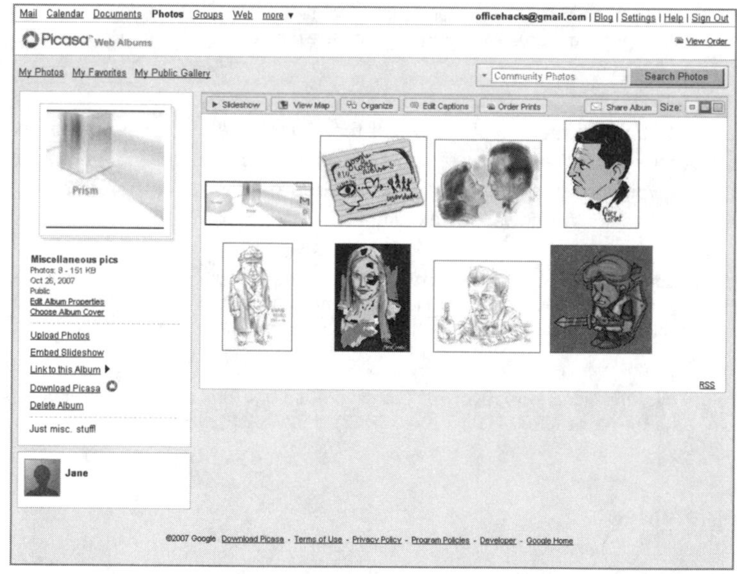

Before adding pictures in Picasa, you are required to create an *album*. Each album is a collection of related photos or pictures, and it has a title, a description, and (optionally) a location. When you create the album, you can set it to be *public* or *unlisted.* A public album can be found by others using the Picasa search tool, so naturally it shouldn't contain any photo content that you don't feel comfortable sharing with the world—and remember that sometimes, things you upload may "survive" on the Web and leave their marks in the future even when you delete them later on. The other option is to make the album unlisted. Unlisted albums won't be made available to strangers, but you can still share their URLs with friends. It's sort of in-between a web page that is password-protected and a web page that is public.

Once you create an album, Google offers you a basic uploader option or an advanced version. To use the advanced uploader, you need to approve a security dialog to install a special browser plug-in.

The advantage of the advanced uploader is an instant thumbnail preview, along with the ability to drag and drop images from your hard disk onto the preview area, as shown in Figure 9-4.

By default, Picasa gives you 1 GB of storage space. Note that you can buy additional storage space as part of Google's Shared Storage service. Just follow the Upgrade Storage link on the upload page; the current rates are $20 per year for 10 GB up to 400 GB for $500 per year, paid with Google Checkout. As a bonus, you will be able to share this storage space with your Gmail account.

Figure 9-4.
The Picasa uploader in its advanced version

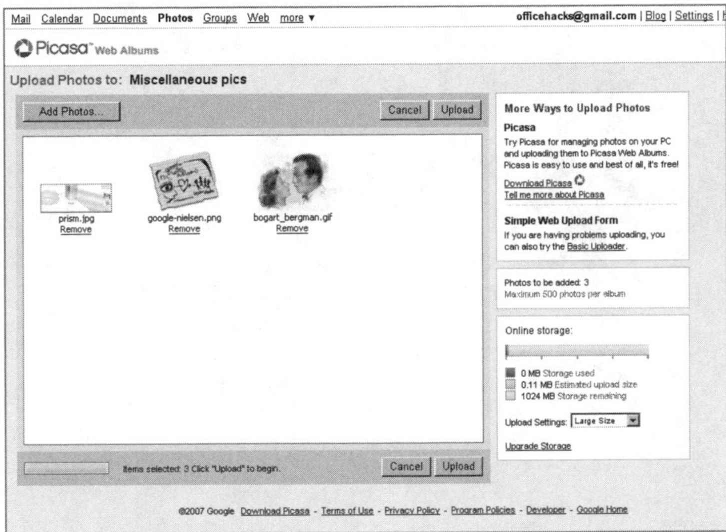

When your photos are uploaded and public, other people can browse them, zoom into them (if your original image is bigger than the default display size), link to the photo, add comments, or order prints. Each album can also be watched as a slideshow. As album owner, you can also add tags and captions, or connect a photo to a real-world location **[Hack #92]**.

HACK 86: Turn a Picasa Photo Feed Into a Screensaver

Arguably the best screensaver is the one that's customized to you, and the easiest way to customize a screensaver is to feed it your existing pictures.

RSS feeds can contain both text and image content. Picasa's Web Albums utilize this to create a photo feed from any album you choose, and you can plug this feed into Google's own screensaver to create a slideshow.

> The Google screensaver is available only for Windows at this time.

Grab Your Picasa Photo Feed

First, locate your Picasa album at http://picasaweb.google.com, as shown in Figure 9-5. If the album is public, the URL will look like the following (where "Jane Doe" is the name, and "Holiday" the album title):

```
http://picasaweb.google.com/jane.doe/holiday
```

Your album page already has an Embed Slideshow feature in the navigation pane, allowing you to include a slideshow gadget into other web pages. But on the bottom right side of the page, you will also find a link called RSS. Right-click it, and copy the link to your clipboard using the menu that appears.

Figure 9-5.
Each Picasa web album contains an RSS link

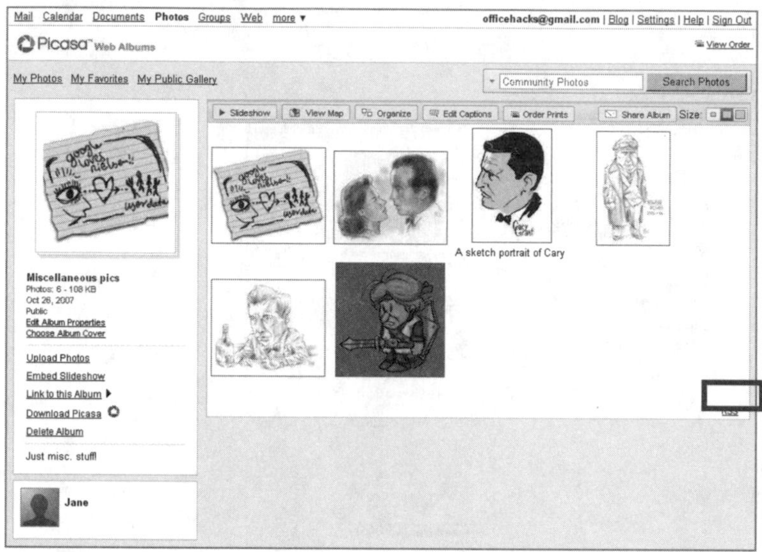

Install and set up the screensaver on Windows

Now, install the Google Pack screensaver, which can render a photo feed into something good-looking. Go to http://pack.google.com and in the software options, uncheck everything but the box reading Google Photos Screensaver. Click Download Google Pack, and accept the terms of service, if you agree with them. Google notifies you a program called Google Updater will be installed. Download and run the executable that you are offered and wait for the installation to complete.

Now open your screensaver settings by right-clicking the desktop, selecting Properties and switching to the Screen Saver tab. Google Photos Screensaver should already be selected in the selection box. Press the Settings button next to it, and in the dialog that opens, click the Configure button to the side of the Photo feeds option, as pictured in Figure 9-6 (this is more flexible than picking the Picasa Web Albums option—but more on that later). Paste your Picasa album's feed URL you noted earlier into the input box and click Add. Uncheck the default Google photo feed, as shown in Figure 9-7, and approve the dialog by clicking Done. Your photo feed is now set up and will rotate your album pictures whenever your screensaver kicks in!

Getting photo feeds from other places

Note that the Google Photo Screensaver also has an option specifically tailored to Picasa web albums only. You will find it in the screensaver's settings dialog, and all you need to do is provide your Google Account credentials, and then toggle whether you want unlisted albums to appear in the slideshow as well. But the general photo feed option also lets you use albums from other galleries—like the ones by photo community Flickr. To give this a try, search for a keyword of your choice at http://flickr.com and check to see whether the results are satisfactory. If they are, you can form the RSS feed URL as in the following example, where "horse" is replaced with your keyword of choice:

```
http://api.flickr.com/services/feeds/photos_public.gne?tags=horse
```

If you have an Amazon.com books/product wish list, you will also be able to grab its photo feed; look for the orange RSS icon on any public wish list page.

Figure 9-6.
The Google Photos Screensaver settings

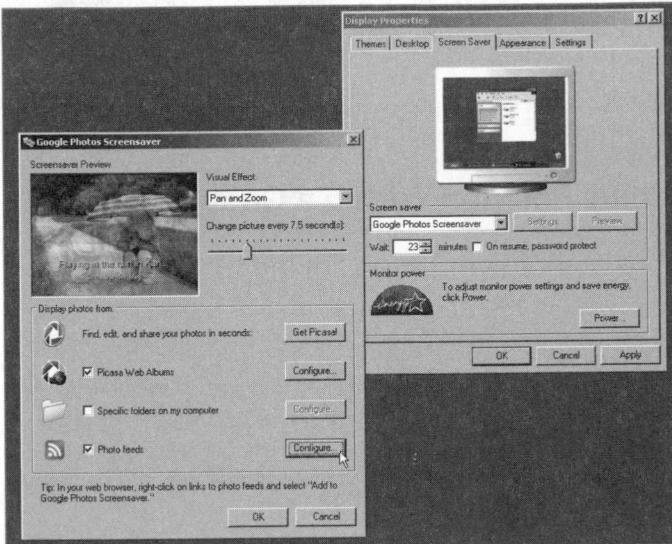

Figure 9-7.
The Picasa feed URL has been added

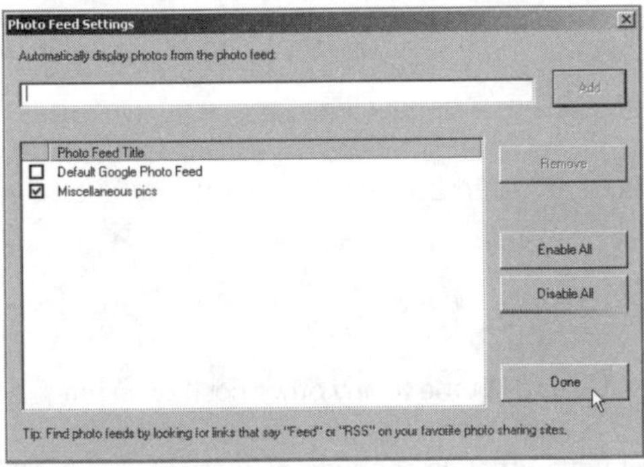

Yahoo! also offers several photo feeds throughout their site. Here are some of them:

- Yahoo! News: Highlights—http://rss.news.yahoo.com/imgrss/441
- Yahoo! News: World—http://rss.news.yahoo.com/imgrss/708
- Yahoo! News: Most emailed—http://rss.news.yahoo.com/imgrss/1756
- Yahoo! Sports—http://sports.yahoo.com/top/photos/rss.xml
- Yahoo! Sports: NBA—http://sports.yahoo.com/nba/photos/rss.xml
- Yahoo! News: Entertainment—http://rss.news.yahoo.com/imgrss/707

At http://images.yahoo.com, Yahoo also offers a photo feed for each of their image search results. For instance, the feed URL when searching for "horse" is (split into two lines):

```
http://api.search.yahoo.com/ImageSearchService/rss/
        imageSearch.xml?appid=yahoosearchimagerss&query=horse
```

By appending and incrementing another parameter, `start` (`&start=0`, `&start=1`, `&start=2`, etc.), you can also subscribe to multiple feeds for a single query to get more photos. For information of additional parameters of this feed, like `output`, `adult_ok`, or `coloration`, please see the Yahoo Image Search Web Service documentation at http://developer.yahoo.com/search/image/V1/imageSearch.html.

HACK 87: Link to a Specific Position Within a Google Video

Don't beat about the bush—not even when linking to video content.

Demetrius is a blogger who regularly points to video content. Today he wants to link to a longer Google Video, which he found using the advanced search options at http://video.google.com/videoadvancedsearch (he restricted results to documentaries with a duration of over 20 minutes). But his blog post discusses only the revealing bit into the twelfth minute of the video, and Demetrius would like to send his visitors straight to that part, too.

Lucky for Demetrius—and you, if you want to point to a specific position within a Google Video—Google offers a feature to achieve this. A normal Google Video URL looks like the following:

```
http://video.google.com/videoplay?docid=-5858262932217432628
```

Play the movie until the part you want to point to, and check the minutes and seconds shown in the video status bar. Let's say that it's reading 12:20 / 1:32:45, meaning that you are seeing minute 12 of a roughly 1.5-hour-long documentary. Now you can append "#12m20s" to the URL—the notation is "m" for minutes and "s" for seconds—like here:

```
http://video.google.com/videoplay?docid=-5858262932217432628#12m20s
```

Note that your visitors are still able to scroll back and forward in time to any other position in the video; this style of linking determines only the starting point at which the video plays back, while saving some time, as it won't load the full video buffer first. Although appending the time works at the Google Video site, it won't work in embedded videos.

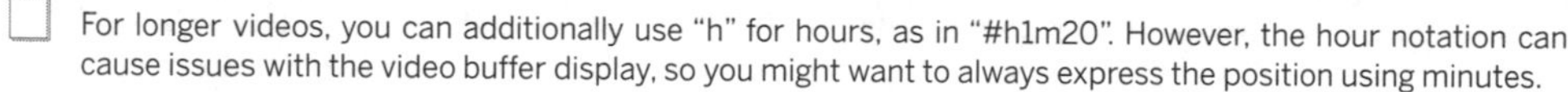

For longer videos, you can additionally use "h" for hours, as in "#h1m20". However, the hour notation can cause issues with the video buffer display, so you might want to always express the position using minutes.

HACK 88: Watch Videos on Your Cellphone

Looking for video content to show around to buddies on the train, in a bar, or everywhere else you can carry a cellphone with you?

YouTube offers you a mobile version of their home page at http://m.youtube.com. When you visit the site for the first time, you will receive a warning message informing you that this is a "data-intensive application" that may incur some extra mobile phone charges unless you have an unlimited data plan. After confirming this warning, you will be presented with a list of videos, each displayed along with a thumbnail, a link, and a rating, as shown in Figure 9-8. There is also a search box, and a list of video categories to visit.

Figure 9-8. YouTube mobile

Clicking a video link takes you to a video page with a larger thumbnail image and a link to watch the video. The actual video is delivered through RTSP, short for Real Time Streaming Protocol. For instance, if Real Player is available on your cellphone, you might be able to view these videos.

However, this does not work with all phones; for instance, it did not work on Internet Explorer for Windows Mobile when tested here.

Also, the iPhone natively supports playback of YouTube videos. If you're not lucky enough to own an iPhone, an alternative for Symbian Series 60 3rd Edition–based phones is the program emTube, which you can download at http://schierwagen.de/blog/support/. The Symbian operating system is commonly used on Nokia, and also some other phones. Another option for watching YouTube videos on Series 60 3rd Edition is the free video management and playback program MobiTubia available from http://mobitubia.com.

HACK 89: Optimize Streaming When Embedding Multiple YouTube Videos

Using a bit of your own JavaScript, improve the download speed when embedding more than a single YouTube video on one page.

Sometimes it makes sense to include a couple of YouTube videos in a single blog post all at once—for instance, when you're writing a post entitled "My 10 favorite music videos on YouTube." Although YouTube already provides some embedding code that you can cut and paste, there's one catch: your visitors, when playing back a video you include on your site, may decide they've seen enough of it; they can then hit the pause button on the YouTube player to start playing the next video in line. However, the old player will still be trying to download and buffer the paused video, causing noticeable delays for any subsequent videos that are being played on the same page (unless the visitor decides to refresh the page, or simply leaves it). As you can imagine, this gets worse with every new video that the visitor starts playing and then pauses.

Some JavaScript is needed here to optimize this default behavior for embedding multiple videos. What you want is to give the visitor the ability to truly cancel a video download without leaving the page.

For reference, this is the current default code to embed a YouTube player (the video ID is highlighted, as this part changes with every video):

```
<object width="425" height="355"><param name="movie" value="http://www.youtube.com/
v/7lyZUt6ueTM name="&rel=1"></param><paramwmode" value="transparent"></param><embed
src="http://www.youtube.com/v/7lyZUt6ueTM&rel=1" type="application/x-shockwave-flash"
wmode="transparent" width="425" height="355"></embed></object>
```

That's quite a bit of code. You will notice that both an `object` and an `embed` tag are being used; the redundancy is caused by the need to support different browsers. However you can simplify this portion by "outsourcing" it into a static JavaScript file which you link in your blog template. You can then include a link reading "Show video," as pictured in Figure 9-9, which triggers the JavaScript function to write the actual embed code to the browser. This is the HTML portion needed (the video ID is highlighted again):

```
<p id="expander1" class="expander">
  <strong>
    <a href="javascript:showVideo(1, '7lyZUt6ueTM')">+ Show video</a>
  </strong>
</p>
<p class="expandee" id="expandee1" style="display: none">
   
</p>
```

Figure 9-9.
Of the three "Show video" links in this forum thread at Google Blogoscoped, the middle one has been expanded. Others can be expanded at the same time; when you collapse a section again, it will stop buffering.

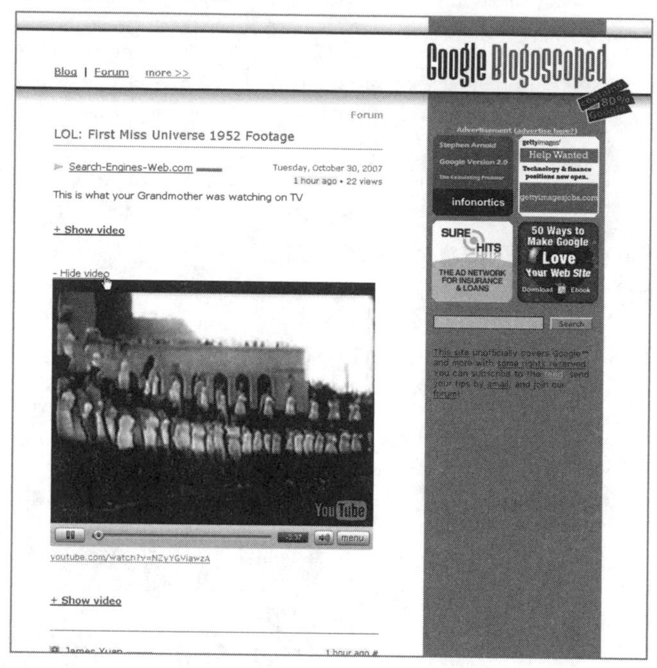

The first parameter shown in the snippet—"1" in this example—is incremented throughout your HTML file to differentiate one HTML block from the next while handling it. As you can see, there is an "expander" and an "expandee," the latter being just a placeholder to carry your embed code. And the following is the JavaScript function to actually show that embed code, along with two general functions to dynamically show and hide HTML elements (note that "element" is abbreviated as "elm" in the code). Include the code by creating an external JavaScript file (in this example, it's named *player.js*), linked from within your HTML `<head>` section using `<script type="text/javascript" src="player.js"></script>`. Alternatively, you can also put it into your blog template for every page, wrapped within `<script type="text/javascript">...</script>`:

```
function showVideo(n, videoId) {
  showElm("expandee" + n);
  hideElm("expander" + n);
  var elm = document.getElementById("expandee" + n);
  if (elm) {
    elm.innerHTML = "<a href=\"javascript:hideVideo(" + n +
      ",'" + videoId + "')\">- Hide video</a><br />" +
      "<object style=\"width: 500px; height: 412px\"><param name=\"movie\" " +
      "value=\"http://www.youtube.com/v/" + videoId +
      "&amp;autoplay=1\"></param>" +
      "<embed src=\"http://www.youtube.com/v/" +
      videoId + "&amp;autoplay=1\" type=\"application/x-shockwave-flash\" " +
      "style=\"width: 500px; height: 412px\"></object>" +
      "<br /><a href=\"http://youtube.com/watch?v=" + videoId +
      "\" style=\"color: #888; font-size: 85%\">" +
      "youtube.com/watch?v=" + videoId + "</a>";
  }
}
```

```
function showElm(name) {
  var elm = document.getElementById(name);
  if (elm) { elm.style.display = "block"; }
}

function hideElm(name) {
  var elm = document.getElementById(name);
  if (elm) { elm.style.display = "none"; }
}
```

As you can see, the `showVideo` function hides the "expander" element but shows the "expandee" element. It will then fill the "expandee" element with the YouTube embed code, and also add a link reading "Hide video" to collapse the video again. The height and width of the player in this example are slightly adjusted to be a bit larger than the default size, but there's another specialty with this embed code: it carries the "autoplay=1" flag, because you don't want your visitors to have to click the play button once more when they've already clicked your "Show video" link.

What happens when the user now presses the "Hide video" link? The following JavaScript will be triggered—and this time, the video buffer stops loading, too, at least in the popular browsers that this has been tested with:

```
function hideVideo(n, videoId) {

  var elm = document.getElementById("expandee" + n);
  if (elm) {
    elm.innerHTML = " ";
  }
  showElm("expander" + n);
  hideElm("expandee" + n);
}
```

HACK 90: Add Subtitles to a Google Video

Allow video viewers to get the message of your film even without hearing any sound. This can be suitable both for hearing-impaired viewers as well as people who watch your videos in an office environment.

Google Video provides the option to add subtitles to any video you've uploaded. To try this, upload a video by going to http://video.google.com and following the "Upload your videos" link. Google accepts the formats AVI, MOV, WMV, MPEG, and Real.

Once you've uploaded your video and it has been approved and processed—this may take some time—you will notice an add button next to the label Captions/subtitles on your Uploaded Videos page. The plain text format of the captions you can enter into Google Video is the time code where the caption begins, followed by the caption itself, followed by the time when the caption ends.

Here is a sample bit, also shown in Figure 9-10:

```
00:00:06.000
I am glad to welcome you to a new show of Animals Today.
00:00:08.900
00:00:15.000
Today we're going to discuss the secret life of dolphins.
...
```

Figure 9-10.
Providing subtitles for Google Video

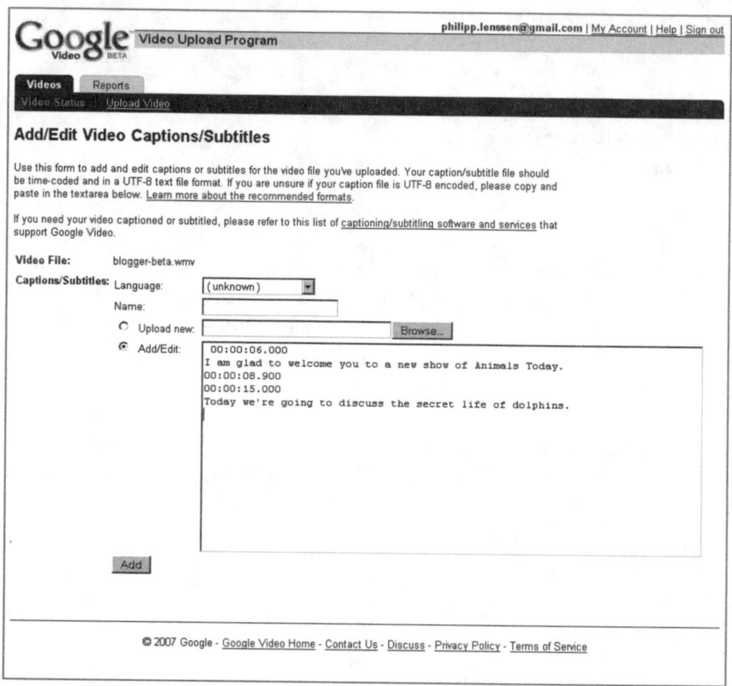

Creating the time codes and captions manually would be too much work in most circumstances. Ideally, you'd be able to see the video and subtitle it by just typing your text below it, in real time. There's a great and free tool available to achieve just that, too: Subtitle Horse at http://subtitle-horse.org.

When you visit Subtitle Horse, you are first required to provide a video URL. Here is a sample URL that I will enter (the video is a tour through Blogger's visual template rearrangement features):

```
http://video.google.com/videoplay?docid=-6552945338831467357&hl=en
```

Click the Submit button and you will find a Flash-based tool to add subtitles to the video, as shown in Figure 9-11. When the video plays, enter captions in the box below it, and press the Return key when you're done. Complete the process for the whole video. Finally, select the Subtitle Horse menu entry reading Import/Export and choose the "export subtitles" option. Choose the player format "video.google" and copy the resulting snippet to your clipboard.

Now go back to the Google Video subtitle submission page, paste your copied text, and hit the Add button. Please note that the subtitles may take a while before they appear in your video. When they do, the result will be similar to the one shown in Figure 9-12.

Figure 9-11.
Subtitle Horse makes creating caption files easy

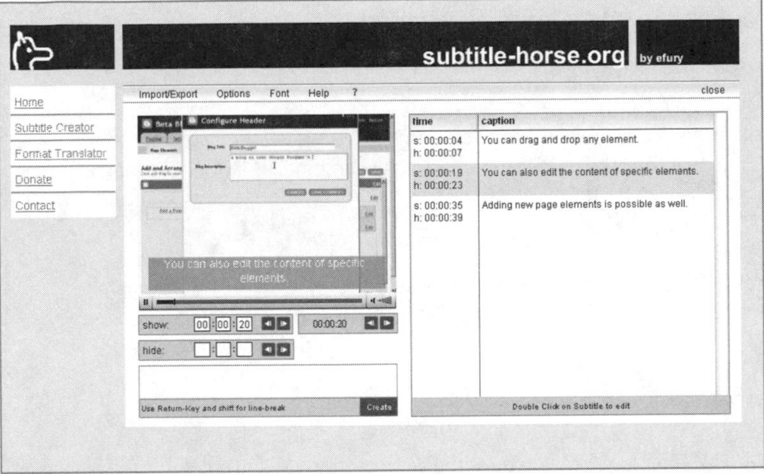

Figure 9-12.
Subtitles on a video showcasing Blogger

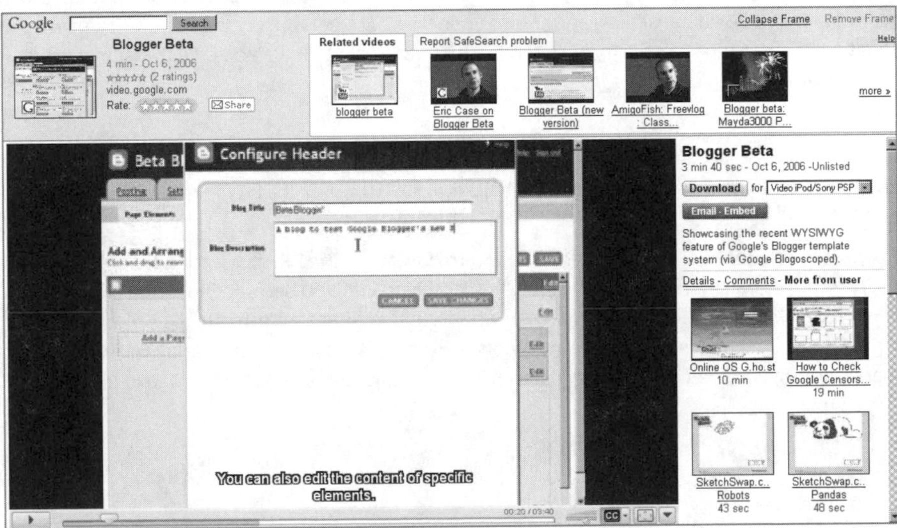

HACK 91: Download a YouTube or Google Video Film for Offline Consumption

Create an offline video library by downloading content from YouTube and Google Video.

Google Video sometimes offers you a link to download a video, but not always. And YouTube never displays this functionality. What if you want to have the video on your local hard disk, so you can watch it without having to wait for the file to buffer, or view it when you're not online?

There's a solution for this: several sites offer a service to download YouTube and Google Video films for offline viewing. The format you will end up with is called FLV (Flash Video), so all you need then is a local FLV player.

First, locate the video address in question. Go to http://youtube.com or http://video.google.com, and jump to a specific video, as shown in Figure 9-13. At YouTube, the URL will look something like the following—copy down the address to convert it later on:

```
http://www.youtube.com/watch?v=4xQja0XMxfg
```

Google Video, on the other hand, searches through different video sites. To find just content uploaded to Google Video itself, use the "site" operator when searching, as in the following example:

```
site:google.com cats
```

Alternatively, you can also select the checkbox below the search box reading "videos hosted by Google." The video address you end up with will be similar to the following one (I've removed unimportant parameters from the URL):

```
http://video.google.com/videoplay?docid=-2068277021797460895
```

Second, download the FLV file. Now that you have the video address, different sites are available to convert the video to a download. KeepVid at http://keepvid.com is one of them, and it has an easy-to-use interface, as shown in Figure 9-14. (Or try a Google search for "download youtube" and you'll find a number of alternatives.) Just paste the video address into the input box and click the Download button. The download link will now appear somewhere below the input box. Click that link and wait for the download to finish. Now rename the video file to have an FLV extension; that is, change it from *get_video* to *get_video.flv*.

> You can also include a KeepVid download button in your browser. Just drag the button at the top right of the KeepVid home page onto your links toolbar. It's labeled "Drag this button onto your links toolbar" in Figure 9-14. Then, when you are on a YouTube or Google Video video page, click the button reading "Keep It!". This will forward you to KeepVid, where you can then pick the download link.

If you're using Firefox, there's an alternative solution to download the FLV file, and it doesn't require a third-party site: you can install the Firebug extension, which lets you see and individually download all the files the browser requests, including Flash videos. Install Firebug from http://getfirebug.com; a browser restart will be necessary. Then, pick Tools→Firebug→Open Firebug from the menu. If a link appears offering you to Enable Firebug, click it as well. Now visit the YouTube page in question and let it load for a bit.

Figure 9-13.
The YouTube video, still online-only

Figure 9-14.
KeepVid converts addresses of YouTube or Google Video films into downloadable files

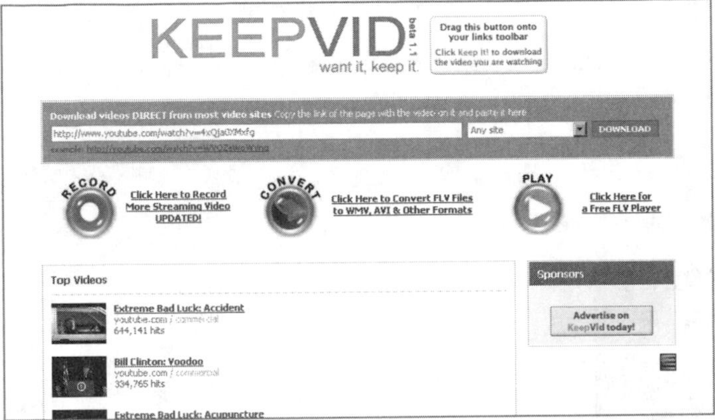

In the Firebug pane, you will notice a list of files appearing. The FLV file in question should be the largest file in the list named *get_video*, as pointed to in Figure 9-15. Right-click this file listing and choose Open in New Tab; your FLV download will now start. (You may want to disable Firebug afterwards, as it can slow down certain sites.) As discussed previously, rename the downloaded file so that it will have an **.flv* extension.

Third, get an FLV player to view the downloaded video. You've got the video file on your hard disk now but chances are that you don't have a viewer for it. You will need to install an FLV player to run the file.

To find an FLV player for your platform, try a Google search for "Windows FLV player," "Mac FLV Player," and so on. For instance, a free FLV player for Windows XP and Vista by a company named Applian Technologies is available at the address http://applian.com/flvplayer/download_flv_player.php. Another Windows player can be downloaded via http://martijndevisser.com/blog/flv-player/. A Mac OS X player called Wimpy is available at http://wimpyplayer.com/products/wimpy_standalone_flv_player.html. If you don't mind going through configuring HTML files to embed the

Figure 9-15.
Firebug reveals the Flash video file that you want to download

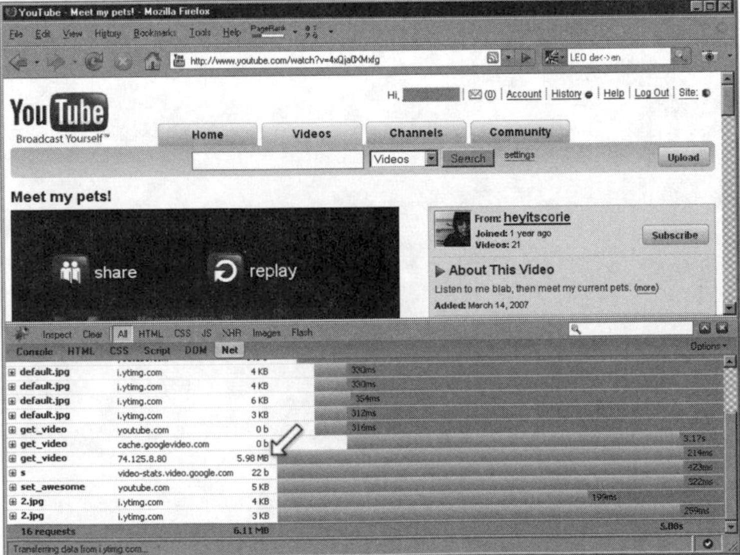

video in, the HTML/Flash-based player available at http://jeroenwijering.com/?item=JW_FLV_Player is an option as well, and it works across different operating systems (as long as you have Flash installed in your browser).

Once installed, you can open your *.flv file with the respective player, as shown in Figure 9-16 using the program by Applian Technologies.

Figure 9-16.
The Applian Technologies FLV player in action (from a video by heyitscorie)

Finding the right videos

Any kind of video content will work with this download hack, but longer films might be especially suited for an offline library. Although YouTube restricts all video content to 10 minutes, Google Video allows longer movies—like full documentaries.

To find such longer films, click on the Advanced Video Search link on the Google Video home page. In the Duration box, choose Long (> 20 min). Under Genre, click the item named "specific genres," if you want to, and check Documentary or Movie (feature) and so on. After hitting the search button, depending on your search settings, thousands of videos will appear. As some of these movie files will be quite large now, an overnight download can make sense. Happy watching!

If you want to edit downloaded FLV videos, you might first want to convert them to a more common format. On Windows you can use the free SUPER converter found at the bottom of http://www.erightsoft.com/SUPER.html to then convert to AVI for editing in the (again free) Microsoft Windows Movie maker at http://www.microsoft.com/windowsxp/downloads/updates/moviemaker2.mspx.

HACK 92: Geotag Your Photos and Share Them on Google Maps

Connect photos to locations, and drop the whole bundle onto Google Maps for easy sharing.

Geotagging is the term for adding location information to images (among other media and data). Maybe that beautiful sunset was photographed in Ibiza, Spain, or the porcelain hamster snapshot is from an antique shop in Chicago. You know, and maybe your friend knows, but the computer programs dealing with your pictures may not know—though if you teach them, they can add a bunch of otherwise unavailable extra services on top of your photo albums.

In Google's Picasa Web Albums (http://picasaweb.google.com), geotagging is easy and visual. Just locate your album and within it, your photo. Now in the bottom right of the page, as shown in Figure 9-17, you will notice a link reading "Add location." Follow this link and a map dialog pops up where you can set the location where the photo was taken. For instance, I've entered "ibiza, spain" into the search box (no quotes), as shown in Figure 9-18, checked the map for accuracy, and confirmed with the Save location button.

Your photo will now display a small map next to it whenever you view it. Repeat this process of geotagging for all of your photos where it makes sense. Note that you will be able to drag and drop the location marker in consecutive dialogs, as your previous location will be saved for future photos.

Now that your images are prepared, you can click the "View album map" link. If your photos are part of a single holiday trip, then they will now be shown along your original route, as depicted in Figure 9-19. Clicking on an individual marker opens a small info box on top of the location containing a larger version of the image, as well as your image caption, if provided.

Figure 9-17.
Your photo in Picasa Web Albums (Photo source: U.S. National Oceanic and Atmospheric Administration.)

Figure 9-18.
The geotagging dialog

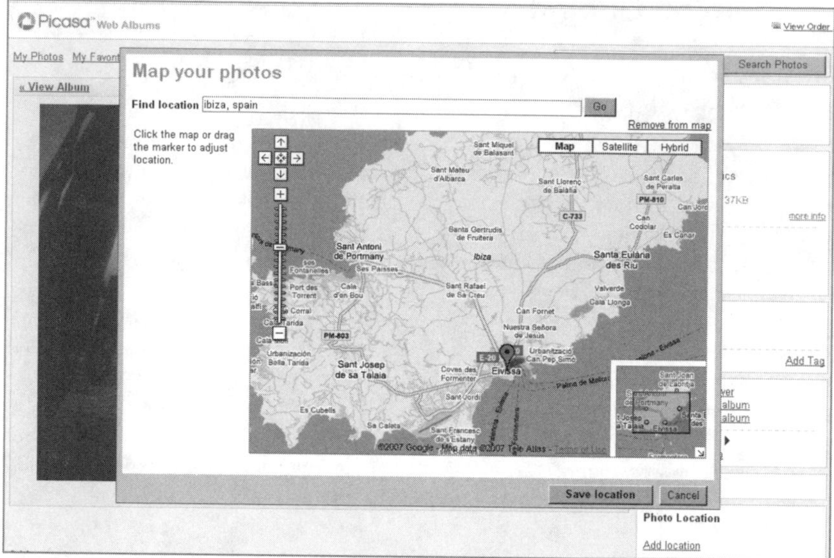

Figure 9-19.
The travel map

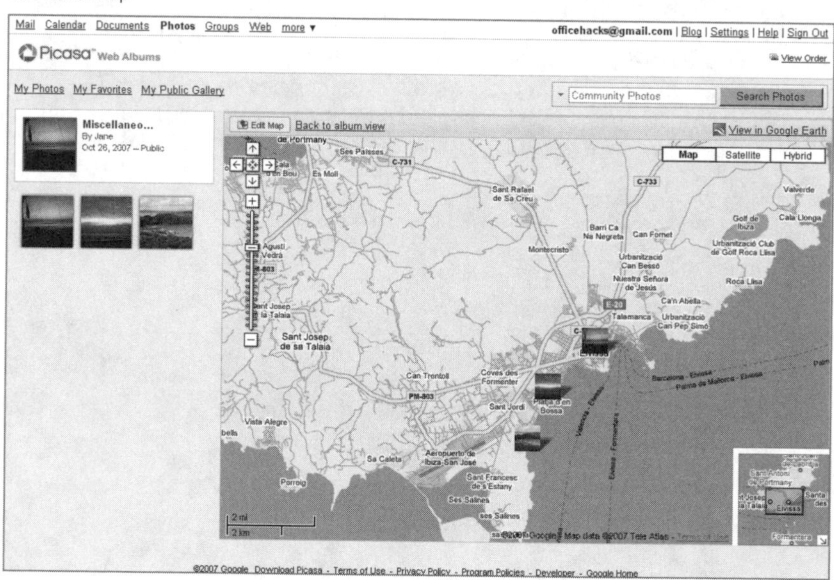

Adding Your Photos to Google Maps

As you can see in Figure 9-19, the photos are already displayed in a Google Maps widget. But you are also able to export the geographical metadata to drop it into the external Google Maps site—and from there, into your own site.

For this step, you need to grab a file of the KML format. KML means *Keyhole Markup Language*; Keyhole was the company that originally developed the program that was later turned into Google Earth, the 3D-view desktop application sibling of Google Maps. You will find the address of the file on your album page as well as your album map page, with the View in Google Earth link. Right-click the link, then use the menu that appears to copy its URL. The address will look similar to the following:

```
http://picasaweb.google.com/data/feed/base/user/officehacks/
    albumid/5125663951730983025?kind=photo&alt=kml&hl=en_US
```

However, instead of adding this to Google Earth, you can also just add it to Google Maps. Go to http://maps.google.com and paste the KML file URL into the search box and hit Search Maps. Google will recognize that you've entered the web address of a KML file and automatically display your photos on the map now. Click "Link to this page" and a new dialog opens. Here you can either select the URL to point others to, or copy an HTML snippet for inclusion on your web site, such as your blog.

Google Maps also supports KMZ files for display as a layer. KMZ is a zipped KML file. To find KMZ or KML files that others have published, you can search Google for "`filetype:kmz | filetype:kml`" (no quotes, and the | character is the vertical line or "pipe" character), and copy the URL shown below the snippet into Google Maps as before (note the URL must be preceded with "http://" when you paste it into Google Maps).

HACK 93: Resize and Customize Embedded Videos

Don't let YouTube limit you to their default video size and colors when sharing content.

To embed a video from YouTube, all you need to do is go to http://youtube.com, search for content, and then copy the embed code into your own site. Here's an example of the embed code, which you can find at the right side of the video player, as shown in Figure 9-20. If you use a rich text editor for your site, make sure to switch to the HTML editing mode before pasting this in:

```
<object width="425" height="355"><param name="movie" value="http://www.youtube.com/
v/4xQja0XMxfg&rel=1"></param><param name="wmode" value="transparent"></param><embed
src="http://www.youtube.com/v/4xQja0XMxfg&rel=1" type="application/x-shockwave-flash"
wmode="transparent" width="425" height="355"></embed></object>
```

Resizing a Video

What if you want to include a different size than the default one YouTube offers you? Just replace all occurrences of the width and height pixel values—here, 425 and 355, respectively, as highlighted earlier—with values of your own choosing. To make sure that the video is resized proportionally, you

WANT EVEN MORE CUSTOMIZING OPTIONS?

With some programming, you can connect to the YouTube JavaScript Player API and embed a custom, so-called chromeless player. Check out http://blogoscoped.com/youtube api/ to get you started.

Figure 9-20.
Copying the embed code for a YouTube video (note that for some videos, embedding has been disabled by the owner)

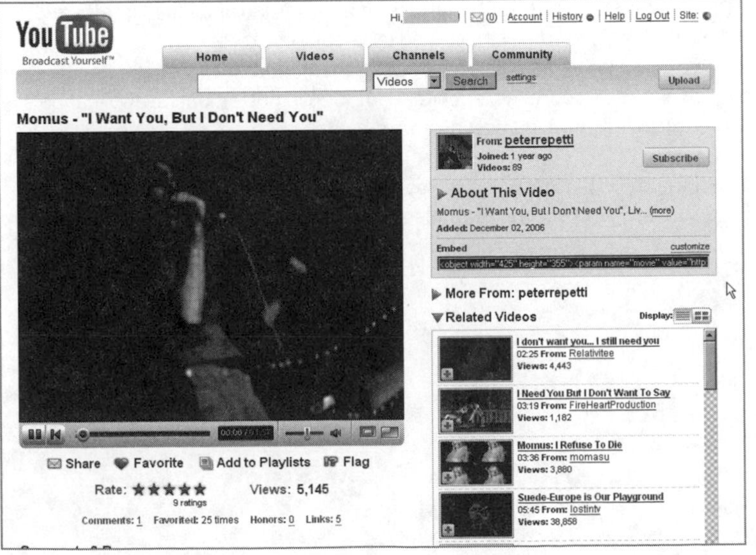

can use any image editing software; just create a new image file of the base size 425 x 355, and then resize the image to a specific width—say, 500. Your image editor will now (usually) be able to adjust the width accordingly, keeping proportions intact. In the case of a width of 500, the height would now be 418, as shown in Figure 9-21.

Figure 9-21.
Resizing an image in PaintShop Pro 4, one of the many available picture editors

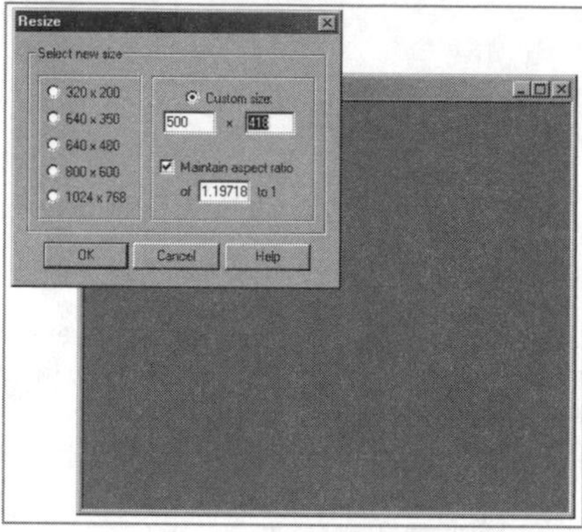

Figure 9-22.
Changing colors and adding borders on a YouTube video

Adding Colors

Next to the embed code at YouTube is a "customize" link to add different colors to the YouTube player. You can also choose to have a border on the player. Here's an example snippet to make an orange interface, including a border, as shown in Figure 9-22 (relevant parameters are in bold):

```
<object width="425" height="373"><param name="movie" value="http://www.youtube.com/v/4xQ
ja0XMxfg&amp;rel=1&amp;color1=0xe1600f&amp;color2=0xfebd01&amp;border=1"></param><param
name="wmode" value="transparent"></param><embed src="http://www.youtube.com/v/4xQja0XMxfg&am
p;rel=1&amp;color1=0xe1600f&amp;color2=0xfebd01&amp;border=1" type="application/x-shockwave-
flash" wmode="transparent" width="425" height="373"></embed></object>
```

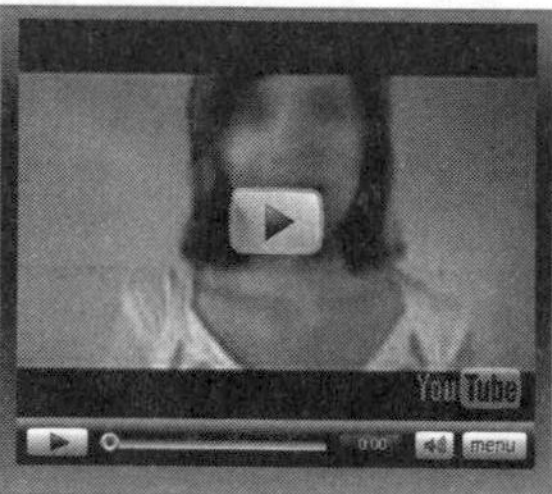

Figure 9-23.
A new color scheme for YouTube's player

However, you can go beyond the color choices that YouTube presents to you in their customization dialog. The parameters `color1` and `color2` are simply two parts of a gradient. The values, like "0xe1600f," are hexadecimal numbers from 0–255 representing red, green and blue. In this case, `0x` just starts the hexadecimal number, followed by `E1`, `60`, and `0F`, meaning 225, 96, and 15 (which is a tone of orange in the additive color model used by web pages). To mix your own colors, check to see whether your photo editor of choice supports hexadecimal notation. If not, an online application like http://mediagods.com/tools/rgb2hex.html comes in handy.

With your new hexadecimal values in hand, you can replace both gradient color pairs found in the YouTube snippet. I picked cyan and black for the example shown in Figure 9-23, playing the video "Meet my pets!" by heyitscorie (http://youtube.com/watch?v=4xQja0XMxfg).

HACK 94: Disguise Your Picasa Identity

Change your Picasa address, and add another login name to your Google account at the same time.

When your Google username is your real name—such as `JaneAnnDoe1980@gmail.com`—then your Picasa Web Album addresses will be along this format, including that name:

```
http://picasaweb.google.com/JaneAnnDoe1980/MiscellaneousPics
```

However, there may be times when you want to share pictures of your album without revealing your full name (or your birth year, for that matter). Picasa already allows you to select a nickname different from your Google name for display on album pages. But the URL, as shown in the example, is still a giveaway.

But there's help, as Romanian Google watcher Ionut Alex. Chitu discovered on his independent blog Google Operating System (http://googlesystem.blogspot.com). First, login to Picasa Web Albums at http://picasaweb.google.com. Click Settings on top. In the section titled Gallery URL, there's a link to the righthand side reading "Want to add a new Google user name?" as pictured in Figure 9-24.

Figure 9-24.
The Picasa Web Albums settings page allows you to change your URL

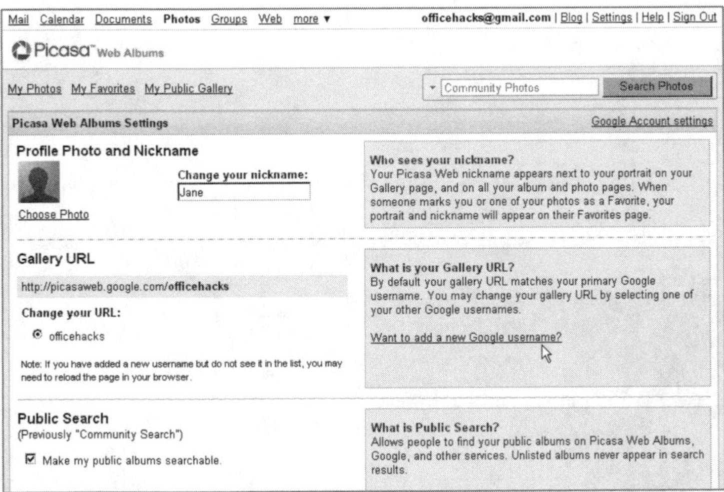

After clicking on this link, you will be forwarded to a dialog where you can provide an alternate user name for this account, like "rogerrabbit", or any other name that's still available. Confirm the change via the Add Username button. In the main settings dialog, select your newly chosen name, and OK the selection by clicking the Save Settings button at the bottom of the page.

You will find that your gallery can now also be reached via an address such as:

```
http://picasaweb.google.com/rogerrabbit/MiscellaneousPics
```

Interestingly enough, now you can also log in to your Google account anywhere by entering your chosen new name (in the example case, "rogerrabbit"). If you feel that your originally chosen user name is too long to repeatedly type during the login process to Google, why not change it to something shorter, if available? Just note that you can only add up to four new names this way.

HACK 95: Display Music Video Lyrics

Sing along with music videos!

YouTube hosts a lot of music videos, as a search for your favorite singer or band will probably reveal. Some of them include subtitles within the video, but what if you want to sing along a video that doesn't include lyrics? A Greasemonkey script for Firefox comes to the rescue (with a tip of the hat to the Google Operating System blog at http://googlesystem.blogspot.com).

First, install Greasemonkey from https://addons.mozilla.org/en-US/firefox/addon/748 **[Hack #42]**. Make sure that the monkey in the bottom right of Firefox is smiling, which means that Greasemonkey is activated (click the icon if that's not the case). Now jump to http://userscripts.org/scripts/show/22569, click the "Install this script" button, and follow the installation process; note that because user scripts can execute their own commands, you should install only scripts you trust.

Next, locate a video clip at YouTube.com. There won't be lyrics available for all videos, but for some; to get this to work, it seems to be crucial that the artist's name as well as the song name are included in the title of the video. For instance, the URL http://www.youtube.com/watch?v=tAtcJ954TjQ—titled "Badly drawn boy – Once around the block"—will do.

Now check the righthand sidebar on the video page. If all went well, an arrow and the word Lyrics will appear. Click this label to expand the lyrics, which will take a moment to load. A successful result, as shown in Figure 9-25, allows you to do a little karaoke (to the potential detriment of your neighbors—but hey, life is short!).

Figure 9-25.
Showing the lyrics of the song next to the video

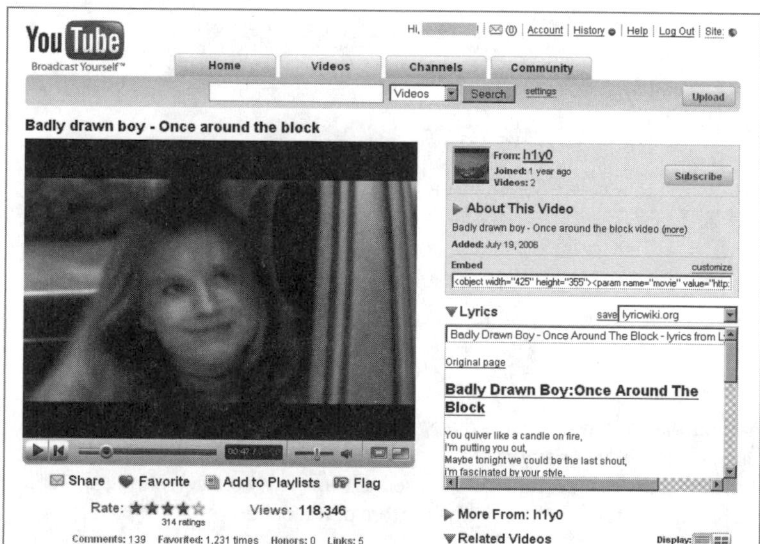

If the lyrics to your favorite video cannot be found, or the wrong ones are displayed, you have the option of choosing another lyrics provider from the checkbox nearby. As a fallback, you can also do a Google search for the artist and song name, appending the word "lyrics", as in "loudon wainwright the swimming song lyrics" (without the quotes).

By default, the lyrics label won't show when you omit the "www" from the YouTube URL. To enable this userscript to work both with "www" and without, choose Tools→Greasemonkey→Manage User Scripts from the Firefox menu. Select YouTube Lyrics in the lefthand list, and add "http://youtube.com/watch?*" to the Included Pages list, as shown in Figure 9-26.

Figure 9-26.
Allowing the user script to work with more URLs

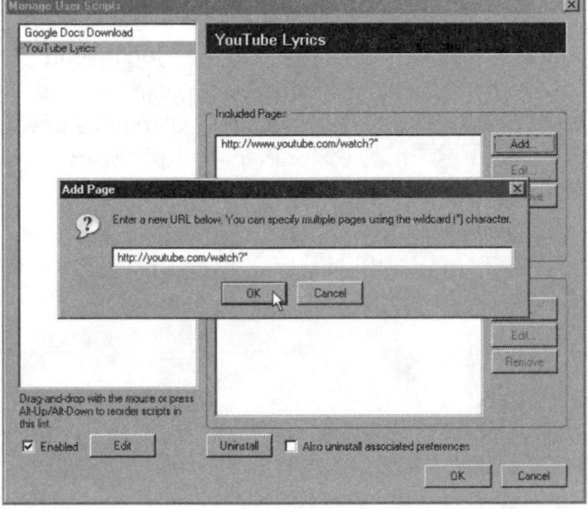

HACK 56: Beyond Google: From Flickr to Vimeo and Blip.tv

Life is a sum of all your choices, as Albert Camus said. And if Google doesn't cut it for you, here's a little help in choosing the right photo and video sharing sites.

There are a lot of media-sharing sites beyond Google's properties. This hack includes a list to get you started. Note that although some of the lesser-known sites for media sharing may have features you prefer individually, viewers of your media may have an easier time understanding interfaces and features of sites that they're already used to. That shouldn't stop you from switching from YouTube to the less well-known Vimeo, for example, but it's worth keeping in mind.

Flickr

Flickr, owned by Yahoo!, is a photo sharing site not unlike Picasa Web Albums. It's been around for longer, though, and has some interesting features not available in Google's competing product. Among the most interesting differences:

- You can tag your photos with a Creative Commons license **[Hack #31]**. People on the site can then search specifically for just the photos with this "sharing enabled" license attached to it, potentially giving your pictures more exposure.
- Groups in Flickr bring together like-minded people for photo sharing on specific subjects. (For instance, a group pool called Clock Works was set up to compile one photo of a clock face for every minute of the day, in chronological order; when run in slideshow mode, this results in an interesting film!)
- If your Flickr photos appear in Yahoo! search results, they will display your username right below them.
- Flickr has its own messaging system on the site, alerting you of new happenings, such as when another Flickr user adds you as a contact.

- A calendar displays the most interesting photos of each day for easy exploration. You can also view photos displayed on a world map.
- The Camera Finder lets you browse photos by specific camera maker and model.
- You can batch-organize your photo collection via drag and drop.
- A photo editor called Picnik lets you retouch your pictures without leaving the browser. You can resize, crop, adjust colors, sharpen your image, remove the red eye effect, overlay text or clip art, and more.

To sign up for Flickr, visit http://flickr.com. You can use your Yahoo! login, if you have one. Once you're logged in, you can start to manage your photos, as shown in Figure 9-27. Once you upload photos, an individual photo page appears, similar to the one shown in Figure 9-28. Flickr is free to use in its basic variant, and offers you a pro account for $24.95 per year, including unlimited storage, photo statistics, and ad-free browsing, among other features. Photo editor Picnik (http://www.picnik.com) is also available in a premium variant, for $24.95 per year.

Other photo-sharing sites include Zooomr (http://zooomr.com), SmugMug (http://smugmug.com), Photobucket (http://photobucket.com) and Fotki (http://fotki.com).

Figure 9-27.
Your Flickr dashboard

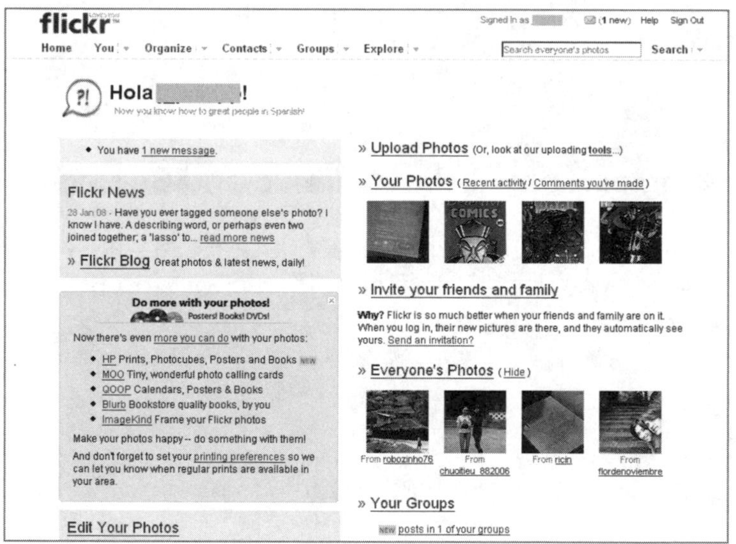

Figure 9-28.
An individual photo page (or in this case, a drawing I made); as owner of the photo, you'll see a couple of buttons on top other visitors won't see, including Edit Photo or Delete.

Vimeo

For video-sharing, take a look at Vimeo.com. Signup is quick, and requires you to confirm a registration mail sent out to you. Then you can share your first video by clicking Upload on top. While the video is uploading, you can edit the film's title, description, and tags, as shown in Figure 9-29.

Figure 9-29.
Uploading a video at Vimeo

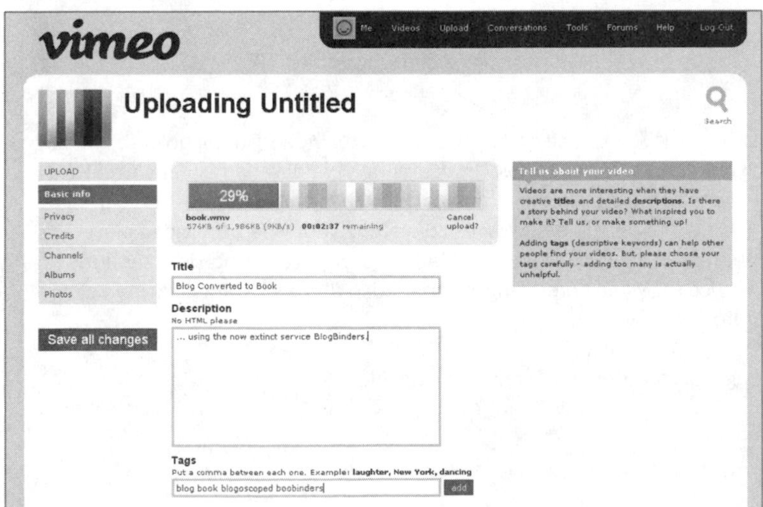

Alternatively, you can also upload videos via email—especially suited for films recorded with your mobile phone. Look for your special email address to send clips to; it's on the bottom right of the upload page.

Your video playback page will have a URL like http://vimeo.com/739349, and appear similar to the one in Figure 9-30. The video page looks neat and uncluttered. On the downside, the video will not automatically buffer or play when you visit the video page—you also won't see any buffering or playback time status unless you hover over the video. As with YouTube, videos can be embedded elsewhere using an HTML snippet.

The Vimeo HTML source code contains a kind of Easter egg in the form of ASCII art. Have a look by right-clicking any page, and selecting View Page Source (or similar) from the context menu!

Figure 9-30.
An individual Vimeo video playback page

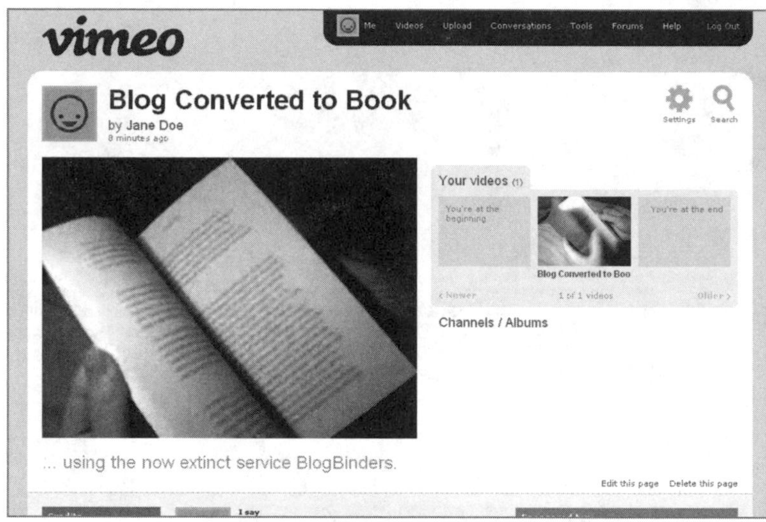

Blip.tv

Blip.tv (yep, that's the URL; http://blip.tv) also lets you upload your video. During upload, you can provide information on your video and also choose from among several variants of the Creative Commons license. Your video URL will be in the format of http://blip.tv/file/705790, displaying as shown in Figure 9-31. Note that until Blip.tv finishes converting your video, the video player may require the installation of an additional Windows Media Player plugin, which is sometimes troublesome in Firefox—once the video processing is done, video playback works fine in Firefox, though, as shown in Figure 9-31.

Some more video sharing sites that you may want to try include:

- Jumpcut (http://jumpcut.com)
- Veoh (http://veoh.com)
- Yahoo! Video (http://video.yahoo.com)
- Viddler (http://viddler.com)
- Eyespot (http://eyespot.com)

Figure 9-31.
The Blip.tv video player

Some video sites I tried, like Revver (http://revver.com) or Spike (http://spike.com, formerly known as iFilm) made it complicated to do quick uploads; during the time of this writing, the uploaded videos were still in a long processing or reviewing phase and did not appear live. Note that some blogging tools include video sharing options as well **[Hack #114]**.

QUICK HACK

GIVEN A SPECIFIC WEB SITE OR PRODUCT, LIKE YOUTUBE, HERE'S HOW TO FIND SIMILAR OFFERINGS

One way to find things that are like YouTube is to search Google.com for "youtube". Below the first result (probably YouTube.com), click "Similar pages." You'll see (mostly) related sites.

Another way to find related sites, services, or products is to check Wikipedia (http://wikipedia.org); sometimes, Wikipedia contains an entry about a web site, listing related web sites at the end of the article, or pointing to a full comparison chart entry on Wikipedia.

Yet another option is to visit Google Sets at http://labs.google.com/sets. Enter "youtube" in the first field, and also some other site mentioned in this section, like "vimeo," in the second field. Press Return, and your list will be expanded to show many more related sites **[Hack #26]**.

Also, sometimes you can search Google for a phrase like "* is better than youtube"—including the quotes—or "i prefer * to youtube" or "* is like youtube" (replace "youtube" with any other site you want to research, as needed). In the results, you'll find competitors listed in bold!

Once you know a set of products or sites within the niche you are researching, you can also combine them into one search query. Go to Google and enter (for example) "youtube spike vimeo", and so on (without the quotes). Sometimes this type of search leads to articles reviewing these services that compare pros and cons. This can work with other things too, so you can also enter (for example) "canon nikon sony kodak olympus" to find camera comparisons. If you get too many unrelated results, add words like "review" or "comparison" to the query.

10 CREATE YOUR OWN HOME PAGE, BLOG, OR GROUP

Google offers several free tools to create your own web presence for the purpose of publishing your articles or discussing topics with a group. You can also combine several of these tools, such as connecting a blog to your discussion group, to create a useful online destination. It's a read-write web, so here's how to write to it, using Google's tools.

Publish Regular News or Perspective with a Blog

If you have a Google Account [Hack #1], you can sign up with Blogger.com and create your own blog (see [Hack #11] and [Hack #109]). This will give you space to post items, recent ones displayed first, with readers able to leave comments on each article.

On your blog you can publish just about anything: your personal life, diary-style; news, with a focus on one topic, or more general coverage of world issues with your own unique perspective; serialized fiction; home-made cartoons, and more. You can also use a blog to "clip" your favorite parts of the web, like showcasing a daily favorite YouTube video of yours by embedding it into the post.

Your blog's address will be either http://something.blogspot.com, where "something" is your chosen blog name (if it hasn't been taken!)—or you can configure Blogger to transfer your blog posts to your own server via FTP (File Transfer Protocol).

Figure 10-1.
The Blogger dashboard after registering and signing in

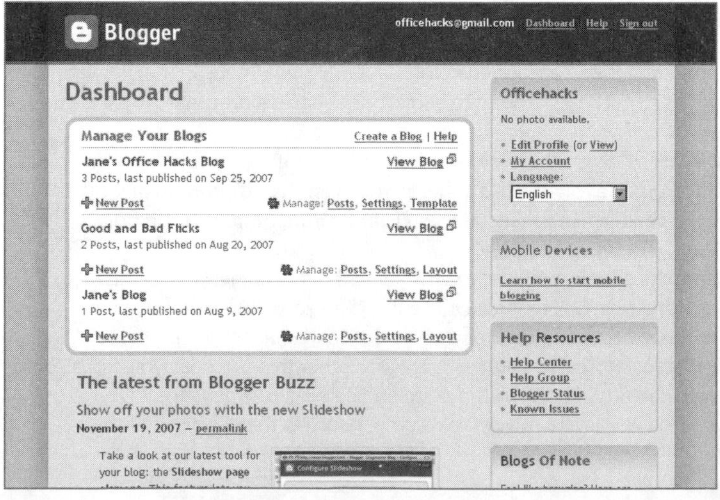

Create Your Home Page with Google Page Creator

Home pages are a little more static and less communicative than blogs, but they can still serve a purpose. For instance, maybe you want to offer a certain download of your finished ebook. Or you want to add a list of Frequently Asked Questions on the subject of flesh-eating plants—a list that might see several amendments in the future, but that won't be moved further down the page by new articles.

Once you have a Google Account set up, you can head straight over to http://pages.google.com to give this a try. The editor is pictured in Figure 10-2 and the results in Figure 10-3. You can see that the editor is mostly WYSIWYG (What-You-See-Is-What-You-Get). Elements can be clicked to edit their containing text. You can adjust font styles, include images, change templates, add Google gadgets, and more.

Figure 10-2.
Google Page Creator in editing mode

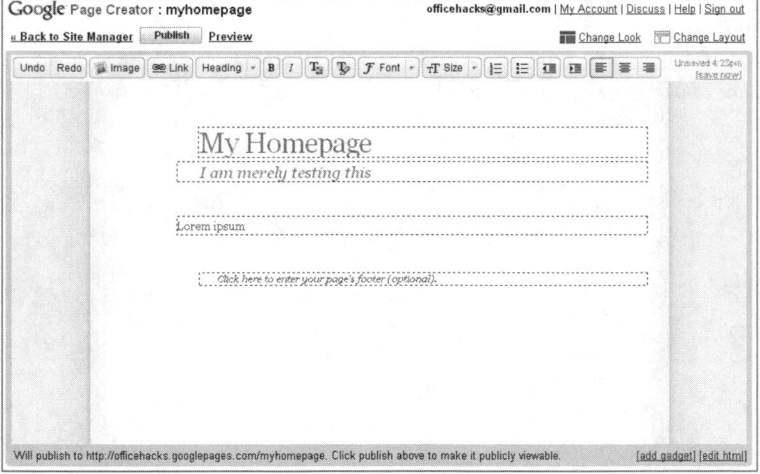

Figure 10-3.
The published page

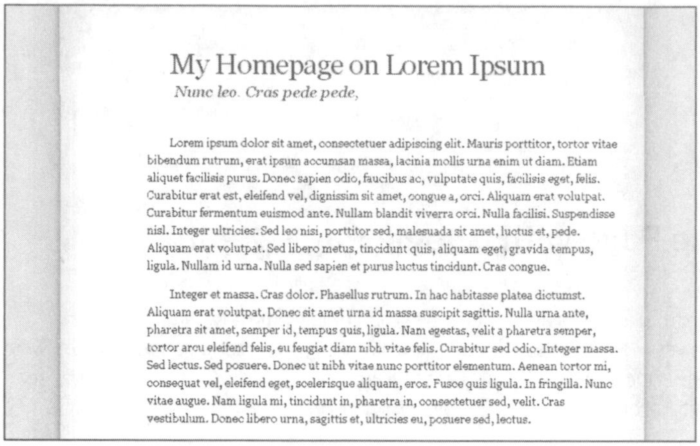

My Homepage on Lorem Ipsum
Nunc leo. Cras pede pede,
Lorem ipsum dolor sit amet, consectetuer adipiscing elit. Mauris porttitor, tortor vitae bibendum rutrum, erat ipsum accumsan massa, lacinia mollis urna enim ut diam. Etiam aliquet facilisis purus. Donec sapien odio, faucibus ac, vulputate quis, facilisis eget, felis. Curabitur erat est, eleifend vel, dignissim sit amet, congue a, orci. Aliquam erat volutpat. Curabitur fermentum euismod ante. Nullam blandit viverra orci. Nulla facilisi. Suspendisse nisl. Integer ultricies. Sed leo nisi, porttitor sed, malesuada sit amet, luctus et, pede. Aliquam erat volutpat. Sed libero metus, tincidunt quis, aliquam eget, gravida tempus, ligula. Nullam id urna. Nulla sed sapien et purus luctus tincidunt. Cras congue.
Integer et massa. Cras dolor. Phasellus rutrum. In hac habitasse platea dictumst. Aliquam erat volutpat. Donec sit amet urna id massa suscipit sagittis. Nulla urna ante, pharetra sit amet, semper id, tempus quis, ligula. Nam egestas, velit a pharetra semper, tortor arcu eleifend felis, eu feugiat diam nibh vitae felis. Curabitur sed odio. Integer massa. Sed lectus. Sed posuere. Donec ut nibh vitae nunc porttitor elementum. Aenean tortor mi, consequat vel, eleifend eget, scelerisque aliquam, eros. Fusce quis ligula. In fringilla. Nunc vitae augue. Nam ligula mi, tincidunt in, pharetra in, consectetuer sed, velit. Cras vestibulum. Donec libero urna, sagittis et, ultricies eu, posuere sed, lectus.

Set Up Your Own Discussion Group with Google Groups

Even more communicative than a blog is a discussion group. Google Groups is the Google app that handles Usenet (an international, distributed bulletin board system) discussion newsgroups. But Google adds their own, non-Usenet groups to the mix, and you too can create one of these. Just click the "Create a group" button shown on the Google Groups home page after you've logged in, as shown in Figure 10-4.

Groups can be both public or private and invite-only, as the set-up dialog displayed in Figure 10-5 illustrates. Once you've created a group, you can edit certain pages in it—like the welcome screen—with the Google Page Creator interface. The result may look similar to the sample group pictured in Figure 10-6.

Figure 10-4.
The Google Groups start page

Mail Calendar Documents Photos Groups Web more ▾
officehacks@googlemail.com | My Groups | Favorites | Profile | Help | My Account | Sign out
Google Groups
Search Groups
Advanced Groups Search
Preferences
Explore groups
What is Google Groups?
Take the tour »
Find out what people are doing with Google Groups
Search for a group
Business
Raghav's Picks
Smellthecheese
Health
...fitness.weights
...health.alternative
Home
...and.bargains
...pond.chat
Arts & Entertainment
Web Design and ...
Safe Havens
Browse all group categories...
My groups
Create a new group in 3 easy steps:
1 Create an account
2 Setup your group
3 Invite people
Create a group...
My profile & stats
officehacks@googlemail.com
Your 7-day activity
None
View your full profile
Create a group - Google Home - Terms of Service - Privacy Policy
©2007 Google

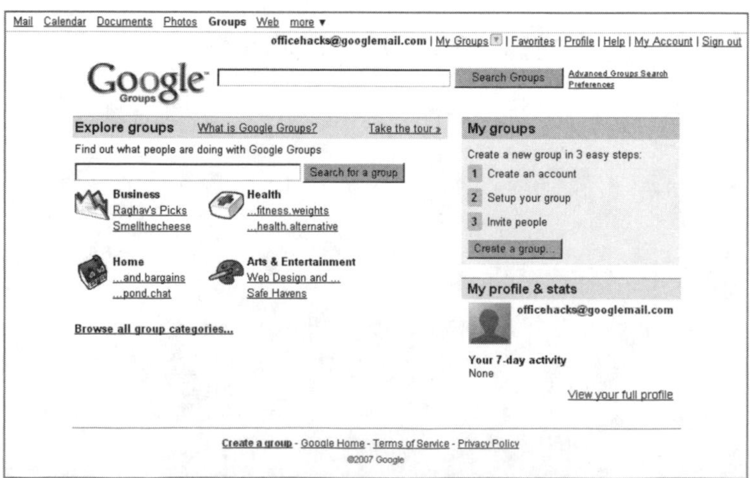

Figure 10-5.
Setting up a group

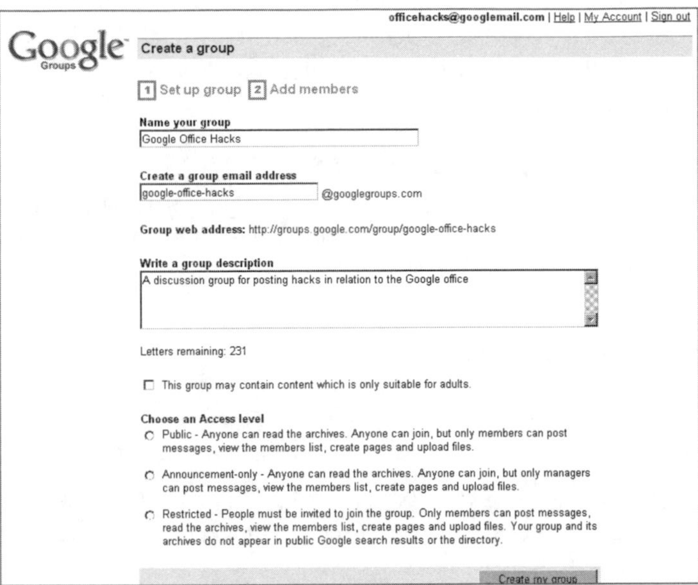

Figure 10-6.
The group's start page

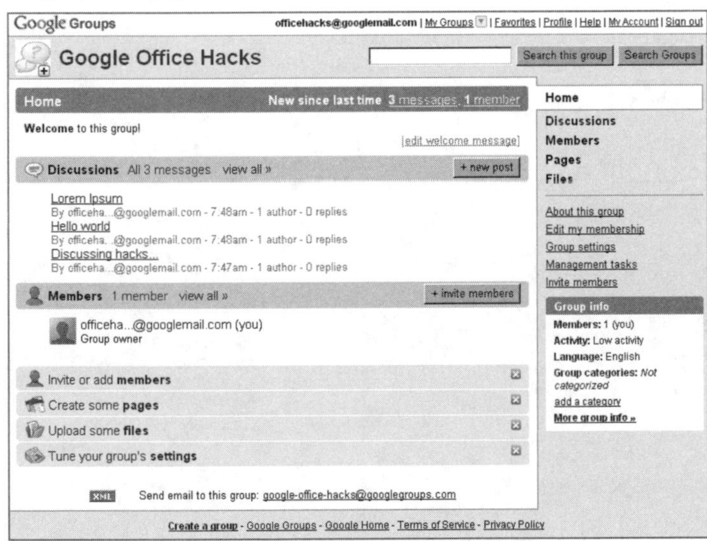

Inviting a new member means that an invitation will be sent to their email account. However, if they are using Gmail, chances are that this invitation will land in their spam folder, where it's likely to be ignored. You can get around this problem by clicking "Invite members" and going to the "Add members directly" tab. Note that, as Google warns on that page, you are supposed to add only people you know and using the feature to send unwanted mails can lead to account deactivation.

HACK 97: Add a Gadget to Your Google Page (or Blog)

Gadgets are the spice of home page cooking: add too few, and your page may taste bland . . . but add too many, and you'll turn people's stomachs. Cook wisely!

Google gadgets—from search tools to weather information to clocks and games—are perhaps best known for being used on the iGoogle home page (see Chapter 6). But many gadgets are also able to live outside that space and migrate to the Google Desktop program, as well as most web pages or blogs, including Google's Blogger, and sites created with Google Page Creator.

Adding a Gadget in Google Page Creator

To see how you can add a gadget to a Google Page Creator page, start by logging in to http://pages.google.com. Click the link reading "Create a new page" and name it anything you want. I'll pick "Global Warming Info Page" for mine, and hit the "Create and Edit" button.

You'll now be entering the edit mode of Google Page Creator. You can switch to a two-column layout first to make some room for the gadget. Click Change Layout on top and select one of the styles offered, for a result like the one pictured in Figure 10-7.

Figure 10-7.
Preparing the page to make place for a gadget

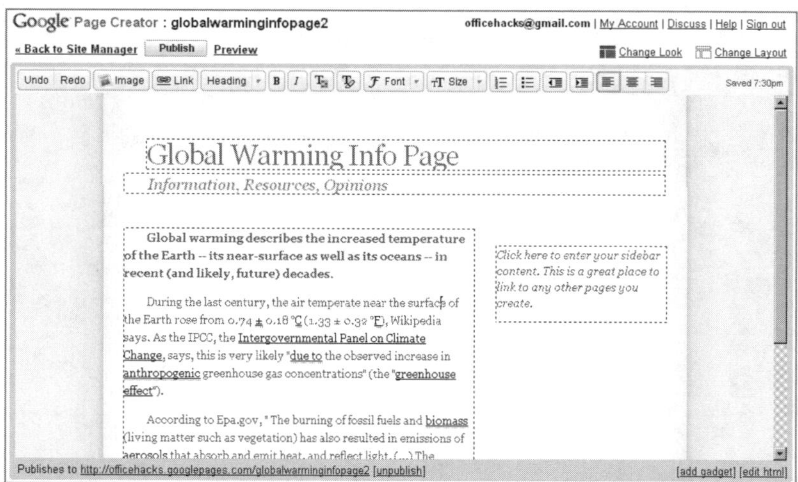

Now click the link "add gadget" in the bottom right to open the gadget directory. Pick the gadget you like by browsing the directory or performing a search. There's so many different gadgets that you can try just searching for your topic at hand—for instance, I've searched for "global warming" to find a gadget called "Global Warming Daily Tip." Select the gadget and configure it if needed, and confirm with OK.

You can now click the Preview link on top to check whether the design appears as you want it to. Make design changes where needed—you may need to select an element and switch to the HTML editing mode at times, for example, to adjust the "width" and "height" attributes of an inline frame element—and you're ready to go live with the page by hitting the Publish button.

Your page is now public, as the one shown in Figure 10-8, at a URL like this one:

```
http://officehacks.googlepages.com/globalwarminginfopage2
```

Figure 10-8.
The published page; to the left side is your own content, and to the right side rests a dynamic gadget

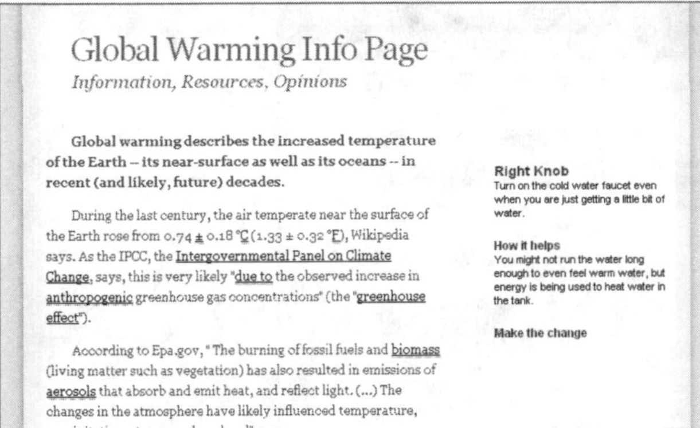

Add Gadgets to Your Blog

If you don't have a blog yet, create one on your topic of choice **[Hack #11]**. Suppose you want to add a gadget to your Blogger blog's sidebar. However, the normal Blogger.com editor won't suffice at this time; instead, point your browser to http://draft.blogger.com for a newer, more experimental version of Google's blog editor. On your dashboard page, click on the Layout link next to your blog.

You're now at the Add and Arrange Page Elements dialog as pictured in Figure 10-9. Click Add a Page Element and in the box titled Gadget, click the Add to Blog button. Now it's again time to locate your favorite gadget; for my sample, I will choose one titled "Environment: Random Graphic of the Day," as shown in Figure 10-10.

After clicking Save Changes in the gadgets dialog, and then clicking Save in the underlying page template editor, you can fine-tune parts of the layout via the Edit HTML link on top. For instance, you can search for "sidebar-wrap" in the HTML source's stylesheet part and then edit the width value to increase this element's size, allowing for wider gadgets. Here's the "before" code:

```
...
#sidebar-wrap {
  width:240px;
...
```

and the "after" code:

```
...
#sidebar-wrap {
  width:340px;
...
```

To accommodate this larger sidebar, you should also increase the width defined in the `#outer-wrapper` style. Your blog, like the one pictured in Figure 10-11, should show that all pages carry the widget you included.

Any content within gadgets, text or otherwise, will not be indexed by search engines when they crawl your page. The reason is that gadget content is delivered via an *IFrame* (an inline frame on the page) that points to content from another server.

Figure 10-9.
Adding a gadget to the main template will affect all of your blog

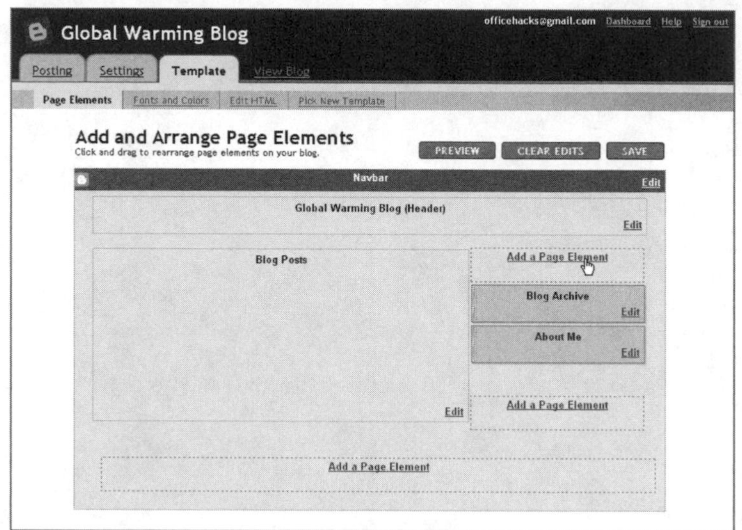

Figure 10-10.
Blogger's "Add a gadget" dialog

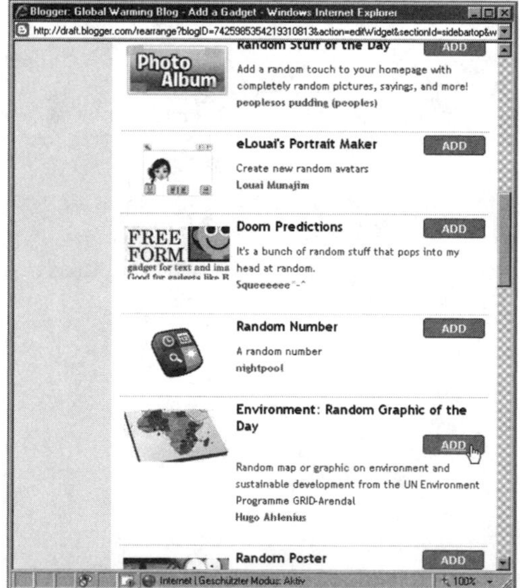

Figure 10-11.
The published blog is now accompanied by a sidebar showing a daily graphic

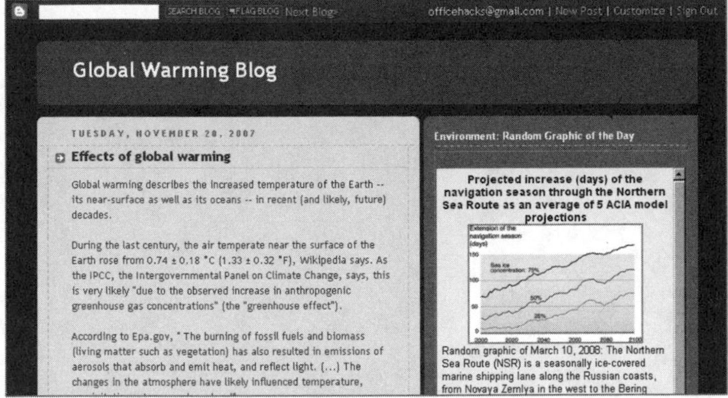

HACK 98: Battle Spam in Your Blog

Adjust the signal-to-noise ratio in your favor.

Spam—unwanted and noisy bulk messages to promote a product, site, or idea—is crawling around every corner of the Web. And it's not just in email, but also in blog comments, blog postings, search results, tag-based photo sites, wikis, and basically everywhere that people (or bots) can write something somehow. And if you run a blog, then identifying and suppressing comment spam may become one of your daily challenges. Just clicking the Trash icon next to spam messages—you need to be logged in to see the icon—is not always enough, so here are a few tips on how to cope.

Disable Comments

First of all, you don't necessarily need to enable comments for your blog. However, this should be a last resort only; a comment-free blog is only half a blog. To disable commenting for visitors, log in to http://blogger.com and switch to the Settings tab of your blog, and then the Comments subtab. In the Who Can Comment field, select "Only members of this blog" from the menu. This can prevent commenting, as long as you don't allow anyone to become a member. (You can also select the "Registered Users" option; this won't disable comments, but it will stop anonymous commenting.)

Enable Comment Moderation

Another defense measure if you face a lot of spam is to enable comment moderation. You will find this setting next to the label "Enable comment moderation" on the Settings→Comments page, as pictured in Figure 10-12. Check the Yes box, provide an email for comment approval requests to be sent to, and confirm your selection by hitting the Save Settings button.

Now, whenever someone tries adding a new comment, you will get an email first, as pictured in Figure 10-13. Only after clicking the Publish link of that mail will the new comment go live.

Figure 10-12.
The settings page for Blogspot blog comments

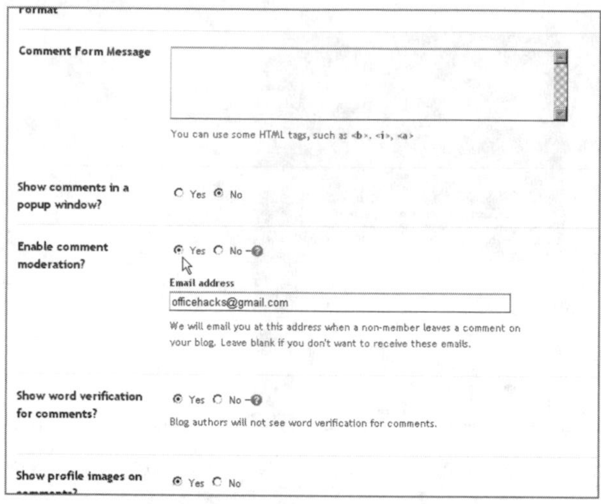

Figure 10-13.
The moderation alert email asks you to approve a new comment

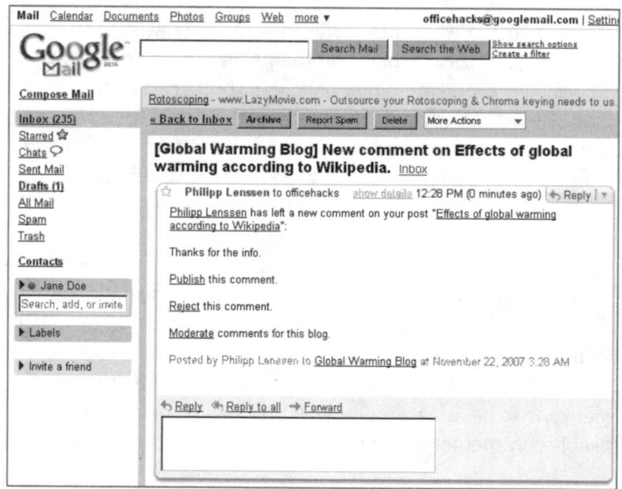

Disable Comments for a Specific Post

Rather than toggling the global comments settings for your blog, you can also simply disable the comments for a single blog posting. Ionut Alex. Chitu, who has a popular blog on Google at http://googlesystem.blogspot.com, says, "If an old post gets more than three to four spam messages in a day, I disable the comments for that post temporarily."

Here's how you can disable comments for a specific older post of yours. Log in to Blogger.com, find your blog on the dashboard, then click the Posts link that appears next to the "Manage:" prompt. Locate the post in question and click the Edit link to its left. Expand the settings for the post via the Post Options link below it, as shown in Figure 10-14, and switch to "Don't allow, show existing." After hitting the Publish Post button, your change will be active.

Figure 10-14.
Switching the comments settings for an individual post

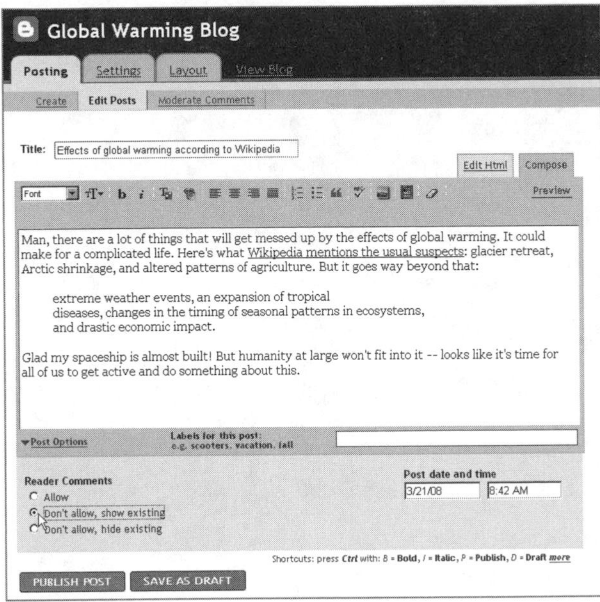

Get Email Notifications for New Comments

If you decide that the moderated comments option is either taking up too much of your time, or removing the feeling of real-time interaction in your blog's comments, you might also want to just get an email notification whenever a new comment is posted. This way, when someone posts a spam comment to one of your posts, it will appear immediately but you will be alerted to it, and you can then delete the comment via the Trash icon next to it.

To activate the notification option, go to the Settings→Comments page for your blog. Enter an email in the bottom field labeled Comment Notification Address and click Save Settings.

Helpful CAPTCHAs

By default, your blog is also protected by so-called *CAPTCHAs*, images displaying characters that the user is then required to type correctly into a box near the image, as shown in Figure 10-15. CAPTCHA is short for "Completely Automated Public Turing test to tell Computers and Humans Apart" but you can think of it simply as a way to "capture" bots, because they may not be able to understand the image, and thus might fail at entering the correct letters. The letters in CAPTCHAs are usually rather distorted to increase the barrier for those bots able to utilize Optical Character Recognition, so sometimes even human users will have a bit of trouble passing the test the first time.

CAPTCHAs are enabled by default, but you can also disable this feature anytime by toggling the checkboxes next to the label "Show word verification for comments" on the comments settings page.

Figure 10-15.
A CAPTCHA in action

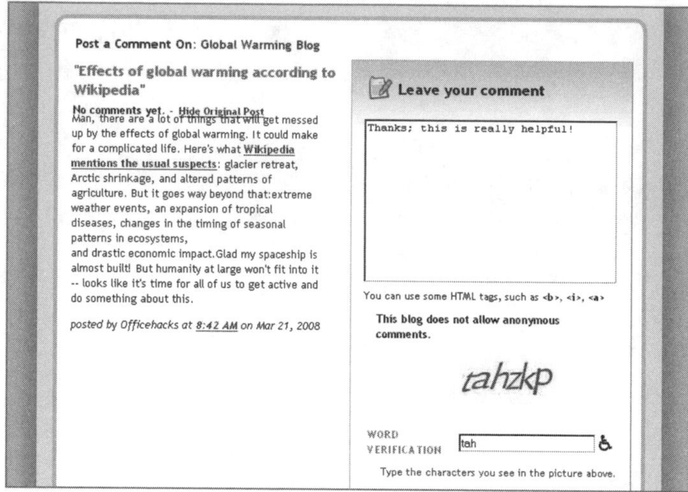

The "nofollow" Value

Your blog is protected by another mechanism, the `rel="nofollow"` attribute value. This HTML attribute differentiates a link posted by you from a link posted by a commenter, disabling that link's value to search engine rankings. As a better search engine ranking for their linked site is what many spammers are after, this may reduce the incentive for spammers to post comments to your blog.

Note that you can't turn off the "nofollow" setting, as it's a global value active for all Blogspot blogs.

HACK 99: Add a Search Engine to Your Home Page

For many occasions, even the best site navigation doesn't beat a quick site search. Make sure to offer one for your site if it contains many pages.

When you create a web site with Google Page Creator (see the introduction to this chapter), unlike with a Blogspot blog, there will be no site search engine added to it automatically. It's still possible to add one manually though using the Google Custom Search Engine (CSE) program. This search allows your visitors, as well as you, to quickly find older pages hosted on the site.

Find Out Whether Your Site Is Already Indexed

For a Custom Search Engine to work as a site search, your web site must already be indexed in Google web search. Unfortunately, there's no simple switch to just activate this, as it may take days to weeks, depending on the popularity of your web site [Hack #130].

To check whether your site is available (and if so, in what depth), perform the following query at Google.com, replacing `example` with your actual subdomain:

```
site:example.googlepages.com
```

So, if your home page's URL is `http://officehacks.googlepages.com/globalwarminginfo`, you'd query Google for `site:officehacks.googlepages.com` or `site:officehacks.googlepages.com/globalwarminginfo`.

Set Up Your Custom Search Engine

If your site is indexed in Google, you can go about setting up a Custom Search Engine for it. Point your browser to http://google.com/cse/ and click the Create a Custom Search Engine button. You will now be asked to provide details like the name for your search engine or its description. Provide the fields as requested, but do not enter any value in the "Search engine keywords" field.

The next crucial part of this form is to provide your domain in the "Sites to search" text field, similar to what is shown in Figure 10-16. With this value provided, you've turned the Custom Search Engine into your own site search service.

Agree to the terms of service if you're OK with them, and click Next to continue.

On the page that follows, click the Finish button. You will be forwarded to a page listing your search engine. Click the link reading "homepage" next to it. You will find a parameter named "cx" in the URL on top, which you will need to copy for the next step. For instance, the engine I just created has the following address:

```
http://www.google.com/coop/cse?cx=014956320774661537761%3Avwo8c4t2l7s
```

so I'm copying the value "014956320774661537761%3Avwo8c4t2l7s". This is the identifier of this custom search engine.

Figure 10-16.
Setting up the Custom Search Engine

Give your search engine a name and provide a brief description.
Search engine name: Global Warming Site Search
for example, Real Climate Search Engine
Search engine description: Searches only the global warming info site
for example, Climate Science from Climate Scientists
Specify some keywords that describe the content or subject of your search engine. These keywords are used to tune your s
Search engine keywords:
for example, climate "global warming" "greenhouse gases"
Search engine language: English
What do you want to search?
Only sites I select.
The entire web, but emphasize sites I select.
The entire web.
Select some sites
Specify a list of web sites to search. You'll be able to edit this list and add more sites later. Tips on formatting URLs.
Sites to search: http://officehacks.googlepages.com
List one URL per line

A CSE can be restricted to search through a specific site (that is, a domain or subdomain), but you can't restrict it to search specific pages or folders only. If your Google Page Creator site collects several unrelated pages, it might make sense to add a new site via the "Create a new site" link on the Page Creator dashboard. This way, you can pick a separate subdomain.

Add a Search Box to Your Google Page Creator Home Page

Now it's time to add a search box to your site. Switch over to Google Page Creator at http://pages.google.com and click on your page to launch the editor. Select an element of your page where you want to add the search box. I'm using a righthand navigation bar element. Click "edit html" below, and type the this HTML into the box—replacing the cx value with your own value, but also replacing the part in your identifier reading "%3A" with a simple colon:

```
<form action="http://www.google.com/cse" method="get">
  <p>
    <input name="q" />
    <input type="submit" value="Search" />
    <input type="hidden" name="cx"
           value="014956320774661537761:dwyc9i7r_ag" />
  </p>
</form>
```

Let's go through the elements of this HTML snippet. The form element sets up a web form to receive user input. The action attribute specifies which site the form should be submitted to (in this case, the Custom Search Engine service). The method get tells the browser to attach parameters to the URL so that the Custom Search Engine will know what's being searched for. The parameters are then provided in the p (paragraph) element; an input field named q for the query, and a hidden input field named cx for the identifier of your custom search engine. A submit button with a label of your choice, such as "Search," is included as well.

Once you've entered the necessary HTML, click the Update button. Now you can go live with your page by hitting the Publish button, for a result similar to the one pictured in Figure 10-17. Note that as this search engine is hooked up to Google's normal web search index, pages that you freshly publish on your site may not appear in the results immediately.

Figure 10-17.
This site now has a site search in the sidebar

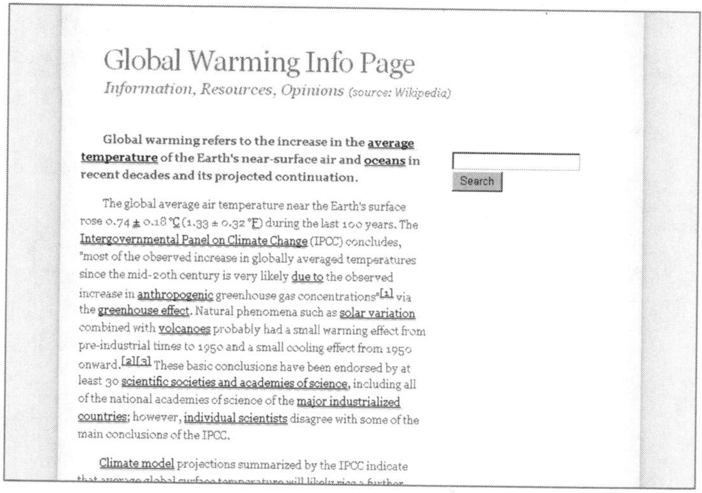

HACK 100: Get a Taste of Blogger's Experimental Features

Unlock Blogger's video embedding, gadgets and more.

"Early adopter" is what the technology industry calls someone who buys new gadgets first, signs up among the first dozen people of every new web site, and in general considers something "old-fashioned" after spotting a second person in the neighborhood using it. Sounds cool, you say? Well, if you want to be an early adopter and you have a blog with Blogger.com, here's what to do: instead of starting your blogging day at http://blogger.com, move to http://draft.blogger.com. Although the design is slightly different than the default, as shown in Figure 10-18, you will still be able to blog as normal. But you will also be able to do more, because Blogger Draft, as it's called, lets you experiment with features not available in the default Blogger version.

Here are a couple of these features as of this time (note that some of these will be rolled out to the normal Blogger over time, and new ones may be introduced to Blogger Draft):

- You can add Google Gadgets to your blog **[Hack #97]**. Find this in Layouts→Add a Page Element.
- Add a Search box to your template. Find this in Layouts→Add a Page Element.

To read out about the latest features available to Blogger Draft users, check out the official Draft blog at http://bloggerindraft.blogspot.com.

Looking for more blog widgets to add? Visit http://assessmyblog.blogspot.com and click on Blogger Hacks on top; you will find ways to add a widget containing the top commenters for your blog, a widget showing popular posts of yours, and more.

Figure 10-18.
Blogger Draft, showing the dashboard view

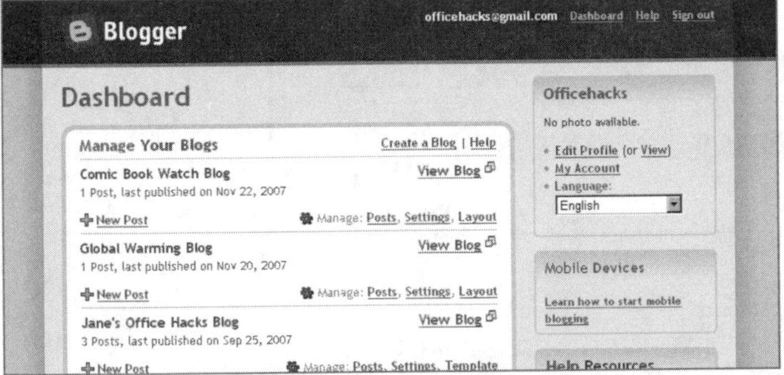

> **QUICK HACK** 
>
> **EXPERIMENT EVERYWHERE**
>
> Google's web search has a similar section where you can play around with as-of-yet unreleased, or merely prototypical, features. It's called Google Experimental and can be found at http://google.com/experimental/ (not to be confused with the Google Labs at http://labs.google.com, though those might be of interest too). You can subscribe to each search experiment individually, such as being able to see results on a time line. It will then show during your normal web searching at Google.com.

HACK 101: Keep a Discussion Thread at the Top of the Group

Put the spotlight on any discussion.

A "sticky" thread in a discussion forum is a thread that will always appear at the top of the list on the overview page, even if more recent threads have appeared since then. If you are the group owner, you will find this feature useful for directing attention to certain topics that you consider especially noteworthy, or of special interest to new members.

You can make a thread sticky in Google Groups if you have the right access permissions for the group (if you are the original group owner—Google differentiates between a group's regular members, managers, and owners, which are roles that you as owner can assign to others).

For example, I've created a group called Comic Book Watcher Group. Using the Group Settings→Appearance tab, I've given the layout an overhaul, as pictured in Figure 10-19. I've also changed the labels' order and text to the right side via the Group Settings→Navigation dialog. Plus, I've made the group private, so no one except invited members will be able to read the discussions, or view the files and pages that are posted in this group.

To set a thread to be sticky, first click on the thread. On top of it, you will find a link reading Options. Clicking it expands the settings; check the "Display this topic first" box, as shown in Figure 10-20, and hit the Save button.

Note that if you can't see this checkbox, and you are logged in, you probably don't have management permissions for this group; contact the group owner to try settle this.

When viewing the threads overview, this particular discussion will now be on top and show a push-pin icon, as pictured in Figure 10-21. You can remove its "stickiness" status later on by toggling the checkbox selection in the options dialog again.

Figure 10-19.
The group's front page

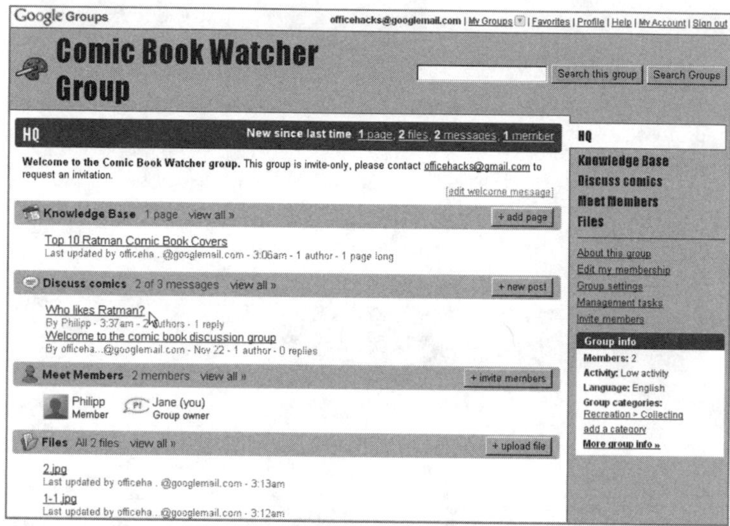

Figure 10-20.
Expanding the options dialog for a thread

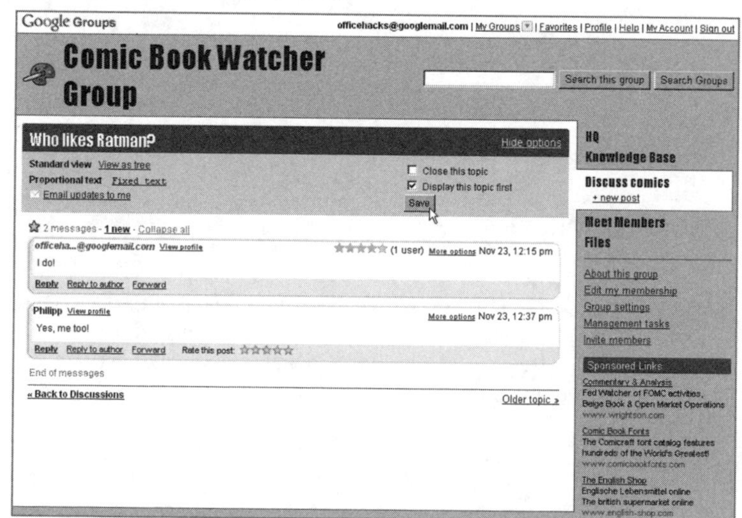

Figure 10-21.
The discussion overview now shows the sticky thread on top

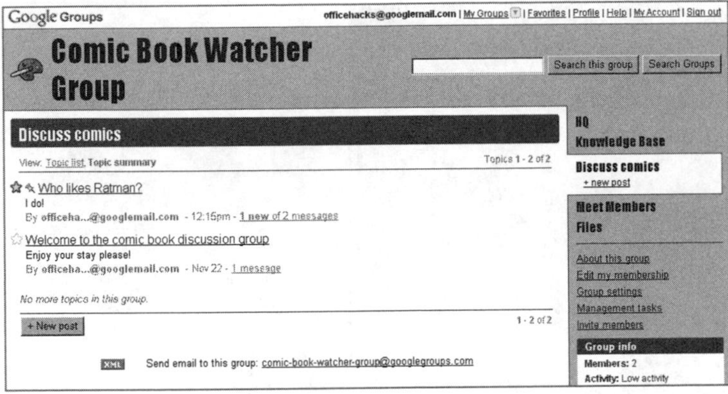

HACK 102: Blog Transparently

Indicate changes in your blog post and credit sources to help maintain an effective conversation around your blog.

Many consider it good blogging style to tell your readers when you make substantial changes after an article of yours went live for some time. This helps keep the conversation transparent. For instance, imagine that someone comments on your article, and then you change it—the comment may now appear odd because the part of your post that it referred to has since changed. The rule of "keeping it transparent" is especially applicable to news blogs, less so for diary-style blogs or fiction blogs.

> There are some ways to find out about changes made to a blog post even if the changes aren't disclosed **[Hack #84]**.

A common indicator for changed text is to use a strikethrough on text you replaced. To try this, log in to Blogger.com and when editing your post, switch to the Edit HTML tab, as shown in Figure 10-22. Let's say that you wrote that George Washington was the second U.S. president, but you've now realized that he was the first. Use the `del` (deletion) and `ins` (insert) tags, as shown in bold:

```
According to Wikipedia, George Washington was a central figure in the founding of the United
States of America, and also the nation's <del>second</del> <ins>first</ins> president.
```

Depending on the template's stylesheet, this text could now appear in one of several different ways; typically, the deletion tag will trigger a strikethrough, as shown in Figure 10-23. You can also just use the `s` (strikethrough) tag.

Figure 10-22.
The Edit HTML tab allows you to make advanced formatting changes to your post

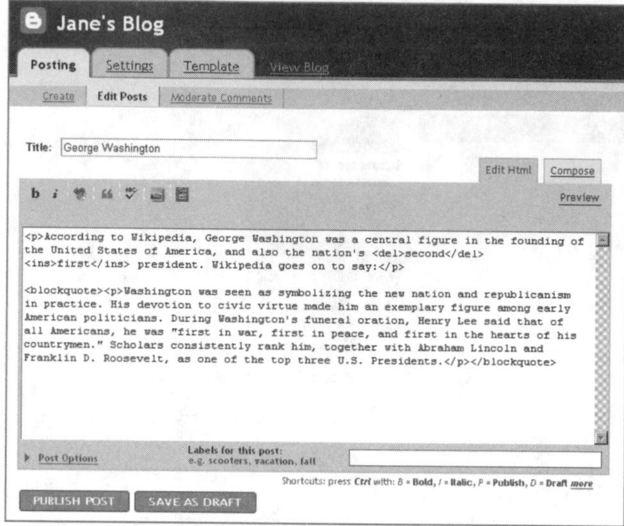

Figure 10-23.
A strikethrough corrects a part of your article while still showing what you originally wrote

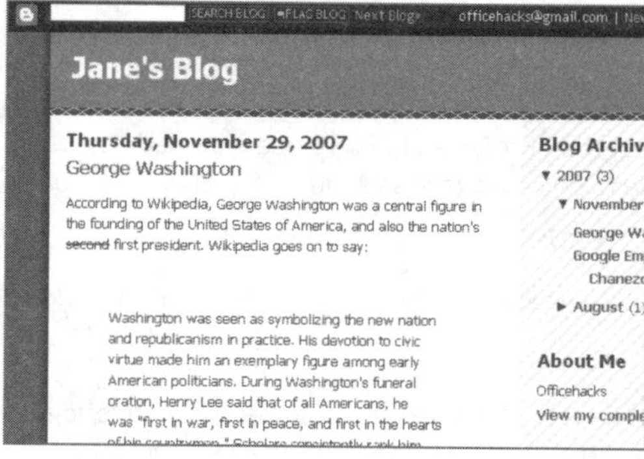

Crediting Your Source

Another good rule for transparency in blogs is to tell your readers where you first saw news or other items you are discussing. A "via" line like the following at the post's end can be used, including a link to the original article:

```
(Via CNN.com.)
```

Now your readers can educate themselves about the kinds of sources you are using in your daily research, and they may also compare your information with the source information to make up their own mind.

Additionally, using the Edit HTML tab, you can style this "via" line a bit. You could use the class `via` on a `p` (paragraph) element, as shown:

```
<p class="via">(Via <a href="http://cnn.com/page/3928.html">CNN.com</a>.)</p>
```

By itself, this will not change the font when you publish the post—you still need to adjust the stylesheet to include a layout definition for the `via` class. In Blogger, click on Template on top.

Now select the Edit HTML tab. Scroll down in the editing field to where the template contains the stylesheet definition; in my template, this part carries the headline "/* Primary layout */", but this may vary from template to template.

Add a stylesheet definition like this one, as also shown in Figure 10-24:

```
.via, .via a { color: rgb(150,150,150) !important; }
```

This instruction means: *every element that carries the class named* `via`*, as well as every* `a` *(anchor/ link) element within, will receive the color red = 150, green = 150, and blue = 150, and this is important, so override other definitions in the stylesheet.* Afterwards, hit the Save Template button. You can now view your blog posting to find that it includes your design changes, as pictured in Figure 10-25.

Hacking the Hack

If you find yourself using the "via" line described in the previous section—or any other HTML construct—in almost every blog post of yours, you can also turn it into a post template. In Blogger, click Settings→Formatting and scroll down to the Post Template field. Enter the base HTML needed to create a new "via" link, as shown:

```
<p class="via">(Via <a href=""></a>.)</p>
```

Click the Save Settings button to finish. This bit of HTML will now be included into the edit box by default whenever you start a new blog post. You then just have to fill in the relevant parts—the URL you want to credit, as well as the site's name—saving you some typing time. In cases where you don't need the HTML generated by the post template, you can simply delete it from the post.

Figure 10-24.
Making a stylesheet change in the template

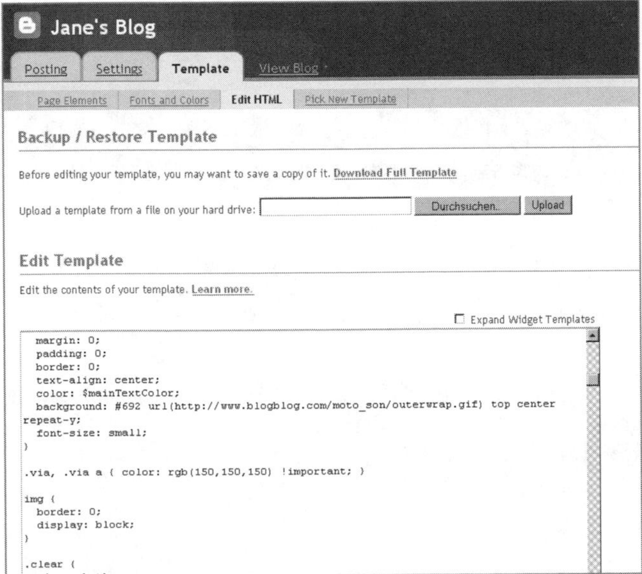

Figure 10-25.
The part reading "Via CNN.com" is all gray now

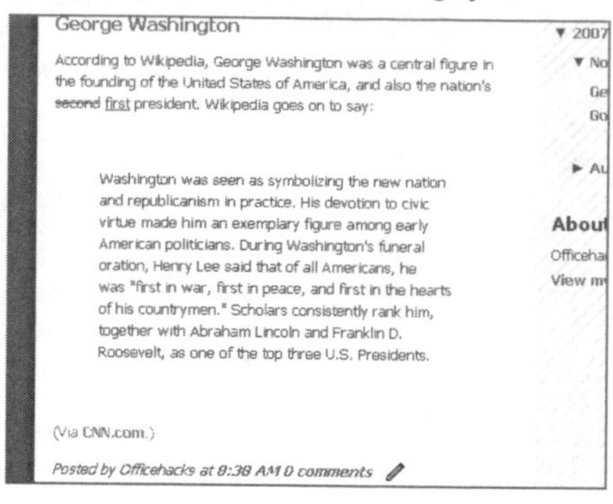

When picking a new class name, try to find a word that describes what the element **is**, rather than **how you want it to appear**. The benefit is that when you decide to make design changes later on, you will need to edit the single stylesheet—but not all of your past posts! So, a class name like `footer` or `warning` or `externalLink` is more effective than a name like `smallGray` or `redUnderlinedParagraph`. However, sometimes juggling dozens of different class names can become complicated, too. If you want to use a specific formatting for one post only, you may also decide to use an *inline* style, like `<p style="color: red">...</p>`. (Note that this style will now show in every medium, even print—a potential downside to inline styles.)

HACK 103: Hide the Blogspot Navigation Bar

Go minimal on your blog design.

Every Blogspot blog by default receives a navigation bar on top, with buttons for switching to the next blog, searching your blog and more, as shown in Figure 10-26. Some users may find this navigation bar useful, but you may still want to disable it—for instance, if you feel that disabling it would improve the layout of your blog.

Figure 10-26.
The Blogspot navigation bar

 Before using tools that modify the appearance of a web site you are using, it is your responsibility to review the most recent terms of service to ensure that your activities do not conflict with those terms (for example, some sites require that you accept ads as part of their terms of use; other display elements may be specified as well).

There is no menu entry to disable showing the so-called Navbar, but you can still hide it. Just switch to your blog's template source by going to the dashboard page and selecting Layout→Edit HTML. In the HTML source text field, scroll down to near the end, and right before the `</body>` tag, include the following:

```
<style rel="stylesheet" media="screen">
#navbar { display: none !important }
</style>
```

What does this mean? Well, `<style>...</style>` encloses stylesheet instructions that define a page's layout; plus, you'll be restricting your instructions to only those layouts that are delivered to the screen (as opposed to, say, the printer) via the `media="screen"` part. The actual layout instruction is now targeting the element of the ID `navbar`, which you define to not display. The `!important` bit tells the browser to override other layout definitions for this element, if they exist.

To save your amended template, hit the Save Template button. You can now check the result by viewing your blog. If there's no navigation bar in sight, your hack was successful.

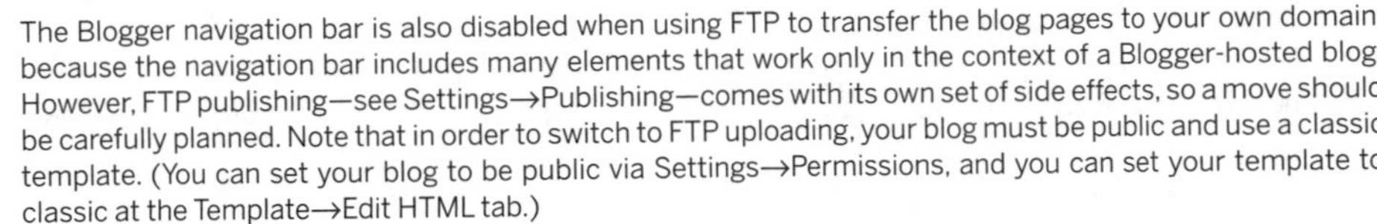

If there still is a navigation bar showing, perhaps Google has since adjusted the way their page design displays the navigation bar. If so, you may need to read the HTML source of your blog's page and adjust your stylesheet instructions accordingly.

The Blogger navigation bar is also disabled when using FTP to transfer the blog pages to your own domain, because the navigation bar includes many elements that work only in the context of a Blogger-hosted blog. However, FTP publishing—see Settings→Publishing—comes with its own set of side effects, so a move should be carefully planned. Note that in order to switch to FTP uploading, your blog must be public and use a classic template. (You can set your blog to be public via Settings→Permissions, and you can set your template to classic at the Template→Edit HTML tab.)

HACK 104: Monitor a Thread for New Posts

When you contribute a post to Google Groups, there may be a delay before it appears. Furthermore, responses to the post may trickle in hours, days, or weeks later. How do you know when that happens? And what if a particular thread in your own group is so emotional that you'd like to get an email whenever someone adds something to it?

One way to keep track of new Groups posts, whether it's your own group or one by someone else, is to check your profile page in Google Groups: it contains links to all the threads you've participated in or initiated. Go to http://groups.google.com, log in, and click Profile on top. In the Recent Activity box, follow the linked threads to check whether there's any news for you.

Another and a more automated option is to subscribe to email alerts for a thread. However, this approach works only for discussion groups hosted with Google, not those groups found on Usenet (which Google also shows on Google Groups). If it's a Google-native group, then you will find a link reading Options (not to be confused with the link reading "More options") at the top of each individual thread. Click it and a menu will open as shown in Figure 10-27. Click "Email updates to me" and you're set. Blogger Ionut Alex. Chitu from Romania adds a caveat, writing "Unfortunately, the notifications are sometimes delayed."

Figure 10-27.
The Google Groups thread options menu

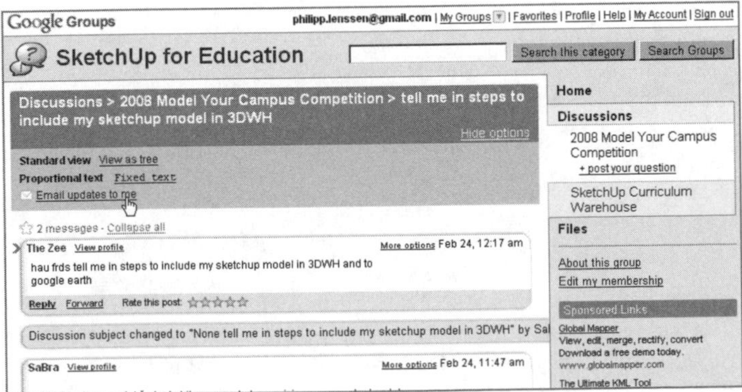

Change Detection Services

How *do* you get email alerts for non-Google-native discussion threads—all those on Usenet? (You can't simply subscribe to a group's RSS feed, as it would show you every new message, not just replies to your question.) The answer comes in the form of what is called a *web page change detection service*. These services let you provide a couple of URLs, and will then email you whenever the page in question was updated. If you provide the Google Groups URL of the Usenet thread to such a service, you will then be able to track it.

Here are a couple of different change detection services, many of them free, to get you started—note that you can get creative and use these services for tracking much more than just Google Groups:

- TrackEngine (http://trackengine.com)
- InfoMinder (http://infominder.com)
- ChangeDetection (http://changedetection.com)

For instance, after registering with TrackEngine, you will be emailed your password. Log in to the site using your email address and password, and you will be offered a bookmarklet to add to your browser **[Hack #16]**. This bookmarklet will read "Track me!"—press it when you're viewing the Google Groups thread in question (Figure 10-28). A pop-up window opens (you may be required to log in again). Switch to the Expert tab, disable the "Use cookies" option at the bottom (otherwise, TrackEngine runs into troubles), and click OK. You will now be alerted via email whenever a response to the thread is posted.

Figure 10-28.
Hitting the "Track me!" button

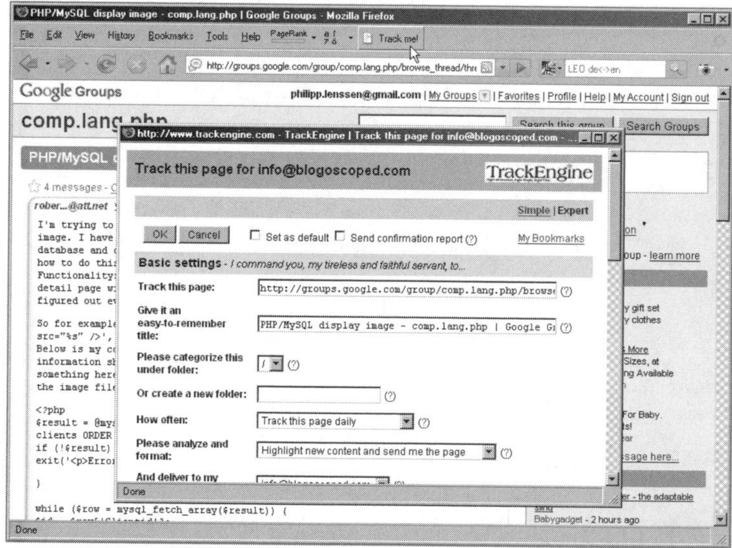

Hacking the Hack

We mentioned earlier how it's impossible to simply subscribe to a group's feed in order to find replies to one specific thread, as that feed would contain posts to any thread in the group. However, with a little Yahoo! Pipes magic, you can actually filter an RSS feed for specific words, to then create a second feed showing just the items you want (in this case, just the replies to the thread you're watching).

First, log in to Yahoo! Pipes at http://pipes.yahoo.com. Next, create a new pipe like this:

1. Under Sources, drag "Fetch Feed" to the work area and specify the URL of the group's XML feed.
2. Under Operators, drag a Filter to the work area, specify "Permit items that match all of the following," and set `item.title` to the subject of the thread.
3. Connect the source to the filter, and the filter to the output, as shown in Figure 10-29. Save the new Pipe, click Back to My Pipes, and click on your new pipe to find its RSS feed.

Now, subscribe to the pipe's RSS feed in your feed reader to be notified of new posts to the thread. You may want to clone and adjust this pipe—which we stored at http://blogoscoped.com/googleappshacks/link/monitor—if you want to subscribe to multiple threads.

— Brian Jepson and Philipp Lenssen

Figure 10-29.
Setting up the Yahoo! Pipe

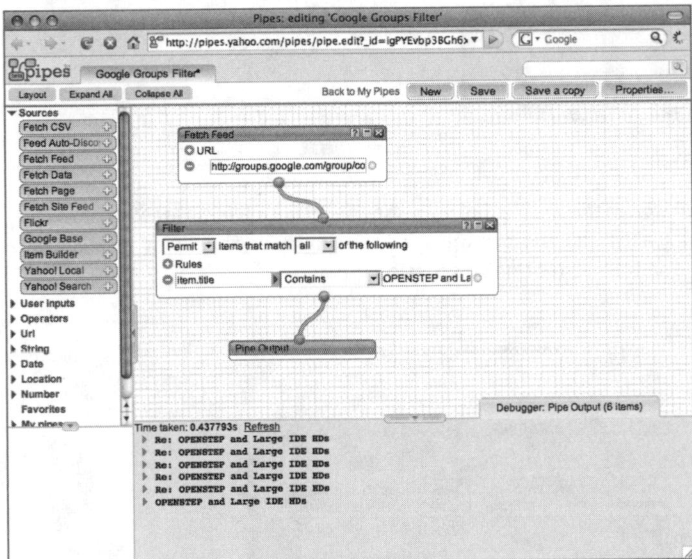

HACK 105: Hide the Ads in Your Google Group

Battle information overflow by hiding ads.

If you maintain or visit a Google group (see the introduction to this chapter), there may be ads showing on the right side of some discussion threads. Although you can't disable them globally for all users—even if you are the owner of the group—you can disable them for yourself if you use the Firefox browser.

 Before using tools that modify the appearance of a web site you are using, it is your responsibility to review the most recent terms of service to ensure that your activities do not conflict with those terms—for example, some sites require that you accept ads as part of their terms of use; other display elements may be specified as well.

To get Firefox, start out at http://firefox.com. Once you've got that installed, there is an add-on for Firefox called Adblock Plus; you can get it by visiting https://addons.mozilla.org/en-US/firefox/addon/1865. Click the Install Now button and follow the instructions. You may be required to restart your browser. When Firefox starts up again, pick one of the available filter lists, as shown in Figure 10-30. The first one in the list includes settings to disable Google AdSense ads, for instance, which are the ones being used over at Google Groups too.

Figure 10-30.
The Adblock Plus configuration dialog after installing

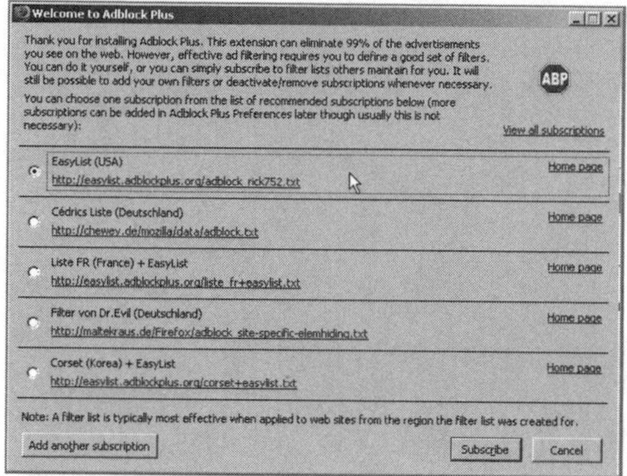

Now you will notice a stop sign icon in the top right of your browser. If your filter is inactive, it will be gray, as shown in Figure 10-31. If activated, the icon will be red and many ads are being disabled, as shown in Figure 10-32 with the sample comic book discussion group.

Figure 10-31.
The Google Groups page with ads

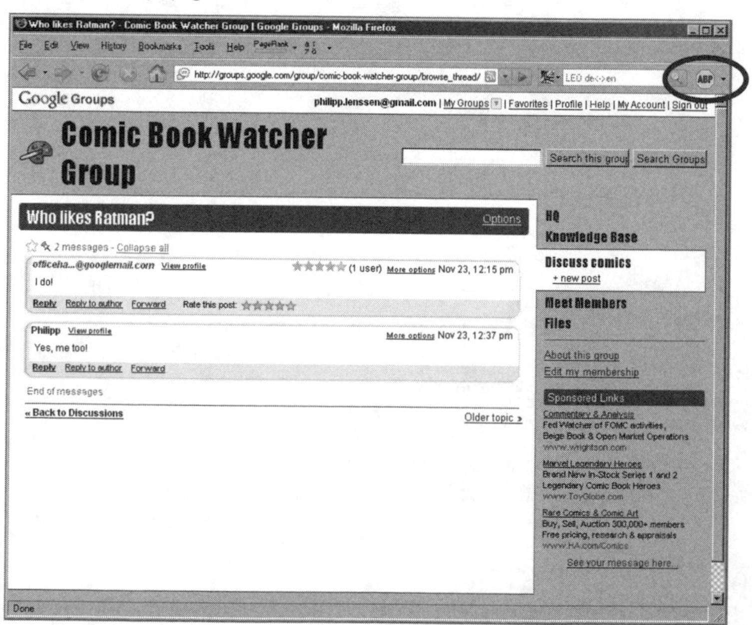

Figure 10-32.
The same page without ads, thanks to Adblock Plus

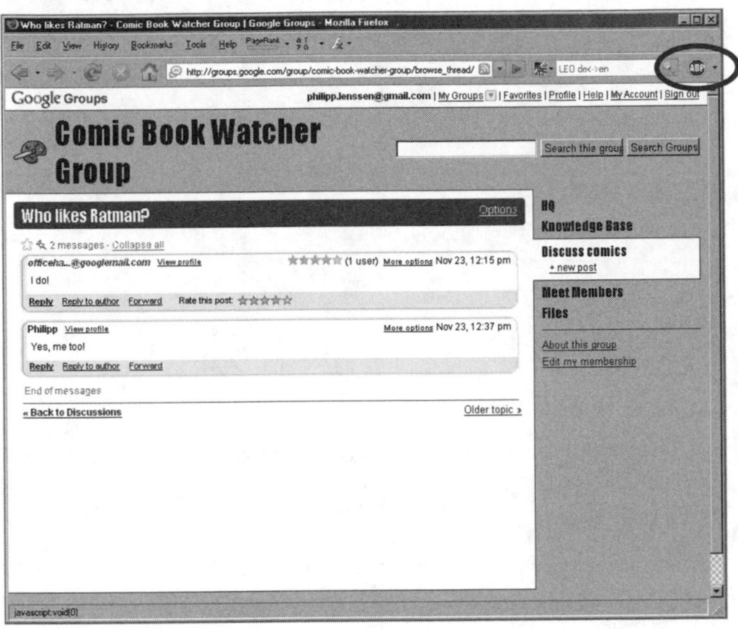

HACK 106: Track Who Links to Your Blog Posts

Feedback helps shape your blog—find it.

Every blog post of yours can be a part of a larger conversation. Perhaps you've written something in reaction to another blog article, and now someone else continues the discussion and writes something at their blog in reaction to your post. To keep track of the "replies" you are getting this way, you can discover posts by others that include a link to your post.

To check for these *backlinks*, you can use Google Blog Search at http://blogsearch.google.com. Note that it won't show all links, but it will show some. When searching, use the `link` operator as in the following query example , where "http://example.com/323.html" would be the permalink to your blog entry:

```
link:http://example.com/323.html
```

If you omit the link operator, Google Blog Search still knows what you mean and will add it automatically.

You will now get a list of blog articles discussing your article, similar to what is shown in Figure 10-33. Click the link reading "Sort by date" in the top right to get the latest reactions first; otherwise, Google will order results by relevance. Note that you can subscribe to these backlinks results via the Atom/RSS links on result pages.

To get a more general list of recent reactions to your blog, you can also simply enter your home page's URL:

```
link:http://example.com
```

Another backlinks tracking tool is Technorati.com. When visiting the site, just enter your blog post's URL into the search box and hit the Search button. Some of the URLs will be the same as the ones Google Blog Search finds, and others may be new.

Figure 10-33.
Google Blog Search tracks the links back to your blog

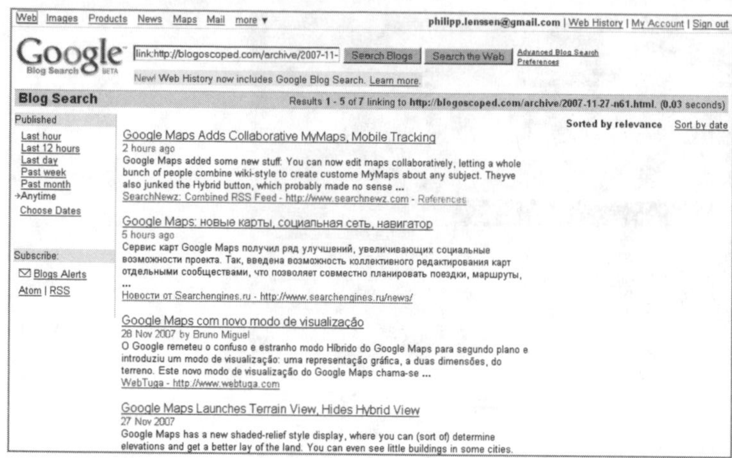

Using Blogger's Backlinks Function

Blogger also offers you a way to show backlinks to your posts right below each post. To enable this feature, click on Settings→Comments at Blogger.com. In the section labeled Backlinks, select Show. Approve the dialog by clicking Save Settings at the bottom.

Other blog systems, like Wordpress.com, also have a feature called "trackback" to allow bloggers to notify your blog system when they discuss a post of yours. This will then result in the link to them being shown below your blog post, as with Blogger's Backlinks function. The downside to trackbacks is that some people might ping your blog's trackback system even when they don't discuss your post, just so that they generate a link to their site in return to increase traffic. (The Blogger Backlinks feature too sometimes falls prey to these "spammers.") At the time of this writing, Google's Blogger does not support trackbacks.

HACK 107: Quickly Share YouTube Videos on Your Blog

Be as lazy as possible when embedding YouTube videos.

If you have a Blogger.com blog and you embed a video from YouTube.com every now and then, you can click the "add video" icon during publishing, as shown in Figure 10-34. However, if you are a more regular video blogger—posting many of your own videos to YouTube, or frequently embedding other people's videos—you can speed up this step.

On the YouTube video page, click the Share link, as shown in Figure 10-35. A dialog will expand below the video with a link reading "Setup your blog for video posting." Click it and you'll be forwarded to a configuration page. Hit the Add a Blog/Site button, pick Blogger as your blog provider—note that this hack also works with some other blog providers, like LiveJournal and WordPress—and enter your Blogger username and password, similar to what is shown in Figure 10-36. A dialog page will now display reading "Fetching your information. Please Wait."

After some seconds, you will be asked to pick the blog you want to add (if your account contains more than one blog). Make your selection and click Add Selected Blogs.

Now, when you click the Share link on a YouTube page the next time, you can immediately share the video by clicking Post to Blog, as pictured in Figure 10-37. By default the new post being created on your blog will also carry the YouTube video's title, as shown in Figure 10-38; entering additional descriptive text for your post is optional.

Figure 10-34.
Blogger's video embed button

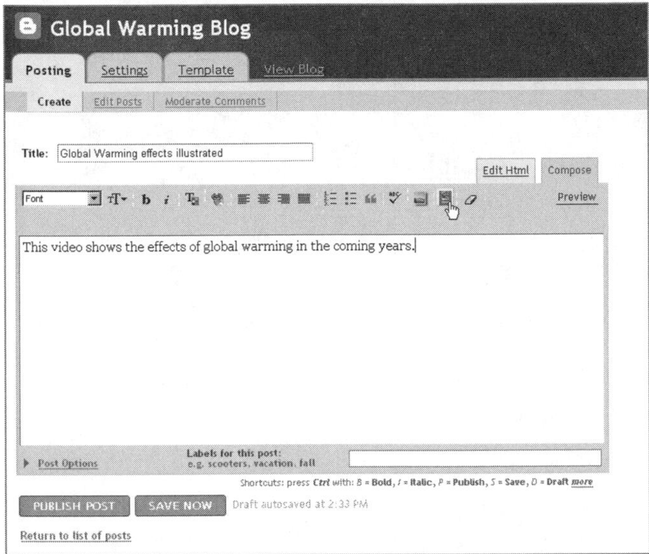

Figure 10-35.
The Share link below YouTube videos

Figure 10-36.
Providing your Blogger account credentials

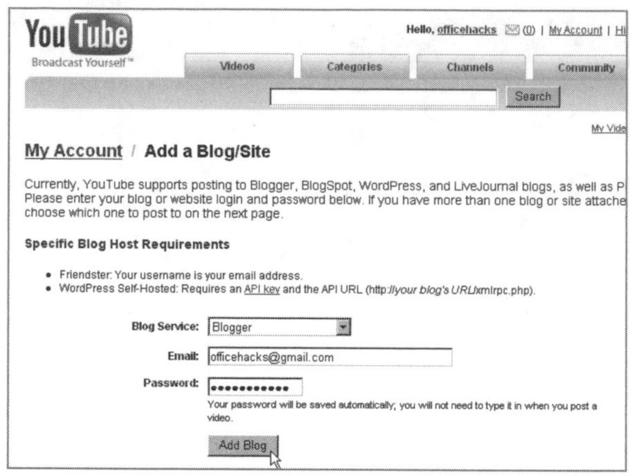

Figure 10-37.
Posting a YouTube video to your blog

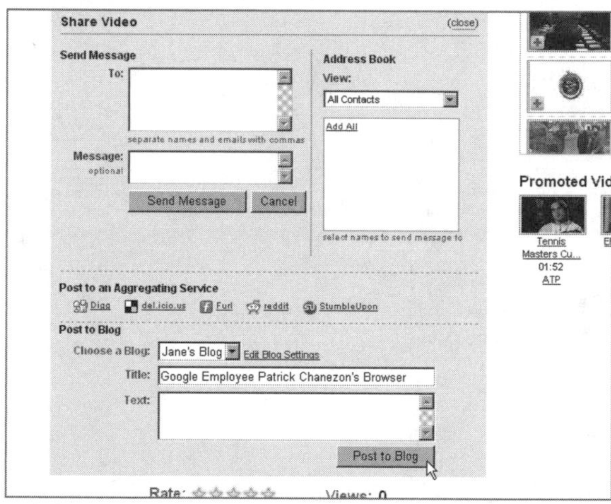

Figure 10-38.
The video is now embedded on the Blogspot blog

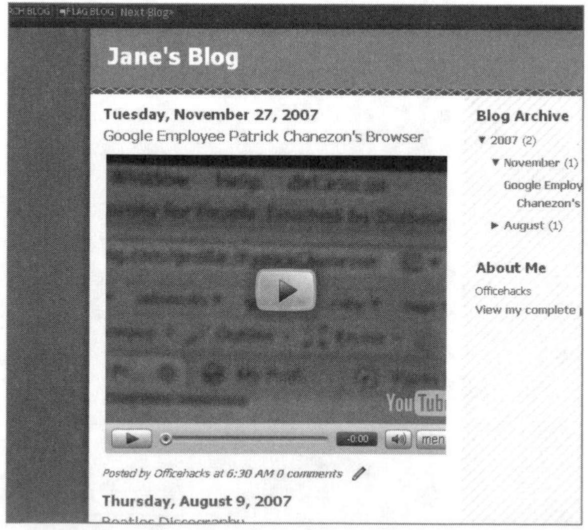

HACK 108: Generate Text Images

If you're a genius with Photoshop or similar tools, you can skip this hack, but if not, here's how to make text with special effects.

When you don't have an image to your blog post and you can't find a fitting Creative Commons licensed image either **[Hack #31]**, you can also generate a new image online. One option is to create an image of a text that describes your post's category, like "Misc. Links," "Fun Sightings," "Tips & Tricks," "Rant," "Politics" and so on. You can also use such an image to add a signature to your post. Generating text images can be helpful for a home page, like one created with Google Page Creator, too. A variety of tools and services are available.

> You can also use the ImageMagick tool described in **[Hack #38]** to create 2D text effects. For more information, see http://www.imagemagick.org/Usage/fonts/

Generate a Signature

Provided that you have a scanner, you can sign a paper, scan it, crop the picture, and add it to your post—the downside being that everyone is now able to swipe your signature. An alternative approach is to generate a signature online. To do so, head over to http://mylivesignature.com/mls_wizard1_1.php and enter your name. You also need to answer a security question. Click Next Step, and you will be able to choose from more than 100 different signature styles, spread out across different pages, as shown in Figure 10-39.

After you've selected an image, the signature creation wizard has you choose a font size, color, and signature slope. Approve your selections and you will end up with a signature image. Right-click it to copy it to your disk; you can now upload it when creating a new blog post (see Figure 10-40).

Figure 10-39.
Picking a font at My Live Signature.com

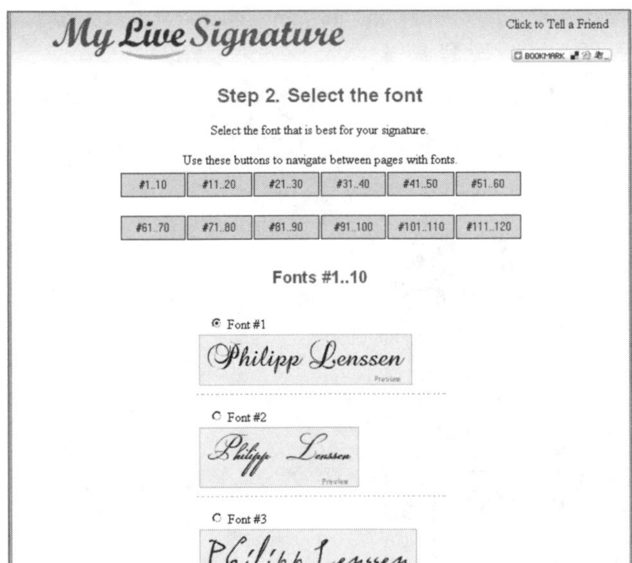

Figure 10-40.
The PNG image as included in the blog post contains a transparent background to smoothly blend in with different designs

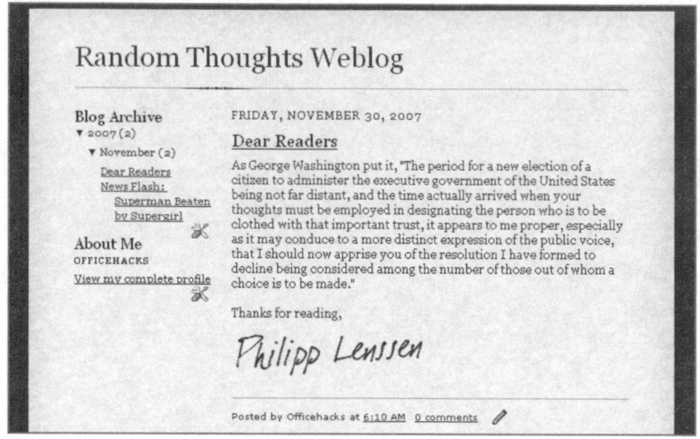

Create 3D Text

A free tool to generate three-dimensional text is available at http://wafu.ne.jp/3dlogo/e3dlogo.html. You can input your words of choice and then toggle an abundance of options. Getting the right result will take some fiddling around with the options and getting used to the interface, and not every image will look good, but if you're shooting for a 3D effect similar to what is shown in Figures 10-41, 10-42, and 10-43, this tool may be for you.

Figure 10-41.
Hacks

Figure 10-42.
Office Hacks

Figure 10-43.
More Hacks

Create 2D Text

At http://interactimage.com, you can also create an image out of different fonts for use in your blog or home page. Just enter some text in the box below the preview canvas and hit the Create button, as shown in Figure 10-44. A variety of settings to the right let you fine-tune your result. If you don't know which font to go for, explore the choices by clicking Font Finder. Once you're done with your image, right-click it to save it.

Figure 10-44.
The Font Image Generator editor

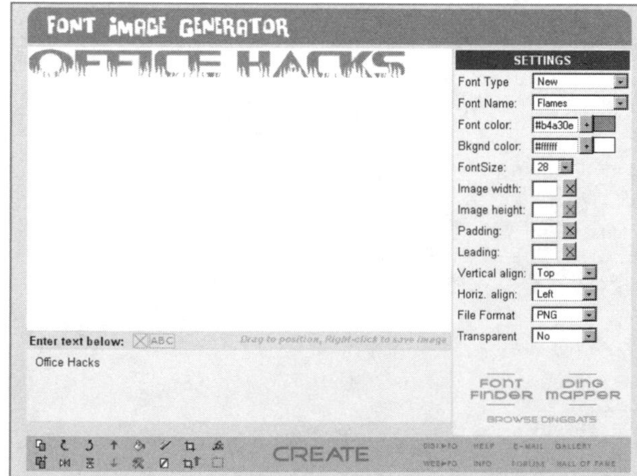

HACK 103: Blog via Email

There is more than one way to create a blog post.

Google Docs **[Hack #11]** isn't the only way to blog outside of Blogger's native editor (see Chapter 10); you can also blog via email. Just go to your blog's email options at Blogger→Settings→Email and enter your own word next to the "Mail-to-Blogger Address" field. Check the Publish checkbox and save the settings, as shown in Figure 10-45. Now you can go to Gmail or whatever email client you use, and write a new mail to your mail-to-blogger address (such as to *officehacks.secretword@blogger.com*) as pictured in Figure 10-46.

Make your secret word for the mail-to-blogger email address something tough to guess, and change it from time to time. Otherwise, a malicious person could create new posts on your blog without your permission. You can think of this custom word as a password, but to be most secure, it's advisable to not reuse a password you use elsewhere for this; you should pick something unique.

Figure 10-45.
Set-up your mail-to-blogger address

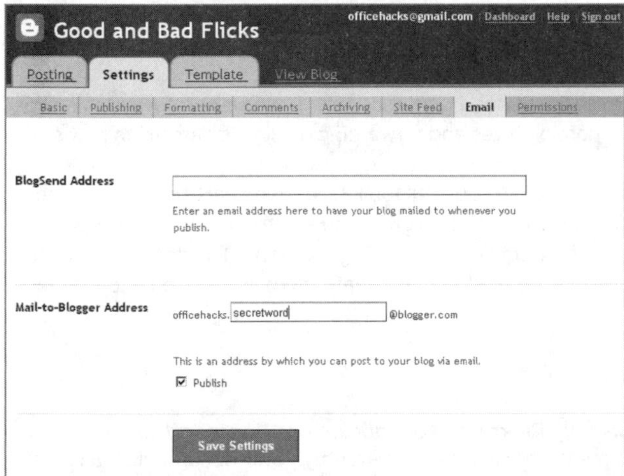

Figure 10-46.
Composing a rich text message in Gmail; the mail subject will turn into the blog post title

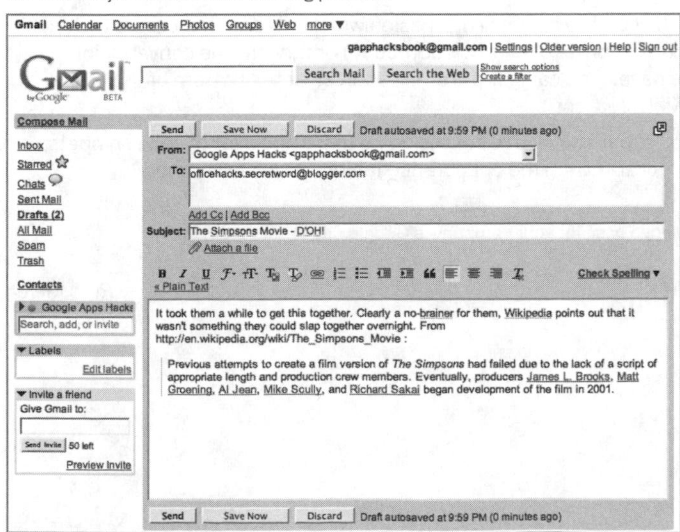

HACK 110: Outsource Your Knowledge Base Hosting

Avoid having to set up and maintain your own intranet wiki and forum.

Google Groups can be useful for business; you can create private knowledge bases full of development resources and use Google's technology and servers to host and search it.

Google Groups' access controls let you create a knowledge base with access limited to yourself, your company, or a set of colleagues. I've created a private group for each technology I use (currently one for Google code and one for C# development). I've invited each of my staff to become part of the group and encourage them to post clever resources like code snippets, and to ask (and answer) tech questions within the forums. I also make sure that everyone forwards email chains with problems/solutions into the discussion forum. Because access is limited to the people you invite, you can post sensitive company questions/answers/code snippets/binaries without fear of public disclosure.

If you plan to access Google Groups from untrusted networks (such as public wireless hotspots), be sure to access it via the SSL protocol: use the https://groups.google.com/group/yourgroupname URL instead of http://groups.google.com/group/yourgroupname.

Also, the centralized archive means that all the members have access to the same information as soon as they've been given access—no more archives and forwarding mailing list emails to new staff.

File hosting gives you somewhere to store cool icons, useful toolkits, or third-party resources. The "Pages" (think of it as your wiki or documentation) section gives you somewhere to put company documentation, like coding guidelines, naming conventions, FAQs, and so on. The documents are collaborative and revision-controlled (like a wiki) so staff can update them as required and everyone can see what's changed and when.

Here are some tips that you might find helpful:

- **Structure your documents.** By selecting "Rearrange your documents" in the "documents" section, you can structure your documents into a sensible hierarchy. "Sub-documents" will be indented underneath their parent and will be shown when you view their parent. Hierarchies can go multiple levels.
- **Add your product or company logo.** Each group lets you include a logo that will be displayed on the top left and in the listings.
- **Discussion posts via email.** If you have an email discussion with someone that covers technical details or any other useful information, bcc (blind carbon-copy) or forward the conversation to the appropriate knowledge bases. You can get the email address at the bottom of the full discussions list (next to the XML feed icon).
- **Make source code readable.** If your knowledge base is going to feature a lot of code snippets, set the default view to `proportional font` in the appearance tab of the group settings.

Another way to set up a knowledge base for your company is Google Sites **[Hack #112]**.

— Reto Meier

HACK 111: Test Your Web Site in Other Browsers

You may have only a single computer physically, but virtually, you can see more.

When you tweak your design by editing the stylesheet or HTML yourself, you may want to test the result on different operating systems and browsers, because for better or worse, not every browser will render your page the same; often, different browsers or versions of those browsers do not support one or another element, or they may interpret it differently.

For Windows users, a great tool to check your site on different systems and browsers is BrowserPool (Mac and Linux versions may come in the future, the service says). You can get it at http://browserpool.de/kc/wob/portal.jsp?lang=en. Click the Free Test Account link to register (see Figure 10-47); enter a username and password, along with your email address, and hit Submit. Check your email inbox to click the confirmation link that was sent to you (you may need to check your spam folder, too, if you don't find the mail from BrowserPool right away).

> Mac and Linux users may want to run a virtualization environment such as VMware or Parallels. Although this requires a Windows license to install Windows under the environment, you should be able to use BrowserPool from within the emulated version of Windows to test all the other versions of Windows you want to use.

Figure 10-47.
Registering with BrowserPool

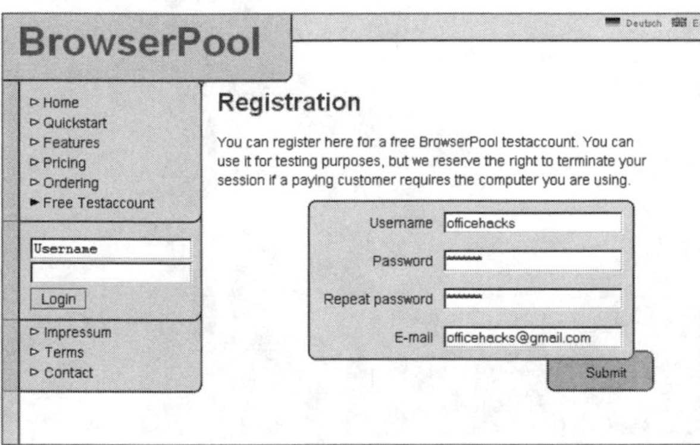

After confirming your new account by clicking the link in the email, you will be able to download *browserpool.exe*. Run the executable to install the program.

Once you start BrowserPool, you can choose between a variety of operating systems and settings, as shown in Figure 10-48. Pick one and a new window opens with your system of choice, as shown in Figure 10-49. You can now fire up a browser within that system to check your blog or home page. If there are any rendering issues with your template amendments, you can now go about fixing them.

Figure 10-48.
The BrowserPool client offers different operating systems with different browsers

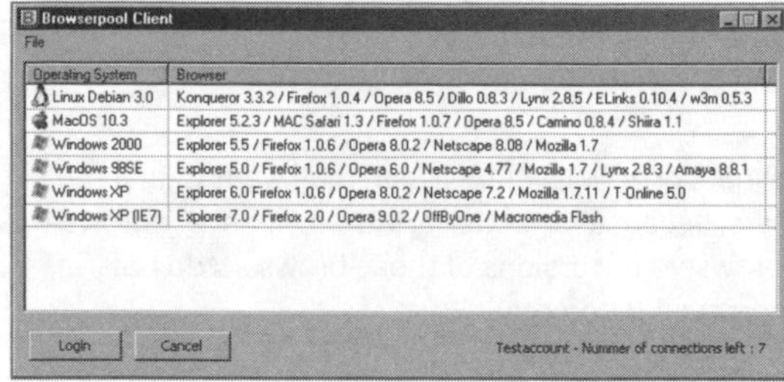

Figure 10-49.
Using BrowserPool to test how a blog layout renders on Mac OS X with Safari

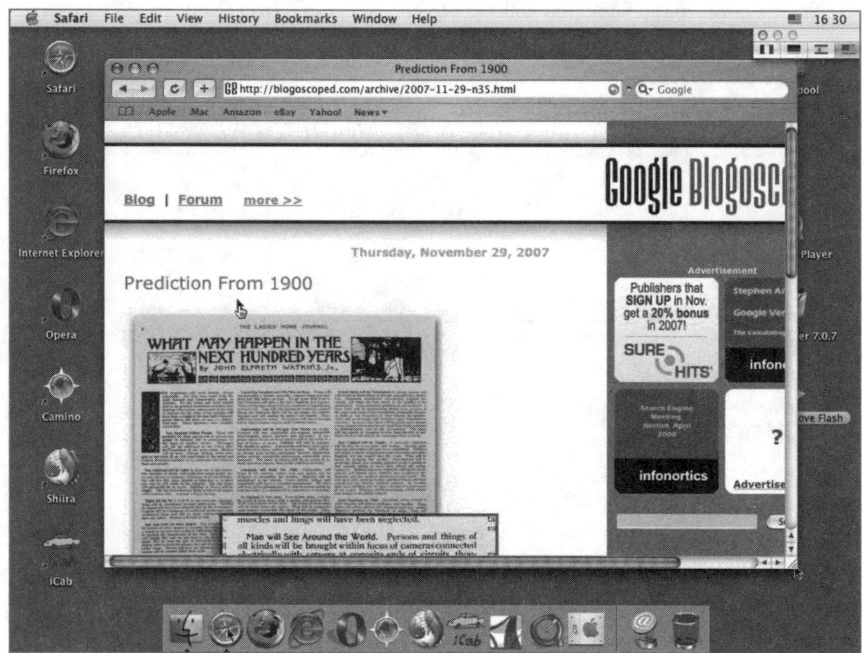

HACK 112: Get a (Google) Site

With some technical knowledge, you can set up custom Google Apps for your organization or team (or private use), and create a Google Site.

Google Sites (http://sites.google.com) is a content management system that includes wiki-like features (like visual on-page editing) as well as project management tools (like the creation of task lists). It's more advanced than Google Page Creator, but also requires a Google Apps account (as opposed to a regular Google account)—and a Google Apps account in turn requires you to have your own domain.

Signing Up with Google Apps

What's a Google Apps account? Google Apps (http://google.com/a/), formerly called Google Apps for Your Domain, is a service that Google offers for businesses, students, schools, and organizations to set up Google-powered applications like Gmail, iGoogle, Google Docs, and more. An administrator for the domain can then configure these tools in certain ways, like setting up a customized design for the iGoogle page.

Even with Google Apps, the data will still be stored at Google in the "cloud." Upsides include not having to manage backups and software updates yourself. A potential downside is that the data is shared with another organization—Google, Inc.—who in some cases, as is true with anything stored with your regular Google Account too, may even be obliged to share data with government agencies (see links to the respective privacy policies at http://google.com/a/help/intl/en/users/privacy.html).

Google Apps comes in standard, premier, and education editions. The premier edition costs $50 per user account per year (at the time of this writing), but the standard edition is free to use. To sign up for the standard edition, point your browser to http://google.com/a/cpanel/domain/new. If you already have a domain, you will be required to enter it in the left field, as shown in Figure 10-50; if you don't have a domain yet, switch to the righthand tab by clicking "I want to buy a domain name" or get a domain name elsewhere (querying Google web search for "domain", "get domain", "hosting", "domain hosting", or similar returns some of the available providers).

Figure 10-50.
Step 1 of 3 for setting up a Google Apps account

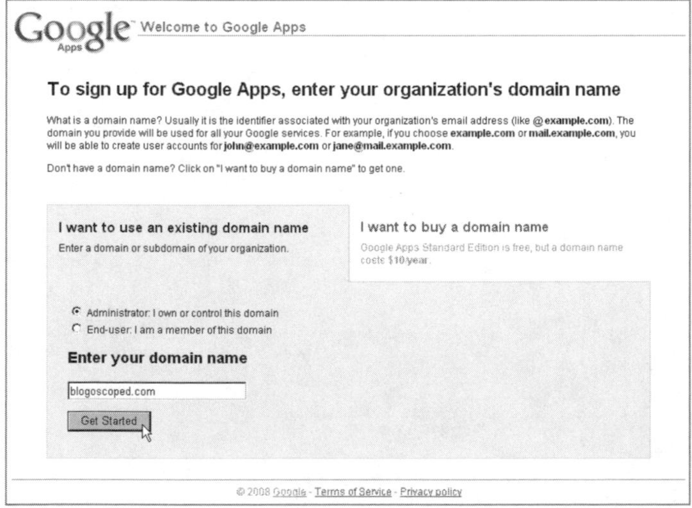

After you've entered your domain into the form—I entered "blogoscoped.com" back in Figure 10-50—click the Get Started button, and complete the registration form that follows, as shown in Figure 10-51. Another form follows requesting you to provide an administrator username and password, and to accept the Terms and Conditions. If you do, click "I accept."

You will now be forwarded to your Google Apps dashboard, as shown in Figure 10-52, and it's time to verify that you are indeed the domain owner. Click "Verify domain ownership" to choose from the available methods to do so. In my case, I'm picking "Upload an HTML file" from the combo box; Google now hands me a verification code, which I'm pasting anywhere into a new file named *googlehostedservice.html*. I'm then uploading that file to the root of http://blogoscoped.com (please consult your web host support if you're unsure how to upload this file to your server's document root). After you start the verification by hitting the Verify button, Google will alert you that it may take 48 hours to complete.

Figure 10-51.
Step 2 of providing your information for Google Apps

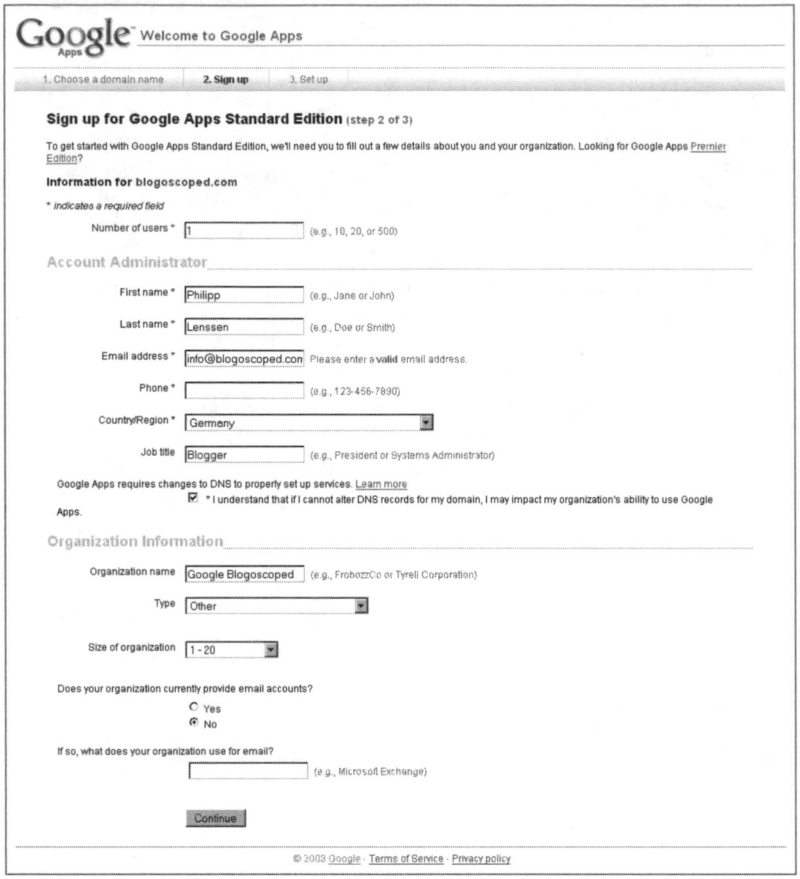

Google Apps — Welcome to Google Apps

1. Choose a domain name | **2. Sign up** | 3. Set up

Sign up for Google Apps Standard Edition (step 2 of 3)

To get started with Google Apps Standard Edition, we'll need you to fill out a few details about you and your organization. Looking for Google Apps Premier Edition?

Information for blogoscoped.com

* indicates a required field

Number of users * [1] (e.g., 10, 20, or 500)

Account Administrator

First name * [Philipp] (e.g., Jane or John)

Last name * [Lenssen] (e.g., Doe or Smith)

Email address * [info@blogoscoped.com] Please enter a **valid** email address.

Phone * [ ] (e.g., 123-456-7890)

Country/Region * [Germany]

Job title [Blogger] (e.g., President or Systems Administrator)

Google Apps requires changes to DNS to properly set up services. Learn more

[x] * I understand that if I cannot alter DNS records for my domain, I may impact my organization's ability to use Google Apps.

Organization Information

Organization name [Google Blogoscoped] (e.g., FrobozzCo or Tyrell Corporation)

Type [Other]

Size of organization [1 - 20]

Does your organization currently provide email accounts?

( ) Yes
(•) No

If so, what does your organization use for email?

[ ] (e.g., Microsoft Exchange)

Continue

© 2008 Google - Terms of Service - Privacy policy

Figure 10-52.
Your Google Apps dashboard, a launchpad to manage the Google Apps offerings like Google Docs, Calendar, Chat, and Google Sites

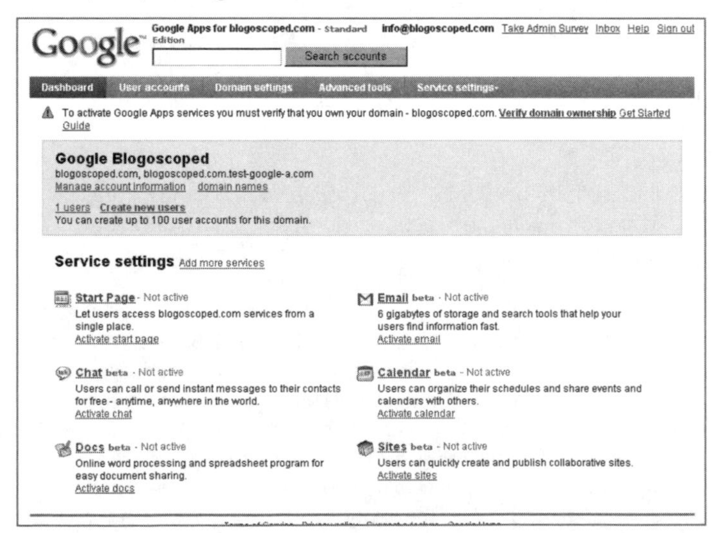

From the dashboard, you can now add services to your Google Apps, or customize the existing ones. For instance, I edited the logo font colors of the custom iGoogle page (which in this case is located at http://partnerpage.google.com/blogoscoped.com), as shown in Figure 10-53.

If you can fully administer your server, you can change the domain that users visit to get to their iGoogle start page. You'll need to create what is called a CNAME record, and which is further explained at http://google.com/support/a/bin/answer.py?answer=47283.

Figure 10-53.
A custom iGoogle home page for Google Apps users

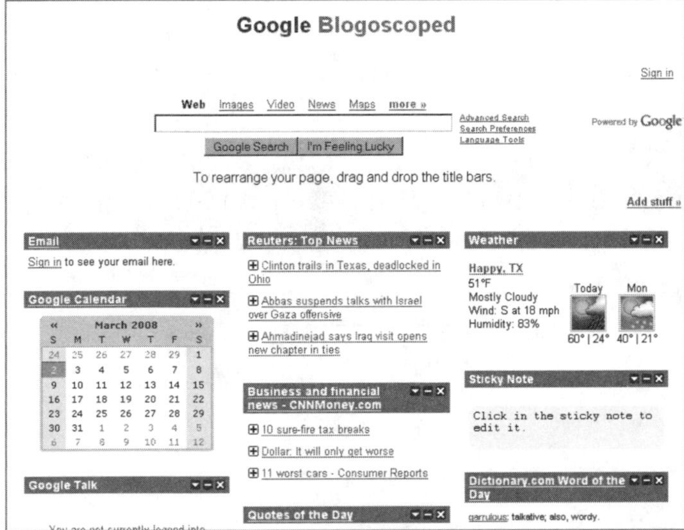

Setting Up Your Google Site

Once you set up your Google Apps account, you will find your Google Sites home page at http://sites.google.com/a/example.com (replace *example.com* with your actual domain). During your first visit, click the Create a Site button. Provide your site name, categories, a site description, a theme, and more.

There are many types of sites you can create, like the home of a local book reading club, a start page for your company's intranet, the home page to a software project, or a page containing your biography, resume, and pictures. Sites can be edited by a team, or by a single person; they can be made public, or invite-only. Take a look at Google's sample project, "Mrs. Richau's Classroom," at http://sites.google.com/a/googleclassrooms.org/mrs-richau/Home, to get an idea of what's possible with Google Sites.

As shown in Figure 10-54, I'm creating a sample site named "Joey's JavaScript Tutorials," offering code downloads, tutorials, and helpful pointers. Click Create Site and you will be dropped on your new site's home page. Outside visitors will see a normal web site, but as you are logged in as administrator, you will now see special buttons printed on the pages for editing pages, creating new pages, or accessing special features, as shown in Figure 10-55. When you create a new page, you are able to choose between a variety of page types and subtypes; for instance, you can create a List named "Overview of All JavaScript Functions" and then set up the subtype "Custom List" (see Figure 10-56). You can also click Site Settings on top to adjust global configurations any time, like your site's overall layout.

Figure 10-54.
Setting up a new Google Sites site

Figure 10-55.
Clicking the Edit button takes you into a WYSIWYG editing mode for the given page

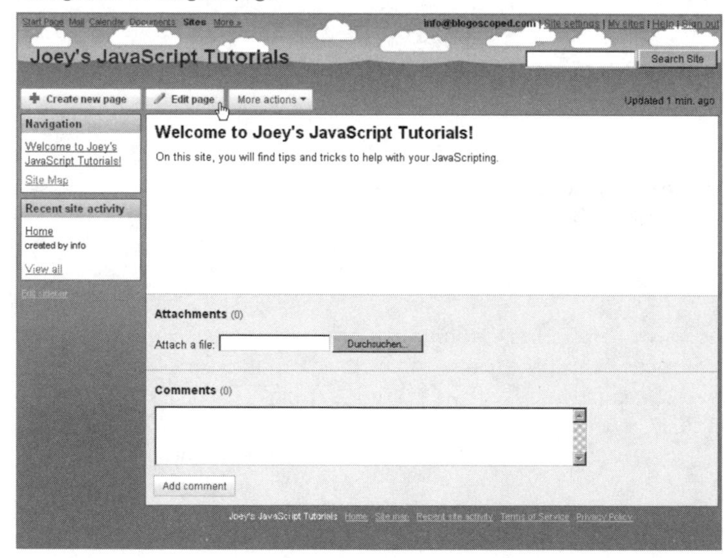

Figure 10-56.
A custom list page starts collecting information on JavaScript functions. An attachment (*alert.rar*) was added as well.

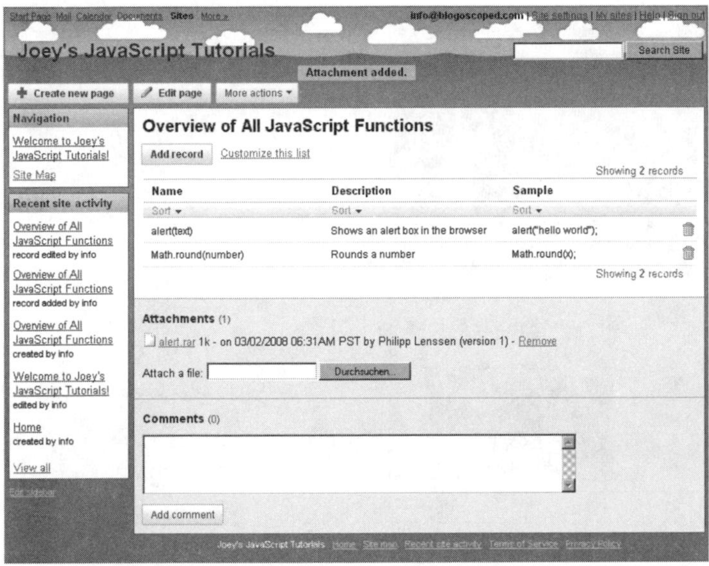

HACK 113: Turn Your Blog Into a Book

The digital world is great for quick and timely info, but you might want to produce something of longer value that you can also physically pass on.

Have you added new posts to your blog at a regular basis over months or years, perhaps even on a single continuous topic? If so, you might want to consider turning your blog into a book. I'm not referring to an ebook, either—though that's a possibility as well—but an actual printed book. This can make a great gift, and it may also earn you some spare change (or more) in commissions.

A while ago, a service called BlogBinders allowed you to turn your Google Blogspot blog semi-automatically into a book. I was able to use it myself while the service lasted, but unfortunately the company has gone out of business now and closed shop. But there's another service available that can achieve the same goal: Lulu.com. If you visit the site, shown in Figure 10-57, you will learn that it allows you to create and sell your content as paperback books, hardcover books, photo books, brochures, calendars, posters, and more.

Print on Demand—How Lulu.com Works

Here's how Lulu works. You have content in a digital format to which you own the copyright. You can now register with the site and upload your document as a Word document, or another accepted format. Your file will be converted to PDF, which you can check for layout consistency. If you approve the change, you can start selling the book through the site. It will be printed on demand, and for every successful order, you will get a commission based on the price you determine to set yourself (though base costs as well as Lulu's commission will be subtracted).

Additionally, you can buy an advanced distribution package at Lulu. This will get your book an ISBN, the bar code shown on books sold at book stores that represents the International Standard Book Number. Plus, the book will then be added to Amazon.com and available to other distributors.

Figure 10-57.
The Lulu home page

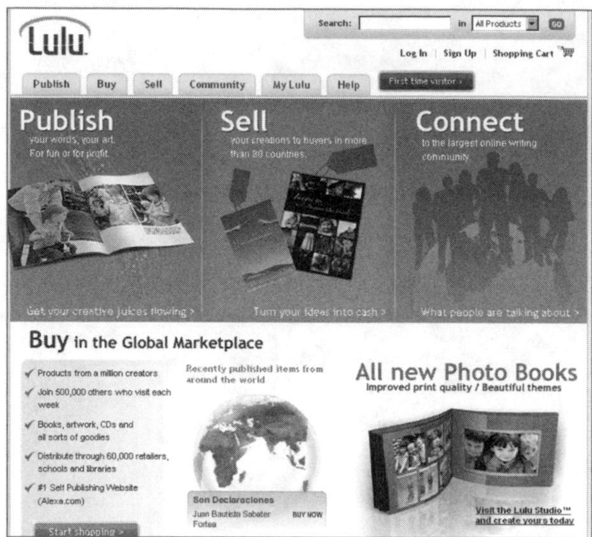

The Technical Steps for the Blog-to-Book Conversion

If the Lulu.com principle sounds easy, indeed it is relatively easy; however, preparing the content to be in the right format for converting it to a Lulu book can be rather challenging. In my experience, unless you know how to produce picture-perfect PDF files yourself using professional tools, preparing the content works best if you're working with an English version of Microsoft Word. Unfortunately, due to the nature of Lulu.com, I found that competing products like OpenOffice.org (and even non-English versions of Microsoft Word) can bring with them conversion headaches at a later point. Lulu offers you book templates to start with; give them a try. You may also want to give doing this with Google Docs a shot, though **[Hack #1]**.

If you settled for a word processor whose output works with Lulu, it's time to go about importing your blog. One of the best approaches for this is to identify which blog posts ought to make it into your book by finding those that have a longer shelf life, or that don't contain too many crucial links, or that are especially well-written or researched. Once you've located each post, you can copy and paste its text into your word processor.

After repeating this process chapter by chapter, and preparing a fitting cover illustration for your blog **[Hack #31]**, you need to check whether the layout of your book survives the conversion to PDF. Once it looks good, you can send yourself a review copy, which may take several days. If the printed book looks good, too, you can approve the book to go live for sale to the public (I did this with my book *55 Ways to Have Fun with Google*, which you can also fully download for free at http://55fun.com). The final PDF generated for you might also make for a good ebook.

How to Write Blog Posts that Stand the Test of Time

Here are some tips to help ensure that your blog posts will be as useful in the future as they are today. These tips are useful both for turning your blog into a book at a later point, as well as optimizing the value of your blog as an archive in general:

- Write about things that you have personal experience in, or that you think may be of more general interest.
- If you link to information crucial to getting your post's point across, also summarize the information in your own words in the post itself. This way, should the external site go down or become extinct—or the link can't be made active, such as in book form—your post is still useful.
- If you talk about an external site in your blog post, use a screenshot of that site to illustrate your point. Doing so will ensure that your article can be understood if the external site is removed or changed.

- Clarify your point by being precise and adding details. Sometimes, this even means stating what may be obvious to you. Otherwise, the in-joke of the day may not be understood by readers—perhaps not even yourself!—some years ahead.
- Use a spellchecker program for your posts. This way, they become more readable. This is especially useful if you convert the blog articles to a book chapter; though people may be used to one or two spelling errors in a blog post, we usually expect a much lower frequency in books.
- Write about a single topic or set of topics. Over time, this will turn you into an expert in that field, rendering your articles all that more valuable (we all like expert advice). Also, this will make it easier to turn your blog into a book, as the book will now have a single theme.
- Use self-explanatory, precise titles for your posts. Otherwise, you might have a hard time digging through your archive to find material for your book.

HACK 114: Beyond Google: From WordPress and FriendFeed to Yahoo's GeoCities

If you feel restricted by Blogspot, Google Page Creator, or Google Groups, look beyond these offerings—there are loads of good (and partly free) alternatives around.

Before deciding which tool is right for you, understand what you're after: a blog, a regular home page, or a discussion forum. A regular home page is better for a few static pages, whereas a weblog is ideal for frequent additions or regularly updated information. If you mainly want to supply a place for a community instead of writing, a forum may be the way to go. And sometimes, mixing and matching among the three is also a good solution—like a web site that combines blog and forum.

Blogging Software

Blog editors can be divided into two camps, roughly: those that run on someone else's server, with no software management needed on your end, and those running on your own server, requiring a bit more administration knowledge. (And then, there's a dividing line between free and paid blog systems.)

One of the most popular blogging platforms is WordPress. You can either download the necessary files from http://wordpress.com to do your own hosting, or get a hosted blog with them on a URL like http://yourname.wordpress.com. It takes only seconds to register with WordPress. Then you can click the New Post button on top, and submit a post with the editor as pictured in Figure 10-58. The result using the default template is shown in Figure 10-59.

Figure 10-58.
The WordPress blog post editor

Figure 10-59.
A published post, hosted at WordPress.com

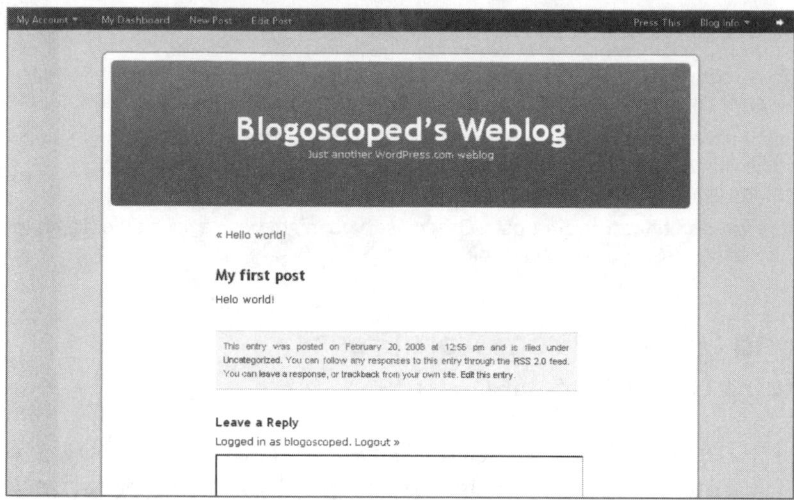

Tumblr (http://tumblr.com) is also a blogging tool, with a refreshingly clean interface supporting quick text blogging or sharing of photos, videos, audio, and more (some also call these blog formats "microblogs" or "tumblelogs" to emphasize their scrapbook nature). Your URL after free signup will be http://yourname.tumblr.com.

Another option for a hosted blog tool is TypePad (http://typepad.com), with your blog URL being *yourname.typepad.com*. You can start out with a free 14-day trial, though even this trial will require you to provide your credit card information. After the two weeks, you can decide if you want to continue with the paid version of the service. At the time of this writing, TypePad pricing starts at $4.95 per month, becoming more costly with higher membership levels.

 When you register for a TypePad trial, note that by default you will be added to the TypePad updates and special offers newsletter. What's more, if you need to amend information in the form—for instance, because you picked a username that exists already—the checkbox selection will always revert to you being subscribed to the newsletter, even when you unchecked it before. If you don't want to receive the newsletter, make sure to uncheck the box every time you submit the form.

The nonhosted sibling of TypePad, created by the same company (Six Apart), is called Movable Type. For personal uses, Movable Type is free to download; a commercial, supported license can be acquired starting at $295.95 (see http://movabletype.com). Another option is to get the Movable Type Open Source version, which can be used for personal and commercial endeavors alike (see http://moveabletype.org).

LiveJournal at http://livejournal.com is another blogging option, with free as well as paid membership levels. More than other services, LiveJournal emphasizes community features like finding new friends. After registering with them—uncheck the "occasionally email me LiveJournal updates" box unless you want those mails—you can start adding blog posts, polls, and more to a URL like http://username.livejournal.com.

Another hosted blog system, this one from Microsoft, is available at http://spaces.live.com and called Windows Live Spaces. If you already have a Hotmail account or a Windows Live ID, you can use it here to sign in. Spaces supports not just creating blog posts, but also adding photo albums. Your blog URL will be http://username.spaces.live.com/blog/, and depending on your template, appears as shown in Figure 10-60.

Figure 10-60.
A Microsoft Windows Live Spaces sample blog

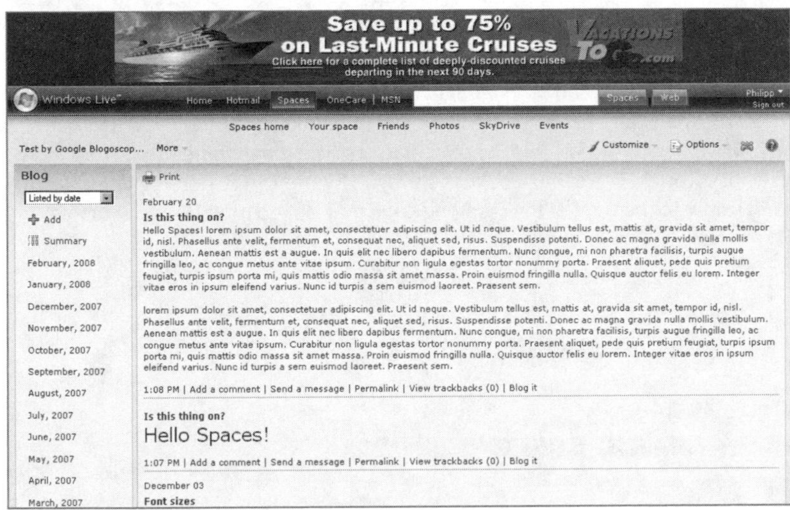

Instead of a blog—or in addition to one—you may also want to try out FriendFeed or Twitter. Twitter (http://twitter.com), for instance, behaves a bit like a mini blog. Instead of longer posts, you just tell people what you're currently doing. FriendFeed (http://friendfeed.com), started by ex–Google employees, also lets you post to a circle of befriended subscribers, and allows you to simultaneously track what your friends are doing or reading. FriendFeed accomplishes this by aggregating feeds from a variety of sources, like Twitter, blogs, YouTube, social news sites (including Digg.com and Reddit.com), and more, as shown in Figure 10-61. Think of it as turning a person into an RSS feed—very simple yet very addictive!

Figure 10-61.
FriendFeed lets you follow the online tracks of interesting people

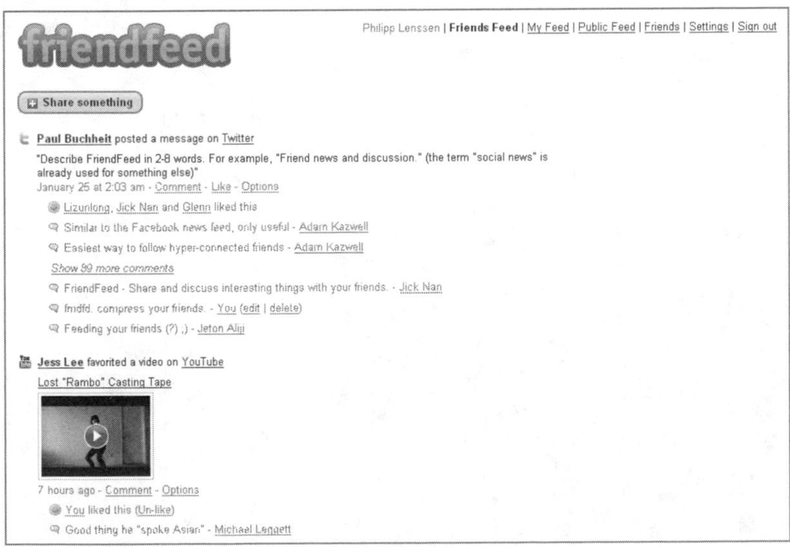

If blogging text doesn't do it for you, consider launching a podcast or video blog. Searching Google for "create podcast," "vlog," and similar can get you started.

Home Page Creators

GeoCities is one of the oldest personal home page creators around. The ad-supported version lets you start for free, too. Get going at http://geocities.com and sign in with your Yahoo! account (first create an account if you don't have one). Afterwards, you can click Create a Web Site to choose between two tools: Yahoo! PageBuilder and Yahoo! PageWizard. The PageWizard is even quicker to use; after picking one of the many templates, as shown in Figure 10-62, and completing the multi-step wizard, your page will appear on http://geocities.com/***username***/***pagename***.html. The layout varies depending on what you picked; a sample page is shown in Figure 10-63. Although the wizard is quick, the ads and scrollbar to the right of the resulting page may be too much for your tastes.

Figure 10-62.
The GeoCities page creation wizard lets you pick a template

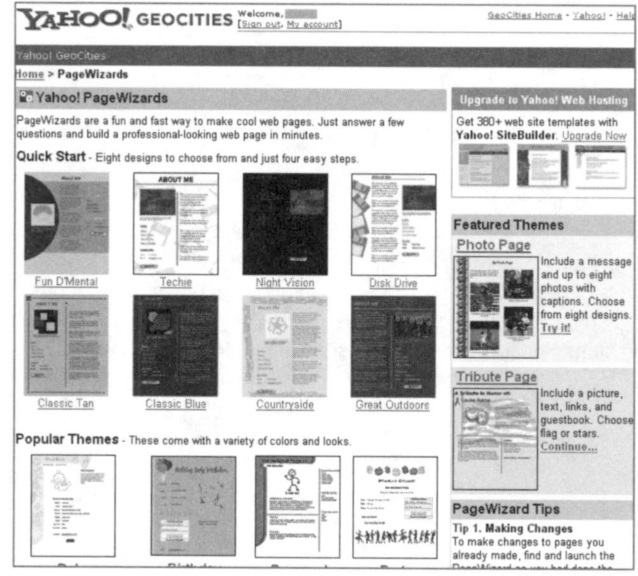

Figure 10-63.
A GeoCities page

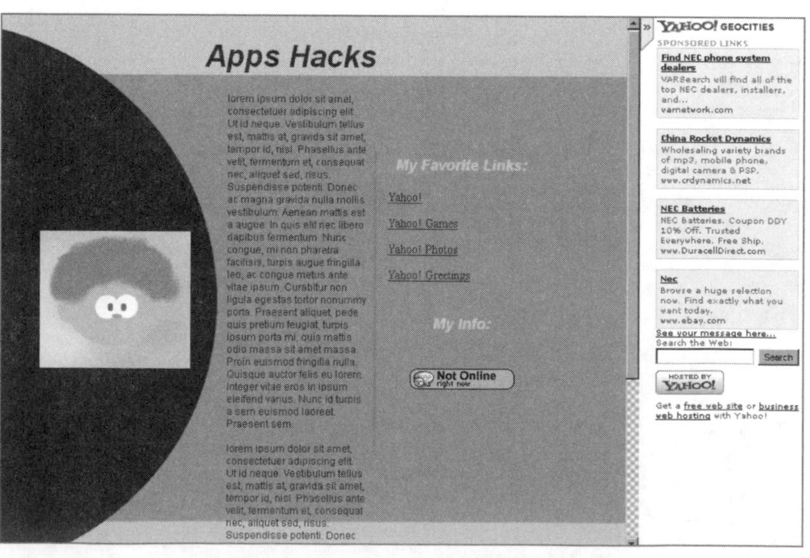

There are many, many more free web apps to create a home page. Domain hosting services also often offer you an integrated tool when you sign-up with them. Querying Google.com for "home page maker," "home page," "hosting," "get website," and so on will yield more alternatives.

Creating a Discussion Group

If you want to maintain your own online discussion group, the free phpBB (http://phpbb.com) may be your tool of choice. Although it requires you to have your own server hosted somewhere, with support for the PHP scripting language and a database like MySQL, it also offers much more fine-tuning options than Google Groups. A sample of a "BB" (Bulletin Board) in use can be seen in Figure 10-64.

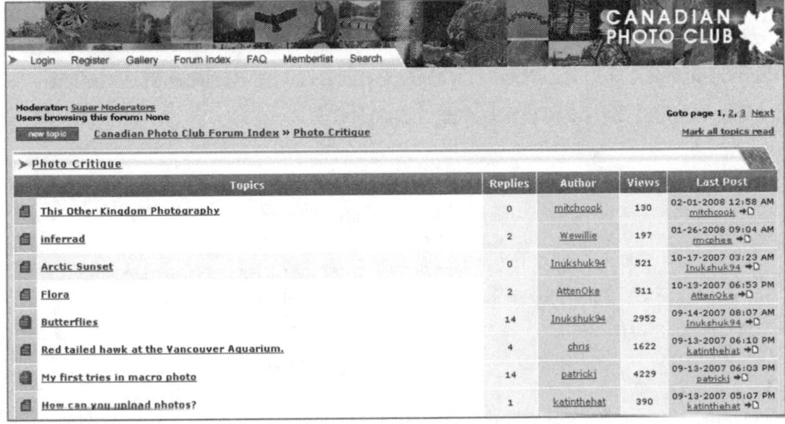

Figure 10-64.
The phpBB-powered forum at CanadianPhotoClub.com

Another paid alternative to creating a discussion group is called vBulletin, available at http://vbulletin.com. Drupal at http://drupal.org, on the other hand, is a full-featured, open source content management and community system, with a forum as just one of its many components.

11 DIVE INTO GOOGLE MAPS, GOOGLE EARTH, AND SKETCHUP 3D

In old maps—drawn on paper—illustrations of dragons were used in all those areas that were yet undiscovered. This visual disclaimer can be roughly translated to, "Looking for territory information in *that* spot? Why, no one wants to go there; that place houses dangerous beasts!" Today, most of those dragons are gone, at least when it comes to this little planet. And we don't have problems folding maps any more, either . . . at least when we use online mapping services like Google's.

Google Maps

Google Maps (http://maps.google.com) is a virtual world map, as shown in Figure 11-1. You can travel to almost any spot on earth, zoom in, and see what it's like there (without all the extra expenses like flight tickets). Google combines such things as location names, satellite or terrain info, panorama photos from street level with data such as user reviews for restaurants, directions, and—for the United States—real-time traffic information. The search box on top is flexible enough so that you can search for both specific cities or countries as well as names of businesses, restaurants, and more.

Special layers—so-called KML (Keyhole Markup Language) files—can be displayed on top of Google Maps to add third-party information.

With a feature called My Maps, you can add your own markers, directions, or areas to Google Maps, and edit your own text for the marker's info box. Google also allows you to grab Google Maps as a

Figure 11-1.
Google Maps. At the top you can see three buttons: Map, Satellite, and Terrain view. In some areas, more buttons are available.

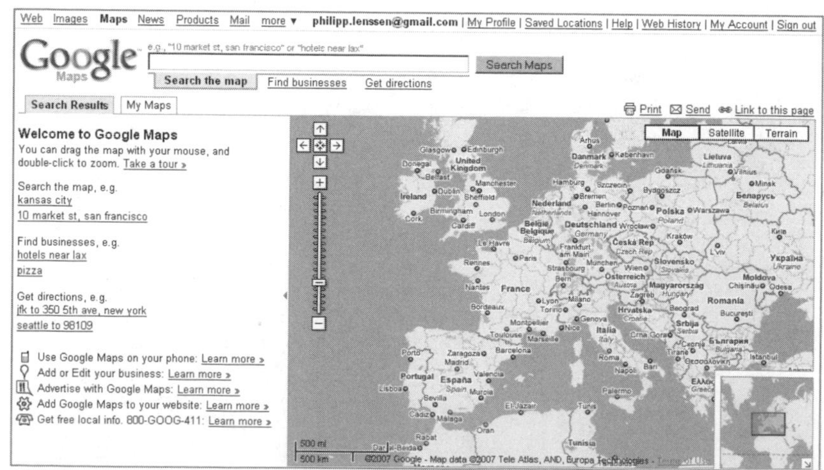

programmable widget for your own blog or home page—this is the Google Maps API in action, which has spawned a great many "maps mashups" online.

Google Maps is also available for mobile phones. This includes directions, and, for some cities in the United States, the display of real-time traffic data to help you avoid traffic jams. To download Google Maps for your phone or PDA, visit http://google.com/gmm from your phone's web browser. If your phone is supported, you'll be able to install it over the air.

Google Earth

Google Earth (http://earth.google.com), pictured in Figure 11-2, is the desktop sibling of Google Maps. After launching it, you'll see that its rotating 3D globe is a bit more fluid than the flat 2D view of Google Maps. Google Earth in its basic version is free, but the paid version lets you generate videos with effects such as seamlessly zooming in to a location—the kind of effect you'd see in TV news coverage.

At this time, Google Earth has the most complete support for Keyhole Markup Language information files—including support for animations. Many organizations have data overlays that you can superimpose on the globe by checking the respective boxes of the Layers pane. A Wikipedia layer adds location-relevant information from the online encyclopedia; the Weather layers allow you to display clouds and forecasts; *National Geographic* magazine provides a layer with regional information, including photos, as well.

Figure 11-2.
Launching Google Earth, software formerly known as Keyhole Earth Viewer

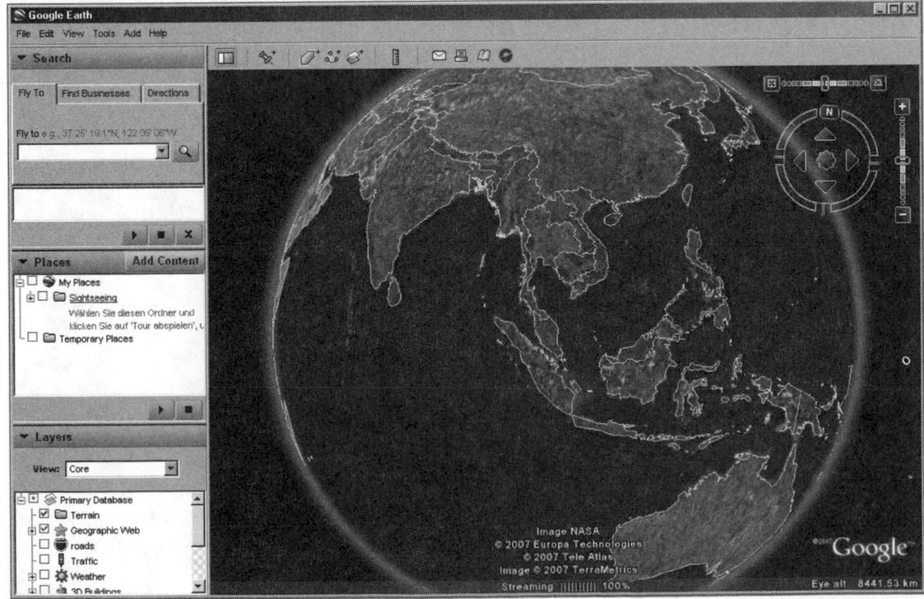

Google SketchUp

Google SketchUp (http://sketchup.google.com) is a 3D program for architects drafting their work, or hobby designers interested in creating a 3D shape. Like Google Earth, SketchUp is not a web application, but instead requires you to install an "offline" client, as pictured in Figure 11-3. The emphasis of SketchUp is on ease of use; although you may not be able to do anything and everything with it, what you can do can often be done very quickly, with little effort. And whatever 3D model you create in SketchUp, you can then include in Google Earth.

A great way to start learning about SketchUp is to follow the online video tutorials at http://sketchup.google.com/tutorials.html. Once you've created something unique and interesting, you can upload it to the Google 3D Warehouse site, a directory of shared 3D models. You can also import any model you find at the 3D Warehouse into your own creations.

Figure 11-3.
The SketchUp 3D editor

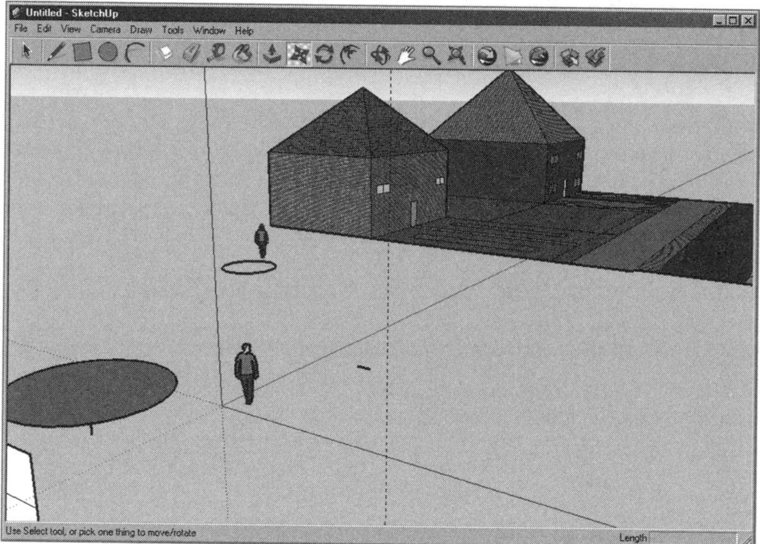

HACK 115: Drop a Google Map Onto Your Site

Take your Google map and run, freeing it from its usual home at the maps.google.com domain.

The easiest way to embed a Google map on your own site is available directly from http://maps.google.com. Just point to any location—you can also zoom in and switch to satellite view, for instance—and then click "Link to this page" on top. A dialog will open that allows you to copy an HTML portion to be pasted into your own site, as shown in Figure 11-4. You can also customize the map size by clicking the "Customize" link in this dialog.

The actual code you end up with consists of an *inline frame*, among other things. An inline frame is a window within the browser window that contains an external site's service; in this case, Google Maps. An example is shown in Figure 11-5, and the accompanying HTML code is in Figure 11-6.

> If you are concerned about using HTML that validates, you need to adjust some of Google's HTML attributes, and also set your document type to "transitional." To validate your HTML, enter your home page address into the official validator provided by the World Wide Web Consortium at http://validator.w3.org. This can help alert you to syntax errors in your code. To learn more about HTML and CSS, visit http://w3.org/TR/html4/ and http://w3.org/TR/CSS21/ respectively.

Figure 11-4.
The Google Maps embedding dialog

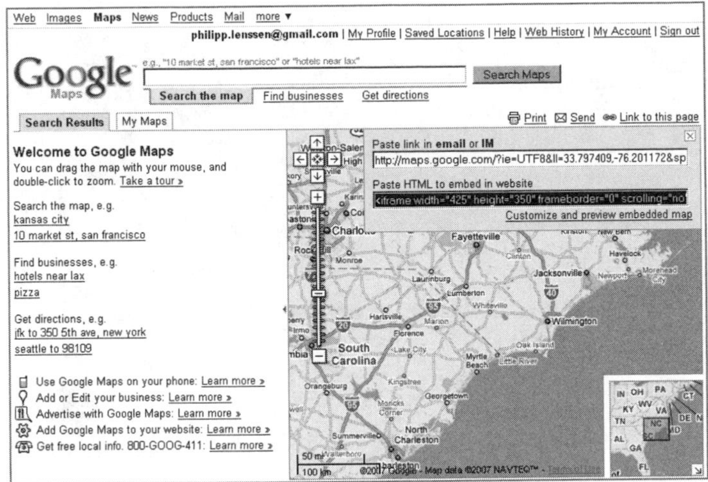

Figure 11-5.
Including the embed code in a sample home page

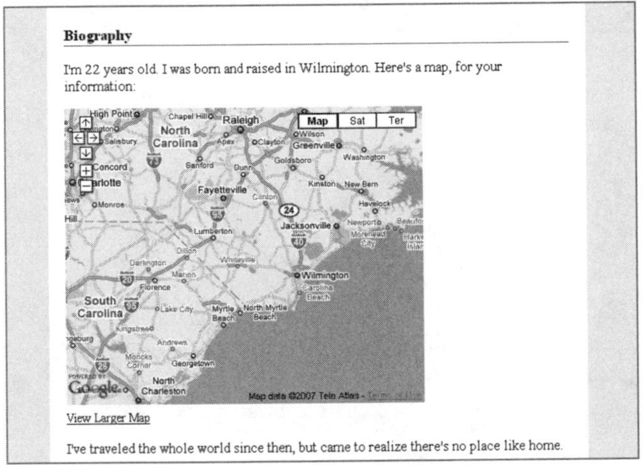

Figure 11-6.
The HTML and Cascading Stylesheet files behind the sample home page

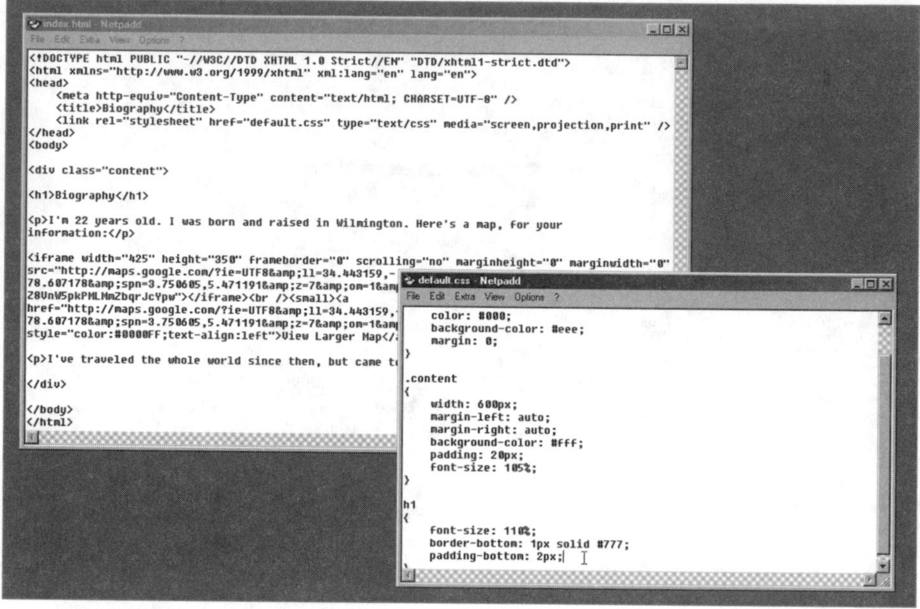

Hacking the Hack

For more control over what your map does and how it appears, you can use the Google Maps API (Application Programming Interface). In addition to understanding basic HTML, you'll need to know some JavaScript.

To get started with the Google Maps API, head over to http://code.google.com/apis/maps/ and click on "Sign up for a Google Maps API key." Read and agree to the terms of service (if you do agree), enter your home page address, and click Generate API Key. Not only will you get your key now—don't forget to make a copy of it for future use—but Google also offers you some sample map code to begin with.

Let's analyze the code, shown here:

```
<!DOCTYPE html PUBLIC "-//W3C//DTD XHTML 1.0 Strict//EN"
   "http://www.w3.org/TR/xhtml1/DTD/xhtml1-strict.dtd">
<html xmlns="http://www.w3.org/1999/xhtml">
<head>
<meta http-equiv="content-type" content="text/html; charset=utf-8"/>
<title>Google Maps JavaScript API Example</title>
<script
      src="http://maps.google.com/maps?file=api&amp;v=2&amp;key=YOUR-KEY"
       type="text/javascript"></script>
<script type="text/javascript">
     //<![CDATA[
     function load() {
       if (GBrowserIsCompatible()) {
         var map = new GMap2(document.getElementById("map"));
         map.setCenter(new GLatLng(37.4419, -122.1419), 13);
       }
     }
     //]]>
```

```
</script>
</head>
<body onload="load()" onunload="GUnload()">
<div id="map" style="width: 500px; height: 300px"></div>
</body>
</html>
```

This HTML will output a blank page with nothing but a small map widget on it. In the `head` section of the HTML, you will see that the Google Maps JavaScript library is referenced (replace "YOUR-KEY" with your actual key value). The `body` includes a `div` element. In HTML, `div` is a generic divisor to wrap just about anything you can think of; in this case, it wraps a map. The `body` element also defines an `onload` event that involves the function `load()`, which runs after the page finishes loading its HTML and images. In the `load()` function, you can see that there's a small check to confirm that the browser is compatible with Google Maps widgets. If that is the case, a new map object is created—it looks for the previously mentioned `div` element with the `id` "map"—and centered to a specific latitude/longitude location, with a specific zoom level.

So far, there's nothing in this sample that an embedding of a simple map inline frame, as shown before, doesn't achieve as well. But once you understand this basic example, you can add advanced features by reading through the tutorials, documentation and examples available at http://code.google.com/apis/maps/documentation/.

For instance, let's say you want to drop a marker of your own on the map. Below the `map.setCenter()` command in the previous example, you can write the following JavaScript to do so:

```
var point = new GLatLng(37.4313, -122.1229);
map.addOverlay(new GMarker(point));
```

Or perhaps you want to add an info window when the user clicks on the map. A so-called *event listener* can be defined for a result like the one pictured in Figure 11-7:

```
GEvent.addListener(map, "click", function() {
    map.openInfoWindow(map.getCenter(),
            document.createTextNode("Thanks for clicking!"));
    });
```

Figure 11-7.
The Google Maps API in (sample) action

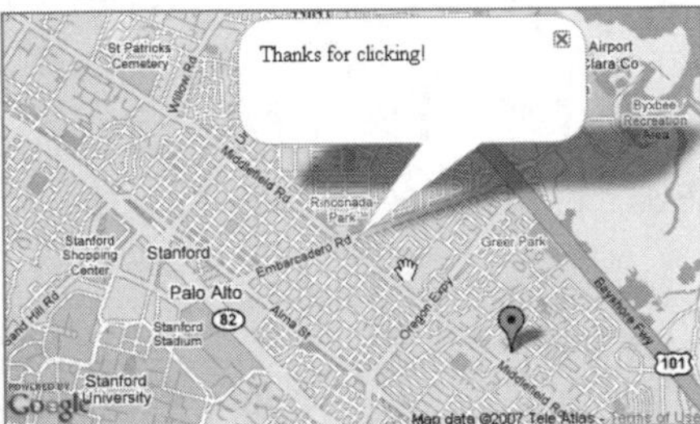

Because these programmable widgets can interact with your own site's data in new ways, they are also called "maps mashups." One such mashup lets you track the location of a package you are waiting for [Hack #83]. Other mashups allow you to create a jogging/hike route, find ski resorts, measure areas, look up zip codes, map your blog visitors' locations, find out where the sun is shining right now (as shown in Figure 11-8), and much more. For a multitude of mashups like these, take a look at "100 Things to do with Google Maps Mashups" at http://gmapsmania.googlepages.com/100thingstodowithgooglemapsmashups. Also, another O'Reilly book, *Google Maps Hacks* (by Rich Gibson and Schuyler Erle, 2006), presents many more ways to utilize the Google Maps API.

Figure 11-8.
The http://daylightmap.com service shows the moving daylight zones

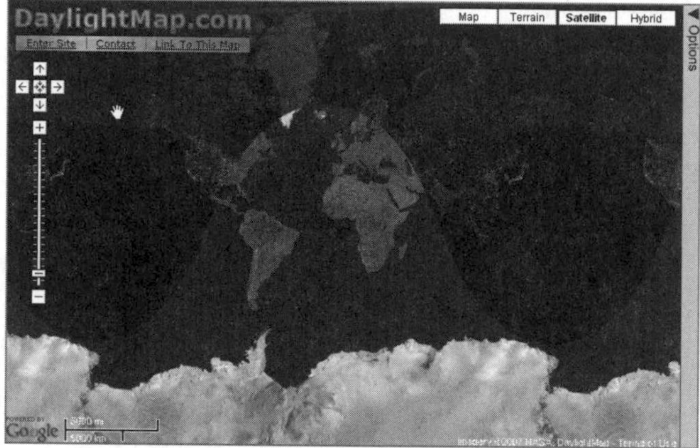

HACK 116: Add a Gadget to Google Maps

Expand the functionality of Google Maps through mapplets.

A "mapplet" is what Google calls a gadget that can be added to Google Maps. Mapplets take the opposite approach from embedding the Google Maps API on your site [Hack #115]; instead of putting a small Google Maps map on your site, you put a small part of your site or service onto Google Maps. Users can then subscribe to your mapplet using Google Maps' My Maps tab.

To get a taste of mapplets, you can subscribe to one yourself. Point your browser to Google Maps (http://maps.google.com) and switch to the My Maps tab on top. Under the headline "Featured content," check the box titled Distance Measurement Tool. This tool will now be activated and you can click any two points on the main map to calculate the distance using kilometers or miles, among other units, including such exotic ones as "Babylonian trade cubit" or "American football field." As pictured in Figure 11-9, I can see that I'm roughly 3,992 miles away from my editor Brian Jepson, who works with me on this book using Google Docs.

Figure 11-9.
The Distance Measurement Tool mapplet

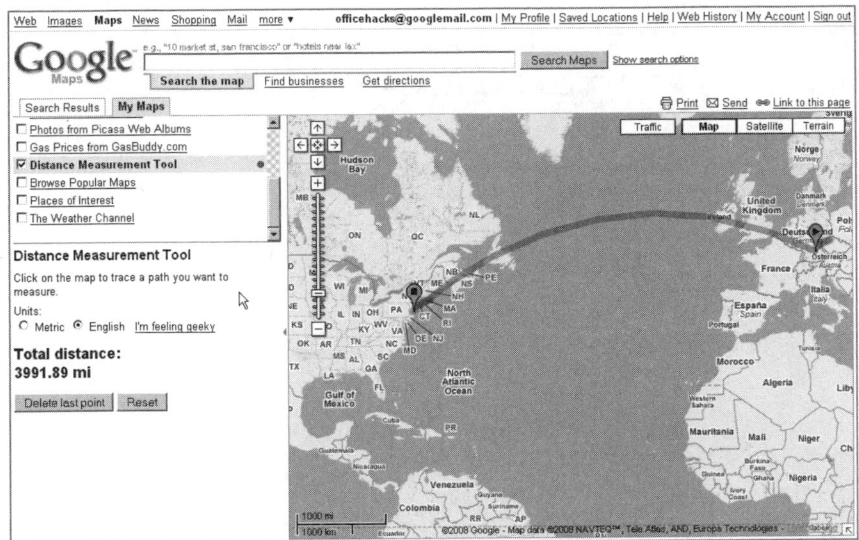

You can find more mapplets by following the "Browse the directory" link on top of the My Maps tab. Note that within the directory, you can use the Add by URL link next to the search box to include mapplets which are not yet in the directory.

Creating Your Own Mapplet

How would you go about writing such a mapplet service yourself? Mapplets are a special form of Google Gadgets **[Hack #60]** that utilize the Google Maps API **[Hack #115]**, so you need to understand a bit of both of these components. Google Gadgets are XML files stored online, and are made up of HTML, stylesheet definitions, and JavaScript; and in the case of mapplets, that JavaScript makes use of the Google Maps API library.

> No matter where a mapplet was originally stored, Google will copy it to their own domain, gmodules.com, before showing it to the user; this caching will last for some time and will keep the load on your server low.

To get an impression of how this all fits together, run the Hello World sample mapplet that Google provides. At Google Maps, click on My Maps, and then click the "Browse the directory" link. Switch to the section Developer Tools on the left, and add the gadget called Mapplet Scratch Pad by clicking the Add It to Maps button, as pictured in Figure 11-10.

Click Back to Google Maps on top, and you will now see that the Mapplet Scratch Pad is enabled. Depending on your screen resolution, the text area of the scratch pad may be quite small, so you may want to copy the code into your own text editor for more comfortable editing, then copy it back each time you want to test or save the code.

At the footer of the scratch pad, you will find a link labeled Hello World (you may need to scroll down in the scratch pad to see it). Click it to load the sample code into the scratch pad, as shown in Figure 11-11. Click the Preview button above the code and you will see how this code displays a green marker with an info window reading "Hello World," as shown in Figure 11-12.

Figure 11-10.
Adding the Mapplet Scratch Pad from the Google Maps gadget directory

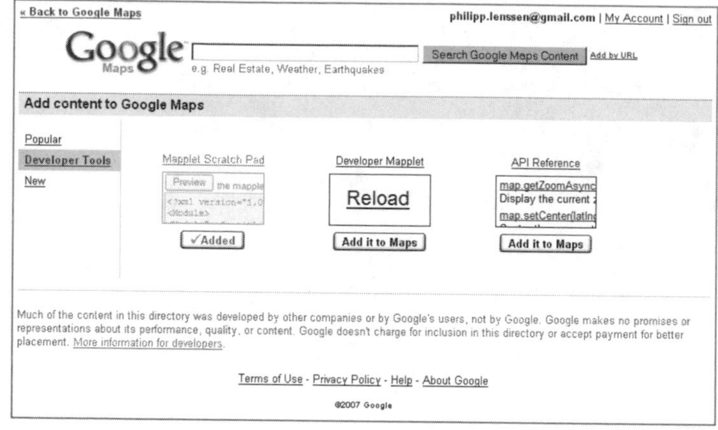

Figure 11-11.
The Mapplet Scratch Pad containing the Hello World sample gadget

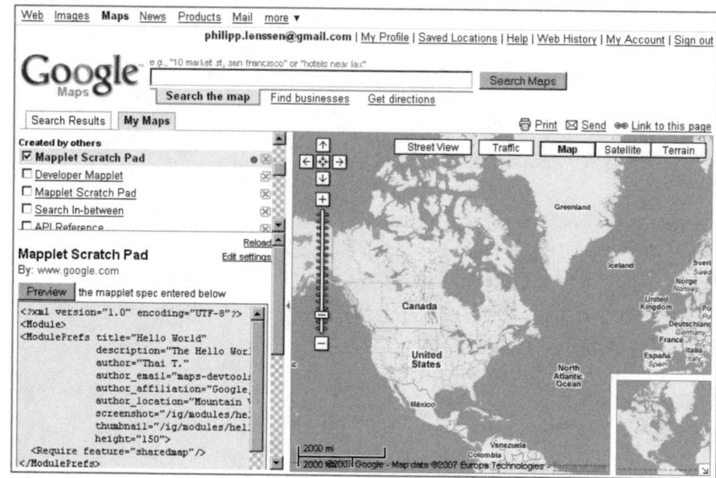

Figure 11-12
Previewing the Hello World gadget

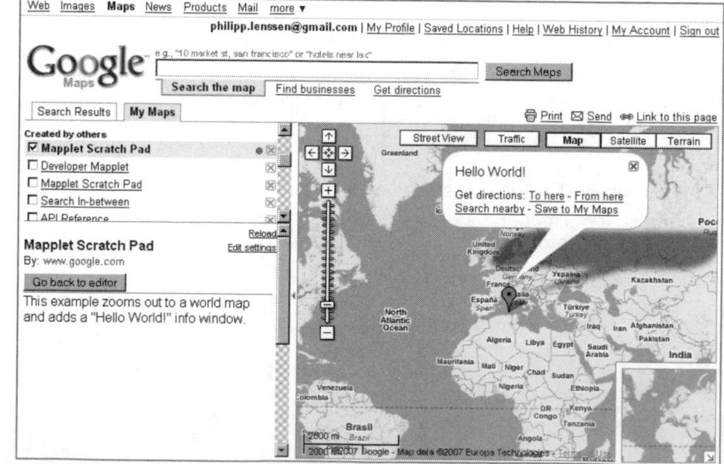

Take a look at the code behind this mapplet, written by Google developer Thai:

```
<?xml version="1.0" encoding="UTF-8"?>
<Module>
<ModulePrefs title="Hello World"
            description="The Hello World of Mapplets"
            author="Thai T."
            author_email="maps-devtools+helloworld@google.com"
            author_affiliation="Google, Inc."
            author_location="Mountain View, CA"
            screenshot="/ig/modules/helloworld.png"
            thumbnail="/ig/modules/helloworld-thm.png"
            height="150">
<Require feature="sharedmap"/>
</ModulePrefs>
<Content type="html"><![CDATA[
This example zooms out to a world map and adds a "Hello World!" info window.
<script>
  // Center the map in the Mediterranean and zoom out to a world view
  var map = new GMap2();
  var point = new GLatLng(37.71859, 6.679688);
  map.setCenter(point, 2);
  // Add a marker to the center of the map
  var marker = new GMarker(point);
  map.addOverlay(marker);
  // Open a "Hello World" info window
  var message = "Hello World!";
  marker.openInfoWindowHtml(message);
  // Make user clicks on the marker open the info window
  GEvent.addListener(marker, "click", function() {
    marker.openInfoWindowHtml(message);
  });
</script>
]]></Content>
</Module>
```

If you've programmed a Google Gadget before, parts of this will look familiar to you. There's the XML declaration on top, setting the character encoding. The `Module` element encloses everything else. The `ModulePrefs` element contains different attributes indicating the mapplet title, the author name, and the location of thumbnail images of the mapplet, among other information. Included in the `ModulePrefs` element is the element named `Require`, which references the `sharedmap` library—this is where the mapplet begins to differ from gadgets included on iGoogle, Google's personalized homepage service.

After the module preferences comes the mapplet code within the `Content` element as a mixture of HTML and JavaScript. The scripted parts are explained in comments from a Google developer: a marker is dropped at the center position of the map, an info window reading "Hello World" is attached to this marker, and an event listener will open that info window when you click anywhere on the map.

You can build on this Hello World sample with your own JavaScript commands now, clicking Preview after each change. Google's mapplets developer guide, available at http://code.google.com/apis/maps/documentation/mapplets/guide.html, goes into more depth with regard to how you can program this framework. You can also learn by viewing the source from any gadget available in the mapplet directory; just click on its linked name, and pick "View source."

HACK 117: Create Your Own Google Maps Layer

Organize location (and time) on top of Google's maps service.

You can add your own layer on top of Google Maps, including routes and markers, areas and info windows. You can share this layer with others and even collaboratively edit the layer with other users.

Creating the Map

To create your own map layer, go to Google Maps (http://maps.google.com) and switch to the My Maps tab on top. Click the "Create new map" link. You will now be asked to name your map, add an optional description, and choose between a public and an unlisted map.

> Unlisted maps are still publicly accessible, but only to people who know the full address—usually, this means only people you shared the map with will see it, but if one of these people has shared the link without your permission, it could be many more people.

For this example, I will create an overview of Barcamp conferences in Germany. (The concept of a Barcamp, a dynamic "unconference" typically discussing technology and the Web, originated in California and has spread to many other places since.) At this time, these conferences don't have a single umbrella organization in Germany, and their home pages are scattered all over the place—by adding a map view, I can make this more user-friendly.

You will notice that when you started creating the map, a set of tools are added in the top left map corner: the dragger tool (the default), the placemark tool, the line tool, and the shape tool. For my conference map, I'm picking the placemark tool. I know there was a conference in Berlin, so I am entering "berlin, germany" (without the quotes) into the search box on top. You can also simply drag your way to the location manually. Once the location is in sight, I put the placemark on it with a single click. An info window pops up, allowing me to add the information for this place. I'm switching to the rich text editing mode, as shown in Figure 11-13, so that I'm able to add links and images as well.

I will also create a new calendar in Google Calendar at http://calendar.google.com, where I'm adding the dates (see Chapter 7), as shown in Figure 11-14. This way, I can cross-link the information: the calendar events can link to my map, and the map placemarks can link to the calendar.

Figure 11-13.
Google's My Maps allows you to add your own placemarks on top of Google Maps

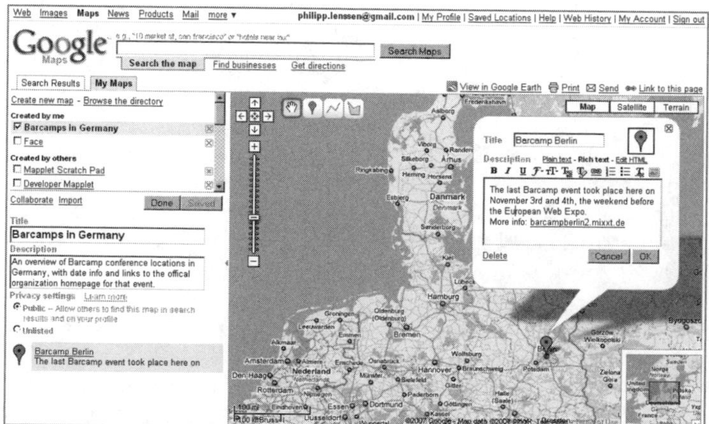

Figure 11-14.
Creating a Google Calendar to store event dates accompanying the custom map

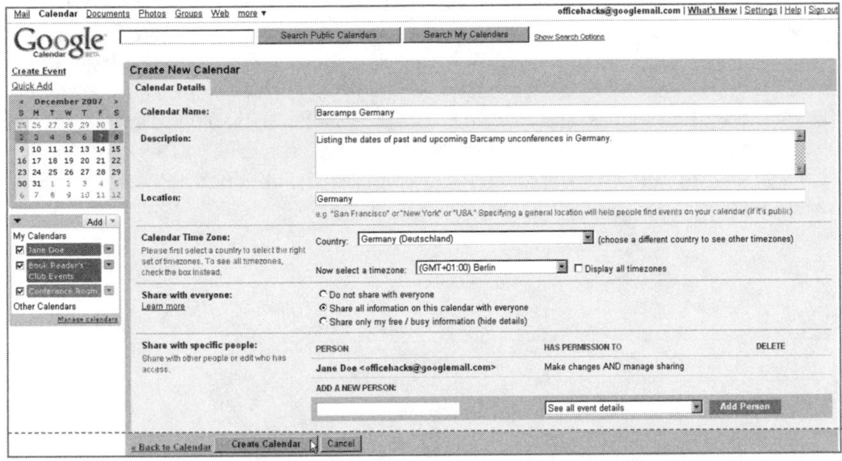

Now I will go about adding the placemarks for the other German locations, like Cologne. I can copy and paste the contents of the first info window's text box to get started with each new placemark, and then just amend what is necessary. When finished, I click the Done button to the left.

Not satisfied with the default look of the placemark icon? While editing a placemark, you can click the icon in the info window to change it. This gives your map a more unique, recognizable feel. There is a variety of default icons available from Google, and you can also add your own image. For best results with custom graphics, keep the icon size to something along the lines of 30 x 40 pixels, and use a PNG file with half-transparent borders. Additionally, you might want to give your icon a distinctive foreground and border color (like blue with a black border) so that it's highly visible on any background. You may also want to give the icon a pointed lower end so that it's clear which location it precisely points to. Take a look at Figure 11-15 for an example of how I converted the Barcamp source logo to a usable placemark icon.

Figure 11-15.
Preparing a good-looking placemark icon in your image editor of choice (here, Corel PhotoPaint); the original logo I picked is green on white, so I'll change it to blue with a black border, similar to the default Google placemark colors.

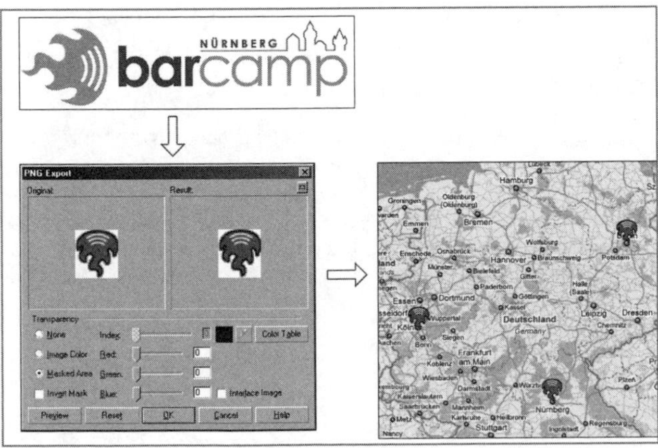

Sharing Your Map

However, your placemarks will *not* be instantly visible now to everyone else using Google Maps; neither will the map instantly appear in the public maps directory. So how do you invite others to your map? Just click "Link to this page" on top—make sure that your map is selected to the left, too—and copy the URL shown. You can share that address with anyone via email, in discussion groups, on your blog or home page, and so on. Someone opening your link will then instantly see your placemarks, directions and shapes, as shown in Figure 11-16, and also be offered to click a Save to My Maps link to permanently add the map to their My Maps tab. And in case you added calendar buttons to your placemark info windows, the other person will have the option to add that calendar to their list of calendars by clicking the calendar button.

Figure 11-16.
Viewing a custom map

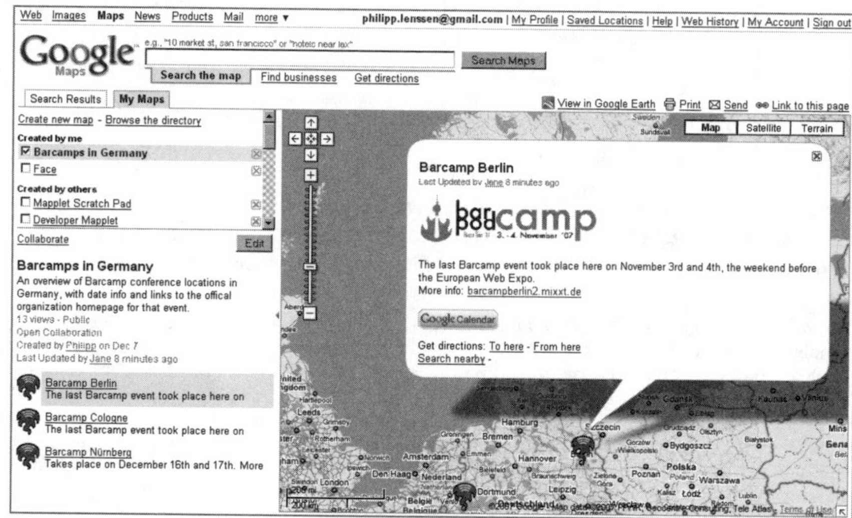

Allowing Others to Edit the Map Along With You

You don't necessarily have to edit a map all by yourself; maybe other members of a group or organization have more information and are willing to help. If so, go into the editing mode for your map once more by switching to the My Maps tab on Google Maps, selecting your custom map from the list, and hitting the Edit button. Now click the link reading Collaborate, and in the dialog that opens up, as shown in Figure 11-17, enter the Gmail email address of your friends or colleagues one by one, separated by commas.

In the advanced permissions, you can choose to allow your friends or colleagues to invite more collaborators. Alternatively, if you want to, you can even allow anyone to edit the map along with you.

People collaborating with you on a map can do anything you can do in terms of editing—that includes, for example, deleting all your placemarks, lines, and areas. However, unless you checked the "Collaborators may invite others" box in your collaboration management dialog, they will not be able to invite new collaborators.

Figure 11-17.
Inviting others to collaborate with you on your My Map

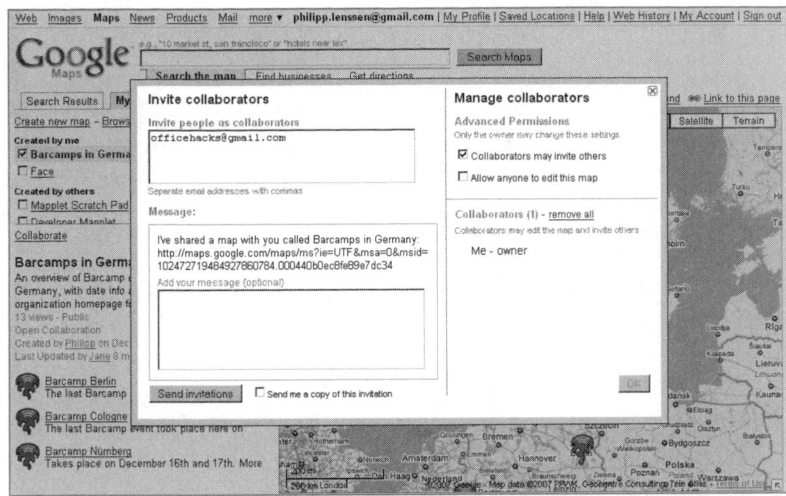

HACK 118: Enable Advanced SketchUp Tools

Expand your toolbox.

When using SketchUp, you can display a variety of tool windows. For instance, you can enable the Shadow Settings window by picking Window→Shadows from the menu. You can also enable a larger tool bar by selecting View→Toolbars→Large tool set (on Mac, View→Tool Palettes→Large tool set).

Another option to display more features is available in the preferences dialog. Choose Window→ Preferences (on Mac, SketchUp→Preferences). Now switch to the Extensions tab via the lefthand pane, as shown in Figure 11-18, and mark Utilities Tools and Sandbox Tools. Press OK (on the Mac, close the dialog box) and you will now have more options, such as the editing of organic terrain shapes. Figure 11-19 shows SketchUp with all these advanced tools enabled.

Figure 11-18.
The System Preferences dialog

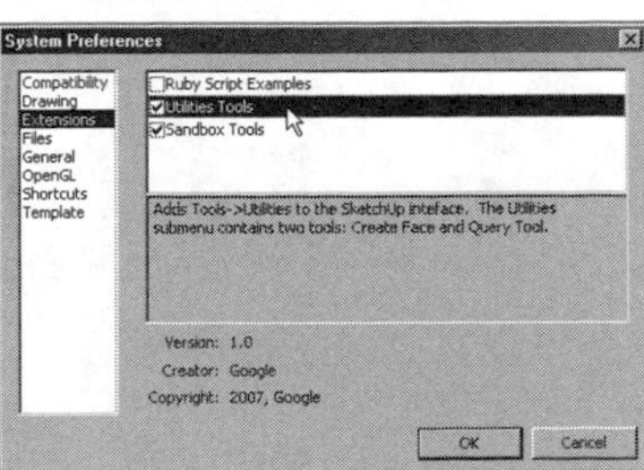

Figure 11-19.
SketchUp with advanced tools enabled

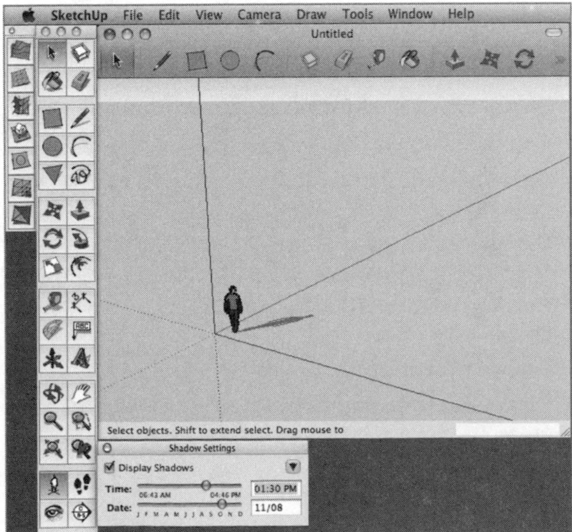

HACK 119: Load Plug-ins Into SketchUp

Extend the native SketchUp functionality using Ruby scripts.

Google SketchUp offers an API (Application Programming Interface) in the Ruby programming language. This way, you can add your own menus to SketchUp, or download third-party plug-ins to extend the functionality of SketchUp.

To give this a try, launch SketchUp and pick Window→Ruby Console from the menu. Many programming introductions start out with showing you how to display the words "Hello world!", so here's how to do it, SketchUp style. Enter the following in the Ruby console command line and press Enter/Return:

```
UI.messagebox("Hello world!")
```

This displays a dialog that displays "Hello world!". Click OK to dismiss the dialog.

To get started with more useful examples, you can delve into the Ruby language (the help file with more pointers can be found in the menu at Help→Ruby Help)—or just download existing scripts. You will find a couple of free scripts at the following URLs:

Ruby Library Depot: http://www.crai.archi.fr/RubyLibraryDepot/Ruby/em_arc_page.htm

Smustard ("The Companion to SketchUp"): http://smustard.com/scripts/

For instance, the first site's Ruby script `balustrade.rb` (by Tomasz Marek) creates a balustrade with custom dimensions. Download the script and drop it into the folder *C:\Program Files\Google\Google SketchUp 6\Plugins* (on Windows) or */Library/Application Support/Google SketchUp 6/SketchUp/Plugins* (on Mac). You can open the file with any plain text editor to take a look at how the balustrade feature is implemented.

To run the file, you first need to load it into SketchUp by typing `load "balustrade.rb"` into the Ruby console, and hitting Enter/Return. If things went right, the console will output "`true`" and you will now find the new menu entry Draw→Balustrade. Click it and provide your desired settings in the dialog, and a balustrade will be added to your model, as shown in Figure 11-20.

 In certain contexts, you may get some harmless warnings from the Ruby module when you load it. As long as you see a "`true`" result in the Ruby console, it should work fine.

Other scripts provided on the aforementioned sites include:

- **Bomb** (Smustard): "Explodes all groups and components in the model"
- **Cab** (Ruby Library Depot): "Creates a cabinet"
- **CameraLines** (Smustard): "Creates a group of lines that connect the eye points of all page cameras"
- **Compo_Spray** (Ruby Library Depot): "Tool to quickly populate the model with components (trees, people, rocks, grass . . .) based on support shapes, options, and constraints"
- **Cutting_Windows** (Ruby Library Depot): "Tool to make the windows/doors automatically cut double-sided walls"
- **GroupByTexture** (Smustard): "Groups faces by texture for export to other 3D software"
- **StrayLines** (Smustard): "Label, Select, Delete, or Show all the open-ended line segments in a drawing"

Figure 11-20.
Running a third-party script in SketchUp

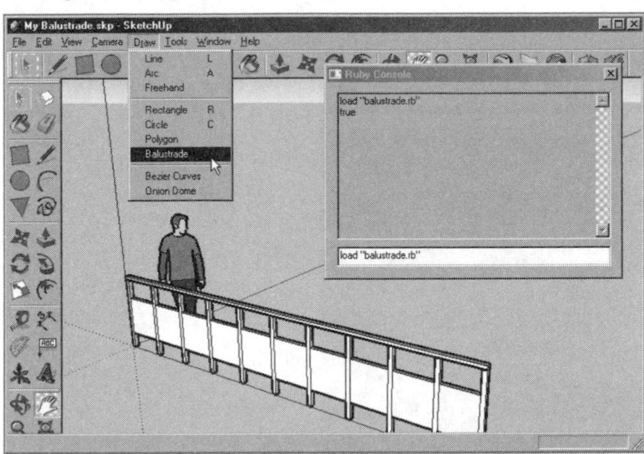

HACK 120: View the Moon and More on Google Maps

Zoom into the Moon, Mars, and other large chunks of matter floating near our home planet.

You've probably used Google Earth or Google Maps to get a better picture of this planet. Other planets are mapped by Google too, though. Curious about the surface of the Moon, for instance? Just go to http://google.com/moon/ and take a look, as pictured in Figure 11-21. You will be able to toggle between different views, and find special background information on the landing of the lunar module *Eagle* during the Apollo mission in 1969, when Neil Armstrong stepped onto the Moon's surface.

In similar vein, Google also has a special Google Maps–style service displaying planet Mars at http://google.com/mars/, as pictured in Figure 11-22.

Also, the desktop program Google Earth—which you can download for free at http://earth.google.com/download-earth.html—contains a special sky view. To see, it pick View→Switch to Sky from the Google Earth menu, for a result as shown in Figure 11-23. Google Sky is also available as a web application at http://sky.google.com.

Google Sky is a powerful tool for locating more than just planets and stars: you can locate deep-sky objects such as nebulae and clusters by searching for their catalog numbers (for example, you can find the spectacular Andromeda Galaxy by searching for NGC 224 or M31). Google Sky also includes overlays from the Hubble Telescope, Chandra X-Ray Observatory, and more. For more information on locating and enjoying these objects, see the *Illustrated Guide to Astronomical Wonders* (by Thompson and Thompson, O'Reilly, 2007).

Figure 11-21.
Google Moon, showing information from the Apollo moon landing

Figure 11-22.
The Google Mars web site

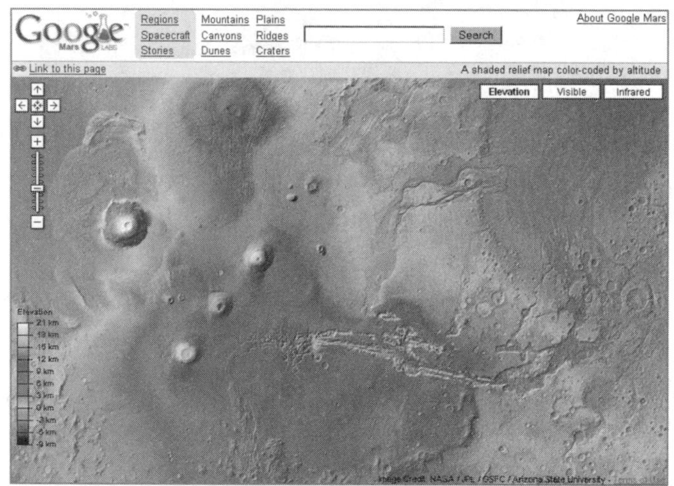

If you're interested in the sky, note that you can also switch to a special background theme on Google displaying imagery of planets. Go to http://igoogle.com and click "Select theme" to the right. Click on the list item Solar System and hit the Save button. Different planets will now show on the Google home page during different times.

Figure 11-23.
Google Sky, as part of the Google Earth program

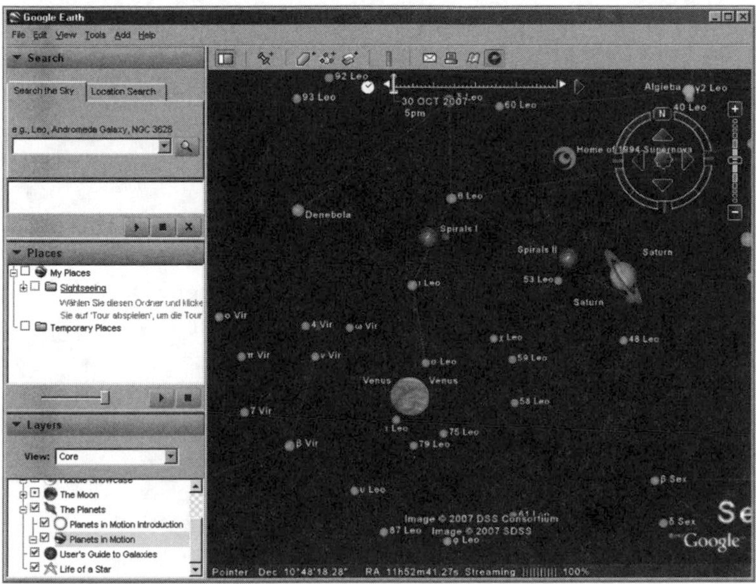

HACK 121: Create Google Maps Overlays On the Fly

A little MySQL and Python puts your locations on the map: you can generate a KML file dynamically with the latest and greatest data.

KML, the Keyhole Markup Language, can be used to describe locations in Google Earth. It's an XML format that Google Maps supports too. You can, for instance, paste the URL of any KML file into the Google Maps search box and hit return; seconds later, the placemarks appear on the map (the same is true for KMZ files, which are zipped KML files).

If you've got geographical data is stored in a database such as MySQL, dropping it on Google Maps won't be a problem. In this hack, I'm using Python to turn a database table into a KML file. To implement this hack, you'll need:

1. Some experience with Python and MySQL.
2. Your own MySQL server on which you can create tables.
3. A recent version of Python, with the MySQLdb and Minidom modules installed (if you don't have Minidom, go to http://pyxml.sourceforge.net).

The Outset

The database table, which is named `places`, has the following data definition. Feed this into MySQL, or whichever database you are using, to create it:

```
CREATE TABLE placemarks
  (id         INT NOT NULL AUTO_INCREMENT PRIMARY KEY,
   name       VARCHAR(255),
   description VARCHAR(255),
   latitude    DOUBLE,
   longitude   DOUBLE);
```

And you can fill it with data using this command:

```
INSERT INTO placemarks VALUES
  (NULL, "Restaurant Tao Tao", "Good Chinese food", 48.775855, 9.176846),
  (NULL, "Restaurant Sushi & Wok", "Good Thai food", 48.776039, 9.176491);
```

If you then issue the command `SELECT * FROM placemarks;` you should see the following:

```
+----+------------------------+-------------------+-----------+-----------+
| id | name                   | description       | latitude  | longitude |
+----+------------------------+-------------------+-----------+-----------+
|  1 | Restaurant Tao Tao     | Good Chinese food | 48.775855 |  9.176846 |
|  2 | Restaurant Sushi & Wok | Good Thai food    | 48.776039 |  9.176491 |
+----+------------------------+-------------------+-----------+-----------+
```

Now, the trick is to get that database into KML. The target KML that you need your Python code to generate is as follows:

```
<?xml version="1.0" ?>
<kml xmlns="http://earth.google.com/kml/2.2">
  <Document>

    <Placemark>
      <name>Restaurant Tao Tao</name>
      <description>Good Chinese food</description>
      <Point>
        <coordinates>9.176846,48.775855,0</coordinates>
      </Point>
    </Placemark>

    <Placemark>
      <name>Restaurant Sushi &amp; Wok</name>
      <description>Good Thai food</description>
      <Point>
        <coordinates>9.176491,48.776039,0</coordinates>
      </Point>
    </Placemark>

  </Document>
</kml>
```

ALL ABOUT PYTHON AND KML

You can learn more about Python at http://docs.python.org/tut/, and find out more about the KML format at http://code.google.com/apis/kml/documentation/kml_tut.html.

The Python script

Start off the Python script by importing the libraries for XML and MySQL handling:

```
#!/usr/bin/python
from xml.dom.minidom import Document
import MySQLdb
```

Now comes the main function: `getKml`, which accesses the database to turn it into XML. Replace the values `YOUR_HOST`, `YOUR_USER_NAME`, `YOUR_PASSWORD`, and `YOUR_DATABASE` with the correct values for your database:

```
def getKml():
    # First, the XML document is created, and a KML root element is appended to it
    doc = Document()

    kml = doc.createElement('kml')
    doc.appendChild(kml)
```

```
    kml.setAttribute('xmlns', 'http://earth.google.com/kml/2.2')

    document = doc.createElement('Document')
    kml.appendChild(document)

    # Now you can open the database connection with your values
    conn = MySQLdb.connect(host   = 'YOUR_HOST',
                           user   = 'YOUR_USER_NAME',
                           passwd = 'YOUR_PASSWORD',
                           db     = 'YOUR_DATABASE')

    cursor = conn.cursor(MySQLdb.cursors.DictCursor)

    # You are now selecting the appropriate values like the place's name and description,
    # to pass them to the addPlacemark function
    cursor.execute('SELECT name, description, latitude, longitude ' +
             'FROM placemarks')
    rows = cursor.fetchall()
    for row in rows:
        addPlacemark(doc,
                document,
                row['name'],
                row['description'],
                row['latitude'],
                row['longitude'])
    cursor.close()
    conn.close()

    return doc.toprettyxml(indent = '  ')
```

The preceding listing called an `addPlacemark` function, which handles generating the necessary XML to show. This is the code for it:

```
def addPlacemark(doc, document, name, description, latitude, longitude):
    placemark = doc.createElement('Placemark')
    document.appendChild(placemark)

    nameElement = doc.createElement('name')
    placemark.appendChild(nameElement)
    nameElement.appendChild( doc.createTextNode(name) )

    descriptionElement = doc.createElement('description')
    placemark.appendChild(descriptionElement)
    descriptionElement.appendChild( doc.createTextNode(description) )

    point = doc.createElement('Point')
    placemark.appendChild(point)

    # Add the <coordinates> element to the <Point> element; coordinate values are longitude,
    # latitude and altitude in this order (though you can leave altitude at zero)
    coordinates = doc.createElement('coordinates')
    point.appendChild(coordinates)
    coordinatesText = str(longitude) + ',' + str(latitude) + ",0"
    coordinates.appendChild( doc.createTextNode(coordinatesText) )
```

Finally, you just need to output the KML to the browser:

```
print 'Content-type: text/xml\n'
print getKml()
```

If the URL of your script is (for example) http://example.com/cgi-bin/map.py, then you can now copy and paste that URL into Google Maps. The result will be similar to the one pictured in Figure 11-24.

Figure 11-24.
The dynamic KML file displayed on Google Maps

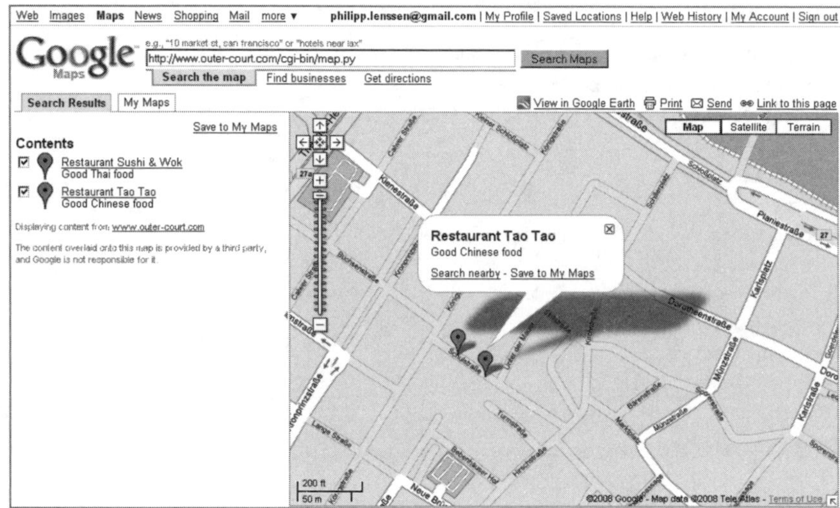

HACK 122: Add a Sky to Google Earth

We know the sky is blue, but it's not always supposed to be *that* blue.

If you create screenshots based on Google Earth views, like the one showing New York in Figure 11-25, you will notice something is awkwardly absent: clouds. Granted, most of us prefer a clear sky to a cloudy one, but a couple of clouds might give the resulting view a more realistic touch.

Here's how to add a sky to Google Earth. Provided that Google Earth is already installed on your system, start out by entering the following in your browser's address bar:

```
http://barnabu.co.uk/files/skydome/skydome-nl.kml
```

When you are asked whether to open this in Google Earth or download it, choose to open in it Google Earth (or, depending on your browser, you may also first need to download it and then open the download).

Once Google Earth is launched and the KML (Keyhole Markup Language) file has finished loading, you will notice a new list entry reading "Skydome" in the Places pane to the left. Check the entry and all of its list children. This will trigger another download, which might take a few seconds.

What is Google Earth loading here? To explain, the skydome is actually a textured 3D model created in Google SketchUp, as shown in Figure 11-26. It's designed by James Stafford, who publishes many more interesting Google Earth models and hacks at his blog, http://barnabu.co.uk. (The cloud texture originated with Philippe Hurbain from France, who has an interest in panoramic

Figure 11-25.
The sky is blue

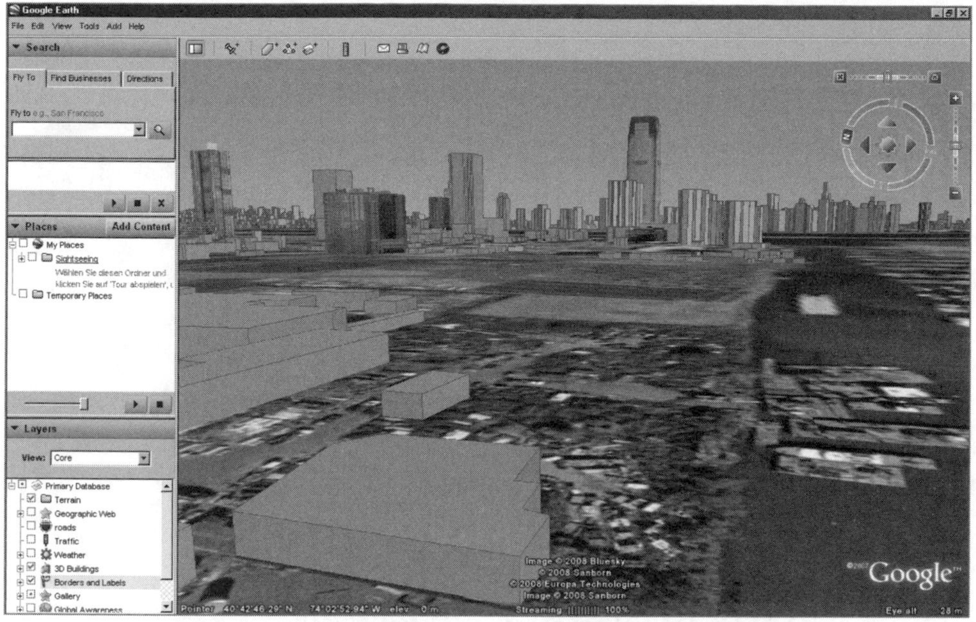

photography, showcased at http://philohome.com/panorama.htm.) Because of this model's large dome shape, which completely "wraps" the outlook towards the horizon, it can serve as a background image in Google Earth.

Now, zoom down onto the location you want to target. Note that the skydome may not be immediately visible. To make it appear, try to tilt your current Google Earth view to the side, or upwards and downwards. Once the dome texture is correctly aligned, the sky will be shown behind other building models, as pictured in Figure 11-27. Or, more poetically expressed in the words of John Milton, "Now glow'd the firmament with living sapphires." And if you want to replace the sky texture with another one, you can follow the steps outlined by James at http://barnabu.co.uk/sketchup-skydome/.

Figure 11-26.
The dome model in Google's SketchUp program

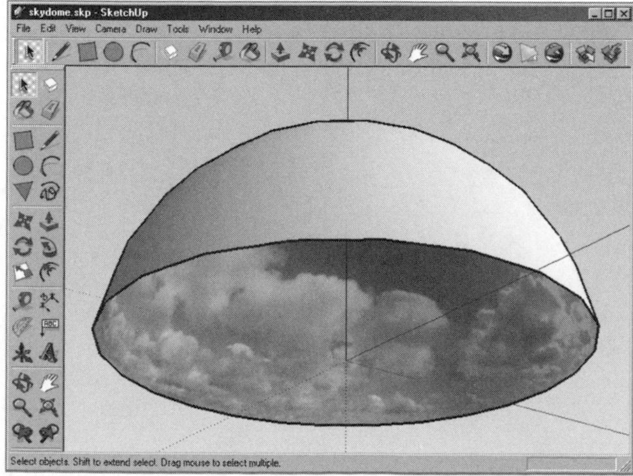

Figure 11-27.
New York with the skydome model properly loaded and aligned

HACK 123: Add Your Business to Google Maps

You're already showing up in web search results, but how do you get yourself into Google Maps search results?

If you have a business—a restaurant, shop, or the like—and you'd like it to appear on Google Maps, you can add it yourself. You first need to go to the Google Local Business Center at http://google.com/local/add/lookup. As pictured in Figure 11-28, you are required to provide information like your address, phone number, and more. In a later step, you can select the category and subcategory of your business, opening hours, accepted forms of payment, and also upload photos.

Once you've done this, your listing needs to be verified by Google. You can choose to receive your code via phone (Google's system will call you and ask for a PIN that was handed out to you), via an SMS, or via a snail mail to the address you provided.

EDIT SOMEONE ELSE'S LOCATION

You can also edit the location of someone else's business if you see that they're not displayed in the precise correct spot (and if the business is not verified yet by the owner); refer to http://maps.google.com/support/bin/answer.py?answer=68474#modify for more. Note you cannot edit listings that are already verified. Also, if you move the marker over 200 meters away from its original location, your change must be approved before it becomes active.

Figure 11-28.
Adding your business at the Google Maps Local Business Center

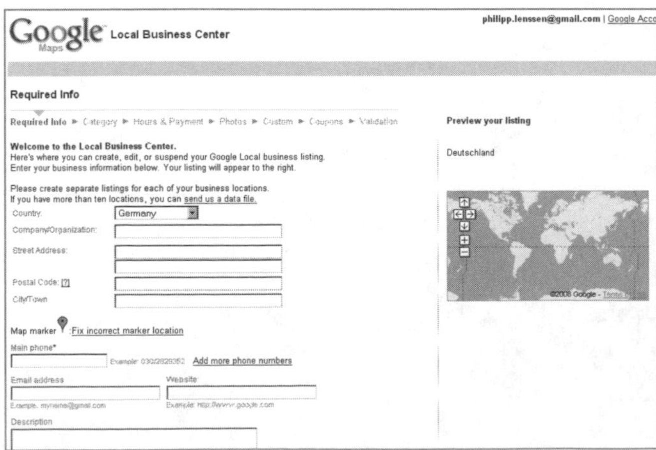

HACK 124: Make Your 3D Model More Sketch-Like

Sometimes computer renderings can look too clean. You can add a more human touch using SketchUp's Styles.

The default rendering mode of SketchUp is already quite refined, as the model by E46LE from the Google 3D Warehouse in Figure 11-29 shows. But what if you want to make your model look more sketchy, true to the name of the program?

If you have the latest version of SketchUp installed, this is easy. Just select Window→Styles from the menu. A dialog opens that lets you apply different sketch rendering modes, like Sketchy Marker, Sketchy Pencil, or Sketchy Charcoal Loose—this one is applied in Figure 11-30.

To fine-tune the rendering, you can now also switch to the Edit tab of the Styles dialog. You can increase the length of extensions drawn to your line, for instance. Experimenting with this feature can be fun and often shows impressive results.

Figure 11-29.
The default rendering shows colors and precise lines

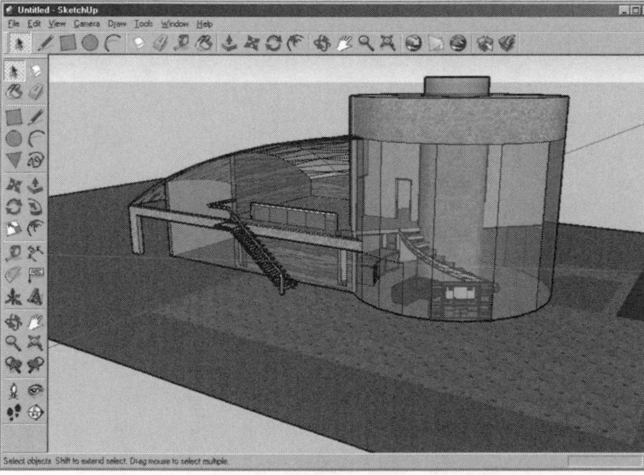

Figure 11-30.
Making a selection from the Styles dialog results in sketchy edges. (This feature was formerly available as a plug-in named Style Builder.)

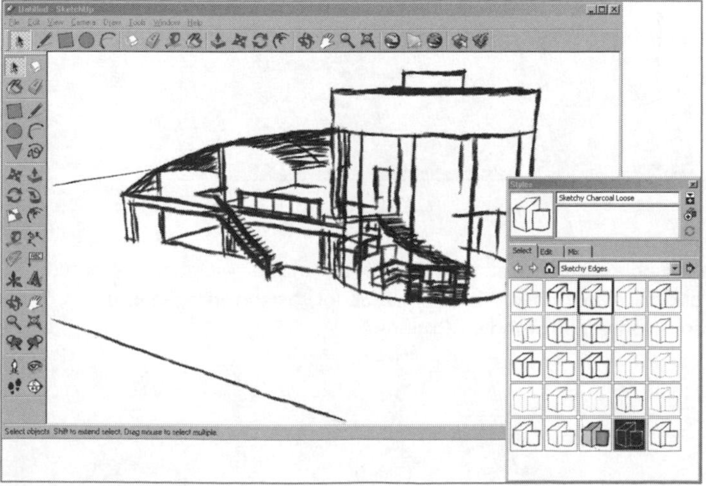

Figure 11-31.
The Google logo, rendered as a sketch

You don't need to restrict yourself to just architecture models, either. As the Google logo modeled by Tyler shows in Figure 11-31, sketchy edges can look good on many models. (Note that this model, as well as the previous one, were downloaded from the Google 3D Warehouse, which you can access by selecting File→3D Warehouse→Get Models.)

HACK 125: Avoid the Clash of Context Menus

Get the best of both worlds by displaying Google Maps' context menu as well as your web browser's context menu—but only one at a time, as needed.

By default, when you right-click a Google Maps area in popular browsers, you will see a context menu pop up, as shown in Figure 11-32. This context menu, showing entries like "Directions from here" or "Zoom in," is served by the web app—Google.com—and not the browser. The browser context menu is instead disabled by Google.

However, sometimes you may want to keep the browser context menu. Not just in Google Maps, but also other Google applications, like Google Docs. In that case, your browser may allow you to prevent web sites from overriding the browser's native context menu. In Firefox, for instance, this is

Figure 11-32.
In the Firefox and Internet Explorer default settings, Google Maps is allowed to suppress the browser context menu when you right-click the page. This way, Google can display their custom context menu layer.

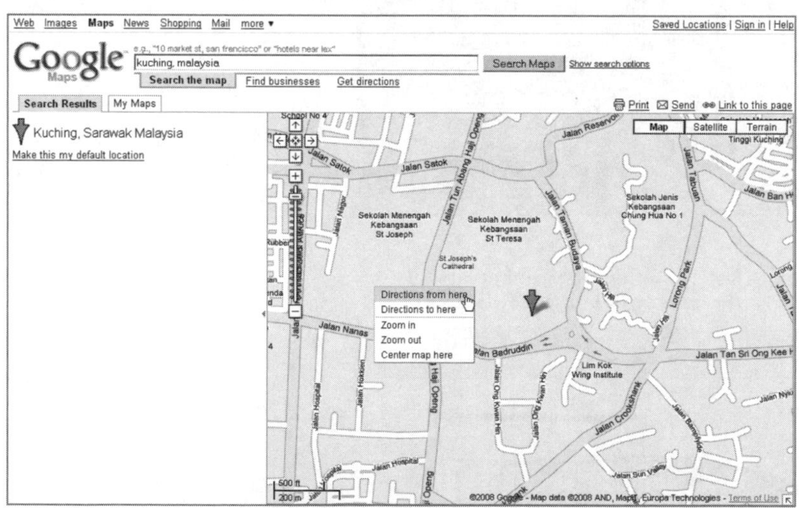

achieved by unchecking the "Disable or replace context menus" box in Tools→Options→Content, then clicking the Advanced button to the right of "Enable JavaScript," as shown in Figure 11-33. (On the Mac, click Firefox→Preferences instead of Tools→Options.)

Figure 11-33.
Preventing scripts from overriding your context menu in Firefox

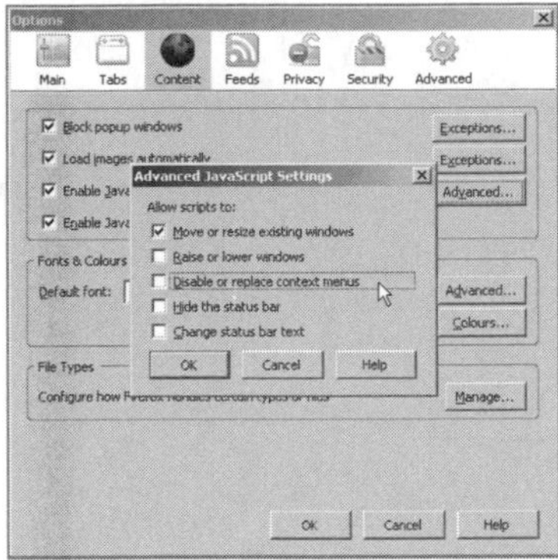

Figure 11-34.
The Firefox context menu hides the Maps menu. What if you *do* want the Maps menu every once in a while, though?

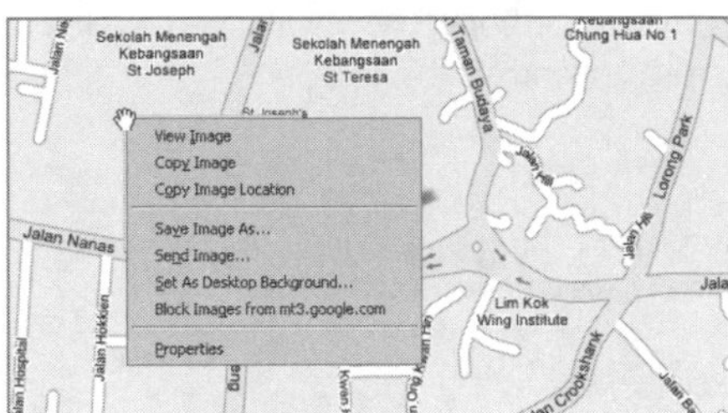

But what if you'd rather have *both* context menus—sometimes one, sometimes the other, depending on the specific circumstances and your task at hand? Take a look at Figure 11-34, which shows what happens when you configure Firefox to disallow web sites to hide the Firefox context menu, and then right-click Google Maps. If you look closely, you will notice that the Maps context menu is still there, albeit almost completely hidden. So how can you force the browser context menu to show but still sometimes hide it to see what's behind? The answer: press Escape after right-clicking the page. This will make the browser context menu disappear, but still leave the web app's context menu open.

HACK 126: Plot Google Calendar Events on a Google Map

If you maintain a public events list using Google Calendar, you can create a version of the calendar's XML feed that will plot your events on a Google Map or in Google Earth.

One way of getting a series of events displayed on a Google Map is to create a Google My Map **[Hack #117]** containing a separate marker for each event. This hack shows you the other way: pulling the events into the map from Google Calendar.

Using a Google Calendar to declare the events that you want to map has the advantage that you can view events by date, using a Google Calendar view, embedded as a calendar or list view in your own web pages using Google Calendar embedding code, or by location, using the Google Map.

Geocoding a Google Calendar XML Feed

When you add an event to a Google Calendar, you can optionally specify a location for that event. Google Calendar will then try to identify the geographical position of that location so that you can view it on a Google Map by clicking on the automatically generated "map" link in the event view for a calendar entry, as shown in Figure 11-35. If you don't add a location, there is no map link provided—instead, you are presented with a "Click to add a location" option.

A feed containing each calendar event as a separate feed item is available from each calendar. The feed format is Atom, used by the Google Data API (GData) framework. To find the calendar's feed, first open the pop-up options menu associated with one of your calendars—there's a drop-down arrow by each calendar name—and select "Calendar settings," as shown in Figure 11-36.

Figure 11-35.
Google Calendar provides a link through to the event location plotted on a Google map

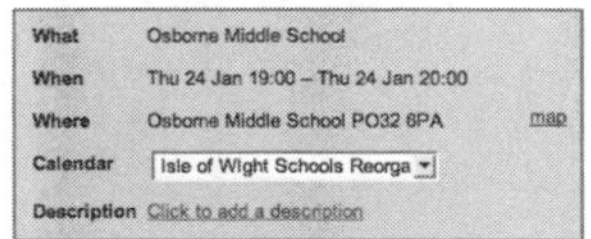

Figure 11-36.
The Google Calendar options menu

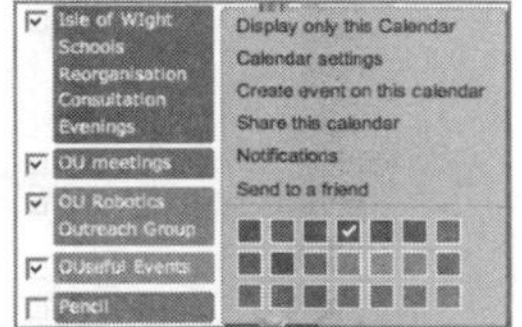

Toward the bottom of the calendar settings are some links to various output feeds from the calendar (Figure 11-37). The public and private feeds are both read-only feeds that can be accessed without logging in to Google Calendar. You have some control over the content of the public feed via the Calendar's sharing settings. The private feed is a full feed, and private only as long as you don't share the URL with anyone else!

Figure 11-37.
Google Calendar "Calendar Settings" page; the feed URLs can be found towards the bottom of the page

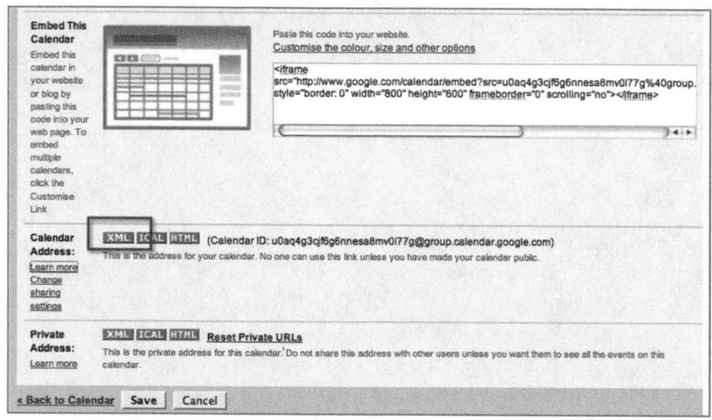

As we know that Google Calendar can generate a map marker from the location of an event, it would seem reasonable to assume that this geocoded information would be made available in the XML syndication feed, essentially defining it as a "GeoRSS" XML file (RSS, like Atom, is a feed format). If that were indeed the case, the GeoRSS feed URL could then be pasted directly into a Google Maps search box, and after clicking the Search button the calendar events associated with particular locations would be plotted on the Google Map, each with their own map marker.

Unfortunately, the location information is not (currently) included in the calendar events feed.

Enter Yahoo! Pipes, and in particular its Location Extractor tool. Pipes is a visual composition tool to mashup and convert various web feeds, and can be used for a variety of hacks **[Hack #135]**.

Creating a pipe is a very visual process—all it takes is a minute or two to create a Yahoo! pipe like the one pictured in Figure 11-38, which accepts the Google Calendar GData XML URL, fetches the feed at that URL, and then uses the Location Extractor to parse the feed, adding longitude and latitude data to a feed item if it is found to contain a location. To run a copy of the pipe on your own Yahoo! Pipes account, feel free to clone the pipe from the pipe's home page: http://pipes.yahoo.com/ouseful/geocal.

If you prefer creating the pipe from scratch, then follow these steps:

1. Create a new (empty) pipe.
2. From the User Inputs menu, drag a URL Input block onto the canvas (a Pipe output block will be automatically added to the canvas, too). The prompt field should contain the label for the textbox on the "home page" for the pipe. The name is the name of the variable in the pipe's URL that will point to the calendar feed;
3. From the Sources menu, drag a Fetch Feed block onto the canvas. Wire the output of the URL input block to the landing point to the right of the textbox inside the Fetch feed block.
4. From the Operators menu, drag a Location Extractor block onto the canvas. Wire the output of the Fetch Feed block to the input of the Location Extractor Block; wire the output of the Location Extractor block to the input of the Pipe Output block.

Figure 11-38.
A Yahoo! Pipe that geocodes an RSS/Atom feed, given its URL. The location extractor actually looks at the title and description tags for possible locations.

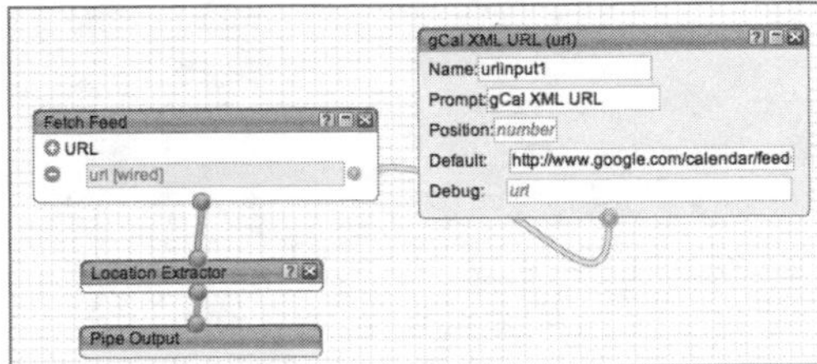

From the "before" and "after" screenshots of Figures 11-39 and 11-40, you can see how the Location Extractor has identified the location and added latitude and longitude coordinates to the feed.

Figure 11-39.
The Location Extractor looks to both the title and the description elements for possible locations. In this case, a UK postcode is contained in the description, which means that there's a good chance that the Location Extractor will be able to identify the location.

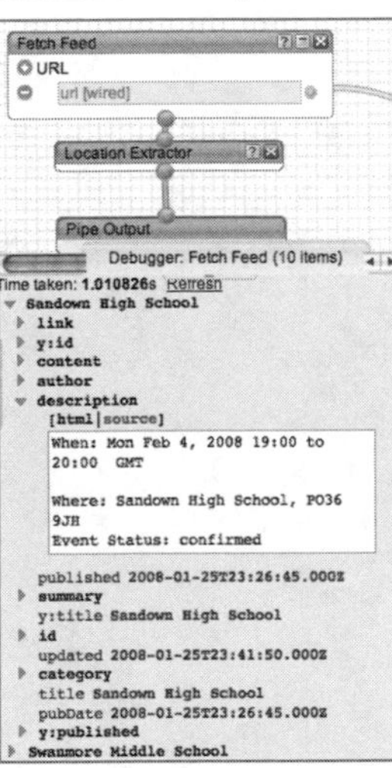

Figure 11-40.
After the Location Extractor block has worked its geocoding magic. Note the appearance of the **y:location** data.

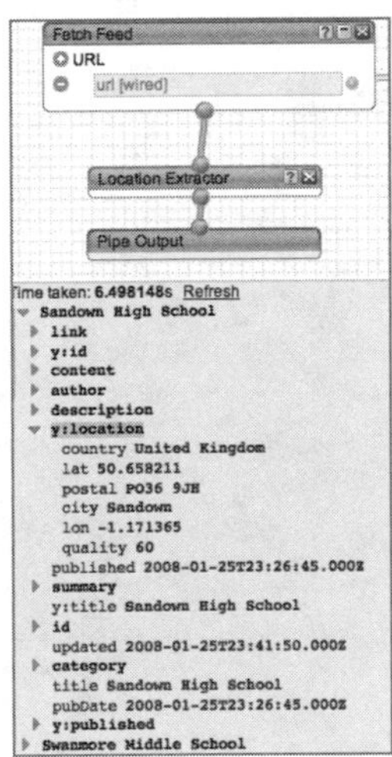

Running the pipe actually displays the events on a Yahoo! map, as displayed in Figure 11-41, but you can also get hold of a GeoRSS or KML feed URL that can then be used to plot the calendar events on Google Maps, or in Google Earth.

Figure 11-41.
The geocal Yahoo! Pipes interface (http://pipes.yahoo.com/ouseful/geocal). Enter the URL of an RSS/Atom feed such as a Google Calendar XML feed and the pipe will geocode the first location it finds within the title and description elements of each feed item.

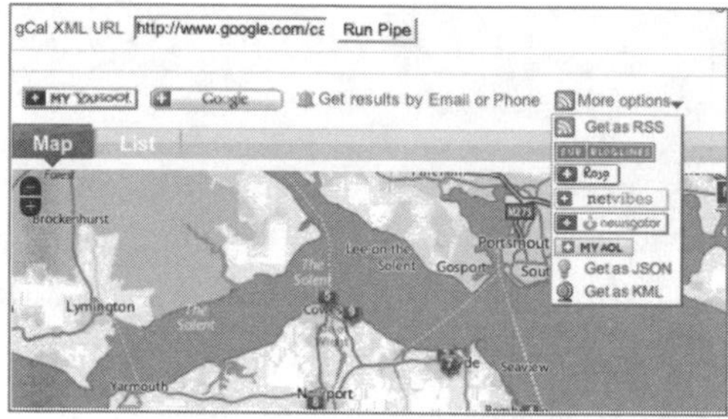

I find it's best to use the "Get as RSS" link, which provides a GeoRSS feed, for Google Maps, and the "Get as KML" link to use as a live Network Link in Google Earth [Hack #122].

When you add the feed to Google Maps or Google Earth, each geocoded item in the calendar feed is listed, along with a corresponding marker on the map, as shown in Figure 11-42.

Figure 11-42.
Google Map plotting the RSS output of the geocal Yahoo pipe. The pipe's KML output can be viewed in Google Earth.

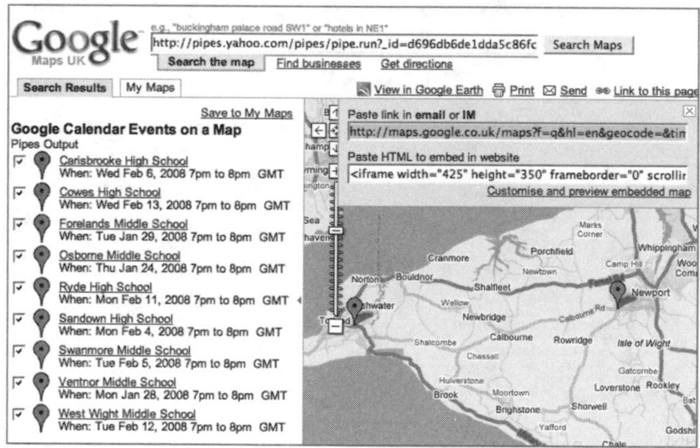

This hack can be applied to either public or private Google Calendar feeds. However, you then trust both Yahoo! and Google not to share the URL of that private feed, which is private only because it's hard to guess.

Viewing Public Google Calendars in Google Earth

As well as viewing your own calendar events on a Google Map, or in Google Earth, you can also view events from other public calendars listed in Google Calendar. You can find public calendars by using the Search Public Calendars button.

Once you have found a public calendar you want to display on a map, just run through the steps listed here:

1. Add the public calendar to your calendar.
2. Grab the XML URL from the Calendar Settings page.
3. Paste it into the geocal pipe (http://pipes.yahoo.com/ouseful/geocal) and run the pipe.
4. Grab the "Get As KML" URL from the Yahoo! Pipe "More Options" menu.
5. Use it as a Network Link in Google Earth.
6. View the dates in 3D geographical glory!

If you find that the location extractor is not working as expected, modify the location of the event. Unfortunately, you can't directly change any of the details in someone else's calendar, unless you manage to come up with another hack to deal with *that* eventuality!

You can also use Google Spreadsheets as source file to generate rich-media placemarks for Google Earth or Google Maps. Google explains the process in a text and video tutorial available at http://earth.google.com/outreach/tutorial_mapper.html.

Want to plot Microsoft Outlook events on the map, too? Try the Windows application Google Calendar Sync, outlined at http://www.google.com/support/calendar/bin/answer.py?answer=89955.

— Tony Hirst

HACK 127: Turn Google Earth Into a Flight Simulator

Google Earth has an interesting feature allowing you to try navigating an airplane.

If you have the latest version of Google Earth installed, then you have more than just a maps program—you also have a flight simulator.

To jump into Google Earth's flight simulator, launch the program and then press Ctrl+Alt+A (Windows) or Command+Option+A (Mac). A dialog, pictured in Figure 11-43, pops up and allows you to choose between a jet fighter (F16) or a propeller plane (SR22). Hit the Start Flight button, and the flight simulator window will fire up (close it any time you want via the "Exit flight simulator" button at the top right, or by hitting Escape on the keyboard).

The full control options for the simulator can be accessed by picking Help→Keyboard Shortcuts from the menu. For instance:

- Increase thrust: Page Up
- Reduce thrust: Page Down
- Rudder left: Shift + left arrow
- Rudder right: Shift + right arrow
- Aileron left: Left arrow
- Aileron right: Right arrow
- Elevator push: Up arrow
- Elevator pull: Down arrow

Figure 11-43.
The flight simulator dialog

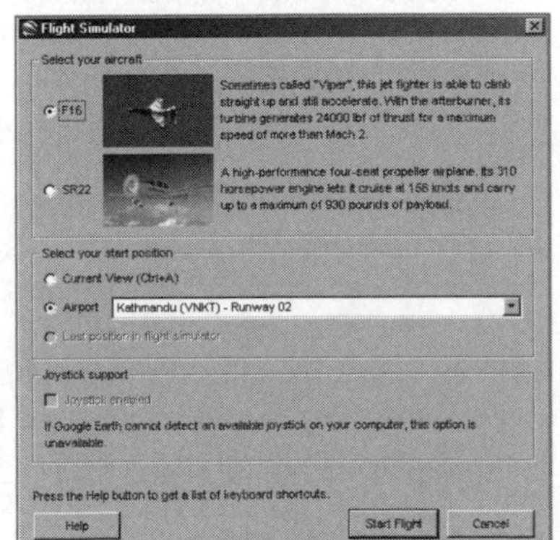

Enjoy the scenery during flight, as shown in Figure 11-44!

Figure 11-44.
Flying!

For more Google Earth goodies, also have a look at Frank Taylor's unofficial Google Earth Blog at http://gearthblog.com.

HACK 128: Beyond Google: The Yahoo! Maps Web Service, Live Maps, and More

Google Maps had quite an effect on the Internet—not just on users, but also on competing mapping products, which after a while tried to improve their service in the direction of the explorative, fast-paced interface Google built.

Yahoo! Local

Google Maps isn't the only good web mapping application, by far. There's also Yahoo! Local Maps at http://maps.yahoo.com, among others. Except for the lefthand side advertisement, the interface is rather similar to Google Maps. A search box can take you straight to a location—you can enter "Rome, Italy" for instance—and you can drag or zoom the map view. A click on the Hybrid button on top displays a mix of street/city labels and satellite imagery, as in Figure 11-45.

Developers may be interested in dabbling around with the Yahoo! Maps web service. It can be found at http://developer.yahoo.com/maps/ and offers not a single API but many APIs under one hood. You need to sign up for an application ID as part of the Yahoo! Developer Network to get started.

The Yahoo! Maps Simple API, for example, allows you to point to a GeoRSS XML file containing your custom map overlay information (note that Google Maps also supports GeoRSS, along with KML files). The Map Image API, on the other hand, returns an XML file containing the URL of an image that you can directly include on your web page. Here's a sample URL and the XML file it returns (snipped and formatted):

http://local.yahooapis.com/MapsService/V1/mapImage?appid=YahooDemo&street=701+First+Avenue&city=Sunnyvale&state=CA

```
<?xml version="1.0"?>
<Result xmlns:xsi="http://www.w3.org/2001/XMLSchema-instance">
http://gws.maps.yahoo.com/mapimage?MAPDATA=gc2rS...U-&amp;mvt=m?cltype=onnetwork&amp;.intl=us
</Result>
```

The resulting image is shown in Figure 11-46.

Figure 11-45.
Yahoo! Local shows Italy's capital

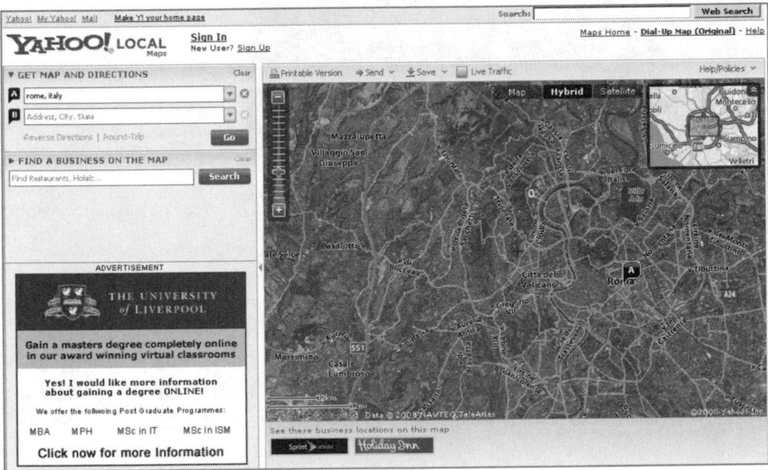

Figure 11-46.
An image returned via Yahoo's Map Image API

MapQuest

AOL-owned MapQuest has been around longer than much of the competition. It used to look different from modern map sites, too, but now offers a new experimental layout at http://beta.mapquest.com that more closely resembles Google Maps. As you can see in Figure 11-47, there's a search box on top, an exploration pane to the left, and a map in the middle right. Dragging the map relocates the view, and a click on the Aerial Image tab toggles from street to satellite maps.

Figure 11-47.
MapQuest's beta site

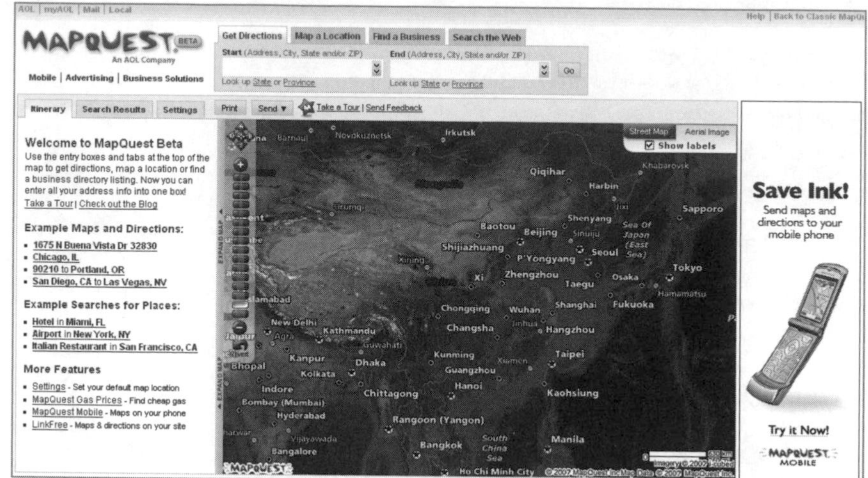

Ask Maps

Ask's maps, available at http://maps.ask.com and shown in Figure 11-48, are organized in ways quite similar to what Google provides. You can search on top or pull down a recent locations box (if you previously searched for something, that is). The map is moved via drag and drop, and zooming can be done by the use of the lefthand slider (or, alternatively, the "+" and "–" keys on your keyboard, or your mouse's scroll wheel). You can also use your keyboard's arrow keys to move about the map.

One interesting feature is Auto-Drive, as Ask calls it. For instance, enter "mountainview, ca to san francisco, ca", without the quotes, and hit Get Map or press Return/Enter. You will now get both driving and walking directions (use the lefthand tab buttons to switch between the two). Plus, you can now press the green arrow below the zoom bar to "play" the route, meaning the marker will automagically move for you, with explanatory speech bubbles popping up on top (like "Turn Left on Ocean View Blvd").

Figure 11-48.
Ask Maps

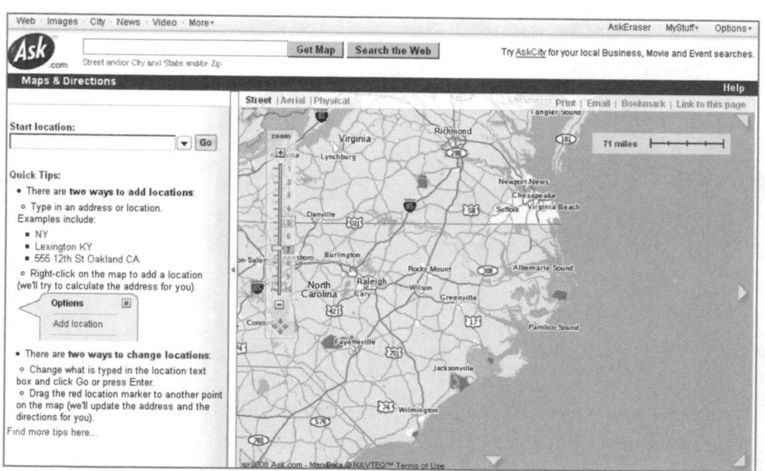

Microsoft Live Search Maps

Microsoft's maps service, located at http://maps.live.com, is part of the Live.com search engine initiative. As with the other services, the map as pictured in Figure 11-49 is zoomable (with the mouse wheel, for instance) and draggable. However, note that—starting centered on the United States—you will hit an invisible wall when moving westward; to move the map to China, for example, make sure that you are dragging rightward to the east.

Microsoft Live Maps also offers a feature reminiscent of Google's placemarks. Called "pushpins," these can be found at Collections→"Add a pushpin" at the top right web app menu.

A special gimmick in Live Maps is the "Bird's eye" button on top. In most locations, it will be "ghosted" and can't be clicked. Zoom closer into some major areas like New York or San Francisco, however, and it becomes clickable. Once clicked, it will offer a detailed and vivid 3D perspective, as shown in Figure 11-50. The view is fixed to be isometric, but can be rotated in steps of 90 degrees using the lefthand rotation icons. To find a list of bird's-eye-enabled cities, point your browser to http://blogoscoped.com/googleappshacks/link/bird.

Figure 11-49.
Microsoft Live Search Maps

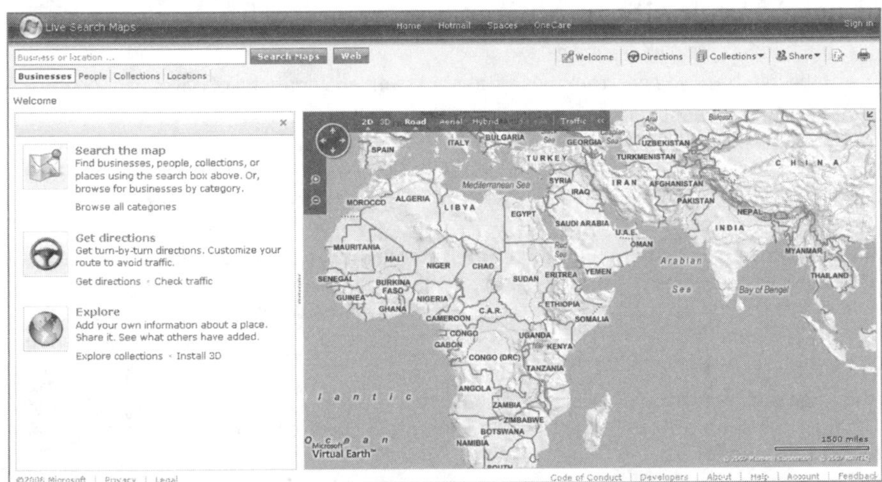

Figure 11-50.
Microsoft's bird's-eye view of New York

12 GOOGLE ANALYTICS AND BEYOND: MARKET YOUR SITE, TRACK VISITORS

Google Analytics, formerly called Urchin, is a web application that tracks your site's visitors. All you need to do is insert a little JavaScript tracker into your web pages, and then wait for the data to trickle in. Looking at numbers and graphs isn't boring once you visualize the crowds that these numbers represent; think of it as a virtual pat on the back for your hard work maintaining your site. What's more, with this data in hand you can go back to your site to optimize it.

Here is some of the feedback you get from these statistics, with explanations of how to act on it:

- **A page is very popular.** Think about why that might be the case. Was your article especially well-written? Was your information hitting on a recent trend? Were you offering a great product? Knowing the reason for this might inspire some changes on the page, or give you ideas for new material elsewhere on your site.
- **A specific search query results in a lot of people finding your site via Google.** Take a look at the keywords people enter, and check out what page they land on when coming from Google—and think about the first impression you're making on them. As the saying goes, your visitors spend 99% of their time on sites *other* than yours. Maybe it's time to emphasize a link, or add an introductory blurb somewhere on the side.
- **Your home page got heavy traffic yesterday.** Check the referrer statistics to find out who linked to you, and track the source of the traffic to find commentary and feedback about your site. React to the feedback, if needed.
- **Your home page got heavy traffic yesterday, but you don't see a spike from any specific referring site.** Perhaps your home page address received a mention in a radio or TV show!
- **People spend mere seconds on most pages, but a full minute on one other page.** Compare the pages in question to find out why there's such a big time difference. Also, use your server log to trace the path they took through your site, retracing your visitors' steps.
- **Your server was sluggish on Monday and you'd like to know why.** Check your stats to look for a peak. Maybe there's a server script with suboptimal performance that needs rewriting?
- **Many people filling out your order form suddenly leave at form page 2 out of 3.** Maybe there's something on page 2 they didn't expect, so check it out and fix it if needed.
- **What, traffic is dropping?** Maybe it's time to take a break from checking stats, and get the word out again—by contacting webmasters, talking to readers or customers, getting involved with the community, or adding great content to your site.

In other words, all of these data points are tools equipping you to do a good job, whether you consider yourself a webmaster, an e-merchant, a news blogger, a web artist, or anything else or in-between. On the following pages, you will find hacks that could improve your mastering of this tool—and thus, your site. Additionally, there are tips and tricks that can help you market your site.

Getting Started with Google Analytics

To log in to Google Analytics (http://www.google.com/analytics/), you need a Google Account **[Hack #1]**.

Analytics makes heavy use of Flash, so if your company network happens to block content for the Flash plug-in, give your sysop a friendly nudge as a reminder that Flash can be used for more than just online games (as a bonus, once your sysop is convinced, you will then be able to play those online games, too).

Figure 12-1.
Setting up a new site with Google Analytics

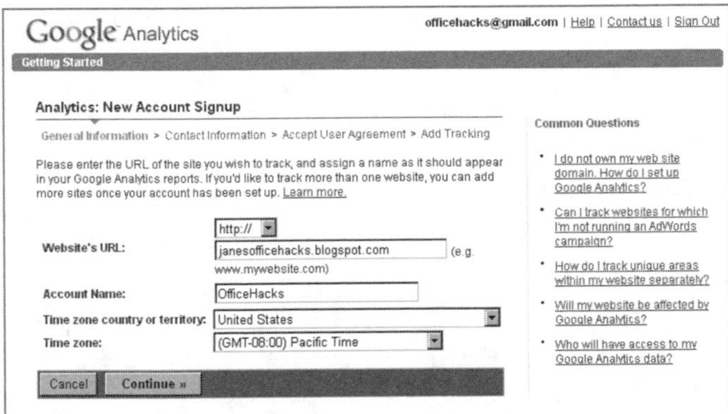

After logging in, you can sign up for a new web site. Enter your URL and provide an account name, as pictured in Figure 12-1. You will then be provided with a tracking code: a JavaScript snippet that you need to add to your site's HTML template. Copy and paste it as directed into your system, and check back later to verify that Google Analytics has detected your tracking code.

Once you've set up your site, you'll start out on your dashboard, as pictured in Figure 12-2. The dashboard can be configured so that you will immediately see those elements that are of most interest to you **[Hack #129]**. For instance, I configure my site's statistics so that I can immediately see the top content by title, the top referring sites (that is, sites that link to the site, a key source of visitors), and the top keywords used to find the site.

Figure 12-2.
The Analytics dashboard gives you a quick overview of your stats

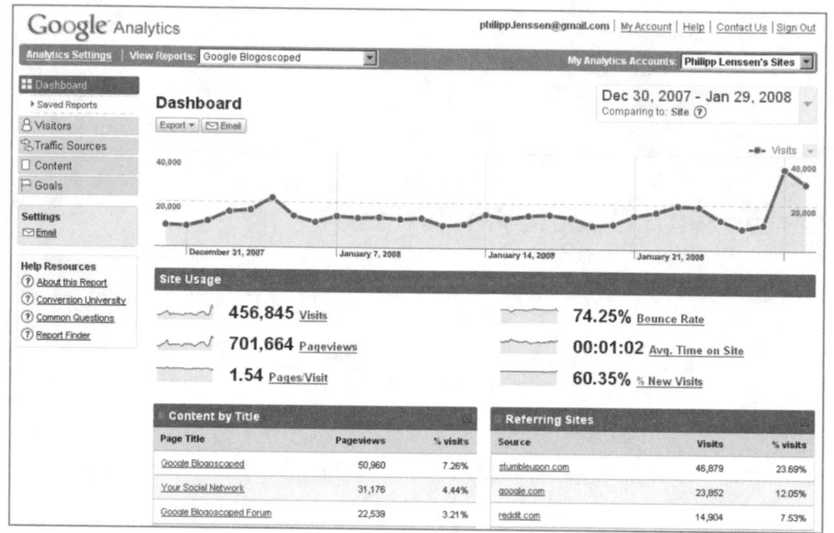

HACK 129: Customize Your Google Analytics Dashboard

Google Analytics has a couple of default boxes when you view a report for one of your web sites. What if you aren't happy with this selection?

At the time of this writing, the Google Analytics dashboard displays a map overlay and a visitors overview box, among others. But what if you already have a good handle on where your visitors come from, making the high-level information contained on the map overlay redundant?

Well, you can just change the dashboard settings. One way to do so is to grab a box and drag and drop it elsewhere on the page. You can also click the X in the upper-right corner of a box to make the element disappear. If you want to add new boxes, instead, first navigate to the Analytics page containing the information you're interested in, such as Content→Content by Title. You can now click the Add to Dashboard button at the top of the page (Figure 12-3). Going back to your dashboard, you will see that the new box has been added, and you can rearrange it on the page like other elements.

Figure 12-3.
Clicking the Add to Dashboard button in Analytics

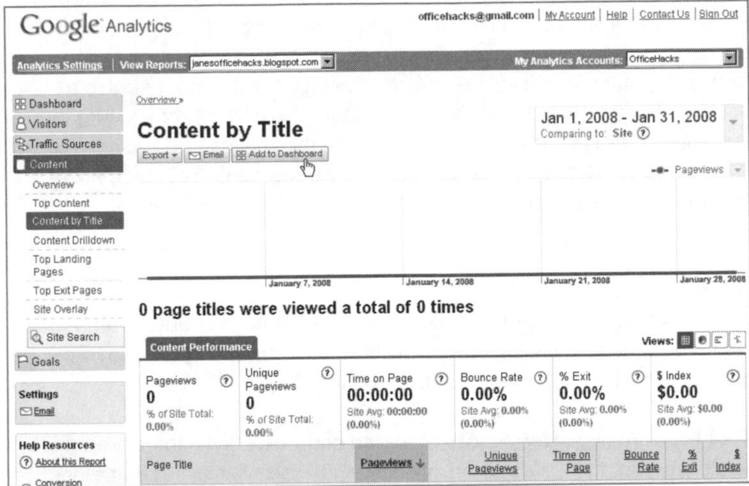

HACK 130: Optimize Your Site for Search Engines

This section is a bit of a nonhack, actually. Hacks are supposed to be quick and clever ways of doing things—the kind of trick that, once known, creates a shortcut to a desired outcome.

And that's the thing with search engine optimization (SEO), the art of trying to rank the pages of your web site well in Google and other engines for a variety of search queries. If SEO were an effortless craft, then millions of us could easily apply it—but there are still only around 10 pages in every search result! This means there will always be competition for this scarce resource.

In addition to that, Google and others work hard trying to prevent any "shortcut" to a precious #1 ranking, unless the site is really good and worthy of that ranking. So in reality, the best SEO tip is this: have a site that's good.

Off-Page Optimization

Offering terrific products, content, or services on your site is a way to make it rank well—because then your site will attract *backlinks*. And backlinks are at the heart of the ranking algorithm of most search engines today.

A backlink happens when someone sees your site and likes it, and then links from their site to yours; this sends you visitors as well as "link love." Google and others, upon finding the link, will check out the authority of the linking site, which then adds to the authority of your site.

People in the past tried the shortcut of creating many sites just for the purpose of linking to their primary web site; this is called a *linkfarm*. Another shortcut, which is costly, is using *paid links*. However, most of these approaches can backfire, in the sense that your site gets banned completely from search engines. The webmaster guidelines of Google can be wrapped up as follows: optimize your site for your visitors, not for search engines.

When Google looks at backlinks, they don't just increase the authority ranking of your site; they also associate the keywords of the link with your page. If lots of blogs link to your site using the words "happy" and "camper" and variations thereof, it may well be that (once time passes), you'll find yourself on top of the search results for "happy camper."

Granted, even if you have great content on your site, sometimes other webmasters, bloggers, online journalists, or online communities may simply not know about that content. In that case, it makes sense to get the word out by getting involved in other communities, sending out relevant tips to webmasters, or contacting bloggers. Always think about how your content, product or service can help *them*, though, by sending out only relevant pointers that you imagine they'll be glad to receive. To know whether they'll likely be glad to receive your pointer also consists of *knowing* them; instead of sending out pointers in bulk (which you should never do), this means that you need to respectfully take the time to first get to know a person or community you want to contact. There's a popular saying in Germany for this—"as you shout into the woods, so the echo returns."

On-Page Optimization

Once you've understood the most important part of the equation, the off-page optimization, you can fine-tune the on-page optimization—meaning everything that takes place on your site (like your HTML template, your titles), not on other people's sites (like backlinks):

Cater for the "long tail" of keywords by offering lots of varied content. Maybe there are only 10 results on each search result page, but there are millions of such top 10 lists—because people look for millions of different things, using millions of different search queries. One way of catering for the long tail of keywords is to ensure that each of your pages has a unique title (and, ideally, rather unique content as well). Another is to add translations of your pages for a multitude of languages, which will generate a multitude of new ways to find you (there are paid online services to which you can submit a text file, and then pick the languages you want it to be translated into by native speakers).

Make your server responsive, and use clean and structured HTML. The best content won't fare well on an unstable technical base, so make it the most stable you can. One way to check your site for errors is to validate it using the World Wide Web Consortium's HTML validator at http://validator.w3.org. You can find out more about HTML and XHTML at http://w3.org/TR/html401/ and http://w3.org/TR/xhtml1/, respectively.

Add only content to your pages that benefits your visitors. You don't need to (in fact, shouldn't) add overlong, keyword-stuffed titles, or hidden keywords, or anything else merely targeted at search engines. One thing you can do, though, is add descriptive text somewhere on a page, like in the footer, that gives a good overview of what the site is about; this text will almost automatically include a wide range of related keywords people may look for.

Treat each of your pages as "microcontent." Microcontent means content that can be understood without knowing further context about your site. The page should be able to "stand on its own." Among other things, it means that a page has a clear concise title, a beginner-friendly introductory sentence, and a readable and permanent URL.

Suppose that the page in question lists favorite Albert Einstein quotes. Well, then its title should be "Albert Einstein quotes" or similar; its first heading should be something like "Quotes by Albert Einstein"; and there might be an introductory sentence along the lines of "The following quips by Einstein are noteworthy both for being prescient, as well as funny." The URL of the page may be http://yourfavoritequotes.example.com/einstein. Furthermore, below the Einstein quotes there could be links to quotes by other famous scientists, a link to a biography of Einstein, and a link to an Einstein discussion board (whether it's on another site or yours). There may also be a photo of young, fuzzy-haired Albert somewhere on the page. In a nutshell, if you would ask yourself the question, "Which is the best single and self-contained page on the Web for someone looking for Albert Einstein quotes?", the answer should be a resounding "Why, this one of course!"

Create a good, simple navigation structure for your site. Every page you want visitors to find indexed in Google should be linked from somewhere (and not within parts of your site that would require Flash, or JavaScript, or frames, either). Keep your site's navigation structure simple and all-encompassing. If you consider a particular page to be of importance, then don't make the navigation path to it overly long, but link to it straight from your home page. On the other hand, also don't oversimplify the hierarchy of pages—because linking to 10,000 of your site's pages from the front page will greatly devalue each individual link.

If your site's topic is often rather dry, consider adding a creative video, fun game, or interesting article somewhere. Even if you have the best content or service in your field, sometimes it takes a little extra to get the word out.

Open up your site and give freely. Consider allowing people to run with your content by making it Creative Commons–licensed (see http://creativecommons.org), by offering gadgets **[Hack #60]** or a developer API (application programming interface), or by turning it into embeddable content via sites like YouTube. Be more water than ship.

Make your site accessible. Accessibility is a broad topic that covers adjusting your site to work with different devices (like mobile phones, printers, text-to-speech engines) as well as different browser settings (like with JavaScript or images disabled) or browsing use-cases (like right-clicking a link to open it in a new window, or using the back button). Indeed, try browsing your site with images and JavaScript turned off. How usable is it? (And as your browser may not allow you to disable certain features, you can also use a text browser like Lynx: http://lynx.browser.org.)

Many things can be done to improve your site's accessibility: use appropriate `alt` text for images where needed, replace frames with a server-side template that emulates frame behavior, or ensure there are no JavaScript-based redirects that break the back button. Replacing a feature that requires a rare plug-in with one implemented in standardized web technologies can make sense as well. For a full accessibility checklist, take at look at http://w3.org/TR/WaI-WEBCONTENT/

Once you consider these issues, you can track the outcome of your work by checking the Google results of keywords relevant to your site, and by checking your stats via Google Analytics or other programs. At this point, don't worry too much about ranking details, though, or expect super-fast results. Also, don't spend hours looking at Google Analytics wondering why the numbers aren't higher yet—rather, improve your site and get the word out. Or, to put it into words commonly attributed to Albert Einstein: "Not everything that counts can be counted, and not everything that can be counted counts."

HACK 131: Track the Traffic of Your iGoogle Gadgets

Get valuable usage statistics for your Google gadget, without paying too much attention to page views.

When you build an iGoogle gadget **[Hack #60]** you probably want to know more about how people use it. Next to getting direct user feedback via email, tracking your gadget statistics is the best feedback.

Before understanding *how* you can track your gadget traffic, you need to understand *what* exactly to track. On normal web pages, one of the most popular values to track is the page view. However, this number is less useful for iGoogle gadgets. That's because your gadget may be included among a dozen other gadgets, triggering a page view whenever the user visits iGoogle—even when your gadget is ignored, and the user is just performing a web search. More useful than the page view may be the actual number of gadget users as well as the amount of interactions with your gadget.

To find the number of users who subscribed to your gadget, just go to your gadget's detail page in the iGoogle directory. You can find it by opening the menu from the top right of your gadget box, and then selecting "About this gadget." If your gadget URL is http://example.com/gadget.xml, then the detail page would be:

```
http://google.com/ig/directory?url=example.com/gadget.xml
```

(If you can't find your gadget in the directory yet, submit it at http://google.com/ig/submit and wait one or two weeks.) On this page, you will now find a text like "243 users", as pictured in Figure 12-4. Compare this to similar gadgets' numbers to get a feeling of how well your gadget is doing.

Figure 12-4.
The number of users is shown on a gadget's detail page (3,993 in this case)

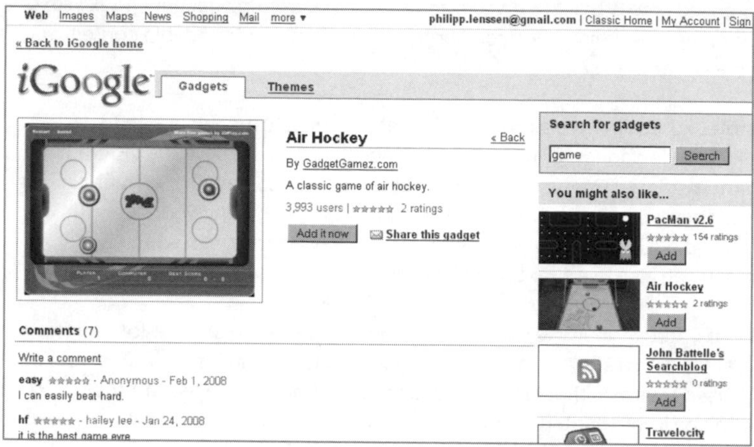

How to best get the number of interactions with your gadget depends on the type of gadget and how you store the gadget XML code.

For instance, if the gadget in question is a game stored on your own server, then you could include an introductory splash screen with a Start button in the module code. The intro screen would be hosted by Google—as its HTML is contained right in the module code—but you'd set up the gadget so that clicking the Start button would request a page from your server. This way, you can use your normal Google Analytics tracking code (see the introduction to this chapter), or any other tracking mechanism you already use on your server, and simply count the page views of the game's page. Here is a sample module, where `example.com` would be your domain:

```
<?xml version="1.0" encoding="UTF-8" ?>
<Module>
  <ModulePrefs title="Anagramania" ... />
  <Content type="html">
    <p>Find anagrams with Anagramania!</p>
    <p><a href="http://example.com/gadgetized/anagramania/">Start</a></p>
  </Content>
</Module>
```

If on the other hand you host all module content within the module code itself, you can make use of a special Google Analytics library available for gadgets. You can then make a call to track page views, or to track specific events in your module, like clicks (please note that some attributes necessary to submit your gadget to the directory, like the author email, have been omitted from this example; see [Hack #60] for a more complete example):

```
<?xml version="1.0" encoding="UTF-8" ?>
<Module>
  <ModulePrefs title="A Clickable Div!" ... >
    <Require feature="analytics" />
  </ModulePrefs>
  <Content type="html">
    <![CDATA[
    <script type="text/javascript">
        // This line tracks the gadget in Google Analytics
        _IG_Analytics("YOUR_ANALYTICS_ID", "/mygadget");
    </script>
    <div onclick="_IG_Analytics('YOUR_ANALYTICS_ID', '/mygadget/click')">
        Clicks on this div will be tracked
    </div>
    ]]>
</Content>
</Module>
```

Note the three bold parts of this XML gadget code. First, the `Require` element prepares the gadget for Google Analytics tracking. Second, a `script` element embeds a call to an Analytics function to register the page view; the value `/mygadget` is a string that you can define yourself that will be shown as a path in Google Analytics reports. Third, the `onclick` event of the divisor element near the end of the module registers when people click the `div`. (You can track other events that are fired, too—not just clicks.)

> The values reading `YOUR_ANALYTICS_ID` in the module code shown in this hack need to be replaced by your actual Analytics identifier. To obtain this ID, log in to Google Analytics. Next to your site's name in the Analytics overview, click Edit. Now click Check Status in the top right. Your tracking identifier will be displayed in a snippet box for easy copy and pasting. It has the form of UA-12345-6.

> Give Google Analytics some time to start showing tracking numbers. The stats do not appear immediately after you set up the tracking.

HACK 132: Create a Firefox Keyword to Skip the Analytics Login Box

Save some seconds (and keystrokes) if you frequently check your stats.

Currently, when you go to http://analytics.google.com, you will be forced to click the Sign In button every time, even when you are already signed in. There are different ways to avoid this to jump straight to your reports overview (or, if you prefer, straight to a single site's reports).

In Firefox, you can add a bookmark keyword. First, log in to Analytics. Now bookmark the page. Right-click the bookmark you've created and select Properties from the context menu that appears. In the properties dialog box, enter they keyword "stats" (or any other word you can easily remember). Click the OK button.

Next time you want to see your statistics, you can just enter "stats" in the browser address bar; as long as you were logged in before, you don't need to reenter your login information this time.

You can also use these bookmark keywords to jump specifically to a single site's report, as shown in Figure 12-5. Just bookmark the page in question, and in the bookmark properties, use a keyword like "mysite stats" (where "mysite" is the name of your site).

Figure 12-5.
Adding a keyword for a bookmark

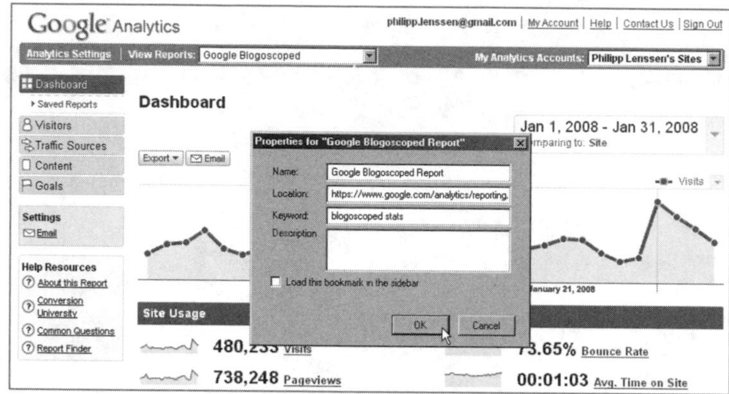

HACK 133: Export Your Analytics Traffic to Google Spreadsheets

Export your traffic data, visualize it, and share it in ways that are not possible within Google Analytics.

Google Spreadsheets (see Chapter 3) accepts Comma-Separated Values data, and Google Analytics exports such CSV data—which means that you can move your site statistics into Spreadsheets.

Exporting the Data

First, go to Google Analytics and find a fitting report that you'd like to export. In this hack, I'm picking Traffic Sources→Referring Sites from the navigation menu. Click the Export button in the top, as shown in Figure 12-6, and click CSV. (There's an Excel icon next to the link, as CSV can also be opened with Microsoft Excel.) Save the CSV file on your disk.

Opening the CSV file with a plain text editor, you will see a portion similar to the following:

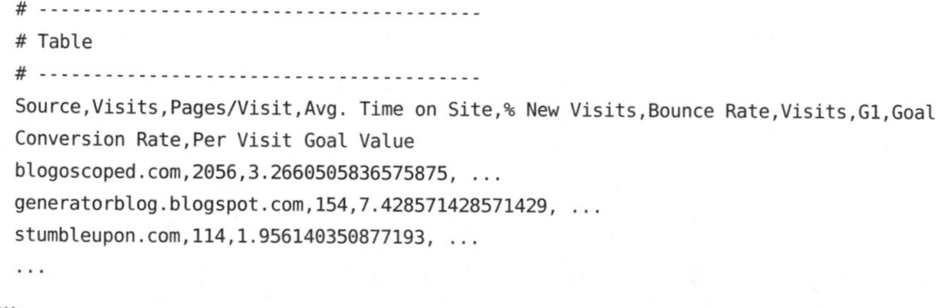

```
# --------------------------------------
# Table
# --------------------------------------
Source,Visits,Pages/Visit,Avg. Time on Site,% New Visits,Bounce Rate,Visits,G1,Goal
Conversion Rate,Per Visit Goal Value
blogoscoped.com,2056,3.2660505836575875, ...
generatorblog.blogspot.com,154,7.428571428571429, ...
stumbleupon.com,114,1.956140350877193, ...
...
```

If you've got a spreadsheet program such as Microsoft Excel installed on your computer, CSV files will probably open within it automatically. To open it in your preferred text editor, launch the text editor first, then use e.g. File→ Open to open the CSV file.

For the purpose of opening it with Spreadsheets, I've decided to delete other data in the CSV file (as the general number of visitors for the time period was included as well) and save it again.

Figure 12-6.
Exporting CSV data from Google Analytics reports

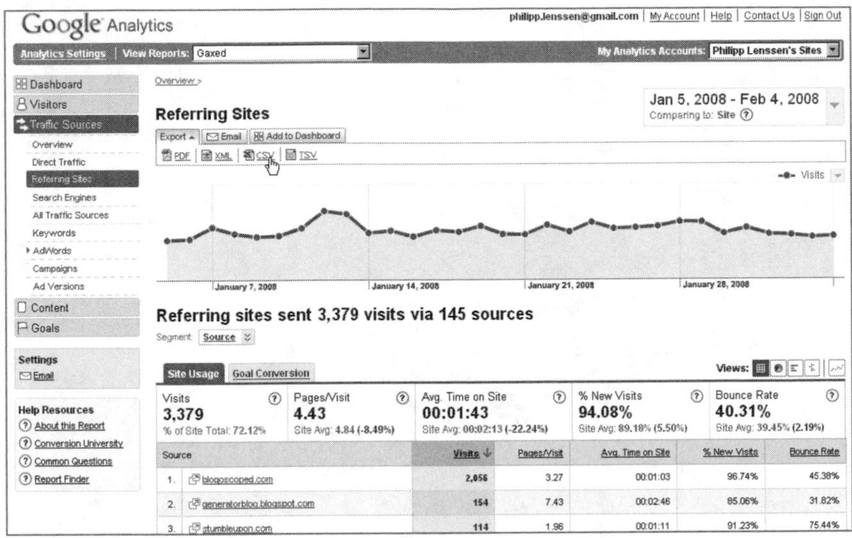

Importing the Data

Now open Google Docs (http://docs.google.com) and click Upload in the top bar. Browse for your Analytics CSV file and click Upload File, as pictured in Figure 12-7. (Google notes that the maximum file size is 1MB.)

Figure 12-7.
Uploading your CSV file to Google Docs

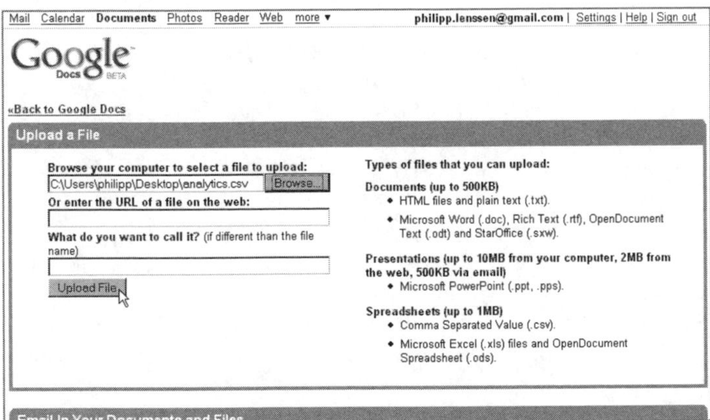

After a while, a Spreadsheets document will open. I've marked the first two columns and added a 3D pie chart, as shown in Figure 12-8. So not only will you be able to create charts *not* available in Google Analytics—you can now also utilize the Spreadsheet's Share tab to let others view just specific traffic data of yours. (Google Analytics has an access manager too, but it won't allow you to specify which traffic data exactly someone is allowed to see; sharing your page views, for instance, will also reveal the most popular search terms used to find your site.)

Figure 12-8.
A 3D pie chart visualizes your referrer stats

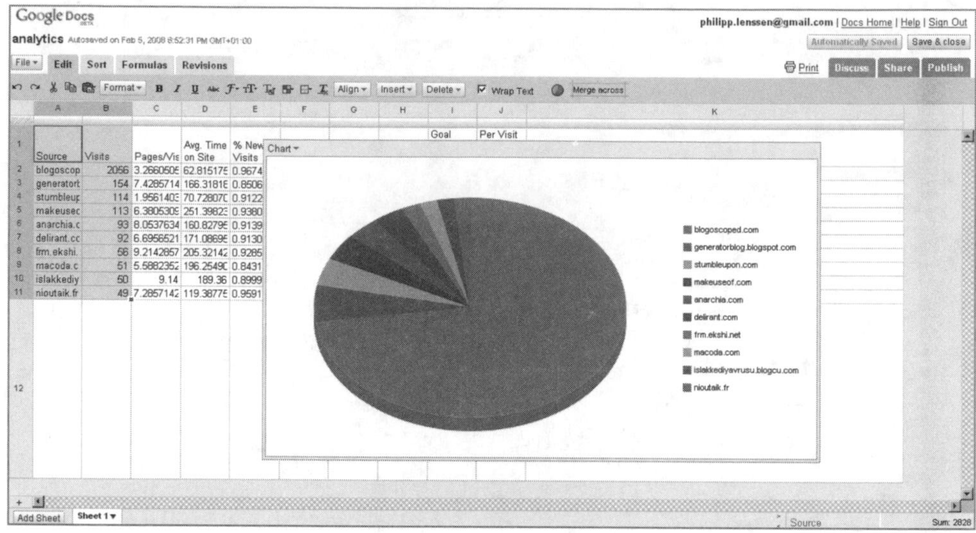

HACK 134: Promote Your Site Using Google Gadgets

Google Gadgets are just one of the many ways to promote your site. Posting content on YouTube, using a Creative Commons license **[Hack #31]**, or publishing an RSS feed, are just a few of the ways to enable people to grab your content and run with it.

If your site offers horoscopes, you can create a horoscope gadget with an option to customize it to one's star sign **[Hack #60]**. If you have a page about horse racing, then you might offer a gadget displaying the latest race results. If your site contains tips for tourists, you could offer a useful gadget showing top spots customized by location, or a Flash game adventure called *Surviving in Rome*. Furthermore, you could offer an iGoogle theme to people **[Hack #61]**.

It's worth keeping in mind that producing a gadget does not guarantee big traffic. Far from it; just publishing a gadget does not automatically make Google users find it, and you may end up with only a couple of subscribers to your content. Google sometimes shows off impressive statistics for popular gadgets, but well, these are the *popular* gadgets, not average ones. And also, gadget views aren't anything like page views, because a gadget is loaded by default every time the user visits the Google home page to perform a search.

Contacting Blogs

One thing that helps to get word out on your content, be it gadgets or other sharable content, is to write to bloggers in a niche related to yours. You can use Google Blog Search (http://blogsearch.google.com) or plain old Google.com to search for keywords like "*horse racing blog*" or "*horse race news*"—if your niche is horse racing—to find some of the community sites for this topic.

When writing to a blogger, it's best to be straightforward and personal, and it's worst—at least from my perspective, mileage of other bloggers may vary—to just send out a traditional press release. Here is an example of a mail I would consider particularly ineffective, and I'll explain the reasons after:

```
Hello,

We would like to inform you of our new virtual reality experience leveraging the latest in
AJAX software, social content, and mobile phone management, to be released next week. Using
HORS-O-RACE, a 3MB desktop program for which we will be glad to provide you a trial version
if you are interested, users can immerse themselves in real-time race tracking information
via our special HORS-O-RACE goggles which ...
```

The email will go on at great length, but you get the idea. What was wrong with it?

- The greeting isn't personal, as it doesn't include the blogger's name. This makes it more likely that the blogger will consider it a bulk mail, and hit the spam button.
- The promotion puts technology before content or use, suggesting that what the application delivers may be less interesting than how it delivers it . . . and if that is the case, it will probably be boring to end users.
- The message is obfuscated by buzzwords, making it harder for the blogger to understand it in the time frame devoted to reading the mail.
- The tool offered requires an installation, which means additional download time, and worse, exposes the blogger's system to risks (like a virus, or auto-updating software that consumes system resource and bandwidth).
- The tool is paid, and includes dependencies—the HORS-O-RACE goggles hardware—which may make this hard for users, who the blogger writes for, to try (notwithstanding the problem that HORS-O-RACE is as of yet unreleased anyway).
- Last not least, the email does not include all the necessary information for the blogger to start writing a review about this right away, should they decide to do so, as the trial version was not included within the first mail.

Here is a much better version of that mail. Bloggers love to get tips and content, so there is no need to beat around the bush by writing eloquent pitches—the blogger will appreciate that you sent a relevant tip, helping to provide content!

```
Hello Jim,

We just released our HORS-O-RACE web app for users to get the latest horse racing
information. It's live at http://example.com/horse-or-race.html ... we're attaching
a couple of screenshots exclusive for you, and hope this is something for your
HorseRaceBlogger.example.com community.

Best,
...
```

This time, the greeting was personal. This time, you've directly explained what the tool does, and provided a public link to a demo. Attached to the mail are a couple of exclusive screenshots, valuable to any blogger who suspects that the same mail might have been sent to a dozen other bloggers (making the blog a mere echo chamber if it's posted). The sentence with an explicit reference to the HorseRaceBlogger community, on the other hand, is one more signal that this mail was prepared by an actual person knowing the recipient, not a spam bot.

HACK 135: Roll Your Own Analytics API for a "Most Popular Posts" Widget

No Google Analytics API? No problem!

If you're like me, you have a blog and use Google Analytics to track visitor activity. Also, you might want a "Most Popular Posts" section on your blog, shown in Figure 12-9, as it's a great way for new visitors to find your best content. The only problem is that this would usually have to be hard-coded, and would therefore need updating periodically after you've checked the Top Content report in Google Analytics, or it would require some server-side scripting and a database to track your page views and show the links dynamically.

Figure 12-9. The goal: a most popular posts widget

Wouldn't it be great if you could somehow use Google Analytics to display the "Most Popular Posts" section on your blog automatically? That would be a huge time-saver for you and would make it much more useful for your visitors, as it would always be up-to-date. Unfortunately, Google Analytics doesn't have an API for that at the time of this writing (there's the Analytics tracker snippet API, but it's for another purpose). But here's a method that doesn't involve any server-side code or screen-scraping. All you need to do is use a few existing free services from Google and Yahoo! and a bit of JavaScript.

> The hack used here will make some of your Analytics data public, a trade-off you may or may not want; details are explained further shortly.

Basic Method

1. **Obtain the tracking data in a usable format.** We can schedule Google Analytics to email this as an XML file on a regular basis.

2. **Make the XML file accessible online.** By emailing an attachment to Google Groups (http://groups.google.com), the file is automatically given a public URL.

3. **Work out the URL of the most recent report.** As Google Groups provides RSS/Atom feeds for all messages, we can easily find the URL of the most recent message and therefore work out the URL of the XML report.

4. **Prepare the data for use.** You need to manipulate the XML and massage it into a handy JSON (JavaScript Object Notation) format that you can use on your blog, which can all be done using Yahoo! Pipes **[Hack #126]**.

5. **Display the links on your site.** With just a bit of client-side JavaScript, you can finally add a self-updating "Most Popular Posts" section to your blog.

There you have it! Using your own Google Analytics data, you can create a completely automated way of displaying your most popular posts to your site visitors.

If you're interested in exactly how I did this, the rest of this hack expands on each step and takes you through the entire process.

Setting Up the Google Group

Because Google Analytics doesn't provide an API, or allow you to link directly to any exported reports, you can use a Google Group to host the files, which you'll schedule Google Analytics to email to you.

When you set up your Google Group, choose the Announcement-only option. Once created, under the "Group settings" menu item, select Access and make sure that the following are checked:

Anybody can view group content. Although it would be preferential to make the group private, that would prevent public access to the feeds for the group, which you'll need later.

Do not list this group. Keeping the group unlisted makes it less likely for someone to stumble across your Analytics reports when searching Google Groups.

People have to be invited. This is so that no one else can post to the group, which would cause issues when trying to retrieve the Analytics message.

Then click Save Changes.

Although you could email your reports directly to the Google Groups email address, each message would then contain an "opt-out" link, because it's not the email address that's registered with Google Analytics. Given that the messages will be publicly available, you'll be using Gmail to forward the messages from the same Gmail address you use for Google Accounts, so that if anyone manages to find the Google Group, they can't stop the scheduled report. Simply create a new filter [Hack #44] and set it up as follows:

- Identify any email with Analytics in the subject that also has attachments.
- Forward the email to your Google Groups email address.
- Skip the inbox, so you don't have automated reports cluttering up your inbox too.

Setting Up Google Analytics

In Google Analytics, under the Content section, view the Top Content report and change "Show rows" from 10 to 50. (You can't configure how many results to include in your report any other way; it just remembers the last setting you selected.) Now click the Email link button near the top of the page, beneath the page title. Select the Schedule tab, then:

- Change the report format to XML.
- Set the date range/schedule to Monthly (unless you have a really active blog, in which case you might want to keep it on Weekly).

Then click the Schedule button at the bottom. To test everything, click the Email button again, select the Send Now tab, choose XML as the format, and click the Send button.

If everything worked correctly, after a few seconds your Google Group should have a Top Content XML report in it!

Yahoo! Pipes

For the next step, you'll need the feed URL for your Google Group. You can get this from the orange XML button at the bottom of your group home page. Choose one of the "New messages" feeds, copy the URL, and head on over to Yahoo! Pipes.

For those that don't know, Pipes at http://pipes.yahoo.com is a really powerful service provided by Yahoo! that lets you fetch data from all over the Web and perform various operations on it, resulting in new or altered XML feeds/JSON output being created, all done using a funky graphical interface—not a line of programming code in sight!

The Yahoo! Pipe I'm using is shown in Figure 12-10 and can be found at:

```
http://pipes.yahoo.com/pipes/pipe.info?_id=6vhLQfPC3BGM7_UDo_NLYQ
```

Figure 12-10.
A screenshot of the Pipe

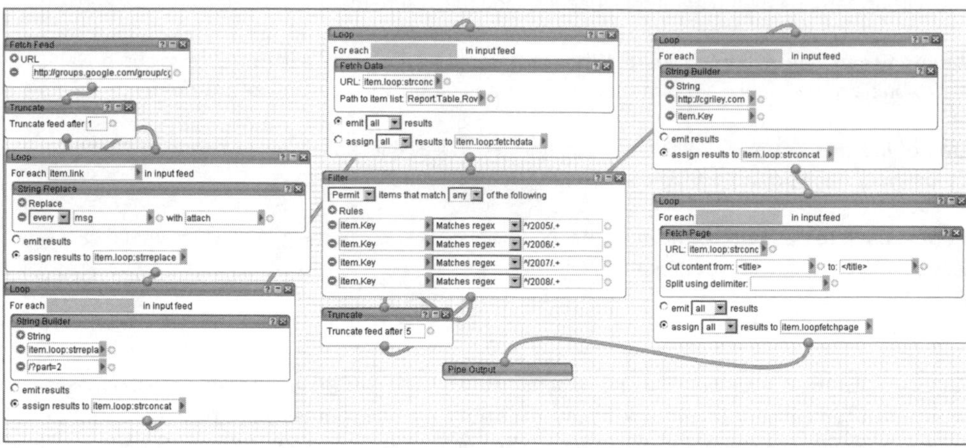

Clone this pipe, (or, if you're feeling ambitious, recreate it using Figure 12-10 as a guide), and make the following changes:

- Put the address of your "New messages" feed into the Fetch Feed box at upper left of the pipe.
- Modify the Filter at the center of the pipe to choose the correct pages from the ones in the report. In Figure 12-10, I've got it set up to match a common URL naming format for blog posts (year first). If you're not getting any results, click on that center Filter, wait for Yahoo! Pipes to refresh the preview at the bottom of the page, and see what you get there. You may need to make some changes to the regular expression on the filter. For example, if all your blog permalinks start with `/blog`, you might change them to `^/blog/2005/.+`, `^/blog/2006/.+`, `^/blog/2007/.+`, and `^/blog/2008/.+` respectively.
- In the Loop in the upper right of the pipe, change the string (http://cgriley.com) to something appropriate for your web site. The idea is to concatenate the URL prefix from your web site with the output you see when you click on the center filter; this results in a valid link that can be clicked on to visit the page.

For those not familiar with Yahoo! Pipes, here's a brief rundown of what you're making the pipe do:

- Grab the Google Groups XML feed and truncate it to leave you with the most recent message.
- Take the message URL and modify it to get the URL of the XML attachment (basically replaces "msg" with "attach" and appends "?part=2").
- Select the report data from the XML attachment and filter out any links that you don't want to include.
- Finally, using the filtered links, fetch each blog post from the web site to retrieve the page title for use in the link and truncate the results to return only the top five.

The result is a JSON file containing the top five most popular blog posts based on the most recent Top Content report sent from Google Analytics to the Google Group. The file is located at http://pipes.yahoo.com/pipes/pipe.run?_id=6vhLQfPC3BGM7_UDo_NLYQ&_render=json. If you've cloned and modified the pipe for your own site, you save the pipe, click Run the Pipe, and then click the More Options button. Right-click the Get as JSON link, and copy its URL to the clipboard.

Displaying Your "Most Popular Posts"

The final step is to take the JSON data returned by Yahoo! Pipes and display the contents on your web site, which can be done using some client-side JavaScript similar to this (replace the bold **6vhLQfPC3BGM7_UDo_NLYQ** with the ID of your pipe):

```
<div id="popularPosts">Loading...</div>
<script type="text/javascript"><!--
function topcontentCallback(obj) {
    var url, title, output, i;
    i = 0;
    output = '<ul>';
    while (i < 5 || i < obj.count) {
        url = "http://www.yoursite.com" + obj.value.items[i].Key;
        title = obj.value.items[i].loopfetchpage[0].content;
        // remove the <title> tags the pipe leaves in:
        title = title.substring(27, title.length-8);
        output += '<li><a href="' + url + '" title="' + title + '">' +
                 title + '</a></li>';
         i++;
    }
    output += '</ul>';
    document.getElementById("popularPosts").innerHTML = output;
 }
//-->
</script>
<script type="text/javascript" src="http://pipes.yahoo.com/pipes/pipe.run?_id=6vhLQfPC3BGM7_
UDo_NLYQ&amp;_render=json&amp;_callback=topcontentCallback"></script>
```

Basically, this makes the pipe execute a JavaScript function on the web page by using a callback on the JSON URL. To learn more about JSON, visit the Yahoo! Developer Network's JSON overview at http://developer.yahoo.com/common/json.html, or the official home of JSON, http://json.org.

This is a simple way of making your Google Analytics data available to use in your own web pages and applications. There are obviously some privacy issues, as your report data is available for everyone to see on Google Groups (which can still be found doing a search, even when you used the "Do not list this group" setting) but if you think that's a worthwhile trade-off for being able to have a maintenance-free top posts section, then the world is your oyster.

And you're not restricted to displaying just your most popular posts. You could also use a similar technique to display your top keywords, referring sites, geographic locations, browsers—and anything else that you can find in Google Analytics!

Have fun mashing up your Google Analytics data!

— Chris Riley

HACK 138: Conduct a User Survey

Get to know your site's visitors by using an interesting Google Spreadsheets feature.

Google Analytics and other number-crunching statistic programs already tell you a lot about your site's visitors. But they're not too good at getting across opinions, insights, or wishes of your visitors in regards to your site. If you want to know more about your visitors, why not conduct a survey and ask them directly?

You don't need to go far to find a survey service: Google Spreadsheets itself allows you to create online forms to poll users. Although certain features, like preventing multiple poll submissions from a single user, are missing at the time of this writing, this may still be good enough for your uses.

Here's how to set up forms in Spreadsheets. Go to http://docs.google.com and pick New→Spreadsheet from the on-page menu. In the spreadsheet window that pops up, click on the title of the document to rename it to something like "Site poll" (once you give it a name, your document will be automatically saved). Switch to the Share tab, and below the "Invite people" heading click the radio button labeled "to fill out a form," as shown in Figure 12-11. Click the "Start editing your form" button and a new form editor window appears.

In the form editor, choose a title for your form and, optionally, a description. Now enter a question; I'm entering "How did you find out about this website?" I'm then choosing the question type "Multiple choice," providing options like "Through a friend's recommendation" or "I found it via Google," as pictured in Figure 12-12.

Figure 12-11.
Setting up the spreadsheet to receive user input

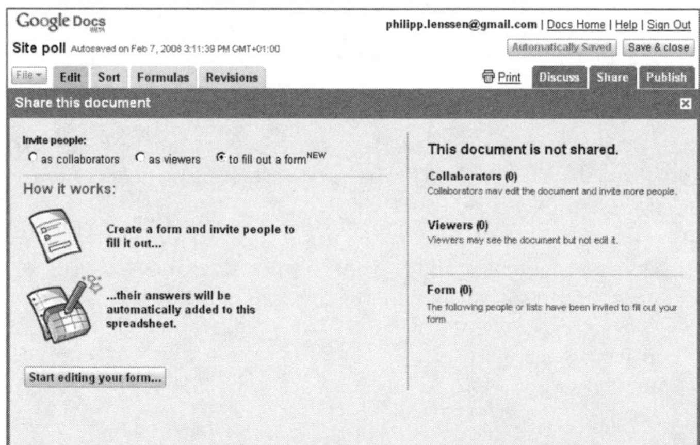

Note that the difference between the answer types "Multiple choice" and "Checkboxes" is that the latter allows for multiple selections to be made all at once ("Multiple choice" only allows a single selection). Another answer type called "Choose from a list" is similar to the "Multiple choice" type, except that it displays a collapsed combo box, thereby saving some space in the form.

Add as many questions and answers as you like—including free-form answers—and progress to the next step by hitting the "Next, choose recipients" button. You can now provide a list of people to send this survey to and click "Invite people"; recipients will see your form right in their email body. For the purpose of this hack, however, the goal is to include the survey on your site. To include it, first right-click the link "Go to live form" in the form editor window and copy its URL to your clipboard.

Figure 12-12.
The spreadsheet form editor

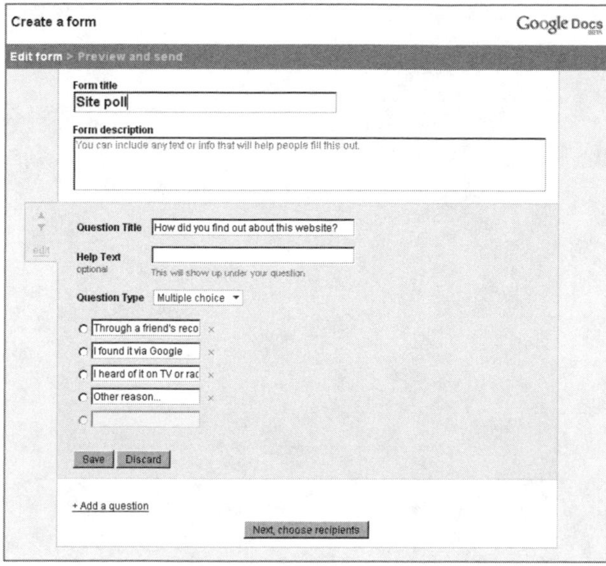

Now you can include an inline frame on your site using that URL, as shown in the sample HTML (note that for more elegant maintenance, in case you repeatedly include such IFrames, you might want to move the sample inline style shown into an external CSS file):

```
<iframe style="border: 1px solid black; width: 400px; height: 400px; overflow: auto"
src="http://spreadsheets.google.com/viewform?key=pvm6FPiylicL4aAD58bv-Tw"><a href="http://
spreadsheets.google.com/viewform?key=pvm6FPiylicL4aAD58bv-Tw">A survey for you</a></iframe>
```

This example displays as illustrated in Figure 12-13. And when your visitors fill out the form, your spreadsheet document will be updated in real time, as shown in Figure 12-14! Now begins the harder part: changing your site and content to accommodate all the user feedback that you'll receive.

Figure 12-13.
The web site poll displayed

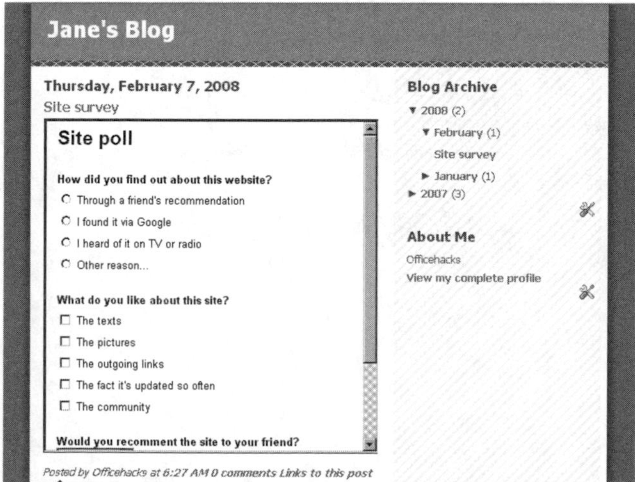

Figure 12-14.
The survey results are automatically integrated into your spreadsheet

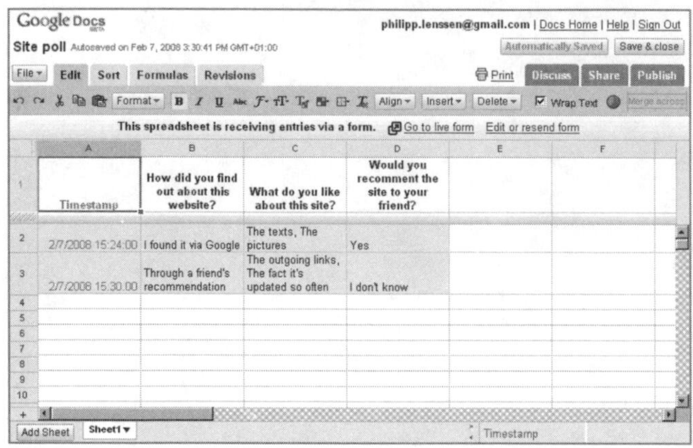

HACK 137: Visualize Traffic with DIY Vector Graphics

Did you know that you can make the browser display vector graphics with just a few lines of code? Welcome to Canvas.

Google Analytics already includes many traffic data visualizations. You can also export your numbers as CSV files **[Hack #133]** and import them into Google Spreadsheets to create new charts.

In this hack, you will learn how to create your own traffic chart using the incredibly cool Canvas framework, which can produce vector graphics and animations with a little bit of HTML and JavaScript. All code referenced in this hack is also available in a single zip file at http://blogoscoped.com/googleappshacks/canvas.zip. Although setting up Canvas may take a little longer than using, say, the Google Charts API **[Hack #4]**, it's also much more flexible, and can even include animated charts.

Draw Something Using Canvas

Canvas is a vector graphics framework which works in most popular browsers today including Firefox, Opera and Safari, and does not require a plug-in like Flash does. Internet Explorer too can render Canvas code, at least with a little tweak you'll see further below. Canvas can be used to have a web page show 2D and 3D drawings, games, charts, applications, animations, and much more.

A longer canvas tutorial is available at http://developer.mozilla.org/en/docs/Canvas_tutorial (explaining how to draw rectangles, curves, imported images, and much more), but let's just see what you need to draw a simple line. First, create a file named *index.html* and open it with a plain text editor. Create a basic page like the following;

```
<!DOCTYPE html PUBLIC "-//W3C//DTD XHTML 1.0 Strict//EN" "DTD/xhtml1-strict.dtd">
<html xmlns="http://www.w3.org/1999/xhtml" xml:lang="en" lang="en">
<head>
  <meta http-equiv="Content-Type" content="text/html; CHARSET=UTF-8" />
  <title>Drawing a line</title>
</head>
<body>
  <h1>Soon, a line will appear!</h1>
</body>
</html>
```

So far, that's all plain (X)HTML. Now somewhere in the `<body>` of the page, put the `canvas` tag:

```
...
<h1>Soon, a line will appear!</h1>
<canvas id="picture" width="600" height="400"></canvas>
 ...
```

Then, in the `<head>` section of the HTML, include a link to a JavaScript file, which you will use to draw the line (you'll create this shortly). Also, insert an `onload` call to the function `main()` in the body tag, as shown here (I'm also adding an inline style; please include your own external style sheet to define the page layout as you see fit **[Hack #18]**):

```
 ...
  <title>Drawing a line</title>
  <script type="text/javascript" src="default.js"></script>
</head>
<body onload="main()" style="background-color: rgb(220,220,220)">
 ...
```

Next, create a *default.js* file containing the following JavaScript, and put it in the same folder as *index.html*:

```
function main() {
    // grab the canvas
    var canvas = document.getElementById('picture');
    var ctx = canvas.getContext('2d');

    // set the color and line width
    ctx.strokeStyle = 'rgba(40,200,180,1)';
    ctx.lineWidth = 8;

    // draw a line
    ctx.beginPath();
    ctx.moveTo(40, 140);
    ctx.lineTo(240, 40);
    ctx.stroke();
}
```

That's not a lot of code—you're grabbing the canvas element using the ID you defined (`picture`), then you're configuring the line style, and then you're moving the line from start point (x and y) to end point. Now open your *index.html* file in a recent version of Opera, Firefox, or Safari, and you will see that a line is drawn, as shown in Figure 12-15! If you can't see a line, it's time to open the debugging window; in Firefox, choose Tools→Error Console from the menu.

Figure 12-15.
Drawing a line using <canvas>

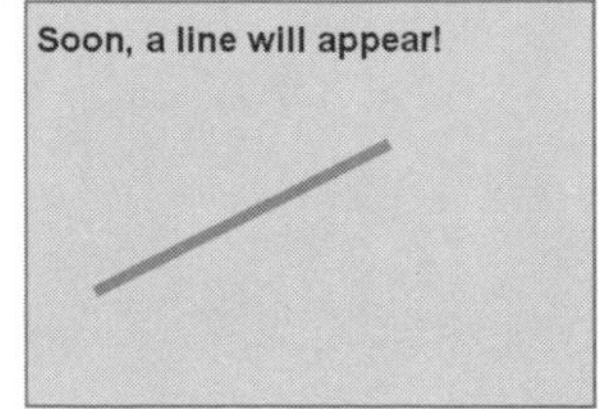

Getting Canvas to Work in Internet Explorer

But wait a second. Didn't I promise this would work in Internet Explorer as well? Now here's the caveat: Internet Explorer doesn't natively support Canvas yet. Before you tear your hair out (or mine), or prepare a nasty letter to O'Reilly asking for your money back, let me explain! Thanks to a bunch of Google developers, it's very easy to get IE7 to support Canvas, because these developers (Emil A. Eklund, Erik Arvidsson, and Glen Murphy) wrote a JavaScript library that emulates Canvas in IE's native vector language, VML (short for Vector Markup Language, not to be confused with VRML, the Virtual Reality Markup/Modeling Language).

You can get ExplorerCanvas from http://excanvas.sourceforge.net by following the links to the download. Drop the JavaScript file in the same folder as your *index.html*, and link it from the HTML as shown here. Using the conditional comments means that you won't be burdening any other browser but IE with the 10 KB the file is made up of, in its compressed file version:

```
...
<script type="text/javascript" src="default.js"></script>
<!--[if IE]><script type="text/javascript"
        src="excanvas.js"></script><![endif]-->
</head>
...
```

Phew . . . you are now ready to open *index.html* in Internet Explorer, too.

Drawing a Traffic Chart in Canvas

Now that you know how to set up Canvas, even if only to draw a simple line, you've opened the door to a whole universe of vector art! Let's use this knowledge to visualize traffic data from Google Analytics. Log in to one of your web site stats at http://analytics.google.com and choose Visitors→ Visitor Trending→Visits. Click the Export button and save the XML download as *stats.xml*.

You can open the XML file in your browser to have a look—it consists of, among other data, point values showing visits for the last 30 days:

```
...
<Point>
  <Value>29,430</Value>
  <Label>January 29, 2008</Label>
</Point>
<Point>
  <Value>24,058</Value>
  <Label>January 30, 2008</Label>
</Point>
...
```

To load this XML file using JavaScript, you can use Ajax (*Asynchronous JavaScript and XML*, a way for web pages to pull remote data without the need for a full page reload). At this point, after changing the files, upload them to your server or run them on a server on your computer—like WAMP, an Apache installation for Windows (http://wampserver.com)—so that the browser will grant the script the rights to grab the XML file. This example won't work if you load it as a `file://` URL.

To continue, I'm amending the files that were previously used for drawing a line (you can also copy the existing files into a new folder and then amend the copies, if you prefer). Replace the entire JavaScript so that it now reads as follows:

```
function main() {
    // grab the XML via Ajax, using different methods, depending on the browser

    var url = 'stats.xml';
    if (window.XMLHttpRequest) {
        req = new XMLHttpRequest();
    }
    else if (window.ActiveXObject) {
        req = new ActiveXObject('Microsoft.XMLHTTP');
    }
    req.onreadystatechange = receiveChart;
    req.open('GET', url, true);
    req.send(null);
}

function receiveChart() {
    // parse the XML into an array, removing commas from
    // numbers, and pass it to drawChart
```

```
        if (req.readyState == 4) {
            if (req.status == 200) {
                var timeFrame = 30;
                var d = req.responseXML.getElementsByTagName('Value');
                var values = new Array();
                for (var i = 0; i < timeFrame && i < d.length; i++) {
                    var visits = d[i].firstChild.data;
                    values[i] = parseInt( visits.replace(/,/g, '') );
                }
                drawChart(values);
            }
        }
    }

    function drawChart(values) {
        // draw the chart while normalizing the display of
        // the lines based on the peak value of the array

        var peak = getMaxValueOfArray(values);
        var canvas = document.getElementById('picture');
        var ctx = canvas.getContext('2d');
        ctx.strokeStyle = 'rgba(40,200,180,1)';
        ctx.lineWidth = 5;
        ctx.beginPath();
        ctx.moveTo(0, canvas.height);
        for (var i = 0; i < values.length; i++) {
            var percent = getPercent(peak, values[i]);
            var x = i * (canvas.width / (values.length - 1) );
            var y = (100 - percent) * (canvas.height / 100);
            ctx.lineTo( Math.round(x), Math.round(y) );
        }
        ctx.lineTo(canvas.width, canvas.height);
        ctx.lineTo(0, canvas.height);
        ctx.stroke();
    }

    function getMaxValueOfArray(values) {
        var max = 0;
        for (var i = 0; i < values.length; i++) {
            if (values[i] > max) {
                max = values[i];
            }
        }
        return max;
    }

    function getPercent(all, part) {
        return all > 0 ? 100 / all * part : 0;
    }
```

Load *index.html* in your browser to see a chart similar to the one shown in Figure 12-16. There are still things left to be done to fine-tune the script, such as:

- Error handling to alert you when something is wrong with the XML.
- Preventing the XML from being cached too quickly in case you want to update it.
- Prettifying the chart or animating it.

but hopefully, this example has you ready to delve deeper into Canvas!

Figure 12-16.
Drawing a Canvas chart based on your Google Analytics statistics

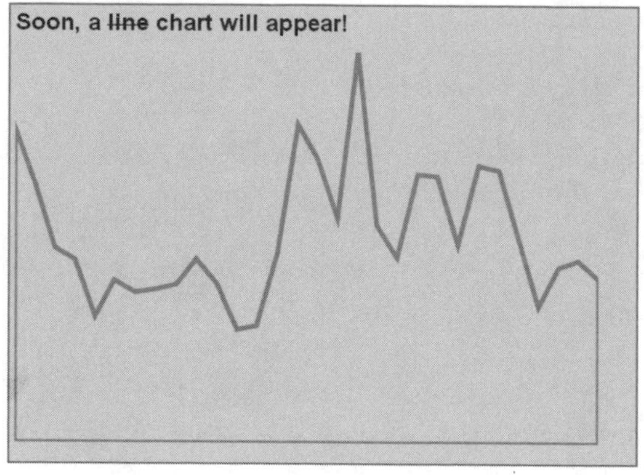

For many more Canvas samples, check out http://developer.mozilla.org/en/docs/Category:Canvas_examples.

HACK 138: Talk to Your Visitors

"Chatback" is Google's name for a live help feature for your site. More than idle chatter, it can be an additional form of communication on your site (complementing things like comment forms, or your About page with contact info like an email address).

Other than measuring your visitors in mere numbers, or conducting a survey **[Hack #136]**, you can also directly chat with visitors to get feedback! Google offers a chat badge that you can post onto your blog or any other web page, making this a simple undertaking, at least technically (taking the time to speak with your visitors, and handling multiple conversations at once, is a different matter).

To get the chat widget, visit http://google.com/talk/service/badge/New and customize the badge by adjusting the title and other options. Your title of choice may be "Talk to me," "Have feedback? I'm listening," "Ask me a question," or anything else. If you edit the configuration, click the "Update badge" button to refresh the snippet. Copy the snippet (see Figure 12-17) and paste it into your blog software's HTML editing tab, or any other home page editor of choice. (For more valid HTML, you may want to escape the ampersand characters in the snippet's URL by writing `&` instead of just `&`.)

If your title is too long for the speech bubble, help is only a few character strokes away: you can adjust the width parameter in the URL, as well as the IFrame's `width` attribute, to expand the length of the badge's speech bubble. The bubble's height can be adjusted too. For instance, you can change the snippet part that reads `w=200&h=60` to `w=400&h=80`, and then change `width="200" height="60"` to `width="400" height="80"`.

Log in to Google Talk (one way is to open http://talkgadget.google.com/talkgadget/popout in your browser), and then go live with your blog post or the changes you made to your home page. The exact way the widget displays depends on your configurations and your online status—if you've set your Google Talk status to "busy," or you're logged out of chat, people won't be able to launch a chat with you from the chat badge.

Now whenever you're available, visitors can launch a chat with you by clicking on the badge. They do *not* need a Google Account to do so. And you will not be able to identify them in any way other than what they may reveal about them themselves, as they will show as "Guest." Figure 12-18, on the other hand, shows what the chat will look like from the visitor's end.

Figure 12-17.
This dialog takes you through creating a Google Talk chatback badge; you can expand and collapse the advanced options via the Edit link

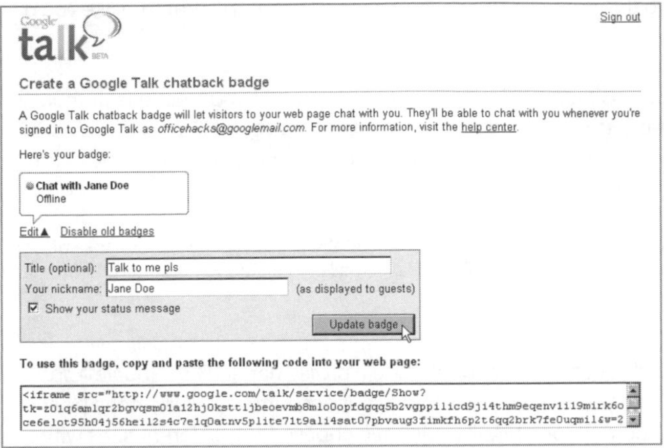

Figure 12-18.
What the chat looks like for one of the visitors to Jane's blog

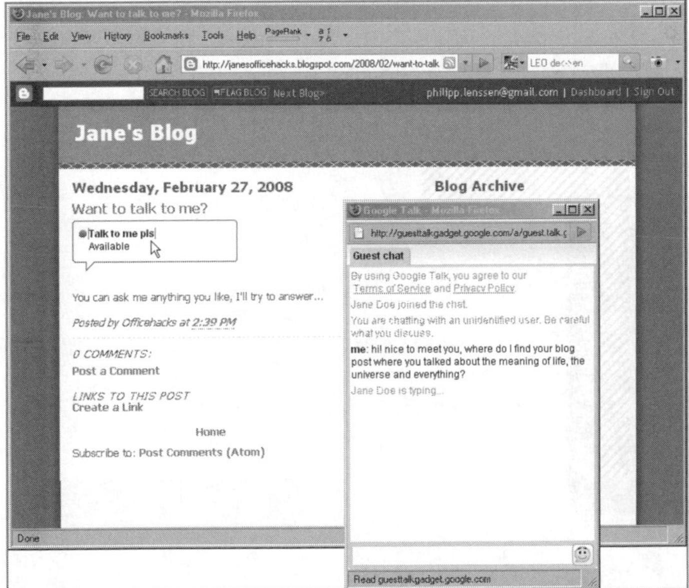

HACK 138: A Different Display for Google Analytics

Google Analytics AIR, also called Analytics Reporting Suite, is a third-party desktop program that visualizes your Google Analytics numbers in quite a different way.

To run Google Analytics AIR, you first need to install AIR, short for Adobe Integrated Runtime. AIR is a framework for creating desktop apps using Flash, HTML, and other technologies, and it's available on different platforms. Download the (currently 11 MB) installation from http://get.adobe.com/air/ and run it. (A hat tip to Siggi Becker for pointing out this hack.)

Now that AIR is installed, download Google Analytics AIR from http://aboutnico.be/index.php/downloads/. There are multiple versions to pick from; I'm using Beta 3, because it's made for the version of AIR that I just downloaded. The file may end up as *download.php* on your system; rename it to *google-analytics.air*. Thanks to this new extension, you can now launch the program like you'd launch other programs.

In the dialog that pops up, as shown in Figure 12-19, hit the Install button (if you trust this author, as always) and follow through with the installation. Afterwards, Google Analytics AIR opens and asks you to choose an account. You can now either see a sample of the program by choosing the demo profile, or add your own Google account.

If you do provide your Google account credentials, again make sure that you trust the author and the software, as with the same password, it's possible to access your Gmail emails, your Blogger blog dashboard, your unlisted Picasa albums and so on.

If you do want to provide your Google account credentials, add a profile name (like "Google Apps Hacks"), your username (like "officehacks@gmail.com") and your account password in the profile dialog. Then hit the "load" button and wait for a bit. You can then choose from different sites within that account, as shown in Figure 12-20. Make a new selection or leave as is, and click "Add profile."

If you opted to see the demo data instead, click "Select profile" on top, select the Test Drive profile, and click "To dashboard."

You will now end up on the dashboard, as shown in Figure 12-21, with a lefthand navigation allowing you to see overviews, map overlays, new vs. returning visitors, visitor loyalty, and more.

Figure 12-19.
Installing the Analytics Reporting Suite

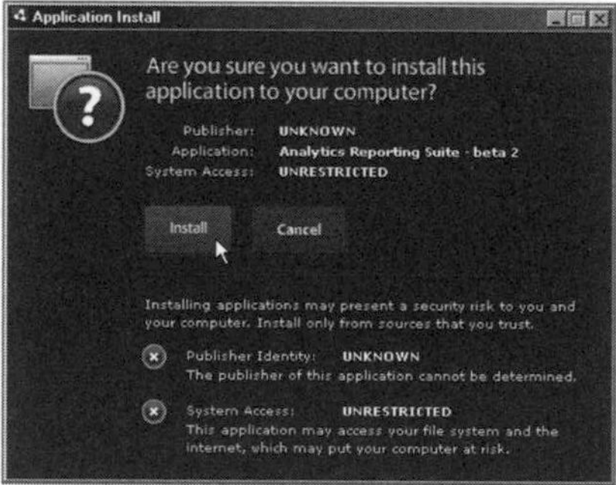

Figure 12-20.
Setting up your profile

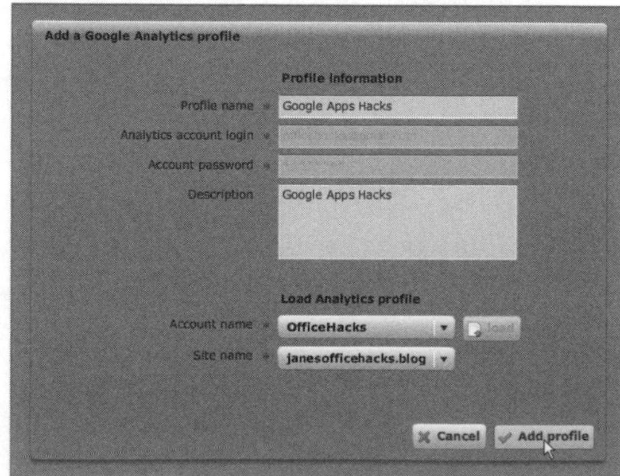

Figure 12-21.
The numbers from the sample account

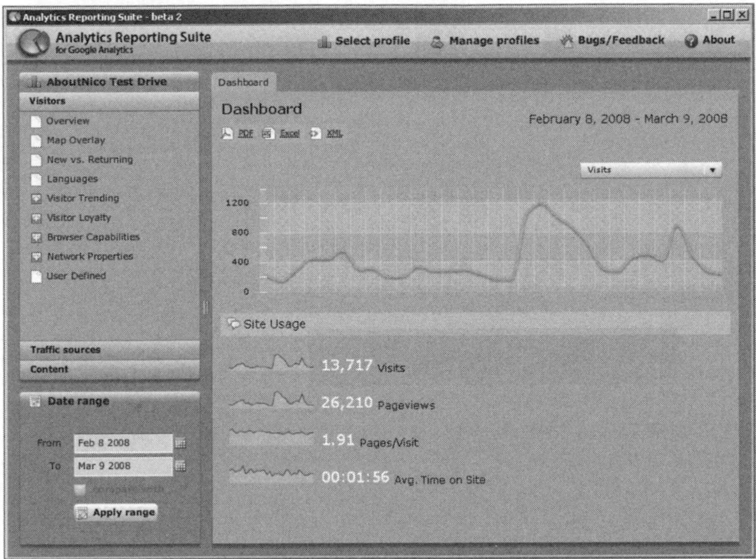

HACK 140: Follow the Online Discussion

Number-crunching apps like Google Analytics are not at all the only tool to track your site and the online discussion that evolves around it.

Statistics show the big numbers first—say, ImportantMajorWebsite.example.com sent 10,000 visitors to your blog post rant—but they often hide how that big site found your page in the first place. This original reason that ended in a traffic peak on your site is the "tipping point." Knowing the tipping point is as important as knowing ImportantMajorWebsite.example.com.

Here are a couple of approaches that will help you understand your site's place in the greater scheme of things, and shed light on the tipping points. You can then read up on what people elsewhere say about your site or service, and react to it accordingly (like improving your site based on the feedback, or, if necessary, clarifying your point of view):

Head over to Google Blog Search at http://blogsearch.google.com and enter your site's URL, or your page's URL, into the search box. Click the Search Blogs button. This will now display blogs pointing to that URL, as shown in Figure 12-22. You can order these results by date, and then move to the last results page, so that you will see the blogs that first linked to your page. The same backlinks discovery can be performed via Technorati at http://technorati.com. (Note that these services usually won't display *all* links which are out there, and they may also sometimes get the date ordering slightly wrong.)

Set up a Google News Alert for mentions of your site's name, or your company or product's name, or your own name. Just go to http://google.com/alerts?t=1 (log in to your Google Account if necessary), type a search term, and click Create Alert. You will now receive emails when certain news sites report on your site.

Note that you can combine several keywords within a single query. If your site is called Acme Inc. and the product is called ACME2000, then the search query can be: *"acme inc" | acme2000 | "acme 2000" | amce2000*. (Yes, including the misspelled product name at the end—as this may be how some news reports accidentally write it!)

Figure 12-22.
Finding out who links to your page

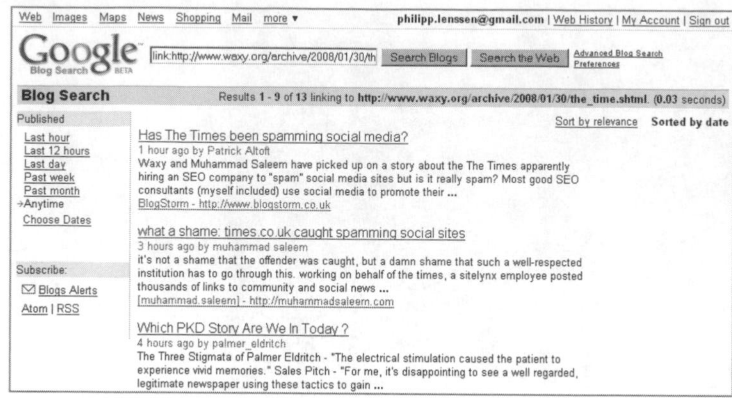

Check your referrer statistics. Log in to Google Analytics at http://analytics.google.com. Click on View Reports to jump to your site in question, and then pick Traffic Sources→Referring Sites from the lefthand navigation. If necessary, expand the list to more than just 10 results by adjusting the Show Rows button at the bottom. You will now find a list of sites that linked to your site and send over their visitors. Click on a domain in the list, and you will see a drill-down of specific subpages on that domain linking to you. You can now click the icon to the left of these subpages to open them in a new window.

Search Google for your site's name, or the keywords of topics you're currently discussing. This will reveal other sites discussing the subject or your site—even when they don't happen to link to your site. To find links, you can also enter `link:example.com` into Google web search (replace "example.com" with your domain).

Searching for keywords related to your area of focus will also retrieve sites and communities which are important in this field, but not discussing or linking your site. It is important for you to know about the ImportantMajorWebsite.example.com's of your field. It will aid your understanding of the online discussion and also offer ideas on where you could potentially get involved. If your site is about the TV series "Heroes," for instance, you might want to search Google for "heroes series," "heroes blog," "heroes forum," and more, to then check the sites topping the results.

Check whether (and how) your content is submitted to social news sites. Social news sites, like Reddit.com or Digg.com, allow their users to submit pointers to any web page. Including yours, of course—and wouldn't it be nice to know about that? Usually, what you can do is head over to the social news site and search for your URL to see if it has been submitted. If searching for URLs doesn't work, you can also often utilize the site's URL submission collision checker (even if you don't plan to submit your site yourself).

If you have a comment system on your site, make sure that you are alerted to new comments made to old posts. Let's say two years ago, you wrote a blog post about the life of long-forgotten astronaut Jonathan R. Humperdink. Nobody seemed interested at the time, but an hour ago a major Hollywood studio announced that they'll turn Humperdink's life into a film—and all of a sudden, interest in the subject, and your article, spikes. Your post will thus get a lot of new comments, but you may not check the comments thread any more. If, on the other hand, your blog is set up so that you will get an alert for each new comment made, you will immediately know of the spike.

To set this up on Google's Blogger.com, switch to Settings→Comments. Scroll down to the Comment Notification Email field, and enter your email address. Hit Save Settings to complete.

HACK 141: Beyond Google: Clicky, Mint, and Others

Google Analytics is just one of many statistics packages available.

Before we delve into the alternatives, there's the need for a word of caution:

Traffic numbers are often incomparable.

Not all statistic packages return the same traffic numbers. Due to differences in handling and wording, there is sometimes great confusion and discrepancy surrounding the values *hits, page views, page loads, visits, visitors, unique visitors, uniques*, and *session*, making these numbers often incomparable between the various tracking programs. For instance, what one program identifies as "visit" may be showing as an inflated "visitor" number in another program. Also, details are easy to miss when adding up numbers—such as the absolute unique visitor numbers of 30 days added up separately being much higher than the absolute unique visitor numbers over a 30-day period taken as a whole (even Google Analytics—which often shows more conservative numbers than many other apps—got this partly wrong in the beginning, though they later announced a bug fix).

If you are asked for your traffic numbers, try to ensure that you are naming your tracker app and provide the exact wording as your interface shows it—including definitions from the app's help file where needed—and that the person asking understands these issues and does not compare numbers from incomparable stats apps. Additionally, try providing values like *average time spent on site* or *pages per visit* if you believe that they help better explain your site and audience.

Here is an overview of some of the values that you may see pop up in your stats cruncher app:

Hit: This is perhaps the least useful value of all, as a *hit* merely describes how often any resource on your server was requested. This includes HTML files but also stylesheets, JavaScript files, image files and so on. This number is often provided by statistic programs working straight on your server log files (not those using a client-side, cookie-based approach).

Page view: A *page view* bundles all hits into a single number. When the visitors stumbles upon a single page of yours, it may trigger 55 hits, but only 1 page view, thus making the value more meaningful (though in the age of behind-the-scenes data polling via Ajax, a page view does not always tell the whole story, either).

Visit: A *visit*, also called a *session*, groups together all the consecutive page views of a user. Usually, a 30 minute time-out between two requests counts as a new visit. So if Joe visits example.com and browses 10 pages within 10 minutes, and then an hour later, Jane visits example.com from the same IP address, 2 visits will be counted.

Visitor: The *visitor* number groups together all the visits from a specific person. This can be done by scripts dropping a cookie on the client computer (which works correctly, as long as the cookie isn't deleted, and as long as the person doesn't visit the site from different computers). Google Analytics calls this the "Absolute Unique Visitor" value, more clearly differentiating its name from the "visit" value other statistic packages may use.

But again—what one program may call a "visit," another may call a "visitor." And one number may not necessarily be more useful than the other. Imagine that you're being asked, "How many cars drive through your home street on a typical day?" To come up with an answer, do you count every car that passes by the street on a given day . . . or do you only count those cars you *haven't seen before* that day, in case people drive through the street once in the morning and once in the evening?

Alternatives or Companions to Google Analytics

With the differences between analytic packages in mind, here are some other ways that you can crunch the numbers coming in from your site:

Clicky (http://getclicky.com): Clicky, as shown in Figure 12-23, displays your traffic numbers in lightweight overviews. They also provide some real-time data via their "Spy" tab, showing you how visitors interact with your site at a given moment. Clicky also supports tracking interactive Ajax or Flash applications, and visualizes data using such approaches as Google Maps mashups or tag clouds.

StatCounter (http://statcounter.com): The free StatCounter service, as shown in Figure 12-24, is a bit more of an "old-school" traffic tracker. After registering and inserting a piece of code from them in your blog or other web site, you'll be able to find out about such things as popular pages, exit pages, keyword analysis, visitor paths, browser usage stats and more. Note that you can decide whether you want the StatCounter tracker widget to be invisible on your site.

Site Meter (http://sitemeter.com): Similar to StatCounter, Site Meter breaks up the different traffic aspects in a lefthand navigation and then visualizes numbers to the righthand content area. The default view is shown in Figure 12-25. The site is ad-supported, like other statistic services, so you'll be seeing banner animations to the top and right (unless you have an ad blocker installed, that is).

VisitorVille (http://visitorville.com): VisitorVille can get its data either straight from your raw server logs, or via a tracker snippet you include in your template. Once data is coming in, it will be displayed in a surprisingly real-time and visual way—by showing your site as a city, as pictured in Figure 12-26, with visitors driving around, or a Google bus delivering a visitor when someone searched for your site (audio clues are attached to these events so that you can partly track your traffic even when the program is minimized, just by listening). When you want to know more about a particular visitor, you can right-click the visitor avatar to open their "passport," showing details like the visitor location, search terms and more—and you can even initiate a chat with them. VisitorVille, available in full 3D or isometric 2D, is paid software (starting at $6.95 per month, depending on your traffic), and also available as a free trial download.

Mint (http://haveamint.com): This stats app costs a one-time $30 per site, which will provide you with a PHP package to set up on your domain (as Mint is not a hosted service). For a live sample demo of Mint, check out http://designologue.com/mint/, as pictured in Figure 12-27.

Figure 12-23.
Clicky

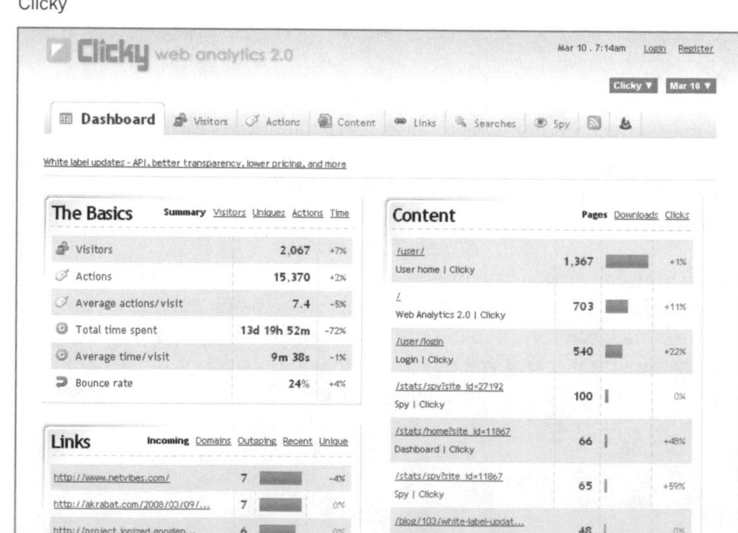

Figure 12-24.
StatCounter

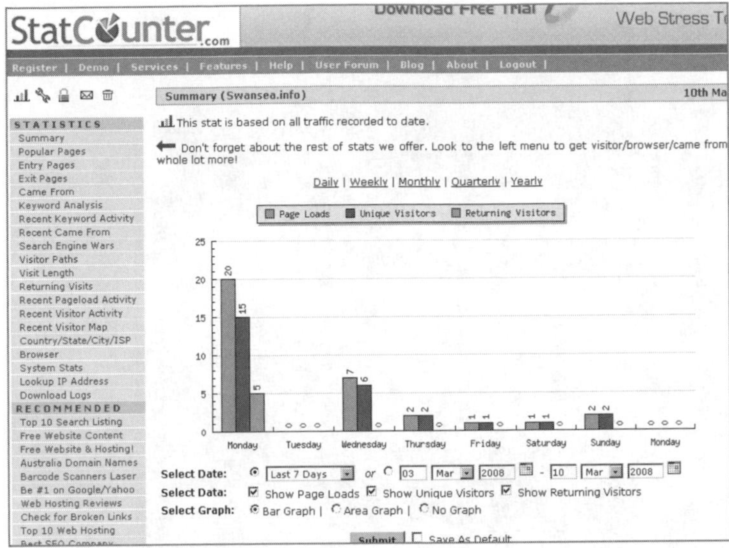

Figure 12-25.
SiteMeter

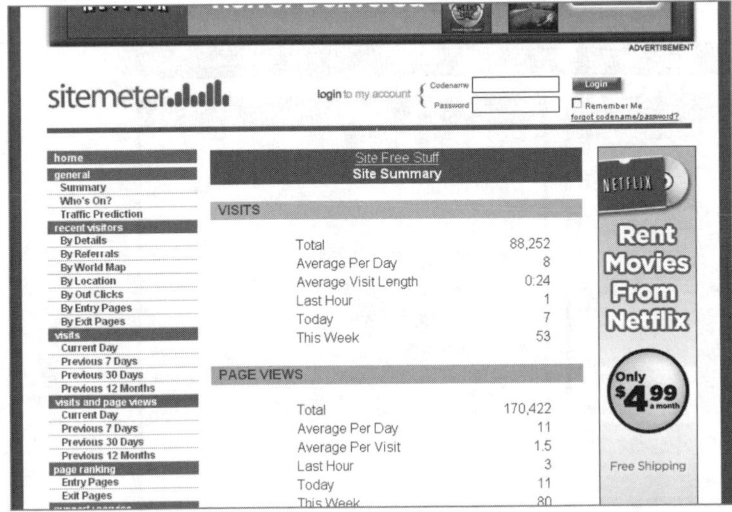

Figure 12-26.
VisitorVille

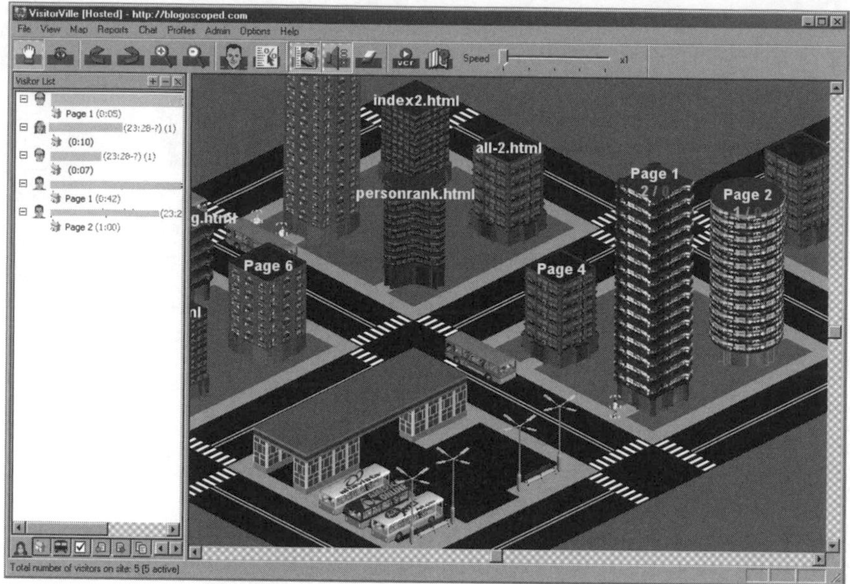

Figure 12-27.
Mint

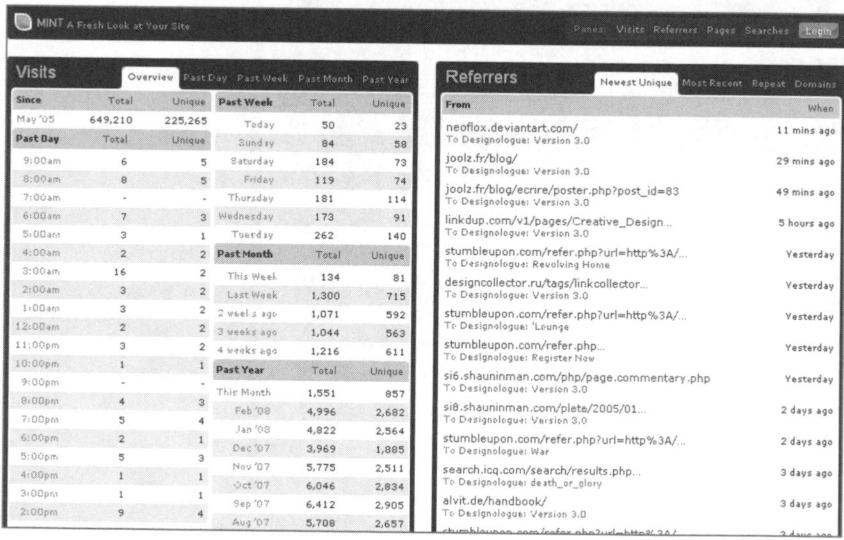

For more tracking programs, also take a look at WebTrends (http://webtrends.com), AWStats (http://awstats.sourceforge.net), MyBlogLog (http://mybloglog.com), OneStat (http://onestat.com), and WebSTAT (http://webstat.com).

Happy webmastering!

CREDITS

About the Author

Philipp Lenssen from Germany is editor and writer behind Google Blogoscoped (http://blogoscoped.com), a news site and community covering Google, search engines, and web technology in general. The blog was started in Malaysia in 2003 and is currently maintained with a great deal of help from people all over the globe. Philipp likes to program, draw or design, and write, and he created or co-created websites like GamesfortheBrain.com, CoverBrowser.com, and SketchSwap.com. When Philipp's not pondering the possibilities the Internet brought us, he's hopefully violently pulled away from his laptop by his wife Shan.

Contributors The following people contributed to this book in the form of hacks:

Tony Hirst from the UK, is a lecturer in artificial intelligence, and blogs about his Google and Yahoo related hacks and more at http://ouseful.info. Since 2001, Tony has been actively involved in educational robotics research.

Brian Jepson is Executive Editor for Make Magazine's Make:Books series, and has written and edited a number of geeky books. He's also a volunteer system administrator and all-around geek for AS220 (http://as220.org), a non-profit arts center that gives Rhode Island artists uncensored and unjuried forums for their work.

Reto Meier (http://blog.radioactiveyak.com) is a developer and technology writer currently living in London. As of lately, the Google Android mobile platform has piqued his special interest.

Chris Riley of http://cgriley.com is a web developer from the UK. In his spare time, he likes to mess about with various web APIs to create interesting and useful mashups.

INDEX

G

H

T

U

V

W

X

Y

Z

Received
JUL -7 14
Mission College Library